Dana Facaros and
Michael Pauls

DORDOGNE & THE LOT

'With understanding, the *petits bonheurs* and sweet surprises begin to add up, secret doors into a part of France where the roots of life are rich and deep'

CADOGANguides

Contents

Maps

About the authors

Dana Facaros and Michael Pauls lived for eight years in a leaky old Quercy farmhouse in the middle of nowhere, and now they're back, at least for a while.

Acknowledgements

Our thanks go out to all the local tourist offices and helpful autochthones who offered us stacks of facts and words of wisdom. Also, great big *bisous* to Lily Delancey Canacee K.C. for her dedicated hard work, and to Carole, Trebor, Tom, Sam, Kate, Victor, Vincent, Jackson I and II, Nigel, Michele, Steve, Tessa, Samson, Merlin, Michel, Leslie, Eunice, Stephanie, Jim, Pam, Norman, Christophe, Shalimar, Raymond, Maraika, Sim, Elisa, Bob, Debbie, Dan, Ixie, Pascale, Kate, Mike, Tom, Sophie, and Jack, for a thousand kindnesses, restaurant discoveries, inspiration *en vrac*, and helping us break all the plates. Special thanks, too, and best wishes to eagle-eyed editor Kate.

About the updater

Linda Rano is a writer living in a village just north of Toulouse with her Parisian husband Max and two children Louise and Miles. She writes about southwest France and, after living there for nearly four years, considers it home.

Cadogan Guides
Network House, 1 Ariel Way, London W12 7SL
cadoganguides@morrispub.co.uk
www.cadoganguides.com

The Globe Pequot Press
246 Goose Lane, PO Box 480, Guilford, Connecticut 06437–0480

Cover and photo essay design by Kicca Tommasi
Book design by Andrew Barker
Cover photographs by John Ferro Sims
Maps © Cadogan Guides, drawn by Map Creation Ltd
Editorial Director: Vicki Ingle
Series Editor: Linda McQueen
Editor: Kate Paice
Proofreading: Claudia Martin
Indexing: Isobel McLean
Production: Book Production Services

Printed in Italy by Legoprint
A catalogue record for this book is available from the British Library
ISBN 1-86011-803-8

Please help us to keep this guide up to date We have done our best to ensure that the information in this guide is correct at the time of going to press. But places and facilities are constantly changing, and standards and prices in hotels and restaurants fluctuate. We would be delighted to receive any comments concerning existing entries or omissions. Authors of the best letters will receive a copy of the Cadogan Guide of their choice.

Dordogne & Lot a photo essay

by John Ferro Sims

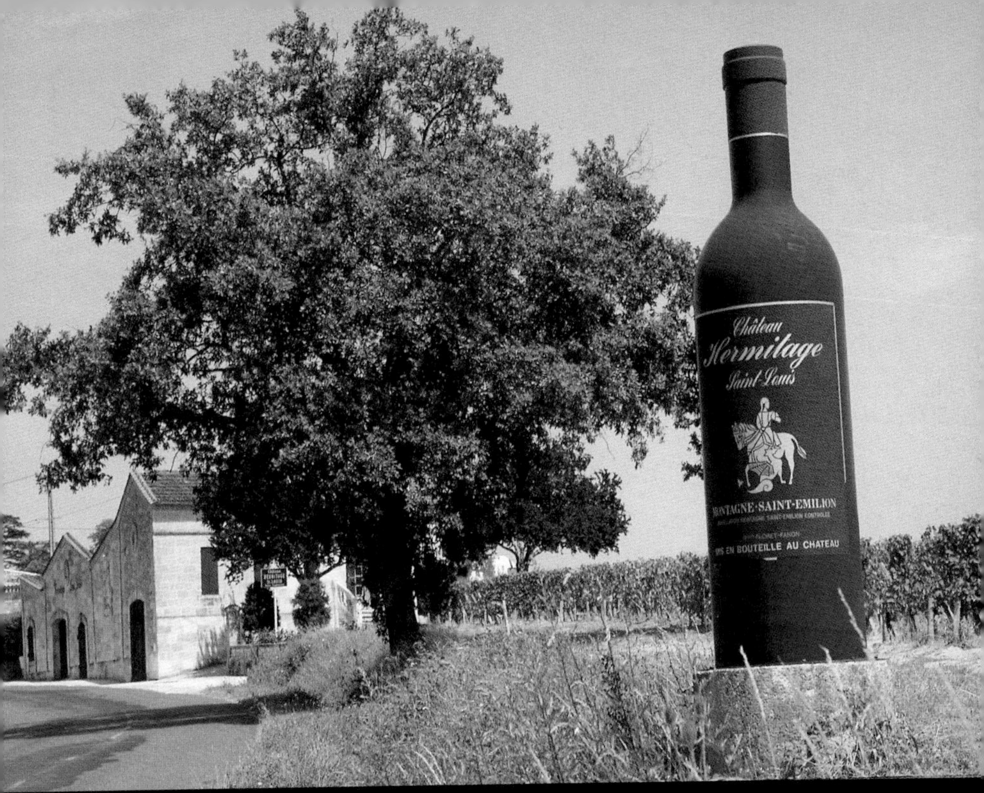
Château
Hermitage
Saint-Louis
MONTAGNE-SAINT-EMILION

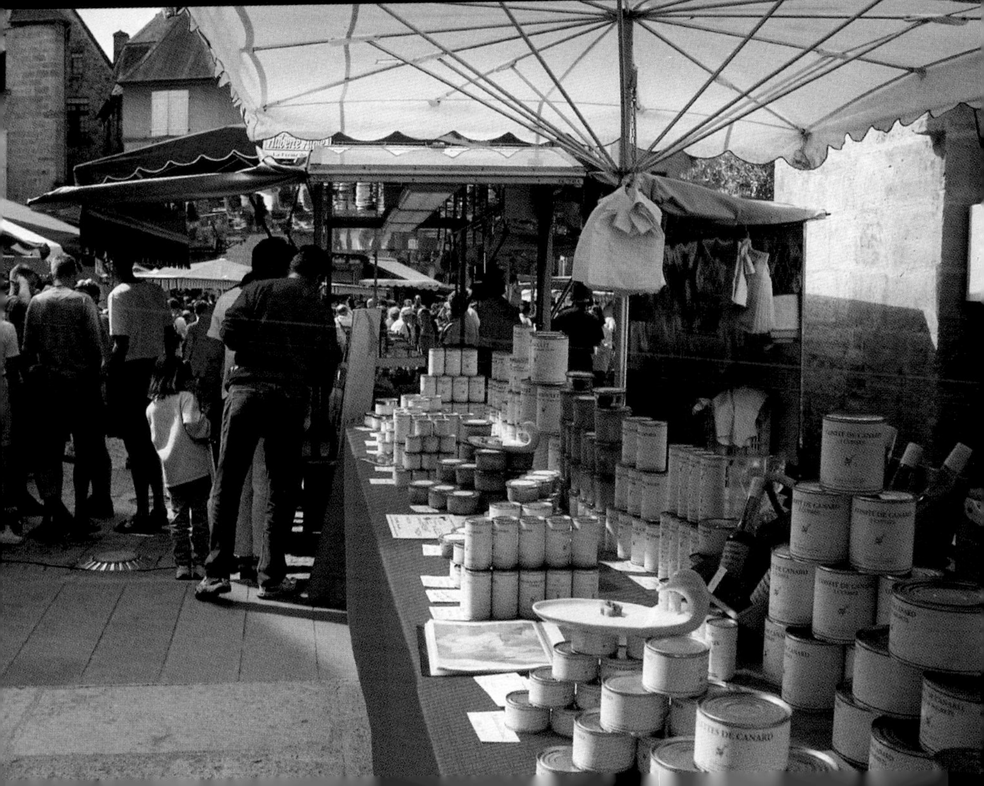

CHÂTEAU
LÉOVILLE BARTON
ST-JULIEN-MEDOC
12 Blles
L.0011
1996
CHATEAU-FIGEAC
SAINT-ÉMILION
FRANCE
1996
CHATEAU
GRAND MAYNE
GRAND CRU CLASSE
SAINT-EMILION
12 Blles
1996
CHATEAU SOUTARD

River Dordogne near Limeuil

Brântome Abbey

The Château de Bonaguil

Bergerac

Chancelade Abbey

Cathedral of St-Etienne, Cahors

Cathedral of St-Front, Périgueux

Wine crates, St-Emilion

Detail, church of St-Pierre, Petit-Palais-et-Cornemps

Villeréal, Lot-et-Garonne

Limeuil

Sarlat-la-Canéda

Stone borie near Cahors

Cathedral of St-Front, Périgueux

Lauze roof

Fishing in the Dordogne, near Trémolat

Château de Biron, Lot-et-Garonne

Vineyard, St-Emilion

Almond-paste 'fruits', Périgueux

Vineyard, St-Emilion

Market, Sarlat-la-Canéda

About the photographer

John Ferro Sims was born of Anglo-Italian parents in Udine, Italy. He worked successfully for five years as an investment analyst before quitting the world of money for a career as a professional photographer which has taken him around the world. He has published 9 books.

Introduction

If southwest France could croon a tune, it would have to be that old Inkspots' hit, 'I don't want to set the world on fire, I just want to be the one you love.' Endowed with the soft, gentle beauty of vine-clad river valleys and oak forests and chestnut, the region presents no overwhelming itinerary of high cultural shrines that demand your awe and homage. But, like all true lovers, it magically opens your eyes to the grace and charm in little things, in everyday life. Of course the southwest has its place in the macrocosm as well – there are a thousand proud châteaux and as many medieval villages, the world's foremost wine region and its very first art, the long secret cave paintings of Lascaux, Font-de-Gaume, Pech-Merle and a score of others.

Apart from Bordeaux and Toulouse, the two great cities that form the limits of this book, nothing much has happened here since the Hundred Years' War. Out of history, out of mind, this region retains something that most of the industrialized world has lost in its mad rush towards modernity. If you talk to an old farmer, he may mention *eime*, the Occitan word for soul similar to the Catalan *seny* – the intangible spirit of the nation, its good sense, its spirit of measure and moderation. The southwest may be the land of mystical troubadours, but it is also the land of France's most reasonable thinkers, of Montaigne, Fénelon, La Boétie and Montesquieu.

For if nothing else, southwest France is a fine place to hear yourself think. The great wine helps, of course, and the delicious regional cuisine puts your digestion in harmony with the universe. The pace of life is slow, and there's time to contemplate that old stone farm on the next hill, blending into the environment naturally and effortlessly. The wall by your chair is covered with eglantine and honeysuckle; the fragrance, the warm sun and the blackbird trilling away just beyond the garden make you delightfully drowsy and once again all plans and outings are postponed. You can't put it off forever, of course – there's a full whack of sights and surprises for you in this book – but the true purpose of this corner of the world is in teaching us all to pause and regain a bit of perspective. Or, as in the words of Montaigne:

> *The value of life lies, not in the length of days, but in the use we make of them; a man may live long, yet live very little. Satisfaction in life depends not on the number of your years, but on your will.*

A Guide to the Guide

This book covers the Aquitaine Basin, a great bay in the ocean millions of years ago and now divided into the *départements* of the Dordogne, Gironde, Lot, Lot-et-Garonne and Tarn-et-Garonne. This is river country *par excellence* – once the Dordogne, Lot, Tarn and Garonne plunge from their sources in the Pyrénées and Massif Central and carve out their steep gorges, we pick them up where they put on their watery brakes to weave gracefully down to the broad estuary of the Gironde and the Atlantic.

If you're driving down from Britain, chances are you'll pass through the verdant valleys and woodlands of the northern *département* of the Dordogne or **northern Périgord**, a lush land dotted with fairy-tale castles and domed Romanesque churches,

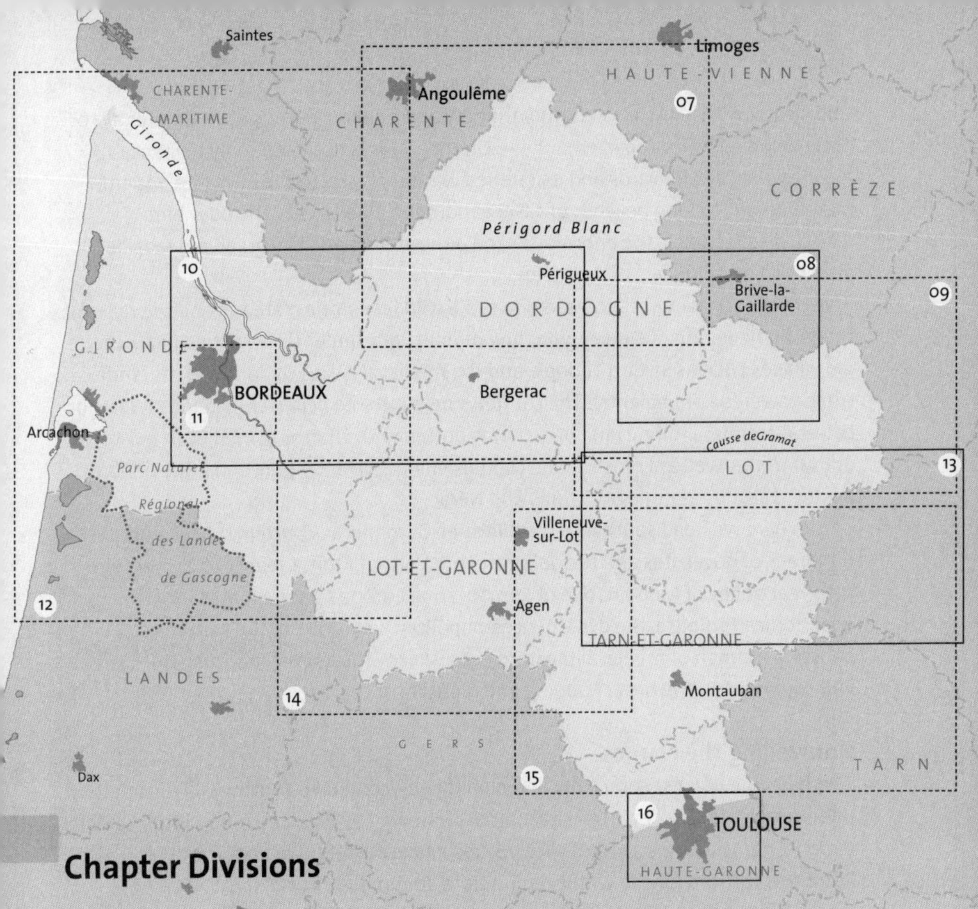

Chapter Divisions

- 07 **Northern Périgord (p.86)**
- 08 **The Vézère Valley (p.120)**
- 09 **Down the Dordogne I (pp.140–41)**
- 10 **Down the Dordogne II (pp.176–7)**
- 11 **Bordeaux (pp.218–19)**
- 12 **Gironde (p.248)**
- 13 **The Lot: Quercy (pp.298–9)**
- 14 **Lot-et-Garonne (pp.348–9)**
- 15 **Tarn-et-Garonne (pp.396–7)**
- 16 **Toulouse (pp.428–9)**

culminating in the astonishing St-Front in the handsome town of Périgueux. The next chapter, still within the Dordogne, delves into the misty past along the enchanting **Vézère Valley**, whose caves and shelters hold the densest concentration of prehistoric art on this planet, including the sublime Grotte de Lascaux.

Next come two chapters following the **valley of the Dordogne river**, first descending from Argentat to Domme, passing by way of some of the busiest tourist attractions in the southwest – the immense chasm and underground river at Padirac, the medieval pilgrimage town of Rocamadour, and the beautiful Renaissance town of Sarlat. The next chapter, Down the Dordogne II, follows the river past the first vineyards, from Bergerac (also home to the national tobacco museum) to lovely St-Emilion and Montaigne's château, ending up at the mighty citadel of Blaye.

Bordeaux with all its 18th-century frippery and fine museums gets a chapter all to itself, followed by its département, the **Gironde**. This is home not only to France's most celebrated vineyards and its rarefied wine châteaux (Mouton, Lafite, Yquem, Margaux) but to long beaches of silver sand, deep pine forests, the busy bird sanctuary at Le Teich, the enormous sand dune at Pilat and the grand old seaside resort and oyster haven of Arcachon.

Next we backtrack east, to head down the wild limestone plateaux and the river **Lot**, covering the region of **Quercy**, wiggling dramatically under cliffs, castles, picturesque old villages such as St-Cirq-Lapopie and the medieval city of Cahors, with its landmark triple-towered Pont Valentré. The Lot flows next into the *département* and chapter of **Lot-et-Garonne**, a rolling land of orchards dotted with charming medieval new towns, or *bastides*, as well as French prune capitals Villeneuve and Agen, and more picture-postcard castles at Bonaguil, Duras and Nérac.

From here we head south into rural **Tarn-et-Garonne**, a *département* decorated with hundreds of dovecotes and the delightful brick city of Montauban, not to mention the great abbey of Moissac, one of Romanesque Europe's greatest masterpieces. Last of all comes **Toulouse**, the dynamic, cosmopolitan 'Ville Rose' of the southwest, boasting a clutch of medieval masterpieces, worthy museums, charming brick streets and squares, and the best shopping and nightlife in this book.

Unravelling the Names

Perhaps the biggest source of confusion for newcomers to southwest France is that underneath the tidy departmental names bestowed by the French Revolution, older regional names have survived—like peeling circus posters, one atop the other. *Aquitaine* sufficed for the whole region from Roman times until the Middle Ages, when things began to get confusing and new names appeared: *Gascony*, for the lands west of the Garonne, and *Languedoc*, for those to the east, while everything owned by the English crown after the marriage of Eleanor of Aquitaine and Henry II became known as *Guyenne*, from the English inability to pronounce Aquitaine properly. Guyenne's borders fluctuated greatly until the end of the Hundred Years' War, and the name survives to this day whenever anyone feels like using it.

Within Guyenne, what is now the *département* of the Dordogne was the county of *Périgord* until the Revolution, and the name is still synonymous with the Dordogne *département*. The Lot, and most of the Tarn-et-Garonne were known (and still are) as *Quercy, Haut* and *Bas*. The Lot-et-Garonne and the Gironde were always the heartland of Aquitaine/Guyenne, although their southern reaches belong to Gascony; Toulouse was the medieval capital of the Languedoc, but in the new division of French regions (since 1981) the name Languedoc migrated to the Mediterranean, eastern half of the territory (to foil any attempts to undo the 13th-century Albigensian Crusade that annexed the south to Paris). This left Toulouse the capital of an artificial region called the *Midi-Pyrenées*, which encompasses the Lot and Tarn-et-Garonne, among others down in the Pyrenées, while the modern region of Aquitaine includes the Dordogne, Gironde and Lot-et-Garonne with Bordeaux as the capital. Get it?

History

03

400,000–600 BC

The southwest gets off to an extremely precocious start, and humanity comes to the Dordogne for its first summer art course

Europeans tend to think of 'early man' as some low-browed troglodyte living in Africa or the Middle East. But the roots of humanity are as deep in Europe as anywhere – going back a million years in some places. Destiny chose this particular corner of France to be the scene of some of the earliest and most significant developments in culture and art. A mere 400,000 years ago, somebody was poking around Périgord and other parts of the southwest, laboriously making flint tools and managing to get a fire lit. The crossing from the Lower to the Middle Palaeolithic occurred in this area about 75,000 years ago; the newcomer was **Neanderthal man** (presumably accompanied by Neanderthal woman). These come across as thick-skulled brutes in most accounts, but were really rather clever, inventing better tools and techniques, and developing the first rituals and burials: the elements of the 'Mousterian culture' in the southwest. The Neanderthals get pushed off the stage at about 40–35,000 years by **Cro-Magnon Man**, or *Homo sapiens sapiens* – us, more or less; books on Cro-Magnon man usually mention with a touch of whimsy that if one of them got on the bus today in a business suit, nobody would notice.

The creations of the Cro-Magnon (named after the hamlet in Périgord where their bones were first discovered) are varied enough for scholars to define distinct **Upper Palaeolithic** cultures. The Perigordian and Aurignacian (35–20,000 BC) left jewellery, finely crafted spear points, and the world's first painting and sculpture (*see* p.53). In the Solutrean culture (20–15,000 BC), people brought their stone tools – axes, spear points, arrowheads, knives, even sewing needles – to a point of perfection. The Upper Palaeolithic reached its height with the Magdalenian culture (15–9000 BC), with the beautiful paintings in the caves at Lascaux and elsewhere. This period was the slow end of an ice age, and it is possible that the people who made Magdalenian art gradually migrated northwards, following the herds of reindeer and other animals they hunted. The **Mesolithic** cultures that followed them (9000–4000 BC) did not paint, nor do much of anything else that was interesting.

Neolithic culture reached the area about 4000 BC, by either migrations or transmission of ideas – a lot of ideas: better tools, the first pottery, sedentary agricultural life, the domestication of animals, and a complex religion. The Neolithic peoples made Europe's first great civilization, and were its first builders. Their dolmens, menhirs, stone circles and tumuli are common all along the continent's coasts, but the Lot and the Dordogne have the greatest inland concentration of them anywhere. The Neolithic age was peaceful, probably matriarchal; they lived in unfortified villages, and evidence of warfare is singularly lacking. Lost so far back in time, hard facts are few, and Neolithic culture leaves us with a tangle of fascinating riddles: the purposes of their megalithic monuments and their siting of them, their considerable achievements in astronomy, and above all the vision of an extremely sophisticated culture, living in close harmony with nature and living well, without metals or technology.

This world lasted for over three millennia in many areas. But the unity of Neolithic civilization was broken c. 2000 BC, with the arrival of new peoples like the metal-working Artenac civilization, around Bordeaux. Over the next millennium and a half the picture grows increasingly confused, as ever more peoples and cultures pass through. The first to have a name, courtesy of later Roman writers, are the **Aquitanii**; they arrived in the 7th century BC (or much earlier, according to some opinions), and they may have been related to the various tribes of Celts who followed them.

600 BC–AD 507

In which Celts and the Romans first bash swords, and later clink glasses

In the 6th–4th centuries BC, new waves of **Celtic** peoples slowly spread over what came to be called **Gaul**. The Romans, when they arrived, found the area inhabited by a number of Gaulish tribes and wrote down their names: the Petrocorii north of the Duranus, or Dordogne, and south of it the Eleuteti and the fierce Cadurcii, who gave their name to Divona Cadurcorum (Cahors) on the Oltis, or Lot. In what is now the lower Lot-et-Garonne lived the Nitiobroges; while the plains around Toulouse were home to the Tolosates and Volcae Tectosages. The region around Bordeaux was occupied by the Biturges Vibiscii, who called themselves the 'Kings of the World'. A culturally complex people who nevertheless preferred pretty jewellery to the less mobile trappings of civilization – like temples and cities – the Celts, or Gauls, did settle a number of small towns, or oppida, which often served as trading stations. Even in this remote age, the 'Gallic isthmus' between the Atlantic and Mediterranean was a busy trade route; tin from Cornwall went one way, and back the other came imports from the Greek world including wine, of which the Gauls were very fond.

Rome's conquest of Gaul was hardly an overnight affair. Julius Caesar, who arrived in 59 BC, gets credit for the job, but Roman influence in the south at least was already strong – a Roman garrison was installed at Tolosa (Toulouse) around the middle of the 2nd century BC. Caesar's invasion came in response to revolts among Gauls who already found Roman control a little too heavy for their tastes. Burdigala (Bordeaux) was captured in 56 BC by Caesar's political partner Crassus, a wealthy magnate who, like Caesar, had bought a command because conquest was not only the path to power but also the only business more profitable to a Roman than city land speculation. The last great effort of the Gaulish nation and its leader, Vercingetorix, ended in total defeat at Gergovia in the Auvergne. The last Gaulish redoubt to fall, Uxellodunum, was somewhere in the Lot or perhaps Périgord (as with Gergovia, scholars are still arguing today over just where Uxellodunum was). The southwest, from the Loire to the Pyrenees, was organized into the Roman province of Aquitania.

Under direct Roman rule, southern Gaul became completely integrated into the Mediterranean economy. The new rulers apportioned out much of the land to Roman investors and veterans of the legions. Among the many new crops they introduced to the area was the grape, and soon the new Gallo-Roman Aquitania was not only meeting its own considerable demand for wine, but actually exporting it to Italy. Some of the *oppida* grew into towns – Tolosa, Burdigala and Divona Cadurcorum among many others; others naturally declined and died, and their ruins can be seen at such places as Mursens and Luzech, in the Lot. Mines and quarries were exploited, and many towns made a good living on manufactures, especially ceramics. By the 1st century AD, the larger towns were looking quite opulent, with forums, temples, public baths and amphitheatres imitating the cities of Italy.

Despite all this, life in Aquitania would not have looked so rosy to the average man. As elsewhere in the western Empire, Roman Gaul was a profoundly sick society, a pyramid with a few fantastically wealthy landowning families at the top, their estates tilled by vast armies of slaves. In the last centuries of the Empire, things got progressively worse. The small middle class in the towns was ground into poverty, as taxes rose and trade declined. Like the equally small class of free farmers, the middle class found itself gradually pushed into serfdom by debt. Not surprisingly, at the end of the Empire large areas of the country were controlled or at least threatened by the *bagaudae* – guerrilla bands out to destroy the system, especially strong in Aquitania.

The **Germanic** raids of the mid 3rd-century were an omen of troubles to come. In 256, the Franks and the Alemanni broke through the Rhine frontier. For two decades, they roamed over Gaul almost at will. Though the legions eventually recovered and drove them out, things would never be the same. The towns suffered most, such as Tolosa and Vesunna (Périgueux), which contracted after the invasions to a fraction of their former size, huddling inside circuits of hastily built walls. By this time the elite had already given up on urban life, and in the 4th century their sumptuous villas grew into cities in themselves; well-defended and self-supporting, these were the centres of what economic life remained in the last days. The fatal invasions came after 407; both **Vandals** and **Visigoths** passed through the region, and after 420 it found itself part of the new Visigothic kingdom, with its capital at Tolosa. Barbarian Franks replaced the barbarian Goths in 507, after the Battle of Vouillé, but this meant little to a part of Gaul that had effectively dropped out of history altogether.

507–1000

In which Aquitania is Frankly demoralized

Christianity had come to the region in the 4th century, as it was being established everywhere as the state religion of the Empire. The first recorded bishops are at Burdigala, in 314. The Church strengthened its power in the 6th century under the newly Christianized **Franks**. The Frankish Merovingian kings held only a tenuous control over most of Gaul, and only brought their army down to meet a foreign invasion, or when tribute was slow in coming; the day-to-day government was usually in the hands of landowners and their younger brothers in the Church. One bright light in the Dark Ages was Cahors. Controlled by a long line of powerful bishops beginning with the legendary Didier, the city survived and somehow prospered through the troubles; Cahors's aqueduct and baths were even restored in the grim 7th century.

Under the Merovingians, Frankish and Roman landowners gradually fused through intermarriage into a new ruling class much like the old one. Over generations their villas began to metamorphose into castles, while the landowners themselves gradually made their logical transformation into feudal barons. The Merovingians created the duchy of **Aquitaine** in the 7th century; for seven centuries the largely independent dukes would be in control of all the western coast from Poitou to the Pyrenees. In this poor backwater, they weren't always up to the task. The **Arabs** roared through from Spain in the early 700s, seizing Bordeaux and dominating the area until Charles Martel beat them at Poitiers in 732. Soon afterwards, the Frankish kingdom under its new **Carolingian** dynasty – headed by Charles's son Pepin the Short – tried to seize the duchy, while the duke, Waiofer, sheltered refugee lords who had been dispossessed by the Carolingians and led the southern resistance to the ambitious new power descending from the north. The result was a bloody war of three decades; Aquitaine was not completely brought under control until 774.

Pepin's son **Charlemagne** found a compromise solution: raising the duchy of Aquitaine into a kingdom, the first 'king' of which was his son Louis; this title lasted only until 877. The height of Frankish power under the Carolingians was a peaceful time for most of France, though it was short-lived. Charlemagne was still warm in his grave when his empire started to disintegrate, and the western shores suffered the visits of the worst barbarians ever: the Normans, or **Vikings**. In 848 they sacked Bordeaux, and all the century their regular raids brought terror and destruction to all the river valleys as far as Toulouse. The bits and shards of Roman civilization that had survived this long now finally faded out. Many people in the 9th century, looking forward to the millennium, were convinced that the end of the world was at hand, when in fact the ground was only being swept clean for something new and better.

1000–1271

The southwest creates a civilization, and the French and English come down to make nuisances of themselves

If the 9th century was the low point for the southwest and many other parts of Europe, the sudden strong impulse of cultural achievement and economic power that followed – the dawning of the **Middle Ages** – is all the more surprising. The Vikings' settling down in Normandy marked an end to foreign invasions, and in a period of relative tranquillity (marked by constant but not-too-serious feudal warfare) the feudal system in the southwest reached its perfection. The crazy quilt of *comtés, vicomtés, sénéchaussées* and *duchés*, interspersed with huge areas where local barons were free to do what they liked within the limits of their feudal oaths, made for a finely balanced anarchy that somehow managed to permit a rapid rebirth of towns, trade, wealth and culture.

In the brilliant 12th century, great abbey complexes appeared under the patronage of local rulers, and new stone churches in the Romanesque style were under way in every town and village – the biggest one in Europe, **St-Sernin**, went up under the wealthy and enlightened counts of Toulouse, the strongest lords of the southwest, who tended all to be named Raymond. Along the coast lived their near-equals, the dukes of Aquitaine; all these were Guillaumes, and the list included **Guillaume IX** (1086–1127), who besides his capable political leadership was one of the first of the troubadours, heralding the rebirth of poetry in Europe. That poetry was written in Occitan, the *langue d'oc*, and it was the pride of an **Occitan** nation, stretching from the Atlantic to the Alps, that was just beginning to become aware of itself when it was overwhelmed by invaders from the north.

Guillaume had a granddaughter, a beautiful and wilful woman whose life would be the stuff of romances, and whose career would change history: **Eleanor of Aquitaine**. She was sole heir to the rich duchy, and when she married Louis VII in 1137, the French crowed for having plucked the biggest feudal plum imaginable. Eleanor did her best with the cold, pious Louis, and even accompanied him on a crusade. Her manifest discontent led inevitably to a divorce, in 1152, and two years later she found a more convivial marriage with Louis's mortal enemy: **Henry Plantagenet**, Duke of Anjou, soon to be Henry II, King of England. Along with Eleanor came the land, and for the next three centuries Aquitaine would be a possession of the English crown. The Plantagenets, in constant need of cash, introduced an intelligent and well-organized administration; if the tax burden was high, the resources were there to pay it. The English proved good rulers, usually sympathetic to local concerns, and they gained a high degree of loyalty from the people of Aquitaine. (One sour note at the beginning came with the depredations of Henry and Eleanor's sons – worst of all Richard the Lion-Heart, a fellow who gets off all too easily in history and legend. Richard battled and pillaged across the region more to line his pockets than to solidify English rule, and in Aquitaine, as elsewhere, he gained a well-deserved reputation as a bloody-minded thug.) Under English control, Bordeaux grew into a city of 30,000 with a new prosperity based on wine; at the height of the trade with England, in 1308, Aquitaine exported almost as much of the stuff as it does today.

Toulouse, under its counts, grew even bigger and richer than Bordeaux, though the city that might have been a natural capital of an Occitan nation instead itself became a victim of imperialism from the north. The French would have made their play for Toulouse in any case, but in the early 1200s fortune provided them with a cause: the presence of the **Cathars**. This heretical sect, which came from the Balkans by way of north Italy, found a perfect haven in the sophisticated, tolerant atmosphere of the Toulousain and Languedoc. In 1209, a sordid deal between Pope Innocent III and the French King Philippe-Auguste paved the way for the **Albigensian crusade**, supposedly directed against the heretics but in reality a naked grab at the lands of the counts of Toulouse. The troops were provided from Paris, a force under the cruel, lucky and always victorious **Simon de Montfort**; this army plundered its way through Quercy and the Agenais before the main event, the total subjection of the south. This was clinched by de Montfort's victory at the Battle of Muret, near Toulouse, in 1213; resistance continued, though, giving King Louis VIII an excuse to bring down another army to finish the job in 1226.

In 1271, the French crown inherited Toulouse by a forced marriage; long before that, fiefs and offices had been handed out to northerners, and the **Inquisition** was introduced, not only to incinerate the few surviving Cathars but to ensure that the free culture that made heresy possible would be extinguished forever.

1271–1453

In which the French and the English continue their quarrels and mischief

Despite the vicious way the French had gone about their conquest, with plenty of bloody massacres *pour encourager les autres*, recovery was rapid. The surest sign of the continuing economic boom was the founding everywhere of *bastides*, planned new towns, usually built on lands that had gone back to forest or swamp during the late Empire and Dark Ages; the first of these was Montauban, a creation of Count Alphonse-Jourdain in 1144. *Bastides* had their political aspect too. Over a score were founded by Alphonse de Poitiers, the first French Count of Toulouse, King Louis's brother and the man in charge of establishing French control over the new conquests. The English in response founded scores of their own *bastides* in Aquitaine.

The vigour of society in these times can be read on any map today; hundreds of town and village names show their origins in the 11th–13th centuries: *bastides* are often named *Villeneuve* or *Villefranche* – free towns with their own charter. Many other names end in *-artigues* or *-essart*, words that denoted reclaimed land, a constant necessity in times when the population was increasing rapidly. A village that grew up around a castle is often named *Castelnau*, and the various places called *Sauveterre* began as *sauvetés*, church foundations that at least in theory were 'safe', exempt from feudal warfare and pillage. The older towns also continued to thrive, notably Cahors, which attracted a number of Italian banking families that fled the disruptions of the Albigensian crusade. The little city on the Lot soon grew into a major financial centre with its own university, and even supplied a pope, John XXII.

England and France, now the only two powers in the region, battled fitfully for a century after the marriage of Eleanor and Henry II, until Louis IX (St Louis) agreed to the **Treaty of Paris** in 1259, formally ceding Périgord and Quercy to the English. From then on the two parties suspiciously eyed one another, in an uneasy truce that occasionally broke out into open hostilities; the French even succeeded in occupying Bordeaux for a decade, until a revolt of the Bordelais threw them out in 1303.

But for all the politeness generally shown by both sides, it was a situation that could not last. In an age when nation-states were dawning, feudal logic no longer worked: as dukes of Guyenne (from the English mispronunciation of Aquitaine), the English kings owed homage to the kings of France – a fine position to be in whenever the two nations' interests were in conflict. The inevitable final showdown began with a quarrel over Guyenne in 1337, and went into the books as the **Hundred Years' War**.

The first decades of the war saw Aquitaine as the major battlefield, without major results until the arrival of Edward of Woodstock, son of Edward III, in 1355. The **Black**

Prince, as he came to be known, ended the war's first round decisively with the Battle of Poitiers (1356), capturing King Jean II among many others. England, now in undisputed control of the southwest, declared their lands a principality free of any claims of French allegiance; the Black Prince ruled it from Bordeaux until his death in 1376.

The next round went to the French, under Bertrand du Guesclin, who recaptured Quercy and most of Périgord by 1369. As the war dragged on, the exhausted combatants found it increasingly difficult to maintain control of events. Both sides hired **mercenary** companies; these got out of hand, and, combined with the other desperados shaken loose from society by constant warfare and disruption, they formed the ***routiers*** ('highwaymen'), armed bands loyal to nothing but their own profit that reduced much of the southwest to anarchy. Coming on the heels of the Black Death (1348–50), which reduced the population by a third in many areas, it caused a time of troubles the region had not known since the days of the Normans.

In the early 1400s, it seemed that France was coming apart once and for all. The English regained all they had lost, and even took Paris in 1420, a time that coincides with the worst ravages of the *routiers* in the southwest. Thanks to **Joan of Arc**, of course, the French soon recovered and prevailed. They blockaded Bordeaux in 1451, and two years later the climactic Battle of Castillon, near Bordeaux, put an end to the wars and to England's continental empire forever.

1453–1594

In which the lobotomized southwest starts arguing with itself over religion

The French moved quickly to consolidate their new possessions. Bordeaux got a big new fortress to watch the citizens, and a *parlement* to scrutinize their morals and political opinions; the city's wine trade with England was ended by royal decree, sending it – along with most of Aquitaine – into economic decline. For both Aquitaine and the Toulousain, French rule meant not only impoverishment, but the enforced death of cultures that had been among the most promising of the Middle Ages. The 1539 decree of Villars-Cotterets mandated the French language in law and government, the first step along the road to the eradication of the *langue d'oc*, which would not be completed until our own time. Before the French came, the south had its own traditions of literature, architecture and art; under a new rigid authoritarianism, directed from Paris, all this withered away quickly. Southwesterners, when able to build, sculpt or write at all, found themselves forced to ape the fashions imported by their governors from the north, and over the generations it became a habit.

The French grip was strong, and with political opposition impossible, the next wave of southern rebelliousness came in the form of religious dissent. **Protestantism** first seeped into the southwest from Calvin's Geneva, and it found its most attentive audience among the industrious middle classes and some of the more enlightened courts. The first Protestant communities appeared in Ste-Foy-la-Grande and Agen about 1532. Soon after, the court at Nérac of the **Albrets**, a powerful noble family of the Agenais, became a centre of humanistic learning and religious heresy (Calvin came to visit). This happened in the reign of the learned Marguerite d'Albret – or rather Marguerite of Navarre, for this ambitious family had, with French help, worked its way to the kingship of that small and woebegone Pyrenean realm.

Protestantism swept across the south, bringing the good news that there was more to life than abject submission to Rome and Paris. With the spirit of the time, civil war was inevitable – the **Wars of Religion**. The conflict gathered steam from 1560, with the massacre of Protestants in Cahors, and the expulsion of Toulouse's Protestant community two years later. Atrocities went both ways; in Gourdon it was the Protestants who were doing the slaughtering. Towns and regions chose sides. Cahors, with its powerful bishops, remained steadfastly Catholic, and fought a continuous battle with Protestant Montauban and Figeac; Protestant Bergerac stomped on Catholic Périgueux as early and as often as possible. The religious rebels found a firm pillar of support in Jeanne d'Albret, daughter of Marguerite and a grisly bigot for the new cause, as Protestant and Catholic armies recaptured the spirit of the Hundred Years' War, prowling the region and looking for enemy towns and souls to burn.

In much of the rest of France it was the same story; now, however, for the first time, the southwest stepped up to centre stage in France's history, thanks to the Albrets and Jeanne's son Henri, who by a complicated set of circumstances just happened to be the heir to the French throne. Henri of Navarre was a good Protestant and a hardy warrior; among other things he sacked Cahors in 1580 with more bloodshed than was really necessary. In two decades of campaigning to win his rightful crown, the Protestant lands of the southwest were his solid base. In the end, though, Henri's good sense and good will made him the man to finally put an end to the Wars of Religion – by the conversion of convenience that finally made him acceptable to the Catholics who were controlling Paris. As **Henri IV**, he ruled well, proclaiming religious tolerance with the **Edict of Nantes** (1598), and earned a secure place for himself as a national hero in the southwest, particularly in his native Gascony.

1594–1789

In which the French do their best to make everyone miserable, and the southwest fights back and loses

With religious troubles out of the way, the southwest was free to return its thoughts to the joys of rule from Paris. Riots and popular revolts had been common enough in the 1500s, usually over oppressive taxes like the *gabelle*, or salt tax. In the sympathetic Henri's reign, the first of a century-long series of peasant uprisings occurred. The movement of the '***Croquants***', in Périgord and Quercy, was more directed at the grasping nobles and their high rents. In 1594 the *Croquants* formed a peasant army in Périgord; the barons organized and beat them, and punished the survivors with memorable ferocity. Henri's successors in Paris heaped more woes on the common folk: more taxes, more forced labour, and lots of revenue agents and troops to enforce them. The early 17th century would have been rough enough without them. High rents and prices, combined with bad harvests, recurring outbreaks of plague (1629 and 1652) and a climate of hatred and everyday violence, the heritage of the religious wars, made further revolts inevitable. In Toulouse, in 1629, things were so bad that even the royal governor, Montmorency, joined the rebels, and Louis XIII had to lead a big army down from Paris to crush them.

From 1637 to 1642, the *Croquants* were back in business again. This time they nearly captured Périgueux, though once again the arms of the king and the nobles had the last say. This would be the last revolt on a large scale, though smaller outbreaks were regular features of rural life up until the Revolution. For the nobles, times were never better, as witnessed by the large number of great châteaux built in this period. At the same time, a lot of the old-style castles were disappearing – pulled down on the orders of Louis XIII's minister Cardinal Richelieu, who didn't want any strong places left that could possibly shelter resistance to the national state. If the countryside was in despair, the two large cities weren't doing too badly. Bordeaux found a new prosperity in the late 17th and 18th centuries, based not only on wine but also on the slave trade with the Americas; the city grew enough to become the third-largest in France. Toulouse in the 16th century was still enjoying a modest boom from the manufacture of *pastel*, dyer's woad, and the building by local initiative of the Canal du Midi in Languedoc (inaugurated in 1681) made the city the centre of a new trade route that crossed the French isthmus. The pastel business dwindled in the face of foreign competition, though, and despite its natural advantages, Toulouse generally continued its long slide into cultural and economic torpor.

For most of the region, hard times continued through the 1700s. Bordeaux could find no better way to profit from the New World than through the slave trade, but the Americas offered many poor Aquitains a way out: tens of thousands emigrated to Canada and the West Indies. Most of the Protestants had already gone, to Prussia and elsewhere, after Louis XIV revoked the Edict of Nantes in 1685. For those who remained, the century was a drowsy era, at least when the peasants weren't revolting. *Intendants* (administrators) from Paris ran everything, and made a few lasting contributions, notably an excellent network of roads (usually embellished with pretty rows of plane trees, still seen in many places today). The *intendants* also dressed up Bordeaux, remodelling the city into a grandiose provincial copy of Paris.

1789–1940

The southwest helps make a revolution, learns to regret it, and then takes a long nap

In 1789, no people in France were more cheerfully assiduous than the southwesterners in smashing up churches and châteaux, finding and burning the tax records and rent rolls. But at the same time, at the National Assembly in Paris, Bordeaux's merchants, and southwesterners in general, were providing most of the voices of moderation and good sense. Their faction, the **Girondists**, stood for liberal reforms and political decentralization. When the radical, Paris-dominated **Jacobin** faction gained control in 1792, the Terror began; the Girondists and their federalist hopes became its first victims. A 1793 federalist counter-revolt in the southwest failed, largely because Toulouse and Montauban wouldn't have anything to do with it; stoutly conservative areas like the Lot were against the Revolution from the start.

The Lot, ironically, loved Napoleon and contributed more than any part of France to his *Grande Armée*, including fine soldiers like Joachim Murat, the son of a village innkeeper, who ended up King of Naples. Jean-Baptiste de Bessières of Prayssac, who was in charge of the occupation of Moscow, briefly claimed the title of Duke of Istria. At the end, though, southwesterners were as tired of Napoleon as anybody else. The Duke of Wellington marched through in 1814, on his way up from Spain. When he arrived at Toulouse, the people hailed him as a liberator.

If the Revolution had been a disappointment, nothing in the century that followed it would be any improvement. Paris-appointed prefects replaced Paris-appointed *intendants*, and the old regional distinctions and boundaries were destroyed in favour of homogeneous *départements*, but through all the 19th-century shifts of the Gallic banana republic/monarchy/empire, no one lifted a hand to help the southwest; nor did the region ever show much energy of its own. Aquitaine and the Toulousain had become the most sluggish and listless of all French provincial backwaters, and anyone with any spunk or talent was off to Paris as soon as he could manage it.

The railway arrived in Bordeaux in 1850; seven years later the line from there to Toulouse and the Mediterranean was finished. Instead of catalysing trade and industry, however, this merely made it easier to leave, and easier for imported goods to flow in and ruin the already hard-pressed southwestern farmers and manufacturers. The farmers did their best, introducing useful new crops such as corn and tobacco, and they managed just barely to survive the 1868 **phylloxera** epidemic that killed off nearly all their vineyards, but prices stayed low and business stayed bad. And all across the southwest, the villages began to dwindle.

Undoubtedly the biggest event of the last century was one that happened elsewhere – the **First World War**. Of the millions who died pointlessly for the glory of France, the southwest contributed more than its share. Many towns and villages lost a third, or even half their young men; in every one you will see a pathetic war memorial or plaque in the church to remind you of France's greatest catastrophe since the Black Death. Between the war and rural abandonment, the southwest declined in population by almost 25 per cent from 1850 to 1950; in some parts of the Lot and other *départements*, the figure was as high as 60 per cent.

1940 to the present

A Nazi interlude, followed by the unexpected return of the English

Though the **Second World War** was less costly and destructive, it was still a miserable and dangerous time for the people of the southwest, however far removed they were from the actual fighting. From the beginning, the Germans seized a strip along the entire Atlantic coast. The 'border' between the occupied zone and Vichy-controlled territory was heavily patrolled, and locals needed special papers to cross it – plenty of people were killed trying to visit their cousins, or sneaking produce over the line to the nearby village market. Deportation of men to forced labour in Germany was a terrible burden, and not all who went ever returned. Another strain, particularly in Périgord, was supporting the wave of refugees from Belgium and northern France who had come down in 1940, but this one the people handled ungrudgingly.

The **Resistance** was not much of a force until 1943, but from then on it operated effectively in the lonely *causses* of Quercy and Périgord, where one of its leaders was the writer and future culture minister André Malraux. In retaliation for their acts of sabotage, the Germans sent the SS Das Reich division on a tour of the southwest in May 1944; these distinguished themselves with wholesale massacres of civilians at Mussidan, in Périgord, Frayssinet-le-Gélat and Montpezat-de-Quercy. Liberation came for most of the southwest in August 1944; Bordeaux's story was much like that of Paris. Colonel Kühnemann, the German commander, was in civilian life a wine merchant with many friends in the city. He had orders to blow up nearly everything on his way out, along with all the bridges as far as Agen, but instead he spent a delicate week dodging the Nazi spooks while successfully negotiating with the Resistance for a peaceful exit. Some German units, trapped at Royan and Verdon on the Gironde, held out almost to the end of the war.

Since the war, the big news has been the unexpected awakening of **Toulouse**. With considerable assistance from the government planners, the city parlayed its early prominence in aviation to become France's forward-looking City of the Air, home of Aérospatiale and the French space agency, a manufacturer of satellites and supersonic airliners. Striving to become the European 'technopole' of the 21st century, Toulouse has also fixed up its historic centre, now sitting well-scrubbed, pink and pretty on the Garonne. Bordeaux, meanwhile, is still Bordeaux, and oddly proud of it.

Large numbers of refugees from the Spanish Civil War, and a wave of *pieds noirs* (French settlers in Algeria, forced out in 1962) have settled in the southwest, adding a touch of diversity not only to the population but to the cuisine – if there's a dinner on at a village festival, school pageant or whatever, it's likely to be paella or couscous. The British invasion of the Dordogne began in the 1960s, when people found out that lovely country homes in that delightful region could be had for a song. That particular song is ended, but the *département* today has one of the largest British expat colonies in France (the largest, officially, is Haute-Garonne, with many professionals and engineers drawn to Toulouse by the aerospace industry). There is also a sizeable British population in Gironde, Lot and Lot-et-Garonne. The Consulate at Bordeaux estimated in 2000 that there were about 25,000 British people living in southwest France – a town's worth. The locals joke that the English are trying to buy back what they lost in the Hundred Years' War; so far, though, relations are generally good.

Politically, the only major change of the postwar era was the Socialist government's 1981 **decentralization** plan, creating the regions of Aquitaine and Midi-Pyrénées. So far the regions have only limited powers, but as the first reverse in seven centuries of Parisian centralism, it brings at least a hope that the southwest may some day finally regain some degree of control over its destiny.

Culture

04

Microtourism

We don't have any Eiffel Towers or Chartres Cathedrals to offer you in this book. Famous, familiar sights are rare in the southwest, and anyone who wants great art will have to look for it in unlikely places like Moissac or Souillac, or in the Palaeolithic caves of Périgord. But the hordes of visitors and expats that prowl this part of France hardly feel the lack. Most of them seem content with the area's wealth of pretty villages and châteaux, along with the wine, fresh air and *confits de canard*, and they might spend a slow weekend in the big towns for a look at a church or a museum.

People who do spend a lot of time down there really need never be bored. Getting the most out of any part of rural France requires learning to look at the country the way the French do – on a small scale. Connoisseurs of every particularity of village and pays, the French are passionately interested in the detail of traditional life and local history. For example, painstaking cartographers have compiled maps showing traditional roof styles in France: where they are high-pitched or shallow, and where the boundary is between slate and canal tiles (except in Périgord, this roughly corresponds to the boundary between the *langue d'oïl* and *langue d'oc* – it's all connected). Other maps display the types of construction used for *pigeonniers*, or dovecotes, notable features of the landscape in the southwest. In some areas they are round, in others square and set on stone pillars, or attached to the house.

Get the locals talking about these subjects and they'll go on for hours, explaining how in some areas only nobles were allowed to keep pigeons, which went out every day and ate all the peasants' grain and so caused the Revolution, which allowed everyone to keep pigeons, and farmers let the poo pile up for their daughters' dowries, but later they planted groves of poplars when a girl was born, because the trees would mature just in time for her marriage, by which time chemical fertilizers had made pigeon droppings less valuable than firewood... You probably get the idea. And by the way, you've probably noticed how the poplars are always planted in orderly quincunxes, like the Place des Quinconces in Bordeaux, but scholars are divided on whether this fashion, invented by King Cyrus of Persia, came into France in the Middle Ages or in the time of Louis XIV...

If you want to play too, the first thing to do is pick up the *Cartes IGN: Série Bleue* map for the area that interests you. Drawn on a scale of 1:25,000, these are the equivalent of the Ordnance Survey or US Geodetic Survey maps. You'll find them in any good newsagent or bookshop; hunters and mushroom-lovers probably account for much of the demand. From the first glance, you'll get a feeling for the traditional life and the slowly evolving fabric of your area: the villages and hamlets, each with its patch of cleared farmland, like islands in the vast green of the forests, along with the works that kept life going: sawmills, remains of old water mills, *pigeonniers*, sandpits and quarries, sources and fountains.

The map will show you some surprises, even if you think you already know the area well. Naturally it will help you find the nearest swimming hole, and some nice places for a walk in the woods, but there will be other surprises too: maybe a dolmen or menhir, a collection of *gariottes* or a fortified tower, or a medieval chapel in an unlikely place that may turn out, like one we found, to have seven devils frescoed on the walls inside. Ruins, by the score, are generally marked on the map without further detail, so take pot luck; ruins can mean anything from bits of a Roman aqueduct to a routiers' stronghold destroyed at the end of the Hundred Years' War, or a barn abandoned by some poor farmer who gave up and moved to the city when phylloxera hit.

Once you get to know the country and its history better, you'll be able to read these maps like a detective. That village surrounded by a circuit of roadside crosses – it must have been a *sauveté* of the Church in the 1100s; the crosses marked the limits within which knights were forbidden to bash each other or molest the peasants. Crosses of all kinds grow thick along the roadsides of the southwest. Around Toulouse people used to believe the Cathars first made them, but in fact many are simply the latest incarnation of markers that go back to Neolithic times (only 200 years ago, a bishop of Cahors was demolishing menhirs and replacing them with crosses, because country people would not stop worshipping secretly at the sites).

Not least among the virtues of rural France is modesty. This doesn't mean a lack of pride in one's region – on the contrary, nearly everyone here is convinced that their particular coin is Paradise on Earth – but rather modesty as an outlook, as a way of life. As historian Emmanuel Le Roy Ladurie has noted, France is the country where bars are called *Au Petit Bonheur* or *Au Petit Profit*. Ladurie and others have developed an equally modest and original way of looking at the past. 'Microhistory', studying a single place and time in the minutest detail, not only flushes out unwarranted generalities and clichés, but adds real depth to our understanding. And a little understanding is all the southwest and its people ask of the visitor. Deeply in love with their country, they are concerned that we learn to appreciate it as they do. With understanding, the petits bonheurs and sweet surprises begin to add up, secret doors into a part of France where the roots of life are rich and deep.

Bertran de Born

East of Périgueux stands the Château de Hautefort, the replacement of the impregnable 12th-century citadel of the war-loving troubadour Bertran de Born (c. 1140–1214). Bertran's career makes mincemeat of the romantic Hollywood stereotype of troubadours as long-haired, love-lorn wimps. Although capable of writing delightfully about love, he liked nothing better than stirring up trouble, which he did through his battle songs and *sirventés*, the topical, satirical songs of the troubadours: 'I want great barons always/to be angry with one another,' wrote Bertran; and elsewhere: 'Peace does not comfort me/I am in accord with war/Nor do I hold or believe/Any other religion.' The minor nobility of Aquitaine listened to his *sirventés*, and agreed; feudal anarchy between overlords offered their only chance for independence and profit. But what assured Bertran's fame is the striking vividness and power of his poetry, capable of enchanting such diverse spirits as St Francis of Assisi, who sang his songs as a wayward youth, and Ezra Pound, who translated many of them so well.

In his day, Bertran was feared by all for his biting satire, so much so that he was blamed for the death of the Young King, Henry Court-Mantel, Henry II's heir and the older brother of Richard the Lion-Heart. The chroniclers tell the story: Bertran through 'ruse and felony' had kicked out Hautefort's co-owner, his own brother Constantine. Constantine appealed to Richard the Governor of Aquitaine as his overlord for justice. Bertran resolved to seek aid in other quarters, and wrote a series of *sirventés* taunting his friend the Young King, whom Bertran knew was sick with jealousy of Richard; the Lion-Heart already ruled Aquitaine and attracted great renown and money for his exploits, while his older brother chafed with little to do (and a small allowance) while waiting to inherit the throne of England. To every noble court Bertran sent songs of a 'lord of little land' and commented that 'It ill beseems a crowned king to live upon a dole and spend but a Norman carter's tax'. Bertran's satires had their doleful effect in the spring of 1183, when a general uprising against Richard's tyranny broke out across Aquitaine. The Young King joined the rebels, at first reluctantly, and then wholeheartedly when Henry II came down in person to aid Richard. The Young King was now fighting not only his brother but his father too, and he raised money for his mercenaries by plundering; after a raid on the holy shrine of Rocamadour, he sickened along the road, and died at Martel.

Grief-stricken, old King Henry blamed Bertran for his son's death, and sent Richard and Alfonso II of Aragon to besiege Hautefort. Bertran scorched the earth before the enemy, so they would have nothing to eat. But when Alfonso asked him as an old friend for sustenance, Bertran offered the Aragonese armies ten days' worth of food for the promise that they would not attack the weakened south wall of Hautefort. Of course that was precisely where the Aragonese unchivalrously began their attack, and Bertran surrendered at once, to spare further damage to his beloved castle.

Bertran was carted off before King Henry, who received him in a towering rage, and determined to have him put to the sword. Then he said: 'Bertran, Bertran, once you said that you never needed more than half your wits. Surely now you need them all!' 'My lord, what I said is true,' Bertran replied in tears. 'Although since the day of the death of your son, the beautiful and valiant Young King, I have lost all my wits, judgment, and mind.' His grief so moved the king that he fainted, and when he recovered he wept and said: 'Ah Bertran, unhappy Bertran, it was only right that you have lost your wits in losing my son, for he loved you more than any other man in the world. And I, for love of him, return to you your liberty, goods, and castle. And I will add 500 marks to rebuild the south wall of your castle. Thanks to this letter from my son Richard, I know of your worthy conduct in the siege of Hautefort. It is as much for your noble acts as a soldier as for your celebrated talents as a troubadour that you have earned today my clemency.'

If Bertran had used his grief to get out of a tight jam, it was nonetheless sincere – his famous *planh* (lament) for the Young King is one of the masterpieces of Occitan literature. But the experience hardly cooled Bertran's heels; out of Hautefort the volley of *sirventés* continued, now lampooning King Alfonso II for playing Bertran false, now egging Richard to battle with verses as vivid as Villon's:

If both kings are bold and fearless,
we'll soon see fields strewn with bits
of helmets, shields, swords and saddlebows,
and bodies split open from head to foot,
and horses wandering about aimlessly,
and lances protruding from ribs and chests,
and joy and tears, and grief and happiness.
The loss will be great, but the gain yet greater.

As the translator Ezra Pound commented, 'This kind of thing was much more impressive before 1914 than it has been since 1920.' Yet for all his love of war, Bertran died in a monastery, from where Dante sent him straight to Hell, inventing for him the interesting punishment of wandering about as a headless trunk, holding his severed head aloft as a lantern. And the head explains to Dante: 'Know that I am Bertran de Born, who gave evil counsel to the Young King and made father and son rebel against one another... Because I parted those who were joined, I carry my brain parted from its roots in this trunk.'

Market Values

The old vans and lorries will start wheezing in some time after eight, unloading prunes and geese and greens and oysters in the morning fog while the children are passing through on their way to school. The stall-holders in French village markets aren't the sort of people to knock themselves out coming at dawn. That's the whole point. The Friday morning market here has probably taken place since the Middle Ages, and today it is a symbol of liberty, and a refuge for everyone from the clock-driven, bureaucrat-infested life of the cities. Free men and women come and go when they damn well please: there are no receipts, and no VAT that can't be avoided; no advertising, no special discount offers, no Styrofoam and no bar codes; just real food, scents, colours and conviviality. European legislation to try and keep fresh food on markets refrigerated has hardly been adopted with vigour, in this country where they like their cheese running off the plate. Perhaps this is that Free Market they're always chattering about in the newspapers.

The village market is the reliable country calendar of France, and all of us down here measure the seasons by the asparagus, spring onions, raspberries, wild strawberries, melons, *cèpes* and chestnuts that rise and pass across its firmament, each at its appointed time. It is also the best way to check on the state of the land. Even vendors who are middlemen, and didn't grow the stuff themselves, are willing to discuss the relative merits and demerits of their produce, with a long discourse on the weather responsible for them if they're not too busy. Farmers who bring in chickens will recount their life stories, and tell you to which special fate in the kitchen they think each of them best suited. If you're not in the mood for such discussions, and even if you're not intending to buy anything, you'll come to the market just the same, for the sensual assault that makes it the climax of the week. Best are the fish stands –

glistening rainbow trout, pink rougets and prawns, inscrutable sea urchins and lithe purple Art Nouveau squids (and a *tielle*, a little Languedocien fish pie, to take home for lunch). Next door are flats of spring flowers, ready for planting, and across the way the green spectrum of the vegetable stand has been arranged with a master's eye for the maximum effect of colour. There's a touch of colour in the market people too, the rosy flush that comes from spending most of their time outdoors.

The French aren't averse to noise. One thing that distinguishes many villages is the vintage air-raid horns that bellow out from atop the mairie to mark midday (when the market closes), as if to say 'Bon appétit!' If they go off unexpectedly, flattening delicate sensibilities for miles around, it's probably to announce a fire; French villages depend on volunteer firemen, that doughty crew that comes roaring up to your house with lights and sirens ablaze just before Christmas with their calendars (if you give them a donation for the calendar, they'll come to your fire). And every village with an alert *syndicat d'initiative* has wired itself for sound, providing a little canned music to regale shoppers at the market in the busy seasons. You may get accordion music, lukewarm rock, or morose Parisian crooners; in Prayssac, the girls at the SI have grown fond of a tape of Ella Fitzgerald with Chick Webb's band. (Ella got her start with Webb, an excellent drummer; his band spent a lot of time in the Apollo and the Cotton Club in the late 1930s. Edgar Sampson provides the arrangements and sax solos.) They play it all the time, and under the plane trees at nine o'clock, in a French village market, everyone seems to think it hits just right.

The music isn't the only eclectic element. In our market, there's a solemn Dutchman with dirt under his fingernails who sells his organic bok choy and Chinese cabbage, Jerusalem artichokes and spiky African melons. Lots of Dutchmen, passionate gardeners from a space-starved country, come down here for a little tranquillity and a little good earth. An Englishman who grew up here provides sweetcorn in late summer – the best you can get in Europe; the seed came from Pennsylvania. Even some of the French have gone exotic. The space cadet at the natural foods stand will sell you popcorn, Canadian wild rice, bulgar or fat-free nacho chips, and just around the corner a lady with a smile like the first sunny day in April is frying Vietnamese *nems* and samosas. Near the librairie, next to the fellow who's cooking a gigantic paella in a 4ft-wide pan, is the notorious Brit Van, with a sign portraying a tin of Heinz baked beans. You can get your Marmite and Bisto here, or a can of Guinness or some home-made scones.

All this may seem a bit disconcerting, if you're the sort given to fantasies about finding a bit of 'unspoiled' rural heaven in deepest France. If that's what you really want, try the Gers or the Aude, fine *départements* both. But the flagrant cosmopolitanism of many of our village markets has done no harm to their more traditional aspects. One can still pick up live geese, or rabbits and chicks in wooden cages, and farm wives still set up folding tables to sell carefully braided strings of garlic and onions, home-made walnut cakes or delicate-looking but potent discs of *cabécou*. Unless a comet collides with the Earth, you can bet that five centuries from now they'll still be doing it (though maybe by then the list of tradititional southwestern specialities will include sweetcorn and *nems*). Not long ago, on a chilly, drizzling day in early autumn, we saw a thoroughly miserable old farmer, staring blankly out from under a flowered umbrella. A shrewish pinchpenny wife had undoubtedly chased him out in the rain to sell the one treasure he had brought, a sinister-looking courgette the size of a steam boiler, precariously balanced on a wooden box with a sign: *5F/kilo*. Five centuries from now, he'll probably still be there too.

Dances with Bears

Onward the kindred Bears, with footsteps rude,
Dance round the pole, pursuing and pursued.

Erasmus Darwin *(grandfather of Charles), in Economy of Vegetation*

Have you ever wondered why children respond so viscerally to teddy bears? One possible reason is pure atavism: way back in the Middle Palaeolithic or Mousterian culture (c. 120,000–35,000 BC) bears often occupied the same caves and shelters as our ancestors, and perhaps not always as dangerous rivals. In the Grotta della Basura on the Italian Riviera, the chamber dubbed the 'Corridor of the Imprints' has fossilized footprints suggesting that bears and people once danced together; in another room a large quantity of bear bones were discovered. And in the 1950s, just above Lascaux at Régourdou, a ritual bear graveyard was discovered; each dead bear had been given 'gifts' of dead animals (*see* p.127).

In the vivid mural art of the Upper Palaeolithic in southwest France, bears (like people themselves) are rarely portrayed among the bison, horses, aurochs and other favourite animal subjects: there's a fine one engraved in the Grotte de Bara-Bahau in Le Bugue (in a cave where bears lived for tens of thousands of years) and another at Lascaux, hidden in the body of the bull, almost as if it were part of a children's find-the-hidden-picture game. Other drawings and engravings are accompanied by bear claw marks. Most suggestive of all are the carvings on staffs found at La Madeleine (Dordogne) and at Massat (Ariège). Few other Palaeolithic works are as explicitly, and mysteriously, sexual: these staffs are the basis for the idea that some of the mysterious symbols in cave art represent male and female principles. Old Eskimo statuettes, from a culture technologically similar to the Upper Palaeolithic, demonstrate an intimacy with bears shocking by the nursery standards of Christopher Robin and Pooh.

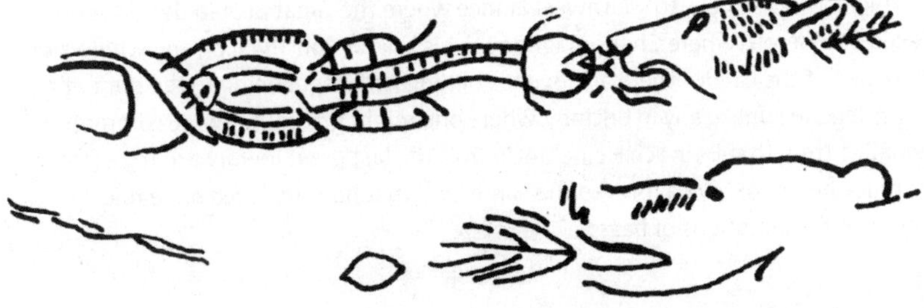

The evidence suggests that our ancestors' relationships with bears were limited to hunting cultures, as in the bear cults that survived into historical times. These were discovered by travellers and scholars in northernmost Japan (the Ainu people) or Siberia, where bears were not only a main source of food and clothing, but were also regarded as the representatives of gods. According to legend, the Ainu descended from the son of a woman and a bear. Ainu hunters apologized profusely when they slew one, and set up bear skulls (where the animal's spirit resides) in a place of honour. When a bear cub was captured, it would be suckled by an Ainu woman and raised with her children until it became dangerous; then for two or three years it would be put in a cage and pampered with delicacies, in preparation for a Bear Festival. Then the bear would be given a huge last meal in a great show of sorrow, as the Ainu apologized and carefully explained to the bear the reasons for sending it to its mountain ancestors. Then it would be ritually strangled and eaten. In commenting on the Ainu in *The Golden Bough*, James Frazer wrote:

> *...the sharp line of demarcation which we draw between mankind and the lower animals does not exist for the savage. To him many of the other animals appear as his equals or even his superiors, not merely in brute force but intelligence; and if choice or necessity leads him to take their lives, he feels bound, out of regard to his own safety, to do it in a way which will be as inoffensive as possible not merely to the living animal, but to its departed spirit and to all the other animals of the same species, which would resent an affront upon one of their kind much as a tribe of savages would revenge an injury or insult offered to a tribesman.*

This may explain why Cro-Magnon hunter-artists made animals vivid, flowing and beautiful, and portrayed themselves as inferior, clumsy stick figures.

Prehistoric relationships with bears may also have something to do with that 'relic of some primeval association of ideas' evident in ancient India and Babylon, in the Book of Job, in Hesiod and Homer and native North American Indian tribes, which have all identified the circumpolar constellation as a bear – the Great Bear, or Ursa Major, which is pursued or watched over by the bright star Arcturus (from the Greek word for bear-keeper). And hence the word for Arctic and Arthur – the early English designated King Arthur's home there in the heavens, and some speculate that the circle, once known as 'Arthur's Wain', described by the stars was the origin of the Round Table. The common English name for the constellation, Charles's Wain, derives from the medieval legendary association of Charlemagne and Arthur.

Which brings us back to southwest France where the Great Bear in the sky is now called a casserole, where Charlemagne took his licks at Roncesvalles, and where along the coast of the Landes there are legends of King Arthur galloping to the hunt at night, legends unlike any in Brittany, where one might guess they were common. It is equally fitting that Heinrich Heine's Atta Troll, the last great literary Bruin (before Winnie-the-Pooh, anyway), roved the same land that has preserved our earliest known representations of bears.

Art Begins Here

Art is art. Everything else is everything else. Ad Reinhardt

Two-thirds of the 115 or so prehistoric decorated caves known in the world are in southwest France. No one will ever know if Upper Palaeolithic art was once as common everywhere, or if the natives of Lot and Dordogne valleys were especially inspired or gifted between 30,000 and 10,000 BC, or if it is only by accident that conditions here were ideal for the preservation of their art – warm valleys with caves rich in sedimentary deposits, that, often thanks to rock slides or other accidents, were long blocked off from light and air.

Created by a people so antediluvian that they are almost impossible to imagine, it is very difficult to look at the works as art in themselves and not as brief, mysterious encounters with another world. Or as P.M. Grand wrote in *Prehistoric Art*: 'The glamour of the sacred is particularly strong in our epoch, which has almost lost sight of the sources of the supernatural. Not to be deceived by this glamour is a major requirement in any investigation of cultures that present to us vastly more questions than answers.' The fact that there may well have been a ritualistic or supernatural motivation behind the drawings and paintings takes nothing away from their aesthetic value; art has always willingly served religion. Forget, too, the Hollywood view of hairy, grunting brutes dragging Raquel Welch around by the hair when they aren't punching dinosaurs; these people were our intellectual equals, with a keen eye for observations, a capacity for abstract or symbolic expression, and imaginative innovations that would take later artists until the 20th century to duplicate. 'This is the infancy of art, not an art of infancy' as the saying goes.

Prehistory itself is a very recent field. Until the 19th century, Upper Palaeolithic artefacts (tools, decorated throwing sticks, carvings in bone or stone, staffs, 'Venuses') were called 'thunderstones', to be dismissed somehow as the 'accompaniments of lightning'. In 1859, the discovery of tools in the same strata as the bones of extinct animals convinced scientists of their great antiquity and led to an increased interest in the field – further fuelled by the publication of Darwin's *On the Origin of Species* the same year. The idea that a stone-tool culture was also capable of the lofty, 'noble' art of painting was much more difficult for many intellectuals. When the first extraordinary murals were discovered in the cave of Altamira in northern Spain in 1879, all but a tiny handful of scholars sincerely believed they were a hoax.

The Doubting Thomases began to change their minds in 1895, with the discovery of the Grotte de La Mouthe in the Dordogne, where along with the paintings and wall incisions a prehistoric lantern was found. A 23-year-old priest named Henri Breuil was invited to trace the drawings, beginning the career of a man now known as 'the father of prehistory'. Once Breuil and his fellow pioneer Denis Peyrony knew what to look for, important discoveries followed quickly; in 1901, the men discovered the reliefs and paintings in Les Combarelles and Font-de-Gaume, both near Les Eyzies. Local children, enthused by the finds in their villages, began to seriously explore the countryside. In 1922 they discovered Pech-Merle in the Lot, in 1940 Lascaux, so magnificent and beautiful that there's the temptation to stand Breuil's description of the cave as 'the Sistine Chapel of prehistoric art' on its head, and say that the Sistine Chapel is the Lascaux of Renaissance art.

One of the many intriguing things about the painted and engraved caves decorated some 16,000 years ago is that they achieve so many of the aims of art in the last half of the 20th century onwards – they suggest far more than they actually show and invite the viewer to participate actively in their meaning; they make admirable use of their environment and the palette that nature presents (bulges in the stone wall give animals a three-dimensional feel, the shadows suggest water, a protrusion becomes the muzzle of a horse); they are not bound as compositions into the artificial rigours of a canvas, much less to any sensation of up and down or north or south. A cave is a natural installation and a natural sanctuary, and it's a shame that Matisse or Joan Miró never had a good crack at one. Most of all, they combine their formal perfection with a function and meaning that, even if the exact nature of it may never be discovered, leaves a powerful and poignant impression even after thousands of years. Nothing means as much or will ever be as immediately close to us as the animal world was to these first artists. The only composition that the 20th century produced that comes close to the powerful impact of Lascaux is Picasso's *Guernica*, a work about new technological advances in death and horror.

Goose Lore and Livers

In the southwest the national bird of France, the strutting cockerel, seems far removed, a symbol rarely seen outside the backyard coop. Instead, visitors are confronted everywhere by giant plywood geese, beckoning clients into tiny shops selling foie gras and confits.

Although it would be heresy to say so in the southwest, the national dish, *confits d'oie*, may have originated in medieval Venice, where one staple was *bigoli con sugo di oca conservato* (fat buckwheat spaghetti with a goose *confit* sauce). In fact, for centuries Périgord pâté was made not of goose, but of partridges stuffed with truffles and chicken livers. In 1726 the partridges got a break when a certain Close de Strasbourg discovered that goose liver with truffles tasted much finer, and the bigger the liver the better. It had already been noted (by the legendary Egyptian savant Imhotep, in 4700 BC) that pigeons that stuffed themselves silly on corn developed swollen, delicious livers, and the concept was extrapolated to geese and ducks (which are much more amenable to *gavage*, or force-feeding). After spending the life of Riley wandering at will in meadows and walnut groves, the geese are fed a three-week adjustment diet of flour, corn, and meat before being enclosed in autumn for three weeks of *gavage* three times a day – traditionally women's work – each bird downing between 66 and 88lbs of corn to create the perfect creamy pink liver weighing up to 3lbs, mostly in preparation for the Christmas holidays and New Year's, when half of

France's foie gras is consumed. Foie gras was also a hit abroad; one of Talleyrand's secret weapons of diplomacy was his chef, who softened up ambassadors and heads of state with pâté de foie gras and a glass of golden Monbazillac.

To the many foreigners (and not a few French citizens as well), *gavage* seems the height of barbarism. They wince at the postcards of geese being force-fed by crafty old women stroking a goose neck with one hand while holding a funnel of corn down its throat with the other; they are horrified that many farms invite visitors to watch, and that many geese willingly waddle over for their corn tipple (they look happier than battery chickens, at any rate). During the Occupation, the Nazis with their delicate sensibilities found the practice offensive and banned *gavage*, with the curious result of making foie gras a proud symbol of the Resistance. In an effort to make *gavage* more humane (but mostly to save the intensive labour involved) attempts have been made to adjust the thymus gland in geese and ducks to make them naturally piggy, but up until now biologically engineered *auto-gavage* has had limited success.

The goose that lays the southwest's golden egg faces an even greater challenge in the form of importers from Romania, Israel and beyond who are flooding the market with phony foie gras, or foie gras incorporating all kinds of fillers, counterfeits that threaten to undermine both the traditional producers and confidence in the product; bad enough that such things happen in Paris, but down here, in the sanctuaries of traditional foie gras, such cheating is blasphemy. Yet anyone passing through the region can't help but notice the disparity between the amount of foie gras on offer, and the actual number of geese and ducks. These days connoisseurs and restaurateurs have to know their sources personally.

But the strange attachment of the area to its fowl fetish goes back centuries before anyone thought to tamper with goose livers. The Basques tell of a race of lovely but goose-footed fairies, the laminak, and Toulouse was the home of the famous Visigothic queen Ranachilde, wife of Theodoric II, *la reine pédauque* or *pé d'aouco*, the goose-foot queen who could swim better than walk and had aqueducts built in Toulouse so she could paddle from her palace to the city. Her story inspired others, like those of Berthe, mother of Charlemagne (d. 783), who was said to have webbed or at least very large feet, and another goosey Berthe, the wife of King Robert the Pious. This couple was excommunicated for a consanguineous marriage, and their incestuous relationship is said to have produced a goose-headed child.

One of the Berthes, at any rate, was customarily represented as a rather domestic queen, telling children tales by her spinning wheel (French tales customarily begin with 'In the time when good Queen Berthe spun...'). Andrew Lang in his researches located the first reference to Mother Goose, *la Mère l'Oye*, in a 1650 book called *La Muse Historique*, predating Charles Perrault's 1697 *Les Contes de ma Mère l'Oye*; in English the first reference to Mother Goose appeared in a fairytale book printed in London in 1729. Perhaps most mysterious of all are the Cagots, a vanished people who lived in the Pyrenees and were said to be albinos, or dwarfs or lepers; in the Middle Ages they were renowned as excellent architects and carpenters, though they were forced to live apart and wear a goose foot around their necks.

The Architecture of Springtime

So it was as though the world had shaken herself and cast off her old age, and were clothing herself everywhere in a white garment of churches.

Ralph Glaber, an 11th-century English chronicler

On a typically rainy autumn afternoon, we saw an old farmer trudging in the mud alongside the road, so we stopped to give him a lift. It turned out he wasn't a farmer at all, despite the beret, overalls and rough-cut walking stick. He was a retired Swiss teacher, and he had decided to spend the rest of his life walking around Europe, looking at Romanesque churches. That made for some good conversation along the way; we compared notes on buildings in Apulia and the Abruzzo, and Templar chapels along the pilgrimage routes in Old Castile. We told him about one unknown church in a tiny nearby village, one with horseshoe arches derived from Muslim Spain and a Celtic spiral carved over the door. He knew about it already.

Such a devotion may seem eccentric, but this fellow was hardly alone. The Romanesque is a bug that bites unexpectedly; no other art and architecture in the West has the same inexplicable capacity to enchant. At first sight, especially if you've been indoctrinated in school, you might think that the products of modern Europe's first artistic urge are mere 'primitives', the first child steps on the way to the Gothic and Renaissance. A closer look reveals an immensely sophisticated art that seems to have sprung, fully formed, out of nothing at the dawn of the Middle Ages. In fact the ideas of Romanesque had been around for a while, breaking out occasionally in unexpected places like Armenia, or Asturias in northern Spain. Only in the tremendous economic upsurge of the 11th century did anyone in Europe really have a chance to build. When they got the chance, they built for the ages, solidly and in good stone. At first sight their works may seem heavy, with the little light that filters through the narrow windows in the afternoon. Not until the late 12th century, with the new Gothic advances, would the technology appear to allow those windows to get bigger. But let your eyes adjust to the shadows for a minute, and you'll see wonders.

'Romanesque', for such a momentous and varied movement in architecture, is as misleading a term as 'Gothic'. Among the few things it has in common with ancient Rome are the use of round arches and a habit of using the basilican plan for churches; large projects, of which the southwest can offer only a few survivors, such as St-Sernin in Toulouse or Ste-Croix in Bordeaux, also often attempt to recapture the monumentality of the Roman manner. But Romanesque has nothing to do with the classical Orders of ancient buildings; rather it depends on a new system of sacred geometry, which probably began with Hagia Sophia in 6th-century Constantinople, and gradually spread across both Europe and the Muslim world. Anyone with a mathematical bent will enjoy looking over the churches or their plans; every point in the ground plans and elevations can be proved with a compass and straightedge, the same way the master masons designed them.

In the springtime of the medieval world, nearly every large region of western Europe developed its own distinctive style. Freedom and fancy were in the air in the 11th and

12th centuries; standards were high and rules few. Provence had its stiff, heavy buildings and octagonal cupolas; the Catalans built similarly, and accentuated their works with elegant towers and brilliant sculpture, while the Auvergne contributed unique patterned façades perhaps inspired by the caliphate of Andalucía. The basic element in Aquitaine is the *clocher-mur*, a west front that rises above the roofline to make a wide belfry, providing a memorable façade and saving the great expense of building a separate tower. There are some eccentricities, like the cave-churches of St-Emilion and Aubeterre-sur-Dronne, cut out of the rock, while Périgord also came up with the most exotic flower of all Romanesque styles, impressive churches with shallow Byzantine domes, an idea brought back from Syria and Palestine after the First Crusade. Many others in Périgord are fortified churches, a testimony to the roughhouse feudal warfare there, though aesthetics may suffer a bit.

Along with the architecture goes its sculptural decoration – the first great age of sculpture since classical Greece. Early medieval society foundthe resources not only to raise all these buildings, but to decorate their portals and columns with a wealth of sculpted detail, even in some village churches. The southwest contributed more than its share, including the most accomplished workshop, the 'School of Toulouse' that created the vibrant, flowing reliefs on the portals of Moissac and Souillac; many consider Moissac's to be the greatest masterpiece of all medieval sculpture.

And what have the French done with this heritage? The Parisian conquest of the Midi and other lands currently French ensured a calculated devaluation of their art and culture. From the Renaissance Italians, the French first learned a rationale for contempt for their greatest buildings, and set off on a path of slavish imitation of the Romans and a submission to academies and rules – a disaster that plagues the national culture to this day. In the philistine 17th and 18th centuries, the tastemakers in the academies considered anything medieval the artistic equivalent of *patois*, especially if it came from the early centuries when the provinces, not Paris, were the vanguard. They spoilt the interiors of thousands of churches, plastering them over with gaudy Baroque frippery and gilded knick-knacks (most of that has been cleared away in the last few decades). There was more to the world of the Romanesque than the Enlightenment ever dreamt of in its philosophy, and in the first days of the Revolution uncomprehending mobs gleefully smashed up some of the finest of medieval sculpture. Casualties included the School of Toulouse's cloisters of St-Sernin and St-Etienne; you can see the surviving fragments in the Musée des Augustins. After the Revolution, scores of churches and monasteries saw duty as barns, warehouses and barracks; many more were simply torn down for their stone.

When the first attempts at restoration were made, the result was often just as unfortunate – the classic example in all France being Paul Abadie's supremely arrogant job on St-Front in Périgueux, in which more was wrecked than restored, while the building was changed out of all recognition. France, surprisingly one of the most backward nations of Europe in historic preservation, has only got its act together in the last few decades. Even in the 1920s, entire cloisters were being sold off or destroyed – a lot of the southwest's best sculpture was purchased for John D. Rockefeller and moved to his Cloisters Museum in Manhattan.

Wandering among the fragments of the early Middle Ages, one often feels like an archaeologist, exploring the enigmatic survivals of a lost civilization. It *is* a lost civilization; we know as little about the inspirations and motivations of early medieval artists as we do about classical antiquity or the Egyptians. The architecture speaks for itself, an inexhaustible vernacular of simple arches, barrel vaulting, pilasters and apses recombined in a thousand different ways. The sculpture is more of a problem; its imagery often reflects concepts that have nothing to do with orthodox religion, or indeed with Christianity at all. Why is the prophet Isaiah dancing at Souillac, and what made the seemingly obscure episode of Daniel in the lions' den the most copied and most significant image in the sculpture of the southwest and Languedoc? And what about the mermaids? In scores of churches around the region, and across Europe, images of mermaids appear in hidden places, sometimes cradling babies, sometimes alone, spreading their forked tails in an unseemly way – any fan of the Romanesque would be reminded of the capital of this strangeness, Italy's Monte Sant'Angelo, where coiled serpents whisper ancient secrets into the mermaids' ears.

The sculpture is the key, though you'll always have to look carefully to find it. When you visit a Romanesque church, even a simple one in a village, scrutinize every corner, inside and out. The great themes of the Life of Christ and the Apocalypse are portrayed for all to see on the portals, but the esoteric bits are in places you wouldn't expect, perhaps to hide them from the casual eye, perhaps in their pride to force us to look all around, and so come to appreciate the work as a whole as they did. The faces are everywhere, especially on the modillons, or corbel-stones around the roofline: hundreds of faces, grimacing, smiling, interspersed with monsters, cats, dogs, boars, unicorns and all the other inhabitants of the medieval imagination. There may be a giant with a club, a dim memory of ancient Hercules, or a fine lady in a small boat (her name is Phaedria, and she symbolizes Desire). On the capitals inside, hunters and lovers, lions and kings stare down at you. The meaning, and even the identity of the characters is often lost to us, though if you could go back to the 1100s a troubadour poet, or a street singer, or a monk with a little Latin might have explained them all. But you can't, and unless you're willing to cut yourself a walking stick and spend the rest of your life at it, travelling and reading and looking, you'll never know.

Cuisine du Terroir

When the French talk about abandoning the charms of nouvelle cuisine for good old country cooking, or *cuisine du terroir*, southwest France is often the first *terroir* that springs to mind. Intensely rural, a land of small traditional family farms, overflowing with the good things of the earth, it serves a hearty *cuisine* of fresh ingredients, so delicious that eating and drinking are two of the most compelling reasons to visit. Indeed, everyone is so pleased with it that it's hard to find a restaurant in the southwest that serves anything else.

The Cuisine of Périgord and Quercy

Yet for all the talk of tradition, the dishes that bring hungry Parisians down *en masse* only date as popular fare from the 19th century; before then, the barons who ruled the land were so rapacious that the peasants' diet was based on red cabbage, chestnuts, turnips, fruit, and fish if they lived near the river, with little meat; hunting was a privilege of the nobility. These days, perhaps to make up for the past, meat is liable to appear in every course except dessert, to the dismay of France's minuscule vegetarian minority. The otherwise calorie- and cholesterol-conscious can take courage from recent studies showing that the basic southwest diet, with all its duck and goose fat ('*sans beurre et sans reproche*', as the great gastronome Curnonsky described it), garlic and red wine, is actually good for you and your heart; heart disease is half the rate it is in the United States. Many natives live well into their nineties.

The best place to tuck into a traditional meal is the *ferme-auberge*, or farm restaurant, one of the delights of southwest France, where most of what you eat has been raised on the spot. A typical meal in a *ferme-auberge* or a good traditional restaurant may start with an apéritif, a kir (maybe with *vin de Cahors* instead of white wine) or a *fenelon* (a delightful cocktail of walnut liqueur, cassis and red wine). Then comes the *tourain* (or *tourin*), an onion and garlic soup cooked in a broth with duck or goose fat and lard, ladled over slices of country bread and cheese. The proper way to finish up the dregs is *faire chabrot*: pour in a dash of red wine, swish it around, and drink it directly from the bowl.

The next dish is generally a pâté, often duck or goose, or *rillons* (the meat left over after preparation of foie gras and *confits*, mixed with a bit of fat to make a smooth paste) or foie gras, the enlarged liver of either a goose or duck (*see* pp.54–5), often studded with a 'black diamond', a bit of truffle it doesn't really need but which jacks the price up even further. Foie gras usually comes prepared in a terrine or half-cooked (*mi-cuit*) in a frying pan, with a bit of lemon or *verjus* (the tart juice of underripe grapes), salt and pepper, white grapes, and served with slices of toasted *pain de campagne* and ideally with a chilled glass of sweet white Sauternes, Loupiac, or Monbazillac. Goose is finer and more delicate; duck is tastier (and cheaper). Other popular starters include a salad of *gésiers*, or gizzards, cooked and sliced, or a plate of charcuterie. In the spring, asparagus often makes an appearance, and sometimes in Périgord you'll see *boutons de scorsonères* – flowers of black salsify – cooked in omelettes. For an autumn delicacy, try an omelette with fresh *cèpes* (boletus mushrooms) or truffles.

Main courses often star yet more duck and goose (and increasingly, believe it or not, ostrich) in the form of *confits*. *Confits* are the southwest's traditional way of keeping meat: thighs, legs, or wings are cooked and then potted in their own fat, and reheated when it's time to eat. *Magrets* (also spelled *maigrets*) are steak-like fillets of duck or goose breast, simply grilled and served with a very light cream sauce with parsley and garlic, or, in the autumn, with fresh *cèpes*. As a fairly recent cut of meat, *magrets* are a fashionable ingredient in new dishes, dressed in fruit sauces, baked in salt, or en croûte. *Cou d'oie*, goose neck stuffed with a truffled minced pork and foie gras, and *demoiselles*, carcasses of fattened ducks grilled on a wood fire, are traditional rural favourites that occasionally make it on to pricey restaurant menus. The duck or goose fat that preserves the confits is the essential ingredient used in the accompanying *pommes de terre sarladaise* – sliced potatoes sautéed in fat, with garlic and parsley, and *cèpes* in the autumn, a combination that lifts the humble spud to culinary heaven (they used to have truffles in them too, back when truffles were still affordable). Another main destination for *confits* is cassoulet, a dish that reaches its epiphany in Toulouse (*see* p.433).

Poultry – free-range Gascon chickens with black feet, or guinea fowl, capon, pheasant and pigeon – is always delicious, occasionally served in a fricassée, in a *ballottine* (a gallatine of rolled poultry and stuffing) or *alicuit*, a traditional Gascon ragoût of poultry giblets (even testicles), wings, potatoes, carrots and onions. Occasionally on the menus of *ferme-auberges* you'll see a *mique*, a dumpling of maize flour cooked in bouillon that was long a staple in old Quercy and Périgord.

Game dishes are few, although there are places that specialize in venison, pheasant, boar and *marcassin* (young boar, served in a *civet* or red wine stew). Beef dishes are fairly rare, outside of *tournedos* in Périgord – fillet of beef accompanied by a rich sauce made with foie gras and truffles. Lamb, especially *agneau de causse*, grazed on Quercy's limestone plateaux, is very popular and prepared in a number of ways (most simply as a *gigot* or leg, roasted with garlic) and served too rare for many Anglo-Saxon tastes. Pork appears in sausages – the omnipresent fat *saucisse de Toulouse*, or thinner chipolatas and spicy merguez – a contribution of the southwest's Spanish immigrants. *Andouillettes* are chitterling sausages; much rarer are pinkish *anguettes*, made with turkey's blood, unappetizing to look at but much appreciated fried in goose fat, with a spoonful of vinegar, garlic, and nutmeg. In the Lot-et-Garonne, pork is often cooked with prunes and wine, in a delicious sweet and savoury combination. Trout, pike (*brochet*, often prepared as *quenelles*, or cakes), and *écrevisse* (crayfish), *sandre* (pike-perch), *alose* (shad) and salmon are the principal fish on the menu, and increasingly you'll see sturgeon, which is delicious smoked (*see* p.118).

The classic salad is made of dandelion leaves (*pissenlit*), or curly lettuce and walnuts, and seasoned with walnut oil, the perfect accompaniment to the most famous cheese of the region, AOC *cabecou* goat cheese rounds from Rocamadour. Another popular cheese from the region is *bleu des Causses*, similar to Roquefort, while the larger weekday markets offer a variety of sheep and cow's milk cheeses produced on family farms.

The locals love their sweets and in some restaurants the desserts are the stars of the show. Traditional specialities often involve walnuts (*tarte aux noix*, walnut tart, *gâteau aux noix*, walnut cake, sometimes coated with bitter chocolate) or prunes (in a *tourtière*, marinated in Armagnac and orange-blossom water and topped with layers of paper-thin pastry called *pastis*, of one part butter to four parts flour). A *flognarde* is a *clafoutis* (batter cake) with pieces of apples, pears or plums; light crispy *échaudés* are flavoured with aniseed liqueurs, *vieille prune* (old prune) or *eau de noix* (made with green walnuts). A *toureau* is a Sunday or holiday bread-like cake in a ring served as a dessert, flavoured with orange-blossom water, lemon, oranges, rum, vanilla and

Grand Marnier, with home-made jam (leftovers are good toasted). Fresh strawberries in season appear in a wide variety of desserts; melons, *pêches de vigne* (peaches grown between vines, now rare), apricots or cherries in Armagnac round off a meal in style.

The Cuisine of the Bordelais

Cross over into the Bordelais and menus take on a whole new cast of ingredients, beginning with the oysters of Arcachon, among the finest in France, traditionally served on the half-shell with buttered bread and little grilled sausages called *crépinettes*. Mussels, *coques* (cockles) and *praires* (clams) are other tasty local shellfish; from the Gironde estuary come *pibales* (tiny baby elvers fried in oil), shrimp, shad (especially as *alose à l'oseille*, stuffed with sorrel and grilled over vine cuttings, which helps dissolve its many fine bones), eels, salmon, salmon trout and, perhaps a bit shocking to the uninitiated, lamprey, a dish so prized that the canons of St Seurin in Bordeaux gave up all their rights to property in the city in 1170 in exchange for 12 good fat lampreys a year (*see* p.245).

If garlic is the totem elsewhere in the Midi, shallots are just as essential to the Bordelais: *à la bordelaise* means topped with a *hachis* of parsley and shallots (but, confusingly, it can also mean accompanied with *cèpes*, or red wine sauce). Chopped shallots attain a kind of epiphany on grilled steaks – the famous *entrecôte à la bordelaise*. A good deal of passion is reserved for *cèpes*, and hunting them in the autumn, especially on someone else's property, leads to huge rows, slit tyres, dog bites and gunshots. There are two kinds: the true *cèpe bordelais* (*cèpe de chêne*) and less tasty *cèpe de pins*. Asparagus, both green and white, is one of the joys of spring in the region, served especially as a starter.

A speciality revived since 1985 is milk-fed lamb, or *agneau de Pauillac*, which holds pride of place among meat dishes along with the beef from Bazas and capons from Grignols; in the autumn, wood pigeon is a favourite dish, although few would countenance the way they are caught – netted a flock at a time in the migrating season. Amongst the sweets, look for *compote de vigneron*, apples melted in red Bordeaux; in the big city itself, try a *canelé*, a delicious pastry made according to a recipe invented by people living around the port of Bordeaux from the remains of flour left in the holds of ships after the main cargoe had been unloaded, then adopted and made popular by the nuns of the Annonciade in the 16th century.

Markets, Picnic Food and Snacks

In most villages, market day is the event of the week, and rightfully so. Brimful of fresh farm produce, and often just as brimful with local characters, they are fun to visit on their own, and become even more interesting if you're cooking or gathering the ingredients for a picnic. In the larger cities they take place every day, while smaller towns and villages have markets just one day a week, which double as social occasions for the locals. Most markets finish up around noon. You'll find that a string bag comes in handy.

Other good sources for picnic food are the *charcuteries* or *traiteurs*, both of which sell prepared dishes sold by weight in cartons or tubs. You can also find counters at larger supermarkets. Cities are snack-food wonderlands, with outdoor counters selling pastries, crêpes, pizza slices, frites, *croque-monsieurs* (toasted ham and cheese sandwiches) and a wide variety of fillings stuffed in long thin crispy baguettes.

Wine

The wine region of Bordeaux, the largest in the world, in the *département* of the Gironde, covers 113,000 hectares and produces 500 million litres a year, enough to launch a battleship. Nearly all of this area is AOC (*appellation d'origine contrôlée*) divided into 57 different *appellations*, including some of the most prestigious in France – Pomerol, Sauternes, Saint-Emilion, Pauillac, Margaux, encompassing about 3,500 red and white *crus*. Each *cru*, or growth results from a unique combination of the soil, climate, location, vine and growers skill. A *premier cru* or *grand cru* is the top of the top, a Château Lafite, Latour, d'Yquem or Ausone that you have to own several oil wells to afford. But even wines not designated as *crus* are now better than ever, thanks to the introduction of new techniques and care.

Similar improvements have been made other AOC wines of the south west – Côtes de Duras, Buzet, Cahors, Bergerac and the sweet white wine of Monbazillac. Many were famous in the Middle Ages, and even preferred to Bordeaux wines, but because they were up river they were denied access to northern markets for centuries – by the Bordelais, of course. If you like to visit wineries or *chais* (a Gascon word meaning the buildings where the wine is stored in oak barrels, before being bottled and laid in the cave or cellar), the ones of the Haut Pays tend to be friendly and easy to get into without reservations for a look around and a taste, often with the proprietor.

Don't neglect the wines with less exalted labels, especially those labelled VDQS (*vin de qualité supérieure*) or *vin de pays* (guaranteed to originate in a certain region – Côtes de Quercy and Vin du Tsar are worth a try), with *vin ordinaire* (or *vin de table*) at the bottom, which may not send you to seventh heaven but is usually drinkable and cheap. *Brut* is very dry, *sec* dry, *demi-sec* and *moelleux* are sweetish, *doux* and *liquéroux* sweet, and *méthode champenoise* sparkling.

If you're buying direct from the producer (or a wine cooperative, or *syndicat*, a group of producers), you'll be offered glasses of wine to taste, each older than the previous one until you are feeling quite jolly and ready to buy the oldest (and most expensive) vintage. On the other hand, many producers (especially in the Haut Pays) sell loose wine à la petrol pump, or *en vrac*; many *chais* even sell the little plastic barrels to put it in. If you want to stock up on loose wine to take home, invest in an inexpensive *cubivin*, a plastic flexible container with a tap, usually housed in a cardboard box; it collapses as you use it and preserves the wine until you get it home and bottle it. *Cubivins* come in various sizes, up to 33 litres; if they're not available in the vineyards, try a hardware or farm store like Gamm Vert.

Travel

05

Getting There

By Air

From the UK and Ireland

The international airports in the region are at **Bordeaux** and **Toulouse**, both of which have direct connections with **London Heathrow** on Air France or **London Gatwick** on British Airways, for about £150 return. You can save money by purchasing your ticket a few weeks in advance, or getting lucky when the rival airlines feel like undercutting each other. Both now also have cheaper flights from **London Stansted** with Buzz, a low-cost subsidiary of KLM, for about £95 return. It can be even cheaper to Toulouse if you don't mind driving an hour from **Carcassonne**: Ryanair fly from London Stansted to Carcassonne's small airport for as little as £60 return, depending on the season. If you're flying from any place but London, it may work out cheaper to fly to **Paris** and catch a domestic flight from there; have your travel agent check both options.

From North America

The only direct flights to southwest France are from **Montréal** on **Air-Transat**, **t** (1877) 872 6728, and **Royal Aviation**, **t** (514) 828 9000 (in France, contact **Nouvelles Frontières**, **t** 05 61 21 74 14), which fly in summer direct to Bordeaux and Toulouse. Otherwise, your best bet is to find a cheap flight to a European hub (**KLM**, by way of Detroit and Amsterdam, is often the cheapest to Toulouse, for instance) and continue from there.

By Train

This is quite pleasant, if sometimes more expensive than the plane, if you do it the nice way, using **Eurostar** for the London–Paris leg of the journey. No matter how you do it, though, you'll have to change trains in Paris (either by metro or taxi), from the Gare du Nord to the Gare Montparnasse or the Gare d'Austerlitz (*see* below). You can order tickets and get information on prices and schedules from Rail Europe Travel Centre, 179 Piccadilly, London W1, **t** 08705 848 848, *www.raileurope.co.uk*; from the Eurostar ticket office 102–104 Victoria St, London SW1, **t** 0990 186 186; at Waterloo International terminal, Ashford international terminal or principal rail stations. In **Australia**: European Travel Office, **t** (02) 92 677 727; in the **USA**: Britain Bound Travel **t** 800 805 8210. Book on-line: *www.eurostar.co.uk*.

The fastest trains from Paris to the southwest are the high-speed **TGVs** (*trains à grande vitesse*), which shoot along at an average of 170mph: the journey from Paris Gare de Montparnasse on the TGV Atlantique to Bordeaux takes 3hrs (for Périgueux, get off at Angoulême and take the connecting bus) then continues to Toulouse by way of Agen and Montauban in slightly under 5hrs. There are also direct trains to Périgueux from Paris Austerlitz, taking around 5hrs. Costs are minimally higher on a TGV, but all require seat reservations which you can make when you buy your ticket or at the station before departure.

Another pleasant way of getting there is by overnight **sleeper** (the slower trains for the southwest all depart from the Gare d'Austerlitz in Paris). Children under four travel free (seat reservations for under fours are 50F); 4–12-year-olds pay half the adult ticket price.

If you plan on making several long train journeys throughout France, look into the variety of **rail passes**; check with the Rail Europe Travel Centre or your nearest French National Tourist Office (*see* p.81). The SNCF also has an agreement with **Avis**, allowing travellers to collect a car at the station at 'preferential prices'; ask when you book your ticket. The **SNCF** website is at *www.sncf.fr*.

By Coach

The cheapest way to reach southwest France, all costs included, is still probably by coach (£96 London–Toulouse return), although under increasing competition from the low-cost airlines. Also, whilst the day-long journey isn't much fun, the coaches do save the hassle of crossing Paris to change trains.

Contact **National Express/Eurolines** at Victoria Coach Station, London SW1, **t** 08705 80 80 80, *www.eurolines.co.uk* (you can't buy tickets on-line). There are at least two journeys a week year round to Cahors, Montauban, Toulouse and Bordeaux, and to Périgueux in summer only.

Airline Carriers

UK and Ireland

British Airways UK **t** 0845 773 3377 (24 hours), *www.british-airways.com*
Dublin **t** 1 800 626 747
France **t** 0825 825 400, *www.british-airways.com/france*

Air France UK **t** 0845 0845 111
France **t** 0802 802 802,*www.airfrance.co.uk*

Buzz UK **t** 0870 240 7070, *www.buzzaway.com*

Ryanair UK **t** 0870 333 1231,
Ireland **t** (01) 609 7881, *www.ryanair.com*

Aer Lingus Belfast **t** 0845 973 7747
Dublin **t** (01) 886 8888, *www.aerlingus.ie*

USA and Canada

Air Canada Canada/USA **t** 888 247 2262, *www.aircanada.ca*

Air France USA **t** 800 237 2747
Canada **t** 800 667 2747

British Airways USA/Canada **t** 800 247 9297

Delta USA **t** 800 241 4141, *www.delta-air.com*

KLM USA **t** 800 374 7747
Canada **t** 800 225 2525

Lufthansa USA **t** 800 399 LUFT, *www.lufthansa.com*
Canada **t** 800 563 5954, *www.lufthansa-ca.com*

TWA USA **t** 800 892 4141, *www.twa.com*

Charters, Discounts and Special Deals

UK and Ireland

Trailfinders, 194 Kensington High St, London W8 7RG, **t** (020) 7937 1234.

Travel Cuts, 295a Regent St, London W1R 7YA, **t** (020) 7255 1944.

Budget Travel, 134 Lower Baggot St, Dublin 2, **t** (01) 661 1866.

United Travel, Stillorgan Bowl, Stillorgan, County Dublin, **t** (01) 288 4346/7.

Try websites such as www.cheapflights.co.uk and www.lastminute.com.

USA and Canada

New Frontiers USA **t** 800 677 0720
Canada, in Montréal, **t** (514) 871 3060, *www.newfrontiers.com*

Travel Avenue USA **t** 800 333 3335, *www.travelavenue.com*

Air Brokers International USA **t** 800 883 3273.

Last Minute Travel Club USA **t** 800 527 8646; Canada **t** 877 970 3500, *www.lastminute club.com*. Annual membership fee gets you cheap standby deals and special rates for major car rental companies in Europe and Europass train tickets.

www.traveldiscounts.com. Members get special rates on flights, hotels and tours .

Student Discounts

Students with ID cards can get reductions on flights, trains and admission fees. Agencies specializing in student and youth travel can help in applying for the cards, as well as filling you in on the best deals.

USIT Campus, *www.usitcampus.co.uk*. 52 Grosvenor Gardens SW1, London, **t** 0870 240 1010; with branches at most UK universities: Bristol **t** (0117) 929 2494; Birmingham **t** (0121) 359 5955; Cambridge **t** (01223) 360 201; Edinburgh **t** (0131) 225 6111; Manchester **t** (0161) 274 3105; Oxford **t** (01865) 242067.

STA Travel, *www.sta-travel.com*. London, 86 Old Brompton Rd, SW7 3LH or 117 Euston Rd NW1 2SX, **t** (020) 7581 4132; Bristol **t** 0870 167 6777; Leeds **t** 0870 168 6878; Manchester **t** (0161) 839 7838; Oxford **t** 0870 163 6373; Cambridge **t** (01223) 366 966 and many other branches in the UK; in the USA, New York City **t** (212) 627 3111; in Australia, Sydney **t** (02) 9361 4966.

Europe Student Travel, 6 Campden St, London W8, **t** (020) 7727 764; non-students as well.

USIT, *www.usitnow-ie*. Aston Quay, Dublin 2 **t** (01) 602 1600; Cork **t** (021) 270 900; Belfast **t** (028) 90324 073; Galway **t** (091) 524 601; Limerick **t** (061) 332 079; Waterford **t** (051) 872 601.

Council Travel, 205 E 42nd St, New York, NY 10017, **t** (212) 822 2700. Specialist in student and charter flights; branches across the USA.

Travel Cuts, 187 College St, Toronto, Ontario M5T 1P7, **t** (416) 979 2406, *www.travelcuts.com*. Canada's largest student travel specialists; branches in most provinces.

By Car

Although the Dover–Calais **ferries** are the most frequent and cheapest, it means going through or around Paris on the abominable *périphérique*, a task best tackled on either side of rush hour. To avoid it and save money on the *autoroutes*, sail instead from Portsmouth, Poole or Plymouth to Caen, Le Havre or Cherbourg; descend by way of the N158/N138 to Le Mans and Tours, and continue on the N10 to Poitiers, from where you can branch off for either Bordeaux, via Angoulême, or Cahors, via Limoges. Another Bordeaux alternative is the *autoroute* A10 from Tours. It's a long day all told, but not difficult, especially if you nap on the ferry; P&O and Brittany Ferries are the main lines. If you're visiting the west end of the region, you could sail to St-Malo (from Portsmouth) or Roscoff (from Cork) and take in Rennes, Nantes, La Rochelle and Saintes, picking up the A10 there towards Bordeaux. If you want to put your car on a **train**, however, the only option in the area is from Calais to Brive and it costs more than it's worth.

Eurotunnel, **t** 0990 35 35 35, *www.eurotunnel.com*, transports cars on purpose-built carriers through the Channel Tunnel between Folkestone and Calais. It is advisable to book in advance although you can just turn up and wait. You will be put on a standby list and given space on a first come, first served basis. There are four departures an hour during peak times. Flexible return tickets start at around £130 if you travel before 7am; the fare is for the car only, regardless of the number of passengers. Check in at least 25mins but no more than 2hrs before departure. Wheelchair users need to inform Eurotunnel staff of their requirements when booking. The British terminal is off junction 11a of the M20, the French terminal off junction 13 of the A16. The journey lasts 35mins.

Drivers with a valid **licence** from an EU country, Canada, the USA or Australia don't need an international licence. A car entering France must have its **registration** and **insurance** papers. If you're coming from the UK or Ireland, the dip of the headlights must be adjusted to the right. Carrying a warning triangle is mandatory; it should be placed 50m behind the car if you have a breakdown.

Car Hire

Look into air and holiday package deals to save money. If you mean to stay three weeks or more, look into the ***Achat-rachat*** system of buying and selling back a new car from Renault, Peugeot or Citroën, booked in advance, with full insurance and warranty. Prices vary widely from firm to firm, and beware the small print about service charges and taxes. In the **USA** try Europe by Car Inc, **t** 800 223 1516; or Renault, **t** 800 221 1052.

Passports and Visas

Holders of EU, US or Canadian passports do not need a visa to enter France for stays up to three months, but everyone else still does. Apply at your nearest French consulate: the most convenient visa is the *visa de circulation*, allowing for multiple stays of three months over a three-year period. If you intend on staying longer, you need a *carte de séjour*, a requirement that may soon be dropped for EU citizens. Non-EU citizens should apply for an extended visa at home, a complicated procedure requiring proof of income, etc. You can't get a *carte de séjour* without this visa.

Getting Around

By Air

The deregulation of the French skies have made for competitive fares, especially if you don't mind flying early or late. **Air France**'s Navette flies every 30mins or so from Paris Orly to Toulouse at 1,200F full economy price, less for people over 60 and under 25, or students under 27. There are other discounts from time to time. Arch-rival **Air Liberté-TATA** has six flights each weekday, fewer on weekends, from Paris (Orly-Sud) to Bordeaux, and 17 flights each weekday to Toulouse; also fewer flights to Agen and Bergerac. For reservations, **t** 0803 805 805 (in France).

Air Littoral links Toulouse and Bordeaux to Italy and other cities in France, often by way of Nice or Montpellier (central reservations, **t** 0803 834 834 in France, **t** (0033) 4 67 20 68 00 from elsewhere).

By Train

For information and reservations on the **French National Railroad** (**SNCF**), contact the stations direct, **t** 0836 35 35 35 (in France), or visit the website at *www.sncf.fr*. From the UK, contact the Rail Europe Travel Centre (*see* p.64). Southwest France has a decent network of trains, although many of the smaller lines have only two or three connections a day, making it rather difficult to see much of the country by rail; in places **SNCF buses** have taken over former train routes. Fares, if not a bargain, are still reasonable, and there are a wide range of **discounts** available, especially if you begin your journey at an off-peak time (*période bleue* or *période normale*, more or less Mon noon–Fri noon, Sat all day, Sun until noon, except on major holidays or summer holidays, or in fact any time when people want to be on the move, when the blue periods shrink accordingly). The old red periods have been eliminated: busy days are now all green or *période de pointe*. In response to complaints about the complexity of the old system, the SNCF has tried to simplify its discounts, but they're still confusing. *See* the grey box below.

Short-distance regional trains are often basic, but long-distance Trains Corails can be delightful when not too crowded. They have snack trolleys and bar/cafeteria cars (the food isn't bad, but it's rather expensive; most stations sell cheaper packed lunches), and some offer play areas for small children.

All tickets must be **stamped** in the little orange machines by the door to the tracks that say *Compostez votre billet* (this puts the date on the ticket, to keep you from using the same one over and over again). Any time you interrupt a journey until another day, you have to re-compost your ticket.

Whether or not you can leave your **luggage** at the station depends on whether or not France is feeling threatened by terrorists. If things have been peaceful, they'll let you use the banks of mechanical lockers (*consignes automatiques*) that spit out a slip with the lock combination when you use them; they take about half an hour to puzzle out the first time you use them, so plan accordingly.

Discount Rail Fares

Billet Séjour If you buy a return or circular ticket and travel at least 1,000km within two months, you get a 25% discount. You have to depart in a *période bleue*.

J30 Book your ticket between two months and 30 days before departure, for nearly 50% off the normal price (not available on lines with supplements).

J8 Book your ticket between a month and 8 days in advance, for about 15% discount (not available on lines with supplements).

Découverte à Deux If two people (related or not) are making a return trip together, they are eligible for a 25% discount in first or second class for journeys begun in blue periods. It also entitles you to a discount if you hire an Avis car from a station, 5% on weekdays and 10% at weekends.

Carte Enfant+ This is issued in the name of a child aged 4–12, costs 350F and allows the child and up to four people who travel with him or her a 50% discount on TGVs and other trains when starting in a *période bleue*. It is valid for one year and allows a discount on Avis car hire.

Découvert Enfant+ This is free, issued in the name of a child aged 4–12, and allows a 25% discount for up to four others on trains departing in a *période bleue*. Again, discount on Avis car hire.

Carte 12–25 Young people aged 12–25, travelling frequently by train, can purchase this card for 270F; it's good for a year and gives 50% discount on travel begun in blue periods.

Carte Découvert 12–25 Young people are eligible for a 25% discount if they buy their ticket in advance and begin travel in a *période bleue*.

Carte Senior People over 60 can purchase a *carte senior* for 290F, valid for a year, offering 50% off blue period travel and 25% at other times, plus 25% when travelling by train abroad if the railway adheres to Rail Plus. Discount with Avis car hire.

Senior Découvert Eligibility for 25% off the journey for those over 60, travelling in *période bleue*. Discount on Avis car hire.

By Bus

Do not count on seeing any part of rural France by public transport. The bus network is barely adequate between major cities and towns (places often already well served by rail) and rotten in rural areas, where more remote villages are linked to civilization only once a week or not at all. Buses are run either by the SNCF (replacing discontinued rail routes) or private firms. Rail passes are valid on SNCF buses and generally coincide with schedules. Private bus firms tend to be a bit more expensive than trains; some towns have a *gare routière* (coach station), usually near the train station, while in others the buses stop at bars or any other place that catches their fancy. Stops are hardly ever marked (although in some areas there are bus stops everywhere, but hardly any buses).

By Car

Unless you stick to the major towns, cycle or walk, a car is the only way to see much of southwest France. This has its drawbacks: high rental rates, quite expensive petrol (though not as bad as in the UK: about 7.5F a litre for regular unleaded at the time of writing), and an **accident** rate double that of the UK (and much higher than the USA). The vaunted French logic and clarity often breaks down completely on the asphalt. Go slow and be careful, especially in country lanes and anywhere in the half-hour before lunch or dinner, when hunger pangs or haste or too many aperitifs can make for risky driving.

Roads are generally excellently maintained, but anything of less status than a departmental route (D-road) may be uncomfortably narrow. **Petrol stations** are rare in rural areas (where they're sometimes connected to supermarkets) and closed on Sunday afternoons and often Monday mornings too. Nearly all serve *super*, *sans plomb* (lead free) and *gasoil* (diesel), the latter much the cheapest. The French have one admirably civilized custom of the road: if oncoming drivers unaccountably flash their headlights at you, it means the *gendarmes* are lurking up the way.

France used to have a rule of giving priority to the right at every **intersection**. This has largely disappeared, although there may still be intersections, usually in towns, where it applies – these will be marked. Watch out for the ***Cedez le passage*** (Give way) signs and be careful. Generally, as you'd expect, give priority to the main road, and to the left on roundabouts. If you are new to France, think of every intersection as a new and perilous experience. Watch out for Byzantine **street parking** rules (which would take pages to explain: do as the natives do, and be especially careful about village centres on market days).

Unless sweetened in an air or holiday package deal, **car hire** in France can be an expensive proposition. Try ADA, **t** 08 36 68 40 02 (in France) or **t** (33) 1 55 46 1999, *www.ada-sa.fr*, which has cars at 99F a day plus 1.45F/km and usual extras.

Speed limits are 130km/80mph on the *autoroutes* (toll motorways); 110km/69mph on dual carriageways (divided highways); 90km/55mph on other roads; 50km/30mph in an 'urbanized area': as soon as you pass a white sign with a town's name on it and until you pass another sign with the town's name barred. Fines for **speeding**, payable on the spot, begin at 600F, but rise rapidly depending on the circumstances, place and speed, and can be astronomical if you flunk the breathalyser (anything more than an *apéro* and a couple of small glasses of wine may take you over). The government is becoming very concerned about the number of fatalities on their roads, so at holidays expect the police to be out. If you wind up in an accident, the procedure is to fill out and sign a *constat aimable*. If your French isn't sufficient to deal with this, hold off until you find someone to translate for you. If you have a breakdown and are a member of a motoring club affiliated with the **Touring Club de France**, ring the latter; if not, ring the police.

By Bicycle

A plethora of tiny rural roads and lack of strenuous mountains make the Dordogne and Lot valleys ideal for a cycling holiday, and a number of companies (*see* list, p.70) are ready to make them even easier by arranging all the hotels along your route and carrying your suitcase for you. French drivers, not always courteous to fellow motorists, usually give cyclists a wide berth; and yet, on any given summer day, half the patients in a French hospital are there from accidents on two-wheeled transport. Wear a helmet. Maps and info are available from the **Fédération Française de Cyclotourisme**, 8 Rue Jean-Marie Jégo, 75013 Paris, **t** 01 45 80 30 21, *www.ffct.org*; in Britain information on cycle touring in France is available from the **Cyclists Touring Club**, Cotterell House, 69 Meadrow, Godalming, Surrey GU7 3HS, **t** (01483) 417 217, *www.ctc.org.uk*.

Air France and British Airways carry bikes free from Britain. From the USA, Canada or Australia most airlines will carry them as long as they're boxed and included in your total baggage weight. In all cases, telephone ahead. Most French trains will carry your bike for free. They are accepted in the luggage racks on TGVs and in the wide areas in Corail coaches if they can be folded or wrapped, with their wheels removed, in special covers available from sport shops such as Decathlon. Otherwise, those trains marked with a bicycle symbol on the timetable should let you put your cycle in the luggage van. SNCF can transport your bike to any location in France for about 300F, within three days.

You can **hire** bikes of varying quality (most of them 10-speed) at some SNCF stations and in major towns and tourist centres. The advantage of hiring from a station means that you can drop it off at another, as long as you specify where when you hire it. Rates run at around 70F a day, with a deposit of 300–400F or credit card number. Private firms hire mountain bikes and better-quality touring bikes by the week.

By *Roulotte*

Several places hire out wooden horse-drawn caravans, or *roulottes*, that sleep up to four for very leisurely exploring of little country lanes. In the Dordogne, you can hire them in Issigeac to explore the Bergerac region, or in Quinsac to visit the Brantôme area: in July and August a week costs 4,600F, in low season prices are as low as 2,890F a week, or 1,300F for a weekend. Book through the Comité Départemental du Tourisme Dordogne-Périgord, 25 Rue Wilson, 24009 Périgueux CEDEX, **t** 05 53 35 50 24, **f** 05 53 09 51 41. In the Lot, you can hire *roulottes* in Aynac from Castel, at the château, **t** 05 65 11 08 02, **f** 05 65 11 08 04, each with a capacity for four adults and a child; or at Serignac from Les Roulottes du Quercy, **t** 05 65 31 96 44.

On Foot

A network of long-distance paths, the ***Grandes Randonnées***, or GRs for short (marked by distinctive red and white signs), take in some of the most beautiful scenery in south-west France. Each GR is described in a Topoguide, with maps and details about camping sites, refuges and ***rando-étapes*** (inexpensive shelters) and so on, available in area bookshops, the larger tourist offices or from the Fédération Française de la Randonnée Pedestre (14 Rue Riquet, 75019, Paris, **t** 01 44 89 93 93). Among the most scenic walking paths are the GR36/6, the Traversée du Périgord, beginning at Angoulème and passing down the Vézère Valley to Cahors; the GR65 Sentier de St-Jacques Cahors–Roncevaux (the southern bit covered in the Cadogan Guide to *Gascony and the Pyrenees*); and the GR8 which follows the Atlantic coast from Pointe de Grave to the Lac de Cazaux. Besides the GRs, each *département* has set up local networks of walking paths through their most scenic regions; the local tourist offices will know them and can tell you which maps and guides you need.

Special Interest Holidays

If you want to combine a holiday with study or a special interest, contact the Cultural Department of the French Embassy, 23 Cromwell Road, London SW7, **t** (020) 7838 2055, or at 4101 Reservoir Road, NW Washington 20007, **t** (202) 944 6400. The Internet is also a rich source of information on specialized theme visits: *www.tourisme.fr* for instance, has a list of unusual and secret ways of seeing the country.

Specialist Tour Operators

Alternative Travel, 69–71 Banbury Rd, Oxford OX2 6PE, **t** (01865) 310 399, **f** (01865) 315 697/8/9. Walking and cycling in the Dordogne, and wine tours in the Bordeaux region.

Andante Travel, The Old Telephone Exchange, Winterbourne Dauntsey, Salisbury, Wiltshire SP4 6EH, **t** (01980) 610 555, **f** (01980) 610 002. Archaeological and ancient history tours to the Dordogne.

Arblaster & Clarke, 104 Church Rd, Steep, Petersfield GU32 2DD, **t** (01730) 893 344, **f** (01730) 822 888. Wine tours of Bordeaux.

Belle France, 15 East St, Rye, East Sussex N31 7JY, **t** (01797) 223 777. Walking, cycling and gastronomic tours in the Dordogne.

Blakes Holiday, Boating, Stalham Rd, Hoveton, Norwich NR12 8DH, **t** (01603) 739 400, **f** (01603) 782 871. Self-drive boating holidays along the waterways of the Dordogne.

Canvas Holidays, 12 Abbey Park Place, Dunfermline KY12 7PD, **t** (01383) 644 000, **f** (01383) 620 075. Guided wildlife tours in the Dordogne.

Crown Blue Line, Crown Travel Ltd, 8 Ber St, Norwich, Norfolk NR1 3EJ, **t** (01603) 630 513, **f** (01603) 664 298. Self-drive cruising along La Garonne, La Baise and Le Lot.

Explore Worldwide, 1 Frederick St, Aldershot, GU11 1LQ, **t** (01252) 760 000. One-week tours mountain biking and rafting in the Dordogne.

Headwater Holidays, 146 London Rd, Northwich CW9 5HH, **t** (01606) 813 333. Cycling and walking tours along the Lot and Célé valleys.

Inntravel, Park Street, Hovingham, York YO62 4JZ, **t** (01653) 628 811, **f** (01653) 628 741. City breaks to Toulouse, cycling tours and riding in the Dordogne.

LSG Theme Holidays, 201 Main St, Thornton LE67 1AH, **t** (01509) 231 713. A French-operated company offering cycling and walking day trips, two-week language courses, painting and drawing, and cookery courses from local chefs in the Dordogne.

Sherpa Expeditions, 131a Heston Rd, Hounslow, Middlesex TW5 ORD, **t** (020) 8577 2717, **f** (020) 8572 9788, *www.sherpa-walking-holidays.co.uk*. Walking and cycling holidays in the Dordogne.

Susi Madron's Cycling For Softies, 2–4 Birch Polygon, Rusholme, Manchester M14 5HX, **t** (0161) 248 8282, **f** (0161) 248 5140. Easy cycling in the Dordogne.

Les Arts Vivants, Château Monferrier, 24330, St-Pierre-de-Chignac, **t** (0033) 5 53 06 75 36, **f** (0033) 5 53 06 08 82. French company running residential holiday courses in the Dordogne, with English spoken, on historical dance, châteaux of the Périgord, weaving, spinning and dyeing.

Practical A–Z

06

Average Maximum Temperatures in °C /°F

	Jan	Feb	Mar	April	May	June
Cahors	11/52	13/55	15/59	17/63	20/68	22/73
Périgueux	10/50	12/54	14/57	17/63	19/66	23/75
Agen	9/48	11/52	15/59	17/63	19/66	23/75
	July	**Aug**	**Sept**	**Oct**	**Nov**	**Dec**
Cahors	26/79	26/79	24/75	20/68	14/57	11/52
Périgueux	25/77	26/79	22/73	18/65	15/59	12/54
Agen	25/77	26/79	21/70	18/65	15/59	10/50

Climate and When to Go

The Aquitaine Basin, shielded from intemperate Continental influences by the Massif Central, has a fairly balmy, humid Atlantic climate, with long hot **summers** broken by heavy thunderstorms.

Early **spring** and late **autumn** usually get the most rainfall—and it can rain for weeks at a time. **Winters** are fairly mild, with only 20–40 days of frost a year, although every 30 years (on average) killer frosts descend: the one in 1956 killed off 95 per cent of the vines; the last one, in 1985, massacred the mimosas.

Of late the weather has been capricious and strange: after five years of drought that produced some of the greatest wine of this century, the autumns of 1992 and '93 saw endless rain and floods, followed by spring-like Januarys and Februarys, and soggy Mays and Junes. In 1996 summer never came; in 1997 April and May were as hot as July, June was as cold and rainy as November, August to October was dry, warm and altogether perfect. December 1999 saw some of the strongest and most destructive storms in France's recent history, ravaging forests around Bordeaux and elsewhere in the country. A hotel we formerly recommended in Petit-Bersac was so damaged it has had to close down, temporarily we hope. You never can tell.

Unless you're coming to learn about the intricacies of preparing foie gras, winter can be a bleak time to visit: hotels, restaurants and sights simply close down, and the skies are often cloudy all day. The first crocuses often show up in January, but, no matter how lovely the weather is, nothing really opens up until the first tourist rush of the year – Palm Sunday and Easter week. May and June, usually warm and not too crowded, are among the best times to visit.

Hot July, August and early September are French school holidays; the southwest is invaded by Parisians and other French as well as thousands of Dutch, German and British holiday-makers. Towns and attractions are crowded, prices rise, and there are scores of village fêtes, fairs, concerts and races.

The region often looks its best in October, when the tourists have gone and everyone is concentrating on the *vendange*; November and December can be dismal, but wild mushrooms, truffles, walnuts and game dishes offer some consolation.

Consulates and Embassies

Australia: 4 Rue Jean-Rey, 75015, Paris, **t** 01 40 59 33 00 (embassy)

Canada: 30 Bd Strasbourg, 31000, Toulouse, **t** 05 61 99 30 16 (consulate; *open Mon–Fri 9–noon*)

Ireland: 4 Rue Rude, 75016, Paris, **t** 01 44 17 67 00 (embassy)

New Zealand: 7 Rue Léonard-de-Vinci, 75116, Paris, **t** 01 45 01 43 43 (embassy)

UK: 353 Bd du Président Wilson, 33073, Bordeaux, Cedex **t** 05 57 22 21 10 (consulate); Victoria Centre, 20 Chemin Laporte, 31000, Toulouse, **t** 05 61 15 02 02 (consulate; *open Mon–Fri 9–noon and 2–5, closed Wed*).

USA: 25 Allée Jean Jaurès, 31000, Toulouse, **t** 05 34 41 36 50 (consulate).

Crime and the Police

Southwest France isn't exactly a high crime area. Isolated holiday homes get burgled, as anywhere else; cars are occasionally broken into or stolen. Generally the police are more annoying than the crooks, especially the mobile *douane* or customs officers; these can turn up anywhere in the interior, and they have nothing better to do than arbitrarily stop cars from outside their *département* and give them the once-over. Report thefts to the nearest *gendarmerie* – not an enjoyable task but the reward is the bit of paper you need for an insurance claim. If your passport is stolen, contact the police and your nearest consulate for emergency travel documents. By law, the police in France can stop anyone anywhere and demand ID; in practice, they only tend to do it to harass minorities, the homeless and scruffy hippy types. If they really don't like the look of you they can salt you away for a long time without any reason.

The **drug** situation is the same in France as anywhere in the West: soft and hard drugs are widely available, and the police only make an issue of victimless crime when it suits them (your being a foreigner just may rouse them to action). Smuggling any amount of cannabis into the country can mean a prison term, and there's not much your consulate can or will do about it.

Disabled Travellers

When it comes to providing access for all, France is not exactly in the vanguard of nations; many Americans who come over are appalled. But things are beginning to change, especially in newer buildings. Contact the **Comité National Français de Liaison pour la Réadaptation des Handicapés**, 236 bis Rue de Tolbiac, 75013 Paris, **t** 01 53 80 66 66, **f** 01 53 80 6667. Hotels with facilities for the handicapped are listed in Michelin's *Red Guide to France*. Also contact **Gîte de France** (main office) for a leaflet on holiday accommodation: Maison des Gîtes de France, 59 Rue St-Lazare, 75439, Paris, Cedex 09, **t** (0033) 1 49 70 75 75, **f** (0033) 1 42 81 28 53.

Specialist Organizations

In the UK

Holiday Care Service, 2nd floor, Imperial Buildings, Victoria Rd, Horley, Surrey RH6 7PZ, **t** (01293) 774 535. For travel information and details of accessible accommodation and care holidays.

Mobility International, 228 Borough High St, London SE1, **t** (020) 7403 5688. Practical advice and information.

RADAR (Royal Association for Disability and Rehabilitation), 12 City Forum, 250 City Rd, London EC1V 8AF, **t** (020) 7250 3222, *www.radar.org.uk*. Publications for every stage of a holiday including planning, transport and accommodation.

Royal National Institute for the Blind, 224 Great Portland St, London W1N 6AA, **t** (020) 7388 1266, *www.rnib.org.uk*. The RNIB Holiday service offers information on a range of issues for the blind and visually impaired and will answer any queries.

Tripscope, The Courtyard, Evelyn Road, London W4 5JL, **t** (020) 8994 9294. Offers practical advice and information on every aspect of travel and transport for elderly and disabled travellers. On request, information can be provided by letter or tape.

In the USA and Canada

American Foundation for the Blind, 11 Penn Plaza, Suite 300, New York, NY 10001, **t** (212) 502 7614, *www.afb.org*. The best source of information in the USA for visually impaired travellers.

Mobility International USA, PO Box 10767, Eugene, OR 97440, **t** (541) 343 1284, **f** (503) 343 6812. Practical advice and information; $20 membership fee.

SATH (Society for the Advancement of Travel for the Handicapped), 347 5th Ave, Suite 610, New York, NY 10016, **t** (212) 447 0027, *www.travel.org/sath*. Advice on all aspects of travel for the disabled, on an ad hoc basis for a $3 charge, or unlimited to members ($45, concessions $25).

In Australia

Australian Council for the Rehabilitation of the Disabled, 24 Cabarita Rd, Cabarita, New South Wales, **t** (02) 9743 2899.

Calendar of Events

February/March

Thurs before Mardi Gras *Fête des Bœufs Gras*, Bazas

Mardi Gras Périgueux

March/April

Late March/early April *Mascarade de Soufflets*, Nontron (even-numbered years)

May

1 Traditional rural fair near St-Aulaye in the Forêt de la Double; also the *Fête de St-Sicaire*, Brantôme

Early in month Flower and strawberry festival, Marmande

2nd weekend *Floralies*, excellent flower show, St-Jean-de-Côle

Usually in May *Fête Folklorique du Grand Fénétra*, Toulouse

Tues before Ascension Thurs *Alors Chante*, five-day festival of French song, Montauban

June

Pentecost Mon *La Ringueta*, traditional games and sports, even-numbered years, Sarlat

Dates vary *Printemps à Cahors*, three weeks of state-of-the-art photographic and video exhibitions with projections on the medieval buildings

Mid-month *Les Epicuriales*, two-week celebration of food, Bordeaux

23 St John's day bonfires, homage to the bull and a week of events, Bazas

July

Late June–early July *Bordeaux Fête Le Vin* (even-numbered years)

Dates vary International folklore festival, two weeks, Montignac

1st Sun *La Félibrée*, Occitan folk festivities, costumes, floats, music and theatre, in a different town in Périgord each year (run by Lo Bornat dau Périgord, 13 Rue Kléber, Périgueux); huge antiques fair, Belvès

Mid-month Blues festival, Cahors; *Festival de la Voix*, Moissac; *Les Estivales*, with markets, concerts, exhibitions, and astronomical observations until the end of the month, Thiviers

14 Big Bastille Day celebrations at Arcachon; regattas on the Dordogne, Bergerac

Festivals

Every single village or town puts on a party at least once a year, usually in honour of its patron saint. These events happen all through the summer, and can be good corny fun. Up go the Christmas lights and flags, the big tables and folding chairs for the feast, and a platform for the band or bands in the main *place* – larger towns can afford both a *bal musette* (accordion waltzes and tangos and French songs for the oldsters) and a local rock band of dubious merit for the teenagers.

There is invariably plenty of *animation* (everything from a local merchant chattering away on a portable microphone, jumping motorcycles, or dogs pulling sleds on wheels to international folklore events). In larger villages, a travelling funfair and/or circus pulls into town for the small fry; there may even be fireworks if the *mairie* has some money to blow.

Food and Drink

Eating Out

Restaurants generally serve between 12 and 2 and in the evening from 7 to 9pm, with later summer hours. In the southwest people tend to arrive early, to have a better choice of dishes, and to get a crack at the specials, or ***plats du jour*** – turn up at 1 for lunch or 8 for dinner and your choice may be very limited. All post menus outside the door so you'll know what to expect; if prices aren't listed, you can bet it's not because they're a bargain. Almost all restaurants have a choice of set-price menus. If you have the appetite to eat the biggest meal of the day at noon, you'll spend a lot less money, especially at pricier places – the best way to experience some of the finer gourmet temples. Eating ***à la carte*** will always be much more expensive, in many cases twice

3rd weekend *Fête de la Madeleine*, lively festival, wine and fun fair at Duras; *Festival de Jazz de Souillac*; Jazz Festival, Montauban
Mid-July–mid-Aug *Festival du Haut Quercy*, Martel
End July Entre-Deux-Mers wine festival, Sauveterre-de-Guyenne
End July–early Aug Theatre festival, Sarlat; *Festival des Nuits Atypiques*, four days of world music in Langon; *Art Lyrique*, opera and recitals in St-Céré and the Château de Castelnau, Bretenoux; Jazz Festival, Andernos

August

1–15 Music and theatre festival at Bonaguil; *Festival International du Mime Mimos*, one of the world's biggest bashes for mimes, in Périgueux (attend at your own risk)
Mid-month Oyster fair, Gujan-Mestras and Arés; jazz, other music and arts festival, Assier; medieval festival, Monflanquin; huge flea market (*brocante*) in Duras; sea festival, Arcachon and Cap Ferret
End of month Festival of the Unusual, every two years, La Tour-Blanche

September

8 Pilgrimage at Rocamadour; music festival, Uzeste
Early–mid-Sept *Piano aux Jacobins*, piano music festival, Toulouse
3rd Sun *Fête du Chasselas*, Moissac; proclamation of the beginning of the *vendanges* by the Jurade, St-Emilion
Mid-month Prune fairs, Agen and Nerac
Third weekend *Journées du patrimoine*, when many private historical monuments open their doors to the public
Late Sept–mid-Oct *Toulouse Les Orgues*, festival of organ music, Toulouse
Last Sun *Fête de la Mongolfière*, Rocamadour: hot-air balloon festival

November

All month Cinema festival, Sarlat
1 Traditional week-long All Saints' fair, La Réole
11 16th-century turkey fair, Varaignes

December

All month *Marchés de gras* (foie gras, fattened duck and goose markets) are held in most towns
Tues afternoons, 2pm *Marchés aux truffes*, Lalbenque

as much; in most average spots no one ever does it.

Menus sometimes include the house wine (*vin compris*), which is usually more than drinkable; in *fermes-auberges* as often as not the bottles or carafes will just keep reappearing until you pass out. If you choose a better wine anywhere, expect a scandalous mark-up. If **service** is included it will say *service compris* or s.c., if not *service non compris* or s.n.c. Some restaurants offer a set-price gourmet *menu dégustation* – a selection of chef's specialities, which can be a great treat. On the other end of the scale, in the bars and brasseries, is the *plat du jour* (daily special) and the no-choice *formule*, which is more often than not steak and *frites*.

A full French meal may begin with an apéritif, hors d'œuvres, a starter or two, followed by the main course, cheese, dessert, coffee and chocolates, and perhaps a *digestif* to finish things off. If you order a salad it may come before or after but never with your main course. For everyday eating, most people condense this feast to a starter, main course, and cheese or dessert. **Vegetarians** will have a hard time in the southwest, but most establishments will try to accommodate them somehow.

When looking for a restaurant, homing in on the one place crowded with locals is as sound a policy in France as anywhere. Don't overlook hotel restaurants, some of which are absolutely top-notch even if a certain red book refuses on some obscure principles to give them three stars. To avoid disappointment, call ahead in the morning to reserve a table, especially at the smarter restaurants, and especially in the summer.

One thing you'll notice in the cities is a growing choice of **ethnic** restaurants, mostly North African (a favourite for their economical couscous – spicy meat and vegetables on a bed of steamed semolina, served with *harisa*, a hot red pepper sauce) or Asian (usually Vietnamese, sometimes Chinese, Thai or Cambodian). There are Italian places, sometimes combined with a pizzeria (the pizza will be all right if there's a proper pizza oven, but with anything else Italian you're taking your chances).

Drinks

Cafés serve drinks, but they are also a home away from home, places to read the papers, play cards, meet friends and just unwind, sit back and watch the world go by. You can sit for hours over one coffee and no one will try to hurry you along. Prices are listed on the *tarif des consommations*: note they go up depending whether you're served at the bar (*comptoir*), at a table (*la salle*) or outside (*la terrasse*).

French **coffee** is strong and black, but lack-lustre next to the aromatic brews of Italy or Spain. If you order *un café* you'll get a small black express; if you want milk, order *un crème*. If you want more than a few drops of caffeine, ask them to make it *grand*. For **decaffeinated**, the word is *déca*; in the summer try a *frappé* (iced coffee). The French only order *café au lait* (a small coffee topped off with lots of hot milk) when they stop in for **breakfast**, and if what your hotel offers is expensive or boring consider joining them. There are baskets of croissants and pastries, and some bars will make you a baguette with butter, jam or honey. If you want to go native, try the Frenchman's Breakfast of Champions: a *pastis* or two, and five non-filter Gauloises. *Chocolat chaud* (**hot chocolate**) is usually good; if you order *thé* (**tea**), you'll get an ordinary bag. An *infusion* or *tisane* is a **herbal tea** – *camomille*, *menthe* (mint), *tilleul* (lime or linden blossom) or *verveine* (verbena). These are kind to the all-precious *foie*, or liver, after you've over-indulged at the table.

Mineral water (*eau minérale*) can be addictive, and comes either sparkling (*gazeuse*) or still (*non-gazeuse* or *plate*). If you feel run-down, Badoit has lots of peppy magnesium in it – it's the current trendy favourite. The usual international commercial soft drinks are available, and all kinds of bottled **fruit juices** (*jus de fruits*). Some bars also do fresh lemon and oranges juices (*citron or orange pressé*). The French are also fond of fruit syrups – red *grenadine* and ghastly green *diabolo menthe*.

Beer (*bière*) in most bars and cafés is run-of-the-mill big brands from Alsace, Germany and Belgium. Draught (*à la pression*) is cheaper than bottled beer. Nearly all resorts have bars or pubs offering wider selections of draughts, lagers and bottles.

The strong spirit of the Midi comes in a liquid form called ***pastis***, first made popular in Marseilles as a plague remedy; its name comes from the Latin *passe-sitis*, or thirst quencher. A pale yellow 90° nectar flavoured with aniseed, vanilla and cinnamon, *pastis* is drunk as an apéritif before lunch and in rounds after work. The three major brands, Ricard, Pernod and Pastis 51, all taste slightly different; most people drink their '*pastaga*' with lots of water and ice (*glaçons*), which help make it more tolerable.

Wine

One of the pleasures of travelling in France is drinking great wines for a fraction of what you pay at home, and discovering new varieties that you've never seen in your local shop. The typical house wines in all three shades of the vinous spectrum, available in all but the snootiest restaurants, are usually very palatable, but if you have your doubts start with just a glass (*un verre*) or the smallest carafe (*pichet*), a quarter-litre. Unless someone else is paying, smart restaurants are the last place to discover new wines, with their prices marked up to triple or quadruple the retail. If you love wine but have to watch expenses, buy it direct from the producers, the *vignerons*. In the text we've included a few addresses for each wine to get you started.

Health and Insurance

The local hospital (*hôpital*) is the place to go in an emergency (*urgence*). If you need an **ambulance** (*SAMU*) dial **t** 15; **police and ambulance, t** 17; **fire, t** 18. **Doctors** take turns going on duty at night and on holidays even in rural areas: **pharmacies** will know who to contact, or else telephone the local SOS Médecins – if

A Guide to Bordeaux Red Vintages

The red wines of one of the largest wine-producing areas in the world are too often categorized under the name 'claret'. This generalization overlooks the wealth of variety to be found in the region, from a Merlot-rich Pomerol to a long-lived, aristocratic St-Estèphe, to a gravelly Pessac-Léognan.

1998: The year initially looked unsuccessful, but Pomerol, St-Emilion and Pessac-Léognan all made marvellous wine, with the Médoc showing greater promise as time goes by.

1997: Soft, charming wines for early drinking, while you wait for the 1996s and 1995s to mature. Initially overpriced, these now offer good value.

1996: Another wonderful vintage – certainly the best since 1990. The Cabernet Sauvignon wines of the Médoc excelled this year, displaying all the attributes of great Bordeaux. The lesser wines are drinking now but the rest should be kept for a couple more years to age majestically.

1995: An outstanding vintage throughout Bordeaux, but particularly in St-Emilion and Pomerol. A very hot summer produced rich, fruit-driven wines that are approachable now but will benefit greatly from cellaring.

1994: Excellent-value wines of good quality that are just approaching maturity. Rain at harvest time prevented this from becoming a truly great vintage, but the wines are very concentrated with sturdy tannins.

1993: A variable year: if a little lighter than an *année de garde*, the most conscientious producers made well-rounded wines with ample fruit for early drinking.

1991: A vintage written off by many critics because of severe frosts in April. However, 1991s have developed into early drinking wines with style and finesse.

1990: Powerful,tannic, fruit-driven wines, with excellent balance. Truly outstanding quality, with many approachable now.

1989: Overall production for this vintage was very high, both in terms of quality and quantity. It was an extremely hot year with rich, deep, opulent wines contrasting with the wonderful, yet more austere, 1988s.

1988: The first of a trio of great years, the 1988s are at an advantage in that they have, in many cases, been overlooked in preference to '89 and '90. They have seriously good ageing potential, possibly lasting longer than the later two vintages, but are still reasonably priced in a market that has seen huge increases.

1985: The rich concentration of fruit enabled many of the wines from this vintage to mature earlier than usual for claret. The top *crus classés* are already proving accessible but further patience will be rewarded.

1983: A delightful vintage, the wines of which are now beginning to open up fully. In comparison to the 1982s, which were highly praised, the 1983s were initially rather overlooked. This is certainly changing now, as the wines show their breeding.

1982: From one of the finest vintages this century, these wines are at their peak now. With rich, luscious fruit, wonderful balance and outstanding concentration. Only the top châteaux will benefit from further keeping.

Reproduced courtesy of Berry Bros & Rudd Ltd, 3 St James's St, London SW1A 1EG, **t** *(020) 7396 9600.*

you don't have access to a phone book or Minitel, dial directory assistance, **t** 12. To be on the safe side, always carry a phone card (*see* 'Telephones', below). If it's not an emergency, pharmacies have addresses of local doctors (including those who speak English), or the nearest outpatient clinic (*services des consultations externes*). Pharmacists themselves are trained to administer first aid, and dispense free advice for minor problems. In cities pharmacies open at night on a rotating basis; addresses are posted in their windows or in the local newspaper. You can ring the doorbell of most rural pharmacies after hours and roust the pharmacist on duty.

Citizens of the EU who bring along their E-111 forms or the equivalent are entitled to the same health services as French citizens. This means paying up-front for medical care and prescriptions; 75–80 per cent of these costs are reimbursed later – a complex procedure for the non-French. As an alternative, consider a travel insurance policy, covering theft and losses and offering 100 per cent medical refund; check to see if it covers extra expenses if you get bogged down in airport or train strikes. Beware that accidents resulting from sports are rarely covered by ordinary insurance. Canadians should check to see if they are covered in France by their provincial health cover; Americans and others should check their individual policies.

Money and Banks

The **franc** is divided into 100 **centimes**. Banknotes come in denominations of 500, 200, 100, 50 and 20F; coins in 20, 10, 5, 2, 1 and ½F, and 20, 10, and 5 centimes. You can bring in as much currency as you like, but by law are only allowed to take out 5,000F in cash although no one ever seems to check. Traveller's cheques or Eurocheques are the safest way of carrying money. The most widely recognized credit card is Visa (*Carte Bleue* in French), which is accepted almost everywhere and will give you cash out of the automatic tellers – as long as you know your PIN number to tap out on the machine . If you plan to spend a lot of time in rural areas, where banks are few and far between, you may want to opt for international giro cheques, exchangeable at any post office.

Banks are generally *open 8.30–12.30 and 1.30–4*; they close on Sundays, and most close either on Saturdays or Mondays as well. **Exchange rates** vary, and nearly all take a commission of varying proportions. Places that do nothing but exchange money (and hotels and train stations) usually have the worst rates or take out the heftiest commissions, so be careful. It's always a good bet to purchase some francs before you go, especially if you arrive during the weekend. France adopted the Euro as official currency in January 1999. The new banknotes and coins will start to appear in 2001 but the old can still be used until the following year. The rate has been set at 6.5595F to 1 Euro.

National Holidays

In France, banks, shops and businesses close on national holidays; some museums also close, but most restaurants stay open. These holidays are:

1 January
Easter Sunday
Easter Monday
1 May
8 May (VE Day)
Ascension Day
Pentecost and the following Monday
14 July (Bastille Day)
15 August (Assumption)
1 November (All Saints')
11 November (First World War Armistice)
Christmas Day

Opening Hours

Most **shops** close down on Sunday and some on Monday. In many towns Sunday morning is when people go to the market. Generally, **markets** (daily in the cities, weekly in villages) are a morning-only affair, although clothes, flea and antique markets can run into the afternoon.

Museums, with a few exceptions, close for lunch, and often on Mondays or Tuesdays, and sometimes for all of November or the entire winter. Most close on national holidays. Hours change with the season: longer summer hours begin in May or June and last through September – usually. Some change their hours every month. We've done our best to include them in the text, but don't be surprised if they're not exactly right. Most give discounts if you have a student ID card, or are an EU citizen under 18 or over 65 years old; most charge admission of 10–30F.

Churches are usually open all day, or closed all day and only open for mass. Sometimes notes on the door direct you to the *mairie* or priest (*presbytère*), where you can pick up the key. If not, ask at the nearest house – they may well have it. There are often admission fees for cloisters, crypts and special chapels.

Post Offices

Known as the **PTT** or ***bureau de poste***, marked by a kind of blue bird on a yellow background, French post offices are open in the cities *Monday to Friday 8am–7pm, and Saturdays 8am until 12*. In villages, offices may not open until 9am and may close for lunch, and shut at 4.30 or 5.

You can receive mail ***poste restante*** at any of them; use the postal codes in this book and it should help your mail get there in a timely fashion. To collect it, bring some ID.

You can purchase **stamps** in tobacconists as well as post offices.

Sports and Activities

All the *départements* publish booklets on the wheres and whens and hows of the sports available in their little realms, and the local tourist offices are also extremely helpful.

Aerial Sports

The cliffs and updraughts especially in the Dordogne and Lot are ideal for **hang gliding** (*parapente*) and **ULMs**, both of which are practised year-round.

You can learn to **parachute**: lessons for beginners (minimum age 15), jumps and gear are available from the Aerodrome de Lalbenque in the Lot (south of Cahors), **t** 05 65 21 00 54; the latter can also take you up in a **glider**, **t** 05 65 22 18 94.

You can look down on the scenery from a **hot-air balloon** (*montgolfière*) from Rocamadour, **t** 05 65 33 71 50, or call Luc Lambert, Libourne, **t** 05 57 74 19 10, or Christian Steisz, Montgolfière du Périgord, La Roque Gageac, **t** 05 53 28 18 58, **f** 05 53 28 89 34 (700F for 30mins or 1,100F an hour).

Another possibility is going up with a pilot in a small three- or four-seater **plane** from the many local airfields scattered around the southwest; rates are a lot lower than you might expect.

Bicycling

Mountain bikes (**VTTs** in French) are very popular in the southwest, and there are a number of places where you can hire them to take off along the specially marked GR hiking and riding paths. Also *see* Travel, pp.68–9.

Contact the cycling centre of each *département* for maps and addresses.

In the Dordogne: Comité Départemental du Tourisme, 25 Rue Wilson, 24009 Périgueux CEDEX, **t** 05 53 35 50 24, **f** 05 53 09 51 41.

In the Lot: Comité Départemental de Cyclotourisme, Labastide Murat, **t/f** 05 65 31 08 02.

Canoeing and Kayaking

Every year, more miles of the southwest's beautiful network of rivers are open to navigation. The Dordogne, the Vézère, the Dronne, the Lot and Célé are justifiable favourites, and operators hire out canoes or kayaks by the week or half-day. You can organize excursions of several days, with returns to base by bus, through UK operators or easily enough in France: each tourist office has lists.

Caves

Speleology, potholing, spelunking – whatever you want to call it, it's very popular, especially in the pocked limestone hills and mountains of the Causse de Gramat in the Lot. For information and keys contact M. Philippe Bonnet at the Comité Départemental de Spéléologie, La Marchande, 46000 Cahors, **t** 05 55 20 99 15.

Fishing

You can fish in the **sea** without a permit as long as your catch is for local consumption. **Freshwater** fishing (extremely popular in this region of rivers and lakes) requires an easily obtained permit from a local club – a *carte vacance* is good for two weeks, between June and September; tourist offices can tell you where to find them. Often the only outdoor vending machine in a town sells worms and other bait.

Ocean-fishing excursions (for tuna and other denizens of the deep) are organized by the day and half-day, arranged in advance; the Arcachon tourist office has numbers.

Gambling

The only **casinos** in this book are in Arcachon and Soulac-sur-Mer, or you can do as the locals do and play for a side of beef, a lamb or VCR in a **Loto**, in a local café or municipal *salle de fête*. Loto is just like bingo, and some of the numbers have names: 11 is *las cambas de ma grand* (my grandmother's legs) and 75, the number of the *département* of Paris, is *los envaïssurs* (the invaders). Everybody plays the **horses** at the local bar with the PMU (off-track betting) outlet.

Golf

You'll find courses at Périgueux, Bergerac, Belvès, Le Bugue and Sarlat (all in the Dordogne); Arcachon, St-Loubès, Lacanau-Océan and Bordeaux (three courses), in the Gironde; Agen, Villeneuve-sur-Lot and Barbaste in the Lot-et-Garonne; at Sauveterre (near Castelnau-Monratier), St-Céré and Lachapelle-Auznac (near Souillac), in the Lot; and also at Toulouse.

Horse-riding

Each tourist office has a list of *centres hippiques* or *centres equestres* that hire out horses. Most offer group excursions, although if you prove yourself an experienced rider you can head down the trails on your own. Each *département* offers treks year-round, at weekends or during the week, with vans organized to take your luggage on ahead and overnight stabling of your horse. The Dordogne has 850km of riding trails; the Lot has 1,500km.

Dordogne: Association Départementale de Tourisme Equestre, 4 et 6 Place Francheville, 24000 Périgueux, **t** 05 53 35 88 88, **f** 05 53 53 42 13.

Lot: Association Départementale du Tourisme Equestre du Lot, BP 103, 46002 Cahors CEDEX, **t** 05 65 35 07 09, **f** 05 65 23 92 76.

Pétanque

Like *pastis* and olive oil, *pétanque* is one of the essential ingredients of the whole south of France, and even the smallest village has a rough, hard court under the plane trees for its practitioners – nearly all male, although women are welcome to join in. It's similar to boules: the object is to get your metal ball closest to the marker (*bouchon* or *cochonnet*). Tournaments are frequent and well attended.

Rugby

Since 1900, rugby, perfectly adapted to the Gascon temperament and physique, has been the national sport of the southwest, and the cradle of most of the players on the national team (although movements to change one of the Six Nations from France to Occitania have so far fallen flat).

Bordeaux, Toulouse and its neighbour Colomiers are among the top teams in France; in some places, especially towards Toulouse, they play heretical 'Cathar rugby' – 13 to a side instead of 15. There's a women's version without tackling called *barette*.

Walking

See 'Getting Around', p.69.

Telephones

Post offices offer free use of a **Minitel** electronic directory; they've done away with most printed directories, and using these slow, cumbersome and complicated technological marvels can be a major nuisance.

Almost all public telephones (except in bars) have switched over from coins to ***télécartes***, which you can purchase at newspaper kiosks, tobacco shops and the post office in 50 *unités* or 120 *unités*.

The French have eliminated **area codes**, giving everyone a 10-digit telephone number, which is all you have to dial within France.

When ringing France **from abroad**, ring **t** 00 33 (the country code) and cut out the first number (in the text this is always '0').

For **international** calls from France, first dial 00, then the country code (UK 44; US and Canada 1; Ireland 353; Australia 61; New Zealand 64), and then the local code (minus any first 0) and number.

For **directory assistance**, dial **t** 12; international directory assistance is **t** 00 33 12 followed by the country code, but note that you may have to wait around for them to ring you back with your requested number.

Tourist Information

A little preparation will help you get much more out of your holiday in southwest France. Check the list of events (*see* pp.74–5) to help you decide where you want to be and when, and book early. If you plan to base yourself in one area, write ahead to the local tourist offices (called either a *syndicat d'initiative* or, more commonly these days, an *office du tourisme*) listed in the text to ask for maps, complete lists of self-catering accommodation, hotels and campsites in their areas, or else contact one of the many agencies in the UK or USA (*see* p.83).

International Tourist Offices

UK: French Government Tourist Office, 178 Piccadilly, London W1V 0AL, **t** 09068 244 123, **f** (020) 7493 6594, *piccadilly@mdlf.demon.co.uk*, *www.franceguide.com*.

Ireland: 10 Suffolk St, Dublin 1, **t** (01) 679 0813.

Australia: BWP House, 12 Castlereagh St, Sydney, NSW 2000, **t** (02) 231 5244, **f** (02) 221 8682.

USA: 16th Floor, 444 Madison Av, NY 10022, **t** (212) 838 7800, **f** (212) 838 7855; 676 N. Michigan Av, Chicago, IL 60611, **t** (312) 751 7800, **f** (312) 337 6339; 9454 Wilshire Bd, Suite 715, Beverly Hills, CA 90212–2967, **t** (310) 271 2693, **f** (310) 276 2835. Nationwide information: **t** 1900 990 0040.

Canada: 981 Av McGill College, No. 490, Montréal, Quebec PQH3A 2W9, **t** (514) 288 4264, **f** (514) 845 4868; 30 St Patrick St, Suite 700, Toronto MST 3A3, **t** (416) 593 4723, **f** (416) 979 7587.

France: Maison de la France, 20 Av de l'Opéra, 75001 Paris, **t** 01 42 96 70 00, **f** 01 42 96 70 11.

Useful Web addresses

There are several excellent websites that provide good general information on the area. Get in touch with a French government tourist office at *www.tourisme.fr*, or try *www.france.com*, *www.beyond.fr*, *www.franceguide.com*, *www.france.com/francescape/top.html*.

For information on accommodation, go to *www.francekeys.com*, or the general site *www.hotelstravel.com*.

For health information, try *www.travelhealth.com*.

Where to Stay

Hotels

Like most countries in Europe, the tourist authorities grade hotels by their facilities (not by charm or location) with stars from four (or four and L for luxury – a bit confusing, so in the text luxury places are given five stars) to one, and there are some cheap but adequate places undignified by any stars at all.

We would have liked to put the exact prices in the text, but in France this is not possible. Almost every establishment has a wide range of rooms and prices – a very useful and logical way of doing things, once you're used to it. In some hotels, every single room has its own personality and the difference in quality and price can be enormous: a large room with antique furniture, a television or a balcony over the sea and a complete bathroom can cost over twice as much as a poky back room in the same hotel, with a window overlooking a parking lot, no antiques, and the WC down the corridor. Some proprietors will drag out a sort of menu for you to choose what sort of price and facilities you would like. Most two-star hotel rooms have their own en suite shower and WC; most one-stars have a choice of rooms with or without. The price-range box below will give you an idea of what prices to expect. The first numbers give the range you'll encounter in 90 per cent of the hotels (there are always exceptions); the second, in parenthesis, the average.

Hotels with no stars are not necessarily dives: their owners probably never bothered filling out a form for the tourist authorities. Their prices are usually the same as those of one-star hotels.

Although it's impossible to be more precise, we can add a few more generalizations. **Single rooms** are relatively rare, and usually two-thirds the price of a double, and rarely will a hotelier give you a discount if only doubles are available (again, because each room has its own price); on the other hand, if there are three or four of you, triples or quads or adding extra beds to a double room is usually cheaper than staying in two rooms. Flowered wallpaper, usually beige, comes in all rooms with no extra charge – it's an essential part of the French experience. **Breakfast** (usually coffee, a croissant, bread and jam for 25F–60F) is nearly always optional: you'll do as well for less in a bar. As usual, rates rise in the holidays and

Hotel Price Ranges

Note: all prices listed here and elsewhere in this book are for a double room.

★★★★ luxe	1,400–3,000F (2,000F)
★★★★	550–1,500F (900F)
★★★	300–600F (400F)
★★	180–390F (280F)
★	140–250F (200F)

summer, when many hotels with restaurants will require that you take half-board (*demi-pension* – breakfast and a set lunch or dinner). Many **hotel restaurants** are superb and described in the text; non-guests are welcome. At worst the food will be boring, and it can be monotonous eating in the same place every night when there are so many tempting restaurants around. Don't be put off by obligatory dining. It's traditional; French hoteliers think of themselves as innkeepers, in the old-fashioned way. In the off-season board requirements vanish into thin air.

Your holiday will be much sweeter if you **book ahead**, especially from May to October. July and August are the only really impossible months; otherwise it usually isn't too difficult to find something. Phoning a day or two ahead is always a good policy, although beware that hotels will usually only confirm a room with the receipt of a cheque covering the first night (not a credit card number). Tourist offices have complete lists of accommodation in their given areas or even *départements*, which come in handy during the peak season; many will even call around and book a room for you on the spot for free or a nominal fee.

Chain hotels (Climat, Formula One, etc.) are in most cities, but always dreary and geared to the business traveller more than the tourist, so you won't often find them in this book. Don't confuse chains with the various umbrella organizations like **Logis et Auberges de France** (*www.logis-de-france.fr*), **Relais du Silence** (*www.relais-du-silence.com*) or the prestigious **Relais et Châteaux** (*www.relaischateaux.fr*) which promote and guarantee the quality of independently owned hotels and their restaurants. Their Internet sites provide useful information on the hotels and offer on-line booking. Many are recommended in the text. Larger tourist offices usually stock their booklets, or you can pick them up before you leave from the French National Tourist Office. Other **Internet** sites you can try are *www.globe-market.com*, which gives access to the French Hotel Guide and *www.chateauxandcountry.com* for castles.

If you plan to do a lot of driving, you could take the English translation of the French truckers' bible, ***Les Routiers***, an annual guide with maps listing reasonably priced lodgings and food along the highways and byways of France (about £1, Routiers Ltd, 25 Vanston Place, London SW6 1AZ, **t** (020) 7385 6644).

Bed and Breakfast

In rural areas, there are plenty of opportunities for a stay in a private home or farm: look for *chambres d'hôte*, often listed separately from hotels with the various *gîtes* in the tourist office brochures (*see* below). Some are connected to *ferme-auberge* restaurants, others to wine estates or a château; average prices are in the 250F-a-night range for a double with breakfast, and payment is almost always in cash only. Local tourist offices can provide you with a list.

Gîtes de France and Other Self-catering Accommodation

Southwest France offers a vast range of self-catering accommodation, from inexpensive farm cottages to history-laden châteaux and fancy villas. The Fédération Nationale des Gîtes de France is a French government service offering inexpensive accommodation by the week in rural areas. Lists with photos for each *département* are available from the French National Tourist office, from most local tourist offices, or in the UK from the official rep: Gîtes de France, 178 Piccadilly, London W1V 9DB, **t** 0891 244 123. Prices range from 1,000 to 3,000F a week, depending very much on the time of year, location and facilities; nearly always you'll be expected to begin your stay on a Saturday. Many *départements* also have a second (and usually less expensive) listing of *gîtes* in a guide called *Cléconfort*.

The **Sunday papers** are full of options, and, increasingly, the **Internet**, which allows you to get in direct contact with the owners. Or try one of the firms listed on the next page. The accommodation they offer will nearly always be more comfortable and costly than a *gîte*, but the discounts holiday firms offer on the ferries, plane tickets, or car rentals can make up for the price difference.

Youth Hostels

Most cities have youth hostels (*auberges de jeunesse*) which offer simple dormitory accommodation and breakfast to people of any age for around 50–80F a night. Most offer kitchen facilities as well, or inexpensive meals. They

Self-Catering Organizations

Companies are springing up offering information and on-line booking only. Try *www.francedirect.co.uk*, who have a large selection of cottages and villas.

In the UK

Allez France, 27 West St, Storrington, Pulborough, West Sussex, RH20 4DZ, **t** (01903) 748 155. Wide variety of accommodation from cottages to châteaux.

Angel Travel Ltd, 34 High St, Borough Green, Sevenoaks, TN15 8BJ, **t** (01732) 884 109. Villas, *gîtes* and flats in Aquitaine.

Bonnes Vacances, Vincent House, Vincent Lane, Dorking, Surrey, RH4 3JD, **t** (01306) 876 876, **f** (01306) 875 875. Villas, cottages, flats.

Bowhills, Mayhill Farm, Mayhill Lane, Swanmore, Southampton, SO32 2QW, **t** (01489) 877627. Farmhouses, watermills, châteaux and cottages in the Dordogne.

Bridgewater Travel, Ackerley House, Roe Green, Worsley, Manchester, M28 2JL, **t** (0161) 703 3003.

Dominique's Villas, 25 Thames House, 140 Battersea Park Rd, London, SW11 4NB, **t** (020) 7738 8772. Large villas and châteaux with pools, etc. in the whole region.

French Affair, 5–7 Humbolt Rd, London, W6 8QH, **t** (020) 7381 8519. Cottages.

French Life Holidays Ltd, Kerry House, Kerry St, Horsforth, Leeds, LS18 4AW, **t** (01132) 390 077. Self-catering in the Dordogne.

Gîtes de France, Brittany Ferries, The Brittany Centre, Wharf Rd, Portsmouth, PO2 8RU, **t** (023) 9289 2200, *www.gites-de-france.fr*.

Holiday in France, 3 Lower Camden Place, Bath, BA1 5JJ, **t** (01225) 310 623. Cottages, farmhouses, châteaux.

Inghams/Just France, Gemini House, 10–18 Putney Hill, London SW15 6AX, **t** (020) 8780 4488, **f** (020) 8780 7705. Self–catering, villas, cottages, apartments, farmhouses and châteaux, many with pools.

Something Special Holidays, Bull Plain, Hertford, Herts, SG14 1DG, **t** (01992) 557 755. Villas, châteaux and *manoirs* throughout the whole region.

Sunselect Villas, 217 Monton Rd, Eccles, Manchester, M30 9PN, **t** (0161) 707 8279. Villas, cottages and private pools.

VFB Holidays Ltd, Normandy House, High St, Cheltenham, GL50 3FB, **t** (01242) 240 310. Gîtes, cottages and flats.

In the USA

At Home Abroad, 405 East 56th St, New York, NY 10022, **t** (212) 421 9165.

Drawbridge To Europe, 5465 Adams Rd, Talent, **t** (888) 268 1148.

Hideaways International, 767 Islington St, Portsmouth, NH 03801, **t** (603) 430 4433.

Overseas Connections, Long Wharf Promenade, PO Box 2600, Sag Harbor, NY 11963, **t** (516) 725 9308.

Prestige Villas, 1140 Post Road, Fairfield, CT 06430, **t** (203) 254 1302.

Rent A Home International, 7200 34th Av, NW. Seattle, WA 98117, **t** (206) 789 9377.

Villas International, 950 North Gate Drive, Suite 205, San Rafael, California 94903, **t** 800 221 2260, **f** (415) 499 9491, *www.villasintl.com*.

are the best deal for people travelling on their own; for people travelling together a one-star hotel can be just as cheap. Another down side is that most are in the most ungodly locations – in the suburbs where the last bus goes by at 7pm, or miles from any transport at all in the country. In the summer the only way to be sure of a room is to arrive early in the day. Most require a Youth Hostels Association membership card; you can usually buy these on the spot, although the regulations say you should buy them in your home country.

UK: YHA, Trevelyan House, 8 St Stephen's Hill, St Albans, **t** 0870 870 8808, *www.yha.org.uk*.

USA: AYH, 733 15th St NW, Suite 840, **t** (202) 783 6161, **f** (202) 783 6171, *www.hiayh.org*.

Canada: CHA, 1600 James Maysmyth Dr, 6th floor, Gloucester, Ottawa, Ontario K1B 5N4, **t** (613) 237 7884.

Australia: AYHA, 60 Mary St, Surry Hills, Sydney, New South Wales 2010, **t** (02) 9261 1111, *www.yha.com.au*.

Another option in cities is the single sex dormitories for young workers, ***foyers de***

jeunes travailleurs et de jeunes travailleuses, which will rent out individual rooms if any are available for slightly more than a youth hostel.

Gîtes d'Etape and *Refuges*

A ***gîte d'étape*** is a simple shelter with bunk beds and a rudimentary kitchen set up by a village along GR walking paths or scenic bike routes. Again, lists are available for each *département*; detailed maps mark them as well. In the mountains similar rough shelters along the GR paths are called ***refuges***, most of them open summer only. Both charge around 50F a night.

Camping

Camping is a very popular way to travel, especially among the French themselves, and there's at least one campsite in every town and village, often an inexpensive, no-frills site run by the town itself (*camping municipal*). Other campsites are graded with stars like hotels from four to one: at the top of the line you can expect lots of trees and grass, hot showers, a pool or beach, sports facilities, and a grocery, bar and/or restaurant, and prices rather similar to one-star hotels. Camping on a farm is especially big in the southwest, and is usually less expensive than organized sites. If you want to camp wild, it's imperative to **ask the permission of the landowner** first, or risk a furious farmer, his equally furious dog and perhaps even the police.

Tourist offices have lists of campsites in their regions, or, if you plan to stay in the Dordogne, you can peruse the web (*www.finest.tm.fr/dordogne-camping*, e-mail *dordogne-camping@finest.tm.fr*). If you plan to move around a lot, the *Guide Officiel Camping/Caravaning* is available in most French bookshops.

Houseboats

You can spend a week or a half-week in the summer on a wide variety of houseboats on the river Lot and Canal Latéral de la Garonne. You don't need a boat licence, and the biggest firm, Safaraid, also hires out bicycles and canoes to make your cruise complete. Write to them at 297 Rue St-Géry, 46000 Cahors, **t** 05 65 35 98 88, **f** 05 65 35 98 89. Other firms are listed in the text.

The Dordogne: Northern Périgord

07

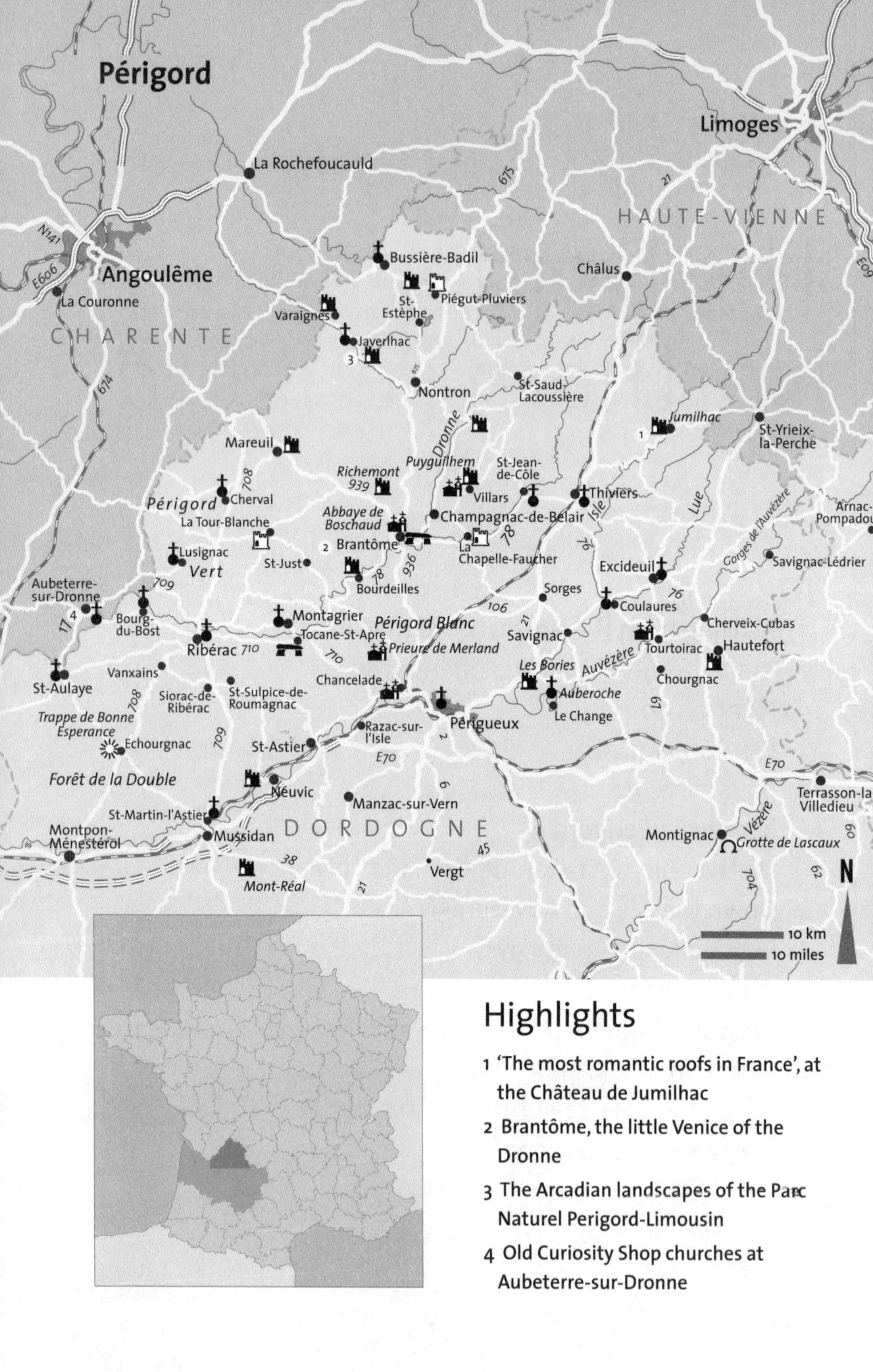

Highlights

1 'The most romantic roofs in France', at the Château de Jumilhac

2 Brantôme, the little Venice of the Dronne

3 The Arcadian landscapes of the Parc Naturel Perigord-Limousin

4 Old Curiosity Shop churches at Aubeterre-sur-Dronne

Petra si ingratis, cor amicis, hostibus ensis
Haec tria si fueris Petra-cor-ensis eris

(A stone to the unpleasant, a heart to the friendly, and iron to the enemy/
If you're all three, then you're a Périgourdin)

Périgord, the old region more or less synonymous with the *département* of the Dordogne, is at once the gateway to greater southwest France and a region with a strong character of its own. Cross its frontiers from the north and simple words like *vin* and *pain* turn into *vaing* and *pang*, the menu fills up with dishes based on duck, goat cheese and walnuts, there's a warmth in the air and in the colour of the very stones. To this add Périgord's unique qualities, its truffles, troubadours and love of medieval domes, its lush green colour and forests, carved by a dozen rivers of exceptional beauty, and you have a countryside as Arcadian as an eclogue, 'the nearest thing to Paradise this side of Greece', as Henry Miller wrote. Ironically, this Paradise is the result of long centuries of war and poverty and neglect. So is much of the architecture that so delights visitors today – nearly a thousand castles and fortified churches, and medieval villages with black stone (*lauze*) roofs and farmhouses that no one ever had the wherewithal to improve.

If Périgord could make a wiseguy from Brooklyn go sloppy, there must be something to it. In fact, so many people agree with Miller that the likes of neo-fascist Jean-Marie Le Pen can complain that what the English couldn't conquer in the Hundred Years' War, they are buying up like crazy in the last few decades. Périgord fulfils a communal dream for a comfortable place, a simpler, rural world of beauty and pleasure. These days the main danger Périgord faces is that of any place that has kept its integrity: of tourism destroying precisely the 'real, authentic' thing it seeks.

The name Périgord comes from the Gaulish nation known as the Petrocorii ('the four tribes'), who according to Caesar sent 6,000 troops to aid Vercingetorix in his final defeat against Rome. From the days of the Vikings to the end of the 16th century, it was governed by counts who make Dracula look like the Queen Mother. Under them, Périgord was subdivided into four baronies (Mareuil, Bourdeilles, Beynac and Biron) which survived until the Revolution, when they were combined to form a single *département*, the third largest in France and renamed after its biggest river, the Dordogne. This first chapter covers the northern section, what is commonly called Green Périgord (after the trees) and White Périgord (after the stones); later chapters take in the great valley of the Dordogne – most of Black Périgord (after either its truffles or the deep shadows cast by its oaks) and the recently designated Purple Périgord, purple, that is, after its wine.

Arriving from the North: Périgord Vert

It was Jules Verne who dubbed northern Périgord 'Green', where deep forests, shady rivers and green limestone hills remain luscious even in midsummer. The region contained in the triangle formed by the three towns of Périgueux, Angoulême and Limoges is now protected as part of the Parc Naturel Régional du Périgord-Limousin.

Getting Around

Two **bus** lines cross this area, one run by CFTA (**t** 05 53 08 43 12) linking Angoulême, Mareuil, Brantôme and Périgueux twice a day, once on Sunday, and the other run by Citram, running twice a day during the week between Angoulême, Mareuil and Ribérac. If you're taking the Bordeaux **train** from Paris, Angoulême is the stop nearest towns in the Dordogne.

Tourist Information

Mareuil: Place des Promenades, **t** 05 53 60 99 85.
Nontron: 5 Rue de Verdun, **t** 05 53 56 25 50.
Varaignes: Château Communal, **t** 05 53 56 35 76. Enquire here about visits to local mills, textiles, slippermakers, and the old royal marine cannon works.

Market Days

Nontron: Wed and Sat.

Where to Stay and Eat

Mareuil ✉ 24340

***__Château de Vieux Mareuil__, Route Angoulême-Périgueux, **t** 05 53 60 77 15, **f** 05 53 56 49 33 (*moderate*). A delightful hotel in a 15th-century castle, set in a 50-acre park, with a 19th-century vegetable garden. The views from the pool are luscious, and the restaurant matches the view (*menus from 160F*). *Closed Oct–April.*

***__L'Auberge de L'Etang Bleu__, **t** 05 53 60 92 63, **f** 05 53 56 33 20 (*moderate*). It overlooks the local, sometimes crowded swimming hole: a blue lagoon in the woods (*menus from 120F*).

Monsec ✉ 24340

Beauséjour, just south of Vieux Mareuil on the D939, **t** 05 53 60 92 45, **f** 05 53 60 72 38 (*cheap*). A Logis hotel-restaurant which, despite its position on a main road, offers comfy rooms and a good, quite busy restaurant, serving southwest food such as *magret de canard au miel et vinaigre à la framboise* (*menus 65–150F*). Terrace overlooking a garden. *Closed Fri night and Sat Oct–Easter.*

La Gonterie ✉ 24310

Le Coudert, south on the D939, **t** 05 53 05 75 30 (inexpensive). Look for signs to the village of La Gonterie and this ivy-covered, charming *chambres d'hôte* belonging to Madame Magrin, a lovely, very friendly lady who will welcome you into her home. From 2001 she will have three bedrooms, two at least with antique furniture and huge bathrooms. The garden has a wild edge to it and is crammed with flowers. *No dinner Sun eve; closed Jan.*

Nontron ✉ 24300

__Grand Hôtel Pelisson__, 3 Place Agard, **t 05 53 56 11 22, **f** 05 53 56 59 94 (*inexpensive*). A traditional hotel in the centre, with rooms equipped for the disabled, an inner courtyard and pool and the best restaurant in Nontron, serving excellent, filling food; note the certificate from Napoleon III dated 1867, proclaiming the inn the official provider of foie gras to the imperial table (*menus 85–260F*). *Closed Sun eve in winter.*

***__Hostellerie St-Jacques__, towards Limoges in St-Saud-Lacoussière (✉ 24470), **t** 05 53 56 97 21, **f** 05 53 56 91 33 (*moderate*). A charming place to stay, with a naff garden but a heated pool and tennis, and a good restaurant (*menus from 120F*). *Closed Sun evening and Mon out of season, and mid-Oct–Mar.*

Varaignes ✉ 24300

Auberge du Vieux-Château, **t** 05 53 56 31 31, **f** 05 53 60 50 87. Set in a restored barn in the centre, this has a good choice of reasonable menus (*65F, lunch only, to 165F*), with a nice choice of classic and regional dishes, all with wine and coffee *compris*. *Closed Mon eve and Tues out of season, and three weeks in the winter.*

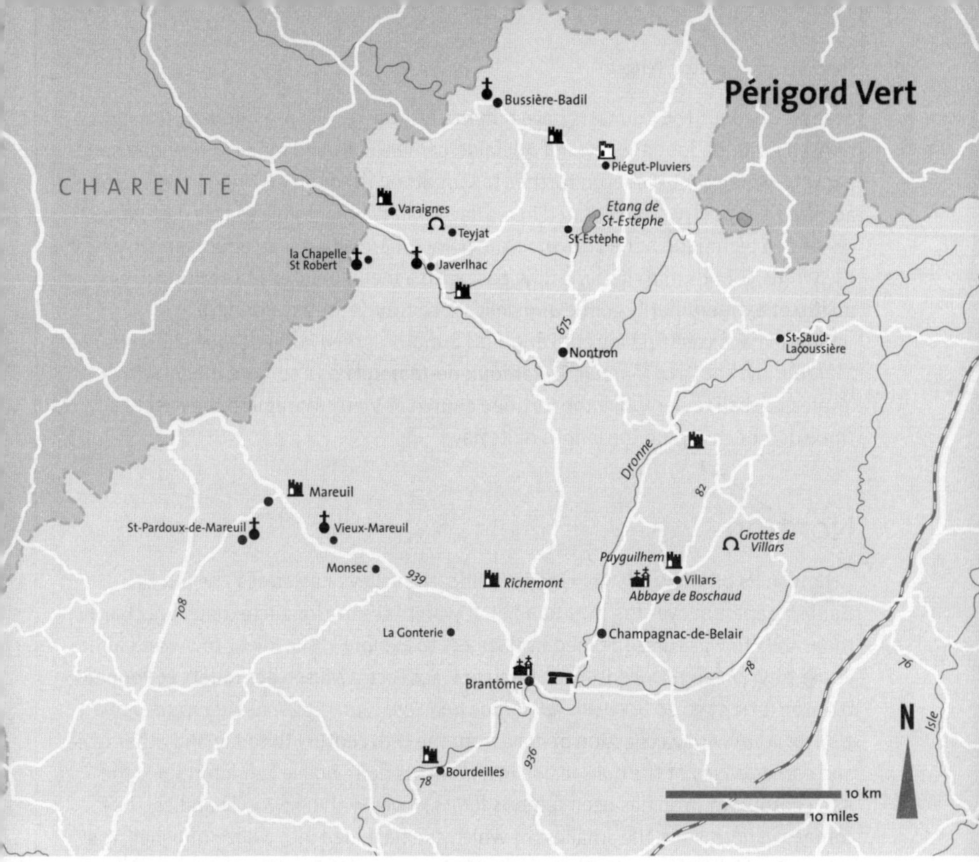

The charter which established the Parc in March 1998 stated the government's aim of developing opportunities and wealth for the local population whilst preserving the area's natural heritage and culture. If you're driving down to the southwest, you may find you have no desire to go any further.

Mareuil-sur-Belle and its Château

If you take the A10 motorway or N10 south to Poitiers, continue south through Angoulême and aim southeast for Périgord, you'll enter the *département* of the Dordogne by way of the ancient fief of the barons of Mareuil. These had their seat at the 15th-century **Château de Mareuil** (***t** 05 53 60 74 13; open April–June 10–12 and 2–6, closed Tues and Sun morning, July and Aug 10–1 and 2–6.30, Sept–mid-Oct 10–12 and 2–5.30, mid-Oct–Nov 2–5, Dec–Mar Sun 2–5.30, closed Tues and Sun morning; adm*), confidently built on a plain and defended by moats filled by the waters of the Belle; inside is a flamboyant Gothic chapel, the dungeons, and Louis XV furniture.

Mareuil was also the home of the troubadour Arnaud de Mareuil, son of a poor castle workman. Arnaud fell deeply in love with the lovely Countess Adélaïde of Béziers, but kept his passion secret by hiring a *jongleur* to sing his love songs. Eventually one of Arnaud's lyrics gave him away, but rather than scorn her humbly-born troubadour, the Countess gave him many gifts – until King Alfonso of Aragón, himself a troubadour and lover of Adélaïde, came to call, and made her send Arnaud packing. Dante sent him even further, to Purgatory, although his only sin was to be admired. His poetry, so celebrated in his day, is nearly impossible to translate, 'the result of a technique honed down to the point where all signs of effort vanish, where the words, sounds and rhythms flow past with a mellifluous ease, resulting in a poetry of extraordinarily gentle and delicate beauty' (Anthony Bonner).

You can have your first look at Périgord's famous domed Romanesque churches near Mareuil: just south of Mareuil, **St-Pardoux-de-Mareuil** has a sombre model with an impressive bell tower, while the fortified church at **Vieux Mareuil** to the east has three domes crowning the length of its nave.

Nontron

High on its promontory, Nontron (in Celtic, 'the valley of ash trees') began as a Gaulish oppidum over the river Bandiat. It won't take too long to exhaust its charms: there are a few picturesque medieval streets to explore in the lower town, and in the upper town, in an 18th-century château in Place Fort, a **Musée des Jouets et Poupées D'Anton** (***t*** *05 53 56 20 80; open April–June and Sept 2.30–5.30, July–Aug 10.30–1 and 2–6.30; adm*) with a collection of dolls from the 18th century to today, and other toys and games. Many of the dolls reside in a fabulous doll's house 22ft long. Since the 15th century Nontron has been famous for its knives with boxwood handles. They come in various sizes, the smallest of which can be folded into a hazelnut shell. You can see and buy them at **La Coutellerie Nontronnaise** (*33 Rue Carnot,* ***t*** *05 53 56 01 55*). These days the town makes a better living from manufacturing neckties and porcelain for Hermès of Paris, examples of which are exhibited and can be bought at the shop on Route de Piégut, 500m north of the tourist office.

In even-numbered years, in late March or early April, Nontron is invaded by the *souffla-culs* (whistle-arses), a hysterical custom dating back to the 13th century. Dressed in nightshirts and nightcaps, the *souffla-culs* march through the streets, squatting here and there to blow their whistles up the nightshirt of the person in front while chanting: 'We are all children of one family; our father was a whistle-maker. No, you're not going to see the colour of my gaiters. No, you're not going to see the colour of my stockings.' The procession ends up with the judgement and fiery death of a dummy symbolizing Carnival.

Around Nontron, on the Limousin Frontier

If you aren't around in time for the *souffla-culs*, other peculiarities, especially geological, await in the countryside north of Nontron, off the D675: eroded formations like the **Roc Poperdu** 3km north, and, another 5km north, the huge **Roc Branlant**, which supposedly rocks when touched. This is set above a stream where a picturesque spill of granite boulders is known as the 'Devil's Chaplet'. Get there by way of the **Etang de St-Estèphe**, a wooded lake with a sandy beach, a favourite retreat in the summer. Further north, the striking, cylindrical 70ft **Donjon de Piégut** stands isolated on a spur, a last memory of the castle wrecked by Richard the Lion-Heart in 1199. A bit further north, where the tip of Périgord is wedged between the Charente and Limousin, detour to medieval **Bussière-Badil** to see its beautiful, fortified 12th-century church of **St-Michel**, a hotchpotch of local Romanesque styles: Limousin in the octagonal bell tower and the flat pendentives under the dome; Charente in the animal and foliage sculptures on the arches of the porch; Périgourdin in the capitals and dome. The whitewashed interior is as impressive as a basilica, although the nave is curiously misaligned with the apse and the walls and columns aren't exactly plumb straight – hence the buttresses added later to keep the thing from falling over. In summer it makes a beautiful setting for a series of concerts.

West of Nontron, on the Limousin frontier, is **Varaignes**, a village that has won an award for its restorations, especially of its 15th-century **château** (sadly minus its magnificent flamboyant portal, sold in the 1920s to an American). The château now houses the **Atelier-Musée des Tisserands et de la Charentaise** (***t*** *05 53 56 35 76; open July and Aug daily 9–12 and 2–6, Mar–June and Sept–Nov daily exc Tues 2–5, Dec–Feb weekends only 2–5*) where you can learn all about the local weaving and textile industries, and in particular how to make the famous (in France anyway) thick and comfy slippers *charentaise*. In nearby **Teyjat**, the **Grotte de la Mairie** (*reserve at Font de Gaume,* ***t*** *05 53 06 86 00; open July and Aug Sat 10–6*) has prehistoric engravings of animals from the late Magdalenian period, discovered back in 1889, only a few years after the findings of the first Cro-Magnon skeletons at Les Eyzies. The old *mairie* has an exhibition in one of its rooms of findings from the cave. South of Varaignes, the 12th-century **church** at **La-Chapelle-St-Robert** is, like Bussières, in a mix of styles, with a dome and lovely bell tower; inside, the apse is supported by sculpted capitals. In the nearby sister village of **Javerlhac**, the older inhabitants keep their ancestral Occitan alive. There is a 13th-century abbey church, a château from the 1400s with a great tubby tower, and the Versailles of all *pigeonniers*, with niches for 1,500 birds.

Brantôme

The main roads from Mareuil and Nontron lead south to Brantôme, a charming town of medieval and Renaissance houses built on an island in the river Dronne. Inhabited since Gaulish times, it has an abbey founded by Charlemagne in 769; he endowed it with the relics of St Sicaire, a slave of Herod who converted to Christianity after participating in the Massacre of the Innocents. Sacked by the Normans in the 11th century, the abbey was rebuilt beside the river against a steep bank. During the Hundred Years' War, it was defended by the barons of Bourdeilles, and it survived the Wars of Religion thanks to one of their descendants, Pierre de Bourdeilles (1540–1614), *abbé* of Brantôme, known in French literature simply as Brantôme.

Brantôme became abbot at the age of 22, and used the abbey's revenues to finance his escapades as a soldier of fortune and lover of court ladies: he accompanied Mary Stuart to Scotland, visited Morocco, Portugal and Venice, and planned an expedition to Peru, only to be frustrated by the Wars of Religion. He rendered a genuine service to his abbey by keeping the Huguenots at bay, diplomatically appealing to the Protestant leader – an old companion-in-arms from his army days. But Brantôme was never content in his role as a churchman, and when Henri III vetoed a promotion the furious Brantôme decided to go to Spain and fight against France, only to be gravely injured falling off his horse. Thus prevented from committing treason, he spent the rest of his life convalescing while writing gossipy, spicy accounts of the people of his time, especially the *Vies des hommes illustres et des grands capitaines* and the scandalous *Vies des dames galantes*, all so true that he left instructions for his heirs to wait 50 years before publishing them, to make sure all his subjects were dead. He is remembered in town with a bust, overlooking the pool of the Fontaine Médicis.

The Abbey

t 05 53 05 80 63; open April–June and Sept 10–12.30 and 2–6, closed Tues; July and Aug daily 10–2; Feb, Mar and Oct–Dec 10–12 and 2–5, closed Tues; closed Jan; adm.

A charming 16th-century dogleg bridge with a Renaissance pavilion, built by a dreamy abbot to watch the reflections in the river water, crosses from the island town to the white pile of the abbey. The 11th-century church, after suffering a string of bad luck and reconstructions, was given the coup de grâce when it was handed over to the 19th-century architect-restorer Paul Abadie, who was never one to preserve when he could rebuild. Only the detached **bell tower** (the oldest in France),

Getting Around

A shuttle Citram **bus** links Brantôme and Périgueux to Angoulême four times a day, linking up to the TGV train to Paris.

Tourist Information

Brantôme: Pavillon Renaissance, **t** 05 53 05 80 52, **f** 05 53 05 80 52. Ask them about walking paths in the vicinity, where to hire mountain bikes, pleasure trips on the river, and canoe trips down the Dronne.

Market Days

Brantôme: Fri; also farmers' market Tues in July and Aug, and truffle market Fri Dec–Feb.

Where to Stay and Eat

Brantôme ✉ 24310

*****Moulin de l'Abbaye**, 1 Route de Bourdeilles, **t** 05 53 05 80 22, **f** 05 53 05 75 27 (*moderate*). Just outside the centre on the Dronne, this dreamy, romantic, ivy-covered hotel-restaurant is spread among several buildings—a converted water mill with a working wheel, a carpenter's house and a *curé*'s residence, set in a delightful garden. The kitchen serves exquisite dishes based on local ingredients, topped off with luscious dessert soufflés (*menus begin at 240F*). *Closed Nov–April.*

*****Hôtel Chabrol**, 57 Rue Gambetta, **t** 05 53 05 70 15, **f** 05 53 05 71 85 (*moderate*). In a handsome old white building right on the river Dronne, this excellent, elegant restaurant serves generous portions of favourites such as *millefeuille de ris de veau au foie de canard et truffe*, as well as wonderful hot desserts, to be ordered at the start of the meal (*menus 165F–500F*). *Closed Sun eve, Mon, 15 Nov–15 Dec and most of Feb.*

****Périgord Vert**, 6 Av de Thiviers, **t** 05 53 05 70 58, **f** 05 53 46 71 18 (*inexpensive*). Another stylish place to stay, this ivy-swathed building is a reliable Logis de France hotel (*meals start at 95F*).

*****Domaine de la Roseraie**, on the Angoulême road at Les Courrières, **t** 05 53 05 84 74, **f** 05 53 05 77 94 (*moderate*). A Relais du

with its Merovingian base, pyramid roof and complex tiers of windows and arches from the 11th century, attests to the abbey's former grandeur. The church lost its dome back in the 13th century, when the Angevins remodelled it; after the Abadie treatment, only a bas-relief of the *Massacre of the Innocents* under the porch and a carved capital, used as a font, survived from the original church. Of the cloister, rebuilt in the 16th century, only one gallery remains. The best bits are the curious *grottes et fontaines sacrées* in the cliff behind the abbey – caves, quarries, shelters, the fountain of St Sicaire, once a pilgrimage site, and the striking Grotte du Jugement Dernier, where the 15th-century monks carved striking reliefs of the *Last Judgement* and the *Crucifixion*.

The abbey has a **museum** filled with the paintings of Fernand Desmoulin, born in Nontron in the 1830s, a friend of Zola and follower of spiritualist Allan Kardec. In this world Desmoulin was known for his portraits of great men like Victor Hugo; in the Beyond, painting in complete darkness with the aid of a medium, he produced strange works in a completely different style.

Besides a stroll through the town and a possible visit to the new **Musée Rêve et Miniatures** (*8 Rue Puyjoli, **t** 05 53 35 29 00; open April–June and Sept–mid-Nov 2–6, July and Aug 10–6; adm*) where a meticulous collector has assembled historic interiors for Lilliputians, there's the ivy-covered **Peyrelevade dolmen**, 1km east of Brantôme on the road to Thiviers, the best preserved of many megalithic monuments in the area, even if it is supported by a crutch of blocks.

Silence hotel, outside the centre. It's set in the middle of a rose garden with seven old-style but well-equipped rooms, a pool, and tennis and riding nearby, as well as a restaurant (*prices start at 169F*). *Closed mid-Nov–mid-Mar.*

Chez Mérillou, Rue A. Maurois, **t** 05 53 05 74 04 (*cheap*). A very pleasant bed and breakfast.

Au Fil de l'Eau, 21 Quai Bertin, **t** 05 53 05 73 65. They offer a good *115F menu*; try the *filets de perche rôtis au ris crémeux et aux amandes. Closed Mon eve and Tues out of season and two months in winter.*

Le Vieux Four, 7 Rue Pierre de Mareuil, **t** 05 53 05 74 16. Set in a cave, they serve some of the best pizzas in Périgord (*about 100F*).

Resto-Grill, 40 Rue Gambetta, **t** 05 53 05 86 25. A stroll away from the tourist hub, they offer quite simple meals in a pleasant, intimate atmosphere. You can eat on a shaded terrace (*menus at 85F and 120F*).

Champagnac-de-Belair ✉ 24530

★★★★**Moulin du Roc**, **t** 05 53 26 86 00, **f** 05 53 54 21 31 (*expensive*). On the Dronne northeast of Brantôme. They offer spacious, beautifully furnished rooms in a charming old mill, with a pool and tennis courts in the grounds, and superb breakfasts; the restaurant does wonders with traditional Périgourdin recipes (*lunch menu 170F, other menus from 245F*). *Closed Jan–Feb, also Tues and Wed lunch.*

Villars ✉ 24530

Le Relais de l'Archerie, Route de Brantôme, **t** 05 53 54 88 64, **f** 05 53 54 21 92 (*inexpensive*). In a little 19th-century château, with small but nice country rooms and a good restaurant, featuring *magrets* and country omelettes (*menus from 80F*). *Closed weekends in Oct–Mar and for a month out of season.*

Bourdeilles ✉ 24310

★★★**Château de la Côte**, at Biras, southwest of the centre on the D106, **t** 05 53 03 70 11, **f** 05 53 03 42 84 (*moderate*). The 15th-century château is lost in the middle of an immense park. There are 14 beautiful rooms furnished with antiques; plus pool, billiards, tennis and helipad, golf, riding, and canoeing nearby. *Restaurant menus start at 160F. Closed mid-Nov–mid-Mar.*

Around Brântome: Richemont, Château de Puyguilhem and Villars

In 1564–8, Brantôme built his **Château de Richemont** to the northwest, in St-Crépin de Richemont; he wrote most of his works here, and declared in his will that no matter what, his family was never to sell it off, but to keep it in his memory. So they have, and have recently opened it for visits. You can see the great man's bedroom and the chapel, where he lies buried under the epitaph he composed (***t** 05 53 05 72 81; open mid-July–Aug 10–12 and 2–6; adm*).

Périgord claims to have a thousand and one châteaux, and of that number, the most splendid is the Renaissance **Château de Puyguilhem** (***t** 05 53 54 82 18; open May, June and Sept till 6.30, July and Aug 10–7, Mar–April and Oct–Dec 10–12.30 and 2–5.30; closed Mon, and Jan and Feb; adm*), northeast of Brântome near Villars. Built in 1524 by the first president of the *Parlement* of Bordeaux, Mondot de la Marthonie, its roofline forest of richly carved dormers and chimneys is as impressive when viewed from within – it looks like the hull of a ship. Saved from total collapse in the 1930s, Puyguilhem has been refurnished with period pieces and Renaissance tapestries; the jewel is the chimney beautifully sculpted with the *Labours of Hercules*.

From Villars, the D82 continues 3km to the **Grotte de Villars** (***t** 05 53 08 80 83; open April and Oct 2–6.30, May, June and Sept 10–11.30 and 2–6.30, July–Aug 10–6.30; adm*), the largest underground network in the Périgord, with 13km explored to date. Unlike most caves in the Dordogne, this combines natural art – brilliant white translucent stalactites and draperies – with prehistoric drawings in magnesium oxide, dating way back to the Aurignacian period (30,000 BC). The authenticity of the blue outline of a galloping horse and 'sorcerer' was confirmed by the dense layer of concretions formed over the pictures. Two kilometres from Villars, out in a meadow, stand the impressive ruins of the chapterhouse and cloister with curiously asymmetrical arches of the **Abbaye de Boschaud** (1154–9), one of four Cistercian foundations in Périgord.

Bourdeilles

From Brantôme, take the lovely D78 and D106/E2 7km southwest along the Dronne for Bourdeilles, seat of the oldest of Périgord's four baronies, so old that the first barons lived back in fairytale times, when they slew griffons and transported themselves to Jerusalem and back by means of an ointment extracted from a dragon's ear. Their **château** (***t** 05 53 03 73 36; open daily exc Tues April–June and Sept–Oct 10–12.30 and 1.30–7, July and Aug 10–7, Feb, Mar, Nov and Dec 10–12.30 and 1.30–5.30; closed Jan; adm*), guarding the frontier between English Guyenne and France, stands in a commanding position over the river, next to a medieval bridge and quaint boat-shaped water mill. In 1259, St Louis ceded Bourdeilles to the English, but not all members of the baronial family agreed to the switch in allegiance, and they built the magnificent octagonal keep, 111ft high which nevertheless failed to keep the English out. In 1376 Du Guesclin took the castle back for France. Brântome was born here, in 1540, and the adjacent Renaissance château was built by his wealthy and widowed sister-in-law, Jacquette de Montbron. Jacquette had invited Catherine de' Medici to visit, and the old medieval keep simply wouldn't do, nor would she trust an architect, but designed the château herself – as far as we know, she was the only woman in the 16th century to do so.

The tour includes both the keep with its four vaulted levels and 9ft-thick walls, and views from the top that make the long slog up worthwhile, as well as the refined château, richly furnished with 16th- and 17th-century furniture from Spain and Burgundy donated by the collectors who oversaw the château's restoration in 1962. Jacquette worked especially hard on her sumptuous **Salon Doré**, its ceiling beautifully painted by Ambroise Le Noble, a member of the Mannerist Fontainebleau school. But when Catherine de' Medici and her Flying Squadron (*see* p.187) swooped through Périgord, she snubbed Bourdeilles, and the furious Jacquette abandoned the building. Amongst the furnishings and paintings, note the 16th-century German *Dormition of the Virgin*, and Burgundian tomb of Jean de Chabannes, the gilt Spanish bed of Emperor Charles V and a tapestry showing his arch rival, François I, with his falconers.

Northeast Périgord

Green and peaceful and full of happy cows, this corner of Green Périgord manages to stay aloof from most of the tourist madness; in the winter the roads are often perfectly deserted.

Up the Côle, to St-Jean-de-Côle and Thiviers

To the east of Brântome, the D78 follows the little river Côle; one of the first villages you'll pass, **La Chapelle-Faucher**, sleeps peacefully on its hill with the ruins of its château, burned a century ago, and its church with a pretty portal, all belying the horrible massacre that happened here in 1569, when the Protestant Amiral de Coigny massacred 300 Catholics, an act avenged three years later by Catherine de' Medici,

Tourist Information

Thiviers: Place Foch, t 05 53 55 12 50.

Market Day

Thiviers: Sat. Tues in the summer, small farmers market. Sat mornings Nov–Mar, *marché au gras*.

Where to Stay and Eat

St-Jean-de-Côle ✉ 24800

St-Jean, **t** 05 53 52 23 20 (*inexpensive*). This simple but sweet place is the only hotel in the town centre.

Doumarias, west on the D78, towards St-Pierre-de-Côle, **t/f** 05 53 62 34 37 (*inexpensive*). A lovely, serene *chambre d'hôte*, in an enormous and well-furnished 16th-century house; there's a quiet courtyard to dawdle in, and inexpensive meals available too (*evening meal from 85F*). *Closed Oct–Mar.*

Auberge du Coq Rouge, in the main square, **t** 05 53 62 32 71. In a 16th-century house, this old-fashioned restaurant is a local favourite, serving sumptuous Périgourdin cuisine at reasonable prices (*menus from 88F; children's menu for 60F*). *Closed Wed and mid-Oct–Easter. Best to book.*

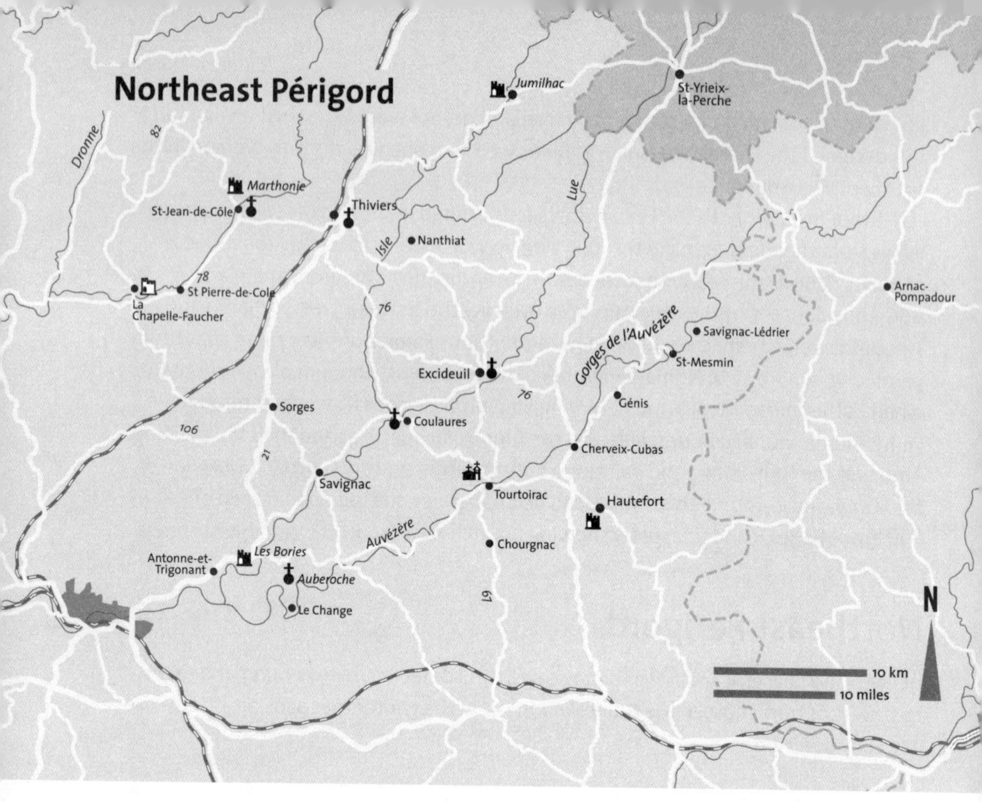

who made sure he was a target of the St Bartholomew's Day massacre in Paris. Northeast, **St-Jean-de-Côle** is as pretty a village as you could ask for, gathered on the banks of the Côle, spanned here by a Gothic humpback bridge, each house crowned by a steep tile roof. It was a busy place in the Middle Ages; the Templars were here, and in the 12th century the inhabitants built themselves a domed church. No one knows how the secrets of dome building were passed on, but in St-Jean they bungled it so often that they settled in the end for a less precarious wooden roof. The bell tower has some delightful carvings, especially one of God modelling Adam out of clay. St-Jean's handsome 15th-century **Château de la Marthonie** was remodelled by the same Marthonie responsible for Puyguilhem; inside is a **Museum of Paper** (*t 05 53 62 30 25; open July and Aug 10–12 and 2–6.30; adm*), with ads and posters.

More excellent Romanesque awaits 7km west in the 12th-century church of **Thiviers**. Built over Merovingian foundations, it boasts a Renaissance porch and capitals sculpted with stone monsters, Samson killing a lion, and Jesus giving St Peter the keys to the kingdom; among the statues there's an unusual *Angel and Vagabond*. Thiviers pays tribute to the goose that lays its golden egg, or rather contributes its gorged liver, at the **Musée de l'Oie et du Canard**, **Maison du Foie Gras** (*t 05 53 55 12 50; open all year; times vary but usually 10–12 and 2.30–5; adm*). Opposite the Maison de la Presse is a **plaque** commemorating Jean-Paul Sartre, who spent his miserable early childhood and summer holidays in the house here with a grandfather who for 40 years refused to speak to his wife because she had no dowry – probably the inspiration for

Sartre's famous remark that 'Hell is other people.' If Sartre hated Thiviers (he wasn't very kind in *Les Mots*), Thiviers returned the favour, and the plaque was only put up after a bitter fight between the *mairie* and the association of *Les Amis de Sartre*.

Around Thiviers: Jumilhac-le-Grand

North and east of Thiviers, the ferny forested frontier of the Limousin is the least populated area in Périgord. Here, like Sleeping Beauty's forgotten castle, at the top of a boulevard, stands the **Château de Jumilhac** (***t*** *05 53 52 42 97; guided tours June–Sept 10–7, night visits possible, Oct–mid-Nov and mid-Mar–April 2–6.30, mid-Nov–mid-Mar by appointment only ; adm*). Antoine Chapelle, the brain behind it, was a master of forges who made such fine cannons for Henri IV that the king knighted him and gave him a former Templar stronghold. Chapelle converted it into a fantasia of towers, turrets and chimneys coiffed with blue slate pepperpots ('the most romantic roofs in France', according to Gustave Doré, who borrowed them for some of his fairytale engravings) topped with an equally fantastic array of forged-iron decorations. Right angles are rare inside as well as out. The Chambre de la Fileuse, built into the thickness of the wall, has naïve murals imitating tapestries, painted for the lady whose portrait is over the door and who had nothing to do but spin when her jealous husband confined her here. The fairy tale of Rumpelstiltskin comes to mind, and indeed the cellars hold a **Musée de l'Or** (***t*** *05 53 52 55 43*), a museum of gold, including pieces in their raw state discovered in the nearby Gallo-Roman mines at Fouilloux.

South of Jumilhac and east of Thiviers, there's some fine countryside along the upper reaches of the river Isle, especially around the D67. **Nanthiat** has a château with a pair of pepperpots of its own, and a handsome Romanesque church, with a rare altar cross in front. Those with a palaeontological bent may be interested in the dinosaur footprints at **La Ferme aux Dinosaures**, La Gironnette, near Savignac, off the D76. The prints are genuine, from about 200 million years ago (***t*** *05 53 62 10 33; open July and Aug Wed and Sun afternoons; adm*).

Down the Isle and Auvézère

After Jumilhac the river Isle loops down to pick up the waters of the Auvézère just before Périgueux. In the 1500s this little mesopotamia was full of iron forges, one of which remains in the wooded gorges of the Auvézère. This is the country of the battling troubadour Bertran de Born, and of fungi worth their weight in gold: truffles.

Excideuil and Around

The busiest market town in the region, Excideuil once belonged to the *vicomtes* of Limoges, who built its vertiginous fortress on a *butte* of Jurassic limestone, a redoubt that three times repelled Richard the Lion-Heart. Its former priory church has a Flamboyant portal and 17th-century retable and overlooks **Place Bugeaud**, named for a local aristocrat who conquered Algeria in the 1840s, and gave the town a fountain.

Getting Around

No trains here, but **buses** link Excideuil and Hautefort to Périgueux and Brive.

Tourist Information

Excideuil: 1 Place du Château, **t** 05 53 62 95 56, **f** 05 53 62 04 79.
Hautefort: Place Marquis Jacques-Françoise de Hautefort, **t** 05 53 50 40 27.
Sorges: **t/f** 05 53 46 71 43.

Market Days

Excideuil: Thurs; medieval market during the weekend closest to 14th July.
Hautefort: Wed.
Sorges: Fri. Truffle market in Jan.

Where to Stay and Eat

Excideuil ✉ 2 4160

****Hostellerie du Fin Chapon**, 3 Place du Château, **t** 05 53 62 42 38 (*inexpensive*). Ten comfortable old-fashioned rooms; well-prepared menus (*from 60F*).

Génis

***Relais St-Pierre**, **t** 05 53 52 47 11, **f** 05 53 62 49 91 (*cheap*). A convenient roadside base for exploring the gorges of the Auvézère, with good and filling food to top you up after a long day's rambling (*menus from 95F*).

Cherveix-Cubas ✉ 24390

****Le Favard**, in the village centre (4km from Hautefort), **t** 05 53 50 41 05 (*inexpensive*). A nice hotel surrounding a round pool, with a popular restaurant; delicious *tourain, pâté de foie gras truffé, country ham, confit de canard*, walnut salad, cheese and home-made dessert.

Sorges ✉ 24420

*****L'Auberge de la Truffe**, N21, **t** 05 53 05 02 05, **f** 05 53 05 39 27 (*moderate*). This excellent, long-established place has had a facelift and a pool, solarium and billiards room have been added. Rooms look out over the garden. The restaurant specializes in truffles, as well as rather less pricey delights (*menus from 80–330F*). *Closed Sun eve.*

****Hôtel de la Mairie**, Place de la Mairie, same phone (*inexpensive*). Managed by Jacqueline Leymarie, the owner of L'Auberge. Cosy, recently renovated rooms.

Antonne-et-Trigonant ✉ 24420

*****Hostellerie de l'Ecluse**, Route de Limoges, **t** 05 53 06 00 04, **f** 05 53 06 06 39 (*moderate*). Attractive rooms, most with a balcony of their own, and a fine restaurant serving memorable dishes such as *suprême de magret de canard aux framboises* (*menus 95F lunch, others up to 250F*).

Le Change ✉ 24640

*****Château du Roc-Chautru**, **t** 05 53 06 17 31, **f** 05 53 06 17 03 (*moderate*). This 19th-century château on the Auvézère offers 11 luxurious rooms, set in a grove of 100-year-old cedars, as well as a pool and tennis (*menus 85–285F*).

Excideuil is on the river Lue, which flows into the Isle at **Coulaures**, a pretty village with a double-breasted Romanesque church containing a 14th-century fresco. The best scenery around, however, is along the Auvézère, beginning at **Cherveix-Cubas**, a village with a **Lanterne des Morts** in its cemetery, a slender version of the mysterious towers in Atur and Sarlat (*see* p.166). From here you can drive, ride, or trek along the delicious **Gorges de l'Auvézère**. Highlights along the way include **Génis**, a village of schist houses, the belvedere at the **Moulin du Pervendoux**, and at **St-Mesmin** the 15-minute walk to the laughing falls of the Auvézère; there's a place to rent kayaks nearby. There is work in progress at **Savignac-Lédrier** to create a tourist site around the old riverside forge, first used in the 15th century. There are to be information panels, buildings to visit and eventually, a museum. Some of this should be in place by the time you read this. At any rate, you can already walk close to the forge.

The Château de Hautefort

South of Cherveix and bossing much of the Auvézère valley stand the high-domed towers of one of Périgord's most famous citadels, the **Château de Hautefort**. In the 12th century a fortress on this spot belonged to the troubadour Bertran de Born (*see* pp.47–8). In 1640 it was rebuilt by a famous miser, Jacques-François de Hautefort. According to the gossip of the day, Jacques-François was the model for Harpagon in Molière's *L'Avare* (though Molière lowered his miser to bourgeois status); when the miser fell ill his doctor prescribed English pills, which brought about his death – they cost so much that Jacques-François couldn't bear to swallow them. His sister, Marie, was the most beautiful woman of her day, nicknamed *Aurore* by the French court. Yet even rarer than her great beauty was her disinterestedness – Marie was both the lover of the melancholic Louis XIII and the best friend of the wife he abhorred, Anne of Austria. Marie's devotion to the queen made her the enemy of Cardinal Richelieu, who went to the extreme of presenting a rival for the king's affections, a young man named Cinq-Mars; when that ploy only resulted in the king having two loves instead of one, Richelieu threatened to leave the king's service himself if Louis didn't dump Marie. She was only reinstated in court after Louis's death in 1643.

In 1836, novelist Eugène Le Roy was born here into a family of château labourers, a background that inspired his most famous work, *Jacquou le Croquant* (1899), describing the abject poverty in which Périgord's peasants lived so that the Hauteforts of the world could afford such dishy spreads (a *croquant* is a local word for a 17th-century peasant rebel; the name invokes a crunching or gnashing of angry teeth). In 1929, the castle passed to the Baron and Baronne de Bastard, who undertook the complete restoration of Hautefort and its gardens. After the baron died, his wife continued alone, finally finishing it in 1968. In the autumn of that same year Hautefort went up in a blaze that could be seen across half of Périgord. But after the shock of losing 39 years of work in one night, the Baronne de Bastard amazed everyone by starting all over again. Now completed, the château is one of the most inspiring in Périgord open to the public, and you can visit the panoramic terraces and the immaculate French **gardens** (***t*** *05 53 50 51 23; open April–June and Sept 10–12 and 2–6, July and Aug 9.30–7, Oct 2–6, otherwise Sun and school winter hols only 2–6, closed mid-Dec–mid-Jan; adm; reduced rates for gardens only*).

The **Hospice** of Hautefort is a Greek cross with a dome echoing those topping the towers. Founded by the parsimonious Jacques-François on his English pill-less deathbed in 1680, the hospital took in precisely 11 old men, 11 boys and 11 young women and was known as the hospital of 33 years, recalling the age of Christ when he died. It now houses a **Musée de la Médecine** (***t*** *05 53 51 62 98; open May, June and Sept Wed, Sat, Sun 10–12 and 2–6, July and Aug 10–12.30 and 2–6; adm*).

Tourtoirac and the Man Who Would Be King

On the Auvézère west of Hautefort lies Tourtoirac, with a damaged 11th-century Benedictine **abbey** behind a lofty *clocher-mur*; the dome of the church survives, along with some delightful carvings on the capitals of the ruined chapterhouse (***t** 05 53 51 12 17; open July and Aug daily 10–12.30 and 2.30–6*). In the village, a plaque on a small shop notes that His Majesty Aurélie-Antoine Ier, King of Araucania and Patagonia, died here on 17 September 1878. In the cemetery, his tomb is marked with a stele and crown, copied by the stonecutter from the king of hearts on a playing card. Aurélie so wanted the French to establish a protectorate in southern Chile that he went off to do it himself. The Chileans thought he was mad, but he never gave up his claim. He left no direct heir, but the faithful have never failed to produce successors to the throne. The **Musée des Rois d'Araucanie** south of Tourtoirac in **Chourgnac d'Ans** (***t** 05 53 50 53 46; open daily exc Tues 10.30–12.30 and 2.30–5.30*) contains books and other information on the king and his claim.

Down the Auvézère in **Auberoche**, a Romanesque chapel with a ruined roof and rain-scoured frescoes is all that is left of a once-mighty fortress that saw the very first battle of the Hundred Years' War. In the summer of 1345, the Earl of Derby installed a garrison here to keep an eye on Périgueux. The Count of Périgord, Roger Bernard, besieged it, and when the beset English tried to send an SOS message to Derby, Roger Bernard jeeringly catapulted the message, with the live messenger tied to it, back into the fortress. Nevertheless, Derby somehow got word, and (according to Froissart) surprised the count's 10,000 men while they dined, capturing 2,000, including Roger Bernard himself. There isn't much left to see in Auberoche, but don't miss the charming water mill downstream at **Le Change**.

Sorges, Périgord's Truffle Capital

North of Auberoche and the river Isle, **Sorges** is the central market for the truffle trade and home of a **Musée de la Truffe** (***t** 05 53 05 90 11; open Tues–Sun 10–11.30 and 2–4.30, July and Aug 8–12 and 2.30–6; adm*) with a truffle path to walk (*guided walks Tues and Thurs at 3.30*) and all you've ever wanted to know about that little black diamond stud in your foie gras. According to the French, in the year 300 the afflicted St Anthony was clawing at the ground in distress when the angels rewarded him with the first truffles. St Anthony, of course, is the patron saint of animals and in art is usually depicted with a pig: for centuries these were used to root for the delicacy. Nowadays their very uncontrolled pigginess has led many truffle-hunters to prefer keen-nosed hounds, whose mothers' teats were rubbed with truffle juice to associate the scent with their first love. Other hunters rely on savvy, keeping a lookout for fine soil looking as if it had been scorched, located in the vicinity of a specially diseased truffle oak, with 'hélomysa' flies circling above. Sorges and the Causses de Thiviers are one of the richest sources of the tasty fungus; in the old days there were so many that the favourite way of eating them was to put them under the ashes in the fire, and wolf them down whole. If you aren't in Périgord in truffle season, you can buy them in little jars (look for them preserved in cognac).

Sorges also has a domed Romanesque church and a 13th-century castle to visit, although you may find the 15th-century **Château des Bories** more rewarding (***t*** *05 53 06 00 01; open July–Sept 10–12 and 2–7; adm*). The last castle on the Isle before Périgueux, it is considered the archetype of all Périgourdin châteaux, with symmetrical round towers, a Gothic kitchen, huge chimney and monumental stair.

Périgueux

Set in a privileged, fertile valley on the river Isle, the capital of the Dordogne *département* is a cheerful city of 35,000 people who produce and market truffles, foie gras and fat strawberries, and print all the postage stamps in France. The old streets around its famous five-domed cathedral have been intelligently restored over the past decades to give the city a lively and lovely heart; another plus is its museum, with its exceptional prehistoric and Roman sections.

History

The first inhabitants of Périgueux, the Petrocorii Gauls, built their *oppidum* on the heights of the left bank of the Isle, by the sacred spring Vesunna. After Caesar defeated their ally Vercingetorix, they settled down to enjoy the *pax romana* and build a brand new town known as Vesunna (or Vésone in French) on the fertile plains of the Isle's right bank. It was the perfect place for a market town. By the 3rd century, Vesunna had 20,000 Gallo-Roman citizens, famous for their ironworking skills.

Vesunna was still in its first bloom when the barbarian Alemanni crushed it under their heels in 275. Raped and pillaged into a state of shock, Vesunna destroyed its own temples and basilicas for the stone to build a wall, contracting itself into the space of a tiny village. As the years (and more barbarians) passed by, this bristling remnant of Vesunna even lost its proud name: it became known as *Civitas Petrocoriorum*, the town of the Petrocorii, or just the Cité, as it's known to this day. Clovis captured the Cité and his successors fought over it; in the Dark Ages, the 24 towers of the wall were converted into donjons by rival factions of gangster-nobles.

The Rise of Puy-St-Front

As the Cité declined, a new *bourg* of artisans and merchants grew up around the nearby hill (*puy*) around the tomb of St Front, a 4th-century follower of St Martial. So many tall tales grew around this Front, or Fronto, that the good burghers can be fairly suspected of false advertising to suck in passing pilgrims: St Front evolved into no less than a personal acquaintance of Jesus who lived in a state of perpetual virginity. Baptized by the hand of St Peter, he was sent to the Cité, where he converted and baptized 7,000 and cured the Count Aurélius of his ulcers. He also managed to be in two places at once, attending the funeral of St Martha at Tarascon whilst saying Mass in Périgueux, a miracle proved by the gloves he forgot back in Tarascon. He chased the devils and dragons out of the pagan temple of Vessuna by blasting open an enormous breach in the walls. Thanks to the pilgrims who stopped at this superhero's

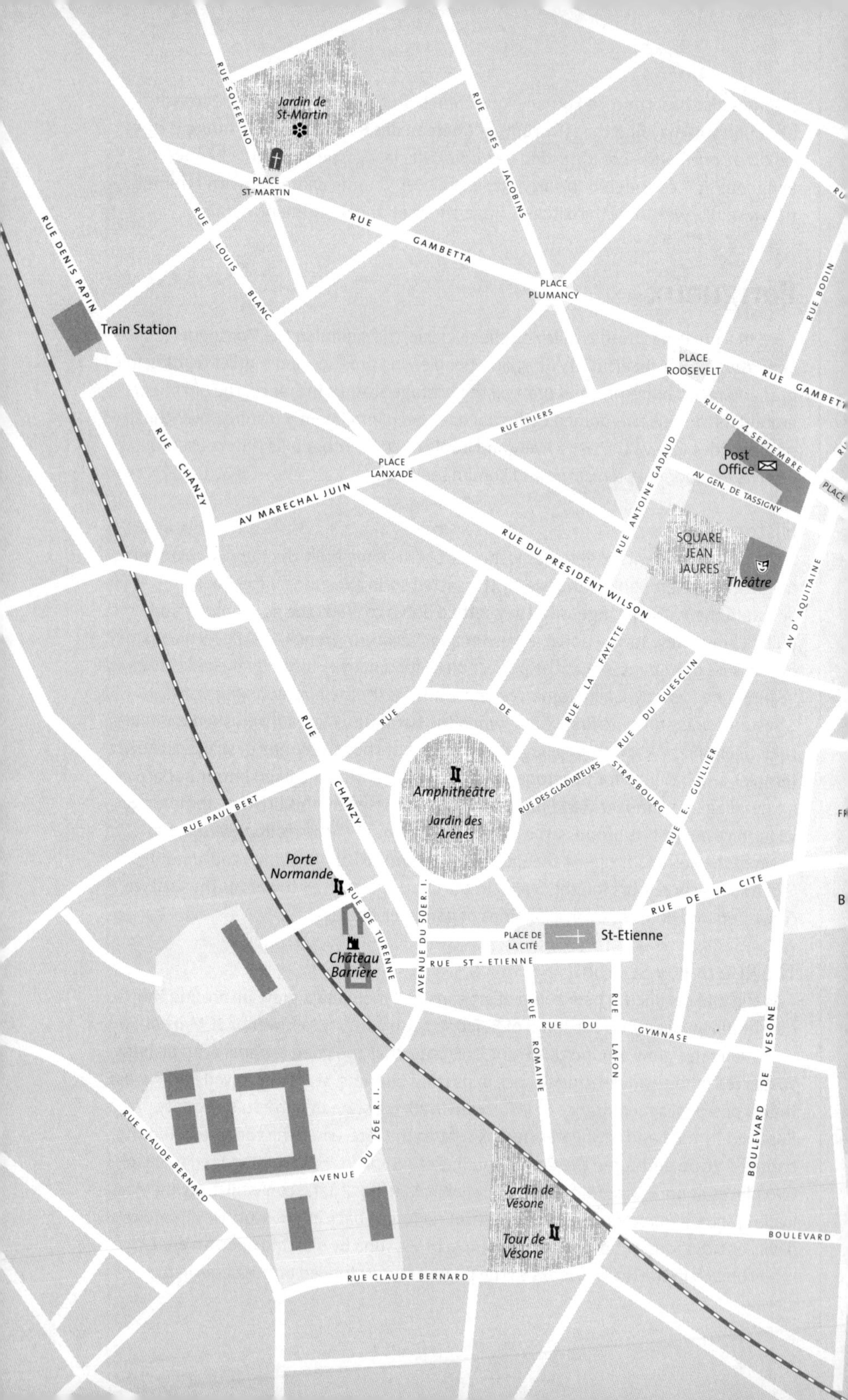

Jardin de St-Martin
RUE SOLFERINO
PLACE ST-MARTIN
RUE DES JACOBINS
RUE GAMBETTA
RUE LOUIS BLANC
RUE DENIS PAPIN
Train Station
PLACE PLUMANCY
RUE BODIN
PLACE ROOSEVELT
RUE GAMBETTA
RUE THIERS
RUE DU 4 SEPTEMBRE
Post Office
AV GEN. DE TASSIGNY
PLACE LANXADE
RUE CHANZY
AV MARECHAL JUIN
RUE ANTOINE GADAUD
SQUARE JEAN JAURES
Théâtre
RUE DU PRESIDENT WILSON
AV D' AQUITAINE
RUE LA FAYETTE
RUE DE
RUE DU GUESCLIN
RUE CHANZY
Amphithéâtre
Jardin des Arènes
RUE DES GLADIATEURS
STRASBOURG
RUE E. GUILLIER
RUE PAUL BERT
Porte Normande
RUE DE TURENNE
AVENUE DU 50E R. I.
RUE DE LA CITE
PLACE DE LA CITÉ
St-Etienne
Château Barrière
RUE ST - ETIENNE
RUE ROMAINE
RUE DU GYMNASE
RUE LAFON
BOULEVARD DE VESONE
RUE CLAUDE BERNARD
AVENUE DU 26E R.I.
Jardin de Vésone
Tour de Vésone
BOULEVARD
RUE CLAUDE BERNARD

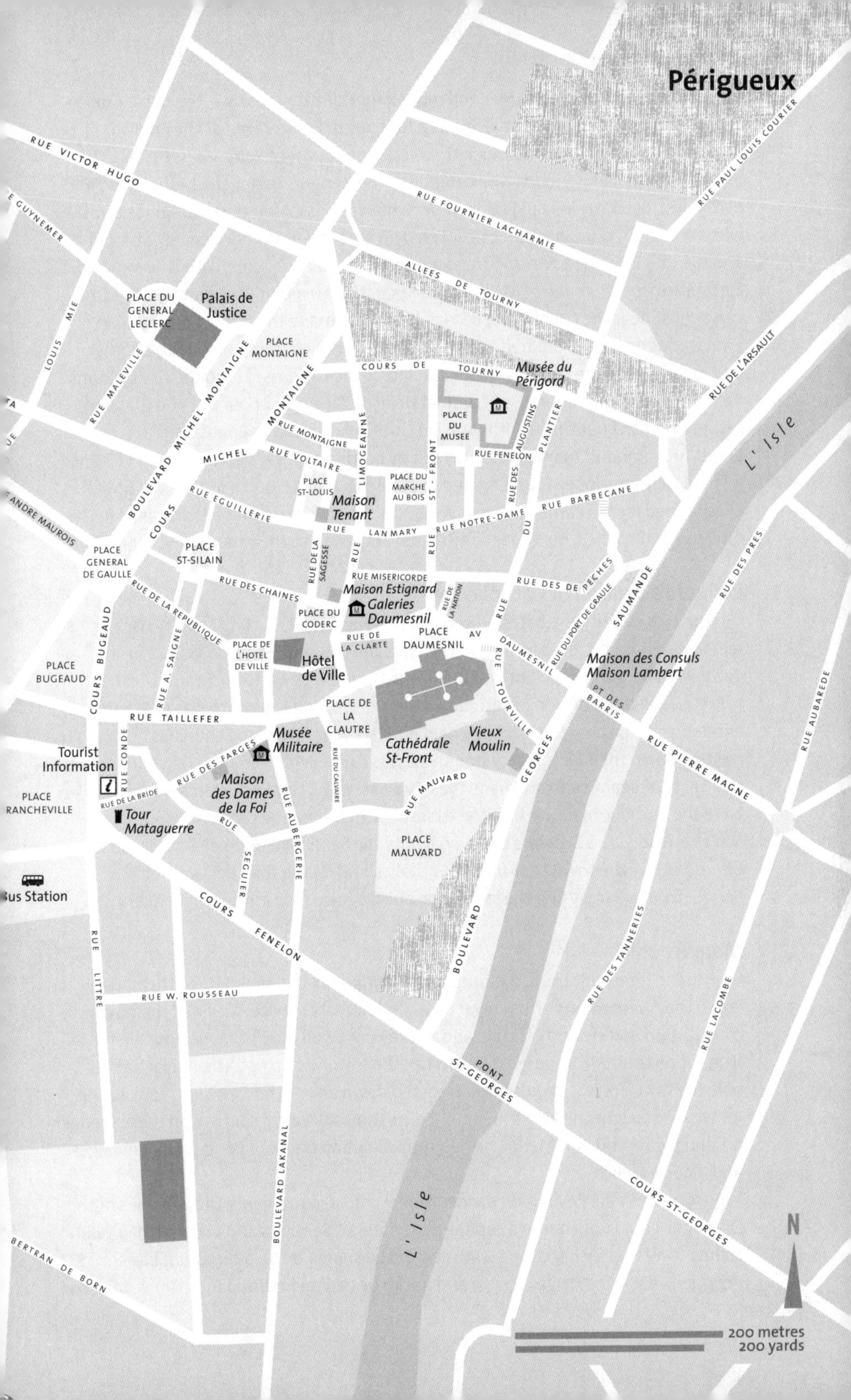
Périgueux
RUE VICTOR HUGO
RUE FOURNIER LACHARMIE
RUE PAUL LOUIS COURIER
ALLEES DE TOURNY
PLACE DU GENERAL LECLERC
Palais de Justice
PLACE MONTAIGNE
COURS DE TOURNY
Musée du Périgord
PLACE DU MUSEE
RUE FENELON
RUE DES AUGUSTINS
PLANTIER
RUE DE L'ARSAULT
L' Isle
RUE MALEVILLE
BOULEVARD MICHEL MONTAIGNE
COURS MICHEL MONTAIGNE
RUE MONTAIGNE
RUE VOLTAIRE
LIMOGEANNE
PLACE DU MARCHE AU BOIS
ST - FRONT
PLACE ST-LOUIS
Maison Tenant
RUE EGUILLERIE
RUE LAN MARY
RUE NOTRE-DAME
RUE BARBECANE
PLACE GENERAL DE GAULLE
PLACE ST-SILAIN
RUE DE LA SAGESSE
RUE MISERICORDE
RUE DES CHAINES
Maison Estignard
Galeries Daumesnil
PLACE DU CODERC
RUE DE LA NATION
RUE DES DE PECHES
RUE DU PORT DE GRAULE
SAUMANDE
RUE DES PRES
RUE DE LA REPUBLIQUE
PLACE DE L'HOTEL DE VILLE
Hôtel de Ville
RUE DE LA CLARTE
PLACE DAUMESNIL
AV DAUMESNIL
Maison des Consuls
Maison Lambert
PT DES BARRIS
PLACE BUGEAUD
COURS BUGEAUD
RUE A. SAIGNE
RUE TAILLEFER
PLACE DE LA CLAUTRE
RUE TOURVILLE
Cathédrale St-Front
Vieux Moulin
RUE PIERRE MAGNE
RUE AUBAREDE
Musée Militaire
Tourist Information
RUE CONDE
RUE DES FARGES
RUE DU CALVAIRE
Maison des Dames de la Foi
RUE DE LA BRIDE
Tour Mataguerre
PLACE FRANCHEVILLE
RUE SEGUIER
RUE AUBERGERIE
RUE MAUVARD
PLACE MAUVARD
BOULEVARD GEORGES
Bus Station
COURS FENELON
RUE LITTRE
RUE W. ROUSSEAU
RUE DES TANNERIES
RUE LACOMBE
PONT ST-GEORGES
COURS ST-GEORGES
BOULEVARD LAKANAL
L' Isle
BERTRAN DE BORN
N
200 metres
200 yards

tomb, bourgeois Puy grew larger and more important than its rival, the noble Cité. In 1182 Puy began its own wall. It also was a firm ally of France against the English.

The English weren't half as much trouble as the counts of Périgord (*see* p.124). One of the worst, Roger Bernard (who catapulted messengers in Auberoche), pillaged and partly destroyed Puy in 1246 just to show who was boss. After this outrage, St Louis, with more than human patience, brokered an agreement that united Puy-St-Front and the Cité into one town and freed it of homage to the counts, with a new motto: *Fortitudo mea civium fides* ('My strength lies in the trust of my fellow citizens'). One can almost hear the counts sneer. St Louis's accord made them more ornery than ever; throughout the Hundred Years' War they weaselled from one side to another, and in 1357, while the French were distracted by the capture of John the Good, Count Archambault V and his brother, Cardinal Hélie de Talleyrand, pounced and grabbed Périgueux with English aid. Although Du Guesclin chased the English out in 1369, Count Archambault managed to stay put by promising loyalty to the crown of France; instead, he took money from England to stir up as much trouble as possible until the exasperated French came back to give him the boot once and for all. His castle in the Cité was demolished, his goods confiscated and given to the canons of St-Front.

Périgord's Bastion of Catholicism

In the 15th century the battered survivors slowly rebuilt, putting the city back on its feet just in time for more trouble in the Wars of Religion. Périgueux was as firmly Catholic as Bergerac was Protestant, but the Huguenots were quicker off the mark: in 1575 they killed the bishop of Périgueux, then, disguising themselves as peasants, entered and captured the city. They held it for six years, wrecking churches and melting down their bells for cannons. Salt was rubbed into Périgueux's wounds when the Treaty of Beaulieu (1576) made the city a safe haven for Protestants; so miserable were the Catholic majority that the triumphal arch they erected for Henri, King of Navarre, read: '*Urbis Deforme Cadaver*'. In pity the Sénéchal André de Bourdeilles offered to buy the town back for the Catholics, and failing that, he captured Périgueux in 1581 by using the same peasant-disguise ruse as the Huguenots.

More Trouble

Since the time of St Louis, the burghers of Périgueux had maintained their privileges. They were exempt from royal taxes and military service; they had their own constitution and elected officials, and to the king owed only 'homage and fidelity'. In 1635, when Louis XIII imposed a tavern tax, the result was a riot. The mayor had to bolt, the tax clerk was murdered and tossed down a well; the *Croquants* took to the forests and fought the king's men until 1641. Louis XIV cast a cold eye on these goings-on, and by the end of his reign, he had rubbed out all traces of Périgueux's privileges and independence.

In 1790, when the Revolution divided France into *départements*, the worthies of the Dordogne could not choose a capital: as Périgueux, Bergerac and Sarlat all had valid claims, it was decided that the status would be shared on an alternating basis. Périgueux drew the longest straw and got to be capital first, and inertia has done the rest to make sure it never went anywhere else. As a kind of footnote to its beleaguered past, Périgueux gave birth in 1846 to Léon Bloy, France's most curmudgeonly Catholic philosopher and author, who celebrated the sinking of the *Titanic* with a huge party in Montmartre 'because it drowned so many Protestants'.

The Cité

Set back from the river, almost forgotten behind the bus terminal in Place Francheville, the Cité is a quiet place far removed from the days of rabid Count Archambault. Although the 19th century systematically razed its walls, tucked between the modern buildings are a handful of Gallo-Roman and medieval souvenirs, especially the 65ft **Tour de Vésone** in the Jardin de Vésone off Rue Claude Bernard. Believed to have been the central *cella* of a circular 1st-century AD Gallo-Roman temple, the great cylinder was originally faced with marble and is topped with brick arches; its walls still bear the breach made by St Front's legendary exorcism, although some say the opening in the wall was made intentionally to admit the rays of the rising sun. Excavations in the area found signs of a pair of basilicas that once marked the entrance to Vesunna's forum; just west in Rue des Bouquets are the ruins of the **Villa de Pompeïus**, from the same period (*ask about guided tours run by the tourist office*). Pompeïus, whoever he was, wallowed in a de luxe set of heated Roman baths; frescoes and mosaics survive as well.

St-Etienne-de-la-Cité

From the Tour de Vésone take Rue Romaine up to the centre of the Cité, where St-Etienne, Périgueux's oldest church, was founded on the site of a Temple of Mars by St Front. In the 12th century it was rebuilt in a style that became the prototype of the Périgourdin domed Romanesque church, with wide Byzantine cupolas not only over the crossing but cupping the length of the nave. Originally St-Etienne had four of these, culminating in a grand carved portal under a huge bell-tower porch; the Huguenots unkindly, and none too neatly, tore off the front half. In 1669 the mutilated structure was no longer deemed worthy to be a cathedral and the status was transferred to St-Front.

The two surviving bays are not only an important lesson in the origins of Périgourdin Romanesque but are steeped in shadowy medieval solemnity, an atmosphere so lacking in St-Front. The first dome, from the early 1100s, is solid and primitive, lit only by tiny windows; the second, from around 1160, is elongated, lighter, and supported by twinned columns. The interior has a fine if incongruous 17th-century wooden retable and a 12th-century Easter calendar; the arch from the tomb of Bishop Jean d'Asside (d. 1169) frames the Romanesque baptismal font.

Rue St-Etienne leads from the church to the **Château Barrière**, a *maison forte*, or strong house, built on the walls of the Cité for a loyal retainer of the counts. Next to the château is a rare 13th-century Romanesque house; across the street the **Gallo-Roman Porte Normande** is a sole survivor of the wall thrown together by the citizens

Getting Around

The **train** station, in Rue Denis-Papin, is 4 hours from Paris (change in Limoges), 1 hr 15 mins from Bordeaux, 3 hours from Agen or Toulouse. Citram **buses** from the station link Périgueux to the Paris–Bordeaux TGV in Angoulême, by way of Ribérac. **Buses** depart from Place Francheville and the station: several companies serve Sarlat, Montignac, Ribérac, Bergerac, and Brantôme; the biggest is CFD, **t** 05 53 08 43 13. The biggest **car park** in the city is up at Place Montaigne, near the Musée du Périgord.

Tourist Information

Rond Point de la Tour Mataguerre, 26 Place Francheville, **t** 05 53 53 10 63, **f** 05 53 09 02 50. In summer they offer guided tours of the historic centre. Ask about *son et lumière* shows and the various summertime festivals in the area.

Market Days

Wed and Sat mornings in Places du Coderc and de la Clautre; same days mid-Nov–mid-Mar, *marché de gras* in Place St-Louis.

Where to Stay and Eat

Périgueux ✉ 24000

On the whole Périgueux's hotels are more geared to travelling *foie gras* salesmen than to ordinary visitors.

★★★**Bristol**, 37–9 Rue Antoine Gadaud, **t** 05 53 08 75 90, **f** 05 53 07 00 49, *www,bristol-france.com* (*moderate*). A modern hotel near Place Roosevelt, with quite spacious and pleasant rooms and the facilities you would expect. Parking available, but no restaurant.

★★**Hôtel du Périgord**, 74 Rue Victor Hugo, **t** 05 53 53 33 63, **f** 05 53 08 19 74 (*inexpensive*). This central hotel offers comfortable Logis de France rooms and an inner garden around an ancient plane tree (*menus 75–170F*).

★★**L'Universe**, 18 Cours Montaigne, **t** 05 53 53 34 79 (*inexpensive*). Near the museum. There's a TV in each room and dining under the arbour in the summer (*meals from 90F*).

Aux Berges de l'Isle, 2 Rue Pierre-Magne, **t** 05 53 09 51 50. On a terrace overlooking the river and St-Front. It serves a refined *pavé de bœuf au foie gras* and luscious desserts (*menus 99–142F*). *Closed Sun eve and Mon.*

Le Roi Bleu, 2 Rue Montaigne, **t** 05 53 09 43 77. A smart place off Cours Montaigne, with

of Vesunna after the invasion of the Alemanni; originally it stood about 35ft high, a jigsaw of columns and temple fragments. The nearby **amphitheatre**, where up to 30,000 spectators cheered gladiators to death, is now practically toothless – as the base for the castle of the bloody-minded counts of Périgord, it had been enthusiastically razed in 1391. Only a few stones and an entrance now enclose a pretty garden and playground.

Puy-St-Front

On the far side of Place Francheville, once the no-man's land between Périgueux's two rival towns, lies the compact and beautifully restored quarter of Puy-St-Front. The tourist office's medieval-Renaissance tour will get you inside some of the courtyards, and into the last remnant of Puy's walls, the **Tour Mataguerre** in Place Francheville. Decorated with fleurs-de-lys, it was repaired in 1477 with the forced labour of men inflicted with the scourge of 15th-century Périgueux – leprosy.

Just to the left of the Tour Mataguerre, Rue de la Bride/Rue des Farges ('forges') was the main road linking the Cité and Puy-St-Front. Some of Périgueux's oldest houses are here, most notably No.4, the 12th-century **Maison des Dames de la Foi**, built by the Templars, inhabited by Du Guesclin, and in the late 1600s occupied by nuns. At the

rather chic selections such as *tartare de saumon fumé aux chips de légumes et langoustines rôties* (*menus 170–450F*). *Closed Sat lunch and Sun and the third week in Aug.*

Le 8, 8 Rue de la Clarté, near to the Cathedral, **t** 05 53 35 15 15. Very good reputation. Serves imaginative regional dishes in its small and lively dining room (*menus 165–400F*). *Closed Sun and Mon; best to book.*

La Picholine, 6 Rue du Puy-Limogeanne, **t** 05 53 53 86 91. Bright and cheerful. Standard southwest dishes are given a Mediterranean touch (*menus 68–130F*).

Le Rocher de l'Arsault, 15 Rue de l'Arsault, **t** 05 53 53 54 06. Tasty *tatin de foie gras* and other regional delicacies in a Louis XIII dining room to the northeast of the centre (*menus 155–450F*). *Closed Sun and for several weeks in summer.*

Hercule Poireau, 2 Rue de la Nation, **t** 05 53 08 90 76. For even older décor, book a table in their vaulted Renaissance cellar north of the cathedral for *Rossini de canard* and other treats at very reasonable prices (*menus 99–220F*). *Closed Sat lunch, Sun and most of Aug.*

There are a number of fine hotels and restaurants a short drive from the centre of Périgueux: besides the ones listed below, *see* Antonne and Le Change, p.98.

Chancelade ✉ 24650

****__Château des Reynats__, **t** 05 53 03 53 59 (*expensive*). This turreted, 19th-century château has been converted into a hotel with attractive rooms. It's close to an 18-hole golf course and has a pretty little park with century trees, pool and tennis courts. The restaurant, with Second Empire fittings but a relaxed, laid-back atmosphere, serves exquisite specialities based on regional cuisine, but with an imaginative touch (*menus 140–350F*). *Closed Mon and mid-Jan–mid-Mar; book.*

__Le Pont de la Beauronne__, 4 Route de Ribérac, **t 05 53 08 42 91, **f** 05 53 03 97 69 (*inexpensive*). A friendly, newish hotel near the golf course. *Menus start at 62F.*

Razac-sur-l'Isle ✉ 24430

***__Château de Lalinde__, **t** 05 53 54 52 30, **f** 05 53 07 46 67 (*moderate*). You can sleep under the mansard roof of this imposing château, set in the midst of a seven-acre park with a pool. Local specialities dominate the menu (*150–300F*). *Closed mid-Nov–mid-Mar.*

top of the street is the **Musée Militaire du Périgord** (***t*** *05 53 53 47 36; open April–Sept 10–12 and 2–6, Oct–Dec 2–6, closed Sun and hols; Jan–Mar Wed and Sat 2–6; adm*), with items on the French military, including some rare mementoes of the colonial wars in this century, as well as memorabilia related to General Daumesnil (*see* below). From here, turn right in Rue Taillefer for **Place de la Clautre**, under the looming bell tower of St-Front. This square, site of the Saturday market, was for centuries a graveyard and the theatre for executions; the last walk a condemned criminal would make in this world was up narrow **Rue du Calvaire**.

The Cathedral of St-Front

This is the fourth church built here, on the summit of the *puy* over the Isle. A 6th-century chapel holding the relics of St Front was replaced in 1074 with a much larger church, to draw in pilgrims on the way to Compostela. In 1120, when this new church burned down, it was decided to build one even larger and more extraordinary. Greek architects, it seems, were hired, and they designed a Greek cross plan under five domes. Their model was Agii Apostoli in Constantinople (now gone), the same design used for another famous church: St Mark's in Venice. By the 19th century this marvel was a rickety disaster waiting to happen. After the Huguenots had damaged it in 1575 and destroyed the tomb of St Front, a streak of thoughtless restorations exacerbated the typical problems of old age, leaving its domes covered with a sloppy hotchpotch of stones and tiles. The famous medieval re-creator Viollet-le-Duc wanted to have a crack at it but his rival Paul Abadie was given the nod in 1852. Abadie loved Romanesque churches so much that he devoured them whole; he demolished much of St-Front and spent the next 50 years rebuilding it. The result is breathtaking from a distance, especially at night when the cathedral is illuminated and reflected in the waters of the Isle. Close up, it is much harder to overlook its newness, the nakedness, the too precise and orderly cut of the stone. Nor was Abadie above adding improvements to the original, especially the pinnacles on the domes; he liked these so well that he stuck their clones on the bulbous domes of his most famous creation, Sacré-Cœur in Paris.

From Place de la Clautre you can see what survives from the church of 1074: the austere façade fitted with the odd Roman fragment, lateral walls that now form an open courtyard, the bottom two-thirds of the 186ft bell tower, two *confessions* (tomb-shrines of saintly confessors) – one under the bell tower and the other under the west dome – and the haunting little **cloister** with the original Romanesque pine-cone crown of the bell tower as a centrepiece. Inside Abadie's church, the most lingering impression is one of vastness (no wonder – it's one and a half times as long as a football pitch). In its minimal decoration it looks more like a mosque. Abadie designed the 'Byzantine' chandeliers, which originally hung in Notre-Dame, for the pompous wedding of Napoleon III; for a franc you can shed light on the enormous 17th-century walnut retable made for a demolished Jesuit chapel.

Medieval Streets around St-Front

The north door of the cathedral opens on to **Place Daumesnil**, the centre of a fascinating web of 15th- and 16th-century pedestrian lanes. The pale stone of their urbane houses was mostly quarried from ancient Vesunna, and residents often leave their gates open to let passers-by admire their beautifully curved inner stairs. Steep, stepped streets descend to the river; houses in Rue du Plantier have terraced gardens (see if you can find the carving of Adam and Eve on one of the stairs), while medieval Rue du Port-de-Graule is lined with tiny boutiques. Down on the quay, in a cluster of 15th–16th-century houses stands the **Maison Lambert** with its Renaissance gallery and the **Maison des Consuls** with flamboyant dormers. The **Vieux Moulin**, perched on a river wall, is a relic of the grain monopoly once held by the canons of St-Front.

Back up in Place Daumesnil, enter the picturesque **Galeries Daumesnil** by way of Rue de la Clarté: these are a set of old courtyards opened up to the public, and named after Pierre Daumesnil, born at 7 Rue de la Clarté in 1776.

Rue Limogeanne and Around

From the Galeries Daumesnil, continue along pedestrian Rue Limogeanne, Périgueux's busiest shopping street since the Middle Ages. Most of the houses here date from the 16th century. No.5, the **Maison Estignard**, is especially lovely with its dormers, mullioned windows and carvings; in the courtyard of No.3, note the bas-relief of a salamander, the emblem of François I. Rue de la Sagesse, parallel to Rue Limogeanne, boasts other fine Renaissance houses; No.1, **Maison Lajoubertie**, has one of Périgueux's most beautiful staircases, carved with the goddess of Love laying aside her weapons. Rue de Sagesse gives into handsome **Place St-Louis**, created by demolishing a block of slums. It has a fountain decorated with a dumpling lady, who probably overindulged in the offerings of the *marché des gras* (fattened geese, ducks, foie gras and truffles) held in this square (*Wed and Sat in winter*). The **Maison du Tenant or du Pâtissier** (1518), on the corner of Rue Eguillerie, has a sculpted porch and an inscription warning that anyone who speaks badly behind people's backs is not welcome inside, for 'The greatest glory is to displease the wicked.'

Musée du Périgord

22 Cours de Tourny, ***t*** *05 53 06 40 70; open weekdays April–Sept 11–6, Oct–Mar 10–5, weekends 1–6, closed Tues and hols; adm.*

Just to the north, the Musée du Périgord is a cut above the average, with something for every taste. The ethnographic collection in the first rooms, devoted to stone-age cultures from around the world (New Caledonia, the Cook Islands, Papua New Guinea and Africa), forms a comparative introduction to the extensive **prehistoric section** upstairs. The prizes here are three extremely rare complete skeletons: the oldest ever found, the Neanderthal *homme de Régourdou* (70,000 BC), ritually buried with the bears near Lascaux (*see* p.127); *homme de Combe-Capelle* (20,000 BC), found near Sergeac; and Upper Palaeolithic *homme de Chancelade*, a mere whippersnapper only 15,000 years old. The collection of tools ranges from the very first cut stones found in the Dordogne, dating back a cool million years, and Upper Palaeolithic carvings and engravings on bone and stone, among them the strange, disembodied *Parade of Bison* from Chancelade and a disc carved with does from Laugerie-Basse. In another

The Peg-legged General

Périgueux's feistiest hero fought with Napoleon in Egypt, lost a leg at Wagram near Vienna, and was given what seemed to be the equivalent of a desk job as commander of the Château of Vincennes in Paris. When the Allies took Paris in 1814, they demanded that Daumesnil surrender Vincennes. 'Tell the Austrians to give back my leg or else come in and get the other one,' he replied. They didn't, and Vincennes remained the only part of France never to surrender to the Allies. After Waterloo, Daumesnil was besieged again, and again he held out, refusing to give over the fort to anyone but a Frenchman. Finally the new king, Louis XVIII, came in person to accept the keys.

During the Revolution of 1830, Daumesnil was still on the job. The hated ministers of Charles X were imprisoned at Vincennes, and when a mob came to lynch them, the old general kept them out too, saying that he'd ignite the powder room if they tried to storm the place. In Cours Michel-Montagne, there's a statue of him pointing with pride at his peg leg.

room, among the Neolithic and barbarian artefacts, are weapons that laid Vesunna low: a bronze Alemanni sword, and Visigothic and Frankish blades.

Downstairs, there are stuffed weasels, snake skins, an Egyptian mummy named Antinoë and a selection of Coptic fabrics. These are followed by the **Gallo-Roman rooms**, filled with fascinating finds excavated from the original Petrocorii *oppidum* and ancient Vesunna: jewellery, frescoes, mosaics, an excellently preserved wooden pump from 15 BC, items from everyday life, a sculpture of the Celtic 'three-horned god', and a 2nd-century BC altar carved with the head of a ram and bull, dedicated to the Eastern cult of Cybele and Attis.

The cloister is lined with some very intriguing if poorly labelled stone fragments from Neolithic to medieval times: a 6th-century Visigothic sarcophagus, a lacy fragment of a Carolingian chancel, and strange faces and slatternly mermaids that once adorned St-Front. The **Beaux-Arts** section begins with ceramics and enamels from Limoges, followed by three rooms of paintings, including the *Diptyque de Rabastens* (1286), a rare work painted on leather from the school of Toulouse; a 16th-century Flemish *Excision de la pierre de folie*, a famous Hieronymus Bosch subject, although here we see doctors simply removing the 'madness stone' from a patient's brain; a fine *Portrait of Fénelon* by Bailleul; a Canaletto; two paintings by the 19th-century Paul Guigou; and works by native Périgourdins, including sculptures by Jane Poupelet, a student of Rodin. In 2001 a new museum will be opened to exhibit items found on local Gallo-Roman sites.

Around Périgueux: Chancelade Abbey

Six kilometres west of Périgueux, **Chancelade** is an enchanting spot with a natural spring and an 11th-century Augustinian **abbey** (***t*** *05 53 04 86 87; open July and Aug daily 2–7*). In 1370 the English gave the monks the bum's rush and converted the abbey into a stronghold that only fell when the great Bertrand du Guesclin personally led the attack, storming up the ladder and splitting open the head of the English captain. You can still see the scars of the battle on the Romanesque **Chapelle St-Jean**. The main **church**, with its arcaded, three-tiered bell tower, was restored in the 1600s, although 13th-century frescoes of Catholicism's two tallest saints, Christopher and Thomas à Becket, have survived the outrages of time and wars. The abbey buildings and lodge can be visited.

In the 12th century, monks from Chancelade founded the **Prieuré de Merlande**, in a forest clearing 6km north off the D2. One of the original two domes was smashed by the English; the rest was fortified in the 16th century and wrecked again in the Revolution. Somehow the capitals on the blind arcading of the choir have survived, with interwoven designs of animals and monsters. South of Périgueux, **Atur** (7km on the D2) has a Romanesque church and a 12th-century Lanterne des Morts (*see* Sarlat, p.166); 21km south on the D8, **Vergt** stands as a rare monument to the seldom-seen constructive side of the counts of Périgord, in this case Archambaut III, who founded this pleasant *bastide* in 1285.

West of Périgueux: the Dronne and Forêt de la Double

The name Dronne may evoke nothing as much as a queen bee's studmuffin, but this is one of the most charmingly bucolic rivers in France. Between the Dronne and the Isle are the gentle rolling hills of the Double forest, crisscrossed by streams that feed moody marshes, created by medieval monks to farm fish for Lent.

Down the Dronne

Tocane-St-Apre, where the D710 running from Périgueux meets the Dronne, is a handsome agricultural village with a good dolmen, the **Pierre-Levée**, the **Musée du Costume et de son Artisanat au XIX Siècle** illustrating 19th-century dress (***t*** *05 53 90 44 94; open May–Sept Wed–Sun 2.30–6.30, Mon 10–1, closed Tues; adm*), and Gallo-Roman excavations that suggest folks have long forded the river here. You should too, following signs for **Montagrier**. The rewards are superb panoramas into the Dronne valley and a 12th-century domed church, **Ste-Madeleine**, with a three-lobed apse and carved capitals; here, on the feast day of the doctor saints Côme and Damien, children

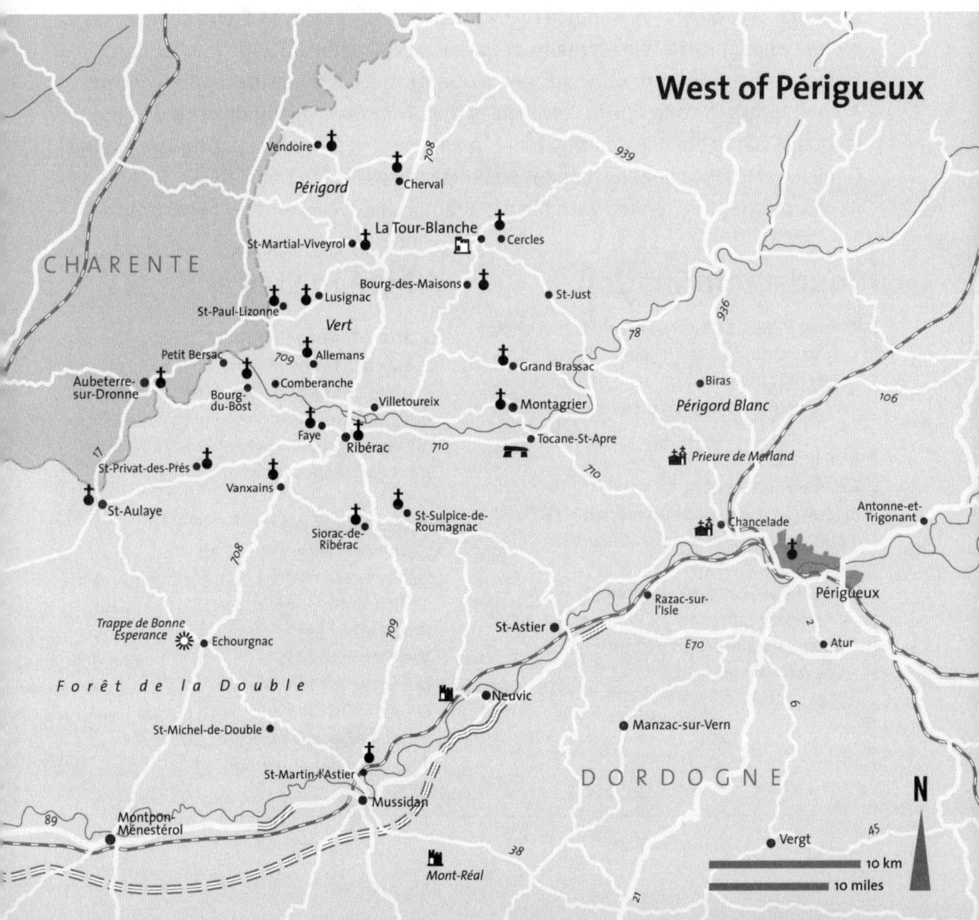

with hernias used to gather for a miraculous cure. From here you have a choice of roads up to **Grand Brassac**, with an even more extraordinary 12th-century **church**, its north portal decorated with two versions of the same enthronement scene, one made to fit the door, and the other, from a larger door, stuck on top of it, while inside three domes hover on pendentives. If you want to enter, Mme Lacour just opposite has the key. **St-Just**, north of Grand Brassac on the D103, has another surprise: silkworms, which you can visit at the 15th- and 17th-century **Magnanerie de Goumandie** (***t** 05 53 90 73 60; open July and Aug 10.30–12.30 and 2–6, mid-May–June and Sept 2–6; closed Tues*) in case you've always wondered about those little mulberry munchers.

Ribérac

As you return to the Dronne and head west for Ribérac, keep an eye peeled for the *cluzeaux* (dwellings cut into the limestone in the Middle Ages). One of the biggest towns in the area, with nearly 5,000 souls, Ribérac is a quiet and demure place that jumps on Friday, its market day. Its restored domed Romanesque Collegiate church **Notre-Dame**, with a handsome apse and bizarre façade, looks more like a school gymnasium than a church; it's used it as a concert hall and for exhibitions (*open mid-June–mid-Sept daily 2–7*). A church up by the river, 12th-century **St-Pierre de Faye**, has a pretty tympanum. Nothing remains of the castle where the quixotic troubadour Arnaut Daniel was born (active 1180–1210). Dante met his shade in Purgatory, where Arnaut speaks the only line in Provençal in the *Divine Comedy* (though this was the language Dante considered using for his great poem before opting for Italian). Arnaut Daniel's verse is so complex that it is well-nigh impossible to translate without losing its charm, but he is credited with the most famous lines ever written by a troubadour:

Tourist Information

Ribérac: Place de Charles de Gaulle, **t** 05 53 90 03 10, **f** 05 53 91 35 13. If you're interested, they produce an informative map of the local *église romanes à coupoles*.

Market Days

Tocane-St-Apre: Mon.

Ribérac: Fri (with a walnut market in Oct and perhaps Nov and a *marché au gras* in Nov–Mar)
Tues May–Sept, farmers' market.
There are night markets in July and Aug but dates vary; call the tourist office for the latest information.

Where to Stay and Eat

Tocane-St-Apre ✉ 24350

Auberge à la Ferme Maigne, on the D103 at Fournieux, **t** 05 53 90 70 35 (*cheap*). A tranquil place to sleep, learn how to ride, or dine on fresh products at very fair prices (*menus from 80F*). Popular with the British.

Ribérac ✉ 24600

****Hôtel de France**, 3 Rue Marc-Dufraisse, **t** 05 53 90 00 61, **f** 05 53 91 06 05 (*inexpensive*). In a 16th-century post house, this family-run hotel is the best and biggest in town. You can dine in the old-fashioned dining room or out in the garden courtyard; it offers a wide choice of fish and duck, with pianoon Sat evenings (*menus from 85F*). *Closed Mon and Tues lunch out of season.*

Ieu sui Arnautz q'amas l'aura,
E chatz la lebre ab lo bou
E nadi contra suberna

(I am Arnaut, who gathers the wind
and hunts the hare with the ox
and swims against the incoming tide)

A Spin around Ribérac

The corner of Périgord north of the Dronne practically bubbles with multi-domed Romanesque churches. The signed circuit begins at **Allemans** (up the D709), passes another church at **St-Paul-Lizonne**, then heads to medieval **Lusignac**, a delightful film-set of a village. Here the fortified church may be domeless, but inside it resembles the Mother of God's attic, filled with clutter, discontinued models of saints, vases of dusty artificial flowers and holy pictures that look as if they were clipped from magazines. The next stop, **St-Martial-Viveyrol**, has remnants of frescoes, while **Cherval** to the northeast has **St-Martin**, the most beautiful of them all, with a cluster of five domes, as many as St-Front itself.

La Tour-Blanche gets its name from the ruined *Turris Alba*, built in the 10th century over a Gaulish fort. Henri IV lodged here for several weeks, although now he'd be more comfortable in the handsome 1617 **Manoir de Roumailhac** in the centre. The 'White Tower' also has a little museum to what the French call 'white iron' or tin, the **Musée de la Ferblanterie** (*t 05 53 91 11 98; open mid-June–Aug 2.30–6*), and a **Musée des Records** (*same tel and opening times as the Musée de la Ferblanterie, exc Sun*) of remarkable objects displayed in the Festival des Records, which takes place every two years in August. The ancient priory of **St-Cybard** at nearby **Cercles** has excellent

Hôtel de l'Univers, 2 Av de Verdun, **t** 05 53 90 04 38, **f** 05 53 90 98 39 (*inexpensive*). Central, smaller, very simple and cheaper. There's a small pool, and each room has a TV.

Le Chevillard, 2km from the centre at Gaynet, on the Bordeaux road, **t** 05 53 91 20 88. An old farm with a large garden; abundant good food at kind prices (*lunch menu 69F, dinner menus 105–165F*). *Closed Mon except in summer and two weeks out of season.*

La Bergerie, 4km north of Ribérac on the D708, signposted, **t** 05 53 90 26 97. A restaurant amongst the corn fields in an old *bergerie* with a pretty patio. The menus are delicious and good value: *joue de porc braisé au Bergerac*, or for dessert apricot cake with almond cream. There is also a good vegetarian menu (*menus 65–220F*). *Closed Tues and Wed except July and Aug; reserve.*

Villetoureix ✉ 24600

Le Vieux Frêne, just as you come out of La Borie, going into Ribérac, on your left, **t** 05 53 91 09 74. In a pleasant spot with a country air and terrace above the river. Simple solid southwest fare (*menus 70–175F*). *Closed Mon except July, Aug and Oct.*

Vanxains ✉ 24600

Ferme Auberge de Farges, head south on the D708, turn left on the D44 and drive another few kms, **t** 05 53 90 91 41 (*cheap*). Book one of their simple rooms for true peace and quiet, and some of the best farm cooking in all Périgord. It's not all duck and goose – there's steak, rabbit, and even some vegetarian dishes (*menus 50–200F*). *Open daily July and Aug; out of season weekends and hols only, closed for a month in winter; book.*

Romanesque carved capitals; also in this village is a garden of orchids, **Les Jardins de Limodore** (***t** 05 53 90 86 83; open to the public around blooming time, April–June Wed and Sat 2–6*) where you can discover 47 species of this beautiful flower.

Bourg-des-Maisons has another good domed Romanesque church; **Vendoire** further northwest has yet another, from the 17th century, with a façade decorated with columns in the style of the nearby Charente. You can drive up to see the ruins of the 13th-century **church** of St-Jean de Grésignac, and learn all about peat at the **Eco-musée de la Tourbe**, with nature trails and boat rides for 50F an hour (***t** 05 53 90 79 56; open May–Sept 10–7, April and Oct Sun 10–6; adm*).

West to Aubeterre-sur-Dronne and its Eglise Monolithique

West of Ribérac and north of the river, you can get a bird's-eye view of the area from the top of Puy de Beaumont, up a little road off the D709, before Allemans. The little bridge at Comberanche will take you back over the Dronne to **Bourg-du-Bost**, with another Romanesque church; from here you can reach **Petit-Bersac**, where archaeologists have uncovered a Gallo-Roman settlement and have collected the finds in a small **Musée Gallo-Romain** (***t** 05 53 90 96 70; open July and Aug 3–6 by appointment; adm*). Another little road leads due south of Petit-Bersac to **St-Privat-des-Prés** where a venerable Romanesque **church** wears a porch and belt of nine blind arches across the façade. St-Privat's **Musée de l'Outil et de la Vie au Village** (***t** 05 53 91 22 87; open July and Aug Tues–Sun 3–6; adm; ask at the* mairie *if it's closed*) is chock-full of tools and curiosities recreating a 19th-century village street, as well as a collection of châteaux and cathedrals, all shrunk to one-hundredth their normal size.

The real attraction in this neck of the woods, however, is 2km into the Charente, at **Aubeterre-sur-Dronne**, 'Dawnland on the Dronne'. A hill town of ivory stone, rising up at the end of a corridor of 150-year-old unpruned plane trees, Aubeterre has more history and mystery than it has room for. Much of it is concentrated in a church cut into a limestone cliff known as the **Eglise Monolithique** (*open 15 June–15 Oct daily 9.30–12.30 and 2–7; other times 9.30–12.30 and 2–6; adm*). First excavations in the cliff began on a small scale in the 5th century, when the rare total-immersion baptismal font was cut into the floor. This early cave church soon became a favourite place for the trump of doom; behind the font a Merovingian necropolis is jammed with a hundred corpse hollows chiselled in the stone, with their little round heads all pointing towards Jerusalem. In the 11th century, Benedictines founded a monastery in front of the cave (completely destroyed by the Protestants in the Wars of Religion) and at some point they acquired an important holy relic of some kind, which they housed in a magnificent stone reliquary built in the form of the hexagonal tomb of Joseph of Arimathea in Jerusalem. To set it off better (no one really knows why) they enlarged the holy precinct of the cave, quarrying deep into rock like rabid termites to create a veritable hall of the mountain king – if St-Emilion's rock-cut church (*see* pp.205–6) is the largest in Europe, Aubeterre's is the tallest in the world, rising 65ft from the ground and supported by two blackened columns as thick as sequoias. A stairway cut in the rock leads to the upper galleries with windows peering down into the shadowy depths; a further stair continued up through the rock to the castle overlooking Aubeterre, enabling its *seigneur* to attend services without having to rub elbows with his subjects.

Outside the door are more tombs, these belonging to medieval monks who chose to face the mysterious reliquary instead of Jerusalem; just under the church floor the rock is pitted like a Swiss cheese with their graves. But an even stranger holy place lies below these, discovered by accident in the 1960s when a truck passing down the street made the pavement cave in. The driver found himself in an ancient *mithraeum* – a subterranean chamber lined with benches on either side, where adherents of Mithras (the favourite god of the Roman legions) would be baptized in the hot blood of a bull sacrificed on ground level; you can see where the gore would have flowed into the chamber through the outlets on either side into the square basin. Mithraism, with its monotheistic tendencies, gave Christianity a run for its money in the early centuries AD, which may account for why the entrance to this temple was so well hidden and why the Christians went to such trouble to create an awe-inspiring alternative above. The new paving in the square was paid for by the late president François Mitterrand, who spent much of his childhood at his grandparents' farm in Aubeterre.

The Eglise Monolithique was an important stop for pilgrims en route to Compostela, a path rife with diversions from dogma, just as the pilgrimage itself was a search for something beyond the daily fare at church. The pilgrims had another important stop in Aubeterre, just up the hill: the 11th-century **St-Jacques**. Although the Protestants smashed it up when they demolished the Eglise Monolithique's monastery, they mercifully spared the magnificent three-arched Romano-Hispano-Moorish façade, partly sunken below the level of the modern pavement and fronting a rebuilt church. Bolted on to the upper left of the façade are the black fragments of an equestrian statue, believed to have been either Charlemagne or Santiago (St James in his Spanish role as a Moor-slaying crusader), or perhaps even Trajan or some other Roman emperor who the Christians found lying around and converted.

The façade itself is very Roman in its arches and registers, while the decoration – its lavishly patterned arches, orientalized reliefs and the foiled arch in the centre – are strongly reminiscent of the work of *mudéjar* craftsmen from Spain in the throes of the *Reconquista*. Although the right arch has been eroded by the weather, the central and especially the left arch are richly decorated with abstract patterns and six panels of the zodiac – although unlike most zodiacs each of the scenes features a fellow sitting in a chair by a cooking fire. The monsters on the capitals are a treat: winking cats with two bodies, biting birds and quadrupeds with silly bearded heads (with extra pairs of heads like grinning balloons strapped to their backs). On the far left side of the left arch, note the centaur with a bow, and on the right a horse with an arrow piercing its neck. Inside is the only other bit the Catholics managed to salvage from Huguenot fury: an 11th-century **statue of the Virgin** holding Jesus in her right arm instead of the usual left, a deviation believed to be mystically significant, although nobody knows exactly how.

Some of the prettiest Dronne valley scenery is in these parts: along the D17 from Aubeterre to **St-Aulaye**, a delightful village at the edge of the Double forest, for instance. It has a rare 11th-century bridge, a Renaissance château, and a Romanesque **church** with a handsome white façade, its three arches supported by fine sculpted capitals. While there, you may want to visit the **Musée du Cognac et du Vin**, and learn all about the Charente's famous brandy (***t*** *05 53 90 81 33; open July and Aug Tues–Sun 3–4.30, out of season Sat only, closed Feb; adm*).

The Forêt de la Double

The emerald forest of La Double, covering some 125,000 acres from the Dronne to the Isle, was long a no-man's-land, a marshy woodland of sand and clay, interspersed with lakes. The trees were all cut down in the 17th and 18th centuries – by barrel-makers, charcoal-burners, glass-blowers and tile-bakers – leaving an impoverished, malarial swamp inhabited by outcasts, memorably evoked in Eugène Le Roy's novel, *L'Ennemi de la Mort*. Napoleon III initiated a scheme to recolonize the forest, draining swamps and replanting the old forest with pines. The population took a brief upturn, but these days it's as empty as ever – a lonesome, poetic place of old farms and nearly abandoned villages, of quiet paths through the trees.

Vanxains, on the D708 between St-Aulaye and Ribérac, is a nearly deserted village that was once the seat of the Vicomte de la Double. It has an elegant, domed Romanesque **church** with fine carved capitals, and a Neolithic line of menhirs at **Sauteranne** that's impossible to find unless you get someone to direct you. In 1747 Vanxains was the birthplace of Suzette Labrouse, 'the Prophetess of the Revolution', who as a child so wanted to see God that she kept a jar of spiders handy, ready to swallow in order to kill herself. Then came the day that God told her to go forth, bring down the greats of the world and remedy the ills of the church. She made her way to Paris, where her naïvety was the butt of many jokes; a satirical comedy called her the 'truffled turkey, the patriotic gift of Périgord to the National Assembly'. She met Marat, Dr Guillotin, Desmoulins and, most disastrously, Robespierre, who persuaded her to go to Rome to tell the Pope to give up his temporal power. The Pope disagreed and locked her up in Castel Sant'Angelo the minute she crossed the border. A few years later the French army in Rome liberated her; she returned to Paris and died in 1821, leaving behind a stash of small bottles filled with mysterious liquids, which to the disappointment of alchemists were never analysed.

To the east along the D43, **Siorac-de-Ribérac** has yet another domed fortified Romanesque church, while the church of **St-Sulpice-de-Roumagnac** 3km further boasts a beautiful 17th-century wooden retable. The D43 continues east towards St-Astier on the Isle (*see* below), with grand views most of the way. Alternatively, some of the marshes south of Siorac are actually little lakes suitable for a swim; the largest is the **Grand Etang de la Jemaye**. Near Echourgnac, in the very centre of La Double, the monks at the **Trappe de Bonne-Esperance** arrived in 1868, and were one of the first positive things to happen to the local economy. Now replaced by nuns, they are locally famous for their cheeses, especially *La Trappe*, which you can purchase at the convent along with other goodies. Just east of Echourgnac one of the last examples of traditional rural architecture in the region, the **Ferme du Parcot**, is open for tours, and doubles as a Double information centre (***t** 05 53 81 99 28; open July and Aug daily 2.30–5.30, May, June and Sept Sun only; adm*). **St-Michel-de-Double**, further south, has other fine examples of 17th-century rural architecture in its **Hameau des Héritiers** and the **Maisons de Gamanson**, close to the Isle.

The Lower Isle Valley

Once past Périgueux, the Isle loses much of its charm; the busy N89 that skirts the south bank of the river between Périgueux and Libourne/Bordeaux is not going to win any beauty contests either. If you want to stop, there's **St-Astier**, 15km from Périgueux, named after the 7th-century hermitage of St Asterius. Part of this, it is believed, is conserved in the crypt of the massive 11th-century church. You can tour St-Astier's subterranean **lime quarries** (***t** 05 53 54 13 85; July and Aug only*). Downriver are the castle and botanical gardens of **Château Mellet** at Neuvic-sur-L'Isle (***t** 05 53 80 86 65; open all year, July and Aug 1.30–7, rest of year 1.30–6, closed mid-Dec–mid-Jan, call first out of season; adm for both castle and gardens, joint tickets available*).

Mussidan, one of the larger villages on the Isle, has twice in its history been singled out for disaster. During the Wars of Religion all the Protestants in the vicinity took refuge there, and fought bravely against the Catholics. They surrendered when their lives were guaranteed, but the Catholics were only joking; many Protestants were hanged, and Mussidan was razed. Henri IV, in honour of the town's sufferings, had it rebuilt. In 1944, the Resistance was very active in the forests that surround Mussidan,

Where to Stay and Eat

Manzac-sur-Vern ✉ 24110

★★Le Lion d'Or, **t** 05 53 54 28 09, **f** 05 53 54 25 50 (*inexpensive*). Big bay windows over the garden and a good-value restaurant, serving sturgeon *civets* and other treats (*menus 115–210F*). *Closed Mon and several weeks out of season.*

Mussidan ✉ 24400

Le Chaufourg, in nearby Sourzac, **t** 05 53 81 01 56, **f** 05 53 82 94 87 (*luxury–expensive*). No stars: the owners say they are 'beyond the system'. An enchanting 17th-century family residence with eight rooms, set in lush leafy gardens with a heated pool; excellent restaurant, often serving sturgeon from Montpon (*open to residents only, meals à la carte, from around 300F*). *Closed Nov–April.*

★★Hôtel du Midi, Avenue de la Gare, **t** 05 53 81 01 77, **f** 05 53 82 90 14 (*inexpensive*). Near the station but very decent. The restaurant provides evening meals (*menus start at about 70F*).

Montpon-Ménestrol ✉ 24700

★★Les Puits d'Or, 7 Rue Carnot, **t** 05 53 80 33 07 (*inexpensive*). Small and welcoming, with a lovely restaurant in the garden, serving delicious regional cuisine (*menus start at 75F*). *Closed Mon all year, Sun eve in Sept–June.*

Auberge de l'Eclade, 2km north on the D730, **t** 05 53 80 28 64. Set in an old barn, with a pretty terrace, offering delicious menus at some of the most reasonable prices in Périgord for the likes of foie gras served in three different styles, and much more (*menus from 80–250F*). *Closed Tues eve, Wed, and several weeks out of season.*

French Caviare

A hundred years ago one of the most abundant fish in the Isle, Dordogne and other tributaries of the Garonne was the *créac*, the native sturgeon (*Acipenser sturio*). Ten feet long, weighing nearly 500lbs each, the luckiest specimens lived to be a hundred. Every June the female would swim up the Gironde with swarms of males to lay between 100,000 and 200,000 eggs in its rivers. In 1890, the story goes that a passing Russian prince was shocked to see local farmers feeding the eggs to pigs and chickens. 'But that is the favourite delicacy of the czar of all the Russias!' he exclaimed. The southwest's caviare industry was born.

At first it was a goldmine. After the First World War, 40 tons of caviare a year were sold; by 1940 production fell to 3 tons. In 1979, the last year that sturgeon fishing was legal, only three *créac* were caught—brought to the verge of extinction by over-fishing, pollution, dredging of the sturgeon's spawning grounds for gravel, and the building of hydroelectric works by the national electric utility, EDF. It is now a protected species, and measures are under way to bring the *créac* back in numbers: EDF has built fish passes to help the *créac* swim up river to lay their eggs, and entrepreneurs are raising the big monsters in tanks along the Isle, Gironde and Garonne. In 1991 a Siberian species, *Acipenser baeri*, that grows up to 7ft in fresh water, was introduced to river tanks, carefully isolated from the *créacs*. So far it has proved a success—producing both caviare in an operation called a 'mini-caesarean', and a million fingerlings a year, raised for meat which increasingly appears on local restaurant menus. Experts say it will take about 15 years before anyone knows if the *créac* itself will make a complete comeback in the rivers it haunted of old.

and the Maquis were in town on 11 June 1944 when an armoured German train pulled up at the station with a machine gun, and a battle began. In reprisals, 52 people were rounded up and executed, the town was pillaged and was on the point of being razed again when the Gestapo chief – unlike the Catholics – decided Mussidan had suffered enough. Mussidan is the site of the **Musée des Arts et Traditions Populaires** (*2 Rue T. Grassin,* **t** *05 53 81 23 55; open June–mid-Sept 9.30–12 and 2–5; Mar–May and mid-Sept–Nov Sat, Sun and hols only 2–6; adm*), with the usual collection of tools and furniture and traditional rooms, and a tractor from 1920, built of parts salvaged from a First World War tank.

Just north of Mussidan, the 12th-century church at **St-Martin-l'Astier** has a very unusual octagonal choir. The partly medieval, partly 16th-century **Château de Mont-Réal**, 7km east of Mussidan just off the D38 (*open July–Sept 10–12 and 2.30–6.30; adm*) belonged to Claude de Pontbriand, who accompanied Cartier to Canada and named the new French town on the St Lawrence after his home in Périgord – or so goes one possible explanation for Montréal's name. A leaflet is available in English at the tourist office in Mussidan. **Montpon-Ménestérol**, famous for its organs (musical, that is), is also the site of one of several new hatcheries that are busily replenishing the Isle with a fish that used to be king of the southwest's waterways: the sturgeon.

The Dordogne: the Vézère Valley

08

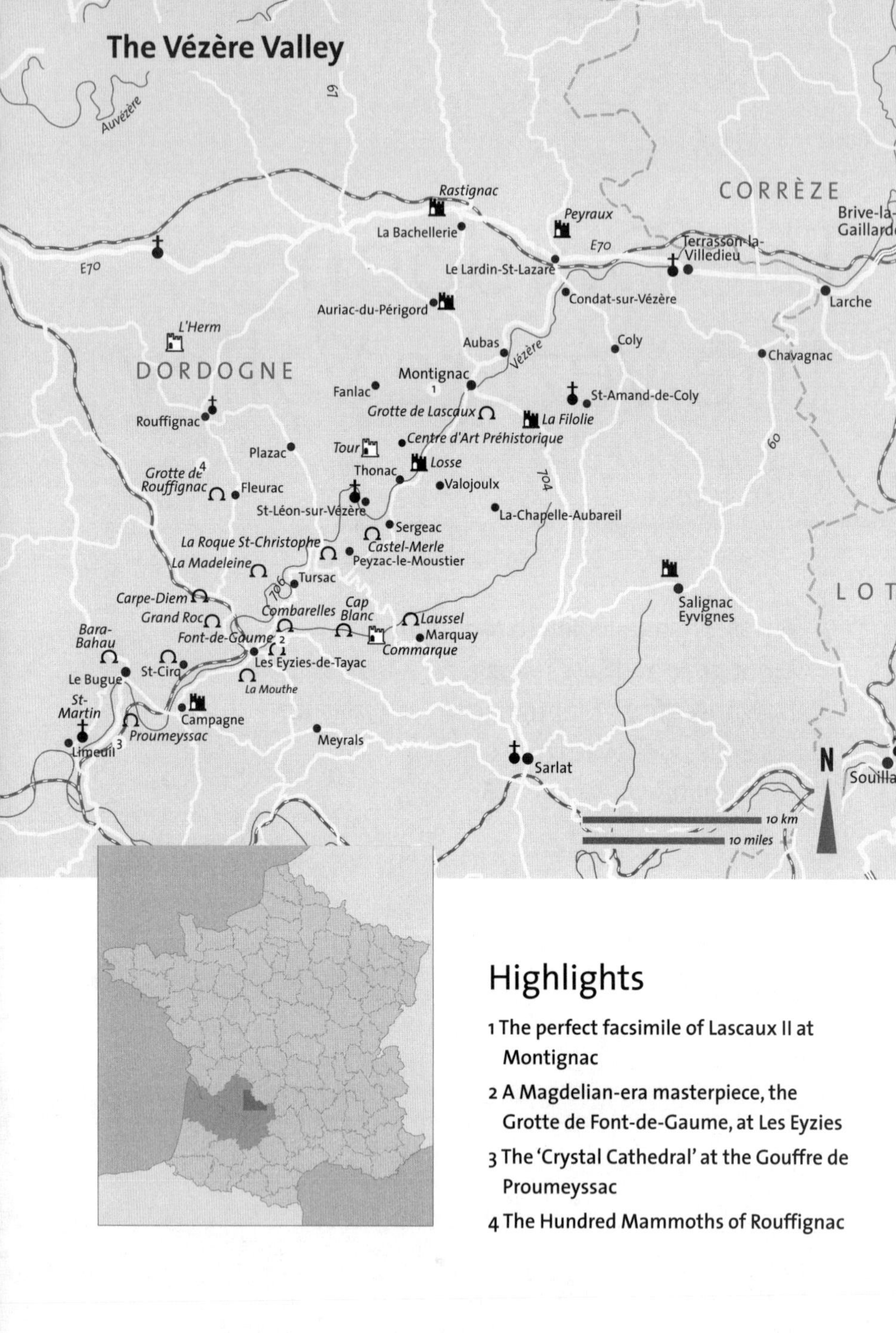

Highlights

1 The perfect facsimile of Lascaux II at Montignac

2 A Magdelian-era masterpiece, the Grotte de Font-de-Gaume, at Les Eyzies

3 The 'Crystal Cathedral' at the Gouffre de Proumeyssac

4 The Hundred Mammoths of Rouffignac

Some 400,000 years ago, when the first people settled on the fair banks of the Vézère, the river had considerably more presence, flowing 100ft higher than it does today. But it was more than gorgeous scenery that attracted these Lower Palaeolithic pioneers – the Vézère's bulging cliffs were amenably pocked with caves and shelters, there was fresh water, river pebbles and flint for manufacturing tools, and, most importantly, thundering herds of bison and reindeer that funnelled down the valley before the glaciers of the last Ice Age. Over the millennia, the hunters turned to art, and left an extraordinary record of their passing in the valley's most secret caves. When the earth heated up, the big game animals retreated northwards, somehow taking all the artistic inspiration with them, and leaving the hunters the slow, Mesolithic drudgery of inventing agriculture.

The Vézère valley yielded the first hint of its prehistoric past in 1862, when a deposit of carved flints and bones was uncovered at a place called La Madeleine. The finds suggested for the first time that mammoths and humanity coexisted at one period, henceforth known as the Magdalenian (*c.* 15,000–10,000 BC). This discovery set off a quest for signs of 'antediluvian man', leading to a torrent of accidental and organized discoveries. One of the most important occurred in 1888, during the excavations for a rail line between Périgueux and Agen, when workers at a hamlet called Cro-Magnon, near Les Eyzies, discovered five Magdalenian-era skeletons, among them a woman, a foetus and a man over 6ft tall, with a long nose, high forehead and a big brain cavity, a race from then on known as *Homo sapiens sapiens*, or Cro-Magnons.

Seven years later the first Magdalenian paintings in France were discovered at Les Eyzies' Grotte de la Mouthe. In 1908, in the caves of Le Moustier, the finding of 70,000-year-old, Neanderthal-like bones of Cro-Magnon's Middle Palaeolithic predecessors and their effects made Mousterian synonymous with Middle Palaeolithic culture (*c.* 80,000– 40,000 BC). All this remained the fare of scholarly journals until the accidental discovery of Lascaux in 1940 electrified the imagination of the entire world.

To date, some 200 Palaeolithic caves, shelters and deposits have been discovered along the Vézère, an extraordinary wealth of finds that has led UNESCO to place the valley on its list of sites to be protected as 'the heritage of humanity'. The sacredness of the place has drawn holy men from the other side of the world – near Le Moustier you'll find one of Europe's most important Tibetan monasteries.

The Vézère also attracts thousands of more worldly visitors every year, whose fiscal well-being is threatened by a score of recent roadside attractions; even worse, the *département* has spent millions of francs to increase tourist access to the river banks, a project that local property owners translated into bonanza profits for firewood, a chainsaw massacre of the lovely old groves that gave the river its special charm.

Down the Vézère: Terrasson-la-Villedieu to Montignac

Most people never make it this far north, and if they do, the Vézère is too busy with roads and train tracks. If you're driving, follow for preference the D60 and D63 between Larche and Terrasson, passing by way of **Chavagnac**, a little village with a Romanesque church guarded by a mighty watchtower.

Terrasson-la-Villedieu

The Vézère spills down the *causse* of Corrèze towards **Terrasson**, a striking medieval truffle and walnut town spanned by the **Pont Vieux**, a 12th-century bridge some 330ft long. Terrasson is built around an abbey founded in the 6th century by a certain St Sour, who according to the story let his two pet doves decide the exact spot. They flew around and around, and when they finally landed, the cry went up: '*Terra sunt*!' ('They've landed!'); hence, supposedly, Terrasson. St Sour's **church**, last repaired in 1889, has, in spite of its name, some sweet 16th-century stained glass; the church of Villedieu has a Carolingian bell. Climb to the top of the old town for the view, and come on Thursday for the lively market. **Les Jardins de l'Imaginaire** (**t** *05 53 50 86 82;*

Getting Around

Public transport is pretty thin on the ground in the Vézère valley. There are **train** stations at Terrasson and Condat-Le Lardin, on the Brive–Périgueux line, and Les Eyzies and Le Bugue can be reached on another line from Périgueux–Agen. There are also daily **bus** connections to Montignac from Périgueux and from Sarlat run by CFTA (**t** 05 53 43 13 08) but that's about it.

Tourist Information

Terrasson: Place Voltaire, **t** 05 53 50 37 56.

Market Day

Terrasson: Thurs.

Where to Stay and Eat

Terrasson-la-Villedieu ✉ 24120

L'Imaginaire, **t** 05 53 51 37 27. The stables of the old Royal Hospital now contain this fine restaurant, whose young chef produces up-to-date cuisine; charming staff too (*menus 175–265F, menu dégustation 310 or 460F, including wine*). *Closed Sun eve, Mon and Tues midday (except July and Aug) and a couple of weeks in the winter.*

Le Lardin-St Lazare ✉ 24570

******Sautet***, Route de Montignac, **t** 05 53 51 45 00, **f** 05 53 51 45 09 (*moderate*). Six generations of the same family have run this hotel but each generation has modernized the old inn to march with the times; fresh modern rooms, tennis, pool, and a good restaurant; delicious *terrine d'oie aux cèpes* (*menus 79–189F*). *Restaurant closed weekends mid-Oct–Mar and Tues and Sat lunch in summer. Hotel closed weekends and several weeks out of season.*

Condat-sur-Vézère ✉ 24570

*****Château de la Fleunie**, **t** 05 53 51 32 74, **f** 05 53 50 58 98 (*moderate*). The luxurious 13th–15th-century château is set in a 106-acre park with tennis courts, pool, driving range, sauna, stables and gourmet meals (*from 135F*). *Hotel closed for two months in winter. Restaurant closed two days a week out of season.*

open April–June and Sept–mid-Oct 10–11.30 and 2–5.30, closed Tues; July and Aug daily 10–11.30 and 2–6) condense defining elements of gardens through the centuries and across cultures onto a six-acre site, with masses of roses, mirrors and synchronized fountains among the trees.

Downriver, **Le Lardin-St-Lazare** offers the 15th-century Château de Peyraux and a 7km detour west to **La Bachellerie** – its name derived, like the English 'bachelor', from *bas-chevalier*, the lowest, youngest order of knights. It is the address of the singular neoclassical **Château de Rastignac** (1811–17) built not for Balzac's immortal social climber, but for the Marquis Chapt de Rastignac, by a Périgordin architect named Mathurin Blanchard. Blanchard studied Victor Louis's works in Bordeaux, but no one knows much else about him, especially how he came up with what looks like the prototype for the rear façade of the White House in Washington. Apparently the resemblance is only a coincidence, but it was enough to infuriate the retreating Nazis in 1944, who got symbolic revenge on Roosevelt by burning the original: what you see today is a careful restoration. It cannot be visited.

Condat-sur-Vézère, a paper-making town, was formerly run as a hospital inn for medieval pilgrims by the Knights Hospitallers. At **Aubas**, the Vézère flows past the classic, severe 17th-century **Château de Sauvebœuf**, built after the 15th-century original was flattened on the orders of Richelieu, to punish the owner for killing a man in a duel. The king's mistress, Marie de Hautefort, was so upset over this scarring of her native Périgord that she had it rebuilt. Her two monumental fountains of 1610 have gone elsewhere, one to New York, another to Clairac (*see* p.370). The village **church** has some fine works, from its 11th-century carved capitals to a pair of 16th-century retables, one in painted wood and the other in stone fragments.

Just before Montignac, the D67 detours 5km north to Auriac-du-Périgord, with its 14th–16th-century **Château de la Faye** built around a medieval keep. The château's chapel of **St Rémy** was famous throughout Périgord; nicknamed St Remédi, the saint was so reputed for his healing juju that all the features of his statue were rubbed off by ill people vigorously rubbing the afflicted parts of their bodies against him.

Montignac and Lascaux

Montignac, once a busy river port, now sits on the right bank of the Vézère, its wooden balconies reflected peacefully across the waters. Although feared for its ferocious counts in the Middle Ages, Montignac rocketed to a sweeter fame in 1940, when a pit used as the occasional dead donkey dump was discovered to house the nonpareil masterpiece of prehistoric cave painting. As extraordinary a sight in its own way is the mutant orange-coloured housing estate blighting the hills south of town.

Château de Montignac and the Counts of Périgord

Montignac had its share of glory and defeats between 15,000 BC and the discovery of Lascaux, most of it centred in the ruined **Château de Montignac** at the top of Rue de Juillet. Now only vertiginous terraces, vaulted casements and a single square tower out of a dozen that originally punctuated its thick walls remain of what was once the most important military castle in the region.

From the 11th to the 14th century, Montignac was the key to Périgord Noir and the chief citadel of the fierce bad counts of Périgord. Their name Taillefer (later Talleyrand) came from an ancestor who made a big impression by slicing a Viking in two with one swipe of his sword. They were unique among the vassals of the kings of France in having absolutely no redeeming virtues; even the hawkish troubadour Bertran de Born stood in awe of them and wrote that one count, Hélie V, was such a cuss that he slept standing up. Hélie was succeeded by his brother Roger Bernard, an ex-priest who thought the best way to govern Périgord was to crush its inhabitants, to 'destroy and pull out their vines' and 'fill their churches with soldiers and pillagers'. Yet the king supported Bernard, appreciating him for his skill at stomping on lesser barons – to the king's mind the fewer nobles the better, especially in this den of cut-throats.

But Bernard's even nastier son, Archambault V, changed sides and swore allegiance to England, and took advantage of a truce to surround Périgord with castles. He captured Domme by surprise, burned the church with all the people inside, then hunted down all the women who escaped, forcing them to cut off their dresses at the waist, for easier raping. Archambault attacked even the monasteries and royal officers, declaring himself the absolute sovereign of Périgord, and to show he meant business he destroyed half of Périgueux. The good folk of Périgord begged Charles VI for relief and in 1394 the king sent down an army to punish Archambault, destroying his fortresses and besieging Montignac for a month. Archambault sued for a truce and offered to pay a huge fine; but as soon as the royal army turned its back, Archambault tortured and hanged the king's commander.

Archambault died before the king could punish him again, leaving an heir – Archambault VI – who proved to be even worse, terrorizing Périgord with murder and mayhem, laughing at royal orders to behave. He didn't laugh so hard in 1397, when once again Montignac was besieged by a thousand men, and Archambault was forced to surrender. The king gave Montignac to his brother, Louis d'Orléans (who had to sell it for ransom money when he was captured at Agincourt) while Archambault hightailed it to London, where he connived and made everyone around him miserable until his death in 1430. By the 18th century, Talleyrand blood had cooled enough to produce a diplomat, the famous sallow-faced Charles (1754–1838), who quit as Napoleon's foreign ministry in protest against his wars, and then after Waterloo successfully negotiated to keep France's old borders.

The town was the last home of Eugène Le Roy, who worked as Montignac's tax collector before he hit the big time with his novel *Jacquou Le Croquant* (*see* p.99). Scenes from his novels, old arts and crafts, and local historical exhibits fill the **Musée Eugène Le Roy**, in the 13th-century hospital shared by the tourist office (***t*** *05 53 51 82 60; open July and Aug 9.30–12 and 2.30–5.30, call for other times; closed Jan; adm*). Nearby, the 18th-century house with columns is by Nicolas Ledoux, the architect of the famous Paris tollhouses. In medieval Rue de la Pégerie is a house Henri IV gave to his mistress, Gabrielle d'Estrées.

Tourist Information

Montignac: Place Bertran-de-Born, **t** 05 53 51 82 60, **f** 05 53 50 49 72.

Market Days

Montignac: Wed and Sat.

Where to Stay and Eat

Montignac ✉ 24290

****Château de Puy Robert**, 2km from Lascaux on the D65, **t** 05 53 51 92 13, **f** 05 53 51 80 11 (*expensive*). A bijou 19th-century neo-Renaissance château complete with turrets, set in a lovely 20-acre park with a pool; luxurious rooms in the Relais et Châteaux tradition, decorated with modern fabrics, English furniture and antiques (*closed mid-Oct–May*). The restaurant uses local ingredients to concoct innovative, exquisite dishes (*menus 250–450F*).

***Le Relais du Soleil d'Or**, 16 Rue du Quatre-Septembre, **t** 05 53 51 80 22, **f** 05 53 50 27 54 (*moderate*). An old inn surrounded by a shady park (itself a historic monument) with a heated pool as well as tennis and riding opportunities. *Closed a month in winter*. In the restaurant traditional southwestern cuisine is given a modern, lighter touch (*menus 120–285F*). *Book*.

***La Roserai**, Place d'Armes, **t** 05 53 50 53 92, **f** 05 53 51 02 23 (*moderate*). In a large 19th-century house, a charming place to stay, where you can forget about the world outside. Attractive gardens with a pool, and good restaurant (*meals 145–215F*). *Closed Oct–March*.

Le Lascaux, 109 Av Jean-Jaurès, **t** 05 53 51 82 81, **f** 05 53 50 04 73 (*inexpensive)*. A simple Logis de France hotel, with a restaurant.

De la Grotte, 63 Rue du Quatre-Septembre, **t** 05 53 51 80 48, **f** 05 53 51 05 96 (*inexpensive–cheap*). Converted from an old house. Riverside terrace, canoeing, and a playground; the restaurant is good and priced right (*menus 60F–195F*), with lots of lovely asparagus in season.

Le Bleufond, on the D65, **t** 05 53 51 83 95. The campsite nearest Montignac. *Open April–mid-Oct*.

Bellevue, in Regourdou, up by Lascaux, **t** 05 53 51 81 29. A fine place to stop for lunch, with good menus (*in the 100F range*). Just beware of coach loads of tourists. *Closed Sat and the odd week out of high season*.

La Chapelle-Aubareil ✉ 24290

La Table du Terroir, **t** 05 53 50 72 14, **f** 05 53 51 16 23 (*inexpensive*). Isolated (but signposted) off the beaten track, 7km south of Montignac, the handsome farm-hotel-restaurant offers panoramic views from its park and hilltop pool, and mini-golf for the kids. In the kitchen the emphasis is on aromatic morel mushrooms, which attain a kind of epiphany in dishes like *foie gras et cou d'oie farci aux morilles*, all based on farm products (*menus 70–220F*). *Closed Nov–Feb*.

St-Amand-de-Coly ✉ 24290

La Gardette, **t/f** 05 53 51 68 50 (*inexpensive–cheap*). Recently renovated, family-run hotel offering six quiet rooms and simple meals (*menus from 70F*). *Closed Oct–Easter*.

Coly ✉ 24120

***Manoir de Hautegente**, **t** 05 53 51 68 03, **f** 05 53 50 38 52 (*moderate*). Three km north on the D62, Coly is the site of the magnificent, ivy-covered 13th-century Manoir, which has 10 antique-furnished rooms to spoil you in comfort; the shady garden is crossed by a trout stream, and there's swimming in the heated pool. Half-pension mandatory in season, but the Périgordian cuisine is excellent—they make all their own preserves. Restaurant open to non-guests by reservation only (*menus from 150F*). *Closed Mon, Tues, and Wed lunch, and Nov–April*.

Lascaux I and II

Guided tours **t** *05 53 51 95 03 (with details of visits in English);* www.culture.fr/culture/arcnat/lascaux/fr/. *Open April–Sept 9–7, early Feb–Mar and Nov–Dec 10–12 and 2–6, Oct 9.30-12.30 and 2-6.30, closed Jan early Feb and Mon Nov–Mar. May–Sept tickets (stamped with a time) can only be bought at a special booth by the Montignac tourist office, afterwards at the site itself. Tours last 40mins. It is 13° in the cave so bring a woolie. Tickets can include admission to Thot Espace Cro-Magnon.*

One morning in September 1940, two local lads and two young refugees from Paris equipped themselves with lanterns and set off up the hill above Montignac, determined to descend into an old dump to find a legendary secret treasure that their elders believed was nothing more than an old folk tale. With difficulty the boys enlarged the overgrown opening and fumbled their way down into a treasure beyond anyone's dreams, one that had been virtually vacuum-sealed when the original entrance was blocked by an ancient landslide.

Within a week the world's authority on Palaeolithic painting, the 73-year-old Abbé Breuil, had made his way to Montignac, and was ravished by what he called the 'Sistine Chapel of Prehistoric Art'. He made Lascaux's young discoverers responsible for guarding the cave – which they did vigilantly, with shotguns. But by the early 1960s it had become clear that the Lascaux's worst enemy wasn't something to shoot at, but the 'white disease' caused by carbonic acid from the breath of a million visitors; within 15 years of its discovery, the masterpiece that had endured for millennia was fading under a film of white calcite deposits. On 20 April 1963 Lascaux was closed forever to the public; although the deterioration has completely stopped, admission is limited to five prehistorians twice a week.

Disappointment at the cave's closure was so universal that the Dordogne *département* financed the 15-year-long construction of **Lascaux II** 650ft below the original. This incredibly painstaking reproduction of the two most beautiful chambers, the **Hall of the Bulls** and the long narrow **Diverticule Axiale** (which comprise 90% of the paintings found in the original cave) was painted by Monique Peytral with the same colours and techniques used 17,000 years ago. Far better than any photograph, Lascaux II reproduces the exuberant life, movement and the clever use of natural protuberances, faults and shadows of the original, although it hardly explains how an artist limited to a lamp of animal fat and juniper twigs could get the proportions of a 16ft bull so perfectly. For Cro-Magnon artists not only drew with the unerring line of a Matisse, but mastered techniques forgotten until recently – note the three-quarter, twisted turn in the animals' heads, the Impressionistic use of perspective in the legs of running horses. Scattered among the animals is a vocabulary of mysterious unexplainable symbols reminiscent of a Joan Miró. And what of the Dr Seuss-ish beast dubbed the 'unicorn', the only known 'imaginary' creature discovered in prehistoric art? Was the painting done for a single religious rite and sealed off, never to be revisted? No signs of habitation were discovered here, and the original entrance to Lascaux I has never been found.

Humble awe is a common response to this magical place, or even a sneaking suspicion that LSD guru Terence McKenna might be right (in his book *Food of the Gods*) that Upper Palaeolithic culture was built around magic psilocybin mushrooms, a healthy psychedelic experience lost with the climatic changes at the end of the Ice Age. Whatever the truth, more than 300,000 visitors a year get a glimpse into the world of their Magdalenian ancestors.

Nearly a kilometre above Lascaux, the privately owned **Gisement du Régourdou** (***t*** *05 53 51 81 23; open daily 11–6, July–Aug 10–7; adm*) has yet to be thoroughly explored. The Cro-Magnon painters of Lascaux ground their red ochres and magnesium oxides here, but the real fascination of Régourdou is its evidence of a Neanderthal bear cult, predating Lascaux by 60,000 years (*see* pp.51–2). In a collapsed cave, 20 bear tombs were discovered: after being ritually cut up, the bear's bones were placed around its skull, sprinkled with red ochre dust and covered with a slab. Around the tombs the fossilized bones of smaller animals were found, presumably funerary gifts to the bear. Fossilized bear turds were found as well. Six feet away from the bear sepulchre, the skeleton of a Neanderthal man was found; the flint tools found here and elsewhere suggest he was left-handed. Some of the findings from the site are in a small museum which includes information on the cult of the bear in prehistory. Five bears are living on the site.

Around Montignac

Six kilometres southeast of Montignac, by the D704, stands one of the Dordogne's dreamiest châteaux, the golden limestone *lauze*-topped **Château de La Grande Filolie** (14th–15th century) – so perfect that, as Périgord novelist Marc Blancpain put it, 'one could believe it grew here, as mushrooms grow in the humid sweetness of an autumn night'. Unfortunately it cannot be visited.

Just as visually striking, the fortified church of **St-Amand-de-Coly**, 6km east of Montignac on the D704, has a massive *clocher-mur* pierced by a shallow arch and topped with a superb roof of *lauzes*, looming like a skyscraper over its narrow valley and hamlet. Built after 1124 as an Augustinian monastery, it lost its cloister and abbey in the Hundred Years' War, but was fortified so well after that calamity that the Huguenots who took shelter here in 1575 withstood six days of close cannon fire. Defensive traces remain inside as well: just under the roof you can see the path from which the monks and villagers could fire down on their besiegers. It is stirring, wholesome Romanesque, unusually built on a slope (the walls of the nave converge slightly, to create a curious perspective). The dome hovers 66ft over the nave: stand under it and sing, and like all true Romanesque churches it rings like a bell.

Downriver from Montignac to Les Eyzies

The ticket to Lascaux II can include **Le Thot Centre de Préhistoire** (***t*** *05 53 50 70 44; same hours. Reservations required: call Semitour Périgord,* ***t*** *05 53 35 50 10. Groups only until the start of July, thereafter the general public can have a go at the activities*), well signposted along the D706. Displays inside reveal the daily lives of the Lascaux artists and there are audio-visuals on Palaeolithic art and on the meticulous creation of Lascaux II, as well as a replica of the tiny chamber at the back of Lascaux, showing a stick man in a bird mask, dropping what looks like a bird decoy as a wounded bison charges and gores him. Another chamber at the back of Lascaux was painted with felines; as a rule, the artists didn't shy away from depicting dangerous animals, but hid them, either at the back or amidst other drawings (see the bear in the Chamber of the Bulls).

Outside are gathered living examples of the subjects of Lascaux – the deer and bulls, and animals that found a last refuge in Poland: European bison and Przewalski's horses, while oxen represent the wild aurochs, which died out in Poland in the 1660s. Even the extinct woolly rhinos and mammoth are animated to wiggle and roar. You can have a go at cave painting yourself on a replica wall, using as far as possible materials that would have been available to the Magdalenians.

Continuing south on the D706, a signposted lane leads to the riverside **Château de Losse**, associated with the Ophelia of Périgord, the fair Hélène of Château de Sauvebœuf, who drowned on her wedding day rather than marry the horrid old *seigneur* of Losse. In 1576, the medieval castle with its moat was converted into an elegant Renaissance palace by Jean II de Losse, governor of Guyenne under Henri IV; it has now been completely furnished with tapestries, porcelains and other 16th- and 17th-century pieces. There are also gardens and a picnic area (***t** 05 53 50 80 08; open mid-April, May and Sept 10–12.30 and 1.30–6, June–Aug 10–7; adm*).

Where to Stay and Eat

Valojoulx ✉ 24290

L'Auberge de Licorne, in the tranquil, honey-coloured square, **t** 05 53 50 77 77, **f** 05 53 51 19 04 (*inexpensive*). The courtyard is bounded by a stream. Peace reigns. *Meals available to guests.*

Moulin La Mailleraie, just up the road, **t** 05 53 51 90 13 (*cheap*). A large rambling building with simple rooms. Your only noise pollution is likely to be the stream.

St-Léon-sur-Vézère ✉ 24290

Auberge du Pont in the centre, **t** 05 53 50 73 07. The 19th-century inn still has its *lauze* roof and serves a tasty *civet d'oie au vin de Cahors* (*menus 90–130F*).

Sergeac ✉ 24290

Auberge de Castel-Merle, **t** 05 53 50 70 08, **f** 05 53 50 76 25 (*inexpensive*). This pretty hotel by the museum has four doubles and serves well-prepared specialities of Périgord on a terrace overlooking the Vézère (*menus 69–190F, and, a rarity in these parts, a vegetarian menu at 87F*). *Open Mar–Oct, closed Mon and a week out of high season. Book.*

Auberge du Peyrol, near Castel-Merle, **t** 05 53 50 72 91. Offers a picture-window overview of the lush Vézère landscape to accompany lush dishes like foie gras in Monbazillac and grilled *magret de canard* with herbs (*menus from 70–220F*). *Closed Mon exc in July and Aug, and Nov–Mar.*

Rouffignac ✉ 24580

Château de Fleurac, southwest of Rouffignac in Fleurac, **t** 05 53 05 95 01, **f** 05 53 05 98 47 (*expensive–moderate*). A 19th-century château with 15 comfortable rooms with period furnishings. *Open Easter–mid-Oct.*

Thonac, the nearest village, is dominated by an immense bell tower, but the main attraction is a leaning tower 2km away on the Plazac road, called the **Tour de Vermondie**. The story goes that a girl was imprisoned here to keep her away from her lover. When he came and sang at its foot, the tower was so moved that it bent over to allow the two to kiss. There are lovely views from here, and towards **Plazac**, a pretty little place in its valley, with a 14th-century church and episcopal palace. Due north of Thonac, the village of **Fanlac** is so perfectly intact that it was chosen as the location for the French TV film based on *Jacquou le Croquant*.

There's a bridge at Thonac crossing the Vézère to Baleinie; upriver from here, the **Ferme des Cabanes** raises geese and ducks and sells all their assorted products, next to some of the most striking dry-stone *cabanes* in the department, believed to date from the 13th century.

Rouffignac, Mammoths and the Château de l'Herm

While travelling in this corner of the Dordogne, you may have noticed that village after village has been twinned with one in Germany. In Rouffignac's case it marks a special act of forgiveness – in 1944, in reprisal for local Resistance activity, the retreating Nazis burned the village to the ground. Only the church of **St-Germain** remained, or at least most of it – the Romanesque apse is rebuilt, but under the bell tower an admirable Renaissance doorway of 1530 survives, its lintel carved with mermaids. If it's open, don't miss the Flamboyant Gothic interior, with elaborate vaulting and twisted columns.

Rouffignac has even greater claims to fame. Five kilometres south, off the D32, is the **Grotte de Rouffignac**, 'the Cave of a Hundred Mammoths' (***t*** *05 53 05 41 71; open April–June and Sept–Oct 10–11.30 and 2–5, July and Aug 9–11.30 and 2–6; adm*). First off, this is the cave to visit if you have trouble walking: a little electric train waits to trundle you 4km down into the bowels of the earth as the guide illuminates the vivid etchings, drawings of mammoths and woolly rhinoceroses, and niches in the clay floor formed by generations of hibernating bears, restlessly spinning. The ceiling of the innermost chamber is an excellent pastiche of horses, mammoths, bison, and an ibex.

Rouffignac is a good example of the way that people sometimes only see what they expect to see. Unlike many caves, its entrance has always been open, and for centuries locals would come down and take scary walks or even Sunday afternoon promenades, leaving their names and dates behind on the walls and ceilings. Only in 1956 did someone notice that the graffiti covered vigorous prehistoric masterpieces. When their authenticity was questioned, a description of them dated 1575 was produced; interestingly, even back then the author sensed that Rouffignac was a sacred place, but somehow mistook the drawings for erotic 'Love's larcenies' of our 'idolatrous forefathers'.

Other signs from Rouffignac point 6km northwest to the sinister **Château de l'Herm** (***t*** *05 53 05 46 61; tours of the interior April–mid-Sept 10–7, mid-Sept–early Nov 11–6; otherwise by appointment only, and appointments sometimes required outside*

July and Aug so call; adm), its savage, ruined towers looming over the trees, a remnant of the Fôret de Barade, once Périgord's darkest wood. Few castles in France are so bloodstained: legend tells of the 13th-century Baron de l'Herm, builder of the two heavy round towers, whose daughter Jeanne fell in love with a page. By a freak accident, the young man accidentally cut Jeanne's hand off when they first embraced; a wax one was made in its place, and in remorse the young husband swore to obey her blindly whenever she raised it. Unfortunately he became a violent drunkard, and came home one day to find her listening to a troubadour. In a jealous rage he would have slain the singer, but Jeanne raised her wax hand, and the troubadour made good his escape – only to hear Jeanne's screams as her husband cut the rest of her to bits.

Windows and openings were cut into the round feudal towers when a third tower was added by L'Herm's later owner, an ambassador of François I named Jean III de Calvimont. Calvimont had spent long periods in Italy, and graced his residence with a Flamboyant Gothic portal guarded by men-at-arms, a superb stone spiral staircase and carved fireplaces, now surreally suspended over the floorless void. Calvimont died a mysterious violent death and left L'Herm to his five-year-old daughter, Marguerite. His widow immediately married a neighbour, Foucauld d'Aubusson, and married the child Marguerite to his diabolical son, François, to make sure the property stayed in the family. But François was already in love with Marie de Hautefort (aunt of the mistress of Louis XIII), and as Marguerite grew older and François's debts grew larger, he had her strangled, beginning a new 80-year-long streak of murders at and around L'Herm involving the Calvimonts, d'Aubussons and anyone remotely connected with them. By 1652, when all the claimants had self-destructed, the château was put up for auction; not surprisingly, no one wanted the cursed place. It was eventually converted into a farm and abandoned in 1862.

Palaeolithic Agglomerations along the Vézère

Back along the Vézère, **St-Léon-sur-Vézère**, now a charming, sleepy backwater off the D706, was once a stopping point for pilgrims to Compostela: its handsome, forthright Romanesque church, built on a Gallo-Roman wall, overlooks the willows weeping into the river and a pedestrian bridge. Inside, only some battered frescoes and reliefs remain of the decoration. The village cemetery has a pint-sized version of Sarlat's *Lanterne des Morts* and some extremely rare *enfeux*, wall niche tombs from the 1200s.

Above St-Léon, you can tour the various cave and cliff dwellings (and cave *pigeonnier*) at **Le Conquil** which some believe were used and fortified from prehistoric times until the Middle Ages. There are now a range of planned activities on the site – demonstrations of how to sharpen a flint, hunt with a bow, paint cave art, etc. – at some of which you can have a go (***t*** *05 53 51 29 03; open April 10–6, May–Sept 10–7*).

St-Léon's bridge leads in a kilometre to the hamlet of **Sergeac** (by car, cross the Vézère further up or downstream), with a pretty Romanesque church of its own and a beautifully sculpted 15th-century roadside 'Hosanna' cross at the entrance to the village. In prehistoric times, the Sergeac area was the most densely populated outside Les Eyzies, with nine known shelters inhabited from 35,000 to 10,000 BC; by coincidence (or not), this favoured spot is exactly on the 45th parallel, halfway between the North Pole and the Equator. Four shelters are open to the public at the **Abri Castel-Merle** on the D65 (*t 05 53 50 79 70; open April–Oct 10–12 and 2–6, closed Sat; July and Aug daily 10–7; adm*). In one were found Magdalenian-era sculptures, and blocks of stone carved with mysterious symbols dated 32,000 BC that may have been part of a portable sanctuary.

The D66 continues south to **Peyzac-le-Moustier**, another hoary site in the annals of prehistory. Excavations begun in 1908 in the **Abri du Moustier** (*currently off limits*) have produced such a wealth of material that the last half of the Middle Palaeolithic era is known as the Mousterian culture (roughly 100,000–35,000 BC).

The bridge from Le Moustier crosses to the curved prow of **La Roque St-Christophe**, a sheer cliff half a mile long, sliced into five shelves, one of which is the largest natural terrace in Europe (*t 05 53 50 70 45; open Oct–Feb 11–4.30, Mar–Sept 10–6.30; adm*). Inhabited from Mousterian times, the hundred or so caves along the tiers were home to up to 3,000 people (the current population of Montignac), who had their own church, cemetery, monastery, and after the 900s, fort, thrown up against the Vikings sailing up the Vézère and later used as a Protestant stronghold.

If after all this, you still can't imagine daily life at the dawn of time, **Tursac** offers its **Préhistoparc** (*t 05 53 50 73 19; open daily Mar–June 10–5, July–Aug 9.30–6.30, Sept–Dec 10–5; adm*), with life-size outdoor dioramas featuring hunters killing mammoths, woolly rhinos and bears. Downriver, over the Lespinasse bridge from Tursac, the excavations at **La Madeleine** (*t 05 53 06 92 49; open daily 10–5, July and Aug 9.30–6.30*) have produced some 600 pieces of *art immobilier*, giving the name Magdalenian to the greatest age of Palaeolithic art. Although the finds are now in Les Eyzies' museum, the path from the parking lot leads to the ruins of a **troglodyte village** similar to La Roque St-Christophe: a 10th-century fort carved into the living rock, a 15th-century chapel, and, on the promontory, a ruined château.

Les Eyzies-de-Tayac, the 'World Capital of Prehistory'

The Vézère and Beune rivers meet at Les Eyzies, where the first known bones of *Homo sapiens sapiens* were discovered just above the train station at a place called Cro-Magnon. As the valley's chief crossroads, with an important prehistoric museum and sites in every direction, Les Eyzies is swamped with summer visitors, all watched over by a lumpish creature representing Cro-Magnon man, sculpted in 1930 by Paul Dardé and a grave insult to the painters of Lascaux.

Getting Around

Les Eyzies station has one **train** a day linking the town to Sarlat, Périgueux, and Agen. **Excursion taxi, t** 05 53 06 93 06. **Parking** in Les Eyzies in season is notoriously frustrating; excursion buses fill the streets like whales in a goldfish pond.

Traffic gets equally congested downriver in **Le Bugue**, the 'Crossroads of Périgord'; it has a station on the same **rail** line and a 24-hour **taxi** service to get you around, **t** 05 53 07 22 97. The **bus** company Rey operates routes around the region, **t** 05 53 07 27 22.

Tourist Information

Les Eyzies-de-Tayac: in the centre, **t** 05 53 06 97 05, **f** 05 53 06 90 79. Although the hours for the sites are accurate at the time of writing, they are prone to change: pick up the latest list and booking requirements here, as well as information on canoe and kayak hire, horse riding and trails.

Market Day

Les Eyzies: Mon.

Where to Stay and Eat

Les Eyzies-de-Tayac ✉ 24620

Expensive

*****Du Centenaire**, Rocher Penne, **t** 05 53 06 68 68, **f** 05 53 06 92 41 (suites can be *luxury*). In the centre yet far from the summer brouhaha, this is a member of the plush Relais et Châteaux group. Along with extremely pleasant rooms, it offers an outdoor heated pool, sauna and gym. What really draws the crowds, however, is the Centenaire's rather formal dining room, where chef Roland Mazère concocts some of the most exquisite meals in the entire region, preparing a daringly different menu of his own recipes based on the freshest local ingredients, accompanied by an *embarrass du choix* from one of the best wine cellars in the Dordogne (*lunch menus from 180F exc Sun, others – excellent value – from 325F*). *Closed Tues and Wed lunch, Nov–Mar.*

Moderate

*****Hôtel Cro-Magnon**, **t** 05 53 06 97 06, **f** 05 53 06 95 45. Founded nearly a century ago by the discoverer of the first Cro-Magnon bones, this creeper-covered hotel is still in the Leysalles family, with the same friendly atmosphere that attracted the first visitors to the Dordogne; the garden annexe near the pool has the nicer rooms. The restaurant, with its old oak beams, is charming both visually and on the palate, where it counts; the cuisine is as traditional as the setting (try the *lotte aux morilles* or *truffe en croustade*; *menus from 140F*). *Closed Wed lunch, mid-Oct–April.*

*****Les Glycines**, by the river, **t** 05 53 06 97 07, **f** 05 53 06 92 19. Pretty rooms in a garden setting, with a pool; the restaurant has its

Musée National de Préhistoire

t 05 53 06 45 45; open daily July and Aug 9.30–7, mid-Mar–June and Sept–mid-Nov 9.30–12, 2–6, mid-Nov–mid-Mar 9.30–12, 2–5; adm.

Tucked under the overhanging cliffs that dominate Les Eyzies, and sharing the terrace with the hapless caveman statue, the 16th-century castle belonging to the barons of Beynac was slowly being cannibalized for its stone when it found a new role in 1918 as a museum – the perfect prehistory apéritif, especially if you are not entirely familiar with the subject; tables and charts help to put the mind-boggling millennia into perspective. If, technologically, humankind got off to a slow, painstaking start (see the flint blades on Level I), the opposite is true in art: the rooms on Level II form a kind of Louvre of prehistory, with the largest collection anywhere of

own kitchen garden and serves fine regional lamb and beef dishes, as well as other Périgordin faves (*menus from 140–280F*). *Closed Sat lunch and Wed out of summer, and from mid-Oct to mid April.*

**Moulin de la Beune, t 05 53 06 94 33, f 05 53 06 98 06. An old mill has been converted into a friendly hotel, with another fine restaurant, where the chef doesn't shy away from adding innovative touches to the area's beloved local recipes.

Inexpensive

**Hôtel du Centre, t 05 53 06 97 13, f 05 53 06 91 63. Bang in the middle of Les Eyzies, this comfortable family-run hotel manages to maintain a modicum of seclusion, thanks to a pedestrian-only square by the Vézère. The restaurant serves mostly regional specialities, indoors or out under the parasols (*from 120F*). *Closed Nov–Mar.*

**Hôtel de France et du Musée, 4 Rue Moulin, t 05 53 06 97 23, f 05 53 06 90 97. Another choice in the centre, built in sturdy stone, this offers the added plus of a shady terrace, and a pool down by the annexe on the river bank. *Closed Nov–Easter.*

**Des Roches, on the road to Sarlat, t 05 53 06 96 59, f 05 53 06 95 54. In a tempting position at the foot of the cliffs with a large lawn, swimming pool and comfortable rooms but no restaurant. *Closed early Nov–Easter.*

Cheap

Les Falaises, 35 Av Préhistoire, **t** 05 53 06 97 35. A good budget choice, with parking and a little garden. *Open all year.*

La Riviere, **t** 05 53 06 97 14, **f** 05 53 35 20 85. Six tidy rooms and a large pool.

Outside Les Eyzies

***Hôtel Lamy, in Meyrals, t 05 53 29 62 46, f 05 53 59 61 41 (*expensive–moderate*). Pretty rooms full of character, bare beams, a garden and pool. *Open all year.*

La Métairie, on the D47 to Sarlat, 7km outside Les Eyzies, **t** 05 53 29 65 32. A big honey-coloured stone building with good-value meals of southwest favourites. You may not fancy eating on the patio, a bit close to the road, but inside is pleasant and peaceful enough (*menus 65–178F*). *Closed Mon lunch and Wed.*

Marquay, ✉ 24620

**Hôtel la Condamine, , t 05 53 29 64 08, f 05 53 28 81 59 (*inexpensive*). A Logis hotel in the countryside, unpretentious, calm and comfortable with a pool and restaurant (*dinner only, menus 80–180F*). *Closed Nov–mid-April.*

**Les Bories,t 05 53 29 67 02, f 05 53 29 64 15 (*inexpensive*). A large country house with a pool and restaurant. *Closed Nov–Easter.*

L'Estérel, **t** 05 53 29 67 10. Dine out on creative *perigourdine* meals in the pleasant country dining room under the beams (*menus 85–195F*). *Closed Nov–March.*

Palaeolithic reliefs and sculpture in stone, bone and ivory. These come in five chief styles. In the Primitive (35,000–25,000 BC) figures are very rare, stiff and roughly shaped; in the Archaic (25,000–15,000 BC), animals were drawn in rigid profile on walls (the Abri Pataud Venus, the animal from Abri Cellier) and the first sculptures in three dimensions were made. The final three styles belong to the Magdalenian era (*c.* 15,000–10,000 BC): the Preclassical, marking the beginnings of the great period of cave paintings; the Classical, marked by a scrupulous attention to proportions, movement and detail, which gradually reveals a decline of spontaneity until reaching the Final period at the end of the Upper Palaeolithic. There are bas-reliefs of shapely Magdalenian women, mammoths butting heads etched on a staff, the famous *Bison licking its Flank* from La Madeleine and the *Aurouchs du Fourneau de Diable*; there are rough carved vulvas and delicate ornate phalluses that make you wonder which sex carved which. Level III has a collection of casts of *art mobilier* found for the most part along the Vézère in the 19th century, including a case of those first subjects of prehistoric sculptors, the lozenge 'Venuses' – buxom, balloon-bottomed beauties common from the Urals to the Pyrenees. Level IV contains casts of Neanderthal and Cro-Magnon skulls, animal bones, and several sepulchres: the remains of bodies covered with ochre and rare seashells. Note especially the Magdalenian **tomb** from St-Germain-la-Rivière in the Gironde, where a young woman was laid out in a foetal position under what looks like a dolmen, surrounded with funerary gifts: shells, tools, ornaments and animal bones. The museum buildings are currently being extended to allow its full collection to be shown.

Under a rocky overhang in the centre of Les Ezyies is the equally remarkable **Abri Pataud** (***t*** *05 53 06 92 46; open July–Aug 10–7; adm*) where Upper Palaeolithic hunters lived on 40 separate occasions over a span of 15,000 years. A **museum** in the nearby shelter contains the finds, including one of the oldest known bas-reliefs, an ibex dated 18,000 BC. Near the station, the Hôtel Cro-Magnon marks the site where *Homo sapiens sapiens* was discovered; here too is the 13th-century **St Martin-de-Tayac**, an imposing fortified church with antique columns on the porch.

Font-de-Gaume

Guided tours daily exc Wed, April–Sept 9–12 and 2–6, Oct–Mar 10–12 and 2–5; adm. Reservations essential in summer: contact the Service de Réservation de la Grotte de Font-de-Gaume, ***t*** *05 53 06 86 00, which also takes booking for other sites around Les Eyzies. Reservations can be made several days in advance.*

Although the Grotte de la Mouthe (where the first cave paintings in France were discovered just south of Les Eyzies) has been closed since 1981, 200 visitors a day are allowed into the Grotte de Font-de-Gaume, a 10min walk east along the D47. Font de Gaume has nothing less than the finest polychrome prehistoric **paintings** open to the general public in France, although as in Rouffignac the cave was visited centuries before the paintings were 'discovered' in 1901.

A path from the ticket booth/shop leads up to the entrance; inside, beyond a narrow passage called 'the Rubicon', the walls are adorned with beautiful paintings and engravings in remarkable flowing lines dating from *c.* 12,000 BC, created with the same drawing and colour-blowing techniques used at Lascaux, and similarly using natural relief to lend volume to the drawing. Although calcite build-ups and graffiti over the years have damaged some of the paintings, others look as if they were made yesterday: magnificent friezes of red and black bison on a light background, reindeer, horses with legs and heads partially formed by natural features in the cave walls. The guide will adjust the lighting in several ways to bring out the extraordinary fullness and depth of the art – it's almost impossible to believe that anyone could make such perfect lines and shading on an irregular stone surface with only a dim smoking lamp of mammoth fat to guide their hand. The partially painted, partially engraved black stag and kneeling red doe are unique in the canon of Upper Palaeolithic art, and only become visible after the guide carefully traces out the lines with a light. The stag is leaning over delicately to lick the doe's brow, an image of tenderness as sublime as it is startling, and one that questions a lot of commonly held assumptions about life 14,000 years ago. (Font-de-Gaume is the rendezvous for visiting Laugerie Haute, *see* below.)

East of Les Eyzies, along the Beune Valley

A kilometre up the D47, the **Grotte des Combarelles** was discovered in the same year as Font-de-Gaume (*reserve,* ***t*** *05 53 06 86 00, open same hours as Font-de-Gaume, closed Wed; adm, buy tickets at Font-de-Gaume*). Some 800 different engravings dated 12,000–10,000 BC have been distinguished in the cave's last 400ft, including 140 horses and 48 rare human representations – hands, masks, women and a seated person. Many are incomplete, most are superimposed in wild abandon, and others only appear when lit from various angles. Most beautiful of all is the reindeer leaning forward to drink from a black cavity suggesting water. A year later and 3km down the road, 100 paintings and engravings were found in the **Grotte de Bernifal**, near the left bank of the Petite Beune, in Meyrals (***t*** *05 53 29 66 39; open July and Aug 9.30–7, June and Sept 9.30–12.30 and 2.30–6; out of season by appointment; adm*). The dominant animal is the mammoth, stylistically similar to the ones in Rouffignac (*c.* 12,000 BC), in the company of many 'tectiform' (roof-shaped) symbols; but the star of the show is a rare, engraved ancestor of the ass.

More prehistory waits around **Marquay**: the **Abri du Cap Blanc** (***t*** *05 54 59 21 74; daily April–Oct 9.30–7; July and Aug 10–7; adm*) has a remarkable, vigorous, 42ft frieze of nearly life-size horses in high relief, following the natural contours of the limestone cliff; the shelter also yielded a Cro-Magnon tomb and tools from the end of the Magdalenian age. Just beyond rise the majestic, romantic ruins of the 12th–13th-century **Château de Commarque**, a castle betrayed to and ruined by the English in the Hundred Years' War; the elegant keep was added in the 16th century. On the cliff opposite, the much-restored 14th-century **Château de Laussel** sits over the Gisement de Laussel (100,000–17,000 BC), which produced the famous relief of the *Vénus de Laussel*, holding her bison horn (now in Bordeaux, but there's a cast in the museum in Les Eyzies).

North of Les Eyzies

Along the opposite bank of the Vézère from Les Eyzies, the D47 is choc-a-bloc with the works of nature and humankind. First, the **Musée de la Spéléologie** (*open July and Aug Sun–Fri 10–6; adm*), set in the natural rock fortress of Tayac, offers summer visitors a look at the formation of caves, and the tools and art of potholing. A number of shelters are scattered in the pretty **Parc Gorge d'Enfer** (***t*** *05 53 06 86 00; open July–Aug 10–8, June and Sept 10–7, other times by appointment*), including the famous **Abri de Poisson** (*opened only on request to the reservation service at Font-de-Gaume*). This has a rare relief of a fish – a salmon over a yard long. It is nearly detached from the ceiling; an enterprising German had sold it secretly to a museum in Berlin, but the French found out just in time and classified the site, preserving the fish *in situ*.

Further along the D47 is a fairy work by Mother Nature, the stalactite Grotte du **Grand Roc**, halfway up a cliff. This cave is known for its extremely rare triangular formations; others resemble coral, some thumb their nose at the law of gravity (***t** 05 53 06 92 70, open Feb–March and Nov–Dec 10–5, April–June and Sept–Oct 9.30–6, July and Aug 9.30–7, closed Jan*). Nearby, you can also tour the **Gisement de Laugerie Basse** (*same hours as Grand Roc; combined adm available*), one of the first shelters excavated, in 1863, and a rich source of *art immobilier*. The adjacent **Abri de Marseilles** was occupied continuously from the Magdalenian to the Gallo-Romans. Although most of the finds have been scattered to museums around the world, a small museum on the site has tools and decorated fragments.

Continuing up the D47, at the **Gisement Laugerie Haute** (*only open on request to the reservation service of Font-de-Gaume*), 42 levels of human habitation have been excavated over the last 120 years, at the bottom of the cliff. When the massive top terrace of the cliff collapsed *c.* 14,000 BC, it had already been home to people for 11 millennia. There are a number of Solutrean (20,000 BC) engravings as well as a sort of carved gutter, an early attempt to solve a problem that would ever after plague humanity – leaking roofs.

Further up near Manaurie, another cave, **Carpe Diem**, has lovely coloured stalactites (***t** 05 53 06 91 07; open April–June and Sept–Oct 10–6, July and Aug 9.30–7, Nov–Dec 10–5*). Lastly, the **Grotte du Sorcier**, discovered in 1956, 5km southwest of Les Eyzies at St-Cirq-du-Bugue (**t** 05 53 07 14 37, *open all year 12–4, mid-May–mid-Sept 10–7*) is also known as the Cave of the Sorcerer, for its rare engraving of a Magdalenian man with a mask-like cartoon face and a body like that of a deer. It also has a dappled horse among other engravings, and a small museum.

To Le Bugue-sur-Vézère

There are even more caves south of Les Eyzies, around Le Bugue. One of the major crossroads of the Dordogne, it can get very busy, and has a few attractions of its own.

Caves, Bears, and Fish

From Les Eyzies, the D706 follows the Vézère down to the village and Romanesque church of Campagne, and the 15th-century **Château de Campagne**, given a William Morris neo-Gothic facelift in the 19th century. There's been no tinkering, however, with the magnificent trees in the château's park and its forest stair, the Chemin des Dames. Unfortunately the château is private (*closed to the public*). Campagne, like so many villages in the area, has its cave to visit, but instead of art or stalactites it is a **Cave Champignonnière** – full of tasty fungi (***t** 05 53 07 01 03; open daily Easter–June and Sept–mid-Oct 10–12 and 2–5, July and Aug 10–6*).

The Vézère flows broadly past **Le Bugue**, a market town full of roadside attractions, including a pair of caves. The prehistoric **Grotte de Bara-Bahau**, 2km to the northwest (***t** 05 53 07 44 58; open all yea, 10–12 and 2–5.30, July and Aug 9–7, closed Jan; adm*), belonged to the bears before graffiti artists moved in some 35,000 years ago. Its

Tourist Information

Le Bugue: Place de l'Hôtel-de-Ville, **t** 05 53 07 20 48, **f** 05 53 54 92 30.

Market Days

Le Bugue: Tues and Sat.

Where to Stay and Eat

Campagne ✉ 24260

****Le Château, t** 05 53 07 23 50, **f** 05 53 03 93 69 (*inexpensive*). Sixteen tranquil rooms furnished with antiques, plus a good restaurant: try the *escalope de foie gras aux fruits rouges* and fillet of trout (*menus from 110F*). *Closed mid-Oct--Palm Sunday.*

Le Bugue ✉ 24260

*****Royal Vézère**, Place de l'Hôtel de Ville, **t** 05 53 07 20 01, **f** 05 53 03 51 80 (*moderate*). Though large, this is less royal than it might be, but houses an excellent restaurant, Les Trois As, with delicious meals, served on a superb terrace over the river (*menus 98–290F*). *Closed Tues and Wed lunch and three weeks in Feb.*

*****Domaine de La Barde**, on the route to Périgueux, **t** 05 53 07 16 54, **f** 05 53 54 76 19 (*moderate*). The fanciest rooms in the area, a pretty garden with a pool, sauna and tennis, and a restaurant. *Closed mid-Oct–mid-April.*

****L'Auberge du Noyer**, at Le-Reclaud-de-Bouny-Bas (it's fun to say) on the D703, **t** 05 53 07 11 73, **f** 05 53 54 57 44 (*inexpensive*). In an 18th-century Périgordin farm with plenty of character; garden, pool, restaurant and riding nearby (*menus from 85F*). *Closed Sat lunch and Nov–mid-Feb.*

****Le Cygne**, Le Cingle, **t** 05 53 07 17 77, **f** 05 53 03 93 74 (*inexpensive*). In a bit of a busy spot but not bad at night. A very good and popular restaurant serving regional favourites (*menus 88–168F*). *Closed several weeks out of season; restaurant closed Sun eve and Mon except in July and Aug.*

****Paris**, 14 Rue de Paris, **t** 05 53 07 28 16, **f** 05 53 04 20 89 (*inexpensive–cheap*). In the centre with simple rooms. *Open all year.*

walls, 'as soft as white cheese' as one prehistorian put it, are covered with rustic flint-blade carvings from the Aurignacian culture; among them are animals (including a rare silhouette of a bear), hand or claw marks, and other mysterious signs. The second cave is a chasm, the **Gouffre de Proumeyssac**, 3km south on the D31E (***t*** *05 53 07 27 47; open Feb, Nov, Dec 2–5, Mar, April, Sept and Oct 9.30–12 and 2–5.30, May and June 9.30–6.30, July and Aug 9–7, closed Jan; wheelchair access; adm*). For centuries protected by demonic legends, Proumeyssac was explored only in 1907; its nickname, the 'Crystal Cathedral', comes from its extraordinary domed chamber of yellow and white stalactites and draperies.

Although freshwater fish lack the glamour of their salty kin, Le Bugue's **Aquarium du Périgord Noir** (***t*** *05 53 07 10 74; open mid-Feb–Mar and Oct–mid-Nov 10–5, April, May and Sept 10–6, June–Aug 9–7, until midnight on Sat; adm*) brings out the charms of pike, sturgeon, eels and turtles in imaginative indoor and outdoor settings; in one hall the fish swim right over your head. A section of exotic fish add a splash of colour. You can plunge under the water in an old-fashioned diving suit and meet the fish face to face (*call for details*). Just beyond, the **Village du Bourant** (***t*** *05 53 08 41 99; open 10–5, May–Sept till 7, closed mid-Jan–mid-Feb; adm*) makes a game attempt to recreate Périgord of a century ago with craft demonstrations such as walnut-oil pressing and the carving of sabots, or wooden clogs – you can understand how one of these tossed into a machine could mother a new word, 'sabotage'. You can also, for free, visit the wild boars at **Les Sangliers de Mortemart** (***t*** *05 53 03 21 30; daily at 3pm June–Sept, during French school holidays, and on weekends*).

From Le Bugue the D31E follows the Vézère to its confluence with the Dordogne at Limeuil (*see* p.187); becoming the D51, the road crosses the Dordogne for Le Buisson, from where the D25 goes to Cadouin (*see* p.184).

Down the Dordogne I

09

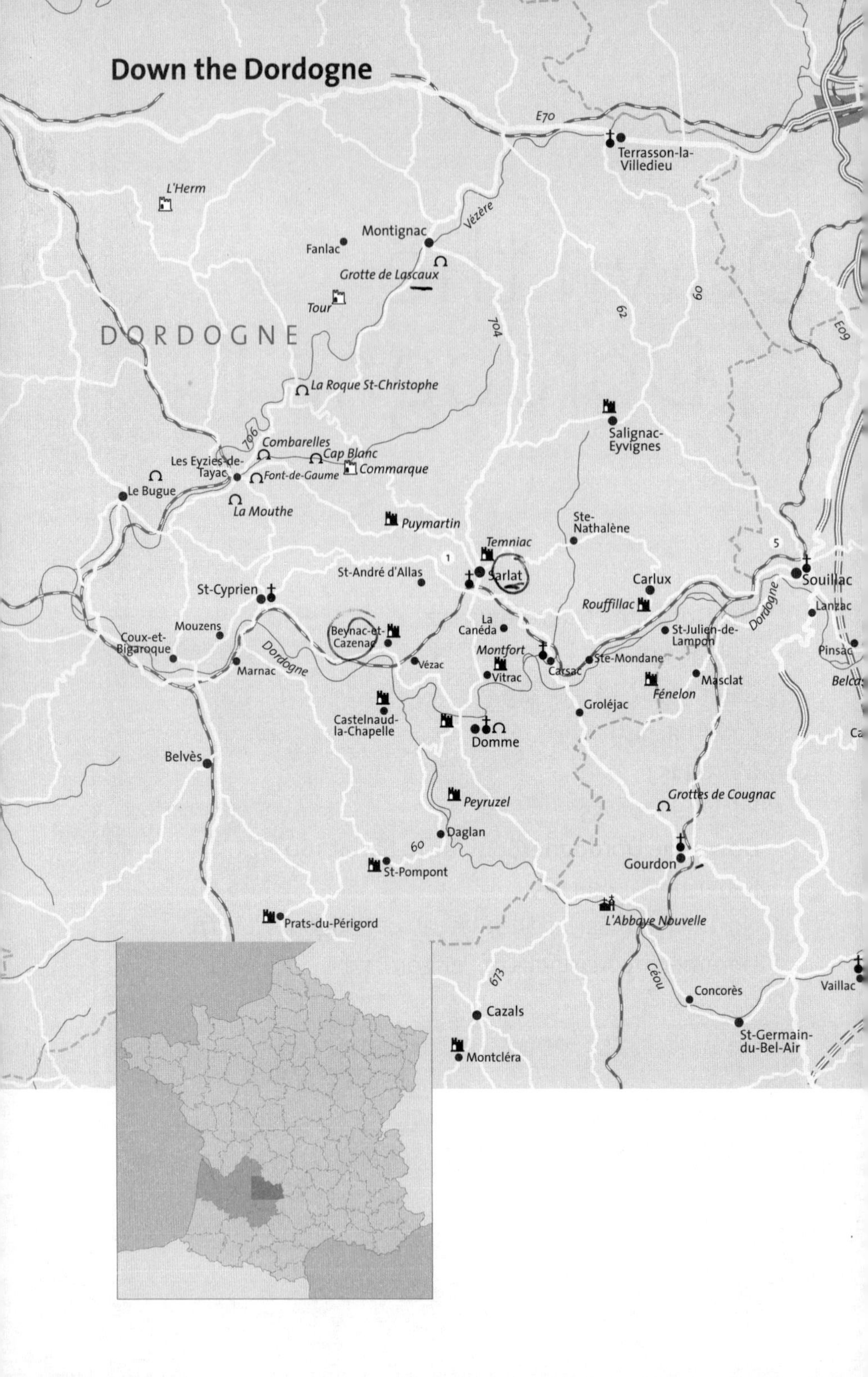

Down the Dordogne
E70
Terrasson-la-Villedieu
L'Herm
Montignac
Vézère
Fanlac
Grotte de Lascaux
Tour
704
62
60
E09
DORDOGNE
La Roque St-Christophe
Salignac-Eyvignes
706
Combarelles
Cap Blanc
Commarque
Les Eyzies-de-Tayac
Font-de-Gaume
Le Bugue
La Mouthe
Puymartin
Ste-Nathalène
Temniac
1
5
St-André d'Allas
Sarlat
Carlux
Souillac
St-Cyprien
Rouffillac
Lanzac
Dordogne
Mouzens
La Canéda
St-Julien-de-Lampon
Coux-et-Bigaroque
Beynac-et-Cazenac
Montfort
Pinsac
Marnac
Vézac
Carsac
Ste-Mondane
Vitrac
Masclat
Fénelon
Groléjac
Castelnaud-la-Chapelle
Domme
Belvès
Peyruzel
Grottes de Cougnac
Daglan
60
Gourdon
St-Pompont
L'Abbaye Nouvelle
Prats-du-Périgord
673
Céou
Concorès
Vaillac
Cazals
St-Germain-du-Bel-Air
Montcléra

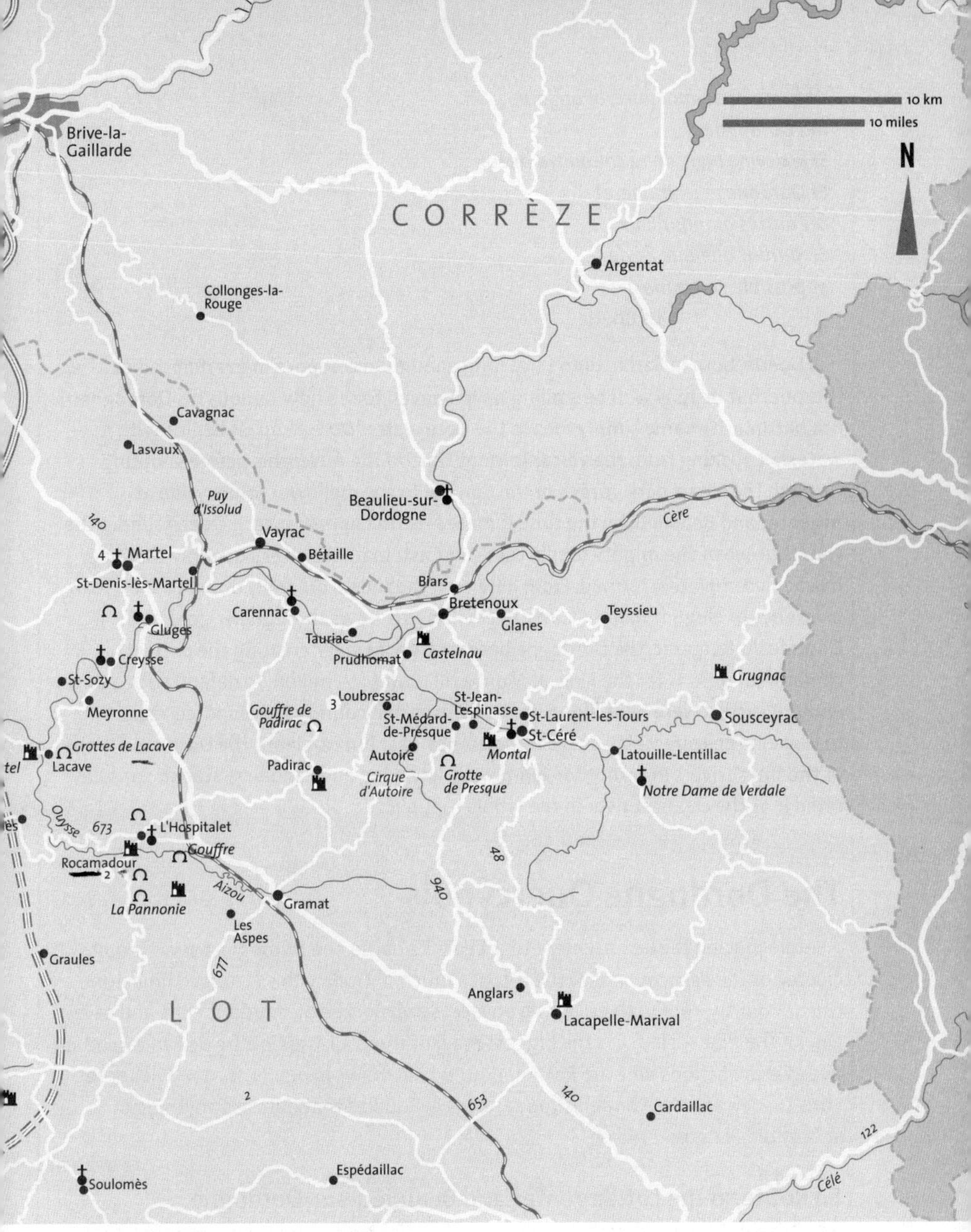

Highlights

1 Golden Renaissance curlicues at Sarlat
2 Vertical Rocamadour, a town stood on its side
3 Guided tours by gondola into the earth's bowels at Padirac
4 The Seven Towers of Martel
5 *Dancing Isaiah* and other Romanesque charms of Souillac

...Laisse, laisse-moi faire, et un jour,
ma Dordogne
Si je devine bien, on te connaîtra mieux
Et Garonne et le Rhône, et
ces autres grands dieux
En auront quelque envie
et possible vergogne
La Boétie

La Boétie, born in Sarlat, didn't live long enough to compose many rhapsodies after this one, but he may well be smiling up in heaven to see how famous his Dordogne has become. Its name simply means the Dore water, '*Dore d'eau*'; it begins with a waterfall gushing from the volcanic Mont Dore in the Auvergne, before shooting through the steep, dark gorges of the Corrèze to the mellower countryside at Argentat and Beaulieu; by the time it makes its first appearance in Quercy, under the watchful eye of the mighty feudal castle of Castelnau, the river's queenly character has been completely formed. From here on it meanders dreamily down to the ocean in a series of elegant hairpin turns, or *cingles*, as it flows through Périgord and Gironde. At Bergerac, the Dordogne becomes a wine river, creating the perfect climatic conditions for the likes of Monbazillac and St-Emilion. To defend such a prize, enough castles were built along its banks, especially during the Hundred Years' War, to make it the Loire valley of the Middle Ages. Last but not least, the Dordogne is one of the finest rivers in France for swimming, kayaking and canoeing: statisticians have rated it as the cleanest river in the whole republic.

The Dordogne Quercynois

Before gracing the *département* that bears its name, the Dordogne flows through Quercy, or the *département* of the Lot. Like much of Quercy this is rugged limestone *causse* country, shot with green velvet valleys and pocked by dramatic cliffs and caves. One of the first such pits is the biggest maw of them all, the Gouffre de Padirac; other five-star attractions here are Rocamadour, which draws in nearly as many visitors as Euro-Disney, and the Romanesque carvings in Souillac that outclass anything in snooty old Périgord.

En Route to the Lot: Argentat and Beaulieu-sur-Dordogne

At **Argentat** the Dordogne suddenly turns from a swift mountain river into a civilized waterway. The Romans founded a port town here, and for centuries the boatmen of Argentat would load timber, cheese, leather, pelts and wine on to their flat-bottomed *gabares* and make their way down to Bordeaux, where the *gabares* themselves would be sold for firewood. The old quay at Argentat has several on display; the town itself, under its sloping *lauze* roofs, has the air of a merry, prosperous pensioner. **Beaulieu**, a lovely town 25km downriver, is even more thoroughly medieval, built around the showcase 12th–13th-century Benedictine abbey church **St-Pierre**, with a magnificent complex tympanum of the *Last Judgement*. This is stylistically similar to the work of the School of Toulouse in Moissac or Soulliac, although here Christ has his arms outstretched in triumph while a carnival of apocalyptic monsters roll below across the lintel, supported by a strange figure Freda White described as 'flowing upward like a flame of prayer'. The whole inspired Abbot Suger, the inventor of Gothic, in his choice of a tympanum for Paris's St-Denis in 1140.

The Château de Castelnau and Bretenoux

The Dordogne bristles with castles, but the oldest, the burnished red **Château de Castelnau** (***t*** *05 65 10 98 00; hour-long guided tours daily exc Tues, summer 9.30–12.15 and 2–6.15, nonstop July and Aug until 6.45, winter 10–12.15 and 2–5.15; adm*) is the most redoubtable of them all, rising high on a conical, 750ft outcropping over the confluence of the Dordogne and the Cère – the spot where the big river flows into the *département* of the Lot. Begun in the year 1000, the building evolved over the centuries, and today the castle is rated the second military castle in France after Pierrefonds in the Oise. That's only fair, for its disdainful lords claimed to be 'the second barons of Christendom'. In 1184, when their liege lord the Count of Toulouse put them under the suzerainty of the nearby viscounts of Turenne, they were so insulted that only after the King of France intervened did they agree to pay the most begrudging tribute to Turenne: one egg, ceremoniously transported by a yoke of four oxen. In 1851 much of the château was damaged by arson, but Jean Mouliéret, tenor at the Opéra Comique, came to the rescue, rebuilding and sumptuously refurnishing one wing; his *objets d'art* and collection of triptyches remain. Inside you can see the Grande Salle, where the Etats du Quercy met, fragments of 11th-century sculpture, the chapel, vaulted cellars and the deep, long-forgotten oubliettes, where seven skeletons were discovered.

Clustered at the foot of the stone behemoth, the hamlet of **Prudhomat-Castelnau** is worth a stop for its 15th-century Collégiale, with Renaissance windows and sculptures. The main urban venture of the lords of Castelnau, however, was the *bastide* of Bretenoux founded on the left bank of the Cère in 1277. Now making some claim as

Vin des Côteaux de Glanes

Just east of Bretenoux, Glanes is the epicentre of one of France's least known *vins de pays*. Grown on the slopes of the mountains of Auvergne, a combination of 45% Gamay-Beaujolais, 45% Merlot, and 10% Ségalin, Côteaux de Glanes was first mentioned in 840 and began to make a comback in a serious way in 1966. In 1976, the growers formed a cooperative, now the Vignerons du Haut-Quercy, t 05 65 39 73 42; to maintain quality, production is limited to 30 hectares. Côteaux de Glanes, red or rosé, can be drunk after the first year, when it has a cherry fragrance; after three to five years it grows spicy, with grace notes of cinnamon and cloves. You can take in most of the winegrowing area, and a good bit of first-rate scenery as well, in a circular tour, continuing east of Glanes to Teyssieu, then continuing down to St-Céré on the little D40.

Getting Around

The main SNCF **rail** line between Paris and Toulouse stops at Brive and usually at Souillac (but check). Get off at Brive to transfer to Bretenoux, Bétaille (4km from Carennac) or Vayrac on the Brive–Aurillac line, or St-Denis-lès-Martel or Padirac-Rocamadour on the secondary Brive–Toulouse line.

Buses link St-Céré with the Gare Bretenoux-Biars, 8km away (*summer only*).

In St-Céré you can hire a **bike** or mountain bike at Rue Faidherbe, **t** 05 65 38 03 23, in Bretenoux at Cycles Peugeot, Av de la Libération, **t** 05 65 38 41 56.

Tourist Information

Bretenoux: Av de la Libération, **t** 05 65 38 59 53, **f** 05 65 39 72 14.
St-Céré: Place de la République, **t** 05 65 38 11 85, **f** 05 65 38 38 71.

Market Days

Bretenoux: Tues and Sat.
St-Céré: Sat. Fairs the first and third Wed of each month.

Where to Stay and Eat

Bretenoux ✉ 46130

****Le Domaine de Granval**, halfway to St-Céré, **t** 05 65 38 63 99 (*inexpensive*). The only hotel in the area, it offers seven well-furnished rooms in a restored farmhouse, set back from the road, with a pool, playground and an inexpensive restaurant. *Closed Mon midday and a month in winter.*

Ferme de Borie, **t** 05 65 38 41 74 (*inexpensive*). A *chambres d'hôte* with a panoramic terrace.

La Croix de Piou, Bd des Tilleuls, **t** 05 65 38 42 62. Very child-friendly, with a box of toys; it serves excellent regional cuisine, or almost any ethnic cuisine you can imagine, if you ring ahead (Russian, Italian, Chinese, American, vegetarian, etc.). The owners picked up their eclectism – most unusual in the Lot – while living in England (*menus 62–167F*). *Closed Sun eve, Mon and holiday eves.*

St-Céré ✉ 46400

*****Le Coq Arlequin**, 1 Bd du Dr-Roux, **t** 05 65 38 02 13, **f** 05 65 38 37 27 (*moderate*). Once the secret headquarters of the British Supply and Intelligence Organization for the local Resistance. The same family, the Bizats, still own the ivy-covered hotel and have recently redecorated the rooms to make them more comfortable than ever. Breakfast

'Jam Capital of Europe' thanks to its two large jam companies, its typical grid plan survives, as do some medieval arcades and houses in **Place des Consuls**, the old market square. It also has one of the nicest swimming holes on the Dordogne, on the Ile de la Bournatelle.

St-Céré and St-Laurent-les-Tours

From Bretenoux it's 9km south on the D940 to **St-Céré**, a charming town romantically set on the banks of the Bave, 'babbler', which tumbles down the *causse* to join the Dordogne. St-Céré reached its peak in the 15th century and has never had any compelling reason to change anything since then. Before it found its destiny as a small art colony, tourist base for the upper Dordogne and centre of a renowned festival of voice in the summer, the visitors to St-Céré were pilgrims, come to visit the relics in the church of **Ste-Spérie**. Spérie, the daughter of the lord of St-Laurent-les-Tours, refused to marry a noble pagan and literally lost her head over him. She picked up her detached noggin and, a tidy soul, gave it a last wash before expiring (794). The

served; but the restaurant is Les Prés de Montal (*see* below), 2km away.

★★★**Trois Soleils de Montal**, St-Jean Lespinasse, **t** 05 65 10 16 16, **f** 05 65 38 30 66 (*moderate*). A large villa in extensive grounds, well respected, with spacious rooms and balconies and the facilities you would expect. The restaurant is Les Prés de Montal (*see* below).

★★★**France**, 181 Av F. de-Maynard, **t** 05 65 38 02 16, **f** 05 65 38 02 98 (*moderate*). Offers cosy modern rooms, a flower garden and pool, and an elegant restaurant with delicious *marmite Quercynoise en croûte* if you like sweetbreads, other dishes if you don't (*menus 120–260F*). *Closed Nov–Easter.*

★★★**Ric**, 2km south in St-Vincent-du-Pendit, **t** 05 65 38 04 08, **f** 05 65 38 00 14 (*moderate*). Only five rooms but they enjoy marvellous views over St-Céré and a beautiful pool. The pretty restaurant serves the classic south-west cuisine with a creative touch (*menus 200–350F*). *Closed every lunchtime except Sun, and mid-Nov–Easter.*

★★**Victor Hugo**, 7 Av du Maquis, **t** 05 65 38 16 15, **f** 05 65 38 39 91 (*inexpensive*). In the centre of town, run by a transplanted Irishman Monsieur Tom; serves lovely *cuisine recherchée* in a 16th-century inn, with nine pretty rooms (*menus 90–200F*). *Closed Mon, in summer also Sun eve, and several weeks out of season.*

Les Prés de Montal, out on the road in Gramat, next to the pool and tennis courts, **t** 05 65 38 28 41. The restaurant for Le Coq Arlequin and Trois Soleils de Montal (*menus 105 and 160F*). *Closed Fri , Tues lunch and Nov–Feb.*

Loubressac ✉ 46130

Château de Gamont, on the D30, **t** 05 65 10 92 03 (*moderate–inexpensive*). An extremely pleasant 17th-century bed-and-breakfast castle, its rooms furnished with antiques. *Open June–Sept; at other times book in Paris,* **t/f** 01 48 83 01 91.

★★**Les Calèches de Py**, at Py-Loubressac, **t** 05 65 39 75 06 (*inexpensive*). A great old stone barn with a superb view over the Château de Castelnau, converted into charming *chambres d'hôte. Closed Nov–Easter.*

★★**Lou Cantou**, **t** 05 65 38 20 58, **f** 05 65 38 25 37 (*inexpensive*). A Logis de France in an old stone building, with lovely views. *Open all year.*

Sousceyrac ✉ 46190

Au Déjeuner de Sousceyrac, **t** 05 65 33 00 56, **f** 05 65 33 04 37. Eight pleasant rooms and an appetizing restaurant, concentrating on local ingredients; the *millefeuille de foie gras* with truffles is unforgettable (*menus 125–240F*). *Closed mid-Oct–mid-April. Book.*

exact spot of her martyrdom is marked with a black grid in front of the altar steps, and her bones lie in the Carolingian crypt, along with a curious Celtic altar, but it's only open on 12 October for her feast day. The rest of the church had to be rebuilt after the Wars of Religion, but there's an interesting *Nativity* in one of the right-hand chapels.

Place du Mercadial, St-Céré's beautiful main market square, is surrounded by half-timbered buildings; the stone benches on the Rue Pasteur corner were for centuries used by fishermen to display their catch. Other medieval-Renaissance houses are everywhere, especially along Rue du Mazel, Rue d'Ollier, Rue St-Cyr, Impasse Lagarouste and Quai des Récollets. On the latter, look for the 18th-century Chapelle des Récollets, decorated with a charmingly painted casement ceiling.

The first artist to establish himself in the area was Jean Lurçat, whose works are on permanent display in St-Céré's **Galerie du Casino** (***t** 05 65 38 19 60; open May–Sept 11–7, rest of year 9.30–12 and 2–6.30, closed Tues and Sun out of season*) and up at the craggy medieval towers of **St-Laurent-les-Tours**. These were purchased in 1945 by

Jean Lurçat and the Renaissance of French Tapestry

After extensive travels in Spain, North Africa and the Middle East, painter Jean Lurçat (1892–1966) spent four decades covering canvases with his memories of the colourful designs of the indigenous peoples he had met, marked by a streak of fantasy and interest in natural forms. In 1939 he was appointed head designer of the Aubusson tapestry factory, a task that marked a turning point both in his career and in the history of French tapestry. For by the 20th century, the proud art of Aubusson, the Gobelins and Beauvais had hit rock bottom, reduced to endlessly reproducing cartoons from the age of the big Louis, themselves servile imitations of paintings. Lurçat's great contribution was to return the art of tapestry to the weavers, creating cartoons that respected the medium and its techniques, combining abstract forms with a return to medieval stylisation (see his famous *Apocalypse* of 1948 in Assy, Haute-Savoie). His main *leitmotiv* at this time, a colourful cockerel or *Coq Arlequin*, was a symbol to restore Gallic pluck after the war.

Lurçat, who had fallen in love with the area while fighting with the Maquis; they now form the **Atelier Musée Jean Lurçat** (***t*** *05 65 38 28 21; open 15 days around Easter, 14 July–Sept 9.30–12 and 2.30–6.30; adm*).

West of St-Céré: Château de Montal to Autoire

Only 2km from St-Céré, the golden **Château de Montal** (***t*** *05 65 38 13 72; open Palm Sun–Oct 9.30–12 and 2.30–6, closed Sat; adm*) was the special project of Jeanne de Balzac, daughter of Robert de Balzac, who had served as governor of Pisa during the wars of Italy. Jeanne, who had accompanied him, was enraptured by the Italian Renaissance, and decided to replant some of it in this corner of *la France profonde* as a surprise gift for her own son, Robert, while he was fighting in Italy; much to Jeanne's despair, he was killed before ever setting eyes on it. After surviving all subsequent wars and the Revolution, the château fell at the end of the 19th century into the hands of a greedy speculator who spent 22 years stripping it of every decoration. In 1908, when only the frame of the staircase remained, an oil tycoon named Maurice Fénaille stepped in, bought Jeanne's château, repurchased as many of its original works as he could, and had copies made of the bits the Americans wouldn't sell back. The sculptures that had been purchased by the Louvre were returned when Fénaille donated the château and all its fittings to the state in 1913.

From the exterior, Montal looks like a typical medieval castle, but once you step inside the rough walls a magical courtyard opens up, decorated with lovely façades, ornate dormers and an imaginative frieze over 100ft long, attributed to the same sculptors who worked in Biron (*see* pp.361–2); note the intertwined initials of Jeanne and her sons Robert and Dordé. Seven of the finest Renaissance portrait busts in France occupy the niches between the windows, and are said to depict accurately the features of Jeanne and her family. The decoration around one of the windows, where legend has it Jeanne often sat, watching for Robert's return, sums up her sorrow – a knight holds a scroll reading *Plus d'espoir* (no more hope). Death accompanies a decapitated youth gripping his skull.

The interior is just as beautiful as the courtyard: the meticulous grand stair in the Italian style, carved in golden cream stone, the grand chimney supporting a heraldic stag with golden antlers, the guard room vaulted with 'basket handle' arches, the walnut table carved from a single tree, the rooms furnished with Renaissance furniture, ceramics, paintings, tapestries and 17th-century German stained glass. Even the graffiti on the walls is quality – left by Léon Gambetta of Cahors, the hero of 1870. After the château you can play the pretty nine-hole golf course, the **Golf des Trois-Vallées** (***t** 05 65 10 83 09; open all year*), with three practice holes, and pitching and putting greens.

From here the D673 ascends past the village of **St-Jean-Lespinasse** with some Romanesque carvings inside its fort-like church, to St-Médard de Presque and the **Grotte de Presque** (***t** 05 65 38 07 44; open mid-Feb–Nov 9–12 and 2–6, July and Aug 9–7; adm*), with chambers full of draperies, stone waterfalls and other geological wonders, most strikingly the 'candles' in the 'Hall of Wonders', brilliant white and 28ft tall. Another 4km down the D673, a right turn will take you to the **Cirque d'Autoire**, where a belvedere overlooks the real, 100ft-high falls of the river Autoire; across the bridge and up the path is a tremendous bird's-eye view stretching from the *cirque* (natural amphitheatre) to the little village of **Autoire** and all the way to the Dordogne valley. Often picked out as an example of a true Quercynois village, Autoire's steep brown-tiled roofs form an exquisite ensemble around its Romanesque/Renaissance church; even in the 1700s various nobles and bourgeois of Paris chose it to build holiday homes. From here the D135 leads to another exceptionally lovely village, **Loubressac**, a 15th-century eagle's nest with sloping brown-tiled roofs and 'one of the finest views in the realm' according to 17th-century writer Savinien d'Alquié, overlooking the confluence of the Bave, the Cère and the Dordogne.

East of St-Céré: the Ségala

The region to the east of St-Céré is called the Ségala, the 'rye land' (*seigle*), where wheat refuses to grow. Limestone gives way to grey granite here on the frontier of the Cantal – the cold spot of France. There are a few things to see in this far corner of Quercy, although the deep chestnut forests, heather and pure air have something to be said for them. One place to aim for is the striking 15th-century pilgrimage church of **Notre-Dame de Verdale**, near Latouille-Lentillac, clinging precariously to the rock face high over the Tolerme gorge – take the narrow road off the D30 to the top and walk down. Further east, old grey **Sousceyrac** is the largest town in the region, once fortified (see the Porte Notre-Dame, topped with a chapel) and ruled by the viscounts of Turenne. They are responsible for the 15th-century **Château de Grugnac**, 1km north, still bearing its charming *lauze* roof; more recent bosses have recently endowed Sousceyrac with the **Plan d'Eau de Tolerme** (8km south), the largest body of water in the whole *département* (*open July and Aug 9.30–6.30*), with windsurfers, rowboats and other activities for a pleasant day by the lake.

Padirac and the Gouffre de Padirac

t 05 65 33 64 56; open April–mid-Oct 9–12 and 2–6, first half of July 8.30–12 and 2–6.30, second half 8.30–6.30, Aug 8am–7pm; adm exp.

A *gouffre* is an immense hole, which is easy to remember if you recall that French trappers named the little burrowing critters they found in America *gaufres*, or gophers. Had a gopher dug the pit in Padirac, it would have to have been the size of the *Titanic* – this chasm plunges down 296ft through the limestone of the Causse de Gramat before forming 13 miles of galleries – or at least that's the length that's been explored so far. But not only is the Gouffre de Padirac spectacularly huge, much of it is spectacularly beautiful. Get there at least 30 minutes before it opens or bring a good book (and sun hat) to survive the enormous queue at the gate. Bring a sweater too: down below the temperature is a constant 13°C (55°F). There are picnic tables and snack bars and restaurants all around if you need sustenance.

For centuries this great opening, 114ft in diameter, was regarded as the entrance to hell itself. The story goes that St Martin was riding his mule through Padirac, downcast at his failure to convert any pagans on the *causse*, when the Devil happened by with a squadron of demons, all bearing sackfuls of condemned souls. Satan offered to hand them over to Martin if the saint could get over an obstacle of his creation. Martin agreed, and Old Nick stomped his foot and opened up a great chasm. Martin said a little prayer and spurred on his mule, which leapt across the abyss (you can still see the hoofprints); the furious Satan gave Martin the souls and leapt with his devils into the pit, which took them straight to hell. In 1889, Edouard Martel, one of the founding fathers of speleology, made the first scientific exploration of the *gouffre*; by 1898 it was opened to the public. Recent investigations have uncovered tools and animal bones from around 50,000 BC, 8km from the entrance.

The 90-minute guided tour starts with a long descent by lifts or stairs into the cool depths of the immense cavity, formed by water dissolving the limestone over millions of years. The chamber was domed until the weight of the roof grew too great and it collapsed; now the floor is covered by a pyramid of rubble. You're left on your own to wander past a spring and down a long underground canyon formed by a river. At the end, there's often another long wait to board the gondolas that row you along the Rivière Plane, the 'smooth river', which flows underground into the Dordogne; in 1996 a diver-speleologist discovered the exact point of its resurgence, under the Cirque de Montvalent. Along this shadowy River Styx (with a little imagination, some of the gondoliers could pass for Charon) the most extraordinary decoration is the *Grande Pendeloque*, or Great Pendant, an enormous stalactite that almost touches the water. When you disembark on the far bank, you may have yet another wait for a guide, who will lead you on foot up the narrow *Pas du Crocodile*, past a 130ft stalactite pillar into the *Salle des Grands Gours*. A *gour* is a natural limestone dam, and here the *gours* create a fascinating series of basins of clear water, flowing one into the other, with a 20ft waterfall and a green lake at the end. Beyond lies another little lake, the *Lac Supérieur*, fed only by rainwater penetrating the limestone. None of this, however,

Where to Stay and Eat

Padirac ✉ 46500

'Knick, knack Padirac/Give the dog a bone...' Though in fact you're more likely to get bland tourist fare.

****Auberge de Mathieu**, 300m from the Gouffre, **t** 05 65 33 64 68, **f** 05 65 33 69 29 (*inexpensive*). Seven comfortable rooms, a pool and a restaurant – try the duck kebabs (*menus from 88F*). *Closed mid-Nov–mid-Feb.*

****Montbertrand**, 2.5km on the St-Céré road, **t** 05 65 33 64 47 (*inexpensive*). Comfortable, with a pool and *confit de canard* (*menus 75–170F*). *Closed mid-Oct–Mar.*

Camping des Chênes, 500m from the Gouffre, **t** 05 65 33 65 54, **f** 05 65 33 71 55. Very popular and shady, with a pool and kayaking; they also have a restaurant (*inexpensive*).

prepares you for the climactic *Salle du Grand Dôme* – an uncollapsed *gouffre*, a majestic vaulted space which soars up to 305ft and in volume could contain two cathedrals of Notre-Dame; as you climb the steps through this fantastical space, with a grandiose view over the lakes, the only way your mind can take in the immensity is to note how tiny all the people are on the far end.

If you emerge from the *gouffre* with some francs still jingling in your pocket after the entrance fees and various tips (no pressure, only if you want) there's exotic flora and fauna to see in the nearby **Zoo le Tropicorama** (***t** 05 65 33 64 91; open May–Sept daily 9–8.30*). They have also opened a permanent exhibition on the history of the *gouffre* and its environment from prehistoric times to the start of the 20th century, **L'Historial du Gouffre de Padirac** (***t** 05 65 33 75 75; open mid-April–Sept 9–7*). Kids can be kept happy at the water activity park **Padirac Loisirs** (***t** 05 65 33 45 15; open late June–early Sept 11–8*).

Carennac to Lacave

This stretch of the Dordogne hugs islets and high cliffs as it flows past several châteaux, a fascinating Romanesque abbey connected with the sweet-tempered archbishop Fénelon, the handsome medieval town of Martel and the splendid stalactite grotto at Lacave.

Carennac

From the river, Carennac presents an enchanting higgledy-piggledy cluster of roofs, walls and turrets around its famous honey-coloured **Prieuré St-Pierre**. Founded in 932 by Frotard, Vicomte de Cahors, the priory was given by the bishop of Cahors to Cluny *c.* 1040. Fortified in the 16th century, it managed to repulse Protestant attacks, fortunately preserving some of the finest Romanesque art in the area: the beautiful 12th-century tympanum over the porch, sculpted by the school of Toulouse with their favourite scene from the *Apocalypse* (Christ blessing in a mandorla), surrounded by the Evangelists and Apostles, divided into registers (as on Cahors cathedral). The frieze below is decorated with an unusual zigzag pattern of animals; in the shadowy

Getting Around

The **Chemin de Fer Touristique du Haut Quercy** runs from Martel to St-Denis just east – not a long haul, but a thrilling one, on the old railway line skirting 240ft cliffs over the Dordogne: the return journey takes 90mins; two departures a day in the summer, **t** 05 65 37 35 81. Accompanied **mountain bike** rides from Saga Team in Carennac, **t** 05 65 10 97 39, and Copeyre in Martel, **t** 05 65 37 33 51. A SNCF **bus** runs between Martel and Souillac: check with the tourist office for details.

Tourist Information

Carennac: in the centre, **t** 05 65 10 97 01.
Martel: Place des Consuls, **t** 05 65 37 43 44.

Market Days

Martel: Wed and Sat *marché aux gras* in Dec and Jan. Fair the 23rd of each month.

Where to Stay and Eat

Carennac ✉ 46110

****Auberge du Vieux Quercy**, **t** 05 65 10 96 59, **f** 05 65 10 94 05 (*inexpensive*). Located in a former post house, with a fair-sized pool, garden and pretty rooms; the restaurant is an idyllic place to linger over a *confit de canard à la ciboulette et au jus de citron* (*menus 90–200F*). Lunch not always served; check first. *Closed Sun eve and Mon out of season, and mid-Nov–mid-Mar.*

****Hostellerie Fénelon**, **t** 05 65 10 96 46, **f** 05 65 10 94 86 (*inexpensive*). At the entrance to the village, with authentic provincial rooms and a pool as well; in the garden dining room, try the *feuilleté de morilles au jus du truffe* if you're flush, but all the menus (*105–290F*) are a good bet. *Closed Fri and Sat midday out of season, and Jan–mid-Mar.*

***Des Touristes**, **t** 05 65 10 94 31 (*cheap*). Eleven basic rooms for a night's flop.

Martel ✉ 46600

*****Le Relais Ste-Anne**, Rue Pourtanel, **t** 05 65 37 40 56, **f** 05 65 37 42 82 (*moderate*). A pretty place, set around a garden courtyard, with a pool; mini-bar, laundry, Jacuzzi and bicycles are offered to guests, but no restaurant. *Closed mid-Nov–late Mar.*

****La Turenne**, Av Jean-Lavayssière, **t** 05 65 37 30 30, **f** 05 65 37 30 30 (*inexpensive*). Simple rooms.

La Mère Michèle, Rue de la Remise, **t** 05 65 37 35 66. A lovely bar and restaurant, serving only the most authentic traditional cuisine (*menus 80–190F*). Owner Michèle must be the biggest felinophile around, and is also a mine of information on the region and various walking paths. She also has a pair of en suite doubles (*inexpensive*) by the garden.

Plein Sud, Place Consuls, **t** 05 65 37 37 77. Reliable pizzas and other inexpensive fare.

Ferme Auberge Moulin à Huile de Noix, at Les Landes, along the St-Céré road, **t** 05 65 37 40 69. The Castagné family combine a recently built but traditional walnut oil press where they make the southwest's favourite salad dressing with a restaurant in a charming 14th-century inn, serving huge portions of traditional cuisine, with plenty of walnut sauces and desserts (*mill open for visits Easter–Oct, daily exc Sun and Mon 9–11.30 and 3–5.30, although you can only see it in action Sat afternoons; in winter call to watch the oil being pressed; menus 78 and 135F; by reservation only*).

****Gilles**, north in Cressensac, **t** 05 65 37 70 06, **f** 05 65 37 77 15 (*inexpensive*). A pleasant country inn with a shady terrace, where you can let time fly by over a nice dish of marinated salmon (*menus 100–270F*).

interior, capitals carved with primitive birds, animals and monsters add to its atmosphere of archaic mystery. The interior has, unusually, a narthex made of columns. A painting of the Evangelists survives in one 15th-century chapel.

The **cloister** (*t 05 65 10 97 01; open June–mid-Sept 10–7, other times variable, phone for details; adm*), with its one Romanesque and three Flamboyant Gothic galleries, was rescued from its fate as a pigsty in 1928. After the Revolution, when most of the carvings were hammered, the villagers sold off the priory's art, except a piece they especially loved, the 15th-century **Mise en Tombeau** (in the **Salle Capitulaire** off the closter), a poignant composition of eight intricately detailed figures. The Virgin's arms reach out stiffly in grief; Nicodemus and Joseph of Arimathea, dressed in Renaissance costumes, hold the shroud, while John, Mary Magdalene and the women in biblical draperies mourn (in the folds you can see the original paint). Here too are 17th-century bas-reliefs on the life of Christ and a moving pietà carved from Carennac's stone.

At the south end of the cloister, the old kitchen, with its monumental fireplace, and refectory have been converted into a conference centre for the commune. During the work a 15th-century mural was uncovered, known as the *Dit des Trois Morts et des Trois Vifs* – three skeletons warning three cavaliers to reflect on earthly vanity. Over one of the fireplaces is a portrait of a dean of Carennac, François de Salignac. In the 17th century, the deanery became a personal fief of the influential Salignac de la Mothe-Fénelon family, who owned châteaux on either bank of the Dordogne; in 1674, the post was inherited by this dean's nephew, François de Salignac de la Mothe-Fénelon (1651–1715), who went on to further glory as the Archbishop of Cambrai.

Besides its priory, Carennac, like any town worth its salt on the Dordogne, also has a château, this one from the 1500s and now housing the **Maison de la Dordogne Quercynoise** (*t 05 65 32 59 19; open daily April–Oct 10–1 and 2–7, July–early Sept 10–7, closed Mon and Sat mornings*) with exhibits on the river, from prehistoric times to the present. Another possible visit is to the **Musée des Alambics et Aromathèque** (*t 05 65 10 91 16; open all year 10–1 and 2–7; demonstrations at 4.30 in summer*), where you can learn all about distilling lavender. The small fry will love a day splashing and sliding around like otters at the **Parc Aquatique La Saule**, towards Betaille (*t 05 65 32 55 75; open June–Aug*).

Around Carennac

Crossing the bridge over the Dordogne from Carennac, a right turn will take you to **Tauriac**, where the church has some well-preserved 15th-century murals of ladies. A left turn at the bridge will lead you to **Vayrac**, and the D119, leading up a steep hill to a site called **Puy-d'Issolud**, a broad plateau that is one of many possible candidates for the lost site of Uxellodunum, where the Gauls made their last stand against Julius Caesar's relentless legions. Ruins on the plateau have been identified as belonging to Celtic fortifications, camps and temples; finds are displayed in a small **Musée Gallo-Romain by the Syndicat d'Initiative** (*t 05 65 32 52 50; open July and Aug, Thurs and Sat 10–12 and 4–7, other days 4–7*).

Fénelon, or the Price of Being a Good Man in Bad Times

If I could come back as anyone, I'd like to be Fénelon's valet.

Voltaire

Known for his gentle eloquence as the 'Swan of Cambrai', young François was bred for the Church from the earliest age and attended the seminary of St-Sulpice in Paris. In 1674, he inherited Carennac from an uncle and was given the special task of bringing Protestant women back to the Catholic fold. Gentle, reasonable, well-spoken and extremely tolerant for his bigoted age, Fénelon was so successful at the task that he attracted the attention of the pious Madame de Maintenon, morganatic wife of Louis XIV and herself a convert to Catholicism. In 1689 she had Louis appoint Fénelon tutor of his grandson and heir, the singularly charmless Duke of Burgundy.

The task took up so much of Fénelon's time that, in spite of tradition, he hardly had the chance to return to Carennac to compose his celebrated allegory for the duke's instruction, *Télémaque*. This book, a lesson in truth, justice and virtue, follows the life of Odysseus' son Telemachus in Salentum, an aristocratic utopia where seven strictly defined classes lived a simple life and dressed according to their station, hence eliminating one of the banes of his time: luxury born from pride and the need to pay for it by soaking the poor. Tradition has it that Fénelon wrote his romance in Carennac's

Martel

Proud, staunchly medieval Martel, the 'City of Seven Towers', resolves under the microscope to a rustic village of 1,400 souls. Severely depopulated over the last century, today many of its empty houses are being restored as summer homes for people from far away. Still, the population isn't nearly big enough for Martel. However small, this is a real city, and, beautiful as it is, it wears a melancholy air with so few around to share its beauty.

Martel means 'hammer', like the three hammers the city wears on its coat of arms, and like the hammer wielded by Charles Martel, scourge of the Muslims; a legend credits the grandfather of Charlemagne with founding the city in the 700s. In 1219, Martel received its charter as a free *commune*, a fief of the viscounts of Turenne; so it remained until 1738, when it was snapped up by the French crown. In central **Place des Consuls** are the covered market and the huge **Palais de la Raymondie**, begun by the Turenne viscounts *c.* 1300, now the town hall and **Musée d'Uxellodunum** (***t** 05 65 37 30 03; open July and Aug Mon–Sat 10–12 and 3–6*), with prehistoric and Gallo-Roman finds from Puy-d'Issolud, old maps and pharmacy jars. Its *beffroi* is the first of the 'seven towers'. Another is the bell tower of **St-Maur**, a fortified but exquisite Gothic church built into the walls that retains a portal from the 12th century with a relief of Christ Pantocrator in the style of Moissac. Superbly restored, it contains excellent stained glass from 1531 with scenes of the Passion, believed to be the work of students of Arnaut de Moles, the master of Auch cathedral. A few sculptural decora-

'Tour de Télémaque'; Ile Barrade, facing Carennac in the Dordogne, was renamed Ile Calypso after the island in the novel.

It was during this period that the unworldly Fénelon became attracted to the quietist ideals of the mystic Madame Guyon, who preached the possibility of abandoning the soul to God's love without any of the outer disciplines or authority of the Church. In 1695, having been recently appointed to the princely post of Archbishop of Cambrai, Fénelon undertook to defend her preachings against the doughty Bishop of Meaux, Jacques Bénigne Bousset, who upheld the authority of the Church. 'It is hard to get a great prelate condemned for trusting overmuch in the love of God,' as Albert Guérard commented, but by 1699 Bousset had succeeded so completely that Fénelon's work had been condemned by the pope.

With that, the king dismissed him from his tutorial post (all of Fénelon's work went down the drain anyway, when the duke died three years before his terrible grandfather). Even worse, *Télémaque* was published in court without its author's permission, and was read by Louis as a satirical comment on his arrogant, bankrupt reign. Fénelon spent the rest of his life as an outcast in Cambrai. Without him, his beloved Carennac fell into ruin and no longer sent him any rents to relieve his poverty. For all that, he asked to be buried there when he died, but the request was denied. As a posthumous apology for Fénelon's treatment from Louis XIV, the regent had *Télémaque* printed; in the 18th century it went into over 180 editions.

tions can be seen in the odd corners; for a puzzle, see if you can find the three sleeping monks – the two angels under blankets don't count.

For the other five towers, you'll need to tour the rest of Martel. It won't take long: there are scarcely more than a dozen streets. One of the towers is the **Maison Fabri**, behind the market, where Henri Court-Mantel died from a fever shortly after his pillage of Rocamadour. The **Tour de Tournamire** at the northern gate doubled as a prison. Beyond this girdle of medieval defences, Martel has modern attractions: the piquant pleasures of **Reptilland**, abode of 86 species of crocs, snakes, spiders and other cold-blooded beasts (***t** 05 65 37 41 00; open July and Aug 10–6, other months Tues–Sun 10–12 and 2–6; closed Jan; adm*); and walnuts. These are serious business here: the big fat tasty variety grown in the three surrounding *départements* (Corrèze, Lot and Dordogne) received their gourmet classification as AOC Noix du Périgord in 1999. One of the best places to learn all about them is just outside Martel (*see* below).

North of Martel, at the northernmost tip of Quercy, is a sleepy corner called the Causse de Martel, napping under its cover of oak and beech forests. The villages of **Cavagnac** and **Lasvaux** both have simple Romanesque churches.

Gluges and Lacave

The Dordogne is at its scenic best between Martel and Souillac, meandering cheerfully through dramatic countryside, and often hemmed in by steep cliffs. Directly south of Martel, the riverside village of **Gluges** fairly cowers beneath one of these lofty rock walls. There's an unusual church, half cut into the rock; the local baron,

Where to Stay and Eat

Gluges ✉ 46600

★★**Hôtel des Falaises, t** 05 65 27 18 44, **f** 05 65 27 18 45 (*inexpensive*). With a perfect setting under the cliffs, beautiful gardens and a restaurant; try the stuffed salmon (*menus from 98F*). *Open end Mar–Oct.*

Camping Les Falaises, t 05 65 37 37 78. One of several lovely campsites by the river.

Creysse ✉ 46600

★★**Auberge de l'Isle, t** 05 65 32 22 01, **f** 05 65 32 21 43 (*inexpensive*). Deservedly popular: lovely rooms, attentive service, a pool and a terrace over a canal, all at reasonable prices.

Meyronne ✉ 46200

★★★**La Terrasse, t** 05 65 32 21 60, **f** 05 65 32 26 93 (*moderate*). The old riverside château of the bishops of Tulle is now a delightful hotel, with modern rooms, shuttle service to the station or airport, and an excellent restaurant where you can suffer the full force of foie gras, *truffles* and *magret* (*menus 100–290F*). *Closed mid-Nov–Feb.*

Camping du Port, near Creysse, **t** 05 65 32 20 40. A lovely riverside site that recently featured in a French soap opera.

Lacave ✉ 46200

★★★★**Château de la Treyne**, just west of town on the river, **t** 05 65 27 60 60, **f** 05 65 27 60 70 (*expensive*). The Relais et Châteaux proprietors have spared no expense to make this 14th-century château set high above the river the showpiece of the region: stately gardens, antique furnishings, tapestries, 16 luxurious rooms with river views, along with a large pool, magnificent stone terrace and a highly rated – and correspondingly expensive – restaurant (*menus 320 and 450F; from 220F at lunch*). *Closed lunchtime Tues–Thurs, and mid-Nov–Easter.* What they haven't succeeded in doing, however, is making their guests feel very welcome.

★★★**Le Pont de l'Ouysse, t** 05 65 37 87 04, **f** 05 65 32 77 41 (*moderate*). This magical hotel, in the same family for four generations, has splendid views of the river under century-old trees. The restaurant here too is formidable, a cuisine as seductive as the environment, with utterly charming service (*menus 180–600F*). *Closed Mon and Tues lunch and early Nov–Feb.*

★**Hôtel des Grottes, t** 05 65 37 87 06, **f** 05 65 37 84 44 (*cheap*). The budget choice.

Camping La Rivière, t 05 65 37 02 04. Another lovely site.

Ferme Auberge et Camping Calvel le Bougayrou, at Clavel (on the D23 towards Meyronne), **t** 05 65 37 87 20. Camping on the arcadian farm; delicious, filling renditions of all the *ferme-auberge* favourites (*menus from 85F*). *Book; open daily exc Thurs in summer, otherwise weekends only, closed mid-Sept–Oct.*

Gérard de Mirandol, built it after his return from the Crusades in 1108. A cave, converted to a fortress in the Middle Ages, can be reached from the village by a stairway carved into the cliff. Gluges is also establishing itself as the home of one of France's most recent tourist fads, corn mazes. Check with the tourist office at Martel for the state of play this year. Another cliff across the Dordogne, the **Cirque de Montvalent**, forms a striking natural amphitheatre; the river formed it ages ago before it chose its present course.

From here, the D23 to **Creysse** follows the river – terrifically scenic, if a bit dangerous; it climbs up and down the cliffs on only one lane. Creysse is an exquisite village built around a Romanesque church, and it attracts more than its share of tourists. Further downstream, well-named **Lacave** can show you one of the most spectacular subterranean wonders of France, open to the public since 1905 (***t** 05 65 37 87 03; open daily April–mid-July 9.30–12 and 2–6, July and Aug 9.30–6.30, Mar and Sept–11 Nov 10–12 and 2–5; adm*). It may not be as famous as Padirac, but Lacave offers some unique sights. From the entrance, you'll travel on a miners' train, then up an elevator into the caverns – a mile of them, including the 'Lac des Mirages', where the reflections of stalactites in the water give the illusion of an underwater city. Some of the caverns are illuminated by back light for strange phosphorescent effects. Lacave excels in unusual formations, 'eccentrics' like the pillar in the shape of a tarasque, the mythical monster of Tarascon, and the 'column of the spiders' feet'. Two kilometres from the caves is the new **Préhistologia – Parc Préhistorique** (***t*** *05 65 32 28 28; open April–June 10–12 and 2–6, July–late Aug 10–6.30, late Aug–mid-Sept 10–12 and 2–5.30, mid-Sept–Oct 2–5*), which tries to tell the history of the world from the Big Bang to Neolithic times, with life-size models of dinosaurs and a reconstruction of a Neolithic village, in a wooded setting. Fun for the kids. From Lacave the D43 continues to Souillac, passing the **Château de Belcastel** in a perfect cliff-top setting over the river to meet one of the most graceful iron bridges you'll ever see, at **Pinsac**; an anonymous engineer of the Ponts et Chaussées, France's national public works office, designed it in the 1930s.

Rocamadour

From Lacave it's 18km of scenery south to Rocamadour, which proudly bills itself as the 'Second Site in France', after Mont-St-Michel. The two share extraordinary, fantastical settings, the very kind of natural sacred, magical places that attract legends like lightning rods. Rocamadour is the medieval French version of a Pueblo village in North America, a vertical cliff-dwellers' town, the beautiful golden stone houses and chapels piled on top of one another over a deep ravine, while far, far below the little Alzou continues its work of aeons, cutting even deeper into the gorge. There are a couple of tempting stops on the way to Rocamadour, if you're heading south from Lacave, or east from the main N20 – **Calès**, a picturesque little hamlet with a midget château, and, a bit further on where the road crosses the blue-green Ouysse, a 13th-century working mill, the **Moulin de Cougnaguet**, fortified against flour thieves and – by the looks of it – against time as well (***t*** *05 65 38 73 56; open for demonstrations April–mid-Oct 10–12 and 2–6, rest of Oct 10.30–12 and 2–5; adm*).

You know you're almost there when the road leads up to **L'Hospitalet**, where everyone stops for the picture-postcard view across to Rocamadour, wedged tight under its overhanging cliff. It is a view that has been enjoyed especially after 1050, when a hostel-hospital was founded by Hélène de Castelnau for pilgrims en route to Compostela. L'Hospitalet was inhabited as early as the Upper Palaeolithic era; its Grotte des Merveilles has, besides stalactites, lakes and other subterranean fancies, mostly fantastical rock formations, and some rather deteriorated artwork (negative hands, animals) that dates back to 20,000 BC (***t*** *05 65 33 67 92; open April–June and Sept–11 Nov 10–12 and 2–6; July and Aug 9–7; adm*). It suggests, if nothing else, that the remarkable site of Rocamadour was a holy place long before any of its stories were written.

Getting Around

Rocamador's **railway** station, on the Brive–Figeac line with occasional trains to Toulouse, Rodez and Paris, is 4km from town and connected by **taxi**; you can hire **bikes** here, but book them ahead in the summer (**t** 05 65 33 63 05). Only the **cars** of visitors with bookings in Rocamadour's hotels are allowed in the village. In July and August the nearer car parks outside the gates fill up fast, when you should park on top at the château or a 600m walk away at L'Hospitalet and walk or take the lifts into town. The **lifts** are also handy if you have difficulty walking (the steps aren't steep, but there are 223 of them), 23F return. A **train** runs between car parking in the valley and the site, 20F there and back, and there to see Rocamadour illuminated.

Tourist Information

L'Hospitalet: the main office, the Maison du Tourisme, is now here, **t** 05 65 33 22 00, **f** 05 65 33 22 01.

Rocamadour: Rue de la Couronnerie, **t** 05 65 33 62 59. Stop here for the hours of the guided tour of the shrines (*June–Sept daily exc Sun morning*). At other times, make arrangements in advance through Pélerinage de Rocamadour, in Rocamadour, **t** 05 65 33 23 23.

Where to Stay

Rocamadour ✉ 46500

Rocamadour has a vast range of hotels, packed together like sardines and all requiring reservations in the summer; one of the advantages of staying is seeing the place first thing in the morning, or in the evening after all the coachloads have departed.

*****Beau Site**, Rue R.-le-Preux, **t** 05 65 33 63 08, **f** 05 65 33 65 23 (*moderate*). The fanciest place in town, in the same family for five generations, occupies a real medieval house. Its decoration is a bit too Ye-Olde-Inn-ish, but this is your chance to sleep in a four-poster bed, if you ask in advance.

*****Domaine de la Rhue**, only a few minutes away on the N140, **t** 05 65 33 71 50, **f** 05 65 33 72 48 (*moderate*). A tranquil hotel with comfortable rooms all in stone and exposed beams; there's a pool; good breakfasts, but no restaurant.

****Ste-Marie**, Place des Senhals, **t** 05 65 33 63 07, **f** 05 65 33 69 08 (*inexpensive*). A simple family place in the heart of things; the more pricey rooms have superb views, and the restaurant is one of the best in town. Leave room for dessert (*menus 76–200F*). *Closed mid-Oct–Easter.*

****Le Troubadour**, Route de Padirac, **t** 05 65 33 70 27, **f** 05 65 33 71 99 (*inexpensive*). A well-kept little hotel with a garden and pool with magnificent views of the *causse*, a few minutes from the centre. *Closed mid-Nov–mid-Feb.*

****Terminus des Pélerins**, Place de la Carretta, **t** 05 65 33 62 14, **f** 05 65 33 72 10 (*inexpensive*). If you want to pay less in the centre, you won't do better than this Logis de France. *Open mid-April–mid-Nov.*

****Lion d'Or**, just beyond the Porte du Figuier, **t** 05 65 33 62 04, **f** 05 65 33 72 54 (*inexpensive*). About as old-fashioned and

Legends and History

The late 11th-century origins of Rocamadour's cult of the Black Virgin are murky enough, and coincide neatly with the founding of the hostel at L'Hospitalet and the sudden flood of passing pilgrims. On the other hand, the Benedictines of Tulle, the promoters of Rocamadour, were hardly the only ones to suddenly find miracles and saintly relics – the money-generating roadside attractions of the Middle Ages – along the busy Way to Compostela. The cult's legitimacy was given a big boost in 1166, when a man's body was discovered buried near the altar. Over the centuries, the story evolved that this unknown was none other than St Zaccheus, the publican who

traditional as it comes, with comfortable rooms and solid Périgord cuisine in the restaurant, which looks out over the Alzou gorge; *tartin de foie gras, foie gras frais, magret sauce aux crèpes*... (*menus 65–210F*).

****Panoramic**, in L'Hospitalet, **t** 05 65 33 63 06, **f** 05 65 33 69 26 (*inexpensive*). A small family-run hotel with a restaurant and pool dramatically looking on to Rocamadour.

****Bellevue,** L'Hospitalet, **t** 05 65 33 62 10, **f** 05 65 33 65 61 (*inexpensive*). A Logis hotel-restaurant. Not much of a view but decent rooms and parking. *Open April–Oct*. Just up the road is the restaurant serving traditional meals (*menus 70–135F*). *Open April–Oct*.

Eating Out

When it comes to dining, Rocamadour is famous throughout the southwest for its creamy, flat cylinders of goat cheese, so special that they've been classified like wine: AOC *cabécou de Rocamadour*. Connoisseurs like them ripe, pungent, and coated with a tawny crust – the perfect accompaniment to a well-aged Cahors, at their very best between June and November. If you and French goat cheese haven't been previously introduced, you may want to try a mild fresh white *cabécou* to start with, or have it grilled – somehow heat takes away some of the immediately goaty impact and leaves a warm, soft, distinct taste delicious as a starter with salad.

Jehan de Valon, the restaurant of the hotel Beau Site, **t** 05 65 33 63 08, **f** 05 65 33 65 23. A great place to try it, in their renovated panoramic dining room, where the same maître d' has been on the job since 1962; the food is exquisite (*menus 115–320F*). *Closed mid-Nov–mid-Feb.*

Château de la Carreta, by the Hôtel de Ville, **t** 05 65 33 62 23. For a simple but tasty lunch.

Chez Anne Marie, by the Hôtel de Ville, **t** 05 65 33 65 81. Filling menus (*70–136F*).

Environs of Rocamadour

****Les Vieilles Tours**, in the countryside 3km west at Lafage, **t** 05 65 33 68 01, **f** 05 65 33 68 59 (*inexpensive*). In a sturdy manor house built between the 13th and 17th centuries and two annexes, with rooms giving on to the garden; there's a pool and choice of breakfasts, including a regional *petit déjeuner* that has nothing petit about it; the restaurant is one of the best in the area (*menus from 125F*). *Closed mid-Nov–Mar.*

******Château de Roumégouse**, 6km east at Rignac (✉ 46500), **t** 05 65 33 63 81, **f** 05 65 33 71 18 (*expensive*). A romantic Relais et Châteaux hotel set in a pretty park with a lovely terrace. The well-known restaurant offers a choice between Louis XIII and Louis XV dining rooms, featuring traditional Quercy foie gras and truffle dishes, and seasonal dishes, beautifully highlighted with fresh herbs plucked daily from the owner's well-tended garden (*affordable menus, from 185F*). *Closed Tues out of season, and Dec–mid-April.*

****Le Petit Relais**, in Calès (✉ 46350), **t** 05 65 37 96 09, **f** 05 65 37 95 93 (*inexpensive*). A pleasant country inn, with a good restaurant and unusual desserts (*menus 78–250F*). *Closed Sat lunch and late Dec–early Jan.*

climbed the tree to see Jesus. Later, he and his wife, St Veronica (of the holy handkerchief), fled Palestine in an angel-powered boat and lived near Limoges; when Veronica died, Zaccheus came here as a hermit and built the first sanctuaries in the cliff-face. The locals called him 'the lover' or *Amator* for his devotion, and hence Roc-Amadour, the rock of the lover or lover of rock. A second attraction was Durandal, the famous sword of Roland; just before he died at Roncesvalles, the hero confided his blade to St Michael, and the Archangel hurled it from the Pyrenees like a javelin straight into Rocamadour's cliff.

Yet always the chief attraction was the blackened, goddess-like statue of the Virgin, whose cult, along with that of chivalry, grew by leaps and bounds at the time of the crusades. Rocamadour's first important patron was Henry II of England, who endowed much of its treasure. His wayward eldest son, the Young King, Henry Court-Mantel – companion of Bertran de Born (*see* pp.47–9) – stole it in 1183 to pay his *routiers* in his war against his own father; he even, some say, replaced the famous Durandel with his own sword. By the time the plunderers reached Martel, the Black Virgin got her revenge, striking young Henry down with a killer fever. Full of remorse, he asked his father's forgiveness, had a halter placed on his neck and laid himself naked in a bed of ashes and died. The Bishop of Limoges refrained from excommunicating the dead man when his grieving father promised to replace Rocamadour's losses.

The story had the same effect as the doings of the royals in today's tabloids, and made Rocamadour more famous than ever. It quickly recovered from pillaging to become one of the busiest pilgrimage shrines in France. Sts Louis, Dominic, Bernard, Anthony of Padua, Engelbert and the blessed Raymond Lull came, as did the kings of France and countless others, especially on the days of pardon and plenary indulgence, when the chronicles say 30,000 thronged into the village to pick up their Get Out of Purgatory Free card. Others who came were less willing: thousands of criminals, Albigensian heretics and men who broke the Truce of God by fighting during Lent were ordered by ecclesiastical courts to make the pilgrimage to Rocamadour, to climb up the famous steps on their knees, to be bound in chains and led to the Virgin to confess and apologize (*amende honorable*) and be purified by the priest. The priest would then strike off the chains, and present the shriven one with a certificate and a little lead medal with a picture of the Virgin to take back home.

Rocamadour suffered a near-fatal setback during the Wars of Religion, when the Huguenot Captain Bessonies came to lay waste and desecrate the shrine, hacking the relics of St Amadour to bits and leaving only the Virgin and her bell intact. After nearly three centuries of neglect, the bishops of Cahors began to restore the shrines in the 1850s – read over-restore – giving the buildings a Disneylandish air that only increases in the high summer, when Rocamadour is swamped by coach parties, and visitors have to queue just to get into the narrow lanes of the village. Arrive early in the morning to avoid the worst; better still, come in the autumn when Rocamadour is at its most magical.

The Village

The holy road from L'Hospitalet enters Rocamadour by way of the 13th-century **Porte du Figuier**, one of four gates that defended the village's one real road. Once in, past a gauntlet of souvenir stands and a waxworks museum, you'll find the lift near the second gate, towered **Porte Salmon**. Beyond, the 15th-century **Palais de la Couronnerie** is now the Hôtel de Ville and tourist office, where two tapestries of local flora and fauna by Jean Lurçat are on display. The street continues through another gate into the **Quartier du Coustalou**, the prettiest and least restored part of the village, with jumbly little houses and a fortified mill.

The **Grand Escalier** into the holy city begins back at Place de la Carretta. The first 144 steps lead up to **Place des Senhals**, where merchants sold lead holy medals (*senhals* in Occitan) stamped with a picture of the Virgin. Rocamadour's oldest street, Rue de la Mercerie, extends from here, with the 14th-century **Maison de la Pomette** at its end. From here, continue up through the gate under the over-restored Fort, sometime residence of the bishops of Tulle. Tulle remained in charge of Rocamadour throughout the Middle Ages, despite attempts by Marcilhac and other abbeys to muscle in on the action.

The Parvis de St-Amadour

At the top of the steps the small square, Parvis de St-Amadour, is the centre of the holy city, where the pilgrim could visit seven churches, just as in Rome, but in a much abbreviated space. These days only Notre-Dame and St-Sauveur are open all year; for the other chapels of St-Michel, Sts Anne, Blaise and Jean-Baptiste, and the Crypt of St-Amadour, you need to take the guided tour.

The 11th–13th-century **Basilique St-Sauveur** makes good use of the cliff for one of its walls. Originally built with two equal naves, another was added to cope with the crowd of pilgrims. Over the altar hangs a painted wooden 16th-century Christ shown crucified on a tree, His right side pierced by the lance instead of the customary left. A Basque-style wooden gallery runs along the side. Steps lead down into another of the seven churches, the simple 12th-century Crypt St-Amadour, where the body of the mysterious hermit was venerated. The Parvis also has the **Musée Trésor Francis Poulenc** (***t** 05 65 33 23 30; open daily 9.30–12 and 2–6, July and Aug 9–7*) with documents and precious works of sacred art – medieval reliquaries from Limoges, stained glass, 17th-century ex votos – all dedicated to the composer Poulenc, an atheist who converted to Catholicism after a vision here in 1936 and used the inspiration to compose his *Litanies à la Vierge Noire de Rocamadour*.

Parvis Notre-Dame

On the other side of St-Sauveur another 25 steps lead up to the holy of holies, the Flamboyant Gothic **Chapelle Notre-Dame**. This dates only from 1479, after a rock crashed off the cliff through the original sanctuary. Inside, darkened by candle smoke, the miraculous Black Virgin still holds court. She is believed to have been carved out of walnut in the 11th century, and sits stiffly on her throne, almost a stick figure; the Christ Child balanced on her knee looks more like Pinocchio than a baby. But the Black Virgin's primitive appearance only heightens her mystic power. The proof is in the pudding, or rather in the ex votos. Many are from Breton sailors, who held the Virgin of Rocamadour in special devotion. Whenever she came through, the miracle would be foretold by the ringing of the 9th-century bell hanging from the roof. Chains from pilgrim petitioners still hang in the back of the chapel. Outside, high in the rock above the door, you can see the supposed **Durandal**, a rusty sword embedded in the stone, fastened by a chain to keep it from falling on someone's head.

Sharing this upper square with Notre-Dame is the **Chapelle St-Michel**, with the overhanging cliff for a roof, decorated on the outside with colourful 12th- or 13th-century frescoes representing the Annunciation and Visitation. The patron of travellers, St Christopher, is painted below; to catch a glimpse of him was good luck, so he was always made extra big. To see the faded fresco of *Christ in Majesty* inside you must take the tour.

Further up, a hairpin walk lined with the Stations of the Cross (or the much easier lift from the Parvis de St-Amadour) takes you up to the ramparts of the **Château** (***t*** *05 65 33 23 23; open April–Oct 8.30–9, Nov–Mar 9–6.30; adm*), built in the 14th century, offering a vertiginous view high over the *causse*. This eagle's nest is also a true one, thanks to the breeding programme for birds of prey at the **Rocher des Aigles** (***t*** *05 65 33 65 45; open April–Oct 10–12 and 2–6, July and Aug 12–6, with regular flight shows*).

Roadside Attractions

Rocamadour, the original medieval roadside attraction, has spawned its own share of secular distractions in the past two decades. In the village centre there's the **Musée du Jouet Ancien Automobile** (***t*** *05 65 33 60 75; open mid-March–Nov 10–12 and 2–6; adm*), with toy cars, including the kind that kids first pedalled in 1910, and a big collection of Dinky Toys too. Or learn all about bees at the **Maison des Abeilles** (***t*** *05 65 33 66 98; open July–early Sept daily 11–7, April–June and mid-Sept–mid-Oct Wed and Sun afternoons only*) with exhibitions and courses on apiculture. In L'Hospitalet, on the Gramat road, you can meet, probably more intimately than you might wish, the 150 Barbary apes and macaques at liberty in the **Forêt des Singes** (***t*** *05 65 33 62 72; open April–June and Sept daily 10–12 and 1–6, July and Aug 10–7, Oct daily 10–12 and 1–5, Nov weekends only 10–12 and 1–5*). Also in L'Hospitalet, there's **La Féerie du Rail**, a huge model 1:87 diorama with 60 trains and a giant sound and light show – the result of nine years' work by a madman named Robert Mousseau (***t*** *05 65 33 71 06; ring ahead for performance schedules*) and an **Aquarium**, by the tourist office, with aquatic creatures from the Lot (*open April, May, Sept and Oct daily 2–6, June–Aug 10–12 and 2–6; otherwise by appointment; adm*). There are even roadside attractions for geologists just south of Rocamadour – the **Gouffre de St-Sauveur**, a round, deep, blue-green pit, and **Gouffre de Cabouy**, the resurgence of an underground river in the canyon of the Ouysse. Or you can float above it all in a *montgolfière* – a hot-air balloon – year-round depending on the weather (***t*** *05 65 33 71 50*).

Down the Dordogne: Souillac to Sarlat

Souillac doesn't look like much from the dusty stretch of the N20 that passes through it, but its church of **Ste-Marie** makes it a mandatory stop to see one of the true jewels of Romanesque sculpture and architecture in the Midi. Souillac's new slogan, 'Gateway to the South', is based on the tradition that cicadas, the totem insect of the French Midi, will only sing once you cross over the 45th parallel; its name, however, comes from the Celtic *souilh*, mud flat, the kind that boars like best – hence the bristling swine on its coat of arms.

Souillac: Dancing Isaiah and Banjo-strumming Automats

The origins of Souillac are fairly typical: a monastery was founded here in the early 900s (reputedly by the beloved smithy saint, St Eloi (Eligius), even though he died in 660) and reached its glory days in the 12th century, when it founded some 150 priories in Quercy, Périgord and the Limousin, and there was money to lavish on a great church. A village grew up around its walls and the monastery took some hard knocks in the wars. A fire in the 1570s finished it off, leaving only the massive 16th-century bell tower of **St-Martin**, with some older fragments of its medieval portal, and the church of Ste-Marie. The philistines of Louis XIV's time worked some outrageous butchery on it, covering over the stately domes with a fake gable roof, destroying one of the finest carved portals in France, and plastering over everything inside, redecorating it in a way they found more tasteful. All that has been cleared away and, though it may still be hard to imagine Ste-Marie in its original splendour, the essentials at least remain.

Its denuded state, in fact, might make it easier to appreciate the authority and perfection of the architecture. Ste-Marie is Romanesque at its most Roman, striving above all for monumental presence. This is best seen outside in the majestic **apse**; one suspects the architect had taken a long look at the palaces and public baths of ancient Rome (some of which were still in good nick in the 1100s). The interior is even better: a single, domed nave, graceful and strong. Of the three domes, the earliest is oddly squared, showing the Islamic origins of the technique; squarish domes like this are rare, though a few turn up in contemporary churches in southern Italy. Sculptural decoration is sparse – some good capitals, including the popular theme of Daniel in the lions' den and a few grimacing faces hidden in unexpected spots.

The surviving fragments of the **portal** have been reconstructed inside the main door. The wild scene on top, showing a fellow with some serious devil troubles, represents *St Theophilus the Penitent*. Archdeacon of Adana (in Turkey), this Theophilus was wrongly thrown out of his office and in revenge sold his soul to the devil; of course the devil got it in writing. Theophilus later repented so sincerely and thoroughly that the Virgin Mary went down to hell and snatched the paper away from the devil for him. The three vignettes in the crowded relief show the signing of the contract, the devil attempting to carry Theophilus away and, above, the Virgin and an angel pulling him up into heaven. Just why this obscure saint should have such a prominent place on the portal is a good question, but then perhaps he isn't so obscure after all – this story is one of the sources for the legend of Faust. Flanking the relief are the two figures without which no French portal would be complete: St Peter (with the keys) and St Paul (with the book).

Outstanding as these reliefs are, the eye is inevitably drawn below to the prophet **Isaiah**. As Freda White rightly noted, 'this statue is alive.' It is commonly called the 'dancing' Isaiah. Poised on one foot, with stone draperies flowing, the composition is unlike anything else produced in the Middle Ages; the carving, in its intricate detail, is a virtuoso display of careful precision. Most striking of all is the extreme stylization: studied and consistent, a vision of form that is the work of a great artist – one of the

Getting Around

Souillac already gets too much traffic from the N20, and it will probably only get worse once the Paris–Toulouse A20 is complete and it becomes the big exit for the Dordogne valley. There are frequent **trains** from Paris, Brive, Cahors and Toulouse, and **bus** services to Sarlat (information **t** 05 65 53 27 50) and Martel (SNCF buses, **t** 05 65 32 78 21). You can also take a tour of the town aboard a little **train** (**t** 05 65 37 83 13).

Tourist Information

Souillac: Bd Louis Jean Malvy, **t** 05 65 37 81 56, **f** 05 65 27 11 45.

Market Days

Souillac: by the handsome old Halles, Fridays. Smaller fruit and vegetable markets on Mon and Wed morning in Place Doussot and Place St-Martin, in July and Aug. Clothes and bric-a-brac market on the first and third Fri of each month.

Sports and Activities

On Avenue Jean Jaurès, the **Musée de la Vieille Prune**, the 'Still Museum', is run by the Distillerie Louis Roque (*t 05 65 32 78 16; open Mon–Fri 8.30–12 and 2–6*), and offers free tastings. **Quercyland** at Les Ondines near Souillac waits to entertain the kids with giant inflatable castles to bounce on, water slides and mini-golf (*t 05 65 37 33 51; open May–mid Sept 10–10*); for adults they offer **canoe and kayak** descents down the Dordogne from an hour to a week in length. Also try **Safraraid**, **t** 05 65 30 74 47 for canoes/kayaks, departing from the campsites at Lanzac and St-Sozy. There's a pretty nine-hole **Golf Club Mas-del-Teil**, at Lachapelle-Auzac, **t** 05 65 27 56 00, with a pool and tennis court; or you can spoil yourself at **Aquareve**, in Rue Morlet, by the Musée de l'Automate, **t** 05 65 32 79 43, with a heated indoor pool, gym, hammam, massage, sauna, vibrosauna, solarium, etc. There are also two places to go riding, the **Club Hippique Souillagais**, Chemin Corpus Christi, **t** 05 65 32 64 62, or the **Ferme Equestre du Bournet**, at Pinsac, **t** 05 65 32 23 94.

Where to Stay and Eat

Souillac ✉ 46200

Lots of people pass through Souillac, and there is a wide choice of places to stay – old two-star inns with a sincere welcome and attractive rooms.

greatest between the Greeks and Donatello. From this he can perhaps be identified as the same man who did the portal at Moissac, or at least an equally talented member of the School of Toulouse. Besides Isaiah and the ruined statue of the patriarch Joseph, one of the side pillars of the portal was saved, swarming with monsters often (though doubtfully) claimed to represent the seven deadly sins, with biblical scenes like the sacrifice of Abraham cleverly mixed in.

Souillac has acquired another attraction of late. Facing Ste-Marie is an ambitious effort called the **Musée de l'Automate**, run in collaboration with the robotic experts of the Cité des Sciences de La Villette in Paris (*t 05 65 37 07 07; Nov–Mar Wed–Sun 2–5; April and May Tues–Sun 10–12 and 3–6; June, Sept and Oct daily 10–12 and 3–6; July and Aug 10–7*). Scores of mechanical dolls, some from as far back as 1870, haunt the premises, eating, drinking, playing banjos, jumping through hoops and doing every other trick that clockwork and circuitry can accomplish, all to special sound and light effects. They have some modern robots to keep them company, including a new high tech **Robot Zoo**, along with exhibits that explain everything you ever wanted to know about the history of automata. The experts who keep them all in good repair also

★★★**La Vieille Auberge**, 1 Rue de la Recège, **t** 05 65 32 79 43, **f** 05 65 32 65 19 (*moderate*). A whiff of Louis XV by the river. Pool, sauna, hammam and Jacuzzi, and rooms equipped with TV and video. The excellent restaurant serves dishes based on the recipes of a century ago, including mountains of foie gras but with a lighter touch (*menus 120–350F*).*Closed for several weeks and some eves out of season.*

★★★★**Grand Hotel**, 1 Allée de Verninac, **t** 05 65 32 78 30, **f** 05 65 32 66 34 (*moderate*). Near the church this charmingly old-fashioned place provides central and comfy enough accommodation. Some of the rooms have balconies. You can go up on the roof for an all-round view. The popular and busy restaurant serves classic dishes (*menus 80–250F*). In the summer the patio out front is a favourite meeting spot. *Closed Nov–Mar.*

★★**Auberge du Puits**, Place du Puits, **t** 05 65 37 80 32, **f** 05 65 37 07 16 (*inexpensive*). The restaurant here has a wide choice of entrées, from tripe to trout, prepared in the same old-fashioned way (*menus 85–250F*). *Closed Sun eve and Mon out of season, and two months in winter; not always open for lunch so call.*

★★**Les Ambassadeurs**, 12 Av de Général-de-Gaulle, the main street, **t** 05 65 32 78 36, **f** 05 65 32 72 70 (*inexpensive*). Simple if elderly rooms, some en suite, and simply prepared but very good local dishes (*menus 85–195F*). Plenty of locals come back week after week. *Open every day.*

★★★**Les Granges Vieilles**, on the D703 from Sarlat, **t** 05 65 37 80 92, **f** 05 65 37 08 18 (*moderate*). The large country house set in a lovely shaded park is a cool haven on a hot day. Some of the rooms are elegant and spacious, others not so much, but all have views on to the park and there is a pool. The restaurant is open midday and evening and you can eat on the patio; menus tend towards the regional but not exclusively so (*85–270F*). Calm assured. Many of the trees in the park were destroyed by the fierce storms in December 1999, but some interesting ones remain, like the large monkey-puzzle.

Le Redouillé on the main road, 28 Av de Toulouse, **t** 05 65 37 87 25. The owner-chef earned his stripes in the Med and is now at home with the very different cuisine of the southwest (*menus from 95–130F*). *Closed Sun eve, Mon and several weeks out of season.*

L'Alouette, in nearby Lanzac, on the N20, **t** 05 65 37 83 66 (*cheap*). A pretty country inn with a pair of doubles and a good restaurant that specializes in beef with truffles (*menus 78–200F*). *Closed Sun eve July and Aug and more frequently out of season; call first.*

make some of their own; you can see these in the fascinating gift shop called Clepsydra. And for something completely different, there's the **Musée des Attelages de la Belle Epoque** (***t*** *05 65 37 07 75; open July and Aug 10.30–1 and 2–6.30, April–June, Sept and Oct 10.30–12 and 2.30–5, closed Mon in April, May and Oct; adm*), right in the centre of town on Rue Paul Chambert, with 60 19th-century carriages on display.

Carlux and Ste-Mondane

As you leave the *département* of the Lot for that of the Dordogne and, more specifically, the corner known as Périgord Noir ('black' for either its truffles or deep forests – no one seems to know which), **Carlux** has a pair of romantic châteaux to look at: a 14th-century castle left ruined by the English in the Hundred Years' War, and, on a remarkable site in a holly oak forest, the 16th-century Château de Rouffillac. Just across the river at St-Julien-de-Lampon is a Gothic church with 16th-century mural paintings. From there the D50 continues west to **Ste-Mondane**.

Mothers are often saints, but few are ever canonized, what with the Church's fantasies about virginity. One who made it into heaven's ranks, however, was

Mondane, the mum of Sarlat's patron, St Sacerdos; she spent her later years in a cave in the riverside village that now bears her name. Although the cave is no longer a pilgrimage site, visitors still pour into Ste-Mondane to see the majestic **Château de Fénelon**, piled on a set of terraces, defended by a triple ring of walls and gate towers, its roofs still covered with their original *lauze* stones (***t** 05 53 29 81 45; guided tours daily 10–12 and 2–6; June–Sept 9.30–7; adm*). Begun in the 13th century, the château was mostly rebuilt in the 1600s as a lordly residence by one of the oldest and most aristocratic families of the Dordogne, de Salignac de la Mothe-Fénelon. The magnificent cedar of Lebanon by the gate was planted to celebrate the birth of François, in 1651, a 13th child but one whose brains soon attracted attention (*see* p.152). Inside, the new owner has refurbished several rooms, using his own collection of arms. There are a few relics of the great man and, in the bedroom where he first saw the light of day, there's a superb 17th-century walnut fireplace.

Carsac-Aillac and the Château de Montfort

Downriver on the D50, **Groléjac** reserves its best features for those willing to get out of the car and walk up its medieval streets, where it conceals a little 18th-century château and a Romanesque church. Near the junction of the Dordogne and the little Enéa stands **Carsac**, a village of 16th–17th-century *lauze*-roofed houses with a domed Romanesque **church**, built in the 11th century. Damaged by the English, the nave and chapels were rebuilt in the 1500s with ogival vaults and capitals carved with unusual classical scenes, including a baby Hercules strangling the serpents that crept into his cradle. When the church was restored in 1940, new works were commissioned from

Where to Stay and Eat

Groléjac ✉ 24250

★★**Grillardin**, **t** 05 53 28 11 02 (*inexpensive*). A simple but pleasant Logis de France with a shady terrace and views. *Open all year.*

Carsac ✉ 24200

Delpeyrat, in the village centre, 1km from the Dordogne and 8km from Sarlat, **t** 05 53 28 10 43 (*inexpensive–cheap*). It may get no stars but it's quiet, well kept and a reasonably priced option; the food is basic but inexpensive and there's plenty of it, and the owners are friendly.

Relais du Touron, **t** 05 53 28 16 70. Puts on a good spread (*menus from 95F*).

Vitrac ✉ 24200

★★**Plaisance**, Le Port, **t** 05 53 31 39 39, **f** 05 53 31 39 38 (*inexpensive*). As pleasurable and relaxing as its name suggests: made of golden stone, with a long garden terrace overlooking the river; canoe rentals, pool and tennis. *Closed mid-Nov–early Feb.*

★★**Hôtel Burg**, Le Port, **t** 05 53 28 33 29, **f** 05 53 28 28 25 (*inexpensive*). A pretty, ivy-covered place by a stream, with modernized rooms, a heated pool, tennis and views. In business since 1801. *Closed mid-Nov–Mar.*

★★**La Treille**, Vitrac-Port, **t** 05 53 28 33 19, **f** 05 53 30 38 54 (*inexpensive*). Right by the river, with a good restaurant. *Closed mid-Jan–early Mar.*

Restaurant de la Ferme (Chez Lacour Escalier), Caudon-de-Vitrac, south of Vitrac on the D46E, **t** 05 53 28 33 35. A lovely old place offering ample portions of *confits*, fillet steak, chicken prepared in a variety of ways, and a delicious Dordogne fish-fry in fishing season; children's menu available. *Temporarily closed but due to open in 2001, menus should be from about 85F.*

Léon Zack: the stained glass and the Stations of the Cross, with texts from Paul Claudel's *Le Chemin de la Croix*.

The **Château de Montfort** (*t 05 53 28 57 80; open June–Sept 10–6, July and Aug 10–7, early Nov park and ramparts only*), high over its river loop (or *cingle*), is one of the most photographed of all the Dordogne's castles. It was named after the ruthlessly effective leader of the Albigensian crusade, Simon de Montfort, although typically for him all he did was burn it to the ground when he captured it in 1214. Still, his name stuck to the spot when the château was rebuilt over the centuries, especially after three sieges by the English in the Hundred Years' War. It is best seen from the road between Carsac and **Vitrac**, the latter village a popular holiday base spread between the crossroads to Sarlat and its medieval core, the old 'Bourg' with a large Romanesque church.

Sarlat-la-Canéda

'*Mon Dieu*, there's nothing here but foie gras, foie gras, foie gras!' muttered an old farmer, brought by his relatives to Sarlat for a Sunday afternoon promenade. Of course he's right: nearly every other boutique glitters with stacks of tiny shiny tins. But such rich stuff fits Sarlat perfectly well, for, cocooned inside its clinking ring of 20th-century sprawl, this golden Renaissance town is architecturally the foie gras of southwest France.

History

It was Clovis, they say, who founded the first church at what is now Sarlat, and Charlemagne who stopped here after Roncesvalles to give it a fragment of the True Cross and the relics of St Sacerdos, Bishop of Limoges. In the 8th century, Pepin, Duke of Aquitaine, added an abbey, and Sarlat grew up around it. It was raging with plague when St Bernard made a memorable visit in 1147 and cured several victims with blessed bread. By the next century, the autocratic rule of the abbot over the increasingly mercantile town had become intolerable to the good burghers, and in 1299, after much strife, the *Livre de Paix* was signed, acknowledging the abbot as boss, but giving the town councillors the authority to run the show. As compensation, Pope John XXII made Sarlat a bishopric in 1317, elevating the church to a cathedral.

Founded as an abbey town, Sarlat has no natural defences and was constrained to add some formidable man-made ones during the Hundred Years' War. In return for defending itself so well against the English, the French simply handed Sarlat over to Edward III in 1360 as part of the ransom for Jean II, although 10 years later du Guesclin and the French won it back by arms. As a reward for its loyalty in spite of it all, Charles VII granted Sarlat enough tax concessions in the 1440s to bring about its golden age and a building boom; nearly all of its *hôtels particuliers*, or town houses, were built between 1450 and 1500 and grace Sarlat with a rare architectural unity.

In 1574, Catholic Sarlat was captured and pillaged by the irrepressible Huguenot Captain Vivans, who got in during Carnival by disguising his troops as harlequins.

Smarting from the embarrassment more than anything else, Sarlat held tight for three weeks in 1587 when it was besieged by the fanatical Protestant Vicomte de Turenne. When their ramparts were damaged, the Sardalais rebuilt them during the night, and when Turenne offered them terms they replied: 'We have a good master and don't want any other.' Turenne went away muttering, ashamed not to have been able by force or ruse 'to take such a town'.

After the Wars of Religion, Sarlat sank gently into the role of a local market town, off the main routes of communications and history. In 1827, the town fathers, hoping to drum up some new business by uncongesting traffic, carved a long straight slice out of its heart to create Rue de la République, better known as the *Traverse*. Further 'improvements' were prevented after 1963, when Sarlat was chosen as one of the first towns to be restored and protected by the state under the *Loi Malraux*.

From Place de la Grande Rigaudie to the Cathedral

Parking is the first hurdle confronting any motorist arriving in Sarlat; the largest and most convenient car parks are south of the *Traverse*, in and around vast Place de la Grande Rigaudie. Here, in 1892, Sarlat erected a statue to its famous son, Etienne de La Boétie, although it unfairly makes the young thinker look like a wimp (*see* below). On the hill beyond him and the courthouse is the **Jardin Publique**, offering a good overview of Sarlat and its many steep *lauze* roofs.

The urban scale becomes immediately more intimate and richly detailed once you walk up Rue Tourny, just north of Place de la Grande Rigaudie. A lane on the right leads into the Cour des Fontaines, with its age-old **fountain**. Clovis founded Sarlat's first church in the second courtyard, a site now occupied by the 12th-century **Chapelle des Pénitents Bleus** (*closed to the public*). Follow the narrow passage to the **Ancien Cimitière**, where 12th–15th-century tombstones have been excavated and arranged on terraces.

A stair from here leads up to Sarlat's great oddity, the **Lanterne des Morts**, a stubby stone rocket built at the end of the 12th century. Its original use has been forgotten – it may have commemorated the miracle of St Bernard, or have been used as a funerary chapel, or perhaps a lantern was lit here during wakes and vigils on the ground floor (there's an upper floor, but it's completely, mysteriously inaccessible). There may even be a confusion over its original name; sometimes it was described as the *lanterne des Maures*, referring to its marked resemblance to Turkish *türbes* and other Muslim mausolea that the crusaders surely saw.

Below stretch the flying buttresses and bulb-topped steeple (locally known as the 'scarecrow') of the **Cathédrale St-Sacerdos**, dedicated to the 6th-century leper-curing Bishop of Limoges. The first church was built at the same time as the Lanterne des Morts and had to be consecrated twice, the second time in 1273, after Sarlat's abbot was shot down while saying Mass by a disgruntled monk with a crossbow. This church was demolished (except for its Romanesque *clocher-porche*) by Bishop Armand de Gontaut-Biron in 1504 in order to construct a much grander cathedral. Unfortunately the project took until the dull 17th century to complete and, although

Getting Around

Direct **trains** to Bordeaux, Les Eyzies, Bergerac and Souillac from Av de la Gare; in July and Aug there are daily links to Bergerac, known as *Autorail Espérance* – a guided tour, with tastings of local products along the way (for tickets and more information, contact the SNCF station, **t** 05 53 59 00 21).

Taxi: **t** 05 53 59 39 65 or **t** 05 53 59 02 43.

There's one **bus** each morning except Sunday to Périgueux (Laribière, **t** 05 53 59 01 48) and another to Souillac (**t** 05 65 53 27 50). For Brive, you need to change at Souillac.

Bike hire from the station, or from Christian Chapoulie, 4 Av de Selves, **t** 05 53 59 06 11.

Tourist Information

Place de la Liberté, **t** 05 53 59 31 45 45, **f** 05 53 59 19 44, *www.sarlat.com*.

Market Days

Wed and Sat.

Where to Stay

Sarlat ✉ 24200

As the capital of Périgord Noir, Sarlat, with its many small hotels, provides a convenient base – as long as you book in advance in the summer.

******Relais de Moussidière***, **t** 05 53 28 28 74, **f** 05 53 28 25 11 (*moderate*). At the west entrance to Sarlat, this traditional stone manor house set on a cliff has been recently converted. The rooms are fairly simple and modern, but the gracious hosts, the 40-acre, exquisite landscaped park with a pool, the duck ponds full of quackers and the two very friendly dogs are better than any fancy antiques. Conveniently nearby are riding stables, golf and tennis courts. *Closed Nov–Mar.*

*****La Madeleine**, 1 Place de la Petite Rigaudie, **t** 05 53 59 10 41, **f** 05 53 31 03 62 (*moderate*). Near the medieval centre, this was converted from a 19th-century town house; rooms are air-conditioned and soundproof, while a private garage conveniently solves Sarlat's parking problems. Owned by a chef, the restaurant serves regional specialities: *civet d'oie* in *vin de Cahors* and such share the menu with lighter, more modern dishes (*menus 115–215F*). *Closed Mon lunch exc July, and Aug and Jan–mid-Feb.*

*****La Salamandre**, 2 Rue de l'Abbé Surguier, **t** 05 53 58 35 98, **f** 05 53 31 22 32 (*moderate*). In a quiet lane in the centre, this began life as a distillery before becoming a comfortable hotel with a garden and pool; 30 (mostly Louis XV) rooms and five flats. *Open all year.*

*****De Selves**, 93 Av de Selves, **t** 05 53 31 50 00, **f** 05 53 31 23 53, *www.selves-sarlat.com* (*moderate*). A classy modern place with airy rooms in pastel colours, some with a terrace. Relaxing gardens and a pool. *Closed for most of Jan and the start of Feb.*

****St Albert et Montaigne**, Place Pasteur, **t** 05 53 31 55 55, **f** 05 53 59 19 19 (*inexpensive*). Fresh, colourful rooms in a pair of old *hôtels* at the south entrance of the old town, with a decent restaurant (*from 100F*).

****La Couleuvrine**, 1 Place de la Bouquerie, **t** 05 53 59 27 80, **f** 05 53 31 26 83 (*inexpensive*). Unusual antique-furnished rooms in a tower in the 14th–18th-century ramparts of Sarlat's walls; the restaurant prides itself on its market-fresh produce (*menus from 98F*). *Closed part of Jan.*

****De Compostelle**, 64–6 Av de Selves, **t** 05 53 59 08 53, **f** 05 53 30 31 65 (*inexpensive*). Modern rooms with private terrace and TV, not far from the centre.

Pierre Henri Toulemon, 4 Rue Magnanat, **t** 05 53 31 26 60 (*inexpensive*). Climb the steps in the street to the big oak doors of this *chambre d'hote* bang in the middle of the old town. The building is classified as a historical monument and the rooms have old furniture – all very atmospheric. *Open all year.*

****Hôtel des Récollets**, 4 Rue J.J. Rousseau, **t** 05 53 31 36 00, **f** 05 53 30 32 62 (*inexpensive*). In a quiet corner west of la Traverse, installed in a 17th-century cloister.

****Hostellerie Marcel**, 8 Av de Selves, **t** 05 53 59 21 98, **f** 05 53 30 27 77 (*inexpensive*). Pleasant rooms in a little, family-owned stone house, although the road can be a bit noisy. *Open Feb–end of Nov.*

Auberge de Jeunesse, 77 Av de Selves, **t** 05 53 59 47 59, **f** 05 53 30 21 27. Within walking distance of the centre, with simple dormitory rooms. *Open Feb–Nov. Book.*

Les Périères, 1km from Sarlat on the D47, **t** 05 53 59 05 84, **f** 05 53 28 57 51. The best camping around, in a beautiful shady park, with a pool, sauna, Jacuzzi, tennis, playgrounds, etc. *Open Easter–Sept.*

Just Outside the Centre

Within a radius of a few kilometres of Sarlat you'll find nearly as many places to choose from, with the added bonus of a little peace and quiet.

****Domaine de Rochebois**, 6km south, on the Route de Montfort towards Vitrac, **t** 05 53 31 52 52, **f** 05 53 29 36 88 (*expensive*). Housed in a suberb château with formal gardens, with amenities like a nine-hole golf course along the Dordogne and a pool. *Closed Nov–late April.*

***La Hoirie**, 2km south from Sarlat at La Canéda, **t** 05 53 59 05 62, **f** 05 53 31 13 90 (*moderate*). A former aristocratic hunting lodge, with 17 comfortable rooms fitted with mini-bar, and a pool in the park.

***Hostellerie de Meysset**, at Argentouleau (2km northwest on the Les Eyzies road), **t** 05 53 59 08 29, **f** 05 53 28 47 61 (*moderate*). The hilltop hotel offers smallish but pretty rooms with country-style furnishings to go with its views over its park, pool and the Sarlat valley; it's equally pleasant from the restaurant terrace, dawdling over delicious confits served with a garlic cream sauce and other treats. *Closed mid-Oct–April.*

Hostellerie La Verperie, just outside Sarlat at La Verperie, **t** 05 53 59 00 20, **f** 05 53 28 58 94 (*inexpensive*). A rambling old house converted into a peaceful, cosy hotel especially suitable for families (pool, games, etc.). Set in a four-acre park. *Closed mid-Nov–mid-Mar.*

La Mas de Castel, at Sudalissant, 2.5km towards Souillac, **t** 05 53 59 02 59, **f** 05 53 28 25 62 (*inexpensive*). New but traditionally styled, offering bright pastel rooms around the pool in the midst of a large garden. *Closed mid-Nov–Palm Sun.*

Eating Out

Despite the tons of foie gras, central Sarlat isn't exactly graced with culinary epiphanies. The best are in the aforementioned hotels.

La Rapière, Place de la Cathédrale, **t** 05 53 59 03 13. A wide choice of dishes at fair prices (*menus from 85F*). *Closed Sun out of season, and Jan–Feb.*

Rossignol, near the Mairie at 15 Rue Fénelon, **t** 05 53 31 02 30. Good-value, regional cuisine (*menus from 90F*). *Closed Wed.*

Criquettamu's, 5 Rue des Armes, **t** 05 53 59 48 10. They do tasty things with foie gras, *magrets* and morel mushrooms (*menus 60–140F*). *Closed Mon exc in July and Aug, and Nov–Easter.*

Le Présidial, near the Place de la Liberté, **t** 05 53 28 92 47. Formerly the site of a royal court, with an elegant dining room and a large patio. There are extravagant regional dishes such as *suprême de pigeonneau en croûte sauce aux truffes*, with a choice of wines from around France, but of course with an empasis on the local (*menus 115–195F*).

Le Relais de Poste, Impasse de la Vieille Poste, **t** 05 53 59 63 13. Good menus, mostly focused on the regional, at reasonable prices (*58–150F*), with a wide wine selection and a range of *eaux-de-vie* made locally. There is a large secluded patio surrounded by walls with plenty of plants. *Closed Sun lunch in summer and Wed rest of the year.*

Chez Marc, 4 Rue Tourny, **t** 05 53 59 02 71. It's so covered in ivy you might not spot the name. Small and popular, serving regional food with a slight something added, hence *civet de canard au vin de noix* and *magret de canard aux fruits rouges* (*menus 55–135F*). *Closed Sun.*

the result is roomy enough, it holds nothing as artistic as the Bishop Armand's own effigy tomb in Biron (*see* p.362).

Place du Peyrou and La Boétie

Adjacent to the cathedral in Place du Peyrou is the former bishopric or **Ancien Evêché** (now a theatre), with handsome, mullioned windows and a top-floor gallery in brick that looks as if it escaped from Italy – not surprising, as it was built by a Florentine cousin of Catherine de' Medici, Cardinal Niccolò Gaddi, who added Bishop of Sarlat to his titles in 1533.

Opposite the cathedral stands the most lavishly ornate town house in Sarlat, the **Hôtel de La Boétie** (1525). The modern entrance is through the wide round arch of a former shop; richly ornamented mullioned windows dominate the upper three floors, squeezed between a vertiginously steep gable. The decoration reaches a curlicue frenzy in the dormer window, in frilly contrast with the sombre *lauzes* of the roof. The *hôtel* was built by the father of the precocious Etienne de La Boétie, who was born here in 1530. A student of the classics, Etienne was aged 18 when he wrote his most original essay, *Discours de la servitude volontaire*, asking why people willingly give up their liberty to support tyrants, when such tyrants could never exist without people willing to give up their freedom, the most precious thing of all. These were radical ideas in the 16th century, and, even when Montaigne published La Boétie's papers after his premature death at the age of 33, he discreetly omitted the *Discours*. It only appeared in 1576 in a collection of 'libellous' Protestant writings, and even then its influence remained dormant until the advent of Rousseau. But most of all, La Boétie is remembered as Montaigne's perfect pal in the latter's beautiful *Essay on Friendship*.

Place de la Liberté and Rue des Consuls

From Place du Peyrou, duck through the medieval alleyway of the Passage Henri-de-Segogne to another of Sarlat's architectural gems, the **Hôtel de Maleville** (now the tourist office). A 16th-century combination of three older houses, with two distinct Renaissance façades – one French, one Italian – it belonged to Jean de Vienne, a local boy who owed his rise to national high office to Henri IV (see the portrait medallions of the king and a woman – either Henri's wife Marie de' Medici, or his favourite mistress Gabrielle d'Estrées). It was later owned by the family that produced Jacques de Maleville, one of the prime authors of the Napoleonic *Code Civile*.

The *hôtel*'s French façade overlooks elongated **Place de la Liberté**, Sarlat's main square and favoured café stop, and address since 1861 of the Distillerie du Périgord, where you can try the original *Pastis Lapouge*, Périgord's own rendition of the famous Marseille apéritif, and a heavenly array of fruit *eaux-de-vie*. The 17th-century Hôtel de Ville is here; next to it, Rue de la Salamandre leads up past 15th- and 16th-century mansions to the handsome **Présidial** and its garden (visible through the gate). The Présidial was the seat of a royal court set up by Henri II in 1552 in defiance of local wishes to administer local justice; note the curious little polygonal lantern on the loggia. It's now a good restaurant by the same name (*see* Eating Out, above). More delights – gabled houses and carved portals – wait along Rue du Présidial and Rue

Fénelon, which brings you back to the northern extension of Place de la Liberté, the Place du Marché.

Here stands the sad carcass of a church with a massive bell tower, **Ste-Marie**, begun in 1365 and completed in 1507. After being used for storing saltpetre during the Revolution, it was sold for a pittance to a speculator, who lopped off its chancel and converted its chapels into shops; before the First World War it served as a post office. Now it forms part of the permanent stage for Sarlat's prestigious late July–early August theatre festival, the **Festival des Jeux de Théâtre**, starring Paris' Comédie Française. The picturesque **Rampe Magnanat**, ascending to the right, has been used by a score of French film directors for their climactic duel scenes, swords clashing before a brooding backdrop provided by the 16th-century Hôtel de Gisson and its hexagonal tower.

On the other side of the Hôtel de Gisson is the old goose market, Place du Marché aux Oies, and the narrow Rue des Consuls. Among the magnificent *hôtels* here, the **Hôtel Selve de Plamon** (Nos.8–10) stands out; it was owned by a prosperous family of drapers, who added a new floor every century or so – early Gothic on the ground floor, Flamboyant Gothic on the first and Renaissance on the second. Opposite is a curious cave-like **fountain** from the 15th century; the river Cuze passed openly under the Hôtel de Plamon as a pestilent sewer until it was covered over in the 19th century.

Across the *Traverse*

The *Traverse* cuts the wealthy Sarlat of splendid town houses from the steeper, more popular and piquant neighbourhood to the west, where some alleys are scarcely wide enough to walk arm in arm. In its intimate scale, the **Chapelle des Pénitents Blancs** in Rue Jean-Jacques Rousseau seems like a walrus. Rue J.-J. Rousseau continues to the lovely, nearly intact 16th-century **Abbaye Ste-Claire**, occupied until the Revolution (*generally open July and Aug*). Further south are Rue du Siège and a stretch of Sarlat's **walls** that survived demolition; here too is the **Tour du Bourreau**, the executioner's tower. In Rue Rousset there's a second tower, the 15th-century crenellated **Tour de Guet**.

Just beyond the boulevards on this west side of Sarlat, there's a **Musée Aquarium** (*Rue du Commandant-Maratuel,* **t** *05 53 59 44 58; open Easter–June and Sept–Nov 10–12 and 2–7, July and Aug 10–7; adm*), with all you've ever wanted to know about creatures that swim and slither in the Dordogne and how Périgourdins have traditionally nabbed them in their flat-bottomed *gabares*. Also on the outskirts, the **Musée de l'Automobile** (*7 Av Thiers,* **t** *05 53 31 62 81; open Nov–early July and late Aug–Oct 2–6.30, most of July and Aug 10–7, Nov–Mar weekends only; ask about possible night visits; adm*) has an accumulation of cars made up to 1940, including the 1926 Le Mans winner, a Lorraine-Dietrich.

Two kilometres north of Sarlat, Pepin the Short built the first citadel on the natural belvedere at **Temniac** in the 8th century (access off the D704, or by way of a marked walking path beginning off Av Brossard). In the 1200s the bishops of Sarlat used the site for a **palace**; it was rebuilt in the 15th century, and today stands in evocative, romantic ruins. The bishops' tower and the pure Périgourdin Romanesque **Chapelle de Notre-Dame**, with its pair of domes and vaulted choir, are nearly intact.

Northeast of Sarlat: the Plateau of Périgord Noir

Sarlat's hinterland is a pretty quiet place these days, but there are a few things worth seeing. At **Ste-Nathalène**, 8km east, a 16th-century watermill, the **Moulin de la Tour**, is still used to produce walnut, hazelnut and almond oils in the old-fashioned way; watch them do it (*every Fri, also Mon and Wed in July and Aug*); otherwise you can just visit the mill and shop (***t** 05 53 59 22 08; open Mon–Sat 9–12 and 2–7*). Roads from Ste-Nathalène run northeast to the 17th-century **Manoir d'Eyrignac**, where the current owner has won prizes for his immaculate restoration of the 18th-century French **gardens**, a perspective of hedges cut into cubes, triangles, circles and spheres (***t** 05 53 28 99 71; open daily 10–12.30 and 2–nightfall or 7pm, June–Aug 10–7; adm*). From here continue northeast to the D61 for **Salignac-Eyvignes**, a picture-postcard Périgord town spread below the 12th–17th-century pepperpot towers of the **Château de Salignac** (***t** 05 53 28 80 06; open July–Aug 10.30–12 and 2–6, but check first; adm*). Built by Archbishop Fénelon's feudal ancestors, the château was hotly disputed in all the region's wars. Terraces now replace the once bristling ramparts; among the highlights inside are two floors of vaulted cellars, the chapel and a Renaissance fireplace.

Eight kilometres northwest of Sarlat, off the D47, the twin-turreted 15th–16th-century **Château de Puymartin** (***t** 05 53 59 29 97; open April–early Nov 10–12 and 2–6, July and Aug till 6.30; adm*), set in a handsome park, was Turenne's headquarters when the Protestants besieged Sarlat, but for better or worse it has had little to do with history since then. Rooms are fitted with 17th-century furnishings, some with Aubusson tapestries – two (without tapestries) take overnight guests. Then, for something completely different, make your way south to **St-André-d'Allas** (4km west of Sarlat); at the stately Château du Roc take the narrow road up to the right for the **Cabanes du Breuil** (***t** 05 53 29 67 15; open Mar–May and Oct–Nov 10–12 and 2–7, June–Sept 10–7, otherwise by appointment; adm*), a hamlet of tiny, dry-stone huts with breast-shaped stone roofs, the kind of place where Asterix or Obelix would feel perfectly at home. In season there is a video, guided tours and demonstrations of dry-stone bulding, by appointment. Similar *bories*, or *gariottes*, exist in Provence and in Ireland, where they're called *clochans*, but whole villages of them are decidedly rare, and these are classified as a historical monument. No one knows who built them, or how long ago; the most likely answer is shepherds, who kept them in good repair over the centuries. There's a very pretty campsite right next to the *cabanes*.

Domme: the 'Acropolis of Périgord'

Lovely, honey-hued Domme is a *bastide* town from the Hundred Years' War, but one whose grid plan was remarkably transplanted on to a bluff-top eyrie over the Dordogne. Philippe III the Bold built it in 1281, and, although he bestowed many

Tourist Information

Domme: Place de la Halle, **t** 05 53 31 71 00, **f** 05 53 31 71 09, mornings only in the winter. Buy cave tickets here. To hire a **canoe** from the little port under Domme, **t** 05 53 28 22 01.

Villefranche-du-Périgord: in the centre, **t** 05 53 29 98 37, **f** 05 53 30 40 12.

Market Days

Domme: Thurs.

Cénac: Tues.

Where to Stay and Eat

Domme ✉ 24250

***__L'Esplanade__, in the centre of Domme by the belvedere, **t** 05 53 28 31 41, **f** 05 53 28 49 92 (*moderate*). Tranquil, recently renovated, with cosy rooms, some overlooking the Dordogne far below. Half-board (*demi-pension*) is mandatory in season – not a terrible penance in the charming restaurant or on its terrace, where some of the richest food in all Périgord is served especially when asparagus is in season (in a flaky pasty with morels) (*menus from 165F, but much more if you splurge with the truffles*). *Closed Mon and Nov–Feb.*

__Les Quatre Vents__, on the D46 towards Sarlat, **t 05 53 31 57 57, **f** 05 53 31 57 59 (*inexpensive*). A modern stone bulding in a quiet park 800m from Domme; it has a pool, and TV in each room, as well as several flats. *Open all year.*

__Relais du Chevalier__, Grand Rue, **t 05 53 28 33 88 (*inexpensive*). Eight comfortable rooms with exposed beams in a 15th-century town house. *Closed Nov–Feb.*

La Porte del Bos, **t** 05 53 28 58 55 (*moderate–inexpensive*). A bed-and-breakfast in the medieval centre, with en suite rooms, a garden, pool and view. *Open Easter–early Nov.*

*__Lou Cardil__, Grand Rue, **t** 05 53 28 38 92 (*cheap*). An attractive inner courtyard to go with its rooms. *Closed Nov–Mar.*

Mazeyrolles ✉ 24550

__La Clé des Champs__, on the D710 5km south-west of Prats, **t 05 53 29 95 94, **f** 05 53 28 42 96 (*inexpensive*). Bright well-equipped rooms in a former goose barn, a swimming pool and tennis, and good home-cooking in the restaurant, featuring flaky apple *tourtière* for dessert (*menus 95–160F*). *Closed Oct–April.*

Petite Auberge, Villefranche (✉ 24550), **t** 05 53 29 91 01 (*inexpensive*). '*Loin de Bruit*', this is well signposted from the centre, on a hill up a quiet country lane. Don't be put off by the corny courtyard: the food is delicious (*menus 70–200F*).

favours on it, he had to resort to threats to get the local peasants to build and settle his baby – only to pay the workers in black leather coins 'minted', or rather cut out, at the Mint in Place de la Rode, Domme's oldest building.

Despite its lofty site and walls, Domme was captured several times: by the English, the counts of Périgord and, in 1588 during the Wars of Religion, by Henri of Navarre's invincible captain, Geoffroy de Vivans – although only on the fourth try, after he laboriously established a secret ammunition depot in a cave halfway up the precipitous, undefended cliff. Then, one black night, after laying coats on the bare rock to muffle the noise of their approach, his troops sprung with a thunderous roar upon the unsuspecting town.

A Roam through Domme

If you approach Domme from the east by way of the D46E, you'll enter the town walls through the best preserved of its three gates, the 13th-century **Porte des Tours** (*afternoon guided tours: see the tourist office*). The narrow gate is framed by two fat guard towers built by Philip the Fair, which were converted into prisons in 1307 when the king ordered the arrest of the Knights Templars; some of them lingered here until 1318, engraving crucifixes and other graffiti you can still see on the wall. Domme's other two gates are equally worth a look: the arched **Porte de la Combe** to the south and the **Porte del Bos**, still grooved for its portcullis.

As with any *bastide*, the focal point of Domme is its central market square, here called Place de la Halle, although no other *bastide* square is quite like this: one side, beyond a **statue** of the Dordogne's literary hero, Jacquou le Croquant, and the church, gives on to the **Belvedere de la Barre**, with panoramic views from Monfort to Beynac. It's also easy to see why the locals hadn't bothered to defend the bluff, even from Vivans. Vivans took care to destroy the church, which is why the current one offers little interest.

However, Place de la Halle boasts other fine buildings: the turreted, asymmetrical **Governor's House** from the 1500s (now the tourist office) and the **Maison Garrigou** containing the **Musée des Arts et Traditions Populaires** (***t*** *05 53 31 71 00; open April–Sept 10.30–12.30 and 2.30–6, July and Aug 10.30–7; adm*), with a mammoth tooth, prehistoric and historical collections and traditional arts and crafts. In the middle, the charming 17th-century stone and timber market offers more than the usual turnips and carrots – the entrance into Domme's very bowels, through the **Grottes de Domme** (***t*** *05 53 31 71 00; open Mar and Oct 2–6, April–June and Sept 9.30–12 and 2–6, July and Aug 9.30–7, also open school hols; adm, tickets from tourist office*). Although the lower part of the cave was used as a refuge for the inhabitants during the Hundred Years' War, the upper part, where fossilized bison and deer bones were found, was discovered only in 1954; beyond is a well-lit stalactite phantasmagoria that ends with a ride in a glass lift up the sheer cliff, depositing you near the Jardin Publique, with the option of walking back to the Belvedere along the cliffside walk.

Just below Domme, some exceptionally lively Romanesque sculpture is concentrated in Cénac's early 12th-century priory of **St-Julien**, located on the edge of town (*open summer only; at other times Sun before 11am*). The Huguenots who smashed it

Les Mai

One thing that may or may not be in Domme when you visit is a tall pine pole in Place de la Halle, decorated with hoops and *tricolores* and a sign reading *Honneur à Notre Maire*; if it's gone down in Domme you may well spot similar poles in other villages or towns, or even next to private homes, reading *Honneur au Patron* or *à Notre Elu*, or with the names of a newly married couple, or perhaps even a newborn baby. They are called *les Mai*, or maypoles, and are erected at boozy confabs known as *la Plantation de Mai*. Once up, they are meant to rot away rather than ever be taken down. The Périgourdins apparently have been planting their maypoles ever since Gallo-Roman times, when a newly elected official would be honoured with a similar pole crowned with a garland. Since the Liberty Trees put up during the Revolution, they have taken on an added republican virtue.

fortunately gave up before reaching the apse: the exterior modillons depict carvings of a man-eating pig, grimacing faces and other oddities, while the interior capitals are vigorously sculpted with a bestiary, Daniel in the lions' den, Jonah and the whale, a monkey-trainer, a naked woman with a snake, and more.

South of Domme to Besse and Villefranche

All is rural tranquillity south of Domme, especially along the D60, fringed by chestnut forests and meadows. The Brigadoon stillness that reigns here (except during the autumn mushroom-hunts) makes the few 'sights' somehow more magical for being unexpected: the elongated old village of **Daglan** with – to the north – its curious, fortified, cross-shaped **Château de Peyruzel** from the 1600s; medieval **St-Pompont**, with a pair of châteaux and a mini-maze of medieval houses huddled beneath the fortified church; and further south, remote **Prats-du-Périgord**, with an even mightier 12th-century church and 16th-century château.

From Prats (Occitan for 'meadows'), follow the signs for **Besse**, an even tinier hamlet, with yet another château and an overbearing fortified **church**, although this one is special: not only has it held on to its *lauze* roof, but also a vigorous sculpted 11th-century porch, a rarity in these parts. French books claim the figures represent the 'Mystery of Redemption' – there's a Garden of Eden scene, possibly an Annunciation (under the six-winged angel), a midget Crucifixion and seven deadly sins, although the hunter on horseback, St Michael killing the dragon and the waltzing horses seem to belong to another story altogether. To guard Périgord's southernmost marches, Alphonse de Poitiers founded the *bastide* of **Villefranche-du-Périgord** in the 1260s. Although the grid plan and a fountain survive from Alphonse's day, Villefranche's central square has taken a lot of licks, leaving only one row of arcades facing the stone-pillared *halle*. The church sharing the square is a more maladroit than usual 19th-century rebuilding of the original; adjacent to the tourist office, the **Musée du Châtaigner**, **Marrons et Champignons**, is devoted to mushrooms and chestnuts (***t** 05 53 29 98 37; open April–Oct 9–12 and 3–6, closed Sun and Mon afternoons; other times Tues and Sun 10–12, Sat 10–12 and 3–6; adm*). Villefranche stands at the frontier of *bastide* country; for more, *see* p.358ff.

Down the Dordogne II

10

Down the Dordogne II

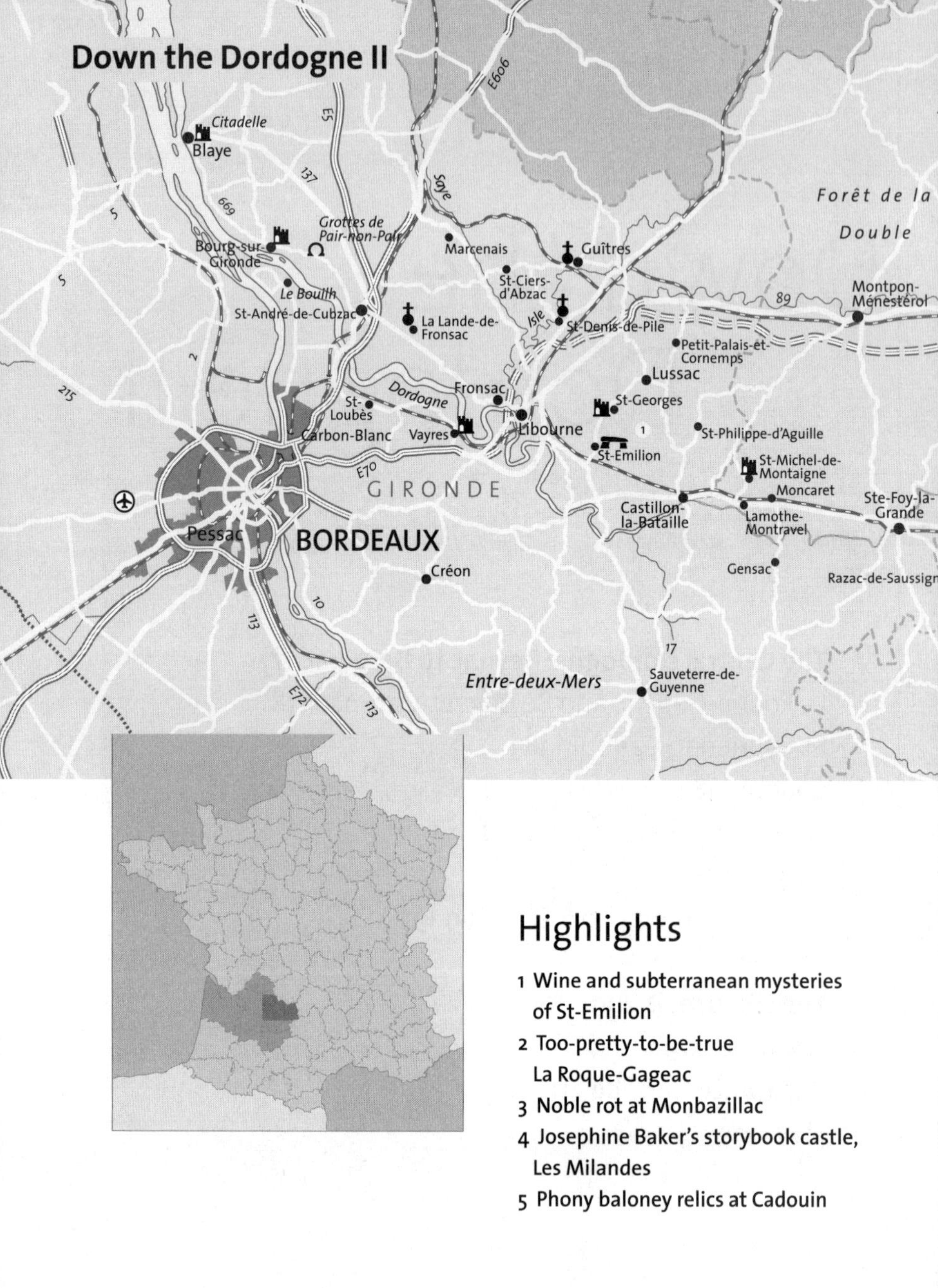

Highlights

1 Wine and subterranean mysteries of St-Emilion
2 Too-pretty-to-be-true La Roque-Gageac
3 Noble rot at Monbazillac
4 Josephine Baker's storybook castle, Les Milandes
5 Phony baloney relics at Cadouin

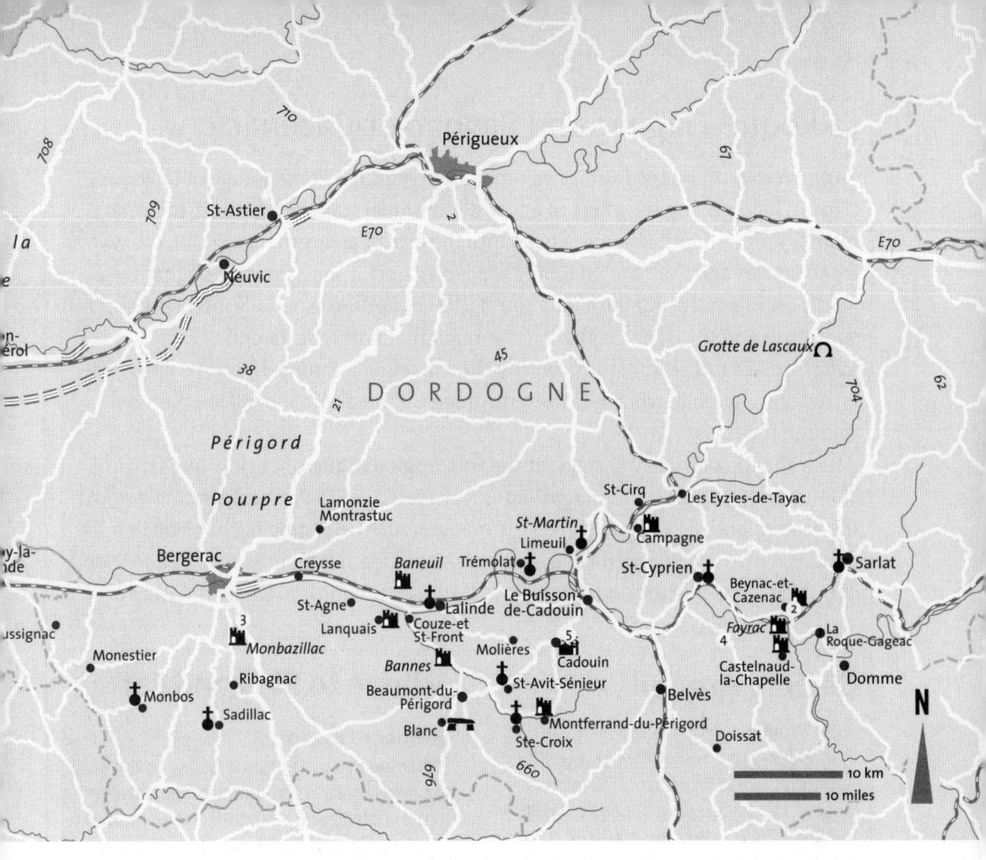

West of Domme and Sarlat the Dordogne bends below celebrated belvederes and beauty spots, some elbow to elbow: from the lofty Château of Beynac, you can count six other châteaux rising along the river, among them the menacing hulk of Castelnaud-la-Chapelle and the whimsical Renaissance château which gave a home to Josephine Baker's 'Rainbow Tribe'. The Dordogne dawdles through walnut country before the Vézère kicks in at Limeuil, and the newly swollen river whiplashes two more times before you see the fine, medieval city of Bergerac and the first vineyards, which will keep it company all the way to the Gironde.

The Central Dordogne: Beynac to Bergerac

This very pretty region has always been a major crossroads, these days for tourists but in the old days for merchants and armies; few of its imposing castles were built for decoration, but the defensive moats, towers and parapets are offset with fairy-tale pointed roofs, sprinkled with fleur-de-lys and topped by spindly weather-vanes.

La Roque-Gageac and Beynac-et-Cazenac

The car park along the river is five times as large as the entire village of La Roque-Gageac, heightening the effect of a two-dimensional stage set. In truth, there isn't room for much depth when you build into the face of an overhanging cliff; the warm stone houses and their brown roofs are piled against it so harmoniously that they hardly seem real. Facing the sunny south (the colours are especially intense at sunset), La Roque-Gageac is sheltered enough that an exotic garden of cacti and palms thrives by the little 16th-century church, set on a throne of rock. Reality does intrude occasionally, when bits from the huge cliff break off and fall like meteors through the roofs.

Near the top of town you can visit the **Fort Troglodytique**, once La Roque's main defence (***t** 05 53 31 61 94; open April–early Nov 10–7, closed Sat except July and Aug*). At the eastern end of La Roque stands the manor house belonging to the village's most famous native son, the 16th-century canon Jean Tarde, a humanist scholar and friend of Galileo who left a moving chronicle of the devastation wrought by the Wars of

Getting Around

The Sarlat–Bordeaux **railway** line runs through here five or six times a day, with stations at Siorac, Le Buisson, Trémolat, Mauzac, Lalinde, Creysse, Bergerac, Castillon and St-Emilion; Le Buisson is also on the main Périgueux–Agen line.

Tourist Information

Beynac: Parking de la Balme, **t** 05 53 29 43 08, **f** 05 53 29 45 67. Ask about walking paths in the area.

Activities

Rise above it all in a hot-air **balloon** from La Roque-Gageac, with Mongolfière du Périgord (**t** 05 53 28 18 58, **f** 05 53 28 89 34). Flat-bottomed ***gabares*** in La Roque-Gageac offer hour-long tours of the cliffs and châteaux on this stretch of the Dordogne (**t** 05 53 29 40 44; *open Easter–early Nov daily 10–6*); others depart from Beynac (**t** 05 53 28 51 15; *open mid-March–early Nov, reserve out of season*). You can also float down the river in a **canoe** and get a bus back: contact Canoë-Dordogne (**t** 05 53 29 58 50, **f** 05 53 29 38 92).

Where to Stay and Eat

Beynac ✉ 24220

★★**Bonnet**, **t** 05 23 29 50 01, **f** 05 53 29 83 74 (*inexpensive*). A traditional hotel between the château and river; the restaurant, with a riverside terrace, is famous for its *truffe en croûte*, a warm pastry containing truffles, smoked bacon and foie gras (*menus from 85F*).

★★**Du Château**, on the road up to the castle, **t** 05 53 29 50 13, **f** 05 53 28 53 05 (*inexpensive*). This tranquil hotel has a restaurant that makes good use of quality ingredients (*menus from 83F*).

★★**Hostellerie Maleville-Pontet**, right on the riverbank, **t** 05 53 29 50 06, **f** 05 53 28 28 52 (*inexpensive*). In business since 1871, this pleasant Logis de France has a terrace right on the beach.

★★**Tavern des Remparts**, **t** 05 53 29 57 76 (*inexpensive*). Only four rooms, but fine views over the castle and ramparts, and tasty food (try the *noisettes d'agneau aux girolles*) served on the terrace or near the big fireplace (*menus 70–120F*). *Closed Nov–Feb.*

Hôtel de la Poste, halfway up the village, **t** 05 53 29 50 22 (*cheap*). Offers a warm welcome and rooms, some with a view. *Closed Nov–Mar.*

Religion in the area. At the the western end, the **Château de la Malartrie** is a convincing reconstruction of the 15th-century original.

It's a few minutes from La Roque-Gageac to **Vézac** and its bridge over the Dordogne and 17th-century riverside **Château Marqueyssac**, in the same family since 1692 (***t*** *05 53 30 22 41; park open daily May, June and Sept 10–7, July and Aug 9–8, mid-Nov–early Feb 2–5; early Feb–April and Oct–mid-Nov 10–6; adm*). Although the château itself is closed to visitors, you can spend a couple of hours walking through some of the prettiest French gardens in the region, with over 150,000 ancient box trees in hedges on panoramic terraces; there's a boutique selling items carved from boxwood, and other attractions and facilities.

Continue a bit further along to **Beynac-et-Cazenac**, although you may have already seen its overpowering **Château de Beynac** from a number of points along the Dordogne (***t*** *05 53 29 50 40; open Mar–May 10–6, June–Sept 10–6.30, Oct–Nov 10–dusk, Dec–Feb 12–dusk; adm*). Barons of Périgord, the Beynacs were every bit as daunting and fierce as their castle appears. When Richard the Lion-Heart made it known that he meant to give their castle to his devoted Captain Mercadier, the Beynacs joined

Vézac ✉ 24220

★★Le Relais des Cinq Châteaux, t 05 53 30 30 72, **f** 05 53 31 19 39 (*inexpensive*). A modern hotel with a pool and superb views over the five surrounding châteaux; owner-chef Jacky knows what's what in the kitchen and does wonderful things with smoked sturgeon, game, and anything else his magic fingers touch; special vegetarian menu too (*menus 80–198F*). *Closed Sun eve and Mon out of season abd a month in winter.*

La Roque-Gageac ✉ 24250

★★La Belle Etoile, t 05 53 29 51 44, **f** 05 53 29 45 63 (*inexpensive*). A modest but welcoming family hotel with a terrace and pretty views of the river and village. Great food, too: try the *tatin de foie gras au jus d'agrumes* (*menus 125–200F*). *Closed Mon and Nov–Easter.*

★★Gardette, t 05 53 29 51 58 (*inexpensive*). A lovely terrace and patio in a garden and a good restaurant with tasty menus (*from 120F*). *Closed Nov–Easter.*

★★Périgord, t 05 53 28 36 55, **f** 05 53 28 38 73 (*inexpensive*). A huge house in large grounds outside the village in peaceful surroundings with a pool, tennis and restaurant (*menus from 98F*). *Closed mid-Nov–mid-Mar.*

La Ferme Fleurie, t 05 53 28 33 39 (*inexpensive–cheap*). A bed and breakfast near the village. *Open Easter–early Nov.*

Le Pres Gaillardou, t 05 53 59 67 89. Highly recommended, with a superb five-course menu beginning with *amuse-gueules*, in a charming stone building partially furnished with antiques (*menus from 100F lunch, 125F eves*). *Closed for a month in winter.*

La Plume d'Oie, t 05 53 29 57 05, **f** 05 53 31 04 81 (*moderate*). Modern and attractive, with big windows over the Dordogne and four pretty rooms to rent. Excellent, light renditions of Périgourdin specialities served with *savoir faire* (*menus 220–350F*). *Closed lunch in Aug. Book in advance.*

Castelnaud-la-Chapelle ✉ 24250

Parc Joséphine Baker, t 05 53 29 52 33, **f** 05 53 28 18 60 (*inexpensive*). Part of Josephine's park on the Dordogne now has a new hotel, with a pool, tennis and mini-golf as amenities, and riding in the vicinity. *Closed Oct–Mar.*

Le Tournepique, t 05 53 29 51 07. Right on the river; dine on the flowery terrace on good things made of duck and walnuts (*menus 75–155F*). *Closed Tues in Sept, and Sat Oct–Mar.*

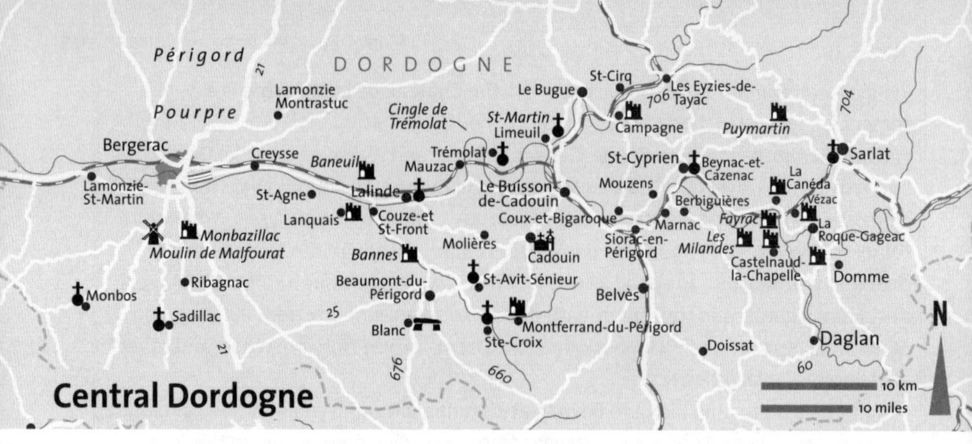

forces with Fortanier of Gourdon, whose father and brothers had been killed by Richard, and who had vowed to seek revenge. In March 1199, when Richard and Mercadier came down with a band of *routiers* to besiege Châlus (a castle just over the border in the Limousin), Fortanier shot an arrow that caught the king in a gap in his armour. Richard died a few days later, and not long after that the Beynacs liquidated Mercadier. In 1214 Simon de Montfort attacked Beynac and its lord, who was nicknamed the '*arca satana*' (Satan's Bow) for being a devoted friend of the Cathar-friendly Count Raymond VI of Toulouse; although he spared Satan's Bow for his loyalty to the King of France, Simon destroyed the château's most imposing towers. During the Hundred Years' War, Beynac fought a constant war against English Castelnaud, just over the river.

The interior has been through numerous transformations: there's a monumental 17th-century stairway, a *Grand Siècle* salon with a sculpted wooden chimney carved with mythologies, a *Sacrifice of Isaac* done with provincial panache, and late 15th-century frescoes in the Oratory (which, stylistically, are only about 400 years behind Tuscany) of the *Last Supper*, the *Pietà* and the *Man of Sorrows*. In the *Last Supper*, note the rare portrayal of the occasion's maître d' – St Martial, the apostle of Limousin and Périgord, and a fitting patron saint for a people in love with food. Behind the castle, the **Parc Archéologique de Beynac** (***t*** *05 53 29 51 28; open July–15 Sept 10–7, closed Sat; adm*) evokes the area's roots from Neolithic to Gaulish times, with reconstructed huts, demonstrations and various workshops such as tool-making.

Castelnaud-la-Chapelle and its Three Castles

Opposite Beynac, the powerful hulk of its eternal nemesis, the **Château de Castelnaud**, stands arrogantly on the limestone cliffs at the confluence of the Dordogne and Céou. First mentioned in 1214, when its Cathar owner was chased out by Simon de Montfort, Castelnaud's rulers, the Caumonts, stuck with the English during the Hundred Years' War, and built the keep as a base from which to terrorize the surrounding countryside. The Caumonts let the Huguenot Captain Geoffroy de Vivans – who was born in the village – use Castelnaud for similar exploits, but by that time the family had moved out of the stark, dark little rooms and narrow stairways of this feudal fort into Les Milandes (*see* below). Appropriately, the castle once again is full of catapults and crossbows in the **Musée de la Guerre au Moyen Age** (*t 05 53 59 31 21; guided tours in French and English; open June–Aug 9.30–7.30, mid-Mar–May and Sept–Oct 10–6, rest of year 10–12 and 2–5; adm, cheaper before 1pm in summer; joint ticket available with Marqueyssac; night visits during high season*). There are audio-visuals on warfare nearly a thousand years ago, plus demonstrations of the weapons, swordfights and so on in summer.

A wooded lane north of Castelnaud follows the river past the privately owned **Château de Fayrac**, which was built between the 14th and 17th centuries and romantically restored in the 19th century. Further on, in its own hamlet, is Castelnaud's third château, **Les Milandes** (*t 05 53 59 31 21; open Jan–Mar and Oct–Dec 10–12 and 2–5, April, May and Sept 10–6, June–Aug 10–7; adm*), a Renaissance beauty built by François de Caumont for his bride, Claude de Cardaillac. They decorated it with frescoes and sculptures, while the chapel filled up with elegant effigy tombs.

Josephine Baker, Châtelaine

In the 1930s, while she was on holiday in the Dordogne, Les Milandes cast a spell on Josephine Baker almost as powerful as the spell Josephine had cast over Paris with her joyful, exuberant versions of the Charleston and Black Bottom, performed in a costume made of nothing but bananas. Of all the black Americans who came to France to escape racism at home, Josephine was the most successful, becoming the highest paid performer in Europe—not bad for someone who was born in a cardboard box in St Louis. She purchased her dream castle and 600 acres to go with it, and used it during the war to hide people wanted by the Nazis, earning a medal for her work in the Resistance. In the late 1940s, after spending millions on the restoration of Les Milandes, she adopted 13 children of every race and creed, her 'Rainbow Tribe', and hosted anti-racism conferences. But her ambitions (which included a 120-acre pleasure garden and amusement park) were unfortunately bigger than her purse, and she and her husband Jo Bouillon fell so deeply into debt that Josephine—it broke her heart—had to sell Les Milandes in 1964 and retire to live in Monaco under the patronage of Princess Grace.

Today the attractions at Les Milandes are more National Trust than interracial trust, but are well worth a visit nevertheless. They include the fireplaces, panelling and carved windows that survived the Reformation fervour, and a museum in the kitchen and other rooms maintained as they were under Josephine's tenure, now a shrine to her memory: there's even a wax Josephine in her famous skirt of upturned bananas. Other exhibits, and summer demonstrations, are devoted to the lordly art of falconry. If you're extremely lucky, the lovely flamboyant Gothic Chapel, where Josephine and Jo were married, may just be open. Just down the lane from the château, a house has on its corner a statue of the Virgin Mary with children, the Virgin carved with Josephine's features. If you take the road down behind Les Milandes you can see the quaint and wistful remnants of her amusement park.

Unfortunately, François and Claude's grandson, raised as a priest, took to his conversion to Protestantism with such righteousness that all these lovely, worldly things were smashed to bits. He married one of the richest widows of his day, and in 1571 fathered a daughter, Anne, before somebody slipped him a few *anamites mortelles* in his favourite mushroom dish. The king made Anne a marquise, and she became such a marriage prize that she was hauled to the altar three times before her 18th birthday.

Tourist Information

St-Cyprien: **t** 05 53 30 36 09.
Siorac-en-Périgord: **t** 05 53 31 63 51.
Belvès: 1 Rue de Filhols, **t** 05 53 29 10 20.
Le Buisson: **t** 05 53 22 06 09.
Beaumont-du-Périgord: Place Centrale, **t** 05 53 22 39 12, **f** 05 53 22 05 35.

Market Days

St-Cyprien: Sun.
Belvès: Sat, and Wed eve farmers' market in July and Aug.

Where to Stay and Eat

St-Cyprien ✉ 24220

★★★**Hôtel de l'Abbaye**, Rue de l'Abbaye-des-Augustins, **t** 05 53 29 20 48, **f** 05 53 29 15 85 (*moderate*). A handsome place to stay, an 18th-century *maison de maître*, with a good restaurant: try the *jambonette de poulet aux langoustines* (*menus from 155F*). *Closed mid-Oct–mid-April.*

★★**La Grande Marque**, at Marnac, just off the road between St-Cyprien and Siorac, **t** 05 53 31 61 63, **f** 05 53 28 39 55 (*inexpensive*). Set in a large park in a quiet, lovely setting over the river; there's a saltwater pool, and an *atelier* for artists—the artist-owners offer courses in sculpture, drawing, painting, and lithography as well. Good food in the restaurant too, with service on the pretty terrace in summer (*menus from 98F*). *Closed Thurs.*

★★**La Terrasse**, Place Jean-Ladignac, **t** 05 53 29 21 69, **f** 05 53 29 60 88 (*inexpensive*). A Logis hotel-restaurant, with a range of rooms of differing standards. Go for the ones in the annexe with the small garden out front. Menus are more interesting the more you pay, but most of it is the usual selection (*92–240F*). There's a comfy sitting room. *Closed Jan and Feb.*

Les Ecuries de la Passée, out on the road to Mouzens, **t** 05 53 29 46 73. A popular restaurant, serving a delicious range of meals, including such treats as *ravioles de langoustines à la crême de basilic* (*menus 86–260F*). *Closed Sun eve and Mon.*

Jardin d'Epicure, just outside St-Cyprien on the D703 towards Sarlat, **t** 05 53 30 40 95. In cheerful surroundings, serving up superb southwest dishes with imaginative flair (*menus 145–280F*). *Closed Wed and occasional lunchtimes, best to phone.*

Coux et Bigaroque ✉ 24220

★★**Le Petit Chaperon Rouge** (head towards the village on the D703, coming off the Sarlat road, and you will find signs), **t** 05 53 29 37 79, **f** 05 53 29 46 63 (*inexpensive*). Hidden up a drive amongst trees. The rooms have old-fashioned comfort, the restaurant is colourful and busy, and the terrace, with plants and fairy lights, looking out over the valley, is lovely. Menus have the usual southwest favourites with different touches, hence the *pavé de turbot aux cèpes, riz basmati* (*98–220F*). Fabrice Constant, the owner and chef, worked in London for several years and can help you out if you need it. Very friendly staff. An excellent place to stay. *Open all year.*

St-Cyprien to Cadouin

The next bridge over the Dordogne is at St-Cyprien, a village overlooking the fertile alluvial plain that has long been the source of its fat, contented air. In the Middle Ages the Romanesque **church** with its bulky 12th-century bell tower had an important relic-magnet for pilgrims – the *Sainte-Epine*, or holy thorn, which monks rubbed against the clothes of sick people. Here you can leave the big river for Les Eyzies and the Vézère, or continue down the big river; the south bank is dominated by forests and walnut orchards, and a famous **abbey**, at **Cadouin**.

Siorac-en-Périgord ✉ 24170

★★Relais du Périgord Noir, Place de la Poste, **t** 05 53 31 60 02, **f** 05 53 28 37 65 (*inexpensive*). A handsome stone building with pleasant if old-fashioned rooms facing on to a flowery garden. The restaurant is good, too. *Closed mid-Oct–mid-April.*

★★L'Escale, **t** 05 53 31 60 23 (*inexpensive*). Relaxing place overlooking a little beach.

★★Auberge de la Petite Reine, **t** 05 53 31 60 42, **f** 05 53 31 69 60 (*inexpensive*). Club-like, with a covered pool, tennis and other sports, including golf lessons at the links, 1km away.

Belvès ✉ 24170

★★Le Belvédère, 1 Av Crampel, **t** 05 53 31 51 41, **f** 05 53 31 51 42 (*inexpensive*). An elegant, renovated hotel in the centre of town, with a terrace; all rooms with bath and TV; good meals with plenty of cèpes (*from 78F, lunch menu 60F*). *Closed Tues out of season, Jan and Feb.*

★Le Home, Place de la Croix-des-Frères, **t** 05 53 29 01 65 (*cheap*). Simple but adequate (*good-value menus from 60F*). *Closed Christmas and New Year and Sun eves out of season.*

Ferme Auberge de La Caussine, Doissat, **t** 05 53 29 94 84, **f** 05 53 29 14 66 (*cheap*). Rooms and a heated pool, chalets and good-value farm-fresh lunches or dinners, including as much wine as you can hold, and coffee too. *Open Easter–Sept.*

Auberge de Nauze, Sagelat, **t** 05 53 28 44 81. The best chef in the area works here. Excellent fish or meat (*menus 98–230F*). *Closed mid-Jan–mid-Feb.*

Le Buisson ✉ 24480

★★★Manoir de Bellerive, Route de Siorac, **t** 05 53 27 16 19, **f** 05 53 22 09 05 (*moderate*). A completely renovated Directoire manor house in a seven-acre park, endowed with such creature comforts as air-conditioning, sauna, tennis and pool; it has a superb restaurant, too, with a chef who concocts mouthwatering fillets of roast duck with honey and vinegar (*menus 150–425F*). *Closed Jan and Feb, restaurant closed Sun evenings, Mon and Tues lunch.*

Cadouin ✉ 24480

★★La Salvetat, 2.5km east of Cadouin on the D54, **t** 05 53 63 42 79, **f** 05 53 61 72 05 (*inexpensive*). A well-restored old farm in a pretty garden setting; swimming pool and other activities. Delicious menus (*from 138F*). *Closed Wed, and Dec and Jan.*

Beaumont ✉ 24440

Des Voyageurs, Rue Romieu, **t** 05 53 22 30 11, **f** 05 53 22 38 99 (*inexpensive*). Pretty little rooms, some with balconies, and a restaurant, Chez Popaul, a great place to fill up on masses of good, solid food—including a celebrated, well-endowed buffet table of entrées (*menus 95–300F; book*).

Chez Laparre, 4.5km southeast, at Labouquerie, just off the Monpazier road, **t** 05 53 22 40 22 (*cheap*). A farmhouse bed-and-breakfast.

Les Remparts, **t** 05 53 22 40 86. Beaumont's award-winning campsite: plenty of shade, tennis, pool, and more.

Belvès and Walnut Country

The bridge from St-Cyprien passes on to the south bank of the Dordogne near **Berbiguières**, a pretty village with a considerable English population and yet another château; just west, **Siorac-en-Périgord** is a busy market and holiday centre (complete with a nine-hole golf course) that uses its 17th-century château as a *mairie*. Just 5km south on the D710, the ancient hill town of **Belvès** with its seven belltowers has been inhabited for donkey's years – its name comes from a local Celtic tribe, the Bellovaques. It went from a fortified Roman *castrum* to a walled English town in the Middle Ages; a ring boulevard now replaces the walls. Within the ring, however, the old plan remains intact, as a kind of proto-*bastide*, the straight narrow lanes lined with Gothic and Renaissance buildings. In the central Place d'Armes stands a last relic of Belvès's defences, the **Tour des Fillols**, and a 15th-century *halle*, supported by 23 pillars, one still bearing the chains from pre-revolutionary days when it doubled as a pillory. The **Musée Organistrum et Vieilles à Roue** (*14 Rue J. Manchotte*, **t** *05 53 29 10 93; visits by appointment*) contains old barrel-organs and the like, Roman bits and bobs and old dolls.

Belvès is best known for its nuts; **Doissat**, some 7km to the southeast, off the D54, has the most extensive walnut plantations in the Dordogne, producing more of them than any other *département* in France. Doissat's partially collapsed château, the last resting place of the dashing Captain Vivans, has a little **Walnut Museum** (*open in summer*).

Cadouin

In 1115, a holy man named Géraud de Salles and a group of canons from Périgueux's St-Front founded a monastery at the end of a wooded valley. Four years later they affiliated themselves to the Cistercians and built a vast Romanesque church and cloister in the Norman style; at the end of the 15th century the cloister collapsed and was lavishly rebuilt by masons from Languedoc and the Rouergue. Why such an ambitious enterprise in the middle of nowhere? Because in 1117 the abbey got hold of a precious gift that put it square on the pilgrimage map of France – the *Saint Suaire*, the cloth used to wrap the head of Christ, a lesser Shroud of Turin.

The Abbey Church and Cloister

t *05 53 63 36 28; open Mar, April and Oct–Dec 10–12.30 and 2–5.30, May, June and Sept 10–12.30 and 2–6.30, July and Aug 10–7; closed Jan and Feb, and Tues in Sept–April.*

The centre of the village is a sturdy Flamboyant **halle** supported on stone pillars, facing the **abbey church**, consecrated in 1154. All the austere decoration of the asymmetrical façade is in triplicate: three flat buttresses, three doorways, three windows and nine blind arches, while the interior, with its three naves and domes, has been stripped naked by Cadouin's 19th-century restorers to reveal the vigorous architecture

Christ's Turban

The legend goes that in the year 68, during the persecutions in Jerusalem, a converted Jew hid the relic to keep it from coming to harm. After he died his two sons—who hadn't converted to Christianity—inherited it, the younger buying the elder's share, after which he enjoyed a famous streak of luck, while the elder knew nothing but misfortune. The cloth remained in the family as a lucky charm and, when the last member died in 660, Christians and Jews in Jerusalem quarrelled over it and put their case before a Muslim judge. He separated the two parties with a bonfire, and threw the cloth in; it proved itself the real McCoy by miraculously not burning, and when it blew over to the Christians' side they got to keep it.

In 1100 Hugues, brother of King Louis the Fat of France, purchased the cloth, and when he died he gave it to his confessor. He in turn passed it on to a priest from Périgord, who returned home with it hidden in a vat of Communion wine. He could not help blabbing his secret, however, and it wasn't long before the newly arrived monks at Cadouin got it off him—in return for the job of watching over the relic. Pilgrims en route to Compostela poured in, as well as Eleanor of Aquitaine, Richard the Lion-Heart, and St Louis, until the Hundred Years' War, when the monks desposited the holy relic in Toulouse's Eglise du Taur for safekeeping. Toulouse, however, refused to give the cloth back, and the Cistercians of Cadouin had to spirit it out of the city by stealth (1456). In 1935, a scientific examination of the cloth showed it to be a fine Egyptian weaving from the 11th century. An even greater embarrassment was the discovery that what for centuries had been considered a decorative border was in fact an Arabic inscription in praise of Allah.

in all its purity. The reliquary holding the *Saint Suaire* originally hung behind the altar in the choir; only the dangling chains remain.

The entrance to the lovely, Flamboyant Gothic **cloister** is just to the right of the church. It took so long to build that even a remote spot like Cadouin fell under the spell of the Renaissance before its completion; while the first, eastern galleries have pinnacles carved with curly kale leaves and thistles, the west gallery, built in the 1500s, is entirely Renaissance. A handout in English explains the scenes carved on the columns, ceiling pendants and doorways, an altogether hearty mix of sacred and profane – an *Annunciation*, scenes from the Last Judgement, Lazarus and Job keeping company with merchants fighting over a goose, an odd four-eyed, three-headed creature, and an anti-feminist trilogy – Samson and Delilah, a scene from the Lays of Virgil, and a courtesan straddling Aristotle (her name is Phyllis; this is from a medieval legend warning against the vanity of scholars). The debunked *Saint Suaire* is displayed with its copper gilt reliquary in the little museum in the Salle Capitulaire.

Cadouin also has a **Musée du Vélocipède** (***t** 05 53 63 46 60; open daily 10–7; adm*) with a rare collection of bicycles from the time they were invented in the early 19th century up to 1947. If you want to return to the Dordogne, the D25 follows the Compostela pilgrimage route to **Buisson-de-Cadouin** with its river-beaches and campsites, the closest point and an important crossroads, where you can catch the D710 for Le Bugue and the Vézère valley.

A Circular Detour Around Cadouin

From Cadouin, consider a little circuit through the woods to the minor but interesting sights in the area: along the D27 to the tiny, unfinished English *bastide* of **Molières**, with a large Gothic church built by a Plantagenet architect, and next to it an exhibit on walnuts. Molières, they say, has a ghost: in the 1360s, Queen Blanca of Castile died here, poisoned by her husband Pedro the Cruel, and she has a habit of wandering the streets. Continue south through the valley of the Couze, dotted with prehistoric *abris*, to charming **St-Avit-Sénieur**, a tiny medieval hamlet around an immense fortified **church** (***t*** *05 53 22 32 27; open daily, guided visits in July and Aug*) from the 11th century, built by Augustinian monks. Despite the terrifying aspect of its towers, the abbey was sacked during Simon de Montfort's crusade; the church's wrecked domes were later replaced with ogival vaulting. Of the abbey, only sections of the cloister, dormitory and *salle capitulaire* survive.

Just west of St-Avit, turn east on the D26, a scenic road passing through the Dordogne's largest wood, the Forêt de la Bessède, to **Montferrand-du-Périgord**, a graceful medieval hilltop village to the southeast, dominated by the ruins of a medieval **castle**. It has a pretty 16th-century *halle* and a little Romanesque church by the village cemetery, although even better is the Romanesque **church** at **Ste-Croix** (take the D26E), with a stern *clocher-mur* and good carved capitals inside.

Some astute navigation on the wiggly narrow lanes, heading northwest of Ste-Croix, will eventually reward with you with the D660 for **Beaumont-du-Périgord**, a *bastide* founded in 1275 by a lieutenant of Edward I, Lucas de Thaney, who honoured Edward's father, Henry III, by laying out Beaumont's wide straight streets in the form of an H. One mighty gate remains of the old ramparts, the **Porte de Luzier**, as well as the striking 13th-century fortified church, **St-Laurent-et-St-Front**, which could probably lick even St-Avit's church in a pitched battle. Yet for all its military features, an effort was made to embellish the west front, with a carved porch and frieze depicting the four Evangelists, a hunt, a king and a mermaid. You can visit the 15th–16th-century **Château de Bannes**, set high on a crag over the Couze valley, replacing an earlier castle destroyed in the Hundred Years' War (***t*** *05 53 61 19 54; guided tours; open July and Aug Wed–Sun 3–6, June and Sept weekends 3–6.30; adm*). One of the southwest's most impressive Neolithic sights, a megalithic gallery known as the **Dolmen du Blanc**, can be seen just over 3km to the south along the D676, on the left side of the road. From Beaumont, the D25 will take you back to Cadouin.

Back along the Dordogne

Before settling down in the western plains around Bergerac, the Dordogne pierces through a last stretch of glorious scenery between Le Buisson-de-Cadouin and Lalinde.

Limeuil and Trémolat

The lords of lofty Limeuil, where the Vézère flows into the Dordogne, defended this important junction with bristling walls, in part intact, along with three mighty gates; the snug village inside, with cobbled streets and stone cottages laced with ivy and roses, is almost too cute to be real (and packed to the gills in July and August). There's a Renaissance statue of the Virgin in the church and, outside the village on the road to Le Bugue, the domed Romanesque **St-Martin** (*open daily 9–6*) was jointly financed in 1194 by King Richard the Lion-Heart and King Philippe Auguste of France as an expiatory chapel for the murder of Thomas à Becket by Richard's dad (see the Latin inscription over the door, asking for God's mercy). Limeuil also has a **Jardin-Musée** (*t 05 53 63 32 06; open July–mid-Sept 10–12 and 2.30–7; adm*), with lovely orchids.

West of Limeuil the Dordogne's most majestic loop is followed by a scenic corniche road called the ***Route du Cingle***. Along the way are a pair of belvederes and **Trémolat**, a charming village whose boundaries exactly match the outlines of a 6th-century estate owned by the parents of Trémolat's patron, St Cybard. Signs of a Carolingian chapel, built to mark the miracles Cybard performed at home, can still be traced in the nave of the fortified 12th-century church; if things got hot, the population retreated into the mighty belltower-keep. Trémolat may look distinctly familiar if you've seen Claude Chabrol's thriller *Le Boucher*, filmed here in 1970. The town has a delightful *plan d'eau* if you need a dip. Don't miss the spectacular views from the Belvedere de Trémolat, just to the west.

Lalinde and Lanquais

The *Route du Cingle* descends through Mauzac to the busy market town of **Lalinde**, a royal English *bastide*, founded by Henry III in 1267 and given a 'solemn charter' and tax concessions that set it up from the start. Lalinde has maintained its grid core, *place* and medieval Bergerac Gate; the town now extends between the Dordogne and the canal built to avoid the *Saut de la Gratusse*, a dangerous stretch of rapids. Before

La Douce Limeuil

In the 16th century, Isabelle de Limeuil, daughter of the *seigneur* of Lanquais (*see below*), put the little town's name on the tip of every tongue in Paris. Rhapsodized by Brantôme as 'La Douce Limeuil', she was one of the loveliest of Catherine de' Medici's bevy of ladies-in-waiting, jokingly known as the 'flying squadron'. As queen mother, Catherine employed astrologers and sorcerers to get her way, and, like the wicked witch in *Snow White*, once sent a poisoned apple to an enemy; nor was she above using the virtue of her 'flying squadron' to seduce great Protestant nobles of France, in the hope that a conquest in the bedroom would translate somehow into a conquest for the Faith. Catherine sent the delightful Isabelle to charm one of the most powerful—the Prince de Condé. When a growing waistline betrayed the fact that she'd succeeded only too well, Catherine sent her home in disgrace. After the baby's birth, Catherine had a change of heart, and gave Isabelle in marriage to a social-climbing Italian banker to whom she owed money.

Tourist Information

Limeuil: **t** 05 53 63 38 90.
Lalinde: **t** 05 53 61 08 55.
Trémolat: **t** 05 53 22 89 33.

Market Days

Lalinde: Thurs; fair on second Thurs of each month.

Where to Stay and Eat

Limeuil ✉ 24510

****Les Terrasses de Beauregard**, Route de Trémolat, **t** 05 53 63 30 85, **f** 05 53 24 53 55 (*inexpensive*). A panoramic hotel-restaurant overlooking the big crook in the Dordogne; good restaurant, with a better-than-average selection of non-meat dishes: *terrine de légumes and soupe aux fruits au Pécharmant* (*menus 90–280F*). *Closed end Oct–Mar.*

Au Bon Accueil, near the top of Limeuil, **t** 05 53 63 30 97 (*cheap*). A sweet little hotel, with a delightful terrace under a pergola and a garden, and good fish fries, *civet de lièvre* and more (*menus 88–160F*). *Closed Nov–Mar.*

Isabeau de Limeuil, Rue de Port, **t** 05 53 63 39 19, **f** 05 53 63 39 50 (*inexpensive–cheap*). A funny little hotel-restaurant on a steep street just up from the riverfront, with loads of character and rooms to match. The restaurant downstairs is popular (*regional dishes 85–170F*) and the room at the back has a huge bulging and tilting stone fireplace. You have to park down the hill and carry bags up but it's not far. Friendly staff. *Open May–mid-Oct*. There is a forge opposite (*open for visits in July–Sept, closed Wed*).

Le Moulin Neuf Paunat, Ste-Alvère (✉ 24510), on the D2 northwest of Limeuil, **t/f** 05 53 63 30 18 (*moderate*). An enchanting, tranquil English-owned bed-and-breakfast, with lovely rooms in the old mill and breakfast served under the arbour.

Trémolat ✉ 24510

******Le Vieux Logis**, by the church, **t** 05 53 22 80 06, **f** 05 53 22 84 89 (*expensive*). Utterly sybaritic: a 17th-century manor with a stunning garden and pool. To quote a reader: 'This is the place that everyone should be compelled to go for at least one night and day before they say anything about France.' So there! The restaurant (in a former tobacco-drying barn or on the terrace) serves the best meals for miles around: heavenly *salade du terroir* and *langoustes*,

the canal was built, boatmen from Lalinde made a good living navigating all the flat-bottomed barges on the river through the rapids, helping their business by warning of a great serpent that gobbled up anyone who foundered. A waterside **Chapelle de St-Front** was built over the worst stretch for heavenly aid, just opposite Lalinde's river terrace. The family that owns the local **Château de Baneuil** occasionally opens the doors to the public (***t** 05 53 24 48 80; open July 1–6*).

West of Lalinde, cross the Dordogne at **Couze-et-St-Front**, where the river water is so clear that from the 15th to the 19th century the village became the area's chief papermaker, producing a very high-quality product which was sold throughout Europe. Along the river you can see vestiges of nearly a dozen old mills. The **Moulins de Larroque et Pombie** still produce handmade paper in the traditional way (***t** 05 53 61 01 75 to enquire about visits*); another, the **Moulin de Couze-La Rouzique**, was restored in 1991 as an *éco-musée* of paper, and contains a rare collection of watermarks and papermaking machinery (***t** 05 53 24 36 16; open April–mid-Oct 2–6.30, other times by appointment*).

From Couze-et-St-Front, the D37 continues to the delightful **Château de Lanquais** (***t** 05 53 61 24 24; open April–June and Sept–Oct 10.30–12 and 2.30–6.30, closed Tues; July*

with an excellent wine list (*210–430F; book*). *Closed Tues and Wed lunch.*

★★★**La Métairie**, west of Trémolat in Millac, **t** 05 53 22 50 47, **f** 05 53 22 52 93 (*expensive*). Ten beautifully furnished tranquil rooms spread through a row of traditional Périgourdin houses in a lovely garden, with a pool and prize views over the Dordogne. Kitchen specializing in Périgourdin treats with a light, modern touch (*menus 140–240F*). *Closed Nov–Mar.*

Lalinde ✉ 24150

★★★**Hôtel du Château**, 1 Rue de la Tour, **t** 05 53 61 01 82, **f** 05 53 24 74 60 (*moderate*). High over the river, in a château begun in the 13th century; seven comfortable rooms with TV, and a pool. The restaurant enjoys a wide reputation for its rich duck and game dishes; in the mushroom season, try the *fricassée de cèpes au beurre de Monbazillac* (*menu 125F lunch, others up to 3,000F*). *Closed Sun eve in winter, Mon except eves in July and Aug, three weeks in Sept.*

★★**Le Périgord**, 1 Place du 14 Juillet, **t** 05 53 61 19 86, **f** 05 53 61 27 49 (*inexpensive*). A Logis hotel, with comfortable rooms, some more appealing than others. Very proud of its chef Philippe Amagat and his extensive range of menus (*from 90F including pork curry to 450F*, offering the traditional tastes of the region, made for everyone at the table). Simple meals at cheaper prices are available to eat on the patio. *Closed for two weeks in Dec–Jan and a week in spring.*

St-Agne ✉ 24520

Ferme Auberge de la Rivière, signposted off the D37, **t/f** 05 53 23 22 26 (*moderate*). The food is fresh and solid southwest, much of it made and prepared on the premises, and you will be given an authentic welcome from Marie-Thérèse Archer who never stops working either on the farm or providing for guests (*menus 100–210F*, the cheaper rates for residents). If you want to stay half-board is obligatory, but this is a pleasure rather than an inconvenience. *Booking required. Open April–Sept.*

La Barabie, up the road at Lamonzie Montastruc, **t** 05 53 23 22 47, **f** 05 53 22 81 20 (*inexpensive*). Pleasant *chambres d'hôte* belonging to Marie-Thérèse's mother-in-law Marie-Jeanne Archer. Marie-Thérèse also provides the meals. A real family affair.

and Aug 10–7; adm). The stout medieval towers were built in the 15th century, and in the 1570s a Renaissance pavilion was added, attributed to the builders of the Louvre; the whole is furnished with antiques and chimneys believed to have been carved by itinerant Italian craftsmen. The 16th-century **Grange** to the right of the château hosts summer Baroque music concerts. Lanquais is also a great place to go riding, with scenic paths in every direction.

To continue west towards Bergerac, recross the Dordogne for the D660, which heads straight and fast across the comparatively dull, flat landscape. In **Creysse** two *gisements* (at Bella Riva) are open to visits by appointment: the Middle Palaeolithic Barbas I and Upper Palaeolithic Barbas II; and at Espace Bella-Riva there is a museum with exhibits on flint tools and Pécharmant, and an aquarium with fish from the Dordogne (***t** 05 53 23 20 45; open 10–12 and 2–6, in June–Oct till 7; adm*). You can also take a ride in a *gabare*. It is here that you'll see the first of the vineyards that the river wears like a green sleeve down to the sea.

Bergerac

Bergerac, known far and wide as the name of a poetic cavalier with a big nose who never even set foot in the town, is a fine little city where swans swim in the Dordogne and a tidy cluster of medieval, half-timbered houses bask by the old river port. It has also been recently christened the 'Capital of Purple Périgord', rectifying the hitherto unfair colourlessness of this corner, in a *département* elsewhere divided into Green, White and Black. The purple is, of course, for *le vin*: this is the only wine-growing part of *département* number 24, where 93 *communes* produce a wide variety of vintages. Perhaps, back in the days when Humphrey Bogart could seduce Lauren Bacall by blowing smoke in her face, it would have been dubbed Nicotine-Brown Périgord: tobacco is still a force to be reckoned with, and the city is not only the home of the national Institut du Tabac but also boasts a unique museum on the much maligned weed, first popularized in France by Catherine de' Medici, who used it to cure her migraines.

History

Medieval *Brageira*, or modern Bergerac, grew up around a feudal castle, but really took off as a town in the 12th century with the construction of a bridge – at that time the only one on the river. As a result Bergerac became the chief crossroads on the Dordogne, and the town naturally evolved into a commercial centre and river port. Like most of France's self-reliant mercantile communities, the Bergeracois converted to Protestanism with gusto. During the Wars of Religion it was known as the 'French Geneva' for its ardour.

The strong religious convictions of its merchants spelt the slow death of Bergerac as a prosperous commercial city. First the walls of the city were destroyed by Richelieu in 1620; in 1681 dragoons forced the Calvinists to convert to Catholicism; in 1685 Louis XVI revoked the Edict of Nantes, denying Protestants the right to worship. By the end of the 17th century, an estimated 40,000 inhabitants of Bergerac and its surrounding pays had emigrated to England and Holland. The city only revived at the end of the 19th century thanks to tobacco, wine and the national gunpowder works.

The National Tobacco Museum

***t** 05 53 63 04 13; open 10–12 and 2–6; closed Sun mornings and Mon; adm. No smoking!*

Although Bergerac occupies both banks of the Dordogne, all the interesting points for visitors are concentrated in the pedestrian area on the north bank. Here restoration work in the last 15 years has uncovered a handsome set of buildings from the 14th–17th centuries – Bergerac's heyday. Some of the finest are in Place du Feu, a pretty square shaded by an enormous old tree, especially the handsome, turreted **Maison Peyrarède** (1604), now the National Tobacco Museum. The museum is chock-full of curiosities on the herb, beginning with documents on its role as the sacred medicine of Aztec gods and a binder of peace agreements among North American

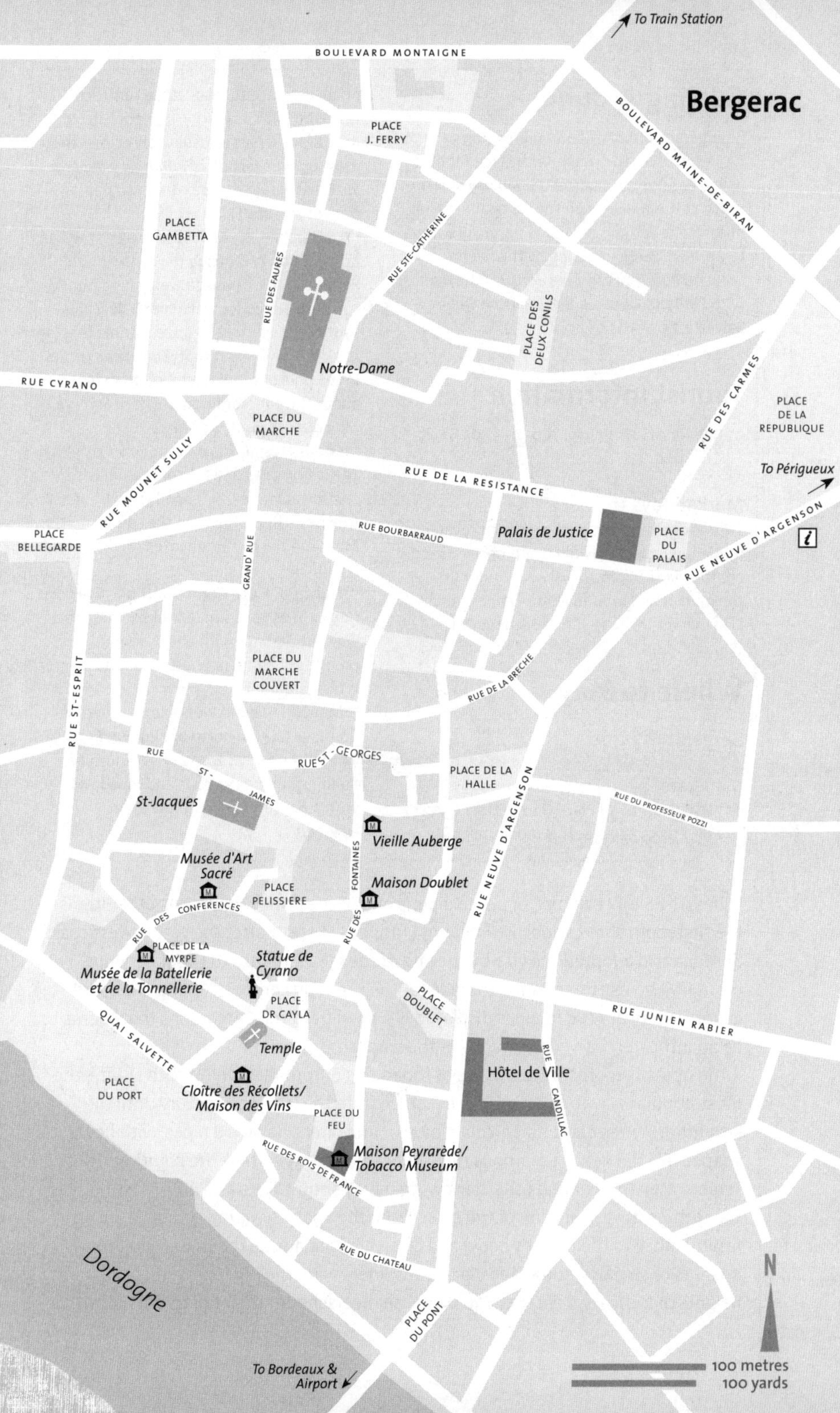
Bergerac
To Train Station
BOULEVARD MONTAIGNE
BOULEVARD MAINE-DE-BIRAN
PLACE J. FERRY
PLACE GAMBETTA
RUE DES FAURES
RUE STE-CATHERINE
PLACE DES DEUX CONILS
Notre-Dame
RUE CYRANO
PLACE DU MARCHE
RUE DES CARMES
PLACE DE LA REPUBLIQUE
RUE MOUNET SULLY
RUE DE LA RESISTANCE
To Périgueux
PLACE BELLEGARDE
RUE BOURBARRAUD
Palais de Justice
PLACE DU PALAIS
RUE NEUVE D'ARGENSON
GRAND' RUE
PLACE DU MARCHE COUVERT
RUE DE LA BRECHE
RUE ST-ESPRIT
RUE ST-GEORGES
RUE ST-JAMES
PLACE DE LA HALLE
St-Jacques
RUE DU PROFESSEUR POZZI
Vieille Auberge
Musée d'Art Sacré
PLACE PELISSIERE
RUE DES FONTAINES
Maison Doublet
RUE DES CONFERENCES
PLACE DE LA MYRPE
Musée de la Batellerie et de la Tonnellerie
Statue de Cyrano
PLACE DR CAYLA
PLACE DOUBLET
QUAI SALVETTE
Temple
RUE JUNIEN RABIER
Hôtel de Ville
RUE CANDILLAC
PLACE DU PORT
Cloître des Récollets/ Maison des Vins
PLACE DU FEU
Maison Peyrarède/ Tobacco Museum
RUE DES ROIS DE FRANCE
RUE DU CHATEAU
Dordogne
PLACE DU PONT
N
To Bordeaux & Airport
100 metres
100 yards

Getting Around

Bergerac's **airport**, Roumanières, **t** 05 53 57 76 03, lies 10km to the south, with three flights a day to Paris on Air Liberté. The **railway** station, north of the centre, is on the Bordeaux–Sarlat line; for the Périgueux–Agen line, go by way of Le Buisson. There's **parking** by the river at Place du Port. You can take a trip on the **river** with Périgord Gabares, leaving from Quai Salvette, **t** 05 53 24 58 80.

Tourist Information

97 Rue Neuve d'Argenson, **t** 05 53 57 03 1, **f** 05 53 61 11 04.

Market Days

Although the stalls in the modern covered market are open daily, Sat mornings and Wed are the big shopping days, with stalls outside the market and around Notre-Dame church. Flea market the first Sun of each month.

Where to Stay

Bergerac ✉ 24100

Moderate

***__Le Bordeaux__, 38 Place Gambetta, **t** 05 53 57 12 83, **f** 05 53 57 72 14. This modern hotel offers a chance to relax in the centre of Bergerac, with its garden and pool; its restaurant serves unusual delicacies—the most upriver version of *lamproie à la bordelaise and aiguillettes de canard au miel* (*menus 110–260F*).

***__La Flambée__, 153 Av Pasteur, **t** 05 53 57 52 33, **f** 05 53 61 07 57. Outside the centre on the Périgueux road, this is a welcoming family-run hotel noted for its kitchen's delicious southwest specialities (*excellent menus from 100–300F*); work off that *feuilleté de truffes* in the pool or tennis court, or rambling about the panoramic park. *Closed Sun eve, Mon out of season, and Jan.*

***__Commerce__, 36 Place Gambetta, **t** 05 53 27 30 50, **f** 05 53 58 23 82. A Logis hotel with comfortable, well-equipped rooms, but ask for one facing away from the square. Menus in the restaurant are fairly standard (*75–118F*).

***__France__, 18 Place Gambetta, **t** 05 53 57 11 61, **f** 05 53 61 25 70. A similar hotel just up the way but perhaps with better sound-proofing; it can also boast a pool, but there is no restaurant.

***__Manoir Le Grand Vignoble__, St-Julien-de-Crempse (12.5km north of Bergerac), **t** 05 53 24 23 18, **f** 05 53 24 20 89. A 17th-century building set amid woods and meadows, with a pool and tennis. *Closed mid-Nov–Feb.*

tribes (the Sioux *calumet*, or peace pipe, is one of the prize exhibits). As other items in the first room show, widespread use in Europe came only after the whole west coast of Africa had adopted the vice by the end of the 1500s, thanks to the slave ships that brought it across the Atlantic to trade for their human cargoes. Among the astonishing variety of African pipes displayed is a bowl from the Cameroons that seems to be an intricately carved biography of the smoker.

The upstairs rooms trace the use of tobacco in Europe, beginning with snuff – the most popular way to take tobacco in France from the late 16th century until the Revolution, when clay and porcelain pipes – and later briarwood pipes, with bowls shaped like the heads of famous men – became the rage. There are paintings by Teniers, Meissonnier and others, showing happy snuff-takers and puffers, but it was the 19th-century invention of the cigar (from the Spanish *cigarra* or cicada, for its resemblance to the insect's body) and cigarette that awoke the masses to the delights of smoking. Cigar and cigarette holders were the rage, some reaching rare heights of intricacy, as in the 1850 Viennese meerschaum cigar holder carved with a

Inexpensive

****Le Family**, 3 Rue du Dragon, near Place du Marché Couvert, **t** 05 53 57 80 90. Central, simple and friendly. Parking is available in a nearby garage.

Eating Out

Expensive

La Tour des Vents, **t** 05 53 58 30 10. Once the Moulin de Malfourat, as well as offering splendid views it serves up well-prepared southwest favourites (*menus 98–258F*). *Closed mid-Jan–mid-Feb, Sun eve and Mon out of season.*

Moderate

L'Imparfait, 8 Rue des Fontaines, **t** 05 53 57 47 92. In the historic centre. Shares top billing with the aforementioned hotels with its fresh sunny cuisine (*menus 118–198F*). *Closed Sun and a month in winter.*

Le Sud, 19 Rue de l'Ancien Port, **t** 05 53 27 26 81. Near the Tobacco Museum. Tasty Moroccan *tajines* and couscous. A full meal runs *100–120F. Closed Sun, Mon, and early June.*

Côté Dordogne, 17 Rue du Chateau, **t** 05 53 57 17 57. Probably the restaurant of the moment in Bergerac. You can eat inside this 17th-century house or on a terrace covered in wisteria. The food is superb and reasonably priced; house specialities include *morue fraîche à l'ail et olives and pigeonneau au foie poêlé* (*menus 100–160F*). *Closed two weeks in Nov, two in Feb, Sun eve and Mon.*

Le Poivre et Sel, 11 Rue de l'Ancien Port, **t** 05 53 27 02 30. Old, timbered and elegant, in a narrow street, surrounded by plants. Eat out on a pretty patio under huge parasols. Culinary delights include *gambas flambés au pastis* and a good choice of large salads (*menus 78–195F*). *Closed for three weeks of the winter.*

Château de Monbazillac, **t** 05 53 58 38 93. The restaurant in the former *chai* is a favourite of local wine barons for its fine classic cuisine, with a long and interesting wine list and summer dining from the terrace (*menus from 145F*). *Closed Mon out of season.*

Ferme-auberge Le Monteil, at Lamonzie-St-Martin, 8km on the road to Bordeaux, **t** 05 53 24 07 59. Well-prepared farm dishes beginning with *tourain à l'ail* and ending up with a home-made dessert (*menus 90–180F*). *Closed Sept. Book ahead.*

Sicilian wedding. One of the last exhibits is a curious machine capable of carving a dozen pipe bowls at once.

The rest of the museum covers the history of Bergerac. Not much has survived all the troubles – some 14th-century ceramics, pharmaceutical jars and other titbits.

Cloître des Récollets

Behind the tobacco museum in Place du Dr-Cayla is Bergerac's 19th-century Protestant Temple, where only occasional services are held for the last die-hard Calvinists. Just behind, on Quai Salvette, the picturesque 16th-century **Cloître des Récollets** has a wooden gallery and lone tree. The Récollets were a Franciscan order founded in Spain in the late 1400s, named, according to the *Catholic Dictionary*, 'from the detachment from creatures and a recollection in God which the founders aimed at'. The order was widespread in southwest France, and Louis XIII charged the Récollets with the task of bringing the burghers of Bergerac back to the Catholic fold; after the Revocation of the Edict of Nantes their methods of persuasion included book-burnings. Today their cloister serves more congenially as the **Maison des Vins** (*t 05 53 63 57 55; open Easter–mid-Oct 10.30–12.30 and 2–6, closed Sun; July and Aug open daily 10–7*), headquarters of the regional wine council: the Cellier de Récollets offers a wide selection of Bergerac vintages and other regional products.

Other City Sights

From Place du Dr-Cayla it's a few steps up to charming, tree-filled Place de La Myrpe and the town's biggest photo opportunity, its statue of swashbuckling **Cyrano de Bergerac**. Cyrano owes his appearance here to Edmond Rostand's tremendously successful 1897 play *Cyrano de Bergerac*. Rostand based much of his character on the real Savien Cyrano (1619–55), born in Paris of Italian parents. A swashbuckling extrovert and poet (the records say nothing of his olfactory appendage), he was appointed as a musketeer in a company of Gascons; better to fit in with that boastful lot, he added Bergerac to his name. He was a celebrated duellist, and published tragedies, comedies, letters and a humorous essay called 'Le Voyage dans la Lune'. Until the early 20th century, all of the real Cyrano's biographers took the Bergerac in his name as fact; but if he is not literally a native son, he will always be one in a literary sense, and anyway Bergerac is grateful for the free advertising.

At the end of Place de La Myrpe in Rue des Conférences the **Musée de la Batellerie et de la Tonnellerie** (*t 05 53 57 80 92; open 10–12 and 2–5.30, closed Sun morning, all Sun*

Monbazillac, and the Other Wines of Bergerac

Although overshadowed by the élite vineyards of nearby Bordeaux, Bergerac has produced wines since the 12th century and exported them to England since 1250. Although quality controls in the 1300s had already strictly defined the planting area, or vinata, and set the date of the harvest, Bordeaux used its position downriver to block Bergerac's vintages and give priority to its own wines until 1511, when the Parlement of Guyenne granted Bergerac a charter guaranteeing access to the Atlantic. By that time, however, Bergerac with its Protestant connections had built up an alternative overland trade with Holland and Scandinavia. And in the 18th century, when the Dutch developed a taste for sweet, heavy wines, or *vins liquoreux*, the best vineyards on the chalky clay hills of **Monbazillac** were converted to the production of a strong white dessert wine using mostly Sémillon grapes, with small quantities of Muscadelle and Sauvignon. Unusually, the vines are planted on the steep, north-facing slopes to take advantage of a microclimate similar to that of the Sauternes and Barsac areas, where autumnal morning mists help to incubate *Botrytis cinerea*, the 'noble rot' that withers the grapes but adds an extra, distinctive sweetness and fragrance that tastes so good when served icy cold with foie gras, melon (with a dash of Angostura bitters) and desserts.

In the 19th century, the reputation of Monbazillac slowly sank, becoming 'the poor man's Sauternes' and then simply cheap plonk. In the 1960s, with the change of fashion to drier wines, Monbazillac's growers uprooted much of the old stock and

out of season, and Mon; adm) holds an interesting collection of models and tools used by vintners, coopers and boatmen in the days of yore, installed in a half-timbered boatsmen's tavern from the 1700s. Just up Rue des Conférences, the little Musée d'Art Sacré occupies a 17th-century **Catholic mission** (*t 05 53 57 33 21; open July and Aug Tues–Sun 3.30–6; rest of year Sun only 3.30–6*). It displays typical Counter-Reformation church paraphernalia and the strange Gallo-Roman *Buste Acéphale de Lauzerte*, a white half-bust of a female – reminiscent in its stylization of ancient Cycladic sculpture – holding its severed head to its abdomen, just like St Denis, the patron saint of Paris. Way before the French Revolution, the Gauls were always ones for chopping off heads, tying them to the tails of their horses or impaling them on stakes in their temples, where they were perhaps used as intermediaries with ancestors in the underworld. Female figures, however, are rare.

Rue des Conférences continues to Rue des Fontaines, with two important buildings: **Maison Doublet**, where the future Henri IV and the agents of Henri III negotiated a truce between Protestant and Catholic forces in 1577, and the 14th-century **Vieille Auberge**, at 27 Rue des Fontaines. Rue de St-James leads from here to long Place Pélissière and the church of St-Jacques, which began in the 12th century as a pilgrim hostel, but was completely rebuilt in the 17th century after the Catholic victory. At the same time the chief Protestant temple, a block up on the Grand Rue, was demolished, to be replaced in 1885 with a metal market pavilion. Further up the Grand Rue stands

replanted new vines, especially Sauvignon, to produce dry white wines and drier, lighter *vins liquoreux*. The result is a lovely golden colour that deepens with age, and a scent of wild flowers mellowing into a distinct 'roasted' flavour when aged. Monbazillac averages 13°, but goes up to 15° in good years—1988, 1989 and 1990 were all superb and may be safely kept, they say, for 30 years. Besides the pavillon by the Château, the Caves de Monbazillac, on the road to Bergerac, t 05 53 63 65 00, has a vast selection (*open daily 10–12.30 and 1.20–7, July and Aug 8.30–7, closed hols*).

Some Monbazillac growers also produce a selection of Bergerac's other AOC vintages, in red, rosé or white. The reds are bright and robust when drunk young, while the whites are the perfect summer drink and an accompaniment to seafood or *hors d'œuvres*. Château Le Bondieu, in St-Antoine-de-Breuilh, t 05 53 58 30 83, produced some of the finest reds in recent years: the '95 is a good buy, and the Haut-Montravel Moelleux Cuvée Gabriel has a strong, very attractive character. To the west, in the minute AOC region of Saussignac that separates Monbazillac from the vineyards of the Bordelais, Château Court-les-Muts in Razac-de-Saussignac, t 05 53 27 92 17, produces a singular, exceptional *moelleux* wine, but only in the best years (the 1994 Saussignac Moelleux with its apricot undertones is excellent). The estate also bottles a good dry red and elegant white AOC Bergerac; one of the best reds is the '88. Château Tour-des Gendres, in Ribagnac, t 05 53 57 12 43, is another reliable vineyard, with an excellent '95 white and a '94 red. Also visit the aforementioned Cloître des Récollets in the middle of Bergerac.

the lofty neo-Gothic bell tower of Notre Dame, a creation of those two busy 19th-century re-creators of the old, Viollet-le-Duc and Paul Abadie. It boasts two 16th-century Italian paintings, donated from the collections of the Duc d'Orléans: *Adoration of the Magi* by Pordenone and *Adoration of the Shepherds* by Godenzio Ferrari, a pupil of Leonardo da Vinci.

Around Bergerac

Just outside the city, on the D660 towards Lalinde, are the laboratories and botanical gardens of the Institut du Tabac at the **Domaine de la Tour**. The institute was created in 1927 to improve the product of the region's nearly 300 growers, who have moved away from brown tobacco to the lighter, low-tar blond. Over a thousand varieties of *Nicotiana* (named after the 16th-century French diplomat Jean Nicot, who introduced tobacco to France) are grown here, and cigarettes aren't their only use – if you're really curious, ask the Bergerac tourist office about arranging a visit.

Six kilometres south of Bergerac on the D13, set high on a ridge, the four-square **Château de Monbazillac** (***t*** *05 53 61 52 52, www.chateau-monbazillac.com; open daily July–Aug 10–7.30, June and Sept 10–7, May and Oct 10–12.30 and 2–6, Nov–Mar 10–12 and 2–5, until 6 in April; closed Jan and Mon in Nov–Mar; adm*) was erected by Charles d'Aydie, Seigneur of Bergerac, in 1550 and – miraculously – essentially remains the same as the day it was built, undamaged and unimproved: a nice compromise between the necessities of defence, with its dry moat, machicolations, towers and parapet walk, and beauty, in its array of rooflines covered in flat brown tiles, dormers and mullioned windows, and graceful fleur-de-lys weather vanes that even managed to escape the Revolution. The owners were Protestants after 1607, made *vicomtes* by Henri IV, and they used the castle as a venue for theological discussions and as a refuge for persecuted pastors, until the *vicomtesse* neatly recanted the day she heard of the Revocation of the Edict of Nantes.

Pécharmant

A great comeback after decades of decline, this pocket wine region is located on the northeastern outskirts of Bergerac, on a south-facing amphitheatre (literally the 'charming hill') of granite sand and rubble topped with clay. Pécharmant is limited to four *communes*, producing a sumptuous, fragrant, tannin-rich red wine that is one of the finest of Bergerac's 12 AOC wines. Made from Cabernet-Sauvignon, Cabernet-Franc and Merlot, with a touch of Malbec for smoothness, it needs at least four years in the cellar before drinking. On the road to Ste-Alvère, Colette Bourgès at Clos Les Côtes, t 05 53 57 59 89, won a gold medal for her Pécharmant in 1992; compare it with the prestige, raspberry-scented wines aged in oaken casks at the superb 17th-century Château de Tiregand in Creysse, t 05 53 23 21 08. The estate also bottles a fine white AOC Bergerac; as an added bonus you can tour the beautiful park (*ring ahead; open Mon–Sat 8–12 and 2–6, closed hols*).

The grounds and two lower floors of the castle are open to the public. There are rooms filled with old Périgourdin cupboards and dressers, antique maps of the area, Flemish tapestries, rare Huguenot books that escaped the book-burnings, prints by engraver Jacques Callot who presaged Goya's series on the horrors of war, collections relating to local celebrities, and the flamboyant dining room made for the flamboyant Comédie Française actor Mounet-Sully. The tour ends with a free glass of Monbazillac's famous wine in the new *pavillon* just outside the château gate; the château is the headquarters for the cooperative of one of Bergerac's most famous vintages. The vicinity of the château is planted with vines (in autumn you can examine the famous noble rot first-hand). Other sections are part of a wine study area, with ancient vines that once grew in the Dordogne, and others from around the world that grow on the 45th parallel.

The **Moulin de Malfourat**, just west of Monbazillac on the D14E, has a famous bird's-eye view over Bergerac's hills and helpful orientation table. It has recently been turned into a good restaurant (*see* above). South of Monbazillac, right between the N21 and D933 (the two major roads from Bergerac into the Lot-et-Garonne), there's a beautiful Romanesque **church** at **Sadillac**, with a dome and excellent animal carvings. There's another, a sturdy, primitive one from the 10th century – one of the oldest in the region – in tiny **Monbos** (west of the D933 just beyond Sigoulès), decorated with a fascinating relief of a hunt.

West of Bergerac to St-Emilion

From Bergerac, the main and often very busy D936 drives west towards Bordeaux, more or less following the route of the Dordogne. If this is your first trip, leave yourself a good day to dawdle on the way – especially in the haunting medieval lanes of St-Emilion.

Ste-Foy-la-Grande and Castillon-la-Bataille

Heading west from Bergerac, **Gardonne**, with a bridge, is mainly of interest as an intersection, with the chance to turn off and take the pretty D4 south towards Duras. Beyond, the road exits the Dordogne *département* for the Gironde at **Ste-Foy-la-Grande**, a bustling market town that was founded as a *bastide* by Alphonse de Poitiers in 1255. Like Bergerac it was a Huguenot stronghold, and to this day it retains a sizeable Protestant population. Although none of the architecture is particularly out of the ordinary, there are some fine half-timbered houses from the 15th–17th centuries, a 13th-century Gothic church, and the arcaded Place Gambetta. In Rue Notre Dame in the port, the **Maison du Fleuve** (***t** 05 53 61 30 50; open July and Aug daily 2–6, May, June, Sept and Oct Tues–Sat 2–6; adm*) has a museum devoted to river traffic and to Ste-Foy's wine, AOC *vin de Montravel*, grown here and in the next town, **Lamothe-Montravel**. You can take a river boat to the museum from the Quai de la Brèche during the summer. A second museum, the **Musée Charles Nardin** (*102 Rue de la République, **t** 05 57 46 03 00; open mid-June–mid-Sept 10–12.30 and 3–7, rest of year*

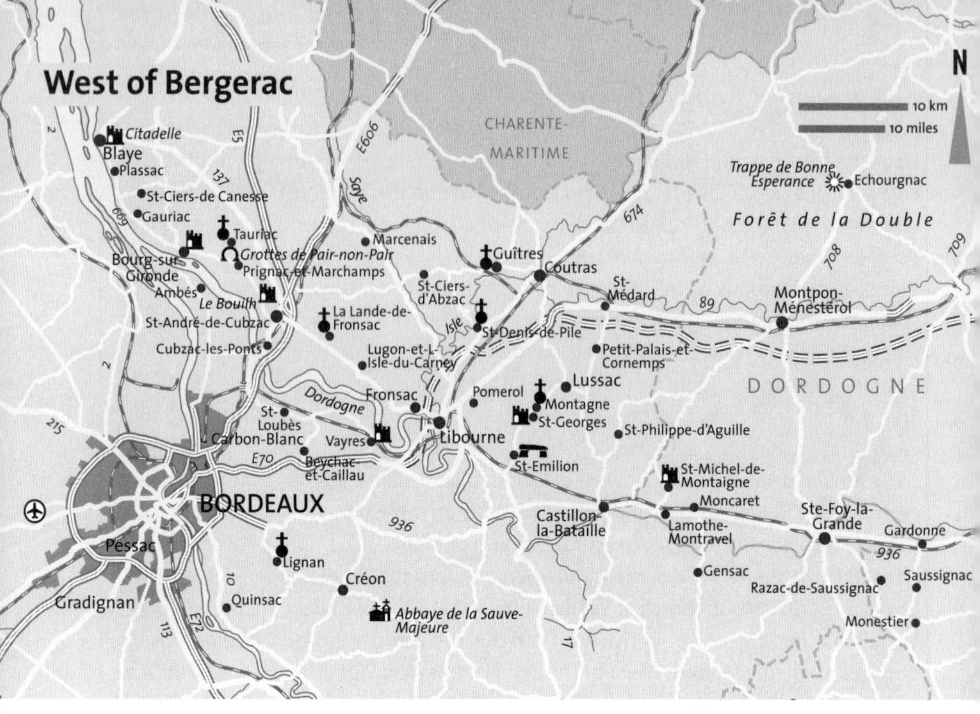

Mon 2–5, Tues–Sat 9.30–12.30 and 2.30–6), is devoted to the area's prehistory up to Gallo-Roman times; there are explanatory cassettes in English so you can tell what's what.

Another small AOC wine area encompasses **Castillon-la-Bataille**; just east of the village, along the D936, is a signpost for the **Monument à Talbot**. This marks the spot where the concluding battle of the Hundred Years' War was fought on 17 July 1453. The English commander, John Talbot, Earl of Shrewsbury, was at Mass when a spy told him that the French, camped near the Dordogne, were retreating. Talbot at once hopped on a horse to see for himself, only to learn that, if the French were retreating, it was only to attack – *reculer pour mieux sauter*. Because he was so conspicuous in his Sunday finest, Talbot was one of the first of 4,000 to die; the monument in the field marks the spot where he was axed down. The battle is relived with sound and light (*late July–mid-Aug weekends*). In town, the **Maison du Vin** eagerly waits to introduce you to the pleasure of *Côtes de Castillon* (6 Allées de la République, ***t*** *05 57 40 00 88; open Mon–Fri*).

There are fine views from points north of Castillon: north, from **St-Philippe-d'Aiguille** and its water tower (*château d'eau*), with an orientation table, although the main reason for heading this way is to continue up to **Petit-Palais-et-Cornemps** to see its lovely and magnificent 13th-century Romanesque church, **St-Pierre**. Though simple in form, the façade is covered with sculptures of animals and birds. On either side of the main door are figures inspired by antique models, especially the relief of the man pulling an arrow or spine from his foot.

Tourist Information

Ste-Foy-la-Grande: 102 Rue de la République, **t** 05 57 46 03 00, **f** 05 57 46 16 62.

Castillon-la-Bataille: Rue Marcel Paul, **t** 05 57 40 27 58, **f** 05 57 40 49 76.

Market Days

Ste-Foy-la-Grande: Sat, this is nothing less than '*One of the Hundred Most Beautiful Markets in France*'.

Castillon-la-Bataille: Mon.

Where to Stay and Eat

Monestier ✉ 24240

********Château des Vigiers**, 5km south of Saussignac, **t** 05 53 61 50 00, **f** 05 53 61 50 20 (*expensive*). This huge 16th-century châteauoffers bucolic Renaissance splendour set among 60 acres of lake and forest, with a large vineyard and 18-hole golf course, pool and tennis; delicious, ot so old-fashioned food in the frescoed dining room (*menus from 425F in the dining room, 180F in the brasserie*). *Dining room closed Tues and Sun, hotel closed most of Dec–Feb.*

Gensac ✉ 33890

****Les Remparts**, 16 Rue du Château, **t** 05 57 47 43 46, **f** 05 57 47 46 76 (*inexpensive*). The site offers lovely views across the valley, the perfect accompaniment to the delights on your plate: try the *médaillon de veau à la crème de thym* (*menus from 145F*). *Closed Sun eve, Mon exc July and Aug, two weeks in Nov and two weeks in Feb.*

Le Belvédère, near La Tourbeille on the D130, **t** 05 57 47 40 33. More lovely views and generous, good-value menus (*from 99F*). *Closed Tues eve, Wed, and Oct.*

Castillon-la-Bataille ✉ 33350

****La Bonne Auberge**, Rue du 8 Mai 1945, **t** 05 57 40 11 56, **f** 05 57 40 21 66 (*inexpensive*). Simple rooms with TV and telephone in each.

Chez Mr et Mme Mintet-Esacalier, at Robin, Route de Belvès, **t** 05 57 40 20 55 (*inexpensive*). Book a room among the vines.

St-Michel-de-Montaigne ✉ 24230

*****Le Jardin d'Eyquem**, in the village centre, **t** 05 53 24 89 59, **f** 05 53 61 14 40 (*moderate*). Five very nice flats in a restored building with a pool in the middle of a vineyard. *Closed Dec–Mar.*

Moncaret and St-Michel-de-Montaigne

In 1887, in **Moncaret** just north of the D936, workmen digging the foundations for a bathhouse next to the church struck their shovels on the rock-hard mosaic floors of the luxurious baths of a 2nd–4th-century AD **Gallo-Roman villa**. The villa was known to the builders of the church, who incorporated a funerary stele into the apse (along with a primitive Carolingian relief of Adam and Eve) and reused some Roman capitals for its columns; other items (vases, tombs, etc.) discovered in the area are now in the museum flanking the excavations. An explanatory sheet gives the fascinating details (***t** 05 53 58 50 18; open daily July and Aug 9–1 and 2–7, April–June and Sept 9–12 and 2–6, Oct–May 10–12 and 2–4; closed hols; adm*). North of Moncaret, swathed in vineyards, the hamlet of **St-Michel-de-Montaigne** stands on the outskirts of the **Château de Montaigne**, purchased by the philosopher's great-grandfather, merchant Raymond Eyquem, in 1477. In 1533, it saw the birth of Michel Eyquem de Montaigne, who was baptized in the village church. In 1885, the château went up in flames, but by good fortune the fire spared Montaigne's home within a home, the round tower where he

Michel de Montaigne

Few men at any time have had the advantage of the wise and gentle upbringing of Michel de Montaigne, the eldest of eight children raised 'without whip or tears' by a Catholic father and Jewish mother. They brought in a tutor to teach him Latin as his first language, and he learned Greek as a child's game. As a young man, he followed the legal and public career destined for him as a court counsellor in Périgueux and Bordeaux; in the latter he met his dear friend La Boétie of Sarlat (*see* p.169). He married in 1565, his wife providing him with such a large dowry that in 1572, when he despaired over the hypocrisy of the law and the horror of the St Bartholomew's Day Massacre, Montaigne could afford to retreat from the world to his château above the Dordogne. He was 39 at the time, and vowed to spend his life doing nothing at all; instead, he wrote three volumes of *Essays*.

The freest French thinker of the 16th century, Montaigne was also the most sceptical, the product of sober, heartfelt sorrow at the dogmas, cruelty and fanaticism of his day. In his writings he reasoned that if human beliefs throughout history have fluctuated so violently, if one age's reason and common sense would inevitably seem ridiculous to the next, then the only sane response to the world was not to believe in its external things and to accept constant mutability and chaos with a smile. '*Que sais-je*?' ('What do I know?') was his motto, and he had it inscribed over the château door. In such a world one could only be true to oneself and live as tranquilly as possible. 'To live properly is our great and glorious masterpiece,' he wrote. In 1580 he went to Italy, where he learned to his surprise and dismay that he had been elected Mayor of Bordeaux in his absence. He reluctantly returned, and was re-elected for another term, an unusual honour, in recognition of his moderation and justice, and his efforts to bring about a reconciliation between Catholics and Protestants.

wrote (and rewrote, and rewrote) his famous *Essays* (***t** 05 53 58 63 93; guided tours Wed–Sun, July and Aug 10–6.30, June, Sept, Oct 10–12 and 2–6.30, otherwise 10–12 and 2–5.30; closed Jan and start of Feb; adm*). There's a minute chapel on the ground floor, its altar painted with a scene of St Michael stabbing the dragon, of which the tolerant Montaigne said: 'I like to light a candle to St Michael, and to his serpent, too.' Stairs wind up to the bedroom on the next floor, equipped with a handy toilet, while upstairs the philosopher installed his famous inner sanctum, a library, where he could sit at his desk surrounded by bookshelves and windows, with a stone armchair niche in the wall for quiet readings. The books are all gone now, but the beams still bear the Greek and Latin maxims Montaigne inscribed on them to ponder; you can see a few he scratched out when he tired of them. He died here after a long illness in 1592, and his heart is buried in the village church.

St-Emilion

Set in a natural amphitheatre surrounded by its famous vines, St-Emilion is a gem, a lovely town mellowed to the colour of old piano keys. A favourite of medieval popes and English kings, it has been restored to much of its old elegance, but leave your high heels at home: lanes called *tetres*, unevenly paved with granite blocks from Cornwall (the ballast of England's wine ships), are so steep that handrails have been installed down their centres. For all that, the town keeps its greatest secrets underground – not only the ruby nectar in its cellars, but Europe's largest subterreanean church, where chthonic fertility cults are covered with a thin veneer of medieval Christianity. Come out of season if possible, or at least late in the day to avoid the crowds of day-trippers, or stay overnight, and see the sights first thing in the morning. In 1999 St-Emilion was classed a world heritage site, the first vine-growing area to achieve this status. It will probably mean more visitors than ever.

History

Known simply as *Ascumbas*, or 'hill', in Gallo-Roman times, the town's destiny was set in motion in the 8th century with the arrival of a Benedictine hermit from Brittany named Emilion. His piety attracted a number of companions, and they enlarged the natural shelters and caves on the site. The largest one was used as a church, slowly excavated until the 11th century to become the Eglise Monolithe. When the founder died, the monastery took his name: *Sent-Melyon* in *langue d'oc*.

As Libourne was not yet founded, the walled town that grew up around the monastery controlled this section of the Dordogne. It received its first charter in 1199 from John Lackland, who also set up a new civil authority of a hundred peers from the bourgeoisie known as the *Jurade*. Up until the time of the Revolution, the *Jurade* was responsible for everything from tax-collecting and the local militia to maintaining the quality of the wine – wine that was imported by the *tonne* to the English court, for, unlike Bergerac just upriver, St-Emilion enjoyed the same export privileges as Bordeaux. English interest was so keen that in 1289 Edward I set the limits of the production area – the same limits used to this day.

St-Emilion, On Your Own

Four of the town's principal sights can only be seen on the tourist office's guided tour (*see* below), but don't fail to take a wander on your own. If you're staying the night, save the tour of the well-preserved town walls for dusk, when the views are at their most romantic.

Entering St-Emilion from the south on the D122, you'll pass a public park built around the **Maison Gaudet**, home of the Girondin deputy Marguerite Elie Gaudet, who managed to flee Robespierre's executions in Paris with seven other Girondins. They hid out for nine months in St-Emilion, in a dark damp tunnel under the garden of Gaudet's sister-in-law, Marie-Thérèse Bouquey. All but one were eventually captured by Robespierre's henchmen and guillotined – ironically, only a few days before 9

Getting Around

There are two **railway** stations nearby: St-Emilion's, 2km away in the middle of the countryside, on the Bordeaux–Bergerac–Sarlat line, and Libourne, 7km away, on the Bordeaux–Paris TGV line. There are several Citram **buses** daily for Bordeaux and Libourne, **t** 05 56 43 68 43. For a **taxi**, **t** 06 09 33 11 58. The country lanes around St-Emilion make for a fun spin on a **bike**; hire one at the tourist office for 90F a day.

Tourist Information

Place des Créneaux, **t** 05 57 55 28 28, **f** 05 57 55 28 29, *www.saint-emilion-tourism.com*. The place to book and start the 45min guided tour of St-Emilion's subterranean monuments (*generally open daily 9.30–12.30 and 1.45–6, July and Aug 9.30–8*). Other tours are available, some in English. They are very helpful.

Market Days

St-Emilion: Sun mornings at Place Bouqueyre.
Lussac: Thurs.

Where to Stay

St-Emilion ✉ 33330

****Château Grand-Barrail**, Route de Libourne, **t** 05 57 55 37 00, **f** 05 57 55 37 49 (*luxury–expensive*). If money's really no object, this is the place: very exclusive prices with attitudes to match; there's a good restaurant (*180F lunch menu, more at other times*). *Closed Feb.*

****Hostellerie de Plaisance**, Place du Clocher, **t** 05 57 55 07 55, **f** 05 57 74 41 11 (*expensive*). This handsome stone building is the most luxurious hotel in town, and the only one with facilities for the disabled; it has an elegant gourmet restaurant and terrace featuring the likes of *langoustines royales* and *mignons de bœuf aux girolles* (*good-value menus from 150F*). *Closed Jan.*

***Palais Cardinal**, Place du 11 Novembre 1918, **t** 05 57 24 72 39, **f** 05 57 74 47 54 (*moderate*). Since 1876, the same family has run this stately classic. It has small but handsome bedrooms, and the advantages of a heated pool; ask for a room overlooking the lovely garden terrace. *Closed Dec–Feb.*

***Le Logis des Remparts**, 18 Rue Guadet, **t** 05 57 24 70 43, **f** 05 57 74 47 44 (*moderate*). Sweet and pretty with a little inner courtyard, rooms complete with bath and TV, and very hospitable staff.

Auberge de la Commanderie, Rue des Cordeliers, **t** 05 57 24 70 19, **f** 05 57 74 44 53 (*inexpensive*). Eighteen rooms, the best overlooking the garden and heated pool.

Logis de la Cadène, 3 Place du Marché au Bois, **t** 05 57 24 71 40, **f** 05 57 74 42 23 (*inexpensive*). Cheapest of all, a handful of rooms, with or without bath.

La Barbanne, 3km north from St Emilion on the Montagne road, **t/f** 05 57 24 75 80.

Thermidor, when Robespierre himself got the chop. Across the road, rising abruptly out of a vineyard, the **Grandes Murailles**, a single 65ft wall with ogival arches, is all that remains of a Dominican monastery built in 1287; as it was outside the town walls, it was destroyed by a marauding French army in 1337.

Just beyond is the main entrance to St-Emilion, the **Porte Bourgeoise**. Take the first left to see the more substantial remains of the once-sumptuous **Palais Cardinal**, built in 1316 by the Cardinal de Ste-Luce, nephew of Pope Clement V – the same who relocated the papacy to Avignon. Continue up Rue Gaudet, where just beyond Place du Chapitre the Dominicans rebuilt their monastery, the **Couvent des Jacobins**, after a donation in 1378 by the English Lieutenant of Aquitaine, Jean de Neville – a donation that had to be reconfirmed several times in the face of opposition by the *Jurade*, who didn't think St-Emilion *intra muros* had room for any more monks. Nevertheless, until

An excellent camp site with a pool and tennis courts.

Lussac

Château de Roques, on the D21 on the road to St-Médard, **t** 05 57 74 55 69, **f** 05 57 74 58 80 (*moderate–inexpensive*). Sleep amid the vineyards at this bed-and-breakfast offering good, copious country cooking (*around 110F*), bikes to rent and free wine-tasting in the great cellars, cut in the living rock. *Closed Jan.*

Château Millaud Montlabert, D243 then D245 towards Pomerol, **t** 05 57 34 71 85, **f** 05 57 24 62 78 (*inexpensive*). There are more rooms amongst the vines in this 18th-century house, pleasantly renovated to create five bedrooms. Independent entrance. Washing machine and small kitchen available for use.

Eating Out

St-Emilion

Local gourmets will tell you that St Emilion's wines go with everything except strong cheeses, and especially well with that Bordelaise favourite, **lamprey**.

In town you'll see many signs for *Macaroons de St-Emilion*, a traditional sweet dating back to the town's long-gone Ursuline nuns; traditional ones are made at **Moulierac**, Tertre de la Tente, **Blanchez**, Rue Gaudet, and **Ertle**, Rue de la Grande Fontaine.

Expensive–Moderate

Francis Goullée, 27 Rue Guadet, **t** 05 57 24 70 49. For food equal to the surroundings: taste-packed Rabelaisian cuisine (*menus 90–240F*). *Closed Sun eve, Mon and late Nov–mid-Dec.*

Le Tertre, Tertre de la Tente, **t** 05 57 74 46 33. After briefly becoming a pizzeria Le Tertre has reverted to its former mission. Dine old-fashionedly well on a broad range of good regional dishes (*menus 115–260F*). *Closed Tues in summer, Mon and Tues out of season.*

Le Clos du Roy, 12 Rue de la Petite Fontaine, **t** 05 57 74 41 55. For dishes that harmonize well with the lifeblood of St-Emilion; try the breast of duck with Granny Smith apples (*menus 150–245F*). *Closed Tues, Wed and several weeks in Nov and Feb.*

Cheap

Amelia Canta, Place de l'Eglise Monolithe, **t** 05 57 74 48 03. A reliable brasserie, with a strategically located terrace (*menus from 75F*). *Closed mid-Nov–start of Feb.*

L'Envers du Décor, Rue du Clocher, **t** 05 57 74 48 31. An excellent-value wine bar with a terrace, where you can try a wide variety of local labels by the glass, with a snack or light meal (*around 100F*). *Closed weekends out of season.*

La Ferme Auberge du Cros Figeac, in a lovely vineyard setting on the road to Libourne, **t** 05 57 24 76 32. Exquisite meats grilled over vines, and a memorable warm foie gras with apple (*menus from 80F, book*).

the Revolution, this church held the town's main pilgrimage attraction: a statue of St Valéry, patron of St-Emilion's vintners (now relocated in the Collégiale). New brides would gently wipe the statue with their handkerchiefs while wishing to become pregnant; Valéry's exact role in the matter was the cause of many pleasantries. Continue straight up Rue Gaudet, passing the 14th-century **Maison Gothique** on the left. The streets fork here: take Rue des Cordeliers for the **Commanderie**, an old Templar post, and the ruined, partially overgrown Romanesque **Cloître des Cordeliers** (*open 10–12 and 2–6.30*), built in 1383 by the Franciscans who had to get a bull from Pope Gregory XI for permission to build in the town walls. In the adjacent chapel, note the carving of two snakes entering a jar, a symbol that goes back to the ancient Greeks. Snakes were commonly used to portray the *daimones*, or genius and identity of a family or tribe; twins were a symbol of fertility; the snake jar may have been like a

St-Emilion and St-Emilion Grand Cru

One of the most annoying problems facing the first Roman colonists of Aquitaine was the fact that they had to import their wine from the Mediterranean. Every year, ever hopeful, they tried new varieties of grapes, but none could cope with the climate and soil—until some time around AD 20, when the Biturige druids of Burdigala (Bordeaux) came across vines called *basilica* with wide-grained wood and fairly loose fruit that the Greeks in Marseille had imported from Epirus (modern Albania). The druids planted them around what is now St-Emilion, where they took so well that the Bituriges, never known for their modesty, renamed the vines *biturica*. Just south of St-Emilion's walls at Château Belair, you can still see where the vines grew in ancient 'flowerpot' rows gouged into rock and filled with soil; adjacent to Château Belair are the ruins of an imperial Roman villa believed to have belonged to the poet and governor Ausonius, whose grandfather and father were said to be druids, and who lent his name to the greatest, most rarefied and smallest of the St-Emilion estates, Château Ausone.

The reputation of St-Emilion soared in the Middle Ages. The French praised it as the *vin honorifique*, the English as the 'king of wines'. No one can really explain why it's so good; the growing area on the north bank of the Dordogne enjoys no special microclimate, and the soil has no prominent characteristic besides its complexity, with clay present in most places – hence the predominant variety (over 60 per cent) is Merlot, which does well in clay, mixed with Cabernet Franc (or Bouchet, as it's called here), Cabernet Sauvignon and/or Malbec. A substantial factor in the creation of this ruby nectar has been some of the strictest quality control in France. Estates were remarkably small to begin with, compared to others in the Bordelais (St-Emilion's *grands crus* extend only 10 to 20 hectares), and in 1921 it was decided to limit the growing area to that decreed by Edward I in the 13th century. In 1948 the medieval *Jurade* of St-Emilion was reincarnated, complete with the swish scarlet caps and robes trimmed in ermine for special occasions; the members announce the *Ban*

cornucopia. The Franciscans must have copied it from the Eglise Monolithe, where it appears twice.

Backtrack to Rue Gaudet and Rue de la Cadène, which soon passes under the 16th-century arch of the **Porte et la Maison de la Cadène**, 'of the chain', by which a street could be quickly closed off in case of emergency. Note the half-timbered house on the left, decorated with a pair of grotesque heads and dolphins. Further up, Rue Gaudet runs into **Place du Marché**, a magnificent urbane stage set built over St-Emilion's first cemetery, its cafés shaded by a Liberty Tree from the Revolution of 1848. Built into the flank of the cliff here is the strange Eglise Monolithe, one of the highlights of the guided tour.

des Vendages, or beginning of the harvest, with a *fête* the night before and a procession to the top of the Tour du Roi with a resounding blast of trumpets over the countryside. The *jurats* also gather for the crucial *Jugement du vin nouveau* in June, to taste each new wine to see whether or not it merits the proud name St-Emilion. You can make your own mind up the first weekend in May, when a dozen châteaux open their doors for free tastings of the previous year's harvest.

What is especially confusing about St-Emilion is the often changing classifications within the *appellation*. The last revision in 1985 divides the châteaux into *premiers grands crus classés A* (of which there are only two, Ausone and Cheval-Blanc), followed by nine others distinguished by *classé B*, followed by 63 *grands crus classés*, all of which have to undergo a second tasting two years or so after the harvest to merit their labels. Below these come the St-Emilion, plain and simple and its eight satellite communities, which came under the authority of the medieval *Jurade* (St-Laurent-des-Combes, St-Hippolyte, St-Christophe-des-Bardes and St-Etienne-de-Lisse are considered the best).

The **Maison du Vin**, Place Pierre-Meyrat, **t** 05 57 55 50 55, **f** 05 57 55 53 10, and the tourist office distribute booklets with up-to-date information on the *chais* open for visits, languages spoken, and their visiting hours—and how much you'll pay for a tasting (the going rate seems to be 15F for one *millésime*, 20F for two, but it varies). Another alternative is take one of the tourist office's afternoon tours (*May–Sept, English translation available*). If you're buying, among the choicest wines now on sale at terrestrial prices are the 1994 *Grands Crus* (Château Croix de Labrie and Château Haut-Villet Cuvée Pomone are exceptional bottles) and the *millésime* '95 (Château de la Grenière and Château Montaiguillon are the ones to look out for). If you take the road to Pomerol you can ogle two of St-Emilion's greatest vintners, Cheval-Blanc and Figeac, the latter with a handsome 18th-century manor house. You can take a quick tour around the vineyards on a tourist train, which leaves from l'Eglise Collégiale (*May–Oct 10.30–6.30*).

The Guided Tour

Generally daily 9.30–12.30 and 1.45–6, July and Aug 9.30–8.

In southwest France the Benedictines were a burrowing order, although the reason they felt compelled to so tediously hollow their churches out of living rock is as obscure as it is remarkable (*see* Aubeterre-sur-Dronne, pp.114–15). They started St-Emilion's **Eglise Monolithe** after Aubeterre, in the 8th century, and when they had attained a cavity measuring 124 by 66ft in the 11th century, they gave it up to construct the Collégiale. It is a primitive, sombre and uncanny place, its nave supported by 10 rough, ill-aligned pillars, unfortunately assisted by an equally monumental scaffolding, jarring and brutal, that shows no sign of ever going away. Its colourful 12th-century murals were almost completely obliterated during the Revolution, when it was used as a saltpetre factory; the only decoration that remains are bas-reliefs: four winged angels, signs of the zodiac, and a dedicatory inscription. Bell ropes from the original bell tower hung through the hole in the ceiling.

Next to the Eglise Monolithe is the entrance to the round **Chapelle de la Trinité**, built in the 13th century by Augustinian monks to the memory of St Emilion, and converted into a coopery during the Revolution. The fascinating wall paintings between the ribs of the apse have recently been restored. An 8th-century sarcophagus and knight's tomb have been placed here, a preview of the adjacent 8th-century **catacombs**, excavated when the Place du Marché cemetery was filled to overflowing with pious souls who longed to spend eternity near the holy relics of Emilion. Bones were deposited through the funnel-like cupola connecting the catacombs with the cemetery of the canons: around the vault you can make out the engraved figures of three corpses with upraised arms, weird zombies symbolic of the Resurrection.

Lastly, the tour takes in the **Grotte de l'Ermitage** where the hermit Emilion lived, a cave that was reshaped over the centuries into a chapel in the form of a Latin cross. The good hermit's one amenity was running water from a natural spring. Worshipped since pagan times, the spring is good for what ails you, especially afflictions of the eye; the story also goes that any young woman who can drop two hairpins into the water in the form of a cross will surely be married within the year. Carved in the stone are St Emilion's 'armchair', where sterile women would sit, praying for offspring, and his bed, which probably originally doubled as his tomb.

The Collégiale

From Place du Marché, walk up steep Tertre de la Tente to Rue du Clocher. To the left in Place des Créneaux, St-Emilion's landmark 11th–15th-century **bell tower** rises up 173ft, the second highest in the Gironde after St-Michel of Bordeaux; for a small fee you can climb the 198 steps for a superb view of the entire town (if it's closed, the tourist office has the key). Here, too, is the entrance to the **Collégiale**, a hotchpotch of a church begun in 1110 – the period of its west portal, Byzantine cupolas, and frescoes of a devil, St Catherine and the Virgin on the right wall of the nave. The north portal has a tympanum adorned with a *Last Judgement* from 1306, with niches that once held high reliefs of the Apostles; in the choir are 15th-century stalls and the treasure, where the relics of St Emilion are currently installed.

From the nearby tourist office you can enter the pretty twin-columned Gothic **Cloître de la Collégiale** (*open summer 9.30–7; adm*). Follow Rue des Ecoles to Rue du Couvent and the austere Norman **Tour du Roi** (*June–Sept 10.30–12.45 and 2.15–8.30; adm*), all that remains of the castle built by Henry III *c.* 1237, with more grand views from the top.

Down near Place Bouqueyre, the medieval quarries of La Madeleine in Rue André Louiseau house the town's new **Musée des Hospices de la Madeleine**, with an excellent display of pottery and ironware made in southwest France from as far back as the 13th century (***t*** *05 57 55 51 65; open daily 10–6; adm*).

Pomerol

Tiniest of all the Bordeaux's great red-wine districts, a mere 3 by 4km, Pomerol produces some of the most distinctive wines in France, noted for their power and bouquet. As in adjacent St-Emilion, the soil is very complex, but its cold, even more clayey nature makes for a more intense and tannic wine; the best vintages take decades to come into their own. Merlot is the predominant grape, making up 95 per cent of the most celebrated of all Pomerols, Château Pétrus, considered the best Merlot wine in the world by wine lovers lucky enough to experience it; the '82 and '83 are said to be among the greatest ever. Unlike St-Emilion and its confusing, constantly changing classifications, Pomerol is simply Pomerol: after legendary Pétrus, the best wines consistently come from La Conseillante, L'Evangile, Trotanoy, Lafleur, Gazin and Vieux-Château Certan. Wines from the gravelly vineyards of nearby Néac and Lalande come under the *appellation* AOC *Lalande-de-Pomerol*; the best are close to the minor Pomerols and are certainly more reasonably priced as well. 1995 was an excellent year, and bottles from Château Moulin de Sales, Château La Croix Bellevue, Château Grand Ormeau, Château La Croix des Moines, Château de Viaux and Château Croix Chenevelle will not disappoint.

The **Syndicat Viticole**,2 Rue du 8 Mai 45, Lalande-de-Pomerol, **t** 05 57 25 21 60, f 05 57 51 82 79, can give you a list of producers and addresses (*open Mon, Tues, Thurs and Fri 2–5*).

You can take a tour of the vineyards in a horse-drawn cart with **Decouverte du Vignoble en Calèche**,**t** 06 84 87 55 45.

In the Environs of St-Emilion

Nearly every little village around St-Emilion has a Romanesque church worth a look. One of the best, **St-Martin-de-Mazerat** (1137), is less than a kilometre west; it has a richly carved south portal, but an amputated bell tower, chopped off on the order of the *Jurats* to prevent the Huguenots from using it to lob cannonballs on St-Emilion. Due west of St-Emilion, overlooking the Dordogne on the D19, is the largest menhir in the Gironde, the 16ft **Pierrefite**. Unlike most menhirs, Pierrefite gets a big summer solstice party – no druids, but old jazz, bonfires, floating candles in the Dordogne, games, food and wine.

Three kilometres north of St-Emilion, the 18th-century **Château St-Georges** is the most beautiful estate in the area, incorporating several towers from the original castle and a magnificent garden stair reminiscent of the one behind Bordeaux's Grand Théâtre. In the village of St-Georges, the 11th-century **St-Georges-de-Montagne** was built on the ruins of a Roman structure and seems too big for its apse; weathered, bizarre heads are carved on the capitals around the door, while others decorate the exterior of the apse. Nearby **Montagne** has another handsome Romanesque church, St-Martin, with a lovely dome and the **Ecomusée du Libournais** (***t*** *05 57 74 56 89; open mid-Mar–mid-Dec daily 10–12 and 2–6; adm*), a better-than-average historical and wine museum with photos, documents, tools and a 2km educational path through a vineyard. **Lussac**, 4km north, produces excellent Lussac-St-Emilion, which you can learn all about in the village's **Maison du Vin** (***t** 05 57 74 50 35; open Tues–Sat 9–12.30 and 2–6.30*).

The Libournais

Continuing down the Dordogne, you'll find more prestigious vineyards surrounding the bustling city of Libourne, which may not rate very high as a place to stay in, but has a surprising secret: in December it's the address of *Père Noël*. All the letters sent by French children end up in his special office here, where 60 elves help him sort the post.

Libourne

In 1269, Sir Richard de Leyburn, of Leybourne, Kent, undertook to build the *bastide* port decreed by Edward, son of Henry III and Duke of Aquitaine. Edward wanted to double the export capacities of Bordeaux, and found the perfect site: a languishing hamlet founded by Charlemagne called Fozera, located on the deep tidal waters of the river Isle just before its confluence with the Dordogne. Named Leyburnia after its founder, the name was gradually gallicized to Libourne as the *bastide* grew into a major port, shipping wine and wood west and sea salt east. After the French sacked Libourne in 1294, the English surrounded the town with high walls and towers; the large cylindrical **Tour Richard**, named after the son of Edward III, still overlooks the Isle at the Grand Port. Here and there you can see old wine warehouses and merchants' houses, mostly from the 18th century, especially in Rue Victor Hugo and Rue Fonneuve. Both lead into the central square of the *bastide*, **Place Abel-Surchamp**, with its arcades, covered market, 16th-century houses and the Hôtel de Ville, built in 1429 and restored when the 19th-century infatuation for neo-Gothic was at its peak. Under its pointy clock tower is the entrance to the **Musée des Beaux-Arts** (***t** 05 57 55 33 44; open Mon–Fri 10–12 and 2–6; adm*), featuring the lively landscape and animal paintings of Libourne native René Princeteau (1844–1914), the first teacher of Toulouse-Lautrec, and a sprinkling of minor works by Le Brun, Bartolomeo Manfredi, Jacopo Bassano, Picabia, Foujita and Dufy. Don't miss the goofy statue on the landing of the monumental stair: La France embracing a bust of the worst Bourbon wastrel, Louis XV.

Libourne's public library or *Médiatheque* (*open Tues, Wed, Fri and Sat*) is installed in the 17th-century cloister of the *Récollets* and contains a rare survivor: *Le Livre Velu* (the 'hairy book', so-called because of its calf-hide cover), a manuscript of 1476 which transcribes the charters and privileges given to Libourne by the kings of England since its foundation.

Getting Around

Libourne is on the main **railway** line from Paris to Bordeaux, with eight TGV stops a day; it also has connections to Périgueux and Thiviers. **Buses** for the surrounding villages depart from the *gare routière* next to the station, **t** 05 57 51 19 28. You can float above the vineyard in a **balloon**: contact **Agence Lambert Voyage**, **t** 05 57 74 19 10.

Tourist Information

Libourne: 40 Place Abel-Surchamp, **t** 05 57 51 15 04, **f** 05 57 25 00 58. Flea market the second Sat of each month.

Guîtres: 4 Av de la Gare, **t** 05 57 69 11 48.

Market Days

Libourne: Tues, Fri, and Sun mornings in Place Abel-Surchamp.

Vayres: Sun.

St-Denis-de-Pile: Thurs afternoons.

Where to Stay and Eat

Libourne ✉ 33500

****Decazes**, 22 Place Decazes, **t** 05 57 25 18 70 (*inexpensive*). A simple place, good for a night. Open all year.

****Des Ducs de Libourne**, Rue des Treilles, **t** 05 57 74 04 47, **f** 05 57 25 08 19 (*inexpensive*). With private parking. *Open all year.*

France, 7 Rue Chanzy, **t** 05 57 51 01 66 (*inexpensive*). Near the station. *Open all year.*

Le Bistrot Chanzy, 16 Rue Chanzy, **t** 05 57 51 84 26. The menu changes with the seasons, but always offers incredibly good value for your francs (*menus 85–95F lunch, à la carte eves*). *Closed Sun, Mon and Wed eves.*

Les Delices de la Mer, 21 Rue Thiers, **t** 05 57 51 94 84. Good for fish lovers; the décor reflects the simple menus of *fruits de mer* and kebabbed and grilled fish (*menus 70–150F*). *Closed Sun eve, Mon and the last two weeks of Aug.*

Les Démons de Bacchus, corner of Av Fonneuve and Rue des Chais, **t** 05 57 25 01 00. For an easy *bistrot*-style meal (*menus 95F and 120F*) and a glass or three of local wine, or just the wine. This ancient stone building seems to be in the process of sliding into the road; lovely stone features inside. *Closed Sat lunch, Sun and end July–mid-Aug.*

Vayres ✉ 33870

****Le Vatel**, **t** 05 57 74 80 79, **f** 05 57 74 71 38 (*inexpensive*). A Logis hotel with comfortable rooms, a pool and restaurant (*menus 75–210F*).

St-Loubès ✉ 33450

****Au Vieux Logis**, 92 Av de la République, **t** 05 56 78 92 99, **f** 05 56 78 91 18 (*inexpensive*). A small, charming place to stay, with an exceptional restaurant—there's a limited selection of dishes, but they're choice: try the fish *soupe de bassin et sa rouille* (*menus 130–260F*). *Closed Sun eve. Book.*

Fronsac ✉ 33126

Le Bord d'Eau, 4 Rue Poinsonnet, **t** 05 57 51 99 91. A wonderful spot for lunch or dinner, on the river itself; charming service and tasty seafood and fresh water fish, as well as duck dishes, and a wide range of sturdy local wines (*menus 100–195F*). *Closed Sun eve, Mon and Feb.*

Lugon et L'Ile-du-Carney ✉ 33240

*****Château du Vieux Raquine**, **t** 05 57 84 42 77, **f** 05 57 84 83 77 (*expensive–moderate*). Sleep in peace and quiet amongst the Fronsac vines. Breakfast available for guests, but there's no restaurant. *Closed mid-Jan–mid-Feb.*

Auberge de la Vieille Chapelle, **t** 05 57 84 48 65. In a charmingly renovated 12th-century chapel which has built up a fine reputation for its meals based on fresh seasonal and local produce (*menus 85–250F*). *Closed mid-Jan–start of Feb, Sun eve and Tues.*

North of Libourne: Up the Isle by Barge or Train

From Libourne, the D910 follows the course of the river Isle north to **St-Denis-de-Pile**, a village named after its 12th-century **church**, with a decorated apse and a painting of *The Visitation* by Le Nain. The **Maison de l'Isle** evokes the world of the river (***t** 05 57 55 44 30; open Mar–Jun Mon–Fri 9–12.30 and 1.30–5.30, July and Aug daily 9–12.30 and 2–6*) and you can also take a leisurely three-hour excursion from St-Denis upstream to **Coutras**, near the confluence of the Isle and Dronne, on the barge *Fleur de l'Isle* (*mid-April–June and Sept–mid-Oct every Sun, July and Aug daily; also Coutras to Penot;* ***t** 05 57 74 29 63 for information and reservations*). The barge calls at **Guîtres**, where you can visit **Notre-Dame**, a church the size of a cathedral begun by the Benedictines in 1080 and finished in the 15th century. Despite fortifications added during the Wars of Religion, it was damaged on a number of occasions and only restored in 1839. The 13th-century grand portal is especially good.

You can hop on another antique form of transport at Guîtres: a **narrow-gauge train**, pulled by a locomotive of 1924, that chugs 15km west to **Marcenais** and back in three hours (***t** 05 57 69 10 69; May–Oct Sat, Sun, Wed or hols, at 3.30; mid-July–mid-Aug sometimes runs Tues and Thurs as well, but ring to check*). The old station at Guîtres has a small train museum to get you into the old railroading mood. In this same area, on the D10 west of Guîtres, **St-Ciers-d'Abzac**'s Romanesque church used to attract pilgrims with weak, stunted children, who came under the protection of St Cyr. Specially venerated here is a massive block of sandstone called La Feyra that once formed part of a Neolithic monument; it is rumoured to turn three times at the ringing of the Angelus.

West of Libourne

Over on the south bank of the Dordogne, **Vayres** is the centre of its own little AOC wine region, *Graves de Vayres*, headquartered at the Château Juncarret (***t** 05 57 74 85 23*). Its most famous castle, however, is purely ornamental: the **Château de Vayres** (***t** 05 57 84 96 58; July–mid-Sept daily 2–6, rest of year Sun and hols only; adm*). Once owned by Henri IV, built on a partially artifical terrace, the château is endowed with a magnificent monumental stairway sweeping gracefully down to the Dordogne and its riverside park. The buildings, essentially 16th and 17th century, are built around a grand court; the refined, decorative east gallery is attributed to Louis de Foix, architect of the famous lighthouse of Cordouan. The 17th-century French gardens were restored in 1939. There are falconry demonstrations on summer afternoons. Downriver, the little *bastide* town of **St-Loubès** gave the world one of its first silent film comedians and one of Charlie Chaplin's inspirations, Max Linder (1883–1925, born Gabriel Leuvielle). He shot three of his films in St-Loubès before shooting himself, and is buried in the village cemetery.

Near Fronsac, the church at **La Rivière** houses a tall 14th-century alabaster statue of the Virgin and Child, while **La Lande-de-Fronsac** to the northwest has a minor architectural jewel in the façade of its church of **St-Pierre**. The tympanum is carved in a rough, oriental style with a scene from the Apocalypse: St John with the Seven

Fronsac and La Lande-de-Fronsac

Just west of Libourne, along the north bank of the Dordogne and high on a limestone plateau separated by the river l'Isle from St-Emilion and Pomerol, are the twin appellations of **Fronsac** and **La Lande-de-Fronsac**, producing another venerable wine (Fronsac was one of Charlemagne's favourite thirst-quenchers). In the 18th and early 19th century, these fresh, generous, supple red wines were pricier and had a better reputation than those of St-Emilion. After a century of near oblivion, they have been making a comeback since the 1980s, thanks to greater care in their elaboration. Merlot again is the dominant grape, with high proportions of Cabernet Sauvignon and Cabernet Franc.

Although the best vintages can be aged for decades, they are also delightfully fruity and ready to drink after four or five years, and go well with chicken dishes. Visitors are welcome at the loveliest estate, the grand 14th-century Château La Rivière, **t** 05 57 55 56 56, with huge limestone cellars (*open daily mid-June–mid-Sept, 9–12 and 2–5*) and at Château Cassagne Haut-Canon, **t** 05 57 51 63 98, in St-Michel-de-Fronsac on a former hunting estate of Cardinal Richelieu (*make an appointment*), bottlers of a wine called La Truffière, recommended with truffle dishes. The handsome white 18th-century **Château Dalem** at Saillans, **t** 05 57 84 34 18 (*by appointment*) has led the way in the rebirth of the wine, exporting it to 16 countries.

More information on tours can be picked up at **La Maison du Vin** in Fronsac, **t** 05 57 51 80 51.

Churches and his vision of 'someone resembling the Son of Man', with seven stars in his right hand, with a double-edged sword coming out of his mouth. There is nothing else like it anywhere in France; no one has any idea who sculpted it, or when.

The Haute-Gironde

The Dordogne grows increasingly wide as it reaches its rendezvous with the Gironde, its last stretch lined with limestone cliffs, yet more vineyards, and a charming corniche road; the famous castle of Blaye at the end marks the frontier of Aquitaine.

St-André-de-Cubzac and Around

There are two last towns to visit along the Dordogne before it meets the Garonne. St-André-de-Cubzac, an important crossroads near the Paris–Bordeaux *autoroute*, was the birthplace of the late Jacques Cousteau in 1910, although the actual house at 83 Rue Nationale is now a chemist's. Just north of town, wrapped in vineyards, the 16th-century **Château de Bouilh** was partially rebuilt to include a pavilion and hemicycle by Victor Louis beginning in 1787, in anticipation of a visit by Louis XVI; these were left unfinished when its marquis was guillotined. There's a neo-Greek chapel, an 18th-century kitchen, and rooms with their original panelling (***t*** *05 57 43 01 45; guided* *tours July–Sept Thurs, Sat, Sun and hols 2.30–6.30; adm*). On the edge of St-André, next to the public park, another, much smaller spread from the 16th century, the **Château Robillard**, has one of the oldest plane trees in France growing at the entrance. The two iron bridges at **Cubzac-les-Ponts** were designed by Eiffel in 1882 and 1889, and later restored by his engineer grandson. The vines you see growing all around here produce white and red Bordeaux and Bordeaux Superieur, including one label from Marsas (north of St-André) with the funniest name of all: *La Pissotière de l'Impératrice*, the Empress's Chamberpot.

From St-André, the scenic D669/E1 snakes along the limestone corniche that characterizes this last stretch of the Dordogne. For centuries this pale limestone was the most sought-after building stone of Bordeaux, especially the stone from the old quarries at **Marcamps**, which are photogenic enough to be used as a set in Robert Hossein's 1982 film, *Les Misérables*. Other old quarries are now used as mushroom farms. **Tauriac** near Marcamps has a 12th-century **church** with Merovingian capitals and two carved tympanums, illustrating the Agnus Dei and a knight.

Just north of the D669 in Prignac-et-Marchamps, earlier residents decorated the **Grotte de Pair-non-Pair** (***t** 05 57 68 33 40; open all year, call for times of guided visits*). Discovered in 1881, the cave yielded a rich store of finds from the Mousterian (80,000 BC) to the Périgordien Supérieur (18,000 BC) – tools of flint and bone, and a great pile of animal bones left over from thousands of prehistoric feasts. Unusually for a dwelling area, it was also decorated with etchings as well as extremely rare Aurignacian paintings (25,000 BC), all tragically washed away in 1899 by an imbecile who wanted to clean them using a hose from a vineyard pump. The etchings, in places scratched one over the other, include mammoths, deer and bison, and most notably a horse in flight, head turned dramatically back towards an unseen pursuer. The cave's funny name, 'Even-Odd', is derived from a village that once stood nearby, lost by its *seigneur* in a game of heads-or-tails.

Medieval **Bourg-sur-Gironde** is a misnomer – it's still on the Dordogne, although just beyond Bourg the river finally contributes its waters to Europe's largest estuary. The white limestone that built Bordeaux was shipped from here. These days, pleasure craft bob in Bourg's port, along with a 19th-century *gabare* that offers day-sailing excursions to Blaye and vice versa in the summer (*contact the tourist office*). There are fine views over the water from the Terrasse du District and the handsome, clifftop **Château de la Citadelle**. Originally home away from home for the archbishops of Bordeaux, this château was reconstructed in the 18th century as a folly. In 1944, the retreating Germans torched it out of spite, but it has been beautifully restored, complete with its gardens of magnolias and pistachios. Since 1995, the grounds have hosted the **Musée Hippomobile** (***t** 05 57 68 23 57; open July and Aug 10–1 and 2.30–7, otherwise variable; adm*), housing a fine collection of landaus, omnibuses, cabriolets, phaetons, gigs and coupés, as well as retired merry-go-round horses.

A second museum, the **Eco-Musée du Bourgeais**, in the centre of town (***t** 05 57 68 42 48; open mid-June–mid-Sept Tues–Sun 3–7*) is devoted to the Grotte de Pair-non-Pair, old trades and traditions, and film maker Emile Couzinet (d. 1964), a native of Bourg.

Getting Around

Citram, **t** 05 56 43 68 43, run **buses** from Bordeaux to Blaye, stopping at St-André-de-Cubzac and Bourg. There's a **ferry** from Blaye to Lamarque in Médoc, **t** 05 57 42 04 49.

Tourist Information

St-André-de-Cubzac: 9 Allée du Champ de Foire, **t** 05 57 43 64 80, **f** 05 57 43 69 63.

Bourg-sur-Gironde: Hôtel de la Juarde, **t** 05 57 68 31 76, **f** 05 57 68 30 25.

Blaye: Allées Marines, **t** 05 57 42 12 09, **f** 05 57 42 91 94.

Market Days

St-André-de-Cubzac: Thurs and Sun.

Bourg: Sun mornings, and the first and third Tues of each month.

Blaye: Wed and Sat, in the avenue leading up to the citadel.

Where to Stay and Eat

St-André-de-Cubzac ✉ 33240

Au Sarment, 50 Rue Lande, 3km north on the same road as the Château de Bouilh, **t** 05 57 43 44 73. In the old stone schoolhouse with tables in the summer on a delightful shady terrace; it's a good place to take the plunge and order *lamprey*, or else opt for the delicious *paupiettes de sole* (*menus from 100F, weekends a bit more*). *Closed Sun eve, Mon and most of Aug.*

Bourg-sur-Gironde ✉ 33710

****La Closerie des Vignes**, at St-Ciers-de-Canesse 8km northwest of Bourg, **t** 05 57 64 81 90, **f** 05 57 64 94 44 (*inexpensive*). A tranquil, charming, modern house surrounded by vineyards, with a park and pool; the restaurant serves delicious smoked salmon quiche and home-made desserts (*menus 140–180F*). *Open April–Oct, serves dinner only.*

Château de la Grave, direction Berson from Bourg, then second to the right and it's signposted, **t** 05 57 68 41 49, **f** 05 57 68 49 26 (*inexpensive*). Sleep like a lord in a genuine castle, restored in Louis XVIII-style and surrounded by vineyards; you can visit the cellars.

Le Troque-sel, 1 Place Jeantet, **t** 05 57 68 30 67. In the centre, with a reputation for its well-prepared seafood (*menus 65–145F*). *Closed Sun eves and Mon.*

La Filadière in Gauriac, on the Corniche road between Bourg and Blaye, **t** 05 57 64 94 05. Overlooking the Gironde; specializes in sturgeon scallops (*menus 90F, weekends 115F*). *Closed Wed out of season.*

Blaye ✉ 33390

****La Citadelle**, **t** 05 57 42 17 10, **f** 05 57 42 10 34 (*inexpensive*). A Logis de France where most of the rooms overlook the swimming pool and the Gironde countryside; the restaurant specializes in locally farmed sturgeon cooked in *Premières Côtes-de-Blaye* (*menus from 150F*).

Le Premayac, 25 Rue du Preymac (near Place de l'Europe), **t** 05 57 42 19 57. For a simpler meal, specializing in grills over vine wood with local wines (*menus from 98F*). *Closed Mon.*

Campsite, **t** 05 57 42 00 20. The small municipal site is inside the walls of the citadel, overlooking the Gironde.

In bakeries you can find the speciality of the town, the ***praslines de Blaye***, or pralines of burnt almonds, invented by the chef of the Maréchal de Plessis-Praslin, governor of the citadel in 1649.

Pick up the key at Bourg's tourist office to visit the fascinating Romanesque crypt with primitive 11th-century carved capitals at Libarde, 1km to the north.

La Corniche de la Gironde: Bourg to Blaye

West of Bourg, the great confluence of the Dordogne and Garonne and estuary islands are watched over by **Pain-de-Sucre**, the local version of Rio's Sugarloaf

Côtes-de-Bourg and Premières Côtes-de-Blaye

The attractive wooded hills around Bourg give way in places for the vineyards of AOC Côtes-de-Bourg. Limestone dominates the soil, and Cabernet Sauvignon and Merlot are the two leading varieties. Like most minor *appellations*, Côtes-de-Bourg wines mature earlier than Bordeaux's *grands crus*, and are often good value: the red '95s are exceptional. Among the finest are **Château Mercier** in St-Trojan, **t** 05 57 42 66 99, **Château Gravette Samonac** in Samonac, **t** 05 57 68 21 16, **Château de Barbe** at Villeneuve, **t** 05 57 42 64 00, **Château Mendoce** at Bourg, **t** 05 57 68 34 95 (the 15th-century property of Diego de Mendoza, François I's maître d'hôtel and cousin of the Mendoza grandees of Spain), **Château Haut-Launay** at Teuillac, **t** 05 57 64 39 44, and the nearby **Château Grand-Launay, t** 05 57 64 39 03.

Some of the old subterranean limestone quarries are now used to store the local bubbly, Cremant de Bordeaux white or pink (and an *appellation* since 1990), produced by Brouette Petit-Fils in the **Caves du Pain du Sucre, t** 05 57 68 42 09. In the centre of Bourg, the **Maison des Côtes-de-Bourg**, Place de l'Eperon, **t** 05 57 94 80 20, has a list of others.

AOC Premières Côtes-de-Blaye is the much larger northern extension of Côtes de Bourg and produces mainly red wine (60% Merlot, 30% Cavernet Sauvignon, and 5% each of Malbec and Cabernet Franc) and a less significant quantity of white (80% Sauvignon, 10% Ugni Blanc and Colombard, and 5% each of Muscadelle and Sémillon). There is even more limestone in the soil here, and the wines are fruity with some body, yet very drinkable when only three or four years old. Again, the '95 reds are a good buy, and the '96 whites are very good, too: the **Cave Coopérative des Hauts-de-Gironde** in Marcillac, **t** 05 57 32 48 33, have fine examples of both; also try **Château Haut-Bertinerie**, in Cubnezais, **t** 05 57 68 70 74, for its blanc '96, and **Château Frédignac** in St-Martin-Lacaussade, **t** 05 57 42 24 93, and **Château Louméde** in Blaye, **t** 05 57 42 16 39, for reds. Many also make a Fine Bordeaux, a double-distilled *eau-de-vie* made from Colombard and Ugni Blanc. For a map and more information, stop at the **Maison du Vin**, 11 Cours Vauban, in Blaye, **t** 05 57 42 91 19, **f** 05 57 42 85 28.

Women growers, in a society called the *Groupement de Developpement Agricole Feminin de Blaye*, have banded together to offer visitors in camping vans free stopovers in their vineyards, as well as a free wine-tasting course; the tourist office has a list of participants.

Mountain. Further up, **Gauriac** has troglodyte houses cut into the limestone, while at **Plassac** you can visit the excavations of three Gallo-Roman villas from the 1st–5th centuries AD and the **Musée Gallo-Romaine** (*t 05 57 42 84 80; open 10.30–12 and 3–7)*. It is interesting to note the development of the Aquitaine style of Roman villas, along with that of their polychrome mosaics; the museum contains wall paintings, bronzes, coins, ceramics and other finds. The same ticket will admit you to Plassac's **Conservatoire Vinicole**, in a century-old wine cellar, devoted to the history of the wines of Blaye. You can admire the corniche from a *gabare*: contact the tourist office at Bourg for information.

Blaye

Occupying a limestone spur overlooking the narrowest, most defensible part of the Gironde estuary, Blaye was inhabited since Neolithic times (5000 BC) but entered history as *Blavia*, a camp of Roman legionnaires, and grew into a town sung by Ausonius. 'The Star and Key of Aquitaine', as its Latin motto proudly proclaims, the town is dominated by a massive 81-acre **Citadelle**, built to defend Bordeaux from the English in 1686–9 by Louis XIV's famous engineer Vauban, along with two other less important forts, on the Ile Pâté and at Fort Médoc. As was so often the case in that era, defending the town entailed its partial destruction – 250 houses were razed to make room for the walls. The greatest loss was the Romanesque Basilique de

Jaufre Rudel

Blaye was firmly marked on love's map even before Marie-Caroline (*see* below), thanks to the extraordinary passion that fired the heart of the handsome troubadour Jaufre (or Geoffroi) Rudel, the Prince of Blaye. Although his triangular castle was engulfed and mostly destroyed by Vauban's enormous citadel, two towers and low walls remain north of the Place d'Armes to give at least some physical credence to his strange and mystical story, well known in the Middle Ages. In 1147 Jaufre heard tell of Melisande, Countess of Tripoli, and, just from the description of her beauty, fell in love with her. He composed many fine songs for her, and begged his liege lord, Count Alphonse Jourdain of Toulouse, to let him accompany him on the next crusade. Seeing how pale he was for love, Alphonse Jourdain reluctantly took him along, but, as they approached the Holy Land, Jaufre became feverishly ill and the Crusaders left him to die alone in a poor fisherman's hut. Suddenly a lovely damsel entered and tenderly took Jaufre's head in her hands, saying, 'You were right to seek me, Jaufre, even if it has cost you your life. I am she whom you have long sought. Rest assured that you will find me as you dreamed.' At that the troubadour smiled and died, and the Countess of Tripoli buried him with the Knights Templars. In grief, she entered a convent and was never seen again. The story inspired writers from Petrarch to Rostand (*La Princesse lointaine*) and Heine, who has the lovers reunited as tender ghosts in a poem from *Romanzero* (1851):

***'Melisande! Was ist Traum?
Was ist Tod? Nur eitel Töne.
In der Liebe nur is Wahrheit,
Und dich lieb ich, ewig Schöne.'***

***('Melisande! What is a dream?
What is death? Just empty sounds.
In love alone is truth,
and I love you, eternal beauty')***

St-Romain, founded in 350, where the famous Roland, lord of Blaye, nephew of Charlemagne and hero of France's greatest medieval epic, *La Chanson de Roland*, was buried in the 8th century after blowing his brains out at Roncesvalles. The foundations of the basilica have recently been excavated; it was an important pilgrimage site on the road to Compostela.

The 146ft-high walls of the Citadel offer excellent views over the estuary and its defences, especially from the **Tour de l'Eguillette** overlooking a cliff; the English (and everyone else) are more than welcome to invade its confines, by foot or zoo train. There's a **Cellier des Vignerons**, full of wine exhibitions (***t** 05 57 42 36 14; open June–early Nov 9.30–12.30 and 2.30–7*), and changing exhibits on the natural and man-made history of the estuary in the **Conservatoire de l'Estuaire** in the Place d'Armes (***t** 05 57 42 80 96; open June–early Nov 1–7, rest of the year 2–6; adm*). A **Musée d'Histoire et d'Art du Pays Blayais** (*currently under restoration, due to reopen 2001*) has been installed in the former commander's quarters, the Pavillon de la Place. It previously contained old plans of the citadel, pharmaceutical jars, and memorabilia of the Pavillon's unexpected 'guest' in 1832: **Marie-Caroline de Bourbon-Sicilie**, Duchesse de Berry, arrested in Nantes while trying to overthrow Louis-Philippe in favour of her son, the Duke of Bordeaux, a pretender to the throne. The flamboyant Marie-Caroline was a political hot potato for Louis-Philippe until the next year, when (though a widow for 12 years) she gave birth to a daughter. Once she was neutralized by the scandal, Louis-Philippe packed her off to Palermo.

Bordeaux

11

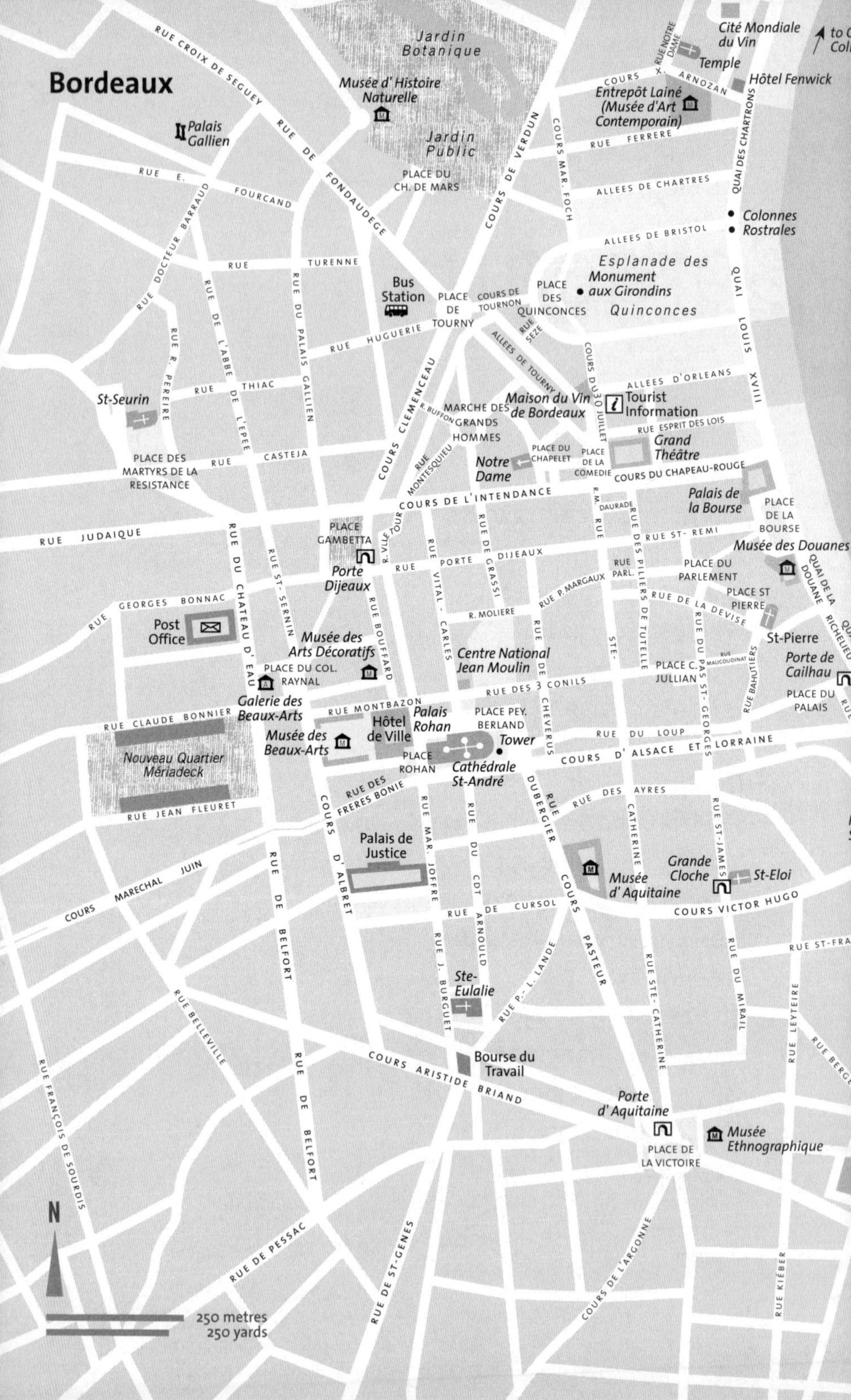

Bordeaux
Jardin Botanique
Musée d' Histoire Naturelle
Jardin Public
Palais Gallien
Cité Mondiale du Vin
Temple
Hôtel Fenwick
to Cité …
Entrepôt Lainé (Musée d'Art Contemporain)
Place du Ch. de Mars
Colonnes Rostrales
Esplanade des Quinconces
Monument aux Girondins
Place des Quinconces
Bus Station
Place de Tourny
St-Seurin
Maison du Vin de Bordeaux
Tourist Information
Marche des Grands Hommes
Grand Théâtre
Notre Dame
Place du Chapelet
Place de la Comedie
Place des Martyrs de la Resistance
Palais de la Bourse
Place de la Bourse
Place Gambetta
Porte Dijeaux
Musée des Douanes
Place du Parlement
Place St Pierre
St-Pierre
Post Office
Musée des Arts Décoratifs
Centre National Jean Moulin
Place du Col. Raynal
Place C. Jullian
Porte de Cailhau
Place du Palais
Galerie des Beaux-Arts
Palais Rohan
Hôtel de Ville
Place Pey. Berland
Tower
Musée des Beaux-Arts
Place Rohan
Cathédrale St-André
Nouveau Quartier Mériadeck
Palais de Justice
Musée d' Aquitaine
Grande Cloche
St-Eloi
Ste-Eulalie
Bourse du Travail
Porte d'Aquitaine
Place de la Victoire
Musée Ethnographique
Rue Croix de Seguey
Rue de Fondaudege
Cours de Verdun
Cours Mar. Foch
Quai des Chartrons
Cours Xavier Arnozan
Rue Notre Dame
Rue Ferrere
Allees de Chartres
Allees de Bristol
Rue E. Fourcand
Rue Docteur Barraud
Rue Turenne
Rue du Palais Gallien
Rue de l'Abbe de l'Epee
Rue R. Pereire
Rue Thiac
Rue Huguerie
Cours de Tournon
Rue Seze
Allees de Tourny
Cours du 30 Juillet
Allees d'Orleans
Quai Louis XVIII
Cours Clemenceau
R. Buffon
Rue Montesquieu
Rue Esprit des Lois
Cours du Chapeau-Rouge
Rue Casteja
Cours de l'Intendance
R. Vile Tour
Rue Judaique
Rue du Chateau d'Eau
Rue St-Sernin
Rue Vital-Carles
Rue de Grassi
R. M. Daurade
Rue St-Remi
Rue des Piliers de Tutelle
Rue Porte Dijeaux
Rue Parl.
Rue P. Margaux
Rue de la Devise
Quai de la Douane
Quai Richelieu
Rue Georges Bonnac
Rue Bouffard
R. Moliere
Rue de Cheverus
Rue Ste-Catherine
Rue du Pas St-Georges
Rue Maucoudinat
Rue Bahutiers
Rue des 3 Conils
Rue Montbazon
Rue Claude Bonnier
Rue du Loup
Cours d'Alsace et Lorraine
Rue Jean Fleuret
Rue des Freres Bonie
Rue Dubergier
Rue des Ayres
Cours d'Albret
Rue Mar. Joffre
Rue du Cdt Arnould
Rue St-James
Cours Marechal Juin
Rue de Belfort
Rue de Cursol
Cours Victor Hugo
Cours Pasteur
Rue St-Fra…
Rue J. Burguet
Rue P.-L. Lande
Rue du Mirail
Rue Leyteire
Rue Berge…
Rue Belleville
Cours Aristide Briand
Rue François de Sourdis
Rue de Pessac
Rue de St-Genes
Cours de l'Argonne
Rue Kiéber
N
250 metres
250 yards

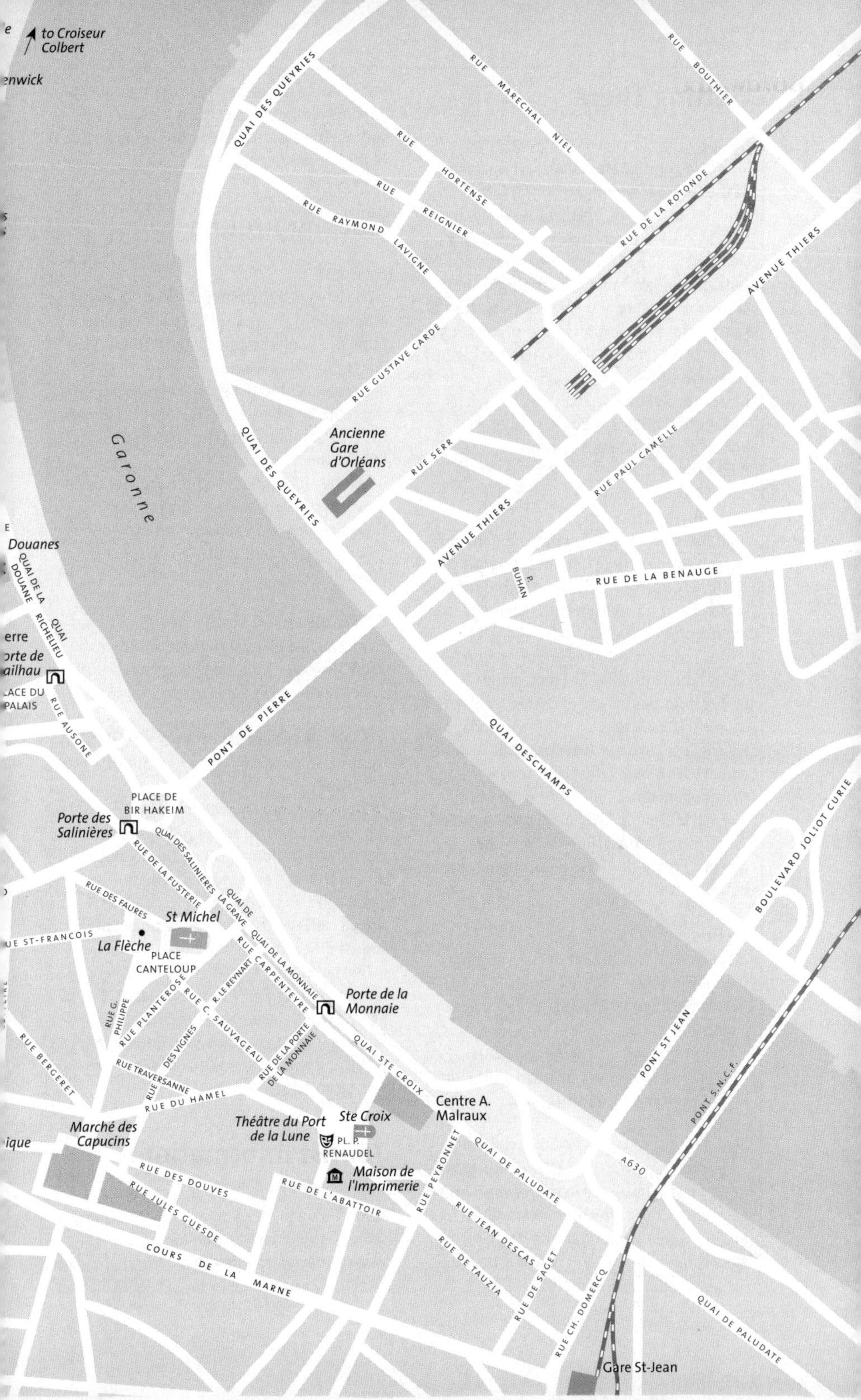
to Croiseur Colbert
Garonne
QUAI DES QUEYRIES
RUE MARECHAL NIEL
RUE BOUTHIER
RUE HORTENSE
RUE REIGNIER
RUE RAYMOND LAVIGNE
RUE DE LA ROTONDE
AVENUE THIERS
RUE GUSTAVE CARDE
Ancienne Gare d'Orléans
RUE SERR
RUE PAUL CAMELLE
P. BUHAN
RUE DE LA BENAUGE
Douanes
QUAI DE LA DOUANE
QUAI RICHELIEU
RUE AUSONE
PONT DE PIERRE
QUAI DESCHAMPS
PLACE DE BIR HAKEIM
Porte des Salinières
QUAI DES SALINIERES
RUE DE LA FUSTERIE
RUE DES FAURES
St Michel
QUAI DE LA GRAVE
La Flèche
PLACE CANTELOUP
RUE CARPENTEYRE
QUAI DE LA MONNAIE
Porte de la Monnaie
R. LE REYNART
RUE C. SAUVAGEAU
RUE PLANTEROSE
RUE G. PHILIPPE
RUE BERGERET
RUE DES VIGNES
RUE TRAVERSANNE
RUE DE LA PORTE DE LA MONNAIE
QUAI STE CROIX
RUE DU HAMEL
Centre A. Malraux
Ste Croix
Théâtre du Port de la Lune
PL. P. RENAUDEL
Marché des Capucins
Maison de l'Imprimerie
RUE DES DOUVES
RUE DE L'ABATTOIR
RUE PEYRONNET
QUAI DE PALUDATE
RUE JULES GUESDE
RUE JEAN DESCAS
RUE DE TAUZIA
RUE DE SAGET
COURS DE LA MARNE
RUE CH. DOMERCQ
A630
PONT ST JEAN
BOULEVARD JOLIOT CURIE
PONT S.N.C.F.
Gare St-Jean

Getting There

By Air

Bordeaux International Airport is 12km west of the centre at Mérignac, **t** 05 56 34 50 50. A shuttle bus, 'Jet' bus, links the airport to the railway station via the tourist office (Place Gambetta: stop M13), and the Barrière Judaïque approximately every 30mins from 6am, from 8.45am at weekends (runs start at 5.30am from the station to the airport, **t** 05 56 34 50 50); alternatively, a taxi into the centre costs 100–180F.

Air France t 0802 802 802
Air Liberté t 0803 805 805
British Airways t 0825 825 400
Buzz t 0155 174 242

By Train

All trains arrive and depart from **Bordeaux St-Jean** station in Rue Charles Domerq, **t** 08 36 35 35 35. TGVs from Paris-Montparnasse take 3hrs; regular trains from Paris-Austerlitz take 4hrs30mins.

Other connections are Périgueux (2hrs); Sarlat (3hrs) by way of St-Emilion and Bergerac; Tarbes by way of Orthez, Pau and Lourdes; TGVs or regular trains to Hendaye by way of Dax, Bayonne, Biarritz and St-Jean-de-Luz, or to Toulouse (2hrs) by way of Agen and Montauban; other trains 3hrs with additional stops in Marmande, Aiguillon and Moissac.

There are also local lines to Mont-de-Marsan, Pointe-de-Grave and, roughly once an hour, to Arcachon.

By Bus

The station for **Citram** buses serving most towns and villages in the Gironde is at Allées de Chartres, **t** 05 56 81 16 82, just off Place des Quinconces.

For information on international bus connections to London, Portugal and Spain, contact **Eurolines**, **t** 05 56 92 50 42.

By Car

Paris has its *périphérique*; Bordeaux has a great ring highway called the *rocade*, which sucks up all the *autoroutes* and national roads and spins them around the city, making it sometimes easier to circumvent it than to penetrate to its centre. There are a number of parking garages in the centre, and near the station; the easiest place to find a spot is the vast Place des Quinconces.

Getting Around

By Bus

The city's **CGFTE** buses (**t** 05 57 57 88 88 for information) are frequent, convenient and huge, prowling the long straight streets like links of metal sausages.

Buy blocks of 10 tickets at kiosks or pay on the bus; from the station, bus 7 will take you to Place Gambetta and the Chartrons; bus 1 follows the river.

Several night buses run from the station, between 9.30pm and 12.30am, the S1 along the quaysides and S7 and S9 through town.

Bus maps are free at the tourist office or railway station.

Other Means

You can hire **bikes** at the station, Bordeaux Vélo, Quai Louis XVIII, **t** 05 56 44 77 31, and Cycles Pasteur, 42 Cours Pasteur, **t** 05 56 92 68 20.

If you fancy your chances on a **motorbike** try Motokits, Hangar 21, Rue Lucien Faure, **t** 05 56 50 50 40.

Cabbies are not allowed to cruise in Bordeaux, but there are 24-hour **taxi** ranks at the railway station and Place Gambetta, and during the day ranks in key locations.

You can also see Bordeaux from a **horse-drawn carriage**, or 1920s **convertible**: call the tourist office for information.

Two **boats** offer trips on the river l'Aliénor, **t** 05 56 51 27 90, and Ville de Boedeaux, **t** 05 56 52 88 88; both leave from the Quinconces landing stage, Quai Louis XVIII. You can even go up in a **balloon** from Quai des Queyries, **t** 05 56 40 20 22.

Tourist Information

12 Cours du 30-Juillet, **t** 05 56 00 66 00, **f** 05 56 00 66 01; there's a branch office in Gare St-Jean, **t** 05 56 91 64 70 (*open June–Sept*); *www.bordeaux-tourisme.com* and

www.mairie-bordeaux.fr provide up-to-the-minute lists of events, visits, hotels and ideas for excursions.

Among the many tourist office initiatives are a wide choice of walking or bus **tours** concentrating on various themes, monuments or neighbourhoods (in English and French), as well as an introduction to wine tasting at the Maison du Vin (2 hours, *charcuterie* and cheese included, 125F); they also run regular half-day excursions to some of the most famous vineyards with tastings – the only way to get into most of them.

If you plan to do lots of sightseeing, you can save money with their ***Bordeaux Découverte*** card, entitling the bearer to discounts, etc. in the city's museums, on excursions and at some theatres. If you plan to spend at least two nights in a two- to four-star hotel, you can also get a discount on the bill, as well as a guided tour of Bordeaux and the vineyards (*Forfait Bordeaux Découverte*).

For information on the *département* of the Gironde, contact the Maison de Tourisme de la Gironde, 21 Cours de l'Intendance, **t** 05 56 52 61 40, **f** 05 56 81 09 99; for all of Aquitaine, the Comité Régionale de Tourisme d'Aquitaine, Cité Mondiale du Vin, 23 Quai des Chartrons, **t** 05 56 01 70 00, **f** 05 56 01 70 07 (call or write first for information).

Post office: 52 Rue Georges Bonnac.

Money exchange: American Express: 14 Cours de l'Intendance, **t** 05 56 44 47 57 (*open Mon–Fri 9–12 and 1–5*).

UK consulate: 353 Bd du Président Wilson, **t** 05 57 22 21 10.

Shopping

Bordeaux has five covered **markets** (*open Mon–Sat mornings*) on Cours Victor-Hugo, Place des Capucins (the most fragrant), Place des Grands Hommes, Place des Chartrons and Place de l'Erme.

If you are there on a Sunday head for the market beside the river at Chartrons.

There is also a bric-a-brac antique market in Place St-Michel (*Sun–Fri*); on Sat it's a farmers' market.

A bottle is the obvious souvenir of Bordeaux: there are **wine shops** and all kinds of vinous paraphernalia. Pedestrian **Rue Ste-Catherine** is Bordeaux's favourite shopping street, especially for clothes.

English **books** are available at Bradley's Bookshop, 8 Cours d'Albret, **t** 05 56 52 10 57.

Bordeaux has two streets devoted to **antiques**: Rue Bouffard around the Musée des Arts Décoratifs and Rue Notre-Dame in the Chartrons, with two-score shops and galleries.

Quartier St-Pierre is another good place to look for old things and curiosities, in particular along Rue de la Devise. Near the Grand Théâtre, buy **pottery** and **candles** at Point à la Ligne, 57 Cours de l'Intendance.

Not far from here is Saunion, 56 Cours Georges-Clemenceau, a must for **chocolate**-lovers, where Thierry Lalet will sell you a selection of his forty-plus fresh and delicious chocolates made next door; the house speciaility is the *guinette*, a cherry soaked in alcohol and covered in dark chocolate.

You can find the famous ***canalé*** cakes, with scrumptious sweet gooey centres and crusty outsides, at Baillardran, 90 Rue Porte Dijeaux, near Place Gambetta.

If you want to stock up on **foie gras** and other southwest staples head for Comtesse du Barry, 2 Place de Tourny.

One of the last remaining shops of its kind in France, founded in 1814, Au Sanglier de Russie, 67 Cours d'Alsace et Lorraine, sells a huge range of **brushes** for absolutely any imaginable household or personal use, featuring extraordinarily exotic animal hairs and woods.

Sports and Activities

Besides the **Jardin Public**, Bordeaux has another lung further west in the **Parc Bordelais** (buses 18 or 14).

Golfers have a choice of three courses on the outskirts of town: the 27-hole Golf de Pessac, 5 Rue de la Princesse, **t** 05 57 26 03 33; the 18-hole Golf Bordelais, Rue de Kater, at Caudéran, **t** 05 56 28 56 04; and the less expensive 36-hole Golf de Bordeaux-Lac, Av de Pernon, **t** 05 56 50 92 72; as well as an indoor course, Golf d'Ornano, 19 Rue Ste-Cécile, **t** 05 56 98 68 93. If you are really interested in playing you can buy a **Golf Pass** from most tourist offices in the area (minimum handicap of 36 required) which gives you five free vouchers with a choice between six courses in Gironde and Dordogne. It is valid for a year and in 2000 cost 990F, **t** 05 56 52 61 40.

Mériadeck has a **bowling** alley and indoor **skating** rink (95 Cours du Maréchal Juin, **t** 05 56 93 11 11). Bordeaux's beloved **rugby** team plays in Bègles just to the south, in the Stade André Moga, **t** 05 56 85 94 01; the first-division Girondins **football** team (who won the French championship in 1999) play in the Art Deco Stade Municipal (1938) in Bd du Maréchal Leclerc, Le Parc Lescure, **t** 05 56 93 25 83.

Where to Stay

Bordeaux ✉ 33000

There is a clutch of pricey new chain hotels at Bordeaux Lac, easily reached off the *rocade* ring road, and a sprinkling of non-chain hotels in the centre.

Expensive

******Burdigala**, 115 Rue Georges-Bonnac, **t** 05 56 90 16 16, **f** 05 56 93 15 06. For luxury and personality in the heart of town. Elegant, air-conditioned rooms all individually styled with wood, stone and marble.

*****Ste Catherine**, 27 Rue du Parlement, **t** 05 56 81 95 12, **f** 05 56 44 50 51. A handsomely restored 18th-century *hôtel* near the Grand Théâtre; the most comfortable hotel in its class, with exceptionally nice rooms.

Moderate

*****Le Majestic**, 2 Rue de Condé, between the Grand Théâtre and Place des Quinconces, **t** 05 56 52 60 44, **f** 05 56 79 26 70. Recently had a complete overhaul: comfortable air-conditioned rooms, with an inner garden, parking garage, but no restaurant.

*****Le Bayonne Etche-Ona**, 4 Rue Martignac, on the corner of the Allées de Tourny, **t** 05 56 48 00 88, **f** 05 56 48 41 60. The 18th-century building on Rue Martignac has been redecorated in a contemporary style; there's another building at 11 Rue Mautrec. All rooms come with TV and minibar.

*****Royal Médoc**, 3 Rue Sèze (just off Place Tourny), **t** 05 56 81 72 42, **f** 05 56 48 98 00. Very comfortable up-to-date rooms and a handy garage.

*****De la Presse**, 6–8 Rue Porte Dijeaux, **t** 05 56 48 53 88, **f** 05 56 01 05 82. Very central, with good soundproofing, and parking nearby. The rooms are decorated simply, but well equipped.

****Les Quatre Sœurs**, 6 Cours du 30-Juillet (near the Quinconces), **t** 05 57 81 19 20, **f** 05 56 01 04 28. Sleep where Richard Wagner slept, before he was run out of town for dallying with the wife of a local politician; rooms, overlooking the street or courtyard, are cosy and furnished with mini-bars.

****Le Continental**, 10 Rue Montesquieu, **t** 05 56 52 66 00, **f** 05 56 52 77 97, *www.hotel-le-continental.com*. An elegant hotel on a pedestrianized street in the centre of town near to the shopping centre at Place des Grands Hommes. The rooms are comfortable, with TVs and telephones.

Inexpensive

****Notre Dame**, 36 Rue Notre-Dame, **t** 05 56 52 88 24, **f** 05 56 79 12 67. A pretty little hotel in a 19th-century building in the quiet Chartrons quarter, which has recently been given a complete facelift.

****La Tour Intendance**, 16 Rue Vieille-Tour (a pedestrian-only lane off Cours de l'Intendance), **t** 05 56 81 46 27, **f** 05 56 81 60 90. Simple and sweet and run by two friendly women; parking available.

****Stars**, 34 Rue Tauzia, **t** 05 56 94 59 00, **f** 05 56 94 21 27. The best choice near the station, a welcoming hotel with shipshape décor, TV and a parking garage.

****Du Théâtre**, 10 Rue de la Maison-Daurade, **t** 05 56 79 05 26, **f** 05 56 81 15 64. Centrally located on a pedestrianized street; fine rooms; parking nearby. No lift.

****Acanthe**, 12–14 Rue St-Rémi, **t** 05 56 81 66 58, **f** 05 56 44 74 41, *www.acanthe-hotel-bordeaux.com*. A pretty sitting room and simply furnished but well-equipped bedrooms; the large family room is the most stylish. Probably most appropriate for those without a car.

Cheap

There are quite a few not very savoury cheap hotels in Bordeaux; if possible, give the dives near the station a miss.

★**Studio**, 26 Rue Huguerie, **t** 05 56 48 00 14, **f** 05 56 81 25 71. Near the bus depot off Place du Tourny. The larger rooms come complete with shower and WC.

Amboise, 22 Rue Vieille-Tour (near Place Gambetta), **t** 05 56 81 62 67. Old-fashioned.

Boulan, 28 Rue Boulan, **t** 05 56 52 23 62, **f** 05 56 44 91 65. Near the cathedral.

Les Gravières, Villenave-d'Ornon (✉ 33140), **t** 05 56 87 00 36. The nearest campsite to Bordeaux, to the south; pleasant and well-equipped but only practical if you have wheels of your own.

Eating Out

Unlike most folks, who pick a bottle to go with their meal, the Bordelais tend to choose a vintage first, then create a menu that will enhance the wine. This concern, and Bordeaux's choice setting between land, river and sea, has led to the invention of a wide choice of specialities from the famous *entrecôte à la bordelaise* to the more rarefied pleasures of lamprey, which like shad, the other local favourite, is 'in season' in April and May.

Although Bordeaux suffered a post-war slump in the kitchen along with its post-war blues in other fields, a new school of chefs in the 1970s brought about a remarkable revival. Best of all, prices have remained reasonable; to dine as well in Paris or along the Côte d'Azur would cost an arm and a leg.

Note that you could starve in August or on Sundays in Bordeaux, when the city's beaneries shut down as tight as a clam.

Luxury

Pavillon des Boulevards, 120 Rue Croix-de-Seguey, **t** 05 56 81 51 02. At the north end of town near the Parc Bordelais, in a sophisticated, tastefully designed house with a veranda in the back garden. Here chef Denis Franc presents delicate, sophisticated dishes based on the absolutely best and freshest ingredients; for a real splurge order the lobster *au Sauternes* (*menus from 220F, lunch only, upwards*). *Closed Sat lunch and Sun, and most of Aug.*

Le Chapon Fin, 5 Rue Montesquieu, **t** 05 56 79 10 10. The oldest restaurant in Bordeaux (since 1800) is still one of the best. During Bordeaux's periods as capital of France it was packed with *tout* Paris, and Sarah Bernhardt and Edward VII stopped by whenever they were in town. Its sumptuous rococo décor (which is unchanged since 1901) and inner garden are a perfect match for the likes of the *marbès de ris de veau et foie gras*, *marmite* of fish and crustaceans with *pistou* – Provençal pesto – or the now celebrated lobster gazpacho, prepared by Francis Garcia; long lists of *grands crus* (*lunch menu 170F, others up to 425F*). *Closed Sun and Mon.*

Les Plaisirs d'Ausone, 10 Rue Ausone, **t** 05 56 79 30 30. In the Quartier St-Pierre. Delicious *à la carte* menu: try the *fricassée de sole et de St-Jacques aux cèpes* (*menus from 170F*). *Closed Sun, Mon lunch and Sat lunch, part of Jan and half of Aug.*

Expensive

Jean Ramet, 7 Place Jean-Jaurès, **t** 05 56 44 12 51. One of Bordeaux's best and classiest restaurants, where chef Ramet prepares both old-fashioned food (braised veal knuckle) and original dishes (*gratin de figues*) to the delight of his fashionable customers (*menus 170–340F*). *Closed Sat lunch, Sun and mid-Aug.*

La Chamade, 20 Rue des Piliers de Tutelle, **t** 05 56 48 13 74. A large restaurant in a charming, warm-coloured 17th-century *hôtel* which exhibits paintings on the wall. Eat downstairs under the vaulted ceiling or on an open balcony. The emphasis is on using products in season and the menus change accordingly, but a bias remains towards the traditional and regional fare, hence foie gras is there all year in various guises. There is a large wine selection (*menus 100–350F, average total spend is 320F per person*). *Open all week, closed two weeks in summer and one in winter.*

Le Vieux Bordeaux, 27 Rue Buhan, **t** 05 56 52 94 36. Dine in their delightful closed court. Famous for the painstakingly high quality of every dish (*menus from 100F*). *Closed Sat lunch, Sun, national holidays and half of Feb and Aug.*

Didier Gelineau, 26 Rue du Pas St-Georges, **t** 05 56 52 84 25. A charming place offering haute cuisine at affordable prices: try the breaded lamb chops with truffles (*menus 130–300F*). *Closed Sat lunch and Sun, and two weeks in Aug.*

La Tupina, 6 Rue Porte-de-la-Monnaie, **t** 05 56 91 56 37. Near St-Michel, this is the bailiwick of Jean-Pierre Xiradakis, master of bringing out the true tastes of ingredients and one of the pioneers in the great Bordelais restaurant revival. A good place to fill up on hearty delights like *émincé de canard* with shallots (*lunch menu 100F, dinner up to 250F*).

Moderate

Dubern, 42–4 Allées de Tourny, **t** 05 56 79 07 70. It seems quite a simple brasserie when you walk in but the upstairs opens into a plush green room with a chandelier. The menus are quite simple, with a range of meat and fish and a good choice of salads. The establishment has just been taken over by the owner of Chez Philippe (*menus 100F and 200F*). *Closed Sun.*

L'Alhambra, 111 bis Rue Judaïque, **t** 05 56 96 06 91. For a delicious beef fillet with a creamy mustard sauce or poached pineapple with kirsch sorbet (*lunch menu 110F, others from 160F*). *Closed Sat lunch and Sun and late July–first half of Aug.*

Gravelier, 114 Cours Verdun, **t** 05 56 48 17 15. This place in the Chartrons offers very toothsome cuisine, especially seafood, prepared with an exotic touch: couscous with tuna and spices, or St-Pierre with ginger (*110F lunch menu, others from 135F*). *Closed Sat lunch and Sun and half of Aug.*

Chez Philippe, 1 Place du Parlement, **t** 05 56 81 83 15. Fish-lovers come to worship here; in season try the *pibale* (*see* p.61) (*menus 100F lunch, others 180F*). *Closed Sun, Mon and Aug.*

Croc-Loup, 35 Rue du Loup, **t** 05 56 44 21 19. A regular clientele come to enjoy imaginative dishes such as ravioli of cuttlefish with coriander, the house speciality bouillabaisse, and *filet de baliste*, a tropical fish raised near Arcachon (*menus 79–165F*). *Closed Sun, Mon, hols and Aug.*

Le Café Gourmand, 3 Rue Buffon, **t** 05 56 79 23 85. An elegant bistro with a turn- of-the-century feel, the walls covered in old family photos. Menus for midday and evening, both good, including *aiguillettes de canard aux pêches* and *moussaka d'agneau à la coriande fraîche*. The desserts are yummy as well, so leave space (*lunch menu from 90F, in the evening most meals are à la carte, or 140F for a selection of meat and fish dishes*). *Closed Sun.*

Le Bistro du Sommelier, 163 Rue Georges-Bonnac, **t** 05 56 96 71 78. Simple meals enhance its wide array of bottles (*menus 80–128F*). *Closed Sat lunch and Sun.*

Le Père Ouvrard, 12 Rue de Maréchal Joffre, **t** 05 56 44 11 58. Lovely imaginative food served in a laid-back atmosphere at kind prices (*menus from 57F*). *Closed Sat lunch, Sun and Aug.*

Restaurant de Fromages Baud et Millet, 19 Rue Huguerie, **t** 05 56 79 05 77. A paradise for anyone who loves cheese and wine, offering 950 wines from all around the world to go with its two hundred types of farm cheese and *raclettes* (*menus start at 110F*). *Closed Sun.*

Le Bistrot de la Port de la Lune, 59 Quai de Paludate, **t** 05 56 49 15 55. A haven for jazz lovers near the train station, it offers a simple but tasty menu to go with the music (*menus from 106F*) and swings until two in the morning.

Malabar, 7 Rue des Ayres, **t** 05 56 52 18 19. One of Bordeaux's better Indian restaurants, with a wide choices of vegetarian dishes (*menus start from 50F*). *Closed Sun, Tues and Aug.*

Cheap

Au Bonheur du Palais, 74 Rue Paul-Louis Lande, **t** 05 56 94 38 63. Excellent, very serious Chinese food, with plenty of seafood (*menus from 68F*). *Closed Sun and Aug.*

La Boite á Huîtres, 36 Cours du Chapeau Rouge, **t** 05 56 81 64 97. If you can't wait to reach the Bassin to slurp down oysters come here, where Eric Matton shares his passion for those shelled delights of the sea so beloved by the French. He only serves the best variety for the time of year, brought down from Brittany, Ile d'Oléron or raised in the local area. There are a few other dishes to choose from too (*menu mostly à la carte, about 50F for six*).

Le Rital, 3 Rue des Faussets, **t** 05 56 48 16 69. Delicious fresh pasta, made daily on location, and lovely fattening home-made desserts (*menus from 50F*). *Closed weekends and the first two weeks in Sept.*

La Casa Pino, 40 Rue Traversanne (St-Michel), **t** 05 56 92 82 88. Considered the best Portugese eatery in the city. *Morue* (dried cod) features, of course. Excellent value (*menu 50F, wine included*). Full of regulars. *Closed Sun and most of July.*

Around Bordeaux

Bouliac ✉ 33270

****Hauterive St-James**, 3 Place Camille-Hostein, **t** 05 57 97 06 00, **f** 05 56 20 92 58 (*expensive*). In Bouliac, to the southeast, 4km from the right bank of the Garonne, is an ultra-screwy post-modern hotel, reminiscent of a local tobacco-drying barn but made of steel intended to rust. It was designed by Jean Nouvel of Périgord (architect of the wonderful Institut du Monde Arabe in Paris) for Jean-Marie Amat, the hotel's owner, celebrated chef and local celebrity.

The sombre rooms, designed for people who never take their sunglasses off, come complete with embarrassing bathrooms by Philippe Starck and electric beds that take some practice to master, but you can escape them in the gym, sauna, Jacuzzi, squash courts or pool and look out over the Garonne, vineyards and Bordeaux.

The hotel's restaurant, in a fine 17th-century stone house, is another story altogether; here Jean-Marie Amat prepares the best meals in the entire Gironde, based on a wide variety of farm-raised poultry, wild mushrooms and fresh seafood, accompanied by a magnificent wine list (*menus at 255F and 400F*). *Closed Jan.*

Le Bistroy, 3 Place Camille Hostein, **t** 05 57 97 06 06. Amat, who doesn't at all mind going over the top, also runs this adjacent restaurant, where you can dine divinely well for less (*à la carte for under 200F*) in carefully cultivated 'destroy'-style surroundings meant to evoke the fall of the Berlin Wall and urban decay. *Closed Jan.*

Le Café de l'Espérance, 10 Rue de l'Esplanade, behind the church, **t** 05 56 20 52 16. Amat has also taken over the village café, where you can dine very well on more simple country cooking for even less (*about 150F*). A king in his realm. *Closed Sun and Mon.*

Pessac ✉ 33600

****La Réserve**, 74 Av de Bourgailh, **t** 05 57 26 58 28, **f** 05 57 25 58 00 (*inexpensive*). In Pessac, 6km southwest, this is the only hotel in the greater Bordeaux area in a park with a lake and swans, along with tennis courts, Jacuzzi and a good restaurant to go with the comfortable rooms (*from 350F*).

Le Cohé, 8 Av Roger-Cohé, **t** 05 56 45 73 72. Specializing in pleasing, old-fashioned French cuisine, with all the frills (*menus 115–350F*). *Closed Sun eve, Mon and Aug.*

Gradignan ✉ 33170

*****Le Chalet Lyrique**, 169 Cours Général de Gaulle, **t** 05 56 89 11 59, **f** 05 56 89 53 37 (*moderate*). An exceptionally comfortable hotel overlooking a terrace more Mediterranean than Bordelais; good restaurant (*à la carte only, around 150–200F*). *Closed Sun and Aug.*

Carbon Blanc ✉ 33560

Marc Demund, 5 Av de la Gardette, **t** 05 56 74 72 28. Dishes based on traditional, bourgeois recipes from the past that perfectly match the old country mansion in a park setting; the menu changes every six months (*menus 145–360F*). *Closed Sat lunch, Sun night and Mon.*

Entertainment and Nightlife

Theatre, Opera and Music

The tourist office has a **calendar** of concerts, opera and ballet in Bordeaux.The premier stage remains Victor Louis' **Grand Théâtre**, Place de la Comédie, for tickets ring **t** 05 56 48 58 54 (*open 11–6, closed Sun and holidays*), followed by the **Théâtre Femina**, 8 Rue de Grassi, box office **t** 05 56 79 06 69. The **Orchestre National Bordeaux Aquitaine** also frequently performs in the Palais des Sports, Place de la Ferme Richemont, **t** 05 56 79 39 61.

The ultra-modern **Espace Culturel du Pin Galant**, out at Mérignac due west of Bordeaux (off Av de la Libération and Av de l'Yser), **t** 05 56 97 82 82, puts on a full calendar of opera, musicals, concerts, jazz, dance, and theatre from around the world, from the dancing monks of Tibet to Offenbach operettas.

For live music of most kinds (rock, reggae, garage, etc.), look at the list of upcoming events at **Le Jimmy**, the best-known stage in Bordeaux, 68 Rue de Madrid, **t** 05 56 98 20 83.

Film

Of Bordeaux's cinemas, the **Trianon Jean Vigo**, Rue Franklin, **t** 05 56 44 35 17, is the most likely to show something good, in the original launguage; also try **UGC**, 20 Rue Judaïque, **t** 05 56 44 02 60.

Clubs and Bars

Bordeaux doesn't have as much nightlife as Toulouse, but there are a few places to check out for a drink or a dance before hitting the sack. For information on what's on get a copy of the bi-monthly *Clubs-et-Concerts* available at newsagents and venues. University students hang out in the bars around Place de la Victoire, especially on Thursdays, when the square fills up with thousands of young people, especially **La Plana** or **El Bodegon**, with rock music turned up to the hilt and videos (*open daily until 2am*).

To top off a late night in Bordeaux, finish up at the Marché des Capuchins near St-Michel for a bowl of onion soup with the workers unloading the produce. Bars here are *open 1–5am*; you could do worse than try **Le P'tit Déj**, 8 Place des Capucins.

Bodega Bodega, 4 Rue des Piliers-de-Tutelle (just off Rue Ste-Catherine), **t** 05 56 01 24 24, offers central tapas and Spanish wine available by the pitcher (*open 11am–2am, closed Sun am*).

Le Bœuf sur le Toit, 15 Rue de Candale, **t** 05 56 91 41 14 (*open daily 7pm to 2am*). Serves a selection of beers and other drinks in a tropical island setting, with occasional free rock concerts.

La Calle Ocho, 24 Rue des Piliers de Tutelles, **t** 05 56 48 08 68 (*open Mon–Sat 7pm–2am*). In St-Pierre you can salsa and mambo to the rhythm of Cuban sounds; the crowd is lively and the place is packed.

La Comtesse, 25 Rue du Parlement-St-Pierre (*open 5.30–2am, closed Sun*). A more sedate place, for a quiet drink.

Dick Turpin's, 72 Rue du Loup, **t** 05 56 48 07 52. A traditional English pub serving British pub food all day.

The **Connemara**, 18 Cours d'Albret, **t** 05 56 52 82 57. A good Irish bar with music, pub games and a restaurant.

Caesar's, Quai Louis XVIII, **t** 05 56 51 99 41. In several places, Bordeaux's former port buildings have been converted into discotheques. This is the most grandiose – a complex including a cabaret revue and top-of-the-pops disco in an imperial Roman atmosphere (*daily 10pm–4.30am*) but currently being renovated so things might change.

Le Nautilus, 122 Quai de Bacalan, **t** 05 57 93 13 20. Plays house and techno, with occasional special evenings (*open Thurs–Sat 11.30pm–5am*).

Le Black Night, 6 Rue Jean Dupas, **t** 05 56 86 34 50. Zouk and salsa to African-Caribbean music (*women in free Fri and Sat before 1am*).

La Macumba, Route du Cap Ferret, **t** 05 56 34 05 48. Out in Mérignac: four rooms with a variety of pop music, and dancing in the garden in the summer (*open Wed–Sun 10.30pm–5am*).

...Bordeaux, squatting in the depths of the Gironde, could be London, Carthage, Rotterdam or New York, could have been Occitan but is only Bordeaux, capital on paper, capital of provincial paper, former satellite of London, and today of Paris... a port that only discovered America at the moment of the slave trade.

Yves Rouquette, *Occitanie*

It's true that Bordeaux, that warm, magic, generous name on the bottle, evokes more than it delivers in the urban flesh. It is a mercantile city that has lost its port; it is both terribly grand and terribly shabby and monotonous, a hallucinatory city of long flat vistas tinted in a thousand nuances of white, from golden cream to unwashed tennis socks. Nearly all its monuments, its squares, its uniform quayside Grand Façade and its proto-Haussmannian boulevards – the very features that made it, 'undeniably, the most beautiful city in France' according to Stendhal – were rammed down Bordeaux's throat by its royal governors. The Bordelais screamed about every one – because they had to pay for them, a terrible imposition even though at the time money was rolling in, thanks to the slave trade. These days, at least, the architecture helps the city earn a few francs as a film set; Bordeaux has played the part of Paris, London, Seville and even Boston in costume dramas.

Bordeaux offers a meaty comparison to Toulouse, the other metropolis of south-west France. Toulouse is confident, rosy and resolutely southern, medieval brick and modern glass, and rather in love with its river ront and canals; Bordeaux is Gothic and 18th-century, splenetic, nostalgic and funky, a stone necropolis that has always looked to the north for tutelage while it made a living from its port. Today the city seems uncertain, divorced from the wide Garonne by a furious funnel of traffic. Like Toulouse, it owes its aeronautics industries to the largesse of Paris; Bordeaux's portion, however, is dominated by the military, and cranks out ballistic missiles instead of glamorous Airbus jets.

In 1857 a Bordelais named Paul-Ernest de Ratier published a pamphlet called *Preuve évidente que Bordeaux n'existe pas*. It is a 'whited sepulchre', a phantom city of phantom beings. 'It has created nothing, it receives everything. It thinks nothing, it hears all, but never listens. It has nothing, it seems to have everything. It is a magnificent scaffold of appearances, of faux-semblants, of colours, of pretexts, of reflections, of illusions.' In response to Ratier's jibes, Bordeaux has in fact finally created something of its very own – GERTRUDE, an acronym for a system that electronically times stop lights to facilitate the flow of traffic. The idea was to save energy; the mentality is very American, to see the heart of a city as an obstacle to pass through as quickly as possible. Or is it because, as Gertrude Stein once said of Oakland, 'there's no there there'?

History

The ancient Greek geographer Strabo was the first to mention the Gironde estuary: in the 3rd century BC, he wrote that a Celtic tribe from Bourges called the Bituriges Vibisci was 'the only foreign people to settle among the Aquitains'. They paid the Aquitains no tribute and occupied the site on the estuary as an emporium. *Bituriges,* after all, translates as the 'kings of the world', a big bold title for a band of tin-traders; their crescent-shaped city, Burdigala, founded at the confluence of the Garonne, the Dévèze and the Peugue, was the 'Port of the Moon' – reflecting not only its crescent shape but also the lunar influence over the tidal changes of the Gironde estuary, 'with its river filled with the boiling tide of the ocean', as Ausone, Bordeaux's famous Gallo-Roman poet, described it. Besides tin, Burdigala helped initiate the barley-beer-swilling Gauls into the joys of wine – imported from southern Italy and the Mediterranean colonies of Greece and Rome by way of Toulouse.

Burdigala knew which side its bread was buttered on, and posed no objection to being captured in 56 BC by Crassus. Quickly Latinized, the Bituriges soon tidied up their helter-skelter trading centre to conform to the basic Roman town grid, with a north–south *cardo* (Rue Ste-Catherine) and east–west *decumanus* (Cours de l'Intendance). To slake the new Gaulish thirst for wine, the traders of Burdigala attempted to grow their own vines, but it took until the year 20 AD to discover the right variety of grape suited to the humid climate (*see* p.204).

Although Vespasian acknowledged Bordeaux's increasing prestige by making it the capital of Aquitaine in place of Saintes (Civitas Santonum), the city had hardly begun to make a name for itself when it was severely mutilated in the barbarian invasion of 276 and retreated into a more defensible *castrum*. Much of the reconstruction was by Christians, devoted to the cult of St Seurin (Severinus), bishop of Bordeaux (d. 420), whose name is confusingly similar to Toulouse's St Sernin, , and whose tomb became the focal point of one of the most desirable burial grounds in the early Middle Ages.

Medieval Bordeaux

In the 7th century the Merovingian king Dagobert made Bordeaux capital of the duchy of Aquitaine. The son of one of his dukes, Huon de Bordeaux, shares a *chanson de geste* with Charlemagne and the 'Elf Oberon'; Huon was followed by a string of 10 Duke Guillaumes (as in Toulouse, there was a wretched lack of originality in given names), who ruled an Aquitaine that stretched from Poitiers to the Pyrenees. The most famous was Guillaume IX (*d.* 1126), the first known troubadour, and one of the bawdiest, as well as grandfather of the great Eleanor, who ended the streak by being the only child of Guillaume X. Eleanor inherited the duchy and gave Bordeaux first to France when she wed Louis VII (1137), then to Anjou and England when she divorced the pious and dour Louis to marry the far more amusing Henry Plantagenet.

Bordeaux blossomed under the English and grew so much that the walls had to be rebuilt twice; for the Bordelais, English rule meant paying fewer taxes and an eager, guaranteed market for their wine. Their beloved duchess Eleanor granted the wine-growers special privileges, privileges that were confirmed by her son John Lackland in 1206, after Bordeaux was besieged by his brother-in-law, the king of Castille. The siege revealed John's inability to defend the city; to keep it loyal he also granted it considerable municipal power – a mayor and councillors, the *jurats*, and in 1214 he went even further with letters of patent that gave the bourgeoisie of Bordeaux the right to sell their wine and other goods duty-free. Under Henry III, Bordeaux's Château de l'Ombrière became the seat of the Seneschal of Aquitaine. Another plus in Bordeaux's eye was the powerful English fleet, able to protect the city's vital sea trade; among the many things brought back by the English crusaders were the maritime laws of ancient Rhodes, which they re-established in Bordeaux.

Medieval Bordeaux was a tough town that produced some tough hombres. One was the archbishop of Bordeaux, Bertrand de Got, who was elected Pope Clement V in 1305 after an 11-month conclave. Clement V stirred the pot like few popes before or since. He earned himself the everlasting hatred of Rome by moving the papacy to Avignon, then colluded with King Philippe IV le Bel to put an end to the powerful and extremely wealthy order of the Knights Templars (Philippe was broke and wanted their possessions, and Clement gave him the moral justification for annihilating the Templars by declaring them heretics). Like any medieval pope, he also diverted as many papal favours as possible to his relatives. He loaded the Curia with 11 Gascon cardinals, who if nothing else kept right on electing popes from southwest France. However, to pay for his extravagances, Clement soaked Bordeaux so badly with tithes and taxes that he had to avoid it when he travelled in Aquitaine.

Philippe IV's grandson, Edward III, opened the Pandora's box that became known as the Hundred Years' War by claiming the French throne. After English victories in Crécy and Calais, Edward III's eldest son, Edward of Woodstock (known as the Black Prince for his fashionable black armour) won the first round of the war at Poitiers (1356), capturing the French King Jean II and his greatest captain, Bertrand du Guesclin, as well as a bouquet of the 'flowers of French chivalry'. In 1360, Jean signed the treaty of Calais, giving Edward III, in exchange for his claims on France, a sure title to the independent duchy of Aquitaine, which then extended from Poitou to the Bigorre. The Black Prince became duke and made Bordeaux his capital, where he minted his own leopard coins. For the French, however, the prince in black armour was definitely the bad guy: not satisfied with the frontiers of Aquitaine, he campaigned to recapture the rest of the 'old duchy of the Plantagenets'. But cash, or rather the lack of it, dealt a death blow to his ambitions; in spite of his string of victories, the financing he needed to continue his campaigns was withheld by the *jurats* and aristocrats of Aquitaine – especially the Armagnacs and the Albrets who, rather than pay the Black Prince's high taxes, turned to France and Charles V. With their encouragement, King Charles began another round of the Hundred Years' War in 1369; the Black Prince, disillusioned, ill and exhausted, died in 1376.

The French finally took Bordeaux in June 1451, an event known in the city annals as the *Male Jornade*, the Rotten Day – 10,000 Bordelais were massacred in the marshlands near the present Pont d'Aquitaine before the city's archbishop Pey Berland was able to negotiate an honourable surrender. The final French conquest in 1453 was so unpopular that the Bordelais rebelled off and on until the end of the 17th century, never forgetting the massacre, or their old rights and trading privileges, and their say in the taxes imposed on them. The French monarchy, rather than try to console the Bordelais, built three fortresses to police them: the enormous Château Trompette (now Place des Quinconces), the Fort du Hâ and Fort Louis. All have long since vanished. The machinery of French power over Bordeaux included a *parlement* of royal appointees and an *intendant*, or governor, also appointed by the king.

Thanks to its position near the Gironde estuary, Bordeaux controlled the export of wines from the *haut pays* (Bergerac, Cahors, Gaillac, etc.), many of which were greatly preferred back in those days when all wines were drunk young. As a sop to Bordeaux (about the only one, too), a law was passed in Paris in the 16th century to block the sale of wine from the hinterlands – none could be shipped down to the sea until all the wine from Bordeaux was sold. Frustrated English drinkers turned to port and sherry. A happier event was the big welcome that Bordeaux gave in 1540 to the hundreds of Jews chased out of Portugal by the Inquisition; by 1753 Bordeaux had seven synagogues.

Bordeaux Booms Again: the Slave Trade and Urban Renewal

At the start of the 18th century, Bordeaux made a living much as it had since the Middle Ages, exporting its claret to the north and supplying passing ships. After Louis XIV's death, new markets opened up in the New World, especially the Caribbean, and merchants from Britain, Germany, the Netherlands, Portugal and elsewhere were on hand to help the Bordelais make fortunes in the triangular trade: glass, fabrics, weapons and gimcracks from Bordeaux were shipped to slave counters in west Africa in exchange for human cargo (one ship, with a nice touch of irony, was named the *Contrat Social*). The slaves were sold in America and the Caribbean for cotton, tobacco, indigo and, most importantly, sugar. Sugar was so fashionable in 18th-century Europe that, imported raw, refined in Bordeaux and re-exported, it brought the city as much money as its wine. The local glass industry took off when it was discovered that wine in bottles survived the journey to America better. By the end of the century, Bordeaux was the first port of France.

To create a city equal to its sweet, intoxicating ambition, Bordeaux's *intendants* started demolishing its poky medieval streets to give the city light and air – in the face of fierce local opposition. Begun by Intendant Boucher, who laid out the Place Royale (now Place de la Bourse), the destruction and re-creation of central Bordeaux was enthusiastically continued under his successor, Louis Urbain Aubert, the Marquis de Tourny. 'Bordeaux being one of the cities in the kingdom where one meets the most foreigners, it is fitting to try to give them a favourable opinion of France...I will make you the most beautiful city in the realm, if you will only have confidence in what I shall propose and help me in the execution.' Tourny laid out wide *cours* or *allées* planted with trees linking his new squares and the first public gardens; to adorn them, 5,000 new buildings went up, including the riverfront Grand Façade.

By the beginning of the Revolution, Bordeaux was the third largest city in France, and one of the most cosmopolitan, with a population of over 100,000. Its close trading contacts with the new United States and the influence of Montesquieu and the Philosophes combined to make the local Girondin party a moderate force at the Convention in Paris. They clashed with the Jacobin fanatics – mainly from the North – who believed in a centralized dictatorship; in 1793, suspected of fomenting a federalist insurrection, 20 Girodin leaders were arrested by Robespierre and died on the guillotine after an all-night fling in the Conciergerie. In Bordeaux the only surviving signs of the Revolution are the quaint, enthusiastic street names engraved into the buildings (Rue de l'Amour d'Egalité, Rue du Peuple Souverain).

Bordeaux in the 19th and 20th Centuries

During and immediately after the Napoleonic wars, Bordeaux hit one of its lowest ebbs: the continental blockade destroyed the city's commerce, the slave trade was abolished in 1815 and the competition of sugar beets undercut the product from its sugar refineries. Ships from the North and Baltic Seas began to sail across the Atlantic without stopping to be provisioned in Bordeaux. The grand urban plans of the *intendants* ground to a halt. It was only with Louis XVIII (and the demolition of the hated Château Trompette, symbol of Paris' tyranny) that Bordeaux began to get on its feet again and build its first ever bridge over the Garonne (1822). Although it had one of the first railways in France (1841) and modernized its quays, little new industry came its way. Inexorably port traffic moved to the north.

In spite of an economy just puttering along and the catastrophic phylloxera that wiped out the vines in 1878, Bordeaux began to spread out; these days the 220,000 Bordelais have the dubious honour of taking up more room per capita than other city dwellers in France, many living in single-storey terrace houses (*échoppes*). With the installation of tramlines in the 1900s the suburbs (now pop. 450,000) fanned out, a situation compared by one Bordelais writer to the universe of Pascal, where 'the centre is everywhere and the circumference nowhere'. Even the vineyards that provided Bordeaux's fermented lifeblood for centuries fell victim – today you'll find some of the most august wine châteaux of France totally immersed in sprawl.

Meanwhile the heart of Bordeaux, so proudly and grandly moulded to fit the French idea of a capital, actually served as one three times, all in circumstances France would rather forget: in 1870, 1914 and 1940. Bordeaux remembers 1914 most fondly, when it hosted *tout Paris* and became one of the chief debarkation points for the American army, while June 1940 leaves the bitter memory of First World War hero Philippe Pétain negotiating the armistice with Hitler, announcing to France over the radio from Bordeaux '*Je fais don de ma personne à la France*' before moving the government to Vichy, because the Germans wanted the Atlantic coast for themselves. The four years and two months under the Occupation left deep scars that were covered up, in Bordeaux as elsewhere, in the name of national unity; there were just too many skeletons, especially in the closets of France's governing *class politique*.

The post-war years were dominated by Jacques Chaban-Delmas, a 31-year-old Resistance general when De Gaulle sent him to sort out Bordeaux in 1946. That year he became a deputy, the next year, mayor; from 1969 to 1972 he served as Pompidou's prime minister and played a role in national politics. Pragmatic, dynamic, foxy and a brilliant manipulator of his own image, Chaban was an updated *intendant*, radically changing the face of Bordeaux with the urban-renewal project of Mériadeck (a flop) and the more successful Quartier du Lac, a congress and leisure complex north of the centre. The best of the old was preserved by the 1966 **Loi Malraux**, which safeguarded 370 acres of 18th-century Bordeaux (especially the Quartier St-Pierre).

Bordeaux found itself in the national news, as official France took its first halting steps to come to terms with its role in the war. The death in 1996 of former President François Mitterrand, whose somewhat shadowy past included service in the Vichy government before he joined the Resistance, has released at least some *mea culpas*, half a century after the fact, notably from President Jacques Chirac. The whole issue – whether or not ever to admit to mistakes – has exacerbated the tension between the democratic right to know what's going on in its elected government (*'la transparence'*) and France's deeply ingrained system of elevating its best and brightest to create a *class politique* that rather smugly knows what's best for the country, even if it occasionally has to resort to the moral low ground to attain its ends. Bordeaux's mayor since 1995, former Prime Minister Alain Juppé, is the intelligent, arrogant, classic product of the *class politique* system; his intense unpopularity on a national level derived not only from the country's record unemployment and economic doldrums, but his inability to grasp the concerns of the typical French citizen.

Bordeaux was the scene of the last trial of a man accused of crimes against humanity in the Second World War. One could well imagine that Mitterrand and the whole of the *class politique* had wished that Maurice Papon would just die and go away ever since his embarrassing past was exposed to the general public in 1983, when two journalists came across his files, but he held on for *14 years* awaiting his day in court (you might recall that France's second last war criminal, René Bosquet, was mysteriously assassinated just before he was about to go on trial). Papon served as general secretary of the prefecture of the Gironde in 1942–4, where the records say he signed for the deportation of 1,500 Jews, in his own words 'only as part of the job'. He wasn't the only one. What is just as dispiriting is Papon's subsequent career as a member of the old boy's club that runs France: in 1945, Paris appointed him *préfet* of the Landes, the department just to the south of the Gironde, although at the same time there were enough members of the Resistance in the area to block the appointment. From 1958 to 1967, however, Papon served as police prefect in Paris, and in 1979 he became Minister of the Budget under Giscard d'Estaing. Some kind of justice was served in the tribunal in Bordeaux in April 1998, when Papon, aged 87, frail and in ill health, was found guilty, as much as it upset certain members of the *class politique*, who saw it as an unneccessary reopening of the wounds best left forgotten.

For all that, it most be said that Bordeaux has seemed a merrier place of late. In 1998, it hosted several World Cup matches, and held its first wine festival ever, **Bordeaux Fête de Vin**, now to be held every two years in June/July. An energetic committee, Renaissance du Vieux Bordeaux, has rehabilitated the old port buildings and warehouses into a new cultural centre, and plans have finally been agreed for the reconstruction of the quaysides; the left bank is in the throes of a seven-year project, under the direction of landscaper Michel Corajoud and his team, to knock down the old warehouses and create a lively waterfront accommodating several means of transport, including trams, where Bordeaux's residents can relax and walk in pleasant surroundings. The industrial right bank should also see some of the action: plans include homes and office buildings to be built around a large public garden. The equally energetic tourist bureau has come up with a host of promotional schemes that bring the city more visitors every year. Meanwhile, Mayor Juppé keeps a discreet low profile, like all French politicians awaiting Fortune's wheel to swing round and give him another chance.

The City

Ste-Croix and St-Michel

From the railway station, spare yourself the anomie of the long, straight, endless Cours de la Marne by proceeding up Rue de Tauzia. The first monuments that beckon in this busy medieval but now genteelly dilapidated neighbourhood are in the vicinity of the former monastery church of **Ste-Croix**. Built in the 12th century, this once had a remarkably exuberant Old Curiosity Shop of a façade that was sadly entrusted in 1860 to Paul Abadie (*see* p.92) who, full of the destructive self-confidence of his time, completely dismantled it and put it back together all wrong. The south tower, portal, figures of Avarice and Luxury, and some carved capitals in the transept survived the Abadie touch; the relics in the parish chapel were reputed in the Middle Ages to cure madness. Note the unusual 15th-century crucifix with a 'bald Christ'. An abbey building of 1672 now houses the school of fine arts, while the new monster along the Quai Ste-Croix proves that Abadie had no patent on dubious taste; this 1980s bunker housing the national conservatory is called the **Centre André Malraux**, a backhanded compliment to the Minister of Culture who passed the national preservation law.

In nearby Place Pierre-Renaudel, an 18th-century sugar refinery has been converted into the **Théâtre du Port de la Lune**. Nearby you can learn about printing and publishing before the advent of computers at the **Maison des Métiers de l'Imprimerie** (*8–10 Rue du Fort Louis, **t** 05 56 92 61 17; open Mon–Wed 2–6 and Sat 9–1; adm*).

Since the time of Charlemagne a church has stood at the site of **St-Michel**, in what is now a lively Portuguese–North African neighbourhood. Its denizens hold a morning flea market under the detached hexagonal bell tower, the 'arrow' or **Flêche** as the Bordelais call it, built 1472–92 and shooting up 377ft, the highest monument in south-west France. It was financed in part by Louis XI, a devotee of the archangel Michael, and over-restored in the 19th century by Abadie. There's a once-celebrated crypt beneath the tower (*guided tours June–Sept daily 3–7*), where Victor Hugo and other 19th-century tourists came to gape at the naturally mummified bodies.

Grimy, Flamboyant Gothic St-Michel was a product of Bordeaux's medieval prosperity, largely built by the city's guilds. It is missing one of its most remarkable features – the original stained glass, blasted away by Allied bombers in the last war. Inside (*open 9–6*), the chapels furnished by the guilds contain the best art: the Chapelle Ste-Ursula in the right aisle has a rare 15th-century sculpture of *St Ursula and the 11,000 Virgins* (she also shelters a pope, emperor and several prelates under her cloak); in the left aisle, note the Chapelle de St-Sépulchre with a beautiful *Descent from the Cross* carved in 1492; the Chapelle Notre-Dame has a Flemish painting of the *Annunciation* (1500); and the Chapelle St-Joseph has nine alabaster Renaissance bas-reliefs on the altarpiece. In 1994 these were rather embarrassingly discovered for sale at an auction in New York; 10 years earlier thieves had made off with them, leaving in their place some run-of-the-mill plaster copies that completely fooled everyone.

From behind St-Michel, Rue de la Fusterie (once lined with coopers' shops) leads to the **Porte des Salinières**, the 'salt' gate built in 1755 by Jacques-Ange Gabriel, although money ran out before it could be festooned with statuary. This overlooks the **Pont de Pierre**, the oldest of Bordeaux's three bridges, built in 1842 and prettily lit at night by a necklace of street lamps. From here continue up busy Cours Victor-Hugo.

The corner at Rue St-James is often mobbed with bargain-hunters at a branch of Paris's famous Tati department store. It's been bustling since the Middle Ages – this was the road to Compostela, and the gate that defended it is known as the **Grande Cloche**, 'Big Bell'. Built next to and dwarfing the odd little church of **St-Eloi**, this gate was part of the second wall built by the English in the 14th century; it figures on the city's coat of arms. Each year its great bell would ring out at the start of the *vendange*. Across Cours Victor-Hugo, the continuation of Rue St-James had, until 1840, a well, where a serpent dwelt that was so horrifying that a mere glance at it meant certain death. One day a soldier, covering his own face and taking a mirror, went down a rope into the well and made the serpent look at itself. It keeled over, the local water problem was solved and the street had a new name, Mirror Street, or Rue du Mirail.

Musée d'Aquitaine

20 Cours Pasteur, ***t*** *05 56 01 51 00; open Tues–Sun and hols 11–6; adm, free 1st Sun of each month.*

Although from the outside it looks like a hard slog, don't be deterred: this is one of the most compelling and beautifully arranged museums in southwest France. Its subject is the history of Aquitaine, and one of its first works is the unique, utterly mysterious 25,000-year-old bas-relief of the *Venus with a Horn* from Laussel in the Dordogne. The horn she holds curves like the moon, her hair is coiffed in 'corn rows' and her outline, even after all the millennia, still bears traces of red ochre, used in Upper Palaeolithic tombs and sacred sites. She keeps company with two other Venuses from Laussel: one an even fatter, saggy-breasted fertility figure with prominent hands, the other a slender dancing form. Another evocative, if less clearly defined relief has two figures holding hands, one above the other, their arms forming the shape of an egg. Among the Neolithic artefacts is a treasure horde – of flint slices – and burials from the Grotte aux 80 Morts at Coux-et-Bigoroque, with a double-trepanned skull. There are pots, swords and jewels from the Metal Ages, a curious face carved on a wooden post from Larrau in the Pyrénées-Atlantiques, and the golden Celtic treasure of coins and a torque from Tayac.

The excellent Gallo-Roman section has another treasure of coins, 4,000 from the time of Claudius found in the Garonne, as well as mosaics, sculptures (note the fragment of a highly stylized relief of horses pounding through water) and a fascinating set of reliefs from everyday life in ancient Burdigala. Ironically, it's the funerary steles that really bring the dead to life: thin-faced Tatiana gazing at eternity with a wry look and wrinkled brow, and the delightful child Laetus, clutching a kitten the way toddlers do, while a rooster at his feet nips at the kitten's dangling tail.

Further on is a legless but still impressive life-size bronze Hercules, and a room dedicated to finds from a mithraeum discovered in 1982 during the construction of a car park in Cours Victor-Hugo. In the 2nd and 3rd century, Mithraism, an all-male, monotheistic religion from the East, posed serious competition to Christianity. A small statue shows the birth of Mithras, rising from earth with the cosmic globe in one hand and a knife to slay bulls in the other; there are statues of Cautes and Cautopatès, his two companions, in Persian costumes, and a rare *Leontocéphale*, a lion-headed man holding keys, his legs entwined with chicken-headed snakes.

Beyond the Early Christian sarcophagi and mosaics are a few strange 11th-century capitals from the Abbaye de La Sauve Majeur, and from La Brède, along with English alabasters, which the Bordelais traded for wine. Montaigne's cenotaph with its Greek inscription stands among the section devoted to French rule. Upstairs are rooms devoted to Aquitaine's last 300 years: its agriculture, industries, port and wine, with the copy of a letter from Thomas Jefferson to the count of Lur-Saluces praising his Sauternes – and a letter from Ronald Reagan to the count's descendant, thanking him for hosting a banquet celebrating the bicentennial of the Battle of Yorktown. There are also ethnographic collections from Africa and Oceania, and the museum has temporary exhibitions on a wide range of subjects linked to world history. The **Musée Goupil**, with photos and engravings from the archives (1827–1920) of the Parisian printer and editor Goupil, occupies one wing of the building.

South of the museum, Cours Pasteur leads down to Place de la Victoire, where the gate, the **Porte d'Aquitaine** (1753), guarded by a pair of sea gods, closes the south end of busy, pedestrian-only **Rue Ste-Catherine**, Bordeaux's main shopping street since Roman times. Fans of Art Deco in its morose, idiosyncratic French version might like to stroll briefly from Place de la Victoire up Cours Aristide-Briand to see the **Bourse du Travail** (1934–8), commissioned by Bordeaux's Socialist mayor Marquet, and decorated with reliefs on the outside and frescoes inside.

Cathédrale St-André

Bordeaux's Gothic cathedral is the fourth church erected on this site since the 6th century, the successor of the church where Eleanor of Aquitaine married Louis VII in 1137. What you see today was built under English rule between the 13th and 15th centuries; in 1440, as the ground was marshy and the architects were reluctant to add more weight to the church, it was given a detached tower, named the **Tour Pey-Berland** after the archbishop who built it. The tower was used as a lead ball factory from 1793 until 1850, when it was repurchased by the archbishop, truncated and crowned with a shiny Notre-Dame-de-Aquitaine. Climb it for a superb view (*open Tues–Sun June–Sept 10–6.30, Oct–May 10–12.30 and 2–5.30, closed hols; adm*).

The cathedral (*open 8–11.30 and 2–6.30*) is built in the form of a Latin cross and supported by an intricate web of buttresses. A fine 14th-century tympanum crowns the north transept door, carved with the *Last Supper*, *Ascension of Christ* and *Triumph of the Redeemer*. The nearby Porte Royale (used by visiting kings and dignitaries) has another, decorated with a throng of saints and a serene 13th-century *Last Judgment*, in which the lids of the open tombs on the lintel add a nice rhythmic touch. The west front, which originally formed part of the city wall, is strikingly bare. The south portal, dedicated to the Virgin, lost its tympanum to make room for carts when the church was converted into a feed store during the Revolution, but carvings of the Wise and Foolish Virgins, angels and apostles have survived; these doors are usually left wide open, as in the Middle Ages, admitting both worshippers and pedestrians making a short cut. The single nave is nearly as long and wide as Notre-Dame in Paris, 410 by 145ft, and was the only place large enough to hold the tremendous pageant on 6 April 1364 when 1,447 nobles came to pay homage to the Black Prince, 'the most magnificent lord of his time'. The wrought-iron grille in the choir is 18th-century, and there are fine statues in the seven chapels radiating from the ambulatory, especially the 16th-century alabaster *Notre Dame de la Nef*. There are regular organ recitals.

Just north of the cathedral, Mayor Chaban-Delmas created the **Centre National Jean Moulin** in 1967 (***t** 05 56 79 66 00; open Tues–Fri 11–6, weekends 2–6*), a collection devoted to the Occupation, Resistance and Deportation, from posters (one with a mother telling her daughter 'Hard Times are Over. Papa's Gone to Work in Germany!') to an ingenious folding motocycle (part of a parachute drop to the Resistance). Upstairs, the office of the Resistance leader Jean Moulin has been reconstructed, containing a collection of his drawings – his cover was running an art gallery in Nice.

Musée des Beaux-Arts

***t** 05 56 10 20 56; open daily 11–6 exc Tues and hols; adm; free 1st Sun of each month. Ring ahead for the 40F guided tour in English.*

There's talk of moving it across the river some day but, when you read this, Bordeaux's cache of paintings will still be in two wings of the large and luxurious **Palais Rohan** at 20 Cours d'Albret, built in the 1770s by the Prince Archbishop Mériadeck de Rohan to replace an insufficiently princely medieval archbishop's palace. To make space for this ecclesiastical bachelor's pad, Rohan got permission from the king to knock over several acres of medieval Bordeaux, and to finance the building by selling off the archbishopric's properties. He kept a close eye on the construction, ensuring the most fastidious fittings, but before he got a chance to move in he was appointed Archbishop of Cambrai. Since 1835, most of the palace has been Bordeaux's town hall (*guided tours Wed 2.30*).

The rest of the spread contains the **Musée des Beaux-Arts**. It has paintings by artists rarely seen in French provincial museums – works by Titian (*Lucretia and Tarquin*); a serene Perugino (*Virgin and Child, with SS. Jerome and Augustin*), in need of a cleaning; a portrait of a senator by Livinia Fontana (1552–1602), a rare female painter from Bologna; a chubby *Magdalen* and equally chubby *Marie dei Medici* by Van Dyck; Rubens' *Martyrdom of St George*; and the jolly *Fête de la Roserie* by Jan Brueghel le Velours. Amid a room of 17th-century, rosy-cheeked portraits and mythologies are a pair of paintings of the cruel world of galley slaves (*Arrivée des Galériens dans la Prison de Gênes* and *Débarquement des Galériens dans la Port de Gênes*) by the

Genoese Alessandro Magnasco (1667–1749), that singularly uncanny 'painter of phantasmagorias' completely out of synch with his time, both in his choice of subject matter (you wonder who would have commissioned these disturbing scenes) and in his technique of quick, nervous, impromptu brush strokes that lend his works their strange light, and his often tormented figures their peculiar phantom-like unreality.

Later paintings from the 18th century include the portrait of *Baron Rockeby* by Reynolds, Dutch landscapes by Ruysdael and co. (favourites of Bordeaux's *nouveau riche* merchants), and a *Nature Morte* by the inimitable Chardin. The next room has representatives of all the grand -isms of the 19th century, from the neoclassical (*L'Embarquement de la Duchesse d'Angoulême* by Gross) and antiquating neoclassical (Guérin's *Hippolytus and Phaedre*, the funniest painting in the collection: the protagonists have identical features and Phaedra looks as if she's just sucked a lemon) to the highly charged Romanticism of Delacroix (*Grèce sur les Ruines de Missolonghi*) and Isabey (*Incendie du Steamer* Austria). There are several glossy snicker-nudge-nudge nudes that first became popular in the decorously porno Second Empire, including Henri Gervex's notorious *Rolla*, inspired by a poem by Alfred de Musset and the source of a tremendous scandal at the 1878 salon (the fact that the naked girl on the bed was neither a goddess nor an allegory, and had left her mussed-up clothing piled to one side, was considered indecent according to the magnificently hypocritical taste of the time). There are paintings by proto-Impressionist Boudin, and Bordeaux native Odilon Redon (1840–1916), introspective precursor of the Surrealists.

Bordeaux produced two other influential artists, whose paintings are displayed in the last room: Albert Marquet (1875–1947), who was a fellow student of Matisse and co-founder of Fauvism before going on to paint his simple landscapes, and André Lhote (1885–1962), represented by his hallmark colourful, geometric compositions on various planes. A lesser-known Bordelais is Impressionist Alfred Smith, whose best works resemble early Monets. Here too is a selection of minor paintings by major 20th-century artists – Matisse, Bonnard, Renoir and Seurat. Temporary exhibitions, are held nearby in the **Galerie des Beaux-Arts** in Place du Colonel-Raynal.

Behind this, and on one of the *axes* so beloved of French urban planners (in this case, aligned with the Palais de Rohan), is the **Nouveau Quartier Mériadeck**, named after the aforementioned cardinal de Rohan (who went on to become an enthusiastic patron of Cagliostro, and play a major role as the big dupe in the Diamond Necklace Affair). Mériadeck was a fragrant slum before it was flattened in 1954 by Mayor Chaban-Delmas, clearing 30 hectares to create the largest single urban renovation scheme in France. Seven hectares were set aside for greenery and fountains, and the buildings facing this central mall were designed in cruciforms (as in the reflecting-glass Préfecture) by planner J. Willerval, to spare pedestrians the sight of Mériadeck's plain-jane skyscraper. As corporate bosses haven't been beating down the doors for office space here, most of Mériadeck is occupied by government bureaucracies, and it shrivels to a desert after dark. It did, however, earn an environmental gold star as the first major project in Europe to make large-scale use of geothermal heating (1981).

Around the corner from the Musée des Beaux-Arts, the excellent **Musée des Arts Décoratifs** (*39 Rue Bouffard*, **t** *05 56 00 72 50; open weekdays exc Tues and hols 11–6,* *weekends 2–6, free 1st Sun of each month; adm*) has a perfect home in a neoclassical *hôtel particulier*, built in 1779 by Bordelais architect Etienne Laclotte; furniture, wallpaper, pharmacy jars and fine ceramics (including some beautiful pieces from Delft), French tin-glazed ware (*faïence stannifière*), wrought iron, paintings, gold- and silverwork, glass and jewellery and costumes all evoke the good life in the 18th and 19th centuries. There are fine engravings of Bordeaux, back when its port and quays were bustling; there are also period documents, famous signatures, and more. In the summer you can eat breakfast, brunch and lunch in the elegant courtyard.

Rue Bouffard continues up to **Place Gambetta** (originally Place Dauphine), laid out with uniform façades by Tourny in 1743; its simple gateway, **Porte Dijeaux**, was added shortly after. During the terror in the autumn of 1793 a guillotine was installed that parted the heads from the rest of 300 Bordelais, including the Girondins who hid out in St-Emilion (*see* p.201); their last words here were muted by the beating drums. The chief of the revolutionaries in Bordeaux was the fiery redhead Tallein, former editor of the *Ami du Citoyen*. Tallein would have given many more Bordelais the chop had it not been for the gentle pleadings of his beloved, soft-hearted Spanish mistress, Teresa Cabarus. When Tallein was recalled to Paris and Teresa was imprisoned by Robespierre, he freed her – by toppling Robespierre himself on the 9th of Thermidor. Legend has it that Tallein's name was among those on a list that an acquaintance accidentally found while rifling through Robespierre's famous sea-green coat, looking for a piece of paper to answer to a bodily need. Tallein and the others on the list joined forces and acted first, so it was Robespierre's head that rolled instead of theirs.

St-Seurin

Northwest of Place Gambetta, **Place des Martyrs-de-la-Résistance** marks the site of a famous Gallo-Roman–Merovingian cemetery. Consecrated, according to legend, by Christ himself in the company of the first saints of Gaul, it was one of several

Ausonius

Near St-Seurin was the Pagus Novarus, city address of Decimus Magnus Ausonius (*c.* 310–94 AD), scion of one of Burdigala's most noble families. After his studies in Toulouse, Ausonius returned to Bordeaux as a professor of rhetoric, with such a reputation that he was appointed tutor of Gratian, son of Emperor Valentian; Emperor Gratian in turn appointed him prefect of Gaul (377). A familiar of St Ambrose of Milan and Emperor Theodosius, Ausonius managed to live blithely through the golden twilight of the Roman Empire, an empire overextended and attacked from all sides, but cosy enough for a patrician to retire in a choice of villas sprinkled across the Gironde, to hunt, fish, grow grapes for wine and write elaborate, exceedingly bland poetry; he might just have left us something more interesting for the interesting times he lived in. His surviving letters to his Bordelais disciple, the poet-saint Paulinus de Nola, are more illuminating than his verse; the two broke their long friendship towards the end of Ausonius's life, when Paulinus austerely rejected his master's conviction that the new religion could be reconciled with the Olympian muses and the sweet worldly life he loved.

supposed burial places of Roland's paladins, slain in the famous ambush at Roncesvalles. The cemetery is long gone, but **St-Seurin**, founded by the city's 5th-century bishop Severinus, still stands, although in an often remodelled and expanded state (*open 8–12 and 2–6.30*). Its antiquity allowed its medieval canons to concoct a number of pretty stories, including a famous one, that Charlemagne chose it as the shrine for Roland's great horn Oliphant after the hero popped out his brains by blowing it too hard. Although Oliphant has sadly gone missing, there are other things to see at Bordeaux's oldest church: the 14th-century porch with lavish sculptures of the Last Judgment and Resurrection, and, hidden behind the undistinguished main façade of 1828, a second 11th-century porch, holding the tomb of St Severinus, supported by carved capitals depicting the sacrifice of Isaac. Inside, a 7th-century sarcophagus does duty as an altar in the Chapelle St-Etienne, and there are beautiful 15th-century alabaster works: the retable in the Chapelle of Notre-Dame-de-la Rose and 14 panels in the choir, on the lives of St Severinus and St Martial, the apostle of Gaul. Note, too, the magnificent 15th-century episcopal throne, curiously made of stone imitating wood, and the sculpted choir stalls: try to find the fat man pushing his stomach in a wheelbarrow, and the man grilling tongues.

The 11th-century crypt (you may have to ask the sacristan to open it) has a fine collection of 6th- and 7th-century sarcophagi, medieval tiles, Merovingian plaques and the tomb of St Fort, supposedly the first bishop of Bordeaux, way back in the 1st century; the Bordelais would bring their young sons to his tomb and touch their foreheads on the stone to make them strong (*fort*) by mystic osmosis. Excavations under the crypt have revealed the 4th-century **Palaeo-Christian crypt** (*guided tours June–Sept daily 3–7; adm*), which goes back to the very origins of Christianity in Bordeaux. Inside are sarcophagi, amphorae and frescoes.

Quartier St-Pierre

From the 3rd to the 12th century, St-Pierre was a separate walled quarter outside the city walls, built around the Palais de l'Ombrière, home of the dukes of Aquitaine and kings of England and, later, the Parlement of Bordeaux. Although the Palais de l'Ombrière was destroyed in 1800, its triumphal arch-gate, the **Porte Cailhau** (*open June–Sept daily 3–7; adm*), still overlooks the river with its asymmetrical turrets and tower. One of only two gates spared by Tourny's demolition squads (the Grande Cloche is the other), it was begun in 1493 to celebrate the Battle of Fornovo, where Charles VIII and the French fought to a draw against the united Italian republics; the nobility of Guyenne played a prominent role. From here you can observe the effect of the 18th-century **Grande Façade** project, conceived by Jacques Gabriel and Intendants Boucher and Tourny to create a homogenous kilometre of architecture from Cours du Chapeau Rouge to Porte de la Monnaie, a regular row of pale stone houses, all the same height, with arcades on the ground floor, each arch with a *mascaron* at its key, topped by two floors of large windows, and a slate mansard roof with stone dormers.

In the Middle Ages the parish of St-Pierre was inhabited by English merchants and craftsmen remembered only in the street names – Rue Maucoudinat ('badly cooked', the address of the tripe butchers), Rue des Bahutiers (cabinet-makers) and Rue des

Argentiers (silversmiths). The presence of the Parlement of Bordeaux from the 15th century on led to the construction of a number of stately 18th-century *hôtels particuliers*, now restored for the most part by the Association pour la Renaissance du Vieux Bordeaux (12 Rue des Faussets). You can see the best of them by walking straight through Porte Cailhau to Rue du Loup (note especially No.71, and also the 200-year-old **wisteria**, in the courtyard in the Hôtel des Archives); cross busy Rue Ste-Catherine, and turn right in Rue de Cheverus (No.8 is now the offices of the *Sud-Ouest*, Bordeaux's paper), and from here turn up Rue Poquelin-Molière. In 1656 Molière and his troupe performed at No.9, then a *jeu-de-paume*, a walled court for court tennis, although after a fire in 1728 it was replaced by a handsome *hôtel particulier*. From here find Rue Grassi and turn right into Rue de la Porte-Dijeaux/Rue St-Rémi.

Rue St-Rémi leads right into the centre of Bordeaux's neoclassical showcase, Jacques Gabriel's **Place de la Bourse**, commissioned by Intendant Boucher in 1735, who wanted to give the city a touch of Parisian class in spite of itself. Originally called the Place Royale, it had for a centrepiece a bronze equestrian statue of Louis XV that was gleefully pulled down and melted into cannons to fire at other kings in the Revolution; today a fountain of the *Three Graces* (1864) holds pride of place, the Graces in this case representing the Empress Eugénie, the Queen of Spain and Queen Victoria. On one side stands the **Palais de la Bourse**, or stock exchange (now the Chamber of Commerce), enlarged in 1862 and 1925, and repaired after bomb damage in 1940; on the other, the **Hôtel des Douanes**, which must be the most grandiose customs house in the world. Installed in its grand, vaulted clearance halls of the former Fermes du Roy (i.e. the king's tax farms) is a museum devoted to a subject that infuriates people to this day – French customs. The **Musée des Douanes** (*1 Place de la Bourse,* ***t*** *05 56 48 82 82; open Tues–Sun 10–6; adm*) traces the history of taxes on imports from the days of the ancient Gauls to displays of more recent uniforms, weapons, weights and measures (including a grand 200-year-old scale) of France's *douaniers*, as well as examples of the forgeries and contraband they've nabbed. Among the originals: Monet's *La Cabanne des Douaniers, effet d'après-midi* (1882).

The Golden Triangle

Bordeaux's Golden Triangle of good taste and luxury shops is formed by Cours de l'Intendance, Cours Georges-Clémenceau and Allées de Tourny. No.57 Cours de l'Intendance was the last address of Goya, the painter, who in 1824 asked permission of Ferdinand VII to settle in Bordeaux with his former nursemaid and mistress. At the time Goya was still the official painter of the Spanish court, but serious illnesses, deafness and political disillusionment had made him ever more reclusive. In his last four years, in the company of his fellow exiles, he turned to a new medium, lithography (*The Bulls of Bordeaux* and *La Laitière*) and evolved a nearly Impressionistic freedom in his handling of paint. He died suddenly in 1828, age 82, while painting a portrait of his friend Molina, and was buried in Bordeaux until 1889, when his remains were transferred to Madrid. Unfortunately you can no longer visit his rooms.

Just off the Cours, in Place du Chapelet you'll find Bordeaux's chief Baroque church, **Notre-Dame** (1684–1707), directly inspired by the Gesù in Rome. Originally a Dominican chapel, its luxurious altar, organ and paintings show a marked change in the Order's taste since the days of Les Jacobins in Toulouse (*see* pp.449–50). Behind it, in the centre of the Golden Triangle, is the iron and glass shopping mall, the **Marché des Grands-Hommes**, rebuilt in 1991 and soon nicknamed the *bouchon de carafe* (the 'carafe stopper'). The east end of the Cours de l'Intendance opens into **Place de la Comédie**, a space that once contained 300 houses, a church and a remarkable Gallo-Roman palace called the Piliers de Tutelle – all demolished in the 17th century by order of Louis XIV, who, after the uprising of the Fronde, wanted nothing to stand in the way of his cannons pointed at the city from the Château Trompette (*see* below).

In 1773, the Maréchal-Duc de Richelieu, great nephew of the famous cardinal, governor of Guyenne and a famous libertine who fathered scores of Bordelais (at one of his dinner parties the only guests were the 29 most beautiful society belles of Bordeaux, masked to permit every indiscretion), felt he wasn't being properly entertained in Bordeaux and rectified the matter by commissioning the **Grand Théâtre** from neoclassical master Victor Louis and making the *jurats* pay for it. If Richelieu rammed the theatre down the city's throat, Bordeaux has since adopted it as its proudest showcase, and in 1992 it underwent a thorough restoration. From the outside it resembles a Greek temple, fronted by a row of mighty Corinthian columns and crowned with statues of goddesses and muses. Louis came up with a number of innovations in its construction, especially the great metal tie-beam (the *'clou de M. Louis'*) that supports the entablature of the peristyle (shades of Soufflot's Panthéon in Paris; France's technically incompetent 18th-century architects had a hard time making their neoclassical stone confections stand up, and by necessity became leading innovators in the use of iron – a habit that culminated in the Eiffel Tower). If it looks fairly restrained from the outside, all sumptuous hell breaks loose within. Louis's vestibule has more columns, Doric this time, supporting a magnificent coffered ceiling, lit by a 62ft cupola; his bold grand stair was copied by Garnier for the Paris Opéra; the auditorium has golden columns and a domed ceiling (repainted in 1919) hung with a massive crystal chandelier weighing 2,860lbs. From the day it opened, this high temple of illusion answered a deep-felt need in business-oriented Bordeaux; every single night it was thronged with merchants who paid a king's ransom to bring down the best players and dancers from Paris.

The Grand Théâtre witnessed a curious ceremony in 1965. A literary feather in Bordeaux's cap, although often begrudged by the feather himself, was novelist François Mauriac (1885–1970), 1952 winner of the Nobel prize for literature. At 22 he fled Bordeaux for Paris, where, at a distance, he could exorcize an unhappy provincial childhood in books such as *Le nœud de vipères* (*The Nest of Vipers*) which didn't exactly endear him to the folks back home. Nevertheless in 1965 there was an official reconciliation of Bordeaux with its native son, in a ceremony in the Grand Théâtre honouring his 80th birthday. But when it was time to give a speech, Mauriac shocked them into silence: 'The honour that you do me at the very evening of my life gives me a great joy, but a grave joy. Dare I say, a sad joy? I love and I hate Bordeaux like myself.'

You can learn and taste the wide variety of Bordeaux *appellations* at the **Maison des Vins de Bordeaux**, on the corner of Place de la Comédie (*3 Cours du 30 Juillet*, **t** *05 56 00 22 66; open daily 8.30–6, Sat 9–12.30 and 1.30–5, closed Sat and Sun out of season*). The labels (Graves, Côte du Blaye, etc.) are generic, but it's a good place to discover some of the nuances between the *appellations*. The tourist office (*see* pp.220–21) sponsors an introduction to wine-tasting here if you want to learn more.

The Esplanade des Quinconces and Around

Just down the Cours du 30 Juillet rises the irresistibly overblown 19th-century **Monument aux Girondins**, a lofty column crowned by Liberty over a fountain mobbed by Happiness, Eloquence, Security, a crowing cockerel and a host of other attractive allegories. Originally statues of the Girondins themselves were planned, but lack of funds kept them from even coming to their own party, as it were. In the fountain basin, two remarkable quadrigas of bronze horses violently rear their sea-monster paws to the sky while expressive figures of Falsehood (holding a mask), Vice (with pig ears) and shameful Ignorance cower under the utterly vacuous gaze of the Republic. The Nazis stripped the fountain of its bronzes in 1943; to everyone's surprise they weren't melted down, but were later found squirrelled away in Angoulême, although they had to wait in storage until the hotly contested mayoral election of 1983, when Chaban suddenly pulled the money out of a hat to restore the fountain.

Stretching out endlessly from here to the river is Europe's largest, and one of its least interesting, squares, the **Place des Quinconces**. When speculators purchased the hated royal Château Trompette and began dismantling it just before the Revolution, their intention was to lay out new streets and build 1,800 new houses. Now half of the square is a parking lot, and in the rest you're hard put to it to find any quincunxes at all. (What's a quincunx, you ask? A pattern like the five on a dice; all French farmers plant their trees in rows like this. Supposedly the fashion was started by the granddad of all gardeners, King Cyrus of Persia.) At the river end, the Place is closed by two columns, the **Colonnes Rostrales**, erected in 1829, decorated with the prows of ships and topped by allegories of Commerce and Navigation.

In 1745, Tourny laid out a promenade lined with linden trees, now called the Allées de Tourny, to give the Bordelais a place to stroll; the houses were designed with uniform façades, but limited to two storeys to allow cannonballs from Château Trompette to fly over them. In 1756, Tourny added the city's first patch of greenery, the **Jardin Public**, which the *intendant* had to promote as something practical to make it palatable to Bordeaux's conservative business class: 'In a commercial city, one must look at such public gardens as very useful, where merchants, often meeting one another there, transact much business. It is like having a second Exchange.' Originally laid out by Jacques-Ange Gabriel in the various perspectives of a *jardin à la française*, it was destroyed by Napoleon's troops. When the garden was finally replanted in 1856, it was designed in the romantic *style anglaise* popularized by Napoleon III, who spent his early years in exile in London. It makes for a delightful wander: on sunny Sundays, expect to see half of Bordeaux here (*open till 9pm summer and 6pm winter*). The Cours de Verdun entrance has a bust of François Mauriac by Zadkine, while nearby you can stroll through the **Jardin Botanique** (*open daily 8–6*). The 18th-century portico inside the garden sees a Sunday morning stamp market; on one of the lawns there's a genuine megalithic cromlech – a dwarf Stonehenge. At the west end of the garden, a *hôtel particulier* of 1778 has housed since 1862 the **Musée d'Histoire Naturelle** (***t** 05 56 48 29 86; open 11–6, weekends 2–6, closed Tues; adm, free 1st Sun of each month*), containing an important collection of Quaternary fossils, many from the Grotte de Pair-non-Pair near Bourg-sur-Gironde (*see* p.212), as well as a selection of stuffed animals from around the world, and mineralogy and geology sections.

Two streets behind the museum in Rue du Docteur Albert-Barraud, a monumental entrance and a few arches known as the **Palais Gallien** is all that remains of the 15,000-seat Roman amphitheatre of Burdigala built in the 3rd century AD. The barbarians, not as keen on gladiator sports as the civilized Gallo-Romans, burned it soon after its construction. Its name comes from a tangled tale that Charlemagne built it as a palace for his wife Galliene; old engravings show that the arena remained fairly intact until the 18th century, when its walls were incorporated into the surrounding buildings; today you have to look down from an aeroplane to trace its oval shape.

The Chartrons

In the 14th century, Carthusians chased out of Périgord found refuge in the swamp north of Bordeaux's walls and drained the land henceforth known as the Chartrons. For centuries, the presence of the massive Château Trompette in the Place des Quinconces kept the Chartrons apart from the rest of Bordeaux, and in the 17th century Flemish wine merchants (then known as *courtiers*), feeling discriminated against by the pro-English *jurats*, set up their own business and quay here. They were soon followed by German, Dutch and Irish traders affiliated with the Hansa of Bruges, and then by the English themselves. The most successful of these merchants, brokers and shippers bought their own vineyards, founding fabulously wealthy wine dynasties, the *aristocratie de bouchon*. Their smug, closed social circle – the source of Anglophile Bordeaux's reputation for snobbery, clubbiness and affected mannerisms (as in replacing many French words with English) – first suffered with the Revocation of the Edict of Nantes. This sent the Protestants among them to seek refuge abroad, although many of them kept up their commercial ties with Bordeaux and helped enlarge the market for its wine across Europe.

The decline of the Chartrons began with the Revolution, when many Chartrons merchants were guillotined and many others moved abroad. Under Napoleon, commerce came to a standstill – for 30 years the Chartrons lived only by fitting out corsairs. Although its commerce revived, it was never the same; if in the 1950s the brokers still had their offices in prestigious but shabby waterfront buildings along the quay, by the 1960s the relocation of port activities to the north, to Bassens and Ambès, and the switch to land transport of wine made even this vestige of the past irrelevant. Ever since then Bordeaux has sought a new role for the quarter while maintaining as much of its original wine business as possible, first by constructing the shiny new (and utterly sterile) **Cité Mondiale du Vin** on the Quai des Chartrons, concentrating on hotels and an ultra-modern conference centre, with exhibitions and shops open to the general public. The snobbiest of the Chartrons nobility lived on the Pavé des Chartrons (now Cours Xavier-Arnozan), paved by Tourny and planted with trees at the same time as he laid out the nearby Jardin Public. Where it meets the quay stands the **Hôtel Fenwick**, built in 1790 for Joseph Fenwick, who managed to combine his duties as the first American consul in Bordeaux with his mercantile activities – represented in the ship's-prow decoration.

One of the success stories of the Chartrons is the restoration of the austere neoclassical **Entrepôt Lainé**, around the corner from Hôtel Fenwick at 7 Rue Ferrère, built in the 1820s, where spices and other goods imported from France's colonies were unloaded, exempt from duty; now its vast spaces are used for the giant-scale exhibitions and installations of the **Musée d'Art Contemporain** (***t*** *05 56 00 81 50; open 11–6, until 8 on Wed, closed Mon and hols; adm, free 1st Sun of each month*), with a charming café. The same building contains the **Arc en Réve Centre d'Architecture** (*same hours*), dedicated to architectural exhibits, often on Bordeaux itself. Not far from these displays of contemporary art are shops dealing in fond old things, in the **Village des Antiquaires**: antiques dealers line Rue Notre-Dame on all sides of the austere Protestant Temple, its only ornament the relief of a Bible exploding out of the clouds.

The old wine trade is remembered in the *hôtel particulier* of Irish broker Francis Burke (1720), now the **Musée des Chartrons**, 41 Rue Borie, between the Quai des Chartrons and Cours Balguerie (***t*** *05 57 87 50 60; open Mon–Fri 2–6; adm*), with a collection of lithographed wine labels and bottles going back to the 1600s. You can also learn about the long-lost wine of the islands – in the old days brokers would load Caribbean-bound ships with 900-litre casks of the finest Bordeaux *crus*, accompanied by a vintner to keep an eye on the evaporation and top up the casks when necessary. This precious cargo was not for the colonies, however; when the ship arrived in the Antilles, wine and vintner stayed on board, and sailed straight back to Bordeaux. The journey improved the wine so much that as *Bordeaux retour des îles* it commanded a premium price in Paris' restaurants. When steamers took over the route, it was found that the wine didn't improve at all; the secret had been the gentle rolling motion of a sailing ship, and *retour*, as it was known by its lovers, went the way of the dodo.

Further north, visitors are welcome aboard the retired battleship the ***Croiseur Colbert***, used by the French navy between 1960 and 1990 (*bus 1; 60 Quai des Chartrons,* ***t*** *05 56 44 96 11; open 10–6, until 8 in July and Aug; adm exp*). At Hangar 16, Quai des Chartrons, opposite Cours du Médoc, is **Cap Sciences** (***t*** *05 56 01 07 07; open Tues–Fri 2–6, weekends 1–7*), an exhibition centre which aims to bring scientific subjects home to the public and introduce us to new scientific innovations and techniques. There is a changing programme of exhibitions and themes. **Vinorama** (*12 Cours du Médoc,* ***t*** *05 56 39 53 02; open Tues–Sat 2–6.30; adm*) is a cornball talking wax museum that explains the history of Bordeaux's wine from Gallo-Roman times to the present, complete with an 'historic wine tasting' of wine made in the Roman style, in the 19th-century style, and so on.

For 50 years, Bordeaux's old docks along Bd Alfred Daney (bus 9 from the station or boulevards) have been disfigured by the Germans' submarine base: a vast indestructible concrete bunker with walls over 15ft thick, the whole in volume equal to

Lamprey (*Lamproie à la bordelaise*)

This is not a recipe for the squeamish, nor one that would have survived Brigitte Bardot's animal rights squads if the beast in question weren't a remarkably uncuddly, ugly, blood-sucking parasite that missed the evolutionary boat back in the night of time, probably because it doesn't seem to have any eyes. Nail a live lamprey to the wall and cut it across the tail, carefully catching all the blood that drains out (for thickening the sauce). Next cut off the poisonous dorsal cartilage (ingesting some by mistake is said to have killed Henri I) and plunge your lamprey into boiling water to make it easier to remove the skin. Slice the delicate white flesh into rounds and add it to a mixture of leeks, onions, chunks of ham and a bottle of St-Emilion that has been stewing for three days. Poach the lamprey in the wine mixture, and add the blood and a touch of chocolate. It comes in tins if you don't feel like doing it yourself.

St Peter's, with 11 huge entrances to U-boat pens, each 300ft long, dug by Spanish, French, Russian and Vietnamese prisoners of war. Since it would take forever to remove the monster, the Bordelais tamed it instead, converting the base in 1993 into a centre for various exhibitions and performances and a unique museum of pleasure boats, the **Conservatoire Internationale de Plaisance** (***t*** *05 56 11 11 50; open Wed, Sat, Sun 1–6.30; adm*). Among the 60 craft displayed are a replica of the *Simon and Jude*, a catamaran of 1662 built by Cromwell's physician, Sir William Petty; one of the first petrol-run pleasure motorboats, built by Daimler in 1889 for Bismarck; the 1989 Cesa world champion and world's fastest sailboat, Sir Timothy Coleman's *Crossbow II*; and the experiment *F1*, designed for the 1992 Americas Cup; as well as an interesting array of antique outboard motorboats. During the winter the old bunkers also contain **Marinexpo** (***t*** *05 56 50 06 14*), evoking the life of Bordeaux's port through the centuries, with ships' models and figureheads. In the summer the exhibits move aboard an itinerant barge. To the west the last swamps of the Chartrons were concentrated in 1960 into an artificial lake, the centre of the **Quartier du Lac**, with Bordeaux's trade fair buildings, congress centre, golf courses, an arboretum and recreational facilities. In 2001 this will also be the site of a new aquarium with flora and fauna of Aquitaine and the Atlantic coast.

Last and least, Bordeaux also has a **Right Bank**. There is a small museum in one of the houses (*open Tues–Sat 10–12 and 2–6.30, Sun 3–6 only*). There have been some attempts to perk it up in recent years, such as the restoration of the old Gare d'Orléans to create a multiplex, and there are plans to do more, but the only real reason for crossing over the Garonne is the views back towards the famous façade.

Pessac

Pessac (bus P from St-André) may be one of many victims of Bordeaux's 20th-century transformation into an octopus, but it is also the site of a landmark experiment to meet the need for new housing and create something architecturally new: Le Corbusier's first project, the **Cité Frugès** in Avenue Henri Frugès. The name commemorates the Bordeaux industrialist whose desire to transform a tract of land he owned near the railway line into healthy, light and airy, affordable housing for 300 families led him to give the young Swiss architect Le Corbusier a crack at practising his theories of urban housing for the post-Cubist era. In 1926 Le Corbusier and his co-builder Jeanneret produced 51 houses for Henri Frugès: geometric modules with rough concrete skins, brightly painted, with hanging gardens on terraces. The houses had many comforts the old *échoppes* of Bordeaux lacked (central heating, running water and adequate sewerage) but the sight of them drove the Bordelais bananas. Frugès was dismissed as a loony, and, when people reluctantly moved in, the first thing they did was try to make Le Corbusier's modules fit their idea of what a house ought to be. In his dismay Frugès never finished the project, although up in heaven he must be gratified to see that his *cité* is now classed as a historic monument and is slowly being stripped of later additions to restore the architect's original intention.

Pessac-Léognan

Since 1987 the northern third of the traditional Graves growing area has been given its own *appellation*, Pessac-Léognan. Its worst enemy is urban sprawl: at the start of the 20th century, the four closest *communes* to Bordeaux (Pessac, Gradignan, Mérignac and Talence) had 119 vineyards. Today there are nine. Yet these, especially in Pessac, only 6km southwest of central Bordeaux, produce some of the greatest wines in the entire *département*, beginning with the prestigious **Château Haut-Brion** (on the P bus route, in Avenue Jean-Jaurès, **t** 05 56 00 29 30) founded in 1550. The elegant finesse of its reds (50 per cent Cabernet Sauvignon, 35 per cent Merlot, 15 per cent Cabernet Franc) were rewarded in 1885, when the property became the only non-Médoc wine to be granted *premier grand cru* status. But Haut-Brion was famous even before then, especially in London. As far as anyone knows, this was the first wine sold under the name of the estate that produced it, rather than under the name of the parish; 17th-century Londoners called it 'Ho-Bryan' and made it such a success that the original owners, the Pontacs, even opened one of London's first luxury restaurants, the 'New Eating House', with a French grocer and wine cellar on the premises. Later owned by Talleyrand, the estate was purchased in 1935 by American banker Clarence Dillon, whose granddaughter, the Duchesse de Mouchy, now runs the company. In 1983 she purchased the equally celebrated **Château La-Mission-Haut-Brion** (**t** 05 56 00 29 30), across the street, which until the Revolution belonged to a mission founded by St Vincent de Paul; it produces a powerful wine equal to the finest from Médoc. Today the two vineyards are green islands in Bordeaux's post-war sprawl, which may be ugly but creates an urban climate that protects the vines from spring frosts and accelerates the harvest, a plus in years of heavy autumn rains. A third vineyard in Pressac (Avenue Pasteur) is the one with the longest continuous history of them all, planted in 1300 by Bordeaux archbishop Bertrand de Got before he became pope, and hence known as **Château Pape-Clément** (**t** 05 57 26 38 38), producing a *cru classé* famous for its intense wines that pack an extraordinarily aromatic tobacco bouquet (visits and tastings available at all three by appointment).

Gironde

12

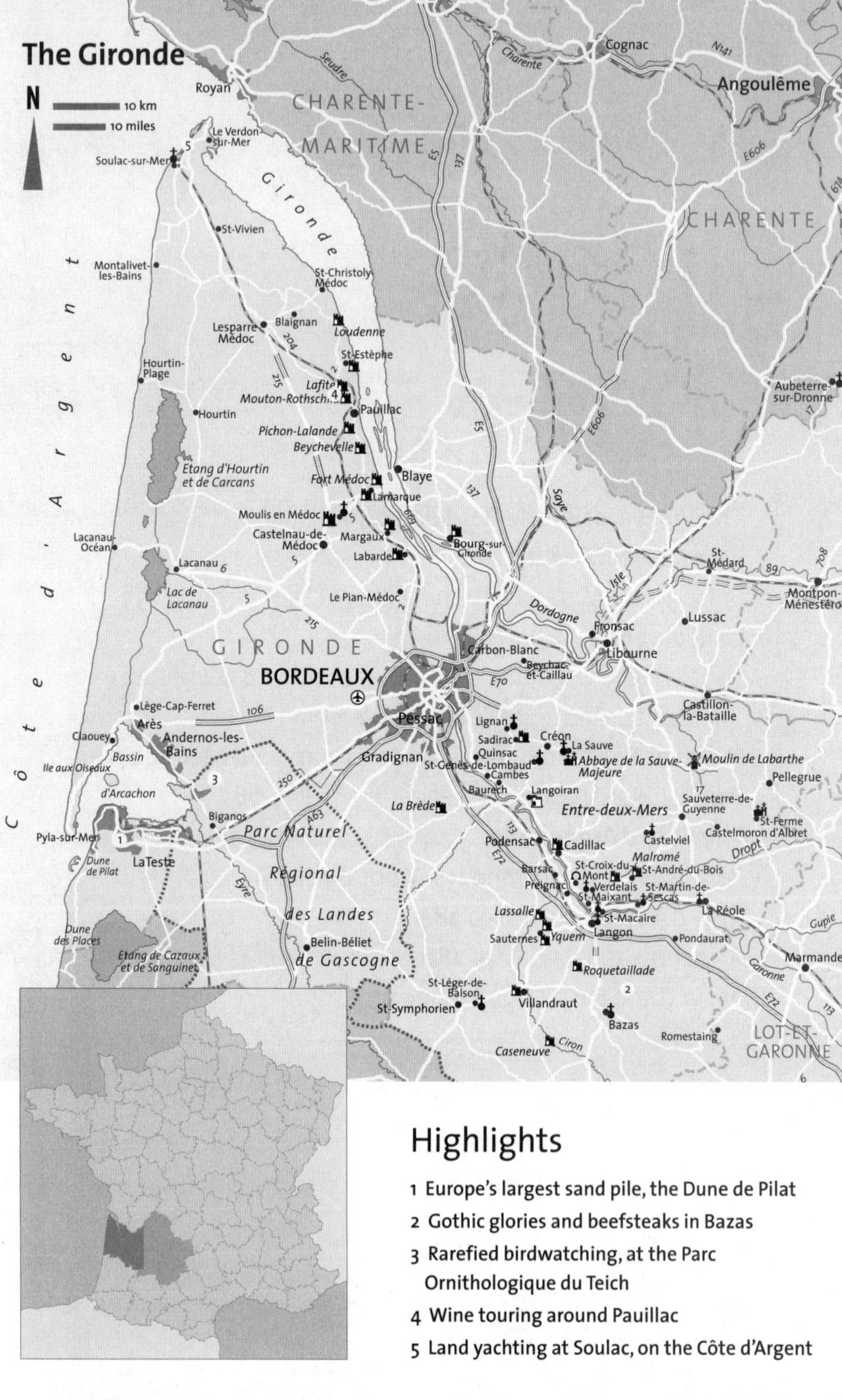

Highlights

1 Europe's largest sand pile, the Dune de Pilat

2 Gothic glories and beefsteaks in Bazas

3 Rarefied birdwatching, at the Parc Ornithologique du Teich

4 Wine touring around Pauillac

5 Land yachting at Soulac, on the Côte d'Argent

Bordeaux's *département*, the Gironde, is chock-full of superlatives. It is the largest in France (6,650 square miles), containing 2,170 miles of rivers and 72 miles of Atlantic coast, the whole lined with fine silver sand scarcely touched by development. In the Gironde, you'll find France's largest two lakes, Europe's largest estuary, its oldest lighthouse, its highest sand dune and the northern fringes of Les Landes, its largest forest – not to mention the largest and, by most criteria, the best vine region in the whole wide world.

The Vineyards of the Bordelais

The nuances and names of the numerous vineyards, *appellations*, growths and other classifications of Bordeaux's wines are befuddling enough even before you go careering off on a wine tour. A look at the map reveals that you can divide the Bordeaux vineyards into four main regions: the **Libournais** along the north of the Dordogne, encompassing the superb *appellations* of Pomerol and St-Emilion, Côtes de Blaye and Côtes de Bourg (*see* pp.204–5, 207, 214); the **Entre-Deux-Mers**, between the Dordogne and Garonne; the **Graves**, south of the Garonne; and the **Médoc**, along the south bank of the Gironde estuary north of Bordeaux.

By the 18th century, much of the best land for growing grapes was consolidated into the hands of Bordeaux's political and legal movers and shakers, the *noblesse de robe*, who built themselves splendid manor houses by their properties. These became the basis for the château system that characterizes Bordeaux's vineyards and gives its wines their prestigious reputation in the consumer's mind (although no one can keep 4,000 names of châteaux straight, and you can bet that wine sellers are well aware that any Bordeaux château that incorporates magic words like Biron and Mouton in its name will be a big seller). Outside Médoc and Sauternes, wine tours reveal that many glorious-sounding châteaux are not only insignificant but even non-existent – most surprisingly in fancy-pants St-Emilion.

The market for Bordeaux red wine and French claret was always big in England (*claret* originally meant white or rosé, but somehow around 1600 the word got twisted into a name for a light red wine, made of white and red grapes). After 1853, with the construction of the railway to Paris, the market began to expand in France as well, especially after the 1855 Paris Exhibition that saw the famous classifications of Bordeaux's Médocs and Sauternes. Bankers (most famously, the Rothschilds) and investors, both French and foreign, bought up estates just in time for the outbreak of phylloxera in 1878. Vines were quickly replanted, grafted on phylloxera-resistant American roots, and good wine was produced again in quantity in 1893. After a brief revival and a few good years, the economy and weather went sour. Excellent wines were produced again in the 1920s, but the prices went out from under them and the market collapsed.

It wasn't until after the Second World War that the vineyards of Bordeaux began to turn a profit again; in the late 1950s enough confidence had returned to allow the experimentation and technological improvements in winemaking that revolutionized

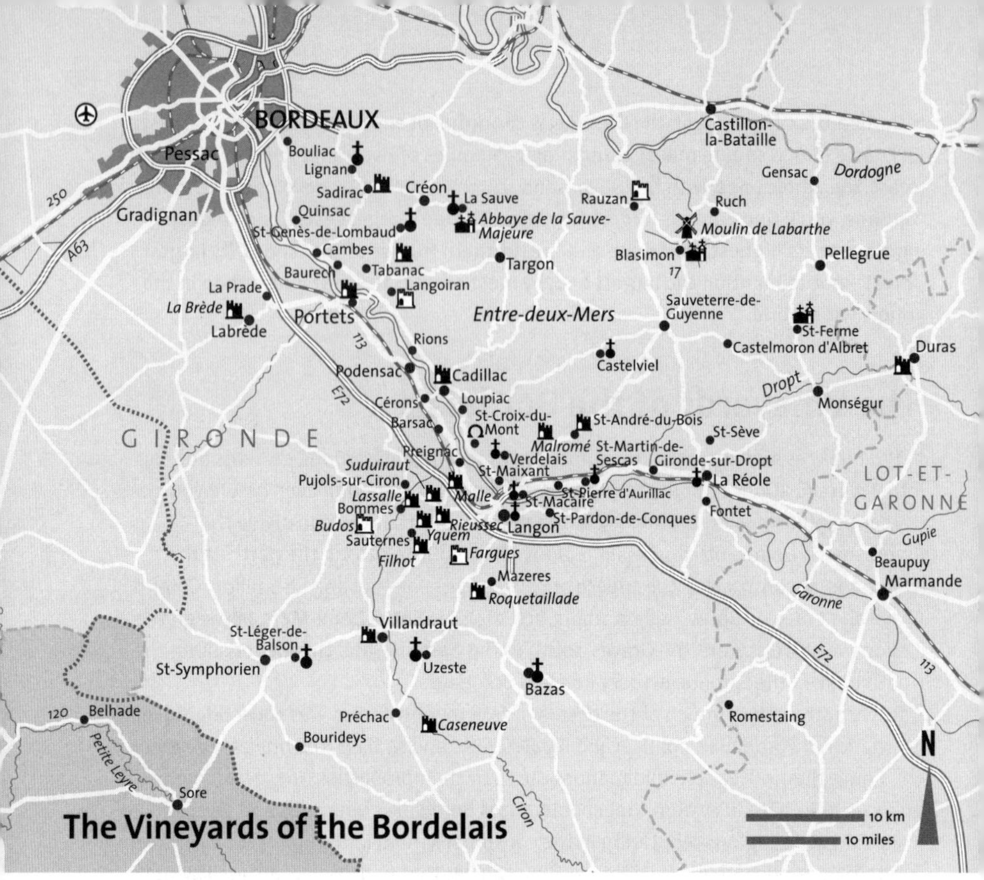

Bordeaux in the 1960s and '70s – most significantly, use of sprays against rot, and adjustments in the temperature of fermentation to an even coolness, especially important for white wines. Even mechanical harvesters are now used in over half the vineyards, enabling vintners to get all the grapes in at the peak moment of ripeness. Now once again investors have moved in to buy up the vineyards – many of them, rather sadly, huge anonymous insurance companies.

An ideal introduction to all Bordeaux wines is offered at **La Maison de la Qualité**, in the Entre-Deux-Mers halfway between Bordeaux and Libourne on the N89, near **Beychac-et-Caillau** (***t*** *05 57 97 19 20; open Mon–Fri 9.30–12.30 and 1.30–5, June–Sept Mon–Sat 9.30–5.30*). This modern building is the fief of those wizards of the nose and tastebud who sniff and gargle each estate's wine every year to see whether it merits the proud name of Bordeaux or Bordeaux Supérieur; for visitors there's a film, free tastings of select wines, commentaries, and advice on visiting the châteaux. The same experts have also opened **Planète Bordeaux**, an inventive and entertaining introduction to the world of Bordeaux wines using the latest technology.

See also p.77 for a guide to vintages. You can study the subject before leaving home at *www.vins-Bordeaux.fr*.

Entre-Deux-Mers

The name comes from *inter duo maria*, 'between two estuaries' (the Dordogne and the Garonne) and by the flat Gironde's standards we're talking highlands – a lovely undulating plateau of soft limestone occasionally reaching over 320ft in altitude, pocked with natural cavities. Its fine, blond stone was quarried to build Bordeaux, leaving behind tunnels converted into mushroom farms that keep the metropolis in fungi. On the whole, however, Bordeaux regards the Entre-Deux-Mers as its backyard Ruritania, a natural base for microtourism, where any village over 2,000 souls seems downright urban; it's one of France's best-kept secrets.

In the Middle Ages, this great wedge of land belonged to the Benedictines, headquartered at the great abbey of La Sauve-Majeure, and they sprinkled the countryside with good Romanesque churches. A century or two later, this peaceful region found itself on the front lines in the Hundred Years' War, which caused such devastation that in the 15th century the French kings repopulated it with northerners speaking

Tourist Information

Sauveterre-de-Guyenne: 1 Rue St-Romain, **t** 05 56 71 53 45, **f** 56 71 59 39.

Blasimon: 14 Place de la République, **t** 05 56 71 89 86.

Monségur: Rue des Victimes, **t** 05 56 61 89 40. At 4 Rue Issartier, you'll also find the tourist office for the entre Entre-Deux-Mers region, **t** 05 56 61 82 73, **f** 05 56 61 89 13.

Créon: 7 bis Rue du Dr Fauché, **t** 05 57 34 54 41.

Market Days

Créon: Wed.

Sauveterre-de-Guyenne: Tues.

Where to Stay and Eat

Créon ✉ 33670

★★★**Château Camiac**, 3km northeast of Créon on the D121, **t** 05 56 23 20 85, **f** 05 56 23 38 84 (*moderate*). A white-turreted château with a score of rooms in a delightful castle surrounded by a park with a pool and tennis court, and meals served out on a magnificent garden terrace in fair weather; try the *barbue* (barbel, a freshwater fish) with leeks and truffle juice (*menus 170–280F*). *Open all year but booking compulsory in Nov–Mar.*

Le Lion d'Or, 2 Place de l'Église, southeast of Créon in Targon, **t** 05 56 23 90 23. Famous for cheap and abundant lunches (*dinner in summer only*) in a relaxed atmosphere (*menus 53–121F*).

Sauveterre-de-Guyenne ✉ 33540

★**De Guyenne**, **t** 05 56 71 54 92, **f** 05 56 71 62 91 (*cheap*). A simple Logis de France, one of the least pricey hotels in the region.

Blasimon ✉ 33350

★★**Château Lardier**, just off the D232, in Ruch, just to the northeast near Blasimont, **t** 05 57 40 54 11 (*inexpensive*). A lovely 17th-century château. Many of the charming rooms are furnished with antiques, and there's a pretty park too. *Closed Nov–Feb.*

Monségur ✉ 33580

Château de la Bûche, 10 Av de la Porte-des-Tours, **t** 05 56 61 80 22, **f** 05 56 61 85 99 (*inexpensive*). An 18th-century building with four charming, renovated guest rooms, as well as a suite for families; good home-cooked meals (*for 120F*).

★★**Grand Hôtel**, overlooking quiet Place Darniche, **t** 05 56 61 60 28, **f** 05 56 61 63 89 (*inexpensive*). Not so grand, but charming and unaffected and *open all year*; good regional cooking in the restaurant (*menus 55–170F*).

Les Tilleuls, Place des Tilleuls, **t** 05 56 61 81 95 (*cheap*). Four rooms with TV; old-style French dining (*midday only, from 60F*). *Closed Sun.*

Entre-Deux-Mers AOC

As Bordeaux's largest producer of dry white wines, to the tune of 99 million bottles a year, much of Entre-Deux-Mers is a rolling emerald sea of vineyards. Of its 165,500 acres of vines belonging to 14 different *appellations*, most are located in the south and along the Garonne valley. The wide diversity of altitudes, soils and influences from its two great rivers make this mesopotamia a patchwork quilt of microclimates, but for many long years Entre-Deux-Mers was considered second-rate – the *blanc* that became plonk in English. Pride, perhaps more than anything else, since the late 1970s has stirred the winemakers (most of whom are natives of the area) to improve the quality, bring out the distinct character of the wines, and lift the *appellation* back up to snuff. As for all white Bordeauxs, Sauvignon is the dominant grape, blended with one or more of the following: Sémillon, Colombard, Ugni Blanc, Merlot Blanc and Muscadelle. Some 60 per cent of the production is sold abroad. Along with white wine, a number of estates produce reds under the *appellation* Bordeaux or Bordeaux Supérieur. At La Sauve, **Château Turcaud, t** 05 56 23 04 41, produces a delightful, floral wine; the cooperative **Les Vignerons de Guyenne** in Blasimon, **t** 05 56 71 55 28, does a fresh, classic pale Entre-Deux-Mers. For a hint of the vast range of this *appellation*, try the elegant cold-fermented wines of the vast 18th-century **Château Bonnet**, further north in Grézillac. On the D139, between Castelmoron d'Albret and St-Ferme, the **Château de l'Aubrade, t** 05 56 71 55 10 (*ring ahead to visit*), has 50 hectares, half white and half red, under five appellations; many have won prizes. Organic Entre-Deux-Mers and Bordeaux *rouge* are produced at the **Château des Seigneurs de Pommiers, t** 05 56 71 65 16, just southwest of Sauveterre de Guyenne, off the D672; the adjacent 13th-century **Château Pouchaud-Larquey,** t 05 56 71 65 16, one of the finest in the area, is being restored, and can be toured along with the vineyard for a small fee (*by reservation*). The **Maison de l'Entre-Deux-Mers** is near to the abbey of La Sauve-Majeure and you can pop in for tastings and to buy.

the *langue d'oïl*, the *gavaches* as the Gascons called them, who settled in tiny hamlets or lone farms that to this day appear regularly every mile or so. The less said about the peninsula of Ambès (the northern corner of Entre-Deux-Mers) the better, unless you hanker after grey urban dilation, modern port installations and defunct petroleum refineries.

Sadirac and Créon

As you drive east from Bordeaux along the D10/D10E a handful of places discreetly bid a detour. The hamlet of **Lignan** was once owned by the Knights of St John, who left behind a little Romanesque **church** with carved capitals and some unusual 11th-century tombs carved out of a single rock. You can also find a **Musée Archéologique** with prehistoric pieces, old pottery and tools and such (***t** 05 56 21 23 58; open Sun 2.30–6.30, till 5.30 in winter; adm*). Further east, **Sadirac**, a pottery-wheeling village since the 14th century, has a pair of Renaissance châteaux and a pair of potters firing up their kilns: you can examine their work at the **Maison de la Poterie** (*Rue de l'Eglise,*

t** 05 56 23 74 84; open Tues–Sun 2–6; adm*), which also exhibits old pots and workshops. The owner of Sadirac's **Château de Belloc** came up with the genial idea of planting the vegetable garden with old-fashioned, nearly forgotten vegetables – **OH! Légumes Oubliés**, which you can not only look at but try, with tastings included in the price of admission (t** 05 56 30 62 00; open mid-April–mid-Dec daily 2–6; adm*).

Further to the southeast lies the Gironde's 'Little Switzerland', a green region sliced by a score of valleys, with **Créon** as one of its chief towns, a *bastide* of 1316 founded by and named after the English seneschal Amaury de Craon, who hoped to dilute the power of the Benedictines at the nearby Sauve-Majeur. Créon retains three sides of arcades in its central square and a church rebuilt in the 16th century, as described in the ornate Gothic inscriptions on the wall of its pentagonal apse. Inside, look for the curiously disproportionate 13th-century statue of the Virgin, which long stood in the niche of the 17th-century *clocher-mur*. Créon's 12th-century priory is now owned by **Mathieu Créations** who manufacture paper by hand, incorporating flowers into the texture of the sheets (***t** 05 56 23 25 66; free tours of the atelier 2–5 by reservation*). Just south of Créon, the church at **St Genès-de-Lombaud** is built over a Roman villa, with a Romanesque portal sculpted with animals and odd little figures.

The Abbaye de La Sauve-Majeure

***t** 05 56 23 01 55; open June–Sept daily 10–6.30, Oct–May 10–12.30 and 2.30–5.30, till 6 on Sun; adm.*

Continue 3km east of Créon for the remarkable ruins of the Benedictine Abbaye de La Sauve-Majeure (*silva major*, the great forest) founded in 1079 by St Gérard de Corbie, who was granted the power of sanctuary and justice by the troubadour Duke Guilhem IX of Aquitaine. By the 1200s it had chapters as far away as England and Aragon. The great Romanesque church dates from this golden age; it was damaged in the Hundred Years' War and Wars of Religion, and picked apart piece by piece by carrion salvagers from the days of the Revolution until 1882, leaving only the skeleton behind. Few skeletons, however, command such presence: three of the twelve massive pillars that supported the triple nave still stand, culminating in a row of five 'bread oven' apses, while the lofty hexagonal bell tower with ogival windows still rises with panache from the fourth bay, fitted with a viewing platform on top. Two carved Romanesque capitals (the sacrifice of Abraham and beheading of St John) are in the second bay, but the most spectacular capitals are in the choir and apses, where the eyes and hair of the figures are lovingly detailed: there are scenes of drinking griffons, fighting centaurs, a battle between an asp and basilisk, and in the apses scenes from Genesis, Daniel in the lion's den and Samson. A pair of others is in the Musée d'Aquitaine in Bordeaux. To see the rest (and the *modillons*, carved by the same hand) you'll have to go the Cloisters Museum in New York. **La Sauve** has an interesting **museum** of its own, located in the former monastery, containing a fine statue of St Gérard in a style reminiscent of Chartres, medallions, 13th-century carved keystones, and documents relating to other religious foundations in the Entre-Deux-Mers.

The statue of St James on the flat *chevet* of La Sauve's parish church of **St-Pierre** is one of the first known to depict the saint in pilgrim's garb, with cockleshells, staff and broad-brimmed hat; next to him stand Sts Peter, Michael and the Virgin and Child. Inside, a Roman capital does duty as a font, and there are some simple, softly faded 13th-century frescoes.

Sauveterre-de-Guyenne and Blasimon

Sauveterre-de-Guyenne, another *bastide* founded by the English (in 1283), has kept its arcaded square and its four fortified gates but not much else of interest; from here, however, the D230 heads west to **Castelviel**, where the south portal of the 11th-century **church** is one of the gems of the region, carved with Virtues and Vices, the Labours of the Months and a bevy of other figures; Deadly Sins and saints appear on the capitals.

From Sauveterre it's 7km north on the D17 to **Blasimon**, site of the castrum *Blavini Mons* that became another *bastide* in 1322, on the orders of Edward II. Outside the centre, the gracefully ruined 12th-century Benedictine **abbey of St-Nicolas** is prettily isolated in the little valley of the Gamage (***t** 05 56 71 89 86; guided tours 15 June–15 Sept 9–5, other times by appointment; adm*). Part Romanesque, part Gothic, and gracefully ruined, the church itself has somehow managed to survive in good nick, complete with a charming Romanesque façade that takes on a magical golden patina at sunset. The sculptures on the portal (1170) are exceptionally finely chiselled – scenes of Vices and Virtues, animals and scenes from the hunt. In contrast, the interior of the church is simple and pure to the point of austerity; the cloister has a handful of good Romanesque capitals. The tour includes most of the old monastic buildings and a little archaeology **museum**, with prehistoric sharks' teeth and relics of a local Druidic cult. Just to the north (on the D17) don't miss the 14th-century **Moulin de Labarthe**, built by the abbots of Blasimon and one of the most picturesque fortified water mills in southwest France.

Northwest of Blasimon, **Rauzan** is huddled under the **Château des Duras** (***t** 05 57 84 03 88; open Tues–Sun 10–12 and 2–7 but this can vary, check with the tourist office at Blasimon; adm*), a castle that originally belonged to England's much-maligned King John before passing to the Duras family. Hotly contested during the various wars, the castle was rebuilt and expanded several times between the 12th and 15th centuries, and has mullioned windows and other details, and a pretty church from the 1200s. Its centrepiece, an impressive 100ft cylinder of a keep pierced with narrow slits for archers, offers lovely views over the village and valley.

East of Sauveterre-de-Guyenne to Monségur

Charming medieval **Castelmoron d'Albret**, just east of Sauveterre-de-Guyenne, is the smallest *commune* in France (not even 10 acres, pop. 64), squeezed behind its walls on a promontory overlooking a little valley – a pretty place to stop, even though there's nothing in particular to see. To the east stands the fortified 11th-century Benedictine abbey of **St-Ferme** (a corruption of St Fermin – he of the bull-running in

Pamplona) (**t** *05 56 61 62 10; guided tours 15 June–mid-Sept, 10–12 and 2.30–7.30, closed Tues; out of season Wed–Sat 9–12 and 2–6*). Although the façade has taken a beating, the interior has an excellent, lively set of capitals illustrating the Old and New Testaments, especially a David and Goliath, a Daniel thrown to a pair of snarling lions, along with two giant heads apparently ready to swallow a squatting man; you may have to ask the sacristan to turn on the lights. The *mairie* is installed in the handsome abbey buildings of 1585, a complex that forms the heart of the peaceful village.

North of St-Ferme there's another *bastide*, 13th-century **Pellegrue**, founded on a rocky spur, with several recently restored churches and three châteaux on the surrounding hills; south of St-Ferme there's another, **Monségur**, capital of *la Petite Gavacherie*, where the inhabitants, brought in from the north in the 15th century to resettle the land, are to this day called *gavaches* or *gabots*. Originally the word meant uncouth mountainmen, or hillbillies, although these days, realizing that everyone is always someone else's hillbilly, this little enclave of northern French descendants living among the twanging Gascons take their nickname in their stride. A walled *bastide*, Monségur was founded in 1265 by Eléonore de Provence, wife of Henri III (the charter she sent, called the *Esclapot*, is preserved in the little museum in the *mairie*); it also has kept its arcaded central *place*, not with the usual medieval *halles*, but a striking 19th-century covered market reminiscent of the old Halles in Paris, as well as several lanes of old half-timbered houses and a simple Gothic church. What it does not have, however, is the famous castle of the Cathars (*that* Monségur is down in the Ariège, in the Pyrenees). Monségur overlooks the river Dropt, and like the *pays de Duras*, just to the east in Lot-et-Garonne (*see* pp.393–4), it busies itself with plums, prunes and prune *eau-de-vie*.

Entre-Deux-Mers: Along the Valley of the Garonne

The most beautiful and dramatic scenery in the Entre-Deux-Mers overlooks the Garonne. Here, where the vineyards produce AOC Premières Côtes de Bordeaux instead of white wine. Medieval Cadillac, St-Macaire and La Réole are the chief towns to aim for, and there is plenty of fine scenery along the way.

Bordeaux to Ste-Croix-du-Mont

From Bordeaux, take the D10 towards **Quinsac**, birthplace of Rosa Bonheur (1822–99), one of France's finest animal painters, an outspoken cigar-chomping, trouser-wearing feminist, and the first woman to be awarded the Grand Cross of the *Légion d'Honneur*. **Cambes**, a small pleasure port to the southeast, has a good Romanesque church with 15th-century English alabasters inside. On the D240 towards Tabanac, you can have a look at the elegant Palladian **Château de Plassan**, generally attributed to Victor Louis and architecturally one of the finest wine châteaux in the Bordelais, the residence and the *chai* (the building where the new wine is stored) built as a harmonious ensemble.

Tourist Information

Langoiran: 4 Place du Docteur-Abaut, **t** 05 56 67 56 18, **f** 05 56 67 56 74.
Cadillac: 8 Place de la Libération, **t** 05 56 62 12 92, **f** 05 56 76 99 72.
St-Macaire: Hôtel de Ville, **t** 05 56 63 32 52.
La Réole: Place de la Libération, **t** 05 56 61 13 55, **f** 05 56 71 25 40.

Market Days

Cadillac: Sat.
La Réole: Sat.

Where to Stay and Eat

Cambes ✉ 33880

La Guinguette de la Varenne, **t** 05 56 21 85 69. On a summer's day, this old building is a perfect place to spend a lazy afternoon on the shady banks of the Garonne. Simple but tasty fare (*around 160F*). *Book at weekends. Phone during winter to confirm opening times.*

Langoiran ✉ 33550

*****Le St-Martin**, by the port, **t** 05 56 67 02 67, **f** 05 56 67 15 75 (*cheap*). Looking as if it escaped from New Orleans, this is a luminous hotel-restaurant-tearoom with huge windows overlooking the Garonne. Eels, shad and lamprey hold pride of place in the spring, *magrets* and *confits* and foie gras the rest of the year (*menus 100–160F*). *Open all year.*

Cadillac ✉ 33410

*****Château de la Tour**, D10, **t** 05 56 76 92 00, **f** 05 56 62 11 59 (*moderate*). Overlooking the Château de Cadillac, this is an inviting, plush place to stay, with a pool and tennis courts in the grounds, and a good restaurant serving the likes of lobster ravioli and elegant desserts (*menus 145–320F*). *Closed Fri eve, Sun eve and Sat Nov–Mar.*

L'Entrée Jardin, 22 Rue de l'Oeuille, **t** 05 56 76 96 96. Opposite the castle, an old stone building decorated inside in deep Wedgwood blue and white, with a patio. The cuisine is mostly local, but not always, and refined: *marbre de foie gras et pruneau à la vinaigrette de truffes* and *filet d'espadon* (*menus 62–150F*). *Closed Sun, Mon and the first half of Aug.*

Au Fin Gourmet, 6 Place République, **t** 05 56 62 90 80. More work-a-day, buzzing with happy locals at lunchtime; serves platefuls of standard regional fare (*menus 65–260F*).

Campsite, near the Lac de Laromet, 3km away, **t** 05 56 62 17 72. A good site.

Just after **Langoiran**, the next village upriver, stands the half-ruined medieval **Château de Langoiran**, a d'Albret property put to the sack in the Hundred Years' War and again in the Fronde; carved chimneys and some murals survive (*open July and Aug daily, Sept–June weekends only, 10–12 and 2–6; for guided tours ask at the tourist office*). The Romanesque church of **St-Pierre-des-Liens** has a beautiful carved 12th-century apse to look at, and there is a pretty Parc de la Peyruche. Little **Rions** was originally peaceful Gallo-Roman *Riuncium*, but found itself square on the frontier between the French and English in the Middle Ages, hence the heavy fortifications that have given it the nickname 'the Carcassone of the Gironde' – the ruins of the citadel and a watchtower survive, along with the **Porte du Lhyan** (1304), defended by an 80ft tower.

Cadillac, a riverside *bastide* of 1280, gave its name to America's biggest dream cars but only by an extremely devious route. A local boy named Antoine Laumet from St-Nicolas-de-la-Grave went off to seek his fortune in America, where he adopted the grander alias of Lamothe-Cadillac. After a busy career up in the Great Lakes country, where he founded Detroit in 1702, he ended up as governor of the Louisiana territory.

St-Macaire ✉ 33490

Résidence Hotelière Les Tilleuls, 15 Allée des Tilleuls, **t/f** 05 56 62 28 38 (*inexpensive*). On the edge of the medieval centre of St-Macaire, offering 11 new studios sleeping 2–6 with kitchenettes, rented by the night, week or month.

L'Abricotier, east of St-Macaire, just off the N113, **t** 05 56 76 83 63. A charming place to dine, with innovative menus and regional specialities from shad to lamprey, depending on the season (*menus 115–220F*). *Closed Mon eve, Tues eve and a month in winter.*

Camping des Remparts, **t** 05 56 62 23 42. A good riverside campsite.

La Réole ✉ 33190

****Les Trois Cèdres**, N 113, in Gironde-sur-Dropt, 4km west of La Réole, **t** 05 56 71 10 70, **f** 05 56 71 12 10 (*inexpensive*). An old-fashioned hotel with 14 rooms; its restaurant serves grilled bass with superb fresh pasta and other delicacies under three cedars on the terrace (*menus 95–200F*). *Closed half of Jan.*

Domaine de la Charmaie, north of La Réole outside St-Sève, **t** 05 56 61 10 72 (*inexpensive*). A charming bed-and-breakfast in a traditional house, with a pool, playground and park; they speak English (*dinners available on request, 120F with wine*).

De l'Abbaye, 42 Rue A. Caduc, **t** 05 56 61 02 64, **f** 05 56 71 24 40 (*cheap*). A little hotel in the centre. *Open all year.*

Le Martouret, 66 Rue du Marouret, **t** 05 56 61 04 81 (*cheap*). Simple rooms.

Auberge Réolaise, 7 Rue Gabriel Chaigne (N113) **t/f** 05 56 61 01 33 (*cheap*). A typical French provincial hotel, with a bar and restaurant. *Closed Nov.*

Les Fontaines, 24 Rue André Benac, **t** 05 56 61 15 25. Named after the fountain in the middle of the restaurant, which adds a refreshing touch to the garden-fresh cuisine; try the bass roasted with potatoes, or the *pot-au-feu* with foie gras, and the scrumptious desserts (*menus 80–240F*). *Closed Sun eve, Mon and a month in winter.*

Le Régula, 31 Rue André Bénac, **t** 05 56 61 13 52. With a pretty pink terrace looking out over the street below, and exhibitions of paintings. Mostly local cuisine (*menus 60–210F*). The 200F menu gives the uninitiated a culinary tour round the region with wines included, mostly from the vineyard at Château Le Luc-Régula up the road. The owners, Monsieur and Madame Bonnier (Monsieur is also chef), are very friendly. *Book. Closed one week in Nov and one in Feb.*

In 1902 a Detroit car-maker took the name Cadillac; it was merged with General Motors in the 1920s, and the rest is history. A full-size Caddy would look like Moby Dick in the main square of Cadillac, and trying to squeeze it under the pretty, lantern-topped 18th-century **Porte de l'Horloge**, the main river gate, would be asking for trouble. But this village does have something even bigger than its eponymous car: the **Château de Cadillac**, built 1598–1620 by Henri III's favourite *mignon* ('cutie-pie', roughly), the fabulously wealthy Nogaret de La Valette, Duc d'Epernon (***t** 05 56 62 69 58; open July and Aug daily 9.30–1 and 2–7, April–June and Sept 9.30–12.30 and 2–6, Oct–Mar 10–12 and 2–5.30, closed Mon; adm*). The story goes that, when Henri IV inherited this proud, dangerous and ruthlessly ambitious toyboy from his predecessor, he made him governor of Guyenne and went out of his way to encourage him to spend as much of his time and fortune as possible building himself this palace. The result is architecturally a meld of the styles popular in the time of Henri IV and Louis XIII, but after damage in the Revolution and a century of duty as a women's prison (until 1928) it has lost some of its original sparkle. Purchased by the state in 1952, the château has great vaulted guard rooms below and painted ceilings above, tapestries from the 13th and 17th centuries (the latter, showing scenes from the life of Henri III, were made here) and, best of all, eight monumental chimneypieces, beautifully sculpted in part by Jean Langlois and decorated with rare marbles, cascades of flowers and fruits, cupids and armour. Also on display are fragments of the grand mausoleum of the ducs d'Epernon, located in a rich marble chapel in the nearby church of St-Blaise, until it was bashed in the Revolution. One wing of the château holds the Cadillac wine confraternity's Maison du Vin.

Wine is also the name of the game in **Loupiac**, the next village, site of the **Villa et Thermes Gallo-Romains** that may have belonged to Ausonius. Inhabited from the 2nd to 5th centuries AD, the baths and plumbing are fairly well preserved, and the whole is covered with colourful mosaic floors, including one in a pretty heart pattern (***t** 05 56 62 93 82; open Sun 2–6*). Another vinous vortex, **Ste-Croix-du-Mont**, sits on an enormous fossilized oyster reef like a great pearl. One of its two châteaux belonged to Pierre de Lancre, a psychotic witch-hunter who terrorized the Basque lands in the 1600s on behalf of the Parlement de Bordeaux. The square in front of the rebuilt Romanesque church enjoys a wide-ranging view of the Garonne valley over the Sauternes; a cave excavated in the petrified oysters offers tastings of Ste-Croix's own golden nectar.

St-Macaire

Perched on its rock over the Garonne, St-Macaire is one of the Gironde's medieval gems, a busy port called *Ligena* in Roman times. In the Middle Ages it assumed the name of its 4th-century hermit Macaire and got a big boost when the kings of England designated it a coin-minting *ville royale d'Angleterre*. In the 18th century the Macariens woke up one morning to find their quays left high and dry when the Garonne slightly altered its course; this took away any economic impulse to modernize its narrow lanes and medieval houses, leaving St-Macaire a village of considerable charm. Another plus is the village's white wine, AOC Côtes de Bordeaux St-Macaire.

Three fortified gates still defend the town, including the **Porte de l'Horloge**, equipped with a watch tower, the town bell and a clock. Best of all is the irresistible, irregular **Place du Mercadiou**, or 'God's marketplace', lined with Gothic arcades and houses in a picturesque variety of styles from the 13th to the 16th centuries. At Place de l'Horloge is an **aquarium** (**t** 05 56 63 95 62) with 350 types of different fish. Sitting atop the village ramparts, **St-Sauveur** was part of a 12th-century Benedictine priory, built on the site of St-Macaire's hermitage. The church has an interesting carved portal and tympanum, and a curious interior plan, ending in a choir shaped like a cloverleaf. Painted murals from the 1400s, wrecked by bumbling over-restorers in the 1850s, decorate the crossing with ghostly memories of their glory: the *Wise and Foolish Virgins*, *St John the Evangelist* and *Christ of the Apocalypse*. St-Sauveur's priory buildings, with their wide-ranging views over the countryside, are a favourite setting for summer fêtes.

Premières Côtes de Bordeaux

This *appellation* begins in the suburbs of Bordeaux and extends along the hills on the north bank of the Garonne to Langon. Although in the 1970s most of the wine produced here was white, fashions have changed and a very pleasant, fruity red wine made from Cabernet Sauvignon and Merlot is now the main product. Conditions vary widely, but in general the wines made to the west are lighter, with less capacity for ageing. Some of the best red wines come from the sun-soaked, well-drained vineyards of the 14th-century **Château de Pic** at Le Tourne in Langoiran, **t** 05 56 67 07 51, **Château Puy-Bardens** in Cambes, **t** 05 56 21 31 14, and the panoramic **Château La Roche** at Baurech, **t** 05 56 21 31 03 – one of the few Bordeaux vineyards run by a woman, here Martine Palau.

Within the Côtes de Bordeaux area, facing Sauternes-Barsac are three small communal *appellations*: Superieur AOC Cadillac, Loupiac and Ste-Croix-du-Mont – all sweet, white dessert wines rated just a notch below Sauternes-Barsac, although they tend to be lighter and fruitier. They are grown on pebbly clay soil on steep hillsides, some 300ft above the Garonne; look for Loupiac's **Château de Ricaud**, producer of a beautifully perfumed sweet wine and a dry white (as well as red Premières Côtes) and **Château Loubens** at Ste-Croix.

Around St-Macaire: François Mauriac and Toulouse-Lautrec

François Mauriac's beloved summer home **Malagar** (3km northwest, in St-Maixant) belonged first to his great-grandfather, and since 1985 to the Conseil Régional d'Aquitaine, who have set up a museum devoted to the life of the author of *Thérèse Desqueyroux*, and allow visitors to ramble in its park (***t*** *05 57 98 17 17; open June–Sept daily 10–12.30 and 2–6, Oct–May Wed–Fri 2–5, weekends and hols 10–12.30 and 2–6*). The 14th-century **Château de Malromé**, 6km northeast of St-Macaire in St-André-du-Bois (***t*** *05 56 76 44 92; open Easter–Oct Sun and hols 2–6, July and Aug daily 10–12 and 2–7; adm*), was completed in the 18th and 19th centuries by the Counts of Toulouse-Lautrec. The scion of the family who became a famous artist often spent his summers with his mother, and died here in 1901 at the age of 37, burned out from alcoholism and syphilis. The château, now the seat of a foundation in his name, displays reproductions of his works in a plush Second Empire setting, and has vineyards. 'I'll drink milk when the cows start eating grapes,' Toulouse-Lautrec would thunder at his doctors, and the château's red Bordeaux Supérieur made of 70 per cent Merlot was one of his favourites; now his posters adorn its labels.

Toulouse-Lautrec is buried, rather uncomfortably for a hard-living, keen-eyed observer of Parisian lowlife, one imagines, in the prim and proper **Basilique de Notre-Dame** at **Verdelais**, just to the southwest. This is the most famous pilgrimage church in the Gironde, with its miracle-working statue of the Virgin (from the 12th or 14th century), and the church has an interesting collection of ex votos from sailors and landlubbers testifying to her powers of intervention in a little **museum** (***t*** *05 56 62 02 06; open summer daily 3–7, winter Sun only 9.30–12.30 and 3–7*). Further up the Garonne, **St-Pierre-d'Aurillac** has a nice river beach and a Merovingian sarcophagus in front of its church, but the most tempting stop between St-Macaire and La Réole is **St-Martin-de-Sescas**, to see the magnificent portal of its 12th-century **church**, with lively carvings of birds, rabbits, trees, leaves and people.

La Réole

In 977, the Benedictines received a charter from the Duke of Gascony to refound a Carolingian-era priory at Squirs on the Garonne, which had been left in ruins ever since the Normans hooliganned their way through in 848. The Benedictines renamed the priory after their Rule (Regulam in Latin). The name was later corrupted to La Réole, and Richard the Lion-Heart gave the priory a set of walls to match its strategic position over the river and to defend its river trade, especially in wine from the *haut-pays*. Pilgrims coming from the Limousin brought additional wealth, and until the English created a rival port, Libourne on the Dordogne, La Réole could proudly claim to be the second town in Guyenne after Bordeaux. Even today it presents a stately river façade, especially with the mass of the 18th-century **Prieuré des Bénédictins** on its riverside terrace. You can easily wander about the old priory, now used for various municipal services – the panelled and stuccoed Louis XV *salle d'honneur* is now the mayor's office, and the impressive vaulted cellars house the library and a little museum of religious art and archaeology (*open July and Aug daily 3–5.30, rest of year Sat and Sun only, same hours*). In nearby Place Rigoulet, the old Benedictine priory church of **St-Pierre** was rebuilt in 1230; it has a pair of pretty Gothic chapels and a painting of the *Marriage of the Virgin* (1666) by Valdés Leal of Seville, a painter better known for his delight in morbid religious gore and corpses. Look for the mermaids carved on the capitals in the nave.

Among the old boutiques and houses in medieval La Réole is the oldest **Hôtel de Ville** still standing in France, built in the early 1200s by order of Richard the Lion-Heart, pierced with irregularly placed mullioned windows, and, below, a *halle* on Romanesque columns with capitals naïvely imitating antique models. Rue Peysseguin is a charming street, with La Réole's synagogue and medieval houses; Bordeaux's *parlement* met between 1653 and 1678 in a handsome 15th-century *hôtel* on Côte St-Michel. In 1230, an English architect under Henry III Plantagenet designed La Réole's **Château des Quat'Sos** ('of the four sisters'), its name referring to the massive round towers at each angle, of which only one is still intact; this castle suffered 12 different sieges, the last in 1629. It remained the personal property of the kings of England until the end of the Hundred Years' War and was always heavily garrisoned; the Black Prince spent a good deal of time here. You can take a cruise on the Garonne aboard *Le Régula*, sponsored by the tourist office (*July and Aug at 3, 4, 5 and 6, on Fri also 7, with a picnic and wine tasting*). The former tobacco factory on the N113 has been given a new role, filled with **Les Musées de La Réole** (***t** 05 56 61 29 25; open July and Aug 10–6, out of season Wed–Sat 2–6 and Sun 10–6; adm*): one featuring a hundred old cars; another on the battles of the Second World War; another displaying antique tractors, harvesters and combines; and a fourth devoted to trains.

The nearby village of **Fontet** has a four-star attraction as well: a group of farm buildings containing the **Musée d'Artisanat Monuments d'Allumettes** (matchstick models) (***t*** *05 56 71 20 45; open 2.30–6, Sun 3–6.30; adm*), including nothing less than the Largest Matchstick Model in the World (of Rheims cathedral), 17ft long and 8ft high, made with 350,000 matchsticks by Gérard Gergeres and proudly displaying its certificate from the *Guinness Book of Records*.

Just north, on the river Dropt, you can look at a pair of attractive water mills: the fortified, 14th-century **Moulin de Bagas**, built by the Benedictines of La Réole, and, 2.5km further up, the Romanesque **Moulin de Loubens** (*they may be open once or twice a year*). The Romans liked the area as well: the ruins of Gallo-Roman villas have been discovered about every 2km along the valley. South on the D12 at **Pondaurat**, visit **Le Grenier à Vimes** and see how osier is cultivated and made into decorative shapes (***t*** *05 56 61 05 78; open Mon–Fri 8–12 and 2–6, Sat by appointment*).

South of the Garonne: the Graves and the Bazadais

Graves is not exactly the name a public-relations firm would choose to sell a region, but it isn't so sombre when you remember that here it has more to do with gravel (*'les Grabas de Burdeus'* originally) than with old boneyards; the greatest vineyards in the *appellation* look as if they're growing out of gravel pits, and in some areas there is a deep rivalry between gravel merchants and vineyard owners, each waiting their chance to pounce whenever any land comes up for sale. The gravel forms a wedge between the river and the deep ferny Landes forest and is endowed with several special microclimates that make it perfect for wine – most famously Sauternes.

Château de La Brède

t *05 56 20 20 49; open 2–5.15 daily exc Tues July–Sept, Easter–June and Oct–early Nov weekends only, 2–5.15 ; adm.*

One Graves estate has been producing good wine since the days of its most celebrated owner, Charles-Louis Secondat, baron of Montesquieu; from Bordeaux, take the N113 and turn off at La Prade for his ivory tower, the Château de La Brède. Montesquieu described it as 'one of the most pleasant places in France, where Nature puts on her dressing gown as she rises from bed'. Montesquieu wore a number of hats in his life, not only as a successful wine grower who sold his Vin de Graves in England but also as a magistrate in the Parlement of Guyenne and, most memorably of all, as a clear-thinking philosopher of the Enlightenment and the author of the best-selling *Lettres persanes*, a satire of French society, and the *De l'Esprit des Lois* (1748), a work proposing the separation of power into legislative, executive and judiciary branches that became the basis for the Constitution of the United States. His descendants still own the stern Gothic castle he was born in, defended by wide, watery moats and preserving Montesquieu's magnificent vaulted library with over 7,000 of his books. His bedroom, left as it was when he died, also doubled as his study; Montesquieu sat writing by the fireplace for so long that one of the firedogs is worn down from his foot resting against it. He created the château's park, its pride and glory, shaded by cedars planted at the time of the American Revolution.

You can top off a visit to the château at the **Jardin Fruitier de La Brède**, Chemin de Mons at Feyteau, and watch how they produce jams out of some unusual ingredients – shallots, onions and Sauternes wine (***t** 05 56 20 22 29; open year-round but call first, closed Sun*).

Portets to Barsac

After La Brède the N113 passes through or very near a collection of villages synonymous with wine, beginning with **Portets**, right on the Garonne. This is the site of the charming Louis XV **Château de Mongenan** (***t** 05 56 67 18 11; open Easter–Sept daily 2–7, mid-Feb–Easter and Oct–Dec Sat and Sun 2–6; adm*), which, besides bottling a fine Graves, offers visitors a Masonic temple and lovely botanical garden, planted after the owner read his Rousseau, with over 1,000 kinds of roses, herbs and medicinal plants; the rooms contain a museum of life in the 18th century, with porcelain, textiles, costumes, dolls and so on. The next town is **Podensac**, home of the famous Bordeaux apéritif Lillet; at the distillery, **Maison Lillet**, on the N113 (***t** 05 56 27 41 41; open mid-June–mid-Sept 9–7, rest of year weekdays 9–4.30*), you can see displays of their famous posters and labels from 1900 to 1930, as well as tastings of Lillet Blanc or Rouge. **Cérons**, still on the N113, offers its **Musée de la Vigne et du Vin** (***t** 05 56 27 11 50; open year round exc Mon and Jan*), full of old equipment, tools and old vintages, with tastings of Cérons' wines; at **Barsac**, we pass into the magic kingdom of noble rot.

The Barsac–Sauternes Circuit

This is a pretty tour of immaculately kept vineyards and castles from every period; on a fine day, consider hiring a bike at Langon's tourist office and doing the trip in reverse. Beginning in **Barsac**, you can pay your respects to St Vincent, patron saint of wine growers, whose church dates from the 16th to the 18th centuries, its Baroque interior a sumptuous feast of woodwork, stuccoes and wrought iron culminating in a wowser of a high altar, carved in 1742. The story goes that up in heaven St Vincent became terribly thirsty for the good French wine he loved, and looked so woebegone that the Boss gave him permission to return to earth for one last wine tour if he agreed to come back to paradise at a certain time. After drinking himself across the country, Vincent's time ran out, but there was no sign of him. The angels found him in the cellars of La-Mission-Haut-Brion (*see* p.246) drinking everything in sight, and so drunk that he was in no state to go anywhere at all, much less to heaven, so they turned him into stone on the spot. And they say he's still there, mitre awry and grapes in hand.

From Barsac, head south to the handsome neoclassical **Château Nairac** (*deuxième cru classé*), built in 1776 by a Huguenot wine merchant, who added the lovely gardens to show off the façade (***t** 05 56 27 16 16; open all year 9–12 and 2–6; ring ahead*). Over the railway line stands the fortified 17th-century **Château Menota**; next is an 18th-

Vin de Graves: Bordeaux's Rive Gauche

A 55km gravelly, sandy ribbon between Bordeaux and Langon, varying from 15 to 20km in width, is the fief of the *appellation* of Graves, a household word in England long before anyone heard of Médoc. As an area it is extremely disparate, but one basically known for its soft, full-flavoured wines. The cheap quality and sulphur stink of the whites produced here for many years gave Graves such a mediocre reputation that many wine buffs learned to dismiss the lot; nor did anyone protest too loudly when Bordeaux developers concreted over vineyard after vineyard. Improvements began with the new Graves classification in 1953, when 13 red wines were given their credentials as a *cru*, or growth. In 1959 they were joined by eight white Graves.

As all of these most prestigious *crus* are concentrated in the north near Bordeaux, in Léognan, Pessac and Talence, a vinous civil war of prestige erupted that resulted in 1987 with a secession of the *crus classés* from the common Graves, in an *appellation* of their own called Pessac-Léognan. The *ne plus ultra* here is Haut-Brion, bang in the middle of Bordeaux's suburbia, along with Mission-Haut-Brion and Pape-Clément (*see* p.246). Other noble names here are Haut-Bailly, Chevalier, Carbonnieux, Fieuzal and Olivier. Visits to these citadels are only possible by elaborate rendezvous; the place to buy them is the **Caves de Léognan** in Léognan, **t** 05 56 21 17 63.

Most of the southern Graves vineyards are concentrated in five *communes*: Langon, St-Pierre-de-Mons, Landiras, Illats and Cérons; the last two also produce wine called AOC Cérons – the demi-sweet intermediary between the dry whites and sweet Sauternes that isn't quite as popular as it used to be. In the past 20 years growers here have changed over in a big way to red wines (mostly Cabernet Sauvignon, which has a surprisingly different character here than in the Médoc) with help from Merlot and Cabernet Franc. While the reds of AOC Pessac-Léognan are famous for their nearly infinite capacity for ageing, those in the southern Graves are light and fruity, generally best drunk after three or four years. Graves *blancs* (Sémillon and Sauvignon, in various proportions) have greatly benefited from the techniques of cold fermentation *en barrique* and work by the *Institut National des Appellations d'Origine*, which has researched vine-cloning in Langon: 1995 was an especially good year for them. Among Graves to look out for are **Château Rahoul** in Portets, **t** 05 56 67 01 12 (especially their elegant whites); the well-structured reds and aromatic whites of **Château Chantegrive** in Podensac, **t** 05 56 27 17 38, owned by Henri Lévêque, who bought his first patch of Graves by selling his stamp collection in 1968; **Château Beauregard-Ducasse** in Mazères, **t** 05 56 76 18 97, located on the highest part of the Graves, home of a good Sauvignon white and an easy-going red; and **Château d'Ardennes** in Illats, **t** 05 56 62 53 80, which uses a variety of traditional and novel techniques to produce a remarkable gamut of exceptional, reasonably priced whites and reds. The **Maison des Vins de Graves**, 61 Cours du Maréchal-Foch, Podensac, **t** 05 56 27 09 25, has tastings, sales and reams of advice; in general the white Graves are an excellent buy (*open Easter–early Nov 8.30–6.30, weekends and hols 10.30–6.30, Nov–Easter Mon–Fri 8.30–5.30, weekends over Christmas 10.30–6.30*).

Tourist Information

Langon: Allée Jean-Jaurès, **t** 05 56 63 68 00, **f** 05 56 63 68 09. They hire out regular and mountain bikes for 75F a day, *mid-May–Sept*.
Villandraut: Place de la Mairie, **t** 05 56 25 31 39, **f** 05 56 25 89 33.
Bazas: 1 Place de la Cathédrale, **t** 05 56 25 25 84.

Market Days

Langon: Fri and Sat.
Barsac: Sun.
Villandraut: Thurs.
St-Symphorien: Wed.
Bazas: Sat.

Where to Stay and Eat

La Brède ✉ 33650

La Maison des Graves, in the village centre, **t** 05 56 20 24 45. Regional dishes that bring out the best of the Graves at kind prices (*lunch menu at 78F, others up to 165F*). *Closed Sun night, Mon and Tues eve.*

Barsac ✉ 33720

*****Château de Valmont**, 22 Rue de la Gare, **t** 05 56 27 28 24, **f** 05 56 27 17 53 (*expensive–moderate*). A pretty château, with 12 rooms of varying degrees of sumptuousness; a pool and good restaurant. *Closed Jan–mid-Feb.*

Sauternes ✉ 33210

Brouquet *chambres d'hôte*, in the centre, **t** 05 56 76 60 17 (*inexpensive*). The only place to stay: three rooms and a pool.
Le Saprien, in the village centre, **t** 05 56 76 60 87. Well-prepared fish and other dishes according to the market, topped off with Sauternes by the glass (*menus 119–219F*). *Closed Sun eve, Mon and Wed eve and 5 weeks in winter.*
Les Vignes, Place de l'Eglise, **t** 05 56 76 60 06. A charming little country inn for an *entrecôte*, properly cooked over *sarments*, omelettes with *cèpes* and other bordelais treats (*menus 65–165F*). *Closed Mon eve and Feb.*

Langon ✉ 33210

*****Claude Darroze**, 95 Cours du Général Leclerc, **t** 05 56 63 00 48, **f** 05 56 63 41 15 (*moderate*). Top of the list: a hotel in a formal

century *gentilhommière* (country seat), **Myrat**, whose owner in 1975 could no longer afford the astronomical costs of making wine and pulled out all the vines, although the new owner has since replanted them (***t** 05 56 27 15 06; ring ahead*). Beyond is **Château Coutet**, a *gentilhommière* built around a medieval tower in the 17th–19th centuries; and a former charterhouse, the **Château Climens**. The last two are Barsac's two *premiers grands crus classés*, and many oenophiles rate Climens as second after Yquem, although they have very different personalities – Climens is fresh and elegant whereas Yquem is above all luscious (***t** 05 56 27 15 33; open for visits Mon–Fri 8–12 and 2–5, closed Aug*). Beyond is **Château Doisy**, a property now divided into three estates, all of which produce excellent *deuxième crus classés*, especially Doisy-Daëne (***t** 05 56 27 15 84; visits Mon–Fri 9–12 and 2–6*).

Follow the D114 along the Ciron and under the A61 towards Pujols-sur-Ciron. Before crossing the Ciron into the Sauternes, you can look at two non-wine châteaux, the handsome 16th-century **Château de Lassalle**, set in a large walled park, and, 4km south, the **Château de Budos**, built in 1308 by a nephew of Pope Clement V in a style similar to Villandraut (*see* below), and now a striking white ruin enjoying a lovely view of the Ciron valley.

18th-century building, with beautiful, sumptuous rooms. Claude Darroze is best known for his delicious terrace under the plane trees, where some of the best traditional Girondin dishes appear – crayfish salads, foie gras, lamprey with leeks and game dishes prepared with a light modern touch, accompanied by a perfect wine list (*menus 220–480F*). *Closed Jan and mid-Oct–mid-Nov. Book.*

★★**Horus**, 2 Rue des Bruyeres, **t** 05 56 62 36 37, **f** 05 56 63 09 99 (*inexpensive*). With a simple, *inexpensive* restaurant. *Open all year.*

Le Chantilly, 24 Rue Pasteur, **t** 05 56 63 57 85, **f** 05 56 76 89 65 (*inexpensive*). The restaurant here is more ambitious. *Open all year.*

Bazas ✉ 33430

★★★**Domaine de Fompeyre**, Route de Pau, **t** 05 56 25 98 00, **f** 05 56 25 16 25 (*moderate*). Overlooking Bazas, a bright, modern hotel with 35 rooms, set in a delightful four-acre park, with a tropical garden, pools, lit tennis court, and billiard room; the lovely restaurant serves lovely food as well (*menus 180–240F*). *Closed Sun eve in winter.*

Hostellerie St-Sauveur, 14 Cours du Général du Gaulle, **t** 05 56 25 12 18 (*inexpensive*). Ten simple rooms (discounts for stays by the week or month).

Château d'Arbieu, just east of Bazas on the D655, **t** 05 56 25 11 18, **f** 05 56 25 90 52 (*moderate*). Four very comfortable bed-and-breakfast rooms, plus a pool and billiards.

Les Remparts, in the Espace Mauvezin, Place de la Cathédrale, **t** 05 56 25 95 24. For the most succulent *entrecôte* in town, and a panoramic view overlooking the Jardin de Sultan. If you aren't a beef eater try the delicious Grignols capon with *cèpes*, game or fish specialities (*menus 75–210F*). *Closed Sun eve out of season, and Mon.*

Houn Barrade, at Cudos, on the D932, 4km south of Bazas, **t** 05 56 25 44 55. This *ferme-auberge* offers farm home-cooking (*80 and 115F menus, menu gastronomique for 140F*); leave room for the *tourtière bazadaise* for dessert. *Open weekends year-round and July–Aug daily; book.*

Villandraut ✉ 33730

★★**De Goth**, Place Gambetta, **t/f** 05 56 25 31 25. A typical provincial hotel, with a good restaurant (*menus 68–149F*). *Closed Mon lunch out of season.*

If you cross the Ciron at Pujols, the first Sauternes vineyard belongs to the spectacular 17th-century **Château de Lafaurie-Peyraguey**, set in 13th-century walls. It's a *premier cru classé*, as is the adjacent **Château Rabaut-Promis**, attributed to Victor Louis. Follow the Ciron and D109/E5 up to **Bommes** and Château de Haut-Bommes, and turn right on the D125E for the hamlet of **Sauternes**, which snoozes away without a care in the world. It has a snooty, disdainful Maison de Vin which you might want to avoid, but a couple of friendly wine shops have opened to sell and tell you about Sauternes. Continue south to the 19th-century Italianate **Château Filhot**, a *premier cru classé*. The stunning park was designed in 1840 and has a *pigeonnier* from the 1600s (*t 05 56 76 61 09; open daily 8.30–12.30 and 2–7*).

North of the village of Sauternes, take the D125 to the D8 and turn right for the hilltop **Château Rieussec**, a *premier cru* recently purchased by the Domaines Rothschild, and the **Château de Fargues**, a *cru bourgeois* that has long been as good as a *premier cru*, owned for 500 years by the same Lur-Saluces who founded Yquem, and who sell nearly all of it in the USA. The magnificently positioned **Château d'Yquem** itself is just north of Sauternes on the D125. It's the one château everyone longs to visit, and now you can (***t** 05 57 98 07 07; visits Sept–July Mon–Fri 2.30–4; call first but be warned – the waiting list is likely to be long*). In the same family for over

Sauternes-Barsac

Celebrated, simply, as the world's finest dessert wine, or by southwestern autochthones as the only proper drink to wash down a foie gras, Sauternes and its twin *appellation* Barsac are golden in tone but bring out the purple prose latent in many a French pen; give them a glass of Château d'Yquem, the closest thing on earth to the nectar of the gods, and you get:

> ***Yquem pushes our sense of taste to the limits of the inexpressible... To taste the apotheosis of taste! The lips make their acquaintance (never a rediscovery, but an endless procession of rebeginnings) with that bewitching freshness. And then, words fail. There doesn't exist, in any language, a way to express the infinite pleasure it consents to offer. Your palate [palais in French] suddenly merits its name. It welcomes the sovereign of beverages. The supreme offering of nature dazzles your mouth. You look across at your friend experiencing the same sensations. The force of communion binds you. A kind of complicity is at work. You read your own expressions on his face. He has become the mirror that reflects your ecstasy.***
>
> ***The nectar descends on you.***
> ***Close your eyes for an instant***
> ***And there you are on the other side of life.***
>
> **Frédéric Dard**

Sauternes and Barsac owe this inimitable quality to the excellence of their *pourriture noble*, or noble rot (*Botrytis cinerea*), nurtured by the autumnal morning mists formed when the waters of the icy little stream Ciron meet the warmer Garonne. Botrytis is a fungus that feeds on overripe grapes, dehydrates them, enhances their sugar content, and puffs them up until they look like brown turds. Unfortunately for the growers of Sauternes-Barsac, this metamorphosis doesn't happen uniformly.

four centuries (the Sauvage-Yquems, who in 1785 married the counts of Lur-Saluces), it made international headlines in 1996 when the family nearly sold it for millions, but in the end couldn't agree. The château itself dates from the 15th–17th centuries. The pale gold wines produced on Yquem's 250 acres have been the quintessence of Sauternes since the 18th century, a position confirmed since the 1855 classification that put it in a class all its own. In some years a rich, dry and more affordable white wine is produced as well, simply called Y (*ygrec*).

From Yquem carry on to the north, turning right on the D116, then left on the D8E for **Château de Suduiraut** (an excellent *premier cru*), built in the style of Versailles for the president of the Bordeaux court, complete with a garden by Le Nôtre. From here continue past the 18th-century **Château Bastor-Lamontagne** and turn right for the one Sauternes bailiwick open regularly for visits, the elegant 17th-century **Château de Malle** in **Preignac** (***t*** *05 56 62 36 86; open April–Oct 10–12 and 2–6.30; visits to the chais by appointment; adm*). Originally the country house of a Bordelais judge, and later of

The most traditional châteaux (like Yquem) harvest the berries literally one by one, selecting each by its degree of noble rot; some years the pickers will go around the vineyard as many as 10 or 11 times. Add to the high cost of labour the risk: because the grapes are picked late in the year, a good rainstorm could make the overripe grapes pop and replace all the carefully cultivated noble rot with common old rot. Another factor is the low density of growth: a good Médoc yields 40 hectolitres per hectare; a Sauternes is allowed 25 maximum. Château d'Yquem averages a mere seven and should be aged a minimum of 10 years before drinking. Because of the noble rot, the vinification requires three grape pressings; during fermentation, the wine needs special attention to maintain a balance between sugar and alcohol, which must be a minumum 12.5 per cent – many are over 14. Hence the extraordinary prices for the finest Sauternes and Barsacs. Conditions in 1989 and 1990 were so superb that in this century you have to go back to the legendary Sauternes of 1928 and '29 to find their match; 1983, '86 and '88 were classic years as well.

The five *communes* of the Sauternes *appellation* lie on the left bank of the Ciron, while Barsac is all by itself on the right bank, where the soil has more limestone and clay, enough to create a subtle difference noticeable to the lucky few who can afford to drink these classiest of dessert wines more than just on special occasions. Like Médoc, Sauternes-Barsacs were classified in the Paris Exhibition of 1855, and have kept their *cru* classifications ever since, although in many cases quality has noticeably gone up or down. While some of the châteaux welcome visitors, prices are too prohibitive for casual tastings; persistence, however, may well be rewarded with a fine Sauternes in the 100F region to put aside for your daughter's or granddaughter's wedding. An excellent place to start is in the centre of Barsac, at the Maison du Vin de Barsac, Place de l'Eglise, t 05 56 27 15 44, which offers comparative tastings of Barsac and Sauternes *grands crus*, and sales at château prices (*open mid-Feb–Dec daily 10–7*).

the Count de Lur-Saluces, Malle with its distinctive breast-shaped towers is one of the few châteaux in France never to have fallen into rack and ruin, and has most of its original furnishings, a pretty set of silhouettes, a fine Italian garden and a nymphaeum decorated with a crazed pebble mosaic depicting figures from the *commedia dell'arte.* Wine-tastings (Malle is a *deuxième cru classé*) are included in the price of admission.

The port at **Langon**, the largest town and capital of the southern Graves, is the highest on the Garonne to feel the tide; note the flood markers posted on the corner of Rue Laffargue. For centuries, until the advent of rail, it was important in shipping wine and other products from the hinterland. Trains between Agen and Bordeaux still stop here, and it even boasts a new 18-hole golf course at St-Pardon de Conques (***t** 05 56 62 25 43*). Its Gothic church of **St-Gervais** contains a surprise: a somewhat atypical Zurbarán (the *Immaculate Conception*, showing the Virgin floating in russet clouds on the heads of two cherubs, her dark mantle flowing all around like a bat-winged storm cloud); the local curé discovered it by accident in 1966. In the **Maison du Paysan**, 1 Allées Jean-Jaurès, are some remains of the 12th-century church of Notre-Dame-du-Bourg: all the beautiful capitals were sold off in 1926 and are now in the Cloisters Museum in New York. You can take a little **cruise** up the Canal des Deux-Mers (*L'Escapade, office 43 bis Rue des Salières, **t** 05 56 63 06 45*).

South of Sauternes: a Detour into the Landes

Landes in French means moors, sand and maritime pines, and once they begin south of the Garonne they don't stop until the foothills of the Pyrenees, constituting the largest single forest in Europe. South of Sauternes or Langon you can dip into the pines; for more, head up the river Leyre from the Bassin d'Arcachon to Belin-Béliet (*see* pp.296–7).

There is already a definite Landaise air about **Villandraut**, the birthplace of Bertrand Got, who went on to become Pope Clement V in 1305. The papacy then wasn't quite the plummy job it is now – in 1305 Rome was in the throes of all-out gang warfare and not a very safe place even for the boss of the syndicate; Clement V's predecessor, Boniface VIII, usually avoided the city, but a rival faction eventually caught up with him and delivered the famous 'Slap of Anagni' across the pope's mug that symbolically put an end to the power of the medieval papacy. The slapper, Sciarra Colonna, was acting for Philippe IV of France, and, when this same wily king invited Clement to move to France in 1308, he jumped at the chance. Before moving the papal court to Avignon and the Comtat Venaissin (a piece of French territory that was the papal spoils of the Albigensian crusade), Clement spent a year here in his strong, moat-belted **Château de Villandraut**, on a plain instead of on a hill and without a castle keep, a style made popular in Wales under Edward I; it became a model for several other 'clementine' castles in the area (***t** 05 56 25 87 57; open daily June and Sept 10–12.30 and 2.30–7, July and Aug 10–7, Oct–May 2–5; adm*). The other thing to do in Villandraut is hire a canoe or kayak for a leisurely paddle under the big leafy trees that line the river Ciron: contact the **Canoe-Kayak Club du Ciron** (*Pont de Villandraut, **t/f** 05 56 25 38 65; open all year*): minibuses will take you 15km up the pretty gorge to Pompejac. They also organize mountain-bike trips.

Just west of Villandraut on the D3, the church at **St-Léger de Balson** has some unusual medieval frescoes of labourers, with comic-strip-like captions over their heads, while further south **Bourideys** awaits as a perfect and utterly tranquil example of a Landes village. **Préchac**, to the northeast, has a late Romanesque church; 4km east, overlooking the gorge of the river Ciron, the irregular polygonal **Château de Cazeneuve** (***t** 05 56 25 48 16; open June–mid-Sept daily 2–6, Easter–May and mid-Sept–Oct Sat, Sun and hols 2–6; adm*) was originally a medieval castle, built in the 11th century by the d'Albrets, then owned by the kings of England, then later by the d'Albrets again; they became kings of Navarre and produced Henri IV, who brought his Queen Margot here for a holiday. The family made the old castle into a pleasure palace in the 17th century, and their descendant, the Duke of Sabran-Pontevès, owns it to this day. It has kept a number of interesting features – the *salles troglodytes* cut into the central court, a Greek nymphaeum (the *Grotte de la Reine*), furnished royal apartments and sculpted chimney-pieces, as well as a mill, lake, bamboo garden and lovely park along the river.

The Pope Clement V tour continues, however, east of Villandraut in the little town of **Uzeste**, founded by Clement's Got (or Goth) ancestors in the 13th century. In 1312 Clement began to pour money into Uzeste for the construction of a small but dignified **collegiate church** (***t** 05 56 25 87 48; guided visits mid-April–mid-Oct Sat and Sun 3–6*), and the next year declared his intention of being buried there, although this wish was granted a lot sooner than he might have hoped. Being in Avignon obliged Clement to go along with Phillipe IV's 1312 scheme of abolishing the Templars and confiscating their enormous wealth to fill the king of France's empty treasury. The demise of the Templars culminated in 1314, when their Grand Master, Jacques de Molay, was burned alive at the stake in Paris, but not before he cried out that both king and pope would follow him to the grave that same year, as indeed they did – the pope from indigestion after eating a plate of ground emeralds, prescribed by his doctor. Clement's monument to himself here in Uzeste suffered when the Protestants took some really good whacks at his church and **tomb** (1315–59): the white marble effigy atop the black slab no longer has a face, although the embroidery of the vestments and anatomy of the dragon at his feet show a great attention to detail. Until the Protestants came, the tomb also sported a black marble baldachin, decorated with alabasters, precious stones and all the sumptuous pomp required by a dead medieval pope. The church's 14th-century *Virgin and Child* was once the object of a local pilgrimage. These days Uzeste is especially zesty around 15 September, when a four-day festival of all kinds of music fills its streets.

Bazas and its Cathedral

For the past 2,500 years, **Bazas** (Gallo-Roman *Cossio*) has been the natural capital of a little region of fertile hills south of the Garonne, once the stomping ground of the Vassates Celts. From the 5th century until the Revolution Bazas even had its own bishop, thanks in part to a unique relic – the blood spilled at the beheading of St John the Baptist, supposedly wiped up with a cloth by a pious woman of Bazas, who just happened to be on the scene and brought the cloth and the new religion back home with her. To shelter the precious relic, a triple church was built on the town's most prominent site, dedicated to Saints John the Baptist, Peter and Stephen. When this threatened to fall over, the present **cathedral** was begun in 1233 by the seneschal of the King of England. Completely contrary to usual practice, the building began with the triple portal (echoing the original triple church) and ended with the choir, and this last bit was only completed thanks to subsidies sent over from Avignon by Clement V. When the rampaging Huguenots turned up to wreck Bazas's pride and joy in 1578, the bishop, Arnaud de Pontac, saved the façade by buying it from the Huguenots for 10,000 *écus*.

It was worth it: you certainly don't get such jammy pieces of theatre in many other places in the Gironde. Around the year 1500, a flamboyant rose window (the petals of which contain the 64 names of the bishops of Bazas), pinnacles, buttresses and a gallery were added to set off the three great 13th-century Gothic doorways. The **central portal** is devoted to the *Last Judgement*, showing the dead climbing out of their tombs, the good souls blithely heading off to the New Jerusalem as some nasty-looking devils corral the wicked into the maw of hell, while stacks of virtues, prophets, angels, martyrs and confessors rocket vertiginously up the five archings. Along the lintel are scenes from the life of Bazas's patron saint, John the Baptist. The **north portal** is dedicated to the *Mission of the Apostles*, especially that of St Peter; here too are *Adam and Eve*, *Cain and Abel* and the *Wise and Foolish Virgins*. The **south portal** belongs to the Virgin, showing her *Coronation*, *Dormition* and *Assumption*. The finely detailed archings here are sculpted with signs of the zodiac, scenes of the Virgin's life and the tree of Jesse. The interior, completely destroyed by the Huguenots in 1578, was carefully repaired by Bishop Pontac, his nephew and great-nephew, only to be devasted again in the Revolution. To fill the space, furnishings, paintings and an 18th-century high altar in coloured marbles were brought in from deconsecrated churches in the area. South of the cathedral you can visit the pretty chapterhouse garden, with a collection of archaeological finds, overlooking the valley of the Beuve.

Part of the cathedral's charm is its magnificent setting, atop the vast, gently sloping **Place de la Cathédrale**. This is bordered by arcades and some fine 16th- and 17th-century houses, most strikingly No.3, the **Maison de l'Astronome** (1530), with ogival arcades and carvings of stars, planets, a blazing comet and a wizard astronomer in a pointy hat. Things get very hot indeed here every 23 June, when strings of bonfires are lit in honour of St John, and the Bazadais leap over the flames and take embers home for luck, as everyone in Europe did a few centuries ago. A bull is symbolically offered to the mayor, for Bazas means beef as much as Sauternes means wine; the town is home of its very own race of cattle, the *bazadaise*.

Besides *entrecôtes*, Bazas also offers visitors a **Musée de l'Apothicairerie**, a pharmacy from the time of Louis XV, and a small **museum** in the former hospital at Rue St-Antoine with a small religious and decorative arts collection (***t** 05 56 25 25 84; open July–mid-Sept, or by appointment; contact the tourist office*). In the Allées Clemenceau you can pick up the pretty **Promenade de la Brèche** along the top of the ramparts, a walkway lined with shady trees with views over the valley. The **Lac de La Prade**, just east on the D9, is a favourite nest spot for herons and other water fowl.

Around Bazas

North of Bazas towards Langon, the last of the Graves vineyards are in **Mazères**, where you have a chance to visit the remarkable **Château de Roquetaillade** (***t** 05 56 76 14 16; open all year 8.30–12 and 2–6, by appointment at weekends; adm*), high on a spur that has had some kind of fort on it since prehistoric times. There are actually two castles, one built in the 12th century and partly ruined, and the other built in the 14th century by a nephew of Pope Clement in the 'clementine' style. In the 19th century, the owners hired the famous restorer Viollet-le-Duc (responsible for Notre-Dame-de-Paris, Carcassonne, etc.) to give it the full medieval treatment, from the exterior down to the furniture, and he seems to have had a grand old time with the

Entrecôte à la Bordelaise

Although nowadays a juicy two-inch-thick rib steak from Bazas is practically synonymous with this dish, until the end of the 18th century this method of cooking was reserved for another kind of meat: rats. Yes, rats, specifically the big fat ones caught prowling the vineyards, their bellies gorged with grapes. Obviously just what you'd expect of a people who lust after lamprey in blood-thickened sauce – but, keeping in mind the Belgian restaurant that has thrived serving rat fricassée for a century, it may taste better than it sounds. An added delight in rat Bordelaise was surely the peculiar pleasure derived from eating one's enemy, in the same way French gardeners eagerly tuck into a dish of *escargots*. In most restaurants, what passes for an *entrecôte à la bordelaise* – a slice of beef with a sauce of shallots and wine – was invented by Parisian chefs in the 19th century (obviously before or after the 1870 siege of Paris, when rat – and cat – were considered great delicacies). To make the real McCoy, grill your *bœuf de Bazas* over a barbecue of vine cuttings (*sarments*): Cabernet Sauvignon for the heat, and, at the last moment, Merlot, which spreads out the smoke. Top it with finely chopped shallots and serve with a side dish of *cèpes* cooked with garlic and parsley.

project. Not one to let an idea go to waste, the grand stairway he built in the castle keep is the one he had designed in the competition for the Paris Opera. There's a farm museum as well, the **Métairie de Roquetaillade**, with a 12th-century dovecote, farm animals, and 100-year-old farmhouse interiors. The wine that bears the château's name belongs to another family and has recently won medals for its reds – especially the 1983, '85 and '86.

North of Bordeaux: the Gironde Estuary and Médoc

Great freighters and tankers promenade along Europe's largest estuary, along with dainty fishing boats equipped with wing nets, skimming over the water like giant dragonflies, nabbing lamprey, shad, eels and crayfish. From March to September the prize catch is elvers, or ***pibales***, only two inches long, a delicacy that can demand as much as 1,000F a kilo on the market and traditionally must be eaten with wooden forks. Islets in the estuary come and go with the tide; refineries and port installations come and go with the economy, and even the vineyards of Médoc took some hard knocks in the 1920s and '30s, only to rebound – the first great year was 1945, in time to celebrate the end of the war. Birdwatchers may want to keep an eye out for purple herons: the only known nesting areas of these rare birds in this region are in the marshlands along the Gironde. The storms in December 1999 wreaked considerable damage to the pine forest in this area but, despite the gaps in the trees and sheared branches, it remains basically intact and you can enjoy the delicious shade from the summer furnace.

Haut-Médoc: Macau, Margaux and Moulis-en-Médoc

Haut-Médoc begins just beyond the northern suburbs of Bordeaux; aim for Blanquefort and get on the main *route des châteaux*, the D2, from which the great plantation houses are nearly all easy to spot. These mostly date from the 18th and 19th centuries and lend Médoc its patina of distinction and big money. Yet resident proprietors are increasingly rare; corporations and foreign consortiums, looking for sound investments, have bought up some of the most prestigious Médoc vineyards, although foreign ownership is nothing new here – in the 18th century three of the finest châteaux belonged to Irishmen named Kirwan, Dillon and Lynch (the last was once mayor of Bordeaux). Note that, while many châteaux welcome visitors, tastings are rarely part of the tour.

The first village of vinous renown is **Macau**, which also produces AOC artichokes and has a little estuary port, where the Bordelais come at weekends to gobble down *bichettes* (little fresh shrimps). At **Labarde**, the next hamlet north, the **Château Siran** (*t 05 57 88 34 04; open for guided tours daily 10.15–6*) and its ample *chais* contain some of the best *cru bourgeois* in the Haut-Médoc – the very best is stocked in a nuclear fallout shelter (head there if the sirens start to wail). Siran's park is famous for its cyclamens that burst into bloom from the end of August to early October; several rooms of the château, once owned by the ancestors of Toulouse-Lautrec, contain works of art – a *Young Bacchus* by Caravaggio and engravings by Velázquez, Rubens and Daumier – as well as 19th-century furniture and ceramics. Another highly rated vineyard in Labarde, 19th-century neo-Renaissance **Château Giscours**, was rebuilt in honour of Empress Eugenie; it welcomes visitors to its *chais* and pretty wooded park, planted in 1881, where you can take in polo matches in the afternoon, on weekends in September (*t 05 57 97 09 09; open 9–12.30 and 2–6*). In **Arsac**, the next *commune* to the west, the **Château d'Arsac**, 'the blue winery' (*t 05 56 58 83 90; visits by appointment only*), is architecturally one of the most striking, beautifully landscaped with a lake, and features exhibitions of contemporary art as well as tastings of its excellent Haut-Médoc.

The wines of Siran and Giscours are in the prestigious communal *appellation* of **Margaux**, noted for the magnificent finesse and delicate perfume of its wines. The **Maison du Vin** in Place La Trémoille dispenses information and sells bottles (*t 05 57 88 70 82; open mid-June–mid-Sept 9–7, out of season 9–12 and 2–6, afternoons only on Mon, closed Sun*) and you can visit the cradle of its celebrated *premier grand cru*, **Château Margaux**, just outside the village (*t 05 57 88 83 83; ring a day ahead to book an hour-long tour of the* chais, *Mon–Fri 10–12 and 2–4, closed Aug and during the harvest*). Here are some of the oldest, most wizened vines in the Médoc, and one of the most severely neoclassical châteaux, designed in 1802 by a student of Victor Louis, set in a pretty English garden. While in the area, have a look at the lovely early 17th-century **Château d'Issan** (*grand cru classé* 1855) set amid the moats of its medieval predecessor: 'For the tables of kings and the altars of the gods', reads the inscription on the gate (*t 05 57 88 35 91; visits mid-June–mid-Sept Mon–Sat 10–12.30 and 2–6, other times ring ahead*). The adjacent **Château Palmer** (1860), another *grand cru classé*

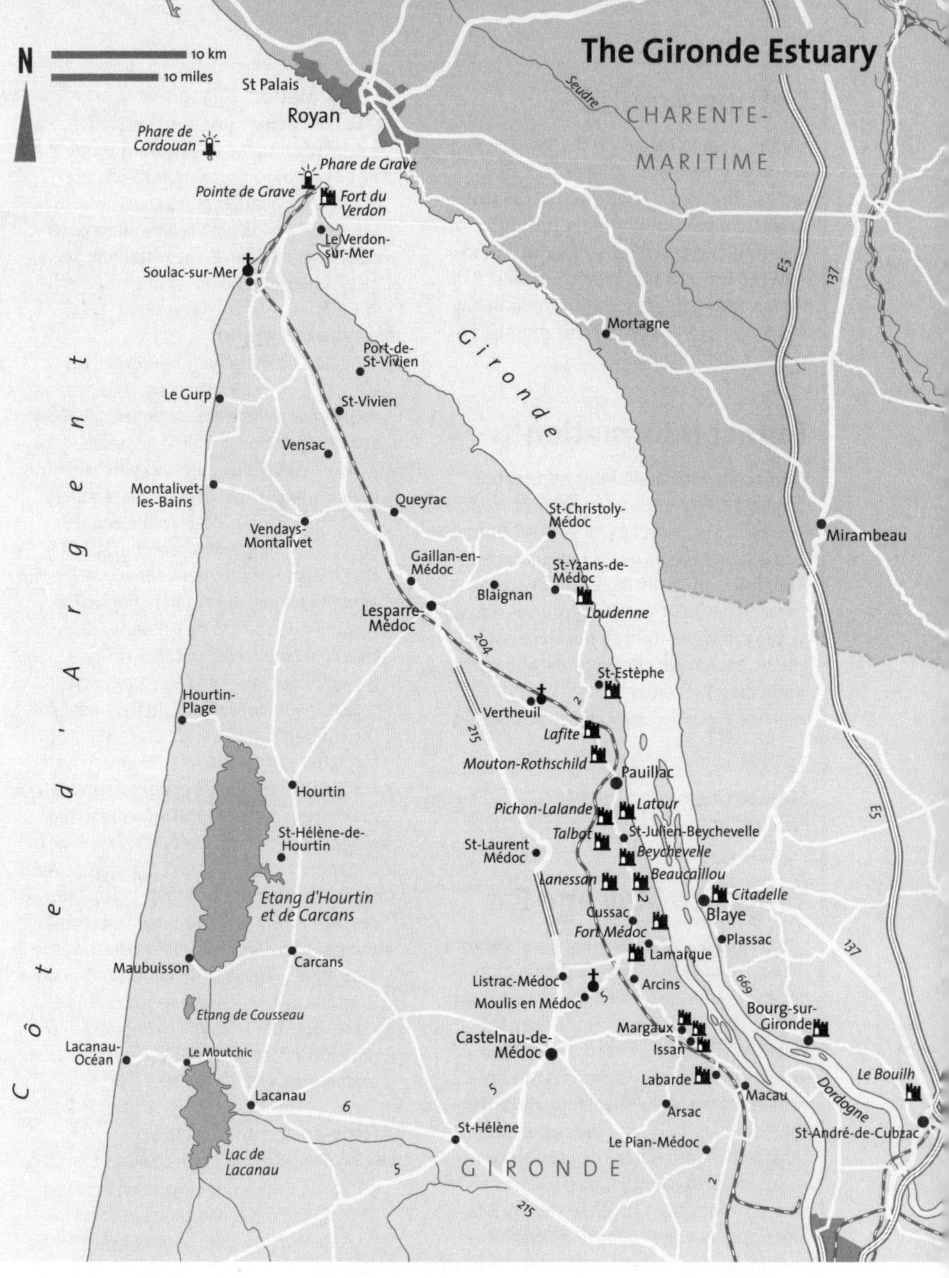

in 1855, was founded by one of Wellington's generals and is still partly British-owned; its wine is often rated just under Château Margaux (***t*** *05 57 88 72 72; open April–Sept 9–11.30 and 2–5, other times ring ahead*).

Moulis-en-Médoc (inland from Margaux and to the northwest) is a charming little village, the seat of the smallest communal *appellation*, where the top wine has been

Getting Around

Trains from Bordeaux on the Soulac line stop in many of the Médoc villages, including Pauillac; the area is also served by Citram **buses** from Bordeaux. If you're driving from the north, there's a **ferry** across the Gironde between Blaye and Lamarque near Fort Médoc, sailing roughly every 90mins in July and Aug, much less often other months, **t** 05 57 42 04 49 for schedules.

Tourist Information

Pauillac: for wine and tourist information, contact the *Maison du Tourisme et du Vin du Médoc*, La Verrerie, **t** 05 56 59 23 38, **f** 05 56 59 03 08. They have a video, hire out bikes, produce a guide listing all the châteaux open to visits, offer tasting courses, and sell over 300 wines from all the Médoc appellations, at château prices, as well as organizing other local activities.

Lesparre: Place Docteur-Lapeyrade, **t** 05 56 41 21 96.

Market Days

Pauillac: Sat.

Where to Stay and Eat

In the old days, one of the spin-offs of wine-making in the Médoc was suckling-lamb. All large vineyards had sheep whose task it was to graze between the rows and keep the weeds down. Lambs, because they bounced around too much and damaged the vines, were confined to the sheepfold, and fed only their mother's milk until they were slaughtered two months later. Their tender pearly meat was a delicacy that died out when chemical herbicides stole the sheep's job. Since 1985, however, *agneau de Pauillac*, raised the old-fashioned way, has made a comeback in local butchers' shops and on restaurant menus. Another speciality is a refined tripe sausage called *grenier médocain*, rarely seen outside the region.

Le Pian-Médoc ✉ 33290

******Le Pont Bernet**, just north of Bordeaux as you drive on to the peninsulas, **t** 05 56 70 20 19, **f** 05 56 70 22 90, *www.pont-bernet.fr* (*moderate*). A rather plush Logis hotel in 15 acres of grounds, with tennis and a pool; near to a golf course. The restaurant serves local dishes (*menus 95–300F*).

Margaux ✉ 33460

********Relais de Margaux**, Chemin de l'Ile Vincent, **t** 05 57 88 38 30, **f** 05 57 88 31 73 (*expensive*). Where Médoc buyers go to swan around and deduct it all as a business expense. Set in an enormous park with lush gardens, and a lovely pool; a glass gallery links the luxurious hotel to the equally beautiful restaurant, where the Japanese chef prepares a succulent *agneau de Pauillac* as well as other classic land- and seafood, accompanied by a wine list and wine prices that could melt a credit card (*menus 195–420F, Sat lunch and Sun 210F only*).

******Le Pavillon de Margaux**, in the middle of the vineyards at Le Caire, **t** 05 57 88 77 54, **f** 05 57 88 77 73 (*moderate*). Fourteen well-equipped rooms and a good restaurant, making good use of local ingredients: *bar rôti médocain et son civet de bigorneaux*, for instance (*menus 89–220F*). *Closed Nov–April.*

Château de Giscours, **t** 05 57 97 09 09 (*inexpensive*). A few bed-and-breakfast rooms.

Auberge Le Savoie, 1 Place Trémoille, **t** 05 57 88 31 76. Rare in these parts for offering good seasonal dishes, a warm welcome and a reasonable bill (*no credit cards*) (*menus from 80F*). *Closed Sun and Mon eve out of season, and several weeks in winter.*

Arcins-en-Médoc ✉ 33460

Le Lion d'Or, Place de la République, **t** 05 56 58 96 79. On the Médoc wine road, between Margaux and Pauillac, this is *gourmand* heaven: look for nothing but Big Authentic Food and plenty of it (*menus 68F at lunch*). *Closed Sun, Mon and July. Book.*

Moulis/Castelnau-de-Médoc ✉ 33480

Château de Foulon, set in the woodlands south of Castelnau, **t** 05 56 58 20 18, **f** 05 56 58 23 43 (*moderate*). This 19th-century château offers five dreamy, perfectly tranquil rooms and the chance to watch swans fluttering across the lawns.

★★**Les Landes**, Place Romain Videau, in Castelnau, **t** 05 56 58 73 80, **f** 05 56 58 11 59 (*inexpensive*). A small and reasonably priced Logis de France, with Bordelais specialities in the restaurant. *Closed Sun.*

Listrac ✉ 33480

Auberge Médocaine, 13 Place du Maréchal Juin, **t/f** 05 56 58 08 86 (*inexpensive*). In the centre; six simple rooms and a restaurant specializing in eel (*menus from 65F, closed Mon out of season*).

Château Cap-Léon-Veyrin Donissan, in the hamlet of Donissan, **t** 05 56 58 07 28, **f** 05 56 58 05 70 (*inexpensive*). For five generations this family has produced an excellent *cru bourgeois*; they also run this small bed-and-breakfast in a comfortable guesthouse in the middle of a vineyard. You can visit the *chais*.

Pauillac ✉ 33250

★★★★**Château de Cordeillan-Bages**, Route des Châteaux, **t** 05 56 59 24 24, **f** 05 56 59 01 89 (*expensive*). Set in a sea of vineyards, this lovely little place has 25 charming rooms in the Relais et Châteaux tradition and the best restaurant in Médoc, where the best local ingredients are enhanced without muss or fuss by a true master chef, Pascal Charreyras; the *ragoût* of asparagus and morels is heavenly. Even for a restaurant patronized by wine merchants and wine-lovers, the selection from the cellar is astounding, thanks to one of France's best sommeliers, Pierre Paillardon, who loves to share his knowledge (*menus 195–480F for dinner*). *Closed Mon, Tues lunch, Sat lunch, and mid-Dec–Jan.*

★★**De France et d'Angleterre**, 3 Quai Albert de Pichon, **t** 05 56 59 01 20, **f** 05 56 59 02 31 (*moderate*). Pleasant riverside rooms in a pretty building, near stands selling *bichettes*, little shrimps lightly flavoured with aniseed.

Blaignan ✉ 33340

Auberge des Vignobles, **t** 05 56 09 04 81. In this village lost amongst the fields of vines, west of St-Yzans, this small stone building offer the chance to eat outside among the trees. Quite simple but good-value meals such as *truite meunière* and *entrecôte aux sarments* (*menus 110–215F*). *Closed Sun eve, Mon and Nov–mid-Mar.*

St-Christoly Médoc ✉ 33340

Restaurant La Maison Du Douanier, 2 Route de By, **t** 05 56 41 35 25. In a quiet village on the estuary northeast of Blaignan, a big house surrounded by buddleia and other flowering shrubs and bushes, where swifts fly in and out of the eaves, and you can eat looking out over the riverbanks. Local cuisine includes *fricassée de poulet des Landes* and *pavé de truite de mer au beurre citronné* (*menus 125–300F*). *Closed Mon May–Sept and Sun eve Sept–Jun.*

St-Julien Beychevelle ✉ 33250

Le St-Julien, 11 Rue de St-Julien, **t** 05 56 59 63 87. Another culinary stop among the wine villages, with a good reputation and a good selection of seafood such as *salade de homard aux herbes du jardin* (*menus 95–350F*).

Lesparre-Médoc ✉ 33340

★★★★**Château Layauga**, 2km from the centre in Gaillan-en-Médoc, **t** 05 56 41 26 83, **f** 05 56 41 19 52 (*expensive*). Seven very pretty rooms in a lovely château, with a pond and lawns set among the vineyards, and a restaurant with a solid emphasis on the best ingredients the southwest can offer – *cèpes*, truffles, foie gras, game and fish – combined in rare fashions. Save room for one of the chef's excellent desserts (*menus 185–450F*). *Closed Feb.*

Médoc, Haut-Médoc and Other Médocs

Geographically a continuation of the Graves, Médoc is a 10km-wide ribbon between the Gironde estuary and the sands of the Landes forests, a thick Quaternary terrace of pink and blue gravel and sand. Although its 1961 *grand crus classés* are today the celebrities of Bordeaux wines, protectionists in the Graves prevented anyone from planting vines in this ideal wine region until the late 17th century, when wealthy Englishmen, insisting on better-quality wines and increasingly buying port, Madeira and malmsey instead of claret, became a force in the market that the Bordelais couldn't afford to ignore. The secret behind Médoc's success and consistency is the unusual depth of its poor, gravelly ridges, which forces the vine roots to go deep in search of water and nourishment; the older the vine (10 years is the minimum age for a Médoc *cru*), the stronger and deeper the roots, and the greater its ability to withstand drought. Equally, in soggy years the perfect drainage of the gravel keeps the roots from getting waterlogged. Because the gravel absorbs heat during the day, damage from spring frosts can often be avoided; the vines are pruned quite short as well. Even in the worst years, a *grand cru* usually comes shining through.

Climate, as always, is another important factor. The vast Gironde estuary regulates the temperature, keeping the Médoc from extremes (the great estates all 'see the water'), while the rains and winds off the Atlantic are tempered by the screen of pine forests of the coast. If away from the waterfront, Médoc's great gravel ridges overlook *jalles*, the wide gullies that both drain the Landes and help moderate temperatures. Another factor is the vast size of the estates – enabling the *maîtres des chais* to adjust the blending and proportions of the grape varieties, depending on the vagaries of the weather. Slow-ripening Cabernet Sauvignon is the chief here,

known as the *Château Chasse-Spleen* ever since Byron commented that a glass of it chases away ill-humours. It is closely rivalled by **Château Poujeaux** (***t** 05 56 58 02 96; offers tastings Mon–Fri 9–12 and 2–6, but ring ahead*); both are *cru grand bourgeois exceptionnel*. Just opposite the Moulis station, **Château Maucaillou** (*cru bourgeois*) is dedicated not only to wine but to teaching people about it; the **Musée des Arts et Métiers de la Vigne et du Vin** (***t** 05 56 58 01 23; open all year 10–12 and 2–6*) pulls out all the stops to initiate you into the cult of the 'blood of the vine', including an optional helicopter ride over the vineyards; you can take a wine-tasting course here and learn about marrying vintages to food at its *école du vin*; meals, too, on request. Moulis also has a 12th-century fortified Romanesque **church** with an ornate apse (carved modillons outside and capitals inside, one showing Tobias carrying a fish); the holy water stoup built into the façade was set aside for lepers.

Listrac and St-Julien

Adjacent to Moulis is another tiny communal *appellation*, **Listrac**. Both Moulis and Listrac are distinguished by their powerful wines, although the fact that they don't

accounting for half the vines grown in Médoc, and forming up to 80 per cent of the *grands crus*; Merlot Noir (around 35 per cent of most Médocs) gives the wine strength and suppleness; a dollop of Cabernet Franc adds its characteristic bouquet.

Médocs have been classified and reclassified more than any wines on this planet. The Paris Exhibition of 1855 classified 60 Médoc vineyards and divided them into five *crus* that, thanks to vested interests, have become fixed in concrete like the hand-prints of the movie stars in Hollywood; when Mouton-Rothschild at last moved up into the first-division *premiers crus* in 1973 it was a major event. Although *premiers crus* shatter the price barriers, the amounts asked for the other four growths tend to reflect current quality rather than the 1855 classifications; hence superior fourth growths that often cost more than second.

In 1920 Médoc estates left out of the Paris rating created a syndicate of their own, the *cru bourgeois*, which, unlike Paris, has undergone a number of adjustments, most recently in 1978. A *cru bourgeois* has to come from a property with a minimum of 17 acres, be bottled on the estate and not in a cooperative, and pass the syndicate's taste test; a *cru grand bourgeois* has to be aged in wooden casks; a *cru grand bourgeois exceptionnel* has to be château-bottled in a *commune* of Haut-Médoc (that is, the half of the region closer to Bordeaux). Besides all these, there are eight small communal *appellations* in Médoc. For all the fussiness, there's more than enough to go around: the average production of the whole Médoc area is 112 million bottles a year. Last but not least, recent studies demonstrate that it's good for your health – Médoc contains bactericidal ingredients that can knock certain viruses cold; plus it speeds up digestion and has a natural beneficial effect on arteriosclerosis. So drink hearty!

'see the water' prevented them from being classified in 1855; the Rothschild-owned **Château Clarke**, one of the rising stars of Listrac, was entirely re-created from scratch in 1973 (***t** 05 56 58 38 00; open June–Sept, ring ahead*). From Listrac, take the D5 down towards the Gironde to see the **Château de Lamarque**, a 12th–14th-century castle that defended the port of Lamarque and Bordeaux from raiders down the estuary until the task was taken over by nearby **Fort Médoc** (***t** 05 56 58 98 40; open April–Oct 10–8 and Nov–Mar 10–5; adm*). Designed by Vauban, Louis XIV's crack fortifications expert, the fort was begun in 1689 and completed only in 1721, owing to the difficulty of building on marshland. Besides the heavily sculpted **Porte Royale**, complete with Louis' sun symbol, you can visit the chapel and museum dedicated to local customs, and take in the view across the estuary to Médoc's sister citadels, at Blaye and the island Fort Pâté. North of Fort Médoc in **Cussac**, signposted off the D2, the eclectic neo-Tudor-Spanish **Château Lanessan** (1870) is the seat of an estate that has been in the same family since 1790; its *chai* was considered the paragon of modernity in the 19th century, and it produces an excellent Haut-Médoc *cru bourgeois supérieur* famous for its long ageing capacity. In the stables (complete with marble mangers), a **Musée du Cheval** displays an interesting collection of early horse-drawn vehicles from the beginning of the century, saddles and other antique horsey gear (***t** 05 56 58 94 80;*

hour-long guided tours of the chais and museum Sept–June 9–12 and 2–7, July and Aug 9–7, last visit at 6; adm).

The Duc d'Epernon, governor of Guyenne and admiral of France (*see* Château de Cadillac, pp.257–8), inherited by marriage the next estate on the grand Médoc tour, which became known as the **Château de Beychevelle** because every ship that passed in the estuary paid its respects by lowering its sails (*becha vela* in Gascon) before paying the admiral his toll. The current handsome white building bearing the name was originally a charterhouse, adapted to its new use in 1757 and decorated with a sculpted pediment (***t** 05 56 73 20 70; tours of the chais July and Aug Mon–Sat 10–5, April, June, Sept and Oct Mon–Fri 10–12 and 1.30–5, Nov–Mar Mon–Fri by appointment*). Nearby **Château-Talbot** is thought to have belonged to John Talbot, Earl of Shrewsbury, loser in the last battle in the Hundred Years' War at Castillon (*see* p.198). Both of these are in the *appellation* of **St-Julien**, wines distinguished for their fruitiness, delicate bouquet and original character; it has the highest density of *crus classés* of any in Médoc, especially the several riverside vineyards of Léoville that once formed the estate of the Marquis de Las-Cases, in the 18th century the most famous property in all Médoc. The most distinctive châteaux here are the 19th-century **Château Ducru-Beaucaillou**, home of a *grand cru classé* in 1855, and the similarly classed 18th-century **Château Langoa-Barton**, which unusually for Médoc has its *chais* under the château (***t** 05 56 59 06 05; open weekdays for tours and tastings by appointment*).

Pauillac, St-Estèphe and Lesparre-Médoc

Before settling into the comfortable position of capital of Médoc wines, with more *premiers grands crus classés* than any other *commune* in the Bordelais, the pleasant town of **Pauillac** was an important port, and home to one of the oldest sailing clubs in France. Before the 1930s, when the estuary was dredged, steamers from France's colonies in the Americas, Africa and Asia would call at the **Ile de Patiras**, in the middle of the Gironde, where passengers would be transferred to and from Bordeaux by smaller craft. Nowadays, instead of exotic steamers there's a marina, and views over the estuary to the looming silhouette of the Braud nuclear power plant. But what people come to ponder at Pauillac is another source of power altogether: the most famous wine châteaux in France, where the purest gravelly ridges produce over seven million bottles a year of the mightiest Médocs of all, full-bodied, presumably non-radioactive wines laced with a distinctive blackcurrant bouquet.

Approaching from the south, don't miss the **Château Pichon-Lalande**, built in the 19th century by the *grande dame* of Bordeaux wine, the Comtesse Lalande, complete with a magnificent view over the riverside vineyards (***t** 05 56 59 19 40; open Mon–Fri 9–11.30 and 2–4, ring ahead*). Further up, the legendary **Château Latour**, a *premier grand cru classé* owned by Allied-Lyons since 1989 (purchase price a record 10,000,000F an acre, for 200 acres), has rarely failed to live up to its status or to lead the way in innovation: in the 1960s it revolutionized the storage of wine in the

Bordelais with the introduction of stainless-steel vats (***t** 05 56 73 19 80; visits by appointment only*). For a break from wine, there's Pauillac's **Le Petit Musée d'Automates**, full of old-fashioned automata (*3 Rue Aristide Briand, **t** 05 56 59 02 45; open June–Sept daily 10.30–7, April, May and Dec Tues–Sun 2–7, Jan–Mar and Oct–Nov Fri–Sun 2–7; adm*).

Just north of Pauillac, **Château Mouton-Rothschild** was purchased by Baron Nathaniel de Rothschild in 1853. He was simply devastated when his wine was not selected as a *premier grand cru classé* in 1855 – an omission corrected in 1973, thanks to the enthusiasm of his descendant, Baron Philippe de Rothschild. In the 1920s Baron Philippe took over a property no one else in the family much cared for and made it his life's work until he died in 1988. One of his first moves was to bottle all of his wine at the château, an idea that seemed eccentric at the time. The neo-Tudor château, while not terribly interesting in itself, has an exquisite English garden.

For oenophiles, the guided tour must be the equivalent of obtaining a private audience with the pope, but is rather easier to arrange (***t** 05 56 73 21 29; open Mon–Fri 9.30–11 and 2–4, last visit on Fri at 3, April–Oct also open weekends and public hols, visits at 9.30, 11, 2 and 3.30; ring ahead; adm*). It begins with the awesomely perfect *grand chai*, Baron Philippe's 'theatre of wine', with its immaculate blond wood barrels lined up with military precision, and the château's collection of wine labels by famous artists (Dalí, Picasso, Warhol, etc.), a tradition begun in 1945. Perhaps because it belongs to the Rothschilds, the bank-vault atmosphere is unavoidable. The tour continues to a rich **museum** of art devoted to wine, *Le Vin dans l'Art* – the oldest pieces are from ancient Mesopotamia – and finishes with a climactic descent into the cellar, the holy of holies, where bottles worth as much as your house and car put together do their silent alchemical work. You can have a taste of the estate's more realistic wines, for a fee.

The big Mouton's eternal rival, the 120-hectare *premier grand cru classé* **Château Lafite-Rothschild** (owned by the Baron's cousins), broods over the Pauillac-Lesparre road from its height – in Gascon *la hite*, hence Lafite (***t** 01 53 89 78 00; visits by appointment Mon–Thurs 1.30–3.30, Fri 1.30–2.30, closed Aug–Oct*). Only a tower survives of the medieval castle, whose lords were in charge of dispensing justice in Pauillac, while the present château dates from the 18th century. In 1868 it was bought by James de Rothschild; his descendants hired the fashionable Catalan Ricardo Bofill to design their extraordinary new round *chais*. Lafite's cellars have bottles going back to 1797.

To the north lies **St-Estèphe**, the last communal *appellation* and one that produces vigorous, deeply coloured wines that differ from Pauillac and other Médocs in their need for extra-long periods of bottle-ageing. This is due to their large quantity of Merlot, which can reach as much as 40 per cent of the vintage, as in St-Estèphe's leading producer, **Château Cos d'Estournel**, just north of Lafite along the D2 (*grand cru classé* in 1855; ***t** 05 56 73 15 55; open Mon–Fri 10–12 and 2–4, ring ahead, tastings for a fee*). This is the most striking landmark along the *route des châteaux*, with its *chai* designed in the 19th century as a replica of the palace of the Sultan of Zanzibar. In this *appellation* you'll also find **Château Calon-Ségur**, another *grand cru classé* dating back to the 12th century and given its heart-shaped device in the 18th century by the Marquis de Ségur because he loved it so much (***t** 05 56 59 30 08; tours and tastings by appointment*). **Château La Haye** (***t** 05 56 59 32 18; open for tours and tastings July–mid-Sept Mon–Sat 10–6, other times same hours but by appointment*), a *cru bourgeois*, was built in 1557 and served as a favourite hunting retreat for Henri II and Diane de Poitiers; their initials are engraved in the very stones. **Vertheuil**, 6km west of St-Estèphe, has an 11th-century abbey **church** endowed with not one but two bell towers and a portal carved with the Elders of the Apocalypse and peasants pruning the vines. The interior, if you're lucky enough to catch it open, has three naves and was redesigned in the 15th century with a striking and unusual barrel-vaulted ambulatory, rib-vaulted choir and choir stalls carved with scenes from monastic life.

North of Loudenne in **St-Yzans-de-Médoc** is one last wine stop: the riverside **Château de Loudenne**, a handsome 18th-century charterhouse in a stunning setting with English gardens, a **museum** of 'The Victorians in Médoc', and guided tours and tastings of the estate's white, rosé and red AOC Médoc (***t** 05 56 73 17 80; open Mon–Fri 9.30–12 and 2–6, June, July and Aug also open weekends 3–6, Sept also open Sun 3–6*). The main town in the area is **Lesparre-Médoc**, which until the end of the 14th century was the seat of the *seigneur* of lower Médoc. His castle crumbled away over the centuries, leaving only an impressive foursquare keep known as the **Tour de l'Honneur** (***t** 05 56 41 06 75; open 15 June–15 Sept Mon–Sat 10–12 and 3–7, otherwise by appointment; adm*), housing a local-history **museum**, with tools and archaeological finds; there are panoramic views from the terrace.

The Côte d'Argent

From Médoc's Pointe de Grave to the Basque lands in the south runs a nearly straight, wide 228km ribbon of silver sand, with the giant rolling waves of the Atlantic on one side and deep green pine forests on the other. Dubbed the Côte d'Argent, the Silver Coast, by a Bordeaux newspaperman in 1905, there is so much sand here that it can be a nuisance (*see* Soulac-sur-Mer), but what the rocky French Riviera wouldn't do for a dune or two! Although we only go as far down as the Bassin d'Arcachon, the oldest resort in the northern half of the Côte d'Argent, it's enough to get a taste of the coast, offering broad sweeping vistas of empty space rare in Europe. If that weren't enough, just on the other side of the dunes is a score of lakes and ponds for calmer watersports, which also happen to lie on one of the Continent's major flyways for migratory birds. The whole is France's greatest outdoor playground: the pleasures of surfing, sailing, fishing, birdwatching, delta-planing, land yachting, canoeing, golfing, cycling, building sandcastles on the beach and slurping oysters draw more and more summer visitors every year.

Pointe de Grave to Vendays-Montalivet

From Lesparre to Soulac-sur-Mer

As you continue north of Lesparre, the vineyards begin to give way to coastal plains at **Queyrac**. Just before St-Vivien, you can visit a rare working windmill, the 1858 **Moulin de Vensac** (*t 05 56 09 45 00; open 10–12.30 and 2.30–6.30, July and Aug daily, June and Sept weekends, Oct–May Sun and hols*). After a few decades of inactivity, the mill has been on the job again since the 1980s, stone-grinding flour (on sale at the mill). From St-Vivien, the D2 leads to the village's small **oyster ports**. The oyster industry began by accident in 1868 when a captain, bringing oysters from Portugal to Arcachon, was waylaid here during a storm for several days and jettisoned his cargo, believing all the oysters had croaked. Enough of the bivalves survived and proliferated to create a profitable cash crop that employed 700 people before 1970, when the Portuguese oyster parasite struck and the new port at Verdon went into full polluting gear.

Legend has it that **Soulac-sur-Mer**, 'the Pearl of the Côte d'Argent', is the descendant of Noviomagus, the fabled ocean port of the Bituriges, which one cataclysmic day in the 6th century sank into the sea. The fact that recent explorations have proved the legend real surprises no one here; Soulac itself replaces an older Soulac that underwent a slower cataclysm, methodically swallowed up by sand in the 18th century. As a result of these roving sand piles, little remains of the medieval port where English pilgrims to Compostela would disembark, except for the **Basilique de Notre-Dame de la Fin des Terres**, Our Lady at the End of the Earth, and even this was buried twice by the voracious dunes, in the 13th and 18th centuries; in 1859, it was exhumed again, just before the top bit of the tower vanished forever, and it now sits tidily in a sand-lined hollow.

Our Lady at the End of the Earth was founded according to fond legend by St Veronica (*see* Rocamadour, p.157). It became a popular pilgrimage site – Louis XI personally made the journey three times – and it was always the first shrine that English pilgrims visited in France. It has a remarkable apse from the 13th century; inside, the polychrome wooden statue of the Virgin worshipped by the pilgrims is still in place, seated with baby Jesus, holding a lily in one hand and a swollen-sailed ship in the other. The carved capitals show Daniel in the lion's den, St Peter in prison, and the tomb and reliquary of St Veronica, who is said to have been buried here before her body was moved to Bordeaux. Three marble columns from the pre-Romanesque church survive in the apse; the stained glass dates from 1954. It is a classed a World Heritage Site.

Soulac also has a small **Musée d'Archéologie**, with some interesting prehistoric and Gallo-Roman artefacts (*28 Rue Victor Hugo, by the tennis courts,* ***t*** *05 56 09 83 89; open June–mid-Sept daily 3–7*). On Bd du Front-du-Mer you can see the lighthouse of Cordouan, 8km away, or play the slots at the casino; just south is Soulac's small resort of **L'Amélie-sur-Mer**, named after a ship that was wrecked here decades ago. The big sand dune here is part of the coastal natural park.

Getting Around

Frequent **trains** in the summer and less frequent but regular ones in the winter link Bordeaux St-Jean or Bordeaux St-Louis to Soulac-sur-Mer, Le Verdon-sur-Mer and Pointe de Grave; there are **bus** links from Lesparre station direct to Vendays-Monalivet and Hourtin in July and August. Some trains are replaced by SNCF **bus** from Pauillac (**t** 05 58 59 00 63). **Ferries** from Le Verdon port to Royan (in the Charente-Maritime) run roughly every two hours, or every half-hour in July and August (**t** 05 56 73 37 73). At Soulac hire quality **bikes** by the week (*April–Sept*) at Cyclo'Star, 9 Rue Fernand-Lafargue, **t** 05 56 09 71 38. In summer, the little **PGV train** runs along the ocean from Pointe de Grave to Verdon and Soulac (*July and Aug daily, June and Sept weekends, call tourist offices for schedules*).

Tourist Information

St-Vivien-de-Médoc: Hôtel de Ville, **t** 05 56 09 58 50.

Soulac-sur-Mer: 68 Rue de la Plage, **t** 05 56 09 86 61, **f** 05 56 73 63 76.

Le Verdon-sur-Mer: Rue François-le-Breton, **t** 05 56 09 61 78, **f** 56 09 61 32.

Vendays-Montalivet: 62 Av de l'Océan, **t** 05 56 09 30 12, **f** 05 56 09 36 11.

Market Days

St-Vivien: Wed.

Soulac: daily.

Vendays-Montalivet: daily in July and Aug.

Sports and Activities

There's no lack of exciting things to do along this shore: Soulac's tourist office can tell you where to parachute, land yacht (*char à voile*), surf, kayak surf, body board, canoe (through the forest from Vensac to St-Vivien), gallop along the sands, or play paintball or tennis; in the evening you can drop whatever money you have left at the **Casino de la Plage**, **t** 05 56 09 82 74. At Vendays-Monalivet, **CAP 33**, **t** 05 56 73 77 28, has facilities for nearly every conceivable sport, including some you may never have heard of before (wave kayaking, speed sailing). They also have instructors, for children as well as adults. Rates are minimal, and you can find them on the sea front.

Where to Stay and Eat

Soulac-sur-Mer ✉ 33780

★★L'Hacienda, 4 Av Périer de Larsan, **t** 05 56 09 81 34, **f** 05 56 73 65 57 (*inexpensive*). A simple Logis de France, centrally located, with a garden courtyard.

★★Des Pins, **t** 05 56 73 27 27, **f** 05 56 73 60 39 (*inexpensive*). Nothing fancy at this simple Logis de France, but pines and sea views, and a beach 100m away; the restaurant is one of the best in the area, serving good reliable food (*menus from 100F*). *Closed mid-Jan–mid-Mar.*

★★Michelet, 1 Rue Bernard Baguenard, **t** 05 56 09 84 18, **f** 05 56 73 65 25 (*inexpensive*). A favourite seaside villa offering 20 pleasant rooms and a warm welcome. *Closed Jan.*

★★Dame de Cœur, Place de l'Eglise, **t** 05 56 09 80 80, **f** 05 56 09 97 47 (*inexpensive*). Pleasant rooms.

★De la Gare, Route des Lacs, **t** 05 56 09 85 60, **f** 05 56 73 63 28 (*cheap*). More economical.

Camping Palace, Bd Marson de Montbrun, **t** 05 56 09 80 22, **f** 05 56 09 84 23. Three-star, along the ocean, with a capacity of 535 campers (*open May–mid-Sept*).

Des Pins, L'Amélie, **t** 05 56 09 82 52. More rustic; two minutes from the beach. *Open June–Sept.*

Montalivet-les-Bains ✉ 33930

★★De l'Océan, **t** 05 56 09 30 05, **f** 05 56 09 39 55 (*inexpensive*). A simple oceanfront place.

★★L'Alberet, Route de Soulac, at Vendays, **t** 05 56 41 71 29, **f** 05 56 41 77 77 (*inexpensive*). A Logis establishment, an updated version of a good old village inn, set in trees and flowers. The restaurant has a pretty terrace and serves old favourites like *escargots* and *coq au vin* (*menus 98–238F*). *Closed Fri and Sun eve out of season.*

Centre Hélio-marin, **t** 05 56 73 26 70, **f** 05 56 09 32 15. Bungalows.

Campsite, a few kilometres inland at Grayan-et-l'Hôpital to the northeast. The largest naturist campsite in France.

Le Verdon and the Phare de Cordouan

From Soulac, the road continues up to the little resort of **Le Verdon-sur-Mer**. Verdon was one of the last places in France held by the Germans in the Second World War; ordered to dig in here, to keep the Gironde and its ports from being used by the Allies, they held out until the April 1945 Battle of La Pointe de Grave. Just before the end they destroyed all Verdon's port installations for ocean liners. In 1967 these were replaced by the rather less glamorous petroleum and container terminals; further up, at **Port Bloc**, is the ferry terminus for Royan (and for the boat for the Phare de Cordouan). Here an ancient forest of holm oak has managed to survive the war to become a popular picnic spot; a dune divides the ocean from the **Marais du Logit**, a shallow wooded lake, filled with waterfowl during the great migrations.

From June to September, *La Bohème II* sails out from Le Verdon-sur-Mer to visit Europe's oldest lighthouse, the **Phare de Cordouan** (***t*** *05 56 09 62 93; call for times and bookings in English; timetable depends on the tide*), sitting on a limestone bump between the Gironde's two main shipping lanes. In the 11th century a tower was built as a first-line defence; and in the 14th the Black Prince made the tower into a lighthouse, manned by a hermit whose job was to feed the fire on the top platform. By 1582 this was falling over, and Louis de Foix, an engineer who had already made himself famous for relocating the mouth of the river Adour, was given the task of erecting a new lighthouse. When good King Henri IV came to power, Louis de Foix decided to give the lighthouse a second role, as a monument to the glory of the monarchy. The result, set on a 24ft pedestal, was an extraordinary Renaissance confection that was completed only in 1611 under Henri's son, Louis XIII. Unfortunately in 1788 this most froufrou of all lighthouses was truncated in order to add a 130ft no-frills utilitarian white cone. To prevent further depredations, Cordouan was designated a historic monument in 1862; in 1981 it even became obsolete as a lighthouse, and was only just spared demolition. Inside, the first of seven floors houses the king's apartments, and the second a chapel, with a pretty cupola and 17th-century windows and an inscription from an era that was a far cry from our multicultural age: '*Un Dieu, un Roy, une Foy, une Loy.*' From here you can climb up another 250 steps to the look-out and lantern for a bird's-eye view of the estuary.

La Pointe de Grave and Down to Montalivet

At the end of the road and the northernmost tip of the Gironde is La Pointe de Grave (or de Médoc), marked by another lighthouse, the 1852 **Phare de Grave**, which you can climb for the view; one room is dedicated to the history of the Phare de Cordouan (***t*** *05 56 09 61 78; open July and Aug daily 10.30–12 and 2.30–6*). Near the lighthouse, a stele commemorating Lafayette's departure for America in 1777 replaces the one destroyed in 1942 by ill-tempered Germans who didn't like people remembering such things.

Most of the Germans who come down to the Médoc coast these days couldn't be more harmless; most of them don't even have any clothes on, but leave them at the gate at one of Europe's largest naturist resorts, the **Centre Hélio-marin**, set up in 1950 at the modest seaside resort of **Montalivet-les-Bains**. Along with the Germans, Scandinavians, Belgians, Dutch and increasingly the French come to strip down, usually with the whole family in tow; unlike with the posey beautiful bodies of St-Tropez, the emphasis at Montalivet is good clean bare-naked fun among sand, sea and pines. There's another naturist centre on the nearby beach of Dépée; if you're not quite ready to let it all hang out, there are designated beaches for '*textiles*' at Montalivet and to the north at **Le Gurp**; yet another naturist camping centre here, **EURONAT**, claims to be the largest in Europe, complete with a thalassotherapy centre. Just in from the beaches, dotted here and there along the coast you can see the crumbling blockhouses and pillboxes from the Germans' Atlantic Wall. Many were originally hidden by the dunes; occasionally you'll find one licked by the tide, covered with barnacles and algae and inhabited by little sea creatures.

Côte d'Argent: the Lakes

More pines, more sand, more water...one of the great selling points of the Côte d'Argent is the proximity of its calm, safe lakes to the Atlantic breakers, popular with windsurfers and sailors who don't want to get too wet. Lacanau, the big resort here, is one of the surfing and wave-skiing capitals of Europe.

Lacs d'Hourtin-Carcans and Lacanau

Lac d'Hourtin and its contiguous twin **Lac de Carcans** stretch 16km from north to south, making it the longest lake in France. There's no road, but a cycle track runs between the Atlantic and the lake, ideal if you want to seek out your own private acre of sand between **Hourtin-Plage**, a small family resort in the north, and **Carcans-Maubuisson**, the sports-orientated resort at the southern end of the lake, with a 15km sandy beach – although beware, it's as dead as a doornail out of season. One of the curiosities of the lake is an insect-eating plant called the *drosèra*; otters, rare in France, are occasionally sighted here. A museum, the **Maison des Arts et Traditions Populaires** (*open 15 June–15 Sept 3–7; adm*), evokes life in the Médoc at the beginning of the 20th century.

South of the big lake, dunes and trees encompass the lovely **Etang de Cousseau**, with 13km of marked paths reserved for cyclists and walkers – it's off limits to cars. There's a wide variety of migratory waterfowl, such as *balbuzards* and water rails, along with boar, deer, aquatic tortoises, genets, European mink and otters. Further south, **Lac de Lacanau** has been a favourite weekend escape of the Bordelais since the early 1900s. They built pleasant summer villas at **Lacanau-Océan**, never guessing that the huge rollers that smacked the beach would in the 1960s begin to attract a new breed of tourist – the cream of Europe's surfing fools. Don't come anywhere near Lacanau in mid-August without a firm reservation in hand: the place is packed to the gills for Europe's surfing championships.

Getting Around

Getting to the lakes by public transport is feasible and not too difficult, at least in the summer. There are six Ouest-Aquitaine **buses** a day from Bordeaux (St-Jean station) to Ste-Hélène, Lacanau, Moutchic and Lacanau-Océan, **t** 05 56 70 12 13. Among the patrol routes laid out by the Germans, now converted into cycling paths, is a 70km trail from Bordeaux (beginning near the Pont d'Aquitaine) to Lacanau; from Lacanau south along the Atlantic to Cap Ferret it's another 40km. You can hire **bikes** in Lacanau at Locacycles, **t** 05 56 26 30 99, or Atlantic 3N, **t** 05 56 03 20 12, both on Av de l'Europe.

Tourist Information

Carcans-Maubuisson: 127 Av de Maubuisson, **t** 05 56 03 34 94, **f** 05 56 03 43 76.

Lacanau-Océan: Place de l'Europe, **t** 05 56 03 21 01, **f** 05 56 03 11 89, *www.lacanau.com*, *lacanau@lacanau.com*.

Market Days

Lacanau town: Tues.

Lacanau-Océan: Wed.

Sports and Activities

There are four places in Lacanau that rent **surfboards** and teach you how to use them, open in the off season as well: try Lacanau Surf Club, Bd de la Plage, **t** 05 56 26 38 84, **f** 05 56 26 38 85, or Surf Sans Frontiers, **t** 05 56 26 22 80, **f** 05 56 03 02 19; or if you know how, hire a board and a wetsuit at Surf City, Bd de la Plage, **t** 05 56 03 12 56.

Hire a horse or pony by the hour at Village Cheval Pierre Durand, **t** 05 56 03 91 00; play tennis, paddle ball, or squash at the Pole de l'Ardilouse, **t** 05 56 26 38 06; play golf at the 18-hole Golf de l'Ardilouse, **t** 05 56 03 92 98; or sail, windsurf, canoe or kayak at Voile Lacanau Guyenne, **t** 05 56 03 05 11.

Where to Stay and Eat

Lacanau-Océan ✉ 33680

★★★**Du Golf**, **t** 05 56 03 92 92, **f** 05 56 26 30 57 (*moderate*). Golfers couldn't be any closer to their beloved links; they get a discount on green fees and there's a heated pool to relax in after a hot round.

★★★**Aplus**, Route du Baganais, **t** 05 56 03 91 00, **f** 05 56 03 91 10 (*moderate*). A hotel and equestrian centre in one, in the middle of the pines, with plenty of ways to keep you fit including a gym. All rooms have balcony and you don't have to ride the horses. The restaurant serves quality meals (*80–145F*).

★★**L'Oyat**, Front de Mer Ortal, **t** 05 56 03 11 11, **f** 05 56 03 12 29 (*inexpensive*). On the seashore, a good bet, and a place where the usual half-board terms are a delight – the restaurant has some of the best food in town. *Closed Nov–Mar*.

★★**L'Etoile d'Argent**, Place de l'Europe, **t** 05 56 03 21 07 (*inexpensive*). Reasonable hotel-restaurant. Special low-season discounts available. *Closed Dec and Jan*.

Airotel de l'Océan, **t** 05 56 03 24 45, **f** 05 57 70 01 87. A campsite in the pinewoods with nearly every luxury, as well as motel rooms, 900 yards from the beach. *Book at least six months in advance for Aug*.

Les Grands Pins, **t** 05 56 03 20 77, **f** 05 57 70 03 89. A campsite even nearer the beach, with heated pool and tennis. *Book at least six months in advance for Aug*.

Le Porge ✉ 33680

La Vieille Auberge, as you come into the village on the D3, **t** 05 56 26 50 40. Tasteful, rustic dining room, with plenty of flowers and charming staff; traditional meals with a good selection of Médoc wines (*mostly à la carte, one menu for 130F*). *Closed Wed and mid-Jan–mid-Feb*.

Arcachon and its Bassin

The straight line of the Côte d'Argent is broken by Gascony's inland sea, the 250km² Bassin d'Arcachon. Not only does it sound like something in your bathroom, but like that fixture the actual amount of water in it varies greatly, when the tide sweeps through twice a day – at low tide, large sections turn into sandy mud pies. The Bassin managed to stay out of history most of the time; the Romans and Rabelais wrote admiringly of its oysters, and in the Middle Ages it belonged to the redoubtable Captals de Buch, English allies in the Hundred Years' War. In the 18th century Louis XVI thought to make the Bassin into a military port and sent down an engineer of the Ponts et Chaussées, Brémontier, to fix the shifting sands. Brémontier built tall palisades 80yds in from the high tide, stopping the wind-borne sand to create barriers: dunes between 30 and 40ft high, which he anchored with a long-rooted grass called *oyat*. To stop the dunes from wandering inland, he spread a mix of seeds of gorse, broom and maritime pines under a network of branches. The gorse sprouted up quickly, and helped hold down the soil as the slower pines established themselves.

For all that, the Revolution intervened before the military port project ever got under way, leaving the Bassin to daydream to the ebbs and flows of its tides until the mid-19th century, when it discovered its double destiny as a massive nursery for oysters and a summer resort for the Bordelais. These days the gargantuan Dune du Pilat, just south of Arcachon, alone attracts at least a million visitors a year. Yet mass tourism has left many corners untouched: the little villages in the back Bassin could be part of a 17th-century Dutch landscape painting, with their ports sheltering the Bassin's distinctive small, shallow-keeled sailing boats called *pinasses* (or *pinassayres*, in Gascon), painted the colour of the owner's house, usually a cool green, light pink or straw yellow.

Arcachon

Arcachon was a small fishing village until 1841, when its life was turned upside down by the building of a railway line from nearby La Teste de Buch to Bordeaux. This new link neatly coincided with the new fashion for sea-bathing launched by the Duchesse de Berry. Private villas went up here and there, but the resort really took off after 1852, when two brothers, Emile and Isaac Pereire, took over the railway line and extended it to Arcachon. The Pereire brothers were descendants of Spanish Jews who found a safe haven in Bordeaux during the Inquisition; their grandfather Jacob was famous for inventing the first sign-language alphabet for deaf-mutes in the 1700s. The Pereire brothers proved just as inventive, but as property speculators, and laid out their new resort with cute winding lanes according to the anglophile tastes of Napoleon III, designed (successfully) to bewilder the uninitiated. The Pereires divided the residential section of their resort into four subdivisions, each named after one of the four seasons. Although Spring and Autumn never really caught on, the **Ville-d'Hiver**, the area best sheltered from the ocean winds and always 3°C/7°F warmer than the rest of Arcachon, attained full fashion status by the 1860s – Gounod,

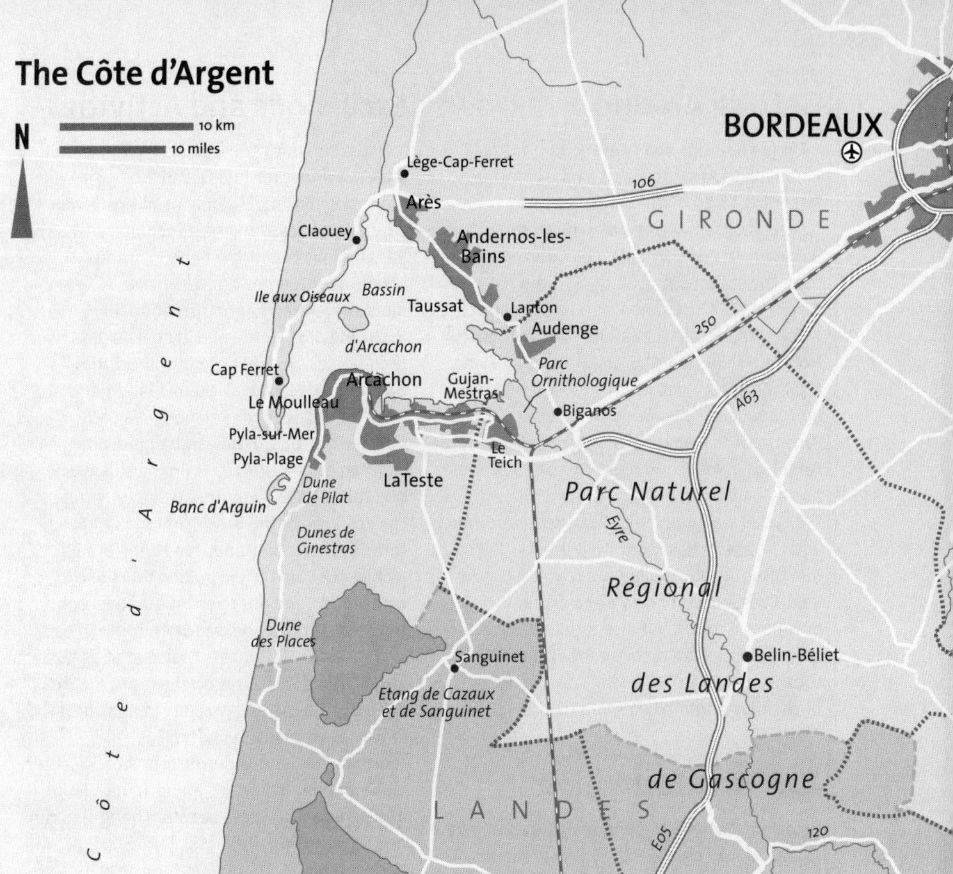

Debussy, Alexandre Dumas, Napoleon III, Marie-Christine of Austria and her future husband Alfonso XII of Spain (who came incognito) were all habitués.

For a centrepiece, the Ville d'Hiver has the **Parc Mauresque** named after its fabulously outlandish pseudo-Moorish casino (1864), inspired by the Alhambra and the Great Mosque of Cordoba – but tragically destroyed by a fire in 1977. Inspired by its fantasy, the usually staid 19th-century Bordelais who built second homes in the Ville d'Hiver let their hair down, indulging in neo-Gothic, Tyrolean, Tudor, pseudo-medieval and other fond fancies; some 200 of these lacy gingerbread villas survive, many now owned by wealthy retirees. Don't miss the fine overall view of the Bassin from the Parc Mauresque gardens, its **Passerelle St-Paul** (over adjacent Allée Pasteur), built by Eiffel in 1862, and the observatory, reached by a 19th-century lift.

The **Ville d'Eté**, facing the Bassin and cooler in the summer, has most of Arcachon's tourist facilities, seaside promenades, sheltered sandy beaches, and the **Musée-Aquarium** (*Rue Professeur-Jolyet, **t** 05 56 83 33 32; open mid-Mar–June and Sept–early Nov 10–12.30 and 2–7, July and Aug 9.30–12.30 and 2–11; closed early Nov–mid-Mar; adm*), with a pretty collection of tropical fish, tortoises, seashells, stuffed weasels and

Getting Around

There are **trains** nearly every hour from Bordeaux to Arcachon, and, in the summer, TGVs direct from Paris-Montparnasse.

Several Citram **buses** a day run from Bordeaux (8 Rue Corneille, **t** 05 56 43 68 43) or from the station, coinciding with the TGVs serving Pyla, Andernos, Arès and Cap Ferret.

The UBA, Union des Bateliers Arcachonnais, from the Thiers (**t** 05 56 54 92 78) and d'Eyrac (**t** 05 56 54 83 01) jetties make frequent half-hour **boat** crossings from Archacon to Cap Ferret, to Andernos, and a range of other trips. For a **taxi** in Arcachon ring **t** 05 56 83 11 11, or **t** 05 56 83 88 88.

Bicycles are a convenient way to get around, and the Bassin has many cycle-tracks; you can hire bikes in all the villages. Arcachon Dingo Vélo, Rue Grenier, **t** 05 56 83 44 09, rents not only normal bikes, but also tandems to quintuplos and an assortment of crazy bikes. Locabeach, 326 Bd de la Plage, **t** 05 56 83 39 64, hires out mountain bikes and scooters.

Tourist Information

Arcachon: Esplanade Georges-Pompidou, **t** 05 57 52 97 97, **f** 05 57 52 97 77. An excellent place to find out about all kinds of activities and tours.

Pyla-sur-Mer: Rond Point du Figuier, **t** 05 56 54 02 22, **f** 05 56 22 58 84.

Market Days

Arcachon: daily, in the covered market in Place de Gracia. Open-air market daily in summer, Wed, Sat and Sun in winter.

Excursions and Activities

Two companies, the UBA (**t** 05 56 54 60 32) and Arcachon Croisiere Ocean (**t** 05 56 54 36 70), make 2hr-long excursions to the **Ile aux Oiseaux** every afternoon, all year round. The Bassin's only island, the Ile aux Oiseaux is government-owned and given over to sea birds as well as oyster farms and sailing boats. In the old days, herdsmen in boats would have their horses swim over to the sweet islet pastures. The Ile aux Oiseaux's landmarks are its picturesque *cabanes tchanquées*, huts perched on stilts. In July and August both companies also offer days on the shadeless, hot, sandy **Banc d'Arguin**, a wildfowl refuge at the entrance of the Bassin; in June sandwich terns by their thousands nest here (bring a picnic). UBA also offers guided tours of the **oyster beds**, and 4hr **river** trips up the cool, forested Leyre (*see* below); both companies, and the Atlantic Princess Croisieres, **t** 05 56 83 39 39, also offer **cruises** up the coast, on the *Arcachon Croisiere Ocean*, including sunset cruises with shellfish platters.

Among the daredevil **sports** practised off the Dune du Pilat are deltaplaning, hang-gliding and parapente, a cross between hang-gliding and parachuting: contact Vol Libre du Pyla, 1 Rue Aurélien Dasson, Gujan-Mestras, **t** 05 56 22 15 02. In the 19th century Arcachon had a sizeable British colony, to which it owes its passion for **golf**. There are three courses and a practice course in the area; the closest is the beautiful Golf Club d'Arcachon, 35 Bd d'Arcachon, **t** 05 56 54 44 00. You can get a bird's-eye view of Arcachon's remarkable setting, from a small **plane** with Aéroclub du Bassin d'Arcachon at La Testre, **t** 05 56 54 72 88, or by **glider** with Association Aeronautique du Bassin d'Arcachon, **t** 05 56 54 15 14, also at La Teste. **Sailing** is popular and a challenge, with

shark skeletons. The Ville d'Eté's most notorious resident was Henri de Toulouse-Lautrec, who had a house by the ocean and liked to swim in the nude, offending the sensibilities of his neighbours. To pacify them, he erected a fence between his house and the beach – then mischievously covered it with obscene drawings. The furious neighbours eventually bought the house and gleefully burned the fence. Their descendants have never really forgiven them. (They should consider the chagrin of the heirs of the young man in the Marquesas Islands, charged with tidying up

strong currents, sandbanks, channels and occasional high winds, and over the course of the year there are a number of **races**, including the *18 heures d'Arcachon* sail race, which takes place in early July. The tourist office has a long list of places to hire your own sailboat, as well as listings for horse-riding, tennis, diving, water-skiing, fishing, cycling and nearly every other sport you can imagine.

Where to Stay

Arcachon ✉ 33120

Hotels in fashionable Arcachon are in general more expensive than anywhere else in this book. If you plan to stay a week or more, you'll go less broke in a furnished room, studio or flat – pick up the fat list at the tourist office. Book months in advance for anything in July or August, when it's hard to find anything under 300F a night.

All of the following have rooms ranging across the *expensive* and *moderate* price categories; if you plump for a sea view, rates rise considerably.

******Arc-Hôtel sur Mer**, 89 Bd de la Plage, **t** 05 56 83 06 85, **f** 05 56 83 53 72. A moderate-sized, modern but stylish hotel where the rooms, all with balconies, overlook either water or garden; heated pool, sauna and Jacuzzi are among the other amenities. *Open all year.*

*****Semiramis**, 4 Allées Rebsomen, **t** 05 56 83 25 87, **f** 05 57 52 22 41. The most charming choice, your chance to stay in a 19th-century Arcachon summer villa in the Ville d'Hiver, complete with painted ceilings and ceramic decorations of the birds likely to be seen at Le Teich. It has a potpourri of 20 rooms, no two alike, and a pool set in a garden of palms, mimosas and acanthus. *Open all year.*

*****Le Richelieu**, 185 Bd de la Plage, **t** 05 56 83 16 50, **f** 05 56 83 47 78. An old-fashioned hotel dead in the centre of town, right across from the beach. *Closed Nov–mid-Mar.*

*****Les Vagues**, 9 Bd de l'Océan, **t** 05 56 83 03 75, **f** 05 56 83 77 16. You can't stay much closer to the ocean. Decorated with a fresh, light touch and with rooms looking right down on the waves. *Open all year.*

****Le Nautic**, 20 Bd de la Plage, **t** 05 56 83 01 48, **f** 05 56 83 04 67. A kilometre from the centre of town; renovated with a Spanish touch; some of the nicest rooms in this category. *Open all year.*

****Les Mimosas**, 77 bis Av de la République, **t** 05 56 83 45 86, **f** 05 56 22 53 40. Tidy if somewhat bland rooms not far from the sea in the Ville d'Eté, a short walk from the train station.

****Marinette**, 15 Allée José Maria de Hérédia, **t** 05 56 83 06 67, **f** 05 56 83 09 59. A large white house in the Ville d'Hiver, with comfortable and pleasant rooms, some with an independent entrance. You can take breakfast on a flowered terrace; no restaurant. *Closed Nov–mid-Mar.*

Pyla-sur-Mer ✉ 33115

*****Haitza**, Place Louis-Gaume, **t** 05 57 52 79 27, **f** 05 56 22 10 23. Simple quiet rooms set in the pine woods, a stone's throw from the beach. *Open April–Sept.*

****La Guitoune**, 95 Bd de l'Océan, **t** 05 56 22 70 10, **f** 05 56 22 14 39. A favourite weekend retreat of the Bordelais; comfortable rooms and an excellent seafood restaurant (*menus from 145F*). *Open all year.*

****Ttiki-Etchea**, 2 Place Louis-Gaume, **t** 05 56 22 71 15, **f** 05 56 22 15 99. Basque style in a peaceful setting overlooking the beach, with a pretty terrace. *Open May–Sept.*

Gauguin's hut after the artist's death. Finding it cluttered with sculptures and paintings, he loaded everything on to his boat and dumped the lot into the Pacific.)

Since 1950, a new crop of villas has gone up on the ocean front in **Parc Pereire**, overlooking Arcachon's best beach, Plage Pereire. As incredible as it seems, in 1922 someone had the chutzpah to drill for oil right in the middle of the park, but instead of black gold discovered at 1,600ft down a natural spring of mineral water, known as **Les Abatilles**, now exploited and bottled in the spa. Further south, along Bd de la

La Corniche, 46 Av Louis-Gaume, **t 05 56 22 72 11, **f** 05 56 22 70 21. By the beach and at the foot of the mighty dune, a neo-Basque wood and brick hotel built in 1932 with spacious balconies and a stairway down to the beach. The restaurant has good seafood and also a selection of southwestern duck confections (*menus from 75F*). *Closed Oct–Easter*.

Côte Sud, 4 Av de Figuier, **t 05 56 83 25 00, **f** 05 56 83 24 13. In a delightful 1940s villa in the pines, a 5min walk from the beach, with an excellent, intimate little restaurant; for something unusual try the *civet d'esturgeon aux huîtres pochées* (*menus 108–165F*). *Closed mid-Nov–Jan*.

Camping La Dune, **t** 05 56 22 72 17. An excellent site south of the dune, witha pool (*open May–Sept*).

Pyla Camping, **t** 05 56 22 74 56. Closer to the beach, also very good, with pool (*open April–Sept*).

Eating Out

Arcachon ✉ 33120

Moderate

Camping Club d'Arcachon, at Abatilles, 1.8km from the centre at Allée de la Galaxie, **t** 05 56 83 24 15, **f** 05 57 52 28 51. In a pine grove (*65–180F*). *Open all year*.

L'Escialler Diego, 12 Bd Veyrier-Montangnères, **t** 05 56 83 84 46. For tasty seafood with a Spanish zing, right on the seafront (*menus 85 and 140F*).

Le Patio, 10 Bd de la Plage, **t** 05 56 83 02 72. Surrounds diners with bright clutter, a waterfall and delicious aromas from specialities such as lobster salad, oysters in flaky pastry, hot stuffed crab and *bouillabaisse océane* (*menu 170F or à la carte*). *Closed Tues and several weeks in winter*.

Les Genêts, 25 Bd du Général-Leclerc, **t** 05 56 83 40 28. Despite its rather downmarket location on a main road opposite the railway tracks, a popular place offering good traditional food (*menus 79–140F*). *Closed Mon, Sun out of season, and several weeks out of season*.

L'Ombrière, 79 Cours Héricart-de-Thury, **t** 05 56 83 86 20. Delicious seafood platters on the garden terrace, as well as duck and veal dishes, and a good selection of wine (*menus from 127F*).

Cheap

La Plancha, 17 Rue Jéhenne, **t** 05 56 83 76 66. Fill up on *gambas à la plancha* and other Spanish-style seafood treats (*under 100F*). *Closed Sun in winter*.

Chez Yvette, 59 Bd du Général-Leclerc, **t** 05 56 83 05 11. Seafood is the obvious thing to eat in Arcachon, and you won't find a fishier place than this seaside restaurant, where fresh denizens of the deep are immaculately prepared; try the fish soup (*menus 98F*).

Pyla-sur-Mer ✉ 33115

Gérard Tissier, 35 Bd de l'Océan, **t** 05 56 54 07 94. A good, quite smart restaurant on the roadside with a pleasant terrace, serving traditional dishes plus fish. Lobster-lovers can splurge on the *homard en fête*, prepared in three different ways. There is a large chimney which works in the winter (*menus 98–265F*). *Closed most of Jan and half of Feb plus Sun eve and Mon out of season*.

Aux Deux Chênes, 56 Bd de l'Océan, **t** 05 57 72 00 68. Cheaper and quicker: the usual array of fast food but also paella, a fish of the day and a few other things on a shaded terrace (*menus 50–100F*). *Closed mid-Dec until the start of Feb*.

Plage, a new **casino** has been installed in the Disneylandish Château Deganne, with a brand-new congress centre, the Palatium, to keep it company. The business centre of Arcachon, near its enormous marina, lacks the unique character of the Pereire's residential districts.

The Dune du Pilat

As the afternoon draws to a close in Arcachon, the thing to do is drive or cycle 8km south, through the resorts of **Moulleau**, **Pyla-sur-Mer** and **Pyla-Plage**. In the pine trees, there's a pay car park to leave your vehicle, and, beyond that, the awesome, terrible, extraordinary sight of that Moby Dick of dunes, the **Dune du Pilat**, at 347ft the highest pile of sand in Europe, at a mile and a half, the longest, and at 550yds the widest. Excavations in this little chunk of the Sahara have found that Pilat began to form 8,000 years ago with the merging of two huge set of dunes, and more or less grew to its present dimensions in the 18th century, when a huge sandbank offshore was destroyed and all the sand was blown here. The name first appeared in 1484. Like all dunes, it's in a constant state of flux, and every year it inches a little further inland at the rate of 17ft a year. A useful stair with 190 steps helps you get to the top of the steep behemoth for an unforgettable view – especially at sunset. If you can't resist the urge to roll and slide and scamper down the ocean-side slope, be prepared to face the torturous return trip back up the slippery sands. Often included in the sundown view are schools of bottlenose dolphins and porpoises, who like to frolic just offshore. South of the sand-monster there's a beach called **Petit Nice** and beyond that a naturist beach, both with lifeguards and snack bars; further south, the **Plage de la Salie Nord** and **Plage de la Salie Sud** are good for surfing.

Around the Bassin d'Arcachon

Ten *communes*, a score of picturesque little ports with wooden oyster shacks, beaches, a river delta and a bird sanctuary, a trip up the Leyre river into the Landes, and a score of rather more commercial amusements await to be savoured around the rim of the Bassin. Try at least once to cross the water the traditional way, in a *pinasse* – trips are offered from the ports of Arcachon, Arès, Andernos and Lège-Cap-Ferret.

La Teste de Buch to Le Teich

Southeast of Arcachon, pines line the Bassin at **La Teste de Buch**. Its name recalls the Captals de Buch who lorded it over the Bassin in the Middle Ages, although in those days pine resin rather than oysters was the cash crop. La Teste has some handsome houses dating back to the 18th century, and includes in its municipal boundaries not only the Dune du Pilat and a racetrack, but also the **Lac de Cazaux**, the second largest in France.

Since 1969, arts and crafts from the days of the Captals have been displayed at the reconstituted **Village Médiéval** at **La Hume**, just east of La Teste (*open mid-June–Aug 10.30–7; adm*), where 50 craftsmen and craftswomen demonstrate their skills, from bookbinding to jewellery-making; there are also shows and games, and even a **Mini-Golf Médiéval**, for putt-putting as in ye knightly days of yore. The same complex has spawned a 'zoo' of domestic animals, the **Parc Animalier La Coccinelle** (*open May and June 10–6.30, July–early Sept 10.30–7.30; adm*), where children can feed the baby

Tourist Information

La Teste de Buch: Place Jean Hameau, **t** 05 56 66 45 59, **f** 05 56 54 45 94.
Gujan-Mestras: 19 Av de Lattre de Tassigny, **t** 05 56 66 12 65, **f** 05 56 66 94 44.
Andernos-les-Bains: 42 Av du Broustic, **t** 05 56 82 02 95, **f** 05 56 82 14 29.
Arès: Esplanade G. Dartiguelongue, **t** 05 56 60 18 07, **f** 05 56 60 39 41.
Lège-Cap-Ferret: 1 Av General de Gaulle, Claouey, **t** 05 56 03 94 49, **f** 05 57 70 31 70.

Market Days

La Teste de Buch: Thurs, Sat and Sun, in the covered market.
Andernos: covered market every morning in summer, Tues, Thurs, Fri and Sat mornings in winter. Outdoor markets in winter in Place du XIV Juillet on Fri, Place de l'Etoile on Tues.

Where to Stay and Eat

La Teste de Buch ✉ 33260

****Auberge Basque**, 36 Rue du Maréchal-Foch, **t** 05 56 66 26 04, **f** 05 56 54 24 67 (*inexpensive*). One of the oldest buildings in La Teste, a Landais-style house of 1776 with a pretty terrace covered with rhododendrons.
Chez Diego, Centre Capital, **t** 05 56 54 44 32. A family of oyster-farmers owns this place, guaranteeing the freshest of oysters and other delicious seafood in pleasant south-of-the-border décor, drawing in hungry clients year-round (*menus 90–140F*).

Gujan-Mestras ✉ 33470

*****La Guérinière**, 18 Cours de Verdun, on the Bordeaux–Arcachon road, **t** 05 56 66 08 78, **f** 05 56 66 13 39 (*moderate*). With a pool and an excellent restaurant (*menus 180–380F*). *Restaurant closed Sat lunch and Sun out of season.*
L'Escalumade, 8 Rue Pierre-Dignac, **t** 05 56 66 02 30. Overlooking the oyster farms, a good honest fish restaurant (*menus 134–250F*). *Closed Mon and Sun eve and several weeks out of season.*
Les Viviers, Port de Larros, **t** 05 56 66 01 04. A wide selection of shellfish and other denizens of the deep, as well as a tasty beef brochette with *cèpes* (*menus about 120F*), served in the light-filled dining room and floating terrace. *Closed Oct–Mar.*
Le Poisson Lune, 184 Av du Maréchal de Lattre de Tassigny, **t** 05 56 66 07 76. Eat on the shaded patio beside a small garden and escape from the road. The Basque chef is proud of the freshness of his fish and will show it to you before cooking; there are several Basque dishes on the menus (*110–350F*). *Open all year.*
La Vache sur le Toit, 2 Route des Lacs, **t** 05 57 52 42 51. A Belgian café offering mussels and chips, beef simmered in beer and other solid Belgian food (*à la carte; mussels, chips and beer for 58F*). It's on a busy corner so you will probably want to eat inside where you can admire the wealth of cow-related paraphernalia.

Biganos ✉ 33380

Chez Marie, 57 Av des Boïens, **t/f** 05 56 82 60 37 (*cheap*). A hotel with restaurant (*menus 57–140F*); not far from the beach. *Open all year.*
***Hôtel de France**, 99 Av de la Libération, **t** 05 56 82 61 08 (*cheap*). A refreshingly cheap choice in the village, a short drive from the beach. *Open all year.*

Taussat ✉ 33148

****Hôtel de la Plage**, 20 Bd de la Plage, **t** 05 56 82 06 06, **f** 05 56 82 51 61 (*inexpensive*). Not in fact on the beach, a Logis establishment with reasonably priced rooms for these parts and a restaurant (*menus from 100F*).

lambs and goats, ride the rides and play the games; and **Aqualand** (*open June–mid-Sept, times vary between 10–6 and 8.30–8; adm*), for a day splashing around in rivers, pools with waves, and every kind of water slide imaginable; plus 14 tennis courts. You can also take a stroll around **Les Jardins du Bassins**, with a patchwork of different garden tapestries (***t** 05 56 66 00 71; open summer 10–12.30 and 2.30–7*).

Andernos-les-Bains ✉ 33510

****Le Rétro**, 20 Av Thiers, **t** 05 56 82 02 10, **f** 05 56 82 37 08 (*inexpensive*). A fairly simple hotel near the beach with a restaurant.

****De la Côte d'Argent**, 180 Bd de la République, **t** 05 56 03 98 58 (*inexpensive*). Ten rooms, no restaurant, a short walk from the beach.

L'Esquirey, 9 Av Commdt Allègre, **t** 05 56 82 22 15. A haven for oyster-lovers – the freshest of bivalves served in a real *cabanon*, along with the freshest, tastiest fish the Bassin has to offer (*up to about 150F*). *Closed Wed and during the week in winter.*

Arès ✉ 33740

Le St-Eloi, 11 Bd de l'Aérium, **t** 05 56 60 20 46. An excellent restaurant in a quiet corner away from the beach, signposted off the main road. A cool spot even on the hottest of days, with a couple of shaded patios. The choice is quite small and the food not fancy but everything is well chosen and well prepared: *filet d'agneau et sa côte, ail confit et jus d'épices* or *lotte escalopées, poêlée à l'huile d'olive, coulis de poivrons rouges* (*menus 90–300F*). Attentive staff. *Closed Mon lunch and Sun eve, all Mon out of season.*

Lège-Cap-Ferret ✉ 33970

Cap-Ferret is the trendiest spot on the Bassin these days, and there are plenty of bars, restaurants and nine campsites, but only a handful of hotels; quite a few people sack out under the stars.

The best ice cream on the whole Bassin is the home-made creation of **Pat-à-Chou**, in Le Grand Piquey, **t** 05 56 60 51 38.

****Sporting Les Dunes**, 119 Av de Bordeaux, **t** 05 56 60 61 81, **f** 05 56 03 61 66 (*inexpensive*). Down at Cap-Ferret, a little duneside and seaside place. *Open Feb–Oct.*

****La Frégate**, 34 Av de l'Océan, **t** 05 56 60 41 62, **f** 05 56 03 76 18 (*inexpensive*). Complete with a pool.

***De la Plage Chez Magne**, in the Port de l'Herbe, **t** 05 56 60 50 15 (*cheap*). A delightful, simple eight-room wooden hotel by the beach, with a good restaurant (*menus from 90F*). *Closed Jan.*

Chez Pierrette, 9 Impasse des Sternes, **t** 05 56 60 50 50. Just south in Le Canon, in a traditional Basque house, with a good reputation for unfussy dishes based on the market and the day's catch; meat specialities as well (*menus 78 and 100F*).

Rond-Point, 2 Bd de la Plage, **t** 05 56 60 51 32. Simple décor but pretensions in the kitchen, which prepares abundant portions of seafood (monkfish sautéed in Vieux Médoc) as well as land food, served inside or out on the terrace (*menus from 100F*). *Open daily July and Aug, closed Mon and Tues out of season, and some weeks Nov–Jan.*

Auberge de Jeunesse, 87 Av de Bordeaux, **t** 05 56 60 64 62. Very popular, with so many customers that many end up under tents. *Open July and Aug only.*

Pinasse Café, 2 bis Av de l'Océan, **t** 05 56 03 77 87, **f** 05 56 60 63 47. Just above the Bassin, a favourite place for lunch (*menus 90–125F*). *Open April–Sept daily, end Feb–Mar, Oct and start of Nov weekends only, closed end Nov–start Feb.*

Chez Hortense, Av du Sémaphore, **t** 05 56 60 62 56. At the end of the peninsula, overlooking the Bassin. Well-prepared if pricey seafood (*menu à la carte, around 200–300F*). *Open in summer and weekends Easter–start of Sept.*

La Hume is part of the Bassin's oyster capital, **Gujan-Mestras**. Here seven little ports crowded with *oustaous* (oyster huts) provide the perfect backdrop for tasting a plate of oysters, or attending the big oyster fair in the middle of August (you can eat them in non-R months now); there's even a little **Maison de l'Huitre**, at the Port de Larros, where you can learn some of their oyster secrets (***t** 05 56 66 23 71; open Mar–Sept daily*

The Oyster's their World

Oysters from the Bassin were popular among rich Romans of Burdigala, who would set up relays to have them brought to their tables in a few hours, where they would slurp them raw with *garum*, the prized and mysterious fish-gut sauce that culinary archaeologists guess was something similar to Vietnamese *nuoc nam*. By the Middle Ages, when the old Roman roads were full of mud and potholes, tastes turned to dried oysters put up in barrels, eaten in a sauce or fried. The Bassin's industry remained small and local, however, until 1850, when once again speedy transport – in the form of the railway – allowed the tasty bivalves to chug posthaste to Bordeaux, and, from 1857, on to Paris – at a time when restaurant diners thought nothing of beginning a meal with 10 or 15 dozen.

Twice, however, Arcachon's bread-and-butter industry was devastated by oyster parasites; the first attack, in 1922, wiped out Arcachon's flat native *gravettes*. These were replaced by *portugaises*, which in turn fell prey to a new parasite in 1970. Since 1972, the oysters farmed in the Bassin belong to two different species – a new *gravette*, a flat hybrid of Charente and Breton oysters, and a parasite-resistant, elongated Japanese oyster, the *huître creuse*, or *gigas*.

Today the Bassin d'Arcachon is the fourth-largest oyster producer in France, but the first in Europe in 'trapping' microscopic oyster embryos and larvae swishing about the sea in search of a home – they simply can't resist stacks of canal roof tiles, bleached in a mix of lime and sand. After eight months clinging to a tile, the baby oysters are moved into calm nurseries in flat cages; the next year, they are moved once more to oyster parks, in fresh plankton-rich waters, where the oyster farmers defend them the best they can against greedy starfish, crabs and other crustaceans, who will nevertheless devour 15 to 20 per cent of the crop over the next three years. In the parks, the oysters are constantly turned, to encourage them to develop a nice shape and a hard shell (although, increasingly, once they reach a certain size they are raised in the sacks they will eventually be sold in, set on shelves at just the right height (*élevage en surélevé*). When at long last they're ready to go on the market, they are placed for up to four days in special pools that trick them into no longer trusting the tide, so that they remain sealed tight while they are shipped and sold by size, from 6 (the smallest) to 0 (the largest and best).

'Now if you're ready, Oysters dear/We can begin to feed,' as the Walrus said. To prepare the little rascals *à la mode d'Arcachon*: count on a dozen oysters per person (or more if you're really greedy), four or more *crépinettes* (small flat sausages cooked in white wine), plenty of thinly sliced rye bread and butter and lots of dry white Graves, properly chilled at 6–8°C (44°F). Open the oysters and keep them cool, then fry or barbecue the sausages just before serving, and eat – slurp down a cold oyster, take a bite of hot sausage with a bit of buttered bread and wash it down with a swallow of wine.

10–12 and 2.30–6.30). The critter on Gujan's coat of arms, however, is the ladybird beetle, the *barbot* in Gascon, a name that goes back to the early days of the phylloxera epidemic, when the locals noticed that their infected vines invariably swarmed with ladybugs. They accused those helpful insects of spreading the plague, while in fact they were gobbling down the real culprits as fast as they could; the priest at Gujan even held *barbot* exorcisms in the vineyards. When the real, much tinier lice-like pests were discovered, the villagers of Gujan became the butt of jokes from their neighbours, who called them the *barbots*. By the 1920s, Gujan learned to laugh at itself, and adopted the ladybug as its own, even naming its rugby team the Barbots.

Le Teich, the Leyre and a Look into Les Landes

At Le Teich, the Leyre (or L'Eyre), one of the most important rivers of the Landes, drains into the Bassin d'Arcachon, forming the kind of marshy delta beloved of migratory waterfowl. In 1972, Le Teich's rare environment of saltwater and freshwater *bayous* was set aside as the **Parc Ornithologique du Teich** (***t** 05 56 22 80 93; open daily 10–6, July and Aug 10–8; adm; bring binoculars, or rent them on the site*). The delta is a favourite stop on the great migration route between Africa and Scandinavia, and a nesting ground for several species, especially grey herons, black cormorants, white storks, black and white oystercatchers, egrets, kingfishers, dabbling garganeys and spoon-billed shovelers. Altogether some 280 different species have been sighted. One of the big success stories has been the return of the mute swan, which vanished from France at the time of the Revolution.

The park is divided into four sections: the vast **Parc de Causseyre**, with several hides and observation posts; the **Parc de la Moulette**, where the geese, swans and ducks are concentrated; the small **Parc des Artigues**, with a collection of ducks from around the world, at liberty, and large aviaries; and the inaccessible **Parc Claude Quancard**, for wading birds (although there are two observation posts). There are three paths to walk, 2.4km, 3.4km and 6km; the longest one does a circuit through all the zones. There's an information centre in the **Maison de la Nature du Bassin d'Arcachon**, and a fine viewpoint over the delta from the **Observatoire du Delta de Leyre**. Next to the park you can visit our smaller winged friends at the **Serre aux Papillons**, a live butterfly zoo in an exotic tropical garden full of orchids (*16 Rue du Port, **t** 05 56 22 62 70; open April–early July 11–6, early July–Aug 10–7, Sept 2–5; adm*). Also in La Teich, **Villetorte Loisirs** (*30 Rue du Pont Neuf, **t** 05 56 22 66 80*) hires out canoes and kayaks to explore the lush waters of L'Eyre.

Le Teich lies in the northern confines of the **Parc Naturel Régional des Landes de Gascogne**, 262,000 hectares (647,000 acres) of forest set aside in 1970. The great pine moors of the Landes may seem monotonous from the car window while you're zooming down the *autoroute* to Spain, but close up they are striking, especially when the heather, gorse or honeysuckle is in bloom and the heady scent of resin fills the air in an aromatherapy overkill. The nearest place to learn about the secrets of the Landes is **Belin-Béliet**, 30km up the river L'Eyre from Le Teich. There's a park information office (***t** 05 57 71 99 99; open all year*), and canoe, kayak and bicycle hire at the

Centre d'Animation du Graoux (*t 05 57 71 99 29*). Belin is a tranquil place, but it can claim a mention in nearly any medieval history book as the birthplace of Eleanor of Aquitaine in 1122, and (some say) of her favourite son, Richard the Lion-Heart (in a now ruined castle on the outskirts of town, marked by a stele). The church of **St-Pierre-de-Mons**, on the outskirts of Belin, was built during Eleanor's reign as a priory on the Compostela road, although its bell tower was only fortified a century later, during the Hundred Years' War, that timebomb left by her French and English marriages. Inside are four archaic capitals, carved with scenes of mysterious import; legend has it that St-Pierre's cemetery, like St-Seurin in Bordeaux and the Alychamps in Arles, has the tombs of Charlemagne's paladins.

The Back *Bassin* Around to Cap Ferret

At **Biganos**, north of the Leyre delta, many of the old picturesque oystermen's *cabanons* have been converted into holiday homes, while the oystermen, one presumes, now work in the local paper mill. The next town, **Audenge** is a sleepy fishing village where the day's catch is trapped in reservoirs left by the retreating tide – a method of fishing that inspired someone to dig similar tide-fed reservoirs for humans to swim in; if the tide is out you can join the locals in the public seawater pools. Next to the north is **Lanton**, with a long beach and a 12th-century church, the oldest on the Bassin. Family-oriented **Andernos-les-Bains**, a lively summer resort with splendid views across the water, and **Arès** both have beaches safe for young children. Andernos holds an important jazz and oyster festival (*end of July/early Aug*) that has featured the likes of Miles Davis and Lionel Hampton.

The northwestern curve of the Bassin is sprinkled with little oyster port-resorts set between the calm waters and rough Atlantic, and all belonging to the *commune* of **Lège-Cap-Ferret**. The prettiest port is **L'Herbe**, an intimate hamlet of wooden houses on tiny lanes, founded in the 17th century. The tourist office at **Claouey** organizes guided tours in the summer. The *commune*'s 35km of ocean beaches culminate in the sandy tail of Cap-Ferret, which has long been doing its damnedest to close off the mouth of the Bassin; in the past 200 years the cape has grown 4km and gobbled up several fashionable villas in its wake. A path leads around to the tip of the cape, with splendid views of the Dune du Pilat, most breathlessly from the top of the 255 steps of the lighthouse (*open June and Sept weekends, July and Aug daily 10–12 and 3–6; contact the tourist office at Claouey*). The cute little narrow-gauge **Tramway du Cap-Ferret** covers the 2km from the end of the road at the Bassin to the ocean beaches, where surfers ride the big rollers expedited by the Bay of Biscay (*t 05 56 60 62 57; 15 June–15 Sept, frequent journeys daily*).

The Lot: Quercy

13

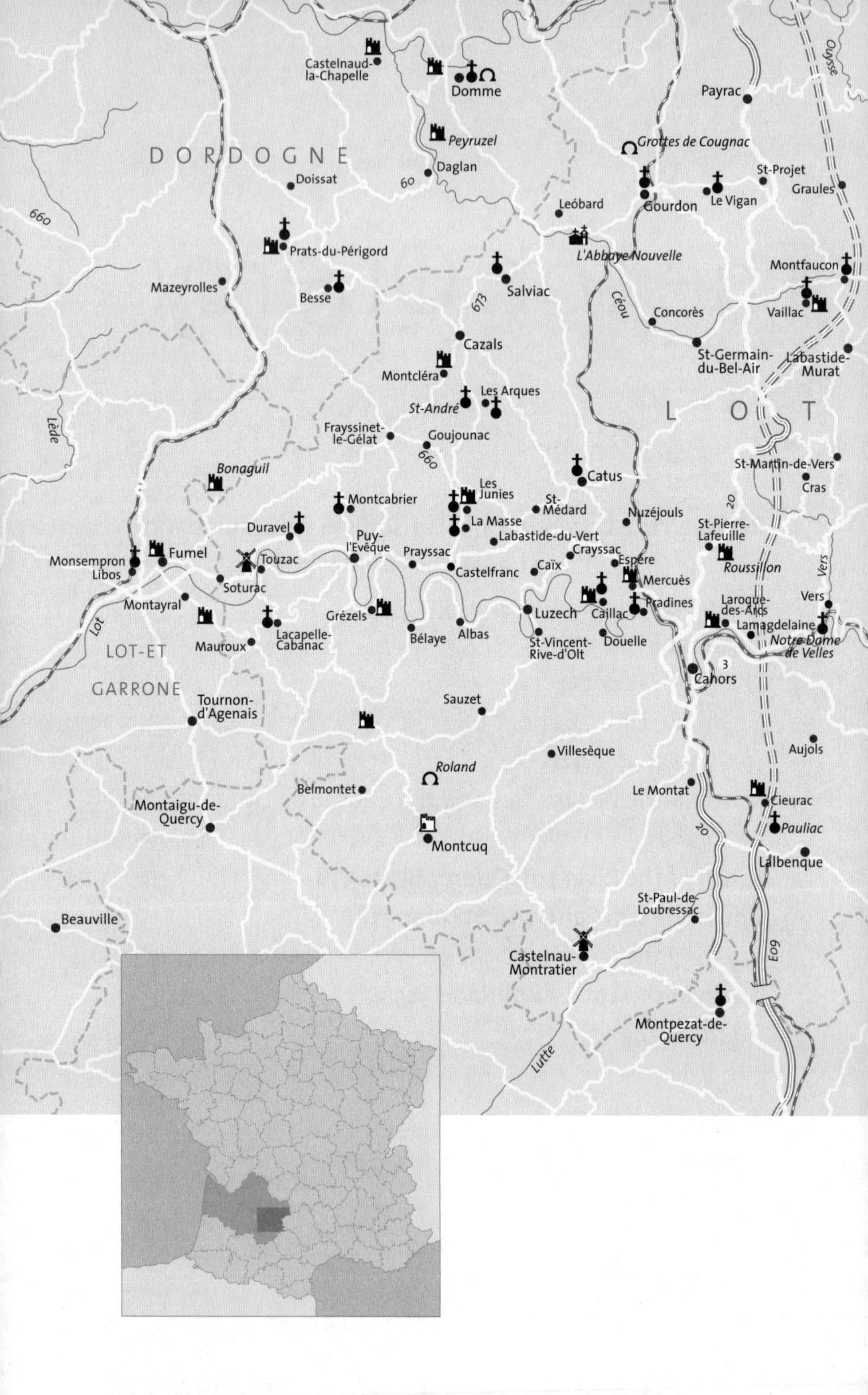

DORDOGNE
LOT
LOT-ET
GARRONE
Castelnaud-la-Chapelle
Domme
Payrac
Peyruzel
Grottes de Cougnac
Daglan
Doissat
St-Projet
Graules
Gourdon
Le Vigan
Leóbard
Prats-du-Périgord
L'Abbaye Nouvelle
Montfaucon
Mazeyrolles
Besse
Salviac
Vaillac
Concorès
Cazals
St-Germain-du-Bel-Air
Labastide-Murat
Montcléra
Les Arques
St-André
Frayssinet-le-Gélat
Goujounac
St-Martin-de-Vers
Cras
Bonaguil
Catus
Les Junies
Montcabrier
St-Médard
Nuzéjouls
St-Pierre-Lafeuille
La Masse
Duravel
Puy-l'Evêque
Labastide-du-Vert
Crayssac
Roussillon
Monsempron
Libos
Fumel
Touzac
Prayssac
Castelfranc
Caïx
Espère
Mercuès
Soturac
Vers
Laroque-des-Arcs
Montayral
Grézels
Luzech
Caillac
Pradines
Lamagdelaine
Notre-Dame de Velles
Mauroux
Lacapelle-Cabanac
Bélaye
Albas
St-Vincent-Rive-d'Olt
Douelle
Cahors
Tournon-d'Agenais
Sauzet
Villesèque
Aujols
Roland
Belmontet
Le Montat
Cieurac
Montaigu-de-Quercy
Montcuq
Pauliac
Lalbenque
St-Paul-de-Loubressac
Beauville
Castelnau-Montratier
Montpezat-de-Quercy
Lot
Lède
Céou
Vers
Ouysse
Lutte
660
60
673
20
3
E09

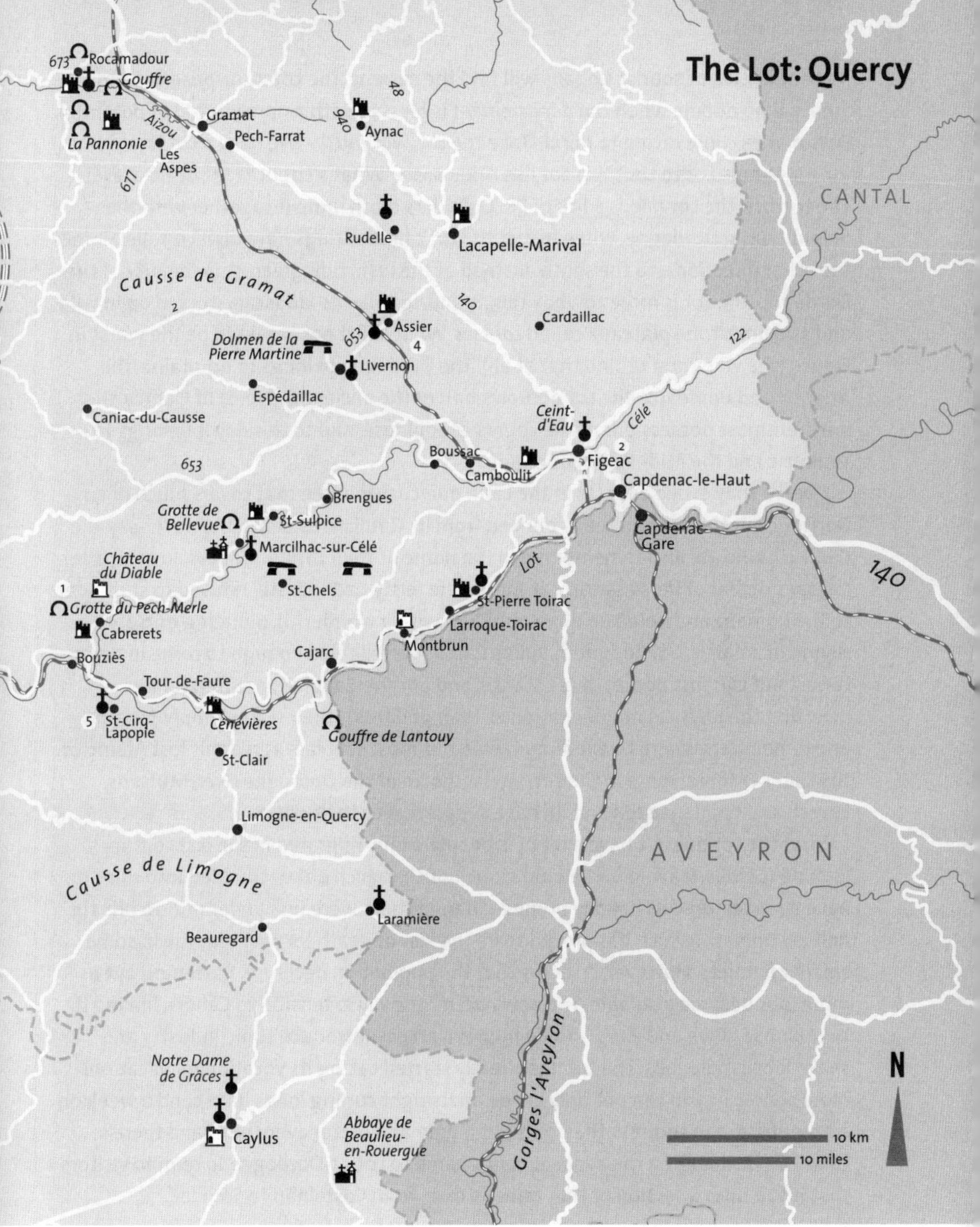

Highlights

1 Winsome spotted horses in the Grotte du Pech-Merle
2 Medieval streets and Egyptian surprises in Figeac
3 The devil-built Pont Valentré and black wine of Cahors
4 Relics of a 16th-century braggart at Assier
5 'An impossible rose in the night', St-Cirq-Lapopie

Connoisseurs of tourist slogans will find the current 'The Lot: A Surprise at Each Step' a limp noodle when the *département* is blessed with a name so full of potential. Possibilities come racing to mind: 'Take the Lot, will you?' – 'We have a Lot to answer for' – 'A Whole Lot to Love' – 'A Lot like Arkansas' – 'What a Lot of ****', or whatever. The truth is, the Lot needs a lick of PR. Outsiders often lump it together with the neighbouring Dordogne, when in fact the Lot's heartstrings have always pulled it in the other direction – to the south. Instead of the lush, tidy, green-shire beauty of the Dordogne, the Lot is more cowboy rough-and-tumble, its landscape tossed up in wild and arid limestone plateaux called *causses*. What soil it has is said to be the worst in France (the vines don't mind that at all). The Dordogne belongs to Aquitaine, the Atlantic and Bordeaux; the Lot occupies half of the ancient province of Quercy, the northernmost possessions of the counts of Toulouse, and to this day it belongs to Toulouse and the Midi-Pyrénées region.

'Quercy' may evoke oaks (as in the Latin *quercus*), the tree that covers much of its territory, but the name is really derived from its Gaulish residents, the never-say-die Cadurcii, who are also remembered in the name of their capital, Cahors. In 51 BC, after Caesar's defeat of Vercingetorix at Alésia, the feisty Cadurcii still refused to surrender to the Romans and holed up at an oppidum with a wonderful, ululating nursery-rhyme of a name, Uxellodunum. Julius Caesar was niggled enough to come in person to sort out this last pocket of resistance, and got the Cadurcii to surrender by diverting the physical manifestation of their goddess – their water supply. Now no one remembers where Uxellodunum was, but most scholars agree this lost Alamo of the Gauls is somewhere in the Lot: Vayrac, north of the Dordogne river, Mursens, Luzech and Capdenac-le-Haut all have supporters to their claim.

What the Lot doesn't have a lot of is people. Many migrated in the last century looking for jobs, leaving behind old stone houses which either tumbled into ruins or have been restored as holiday homes – in 1994 there were just under 14,000 private holiday homes – which has proved to be the kiss of death for everyday life in some smaller hamlets. However, it seems that the population decline is flattening out as more jobs become available. The new A20 motorway extension to Cahors, linking it to Toulouse, Brive and Paris, should improve access, introduce some industry and shake loose more jobs. The Lot has already started taking its vocation for vacations more seriously: you can not only canoe on its tight curling loops but spend a week on a houseboat; the summer fireworks get bigger and better every year; and there's even talk of changing the *département's* name to Lot-et-Dordogne to remind visitors that it too rules a section of that famous river, from Castelnau to Souillac.

Between the Dordogne and Lot Rivers: the Causse de Gramat

The largest and wildest of Quercy's rocky and arid limestone plateaux, the Causse de Gramat is the upper crust of an extraordinary subterranean world of lakes and rivers, accessible to earth-dwellers through caverns, little canyons and *gouffres*,

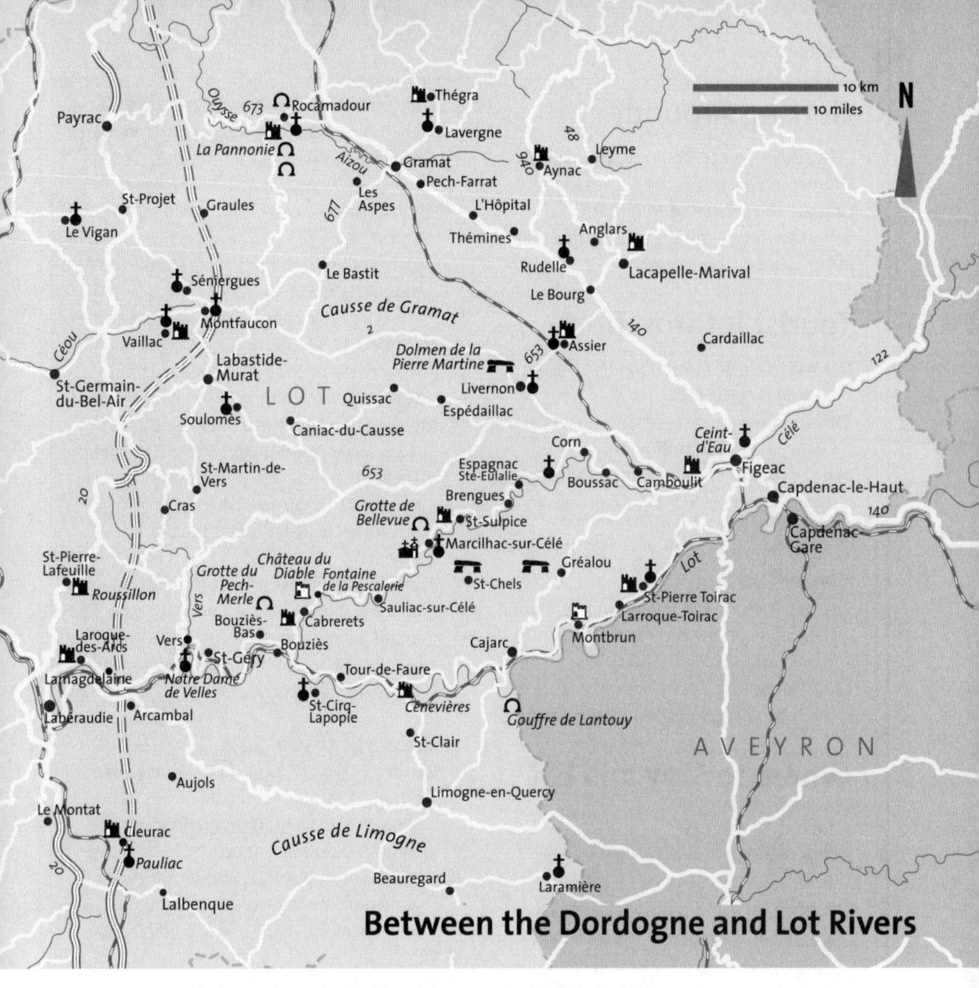

Between the Dordogne and Lot Rivers

including the spectacular pit of Padirac (*see* pp.148–9). The *causse* itself has a peculiar fascination in the spring and early summer, when the scrub oak and juniper, wild flowers, eglantine and honeysuckle soften the deserted landscape; the odd-looking flocks of the *causse* – a local breed of sheep called the *caussenarde* whose eyes are protected from the sun by natural black spectacles – forage in the shade, butterflies flutter by and the dark shadows of buzzards and kestrels slowly make their loops across blue-grey horizons. The limestone soaks in the sun as it soaks in the rain, and the heated scent of juniper in a clearing is like inhaling from a vat of gin. Holiday people fill the houses, and the cafés and restaurants are open, which can be a welcome sight after you've travelled for miles without passing any sign of human life.

Come in the winter, and the *causse* becomes a study in desolation, the colour drained out of it, the oaks clinging dismally to their brown leaves in the sodden mists. The villages seem sad and empty, or locked up altogether; the buzzards and kestrels are still there, but now they seem sinister as they circle over silent, overcast ridges.

Getting Around

The Brive–Figeac–Toulouse **trains** stop in Gramat as well as nearby Rocamadour. Gramat and Labastide-Murat are also linked by **bus** to Figeac: call the tourist office for information on bus connections.

Tourist Information

Gramat: Place de la République, **t** 05 65 38 73 60, **f** 05 65 33 46 38.

Labastide-Murat: Place Mairie, **t** 05 65 21 11 39, **f** 05 65 21 13 18, summer only.

Ask at any tourist office for the excellent *département*-wide practical guide, *Key to the Lot*.

Market Days

Gramat: Tues, Fri and Sun mornings, Place de la Halle; fairs on the second and fourth Thurs of each month.

Labastide-Murat: Sun 9–12, and a huge fair on the second and fourth Mon of each month.

Where to Stay and Eat

Gramat ✉ 46500

★★★**Le Lion d'Or**, 8 Place de la République, **t** 05 65 38 73 18, **f** 05 65 38 84 50 (*moderate*). Central, solid and comfortable, *Le lit on dort* (get it?) also has one of the Lot's best-known restaurants, with a seasonally changing menu and a cellar full of *vin de Cahors* (*menus 130–400F*). *Closed Mon lunch Nov–Mar, and mid-Dec–mid-Jan.*

★★**Le Relais des Gourmands**, 2 Av de la Gare, **t** 05 65 38 83 92, **f** 05 65 38 70 99 (*inexpensive*). Cheerful rooms surrounded by greenery and a restaurant with a growing reputation for the chef's tasty versions of local ingredients; try the delicious duck *confits* with potatoes fried with *cèpes* (*menus 65–200F*). There's a pool, and even a box of toys on hand for little kids. *Closed Mon, Sun in the winter, and hols in Feb.*

★★**Du Centre**, Place de la République, **t** 05 65 38 73 37, **f** 05 65 38 73 66 (*inexpensive*). If you're just staying overnight, these simple modern rooms are fine.

★★**De Bordeaux**, 17 Av du 11 Novembre, **t** 05 65 38 70 10, **f** 05 65 38 76 46 (*inexpensive*). A very reasonably priced hotel, with a restaurant serving good, filling meals (*menus 65–420F*).

Moulin de Fresquet, in a park less than a km from the centre, **t** 05 65 38 70 60 (*moderate*). There are five pleasant bed-and-breakfast rooms in this 17th-century water mill; the restaurant is just as pleasant. *Closed Nov–Mar.*

Pizzeria Rigalou, in Carlucet (14km southwest of Gramat on the D50), **t** 05 65 33 17 89. Tasty pizzas served in a rustic setting, as well as brochettes and other meals (*menus from 60F*). *Open all year.*

Thégra ✉ 46500

Giscard, **t** 05 65 38 77 31. If you want to eat amongst locals, the middle of this quiet village seems a thousand miles from the throngs of tourists at nearby Padirac. It's not smart smart but solid and country with good honest southwest dishes at reasonable prices (*65–145F*) and friendly service.

Labastide-Murat ✉ 46240

★★**Hôtel Climat de France**, Place de la Mairie, **t** 05 65 21 18 80, **f** 05 65 21 10 97 (*inexpensive*). A member of a small, reliable chain of hotels, with 20 rooms in a handsome 13th-century château.

Le Cloitre, in nearby Montfaucon, **t** 05 65 31 11 80. Excellent inexpensive food in a lovely setting.

Gramat

Gramat on the river Alzou is the pleasant if not very remarkable capital of the *causse*, with only a 15th-century clock tower and a watchtower that recall the town before the Wars of Religion; Gramat's baron, Gontaut d'Auriolle, was an ally of Henri IV, but, unfortunately for the town's historical preservation, everyone else in the vicinity remained Catholic. These days Gramat serves as Rocamadour's tourist overflow tank, but also as a base for the many potholers who come to explore the pocked *causse* and, more unexpectedly, for pewter-makers – **Les Etains Arsène Maigne** (*Faubourg St-Pierre, **t** 05 65 38 74 94; open daily*) – and police-dog trainers. The Gendarmerie's **national kennels** are here, now officially known as the Centre de Cynophilie as if it were some kind of New Age cult; you can watch the cops and their best friends do their stuff here (***t** 05 65 38 71 59; June–Oct Thurs 3.30*). Besides police dogs, you can visit 250 different European animals and birds (including a wide selection of rare chickens and pigs) in a wooded park on the *causse*, a few kilometres from the centre at Gramat's **Parc Animalier de Gramat** (***t** 05 65 38 81 22; open Easter–Sept daily 9–7; Oct–Easter 2–6; adm*).

The environs of Gramat are full of little wonders, easily explored by bike. One of the most important tumuli in the Lot, known as the **Etron de Gargantua** ('Gargantua's turd'), is just east (on the D15) and covered with flowers that don't grow anywhere else (the name Gramat comes from the Celtic *grammat*, or tumulus – there used to be one as big as the *etron* in the middle of Place de la République). Other neolithic sites in the vicinity include good **dolmens** at **Pech-Farrat** (east off the N140), **Ségala** (up the Alzou from Gramat) and **Les Aspes**, to the west on the D39. Les Aspes is also near an impressive *gouffre* at Ligue de Biau (enquire about access at the Gramat tourist office). At **La Pannonie**, off the D39, the vast Mansart-roofed **Château de la Pannonie** was begun in the late 1400s as the pleasure dome of a Rocamadour merchant, and has a fine set of windows and dormers. Northeast of Gramat, **Lavergne** has an impressive *pigeonnier*, unusually built over a gate; the apse of the village's Romanesque church has *modillons* carved with lively human and animal faces. Another 2.5km to the north, **Thégra** has a harmonious 15th-century château.

South to Labastide-Murat

Further afield (10km south of Gramat on the D677), **Le Bastit**, once an important Templar commandery serving passing pilgrims, has one of the *causse*'s most spectacular *avens* (natural wells), the **Igue de la Vierge**. To the southwest, **Montfaucon** is a charming hilltop *bastide*, erected by Edward II in 1292 on the English front line as a foil to the new French town of Labastide-Murat; if the **church** is open, pop in to look at the 17th-century altarpieces. Two kilometres north of Montfaucon, **Séniergues** is a minor gem, a picturesque rural hamlet with a 12th-century Romanesque **church** and splendid views all around; **Vaillac**, 3km south, is the seat of a formidable feudal **castle** and Romanesque **church**, where recently a medieval relief of the Virgin of Rocamadour was discovered. The fine *causse* country in this area has been sliced by the new A20 motorway from Brive to Cahors, a project that many Lotois vigorously opposed, knowing well that one of the great charms of the area is or, rather, was precisely its lack of motorways.

The agricultural centre of the south *causse* is **Labastide-Murat**, founded in the 13th century by Fortanier, the *seigneur* of Gourdon, and named after him until 1852, when the town decided to rename itself to honour a hometown boy who spread his name across Europe at the beginning of the 19th century. Yet despite his adventurous career, Murat never forgot the folks back home. He built a château for his brother

The King of Naples

Born in 1767, the son of the local innkeeper, young Joachim Murat began his military career by being kicked out of the army for unruly behaviour. The advent of Napoleon gave him a second chance in the wars of Italy and Egypt, where as Bonaparte's aide-de-camp Murat distinguished himself with gut-busting courage and bravado; his subsequent promotion gave substance to Napoleon's saying that each of his soldiers carried a marshal's baton in his knapsack. Murat was the engineer of the great French victory at Marengo, and nudged his destiny along by loyally supporting Napoleon at the *coup d'état* of 18 Brumaire (a gesture rewarded with his marriage to Caroline Bonaparte in 1800); in 1808 he crushed the May insurrection in Madrid with a brutality immortalized in Goya's paintings of the French firing squads. Pleased, Napoleon gave him the throne of Naples, then called upon him to lead the cavalry of the Grande Armée into Russia in 1812. After the defeat, Murat tried to talk the allies into letting him keep Naples, and when they refused he sailed over to grab it for himself (1815). But Murat had grieviously miscalculated his popularity; when he landed in southern Italy and announced to the first peasants he met that their king had returned, they tried to kill him; a Bourbon army arrived shortly after, arrested him and shot him on the spot.

André – a rare example of the Empire style in this neck of the woods – and sent letters to his mum, displayed in the **Musée Murat** (in his father's *auberge*); amongst the period furniture and other memorabilia is a giant family tree showing Murat's relationship with most of the crowned heads of Europe (***t** 05 65 21 19 23; open July–Sept 10–12 and 2–6; adm*). Three kilometres southeast, **Soulomès** was one of several Templar commanderies or priories in the region, and the village's 14th-century Gothic **church** has a Templar baptismal font and unusual frescoes on the *Life of Christ* – scenes of Jesus taking a stroll with Mary Magdelene, Doubting Thomas, and the resurrected Christ with a knight of St John, a member of the Order that inherited most of the Templars' property after their suppression in 1312.

From Labastide-Murat the scenic D32 heads south through the narrow valley of the little river Vers, its clear waters reflecting the deep, steep greenery of its banks. It was favoured by those most picky of water connoisseurs, the Romans; the valley's gem of a village, **St-Martin-de-Vers**, has the beginnings of the ancient aqueduct carved in the rock that once descended to slake the thirst of Cahors – the best parts of it are south, around the village of Vers (*see* p.323), where the little river flows into the Lot. Closer to St-Martin, to the west, **Cras** lies at the foot of the road up to the haunting, scanty ruins of the **Oppidum de Mursens**, a possible Uxellodunum candidate.

Into the Heart of the Causse de Gramat

To explore the wildest, most desolate part of the Causse de Gramat, the **Désert de La Braunhie**, head south of Gramat towards Cabrerets, or take the small roads east of Labastide-Murat. On the west edge of La Braunhie, **Caniac-du-Causse** has, under its modern church, a 12th-century **crypt** containing the 11th-century reliquary of St Namphaise, a friend of Charlemagne who fought against the Saracens in Quercy and then returned to live as a hermit, wandering about excavating drinking holes for the flocks of the *causse*, earning himself the sincere devotion of Lotois shepherds. The local answer to fertility drugs is to crawl under his reliquary. There are traces of a Roman road nearby.

Some things do grow in the La Braunhie desert – eglantine, juniper, twisted little oaks, gorse, brambles and other prickly thorny things. East of Caniac, you can visit its most dramatic feature, the **Gouffre de Planegrèze**, a pit descending 890ft into one of the *causse*'s innumerable underground rivers. Unlike at Padirac, you can't descend into the chasm, but explanatory panels tell you what's down there. A path carved out of the stone links the pit to a dolmen nearby, as if it were part of the sacred site.

Other picturesque, sleepy villages to aim for in these lonesome wastelands include **Blars** (south of the D653 to Figeac), with a domed Romanesque church with carved capitals and reliefs, **Quissac** and **Espédaillac**, the former with a *pietà* in its church from the 1600s. Just northwest of **Livernon**, the larger town on the east end of the Causse de Gramat, you can see the biggest dolmen in the entire *département*, the **Pierre Martine** (off the D2; walk through the scrubby trees to the end of the field). Its table stone stretches nearly 22ft long, but, massive as it is, it would wiggle at the touch of a finger until 1948, when it cracked; now concrete blocks support it. You can scramble over the stone wall nearby to see a second, slightly smaller dolmen in the next field. If you aren't afraid of getting lost, leave the path between the road and the Pierre Martin to see what must have been the quarry of a score of megalithic monuments – the limestone gouged out and still scoured bare. Livernon's **church** has a beautiful fortified Romanesque bell tower, and there's a pretty fountain in the centre called the Boudoulou, but there's not much else to stop for; from here the stately D653 leads to Assier (*see* below).

Gramat to Figeac: the Limargue

The main N140 between Gramat and Figeac rather neatly separates the *causse* from the Ségala south of St-Céré towards Figeac, running along a broad swathe of land known as the Limargue – a lush micro-region of chestnut forests and meadows of wildflowers. It has some charming villages, and the remains of one of the most blustering castles ever built.

Aynac and Lacapelle-Marival

The N140 traces an important pilgrim route to Rocamadour, remembered in **L'Hôpital** 7km from Gramat, where the Knights of St John ran a hostel, of which a chapel survives. Further southeast, tiny **Thémines** has its fine *halle* with a *lauze* roof, while, yet further along, **Rudelle** is a rather dilapidated 13th-century *bastide*, defended by an astonishing battlemented **church** built by Bertrand de Cardaillac that looks

Tourist Information

Lacapelle-Marival: Place de la Halle, **t/f** 05 65 40 81 11, summer only.
Assier: Route de Lacapelle, **t** 05 65 40 50 60.

Market Days

Lacapelle-Marival has a farmers' market on Tues afternoons and Sun mornings, fairs the second and fourth Mon morning of each month.

Where to Stay and Eat

Lacapelle-Marival ✉ 46120

****La Terrasse**, by the château, **t** 05 65 40 80 07, **f** 05 65 40 99 45 (*inexpensive*). Thirteen rooms in a fairly nondescript building, with a newly remodelled dining room with panoramic views of the castle and laughing brook below. The food is lovely: try the *ris de veau au jus de cèpes* (*menus 78–215F*). *Closed Sun eve, Mon out of season and Jan–early Mar, Mon lunch only in summer.*

Le Glacier, in the centre, **t** 05 65 40 82 67 (*inexpensive–cheap*). Slightly cheaper rooms.

Mas de la Feuille, in Le Bourg, on the N120, **t/f** 05 65 11 00 17 (*inexpensive*). Three rooms in a beautifully restored old farmhouse; meals can be provided.

Les Tragners, Le Bourg, on the N120, **t** 05 65 40 82 40. A working farm with five very pleasant bed-and-breakfast rooms. Meals on request.

Cardaillac ✉ 46100

Chez Marcel, **t** 05 65 40 11 16 (*cheap*). This has been a local institution for decades – one that could almost be part of the village museum. The secret, time-tried formula: plentiful, well-prepared authentic cuisine at the best prices around (*four menus, all under 200F*). *Closed Sun eve and Mon out of season.* There are five simple rooms to rent.

more like an overgrown rook from a chessboard than a house of God. For a scenic detour, take the D40 north from Thémines up to **Aynac**, once a lead-mining centre, where a **château** was built in the 16th century by the bastard son of the Vicomte of Turenne, its four corner towers crowned with breast-shaped slate-coated cupolas; the delicate bas-relief over the door fits in perfectly, even though it was carved in 1895. Aynac's Romanesque church is also worth a look, with its octagonal tower and carved capitals. All in, though, the most extraordinary thing about Aynac is the average height of its inhabitants, who get an entry in the French Guinness Book of Records – in the 1980s five out of 710 measured at least 6ft 6in. A skeleton found near the château was just short of 8ft.

For a pretty drive from Aynac, circle around on the D39 to Leyme, then follow the D48 down to **Lacapelle-Marival**, the major town in these parts, and an attractive one of sunwarmed limestone and old towers. It grew up around an 11th-century chapel, and after the next century was defended by the Cardaillacs' **Château de Lacapelle-Marival** (*open daily July–mid-Sept 10–12 and 3–7; adm*), one of that powerful family's principal residences, which they built smack in the middle of the village, to use its walls as an outer ring of defences; you can stroll along its parapet walk and take a look at its medieval frescoes. The tiny *halle* on sandstone pillars squeezed into the village centre dates from the 1400s. There's another good Romanesque church at **Anglars** (12th-century, with a fortified bell tower) and another with interior carvings at **Le Bourg**, down at the N140 crossroads.

Assier and its Cannonballing Egomaniac

The pleasant, tidy *commune* of **Assier** straddles the dramatic division between the Limargue and the Causse de Gramat. In the 16th century, much of what you see, or at least 2,500 acres of it, belonged to the irrepressible braggart Galiot (Galahad) de Genouillac (1465–1546), François I's Captain General of Artillery, Master of the Horse and Lieutenant General of Guyenne. In 1515 Galiot helped the king beat the redoubtable Swiss pikemen at the Battle of Marignano by blowing them away, on a massive scale, with cannons – the first time anyone ever employed them so in battle. As Galiot bought up the largest property in all Quercy, he made two rich marriages to help finance a building programme that was pharaonic for the Lot in 1526: a Loire Valley-style château in an immense quadrangle, numerous windmills and barns, a vaulted, 180ft stable (still standing in the village), a forge, a church, the Rockefeller Center of *pigeonniers*, and a *jeu de paume* for court tennis matches. The pile was inherited by the dukes of Uzès, who cared little for it, and by 1786 it had reached such a state of decay that the owners let builders cannibalize it for a small fee; wherever you see a carved stone incorporated in a local house, you can bet it came from the château. When Prosper Mérimée, inspector of historical monuments, came to Assier in 1841, he was touched by the romantic ruin of Galiot's pride and put it on his register to prevent the rest from going to hell. Only the relatively simple west wing of the quadrangle, the guards' quarters, remains of the once enormous **Château d'Assier** (***t*** *05 65 40 40 99; open July and Aug daily 9.30–12.30 and 2–6.45; April–June and Sept 9.30–12.15 and 2–6.15, closed Tues, Oct–Mar 10–12.15 and 2–5.15, closed Tues; adm*).

The exterior façade of this wing is framed by two of the château's original four towers, one sheathing Galiot's humble medieval birthplace. The once ornate dormers have all been stripped off, except for one on the left; the niche over the entrance once held an equestrian statue of Galiot. The interior façade, however, is still a handsome Renaissance work; large stone-framed windows alternate with walls bearing medallions of Roman emperors, while bands of a frieze show swords and cannons relating to Galiot's deeds or those of Hercules, with whom Galiot fancied a resemblance. The interior, described by Brantôme as 'the best furnished in France with its vast piles of silver, tapestries and silks', now contains only one of its former score of grand stairways, this one decorated with a handsome pilaster carved with grotesques, Hercules and the Nemean Lion and Galiot's trophies. A pendant in the vault, showing Hercules wrestling with Ateneus, is inscribed with Galiot's motto: *J'aime fort une* (a play on words, meaning either 'I love fortune' or 'I love one very much' – in Galiot's case, read this as Looking Out for Number One). There's an exhibit on Galiot's career, and a hologram of his armour sent over by the Metropolitan Museum in New York.

The man's overweening self-esteem is most manifest today in the **church** he built in the middle of Assier between 1540 and 1549 as a personal shrine to himself and his weaponry. Although Gothic in form, the decoration is Renaissance: the fascinating sculpted frieze that encircles the exterior is devoted to cannons, battles and artillery, with nary a Christian symbol in sight (reminscent of Venice's Santa Maria Zobenigo) although in the tympanum over the door we see the Virgin looking quite pleased to accept Galiot's sword and insignia from an angel, while two other angels unfurl banners reading *Vivit d. Jac. Galeotus!* ('Long live Galiot!'). Inside, under the lovely star vaulting, is Galiot's tomb, topped with a statue of you-know-who in his battle gear, leaning nonchalantly against a cannon, with a braggart's epitaph and his *J'aime fort une* motto. The old warrior died peacefully in bed at age 81 and, according to the dictates of his will, 500 priests were gathered together from miles around to give him a rousing send-off at his funeral. On the Lacapelle–Marival road, you can still see Galiot's 38ft-high pigeon tenement with 2,300 varnished nests, each one representing an acre of his realm.

Cardaillac

Cradle of one of the oldest and most powerful families of Quercy, the name Cardaillac once made people tremble in their boots, but today it means only a delightful old *village perché* where dogs snooze in the middle of the lane, just 3km off the N140. Only two towers and few walls of its mighty 12th-century citadel have survived the demolition of 1629, ordered by Cardinal Richelieu to punish Cardaillac for being a Protestant safe haven – Jeanne de Cardaillac, mother of Madame de Maintenon and future mother-in-law of Louis XIV, was an important Reformation figure. Another important member of the family was Hugues de Cardaillac, who wrote a code regulating the use of cannons in warfare (1346) – a code that his neighbour Galiot probably broke when he blasted the Swiss at Marignano. The village has marked out a walk through the *quartier du fort*, the site of the old citadel on its rocky spur, still dominated by the Cardaillacs' 70ft **Tour de Sagnes** which you can (sometimes) climb for the grand views.

Cardaillac also has the unique **Musée Éclaté** (***t*** *05 65 40 10 63; open Tues–Fri, July and Aug 3–6, Sept just one visit at 3*), with artefacts related to Cardaillac's history, crafts, and traditions, not confined in the walls of a single building but *éclaté* ('burst open') and displayed where they belong, in the old school, bakery, farm buildings, etc. The villagers founded the museum and provide an enthusiastic narration – it's one of the most fun and enlightening of Good Old Days museums (if you understand French).

Figeac

Figeac, the metropolis of the Célé valley, has more than one feather in its cap. It gave the world Jean-François Champollion, the linguistic wizard who cracked Egyptian hieroglyphics, and Charles Boyer, the archetypical French lover of the silver screen (and the inspiration for Warner Bros' cartoon skunk Pepe le Pew). Figeac is the second city of the Lot, with all of 11,000 people; it has more obelisks than Paris, and lays fair claim to flexing the *département*'s industrial muscle, thanks to the aeronautics manufacturer Ratier. But for the casual unsuspecting visitor, it's Figeac's medieval heart of golden sandstone that comes as the most charming surprise of all – if none of the individual buildings make the architectural textbooks, some 700 have been intelligently restored in the past decade to create a delightful ensemble.

History

The story goes that Pepin the Short was resting on the banks of the Célé in 753 when he saw doves suddenly fly up in the form of a cross. He founded a church on the site (the ancestor of St-Saveur), which, the legend continues, was consecrated two years later by Pope Stephen II himself. The abbey that grew up around it linked itself with Cluny, and drew in its share of pilgrims en route to Rocamadour or Compostela. As was so often the case, the 11th and 12th centuries saw the hamlet around the abbey expand into a sizeable commercial town that chafed at being bossed around by an abbot, and in 1302 Philip the Fair liberated it, replacing monastic rule with that of seven consuls, one for each quarter, with a *Viguier* in charge of administering royal justice in the town. It was the beginning of Figeac's prosperity; apparently, like their brethren in Cahors, they were known for cutting a close deal.

As in many mercantile towns, Protestantism made many converts in Figeac, although the Calvinists only took control in 1568 when their captain bribed the wife of a consul to steal her husband's keys while he slept and toss them over the gate. In 1598 the Edict of Nantes made Figeac a Protestant safe town; Henri IV's brilliant minister, the duke of Sully, took refuge here after the king's assassination. Sully remained Henri IV's right-hand man (and a Protestant) even after the king decided that Paris was worth a Mass; as the powerful superindentent of finances he performed the seemingly impossible task of filling the king's war chest, promoting agriculture and building roads all across France while lowering taxes and balancing the budget. In his retirement he wrote the *Memories of wise and royal economies of the state of Henry the Great*, which subsequent superintendents of finances would have done well to study, rather than abet France's kings down their extravagant road to ruin and revolution.

If the Calvinists damaged much of Figeac's ecclesiastical patrimony, the Nazi SS in 1944 cruelly struck at the inhabitants themselves, deporting nearly every able-bodied man not employed by Ratier, which at the time made parts for the Luftwaffe. Of the 540 who went, only 395 returned from the labour and concentration camps at the end of the war.

Place Vival and Around

There may be no canals, but there's something vaguely Venetian about Figeac, beginning with its medieval street plan, full of curving lanes and irregular, asymmetrical little squares, offering a wealth of visual surprises for the pedestrian. The stone houses are so tall and densely built that many are topped with covered rooftop terraces that the Venetians call *altane* and the Lotois call *soleihos*, which not only offered city-dwellers a breath of fresh air but came in handy for drying textiles for sale as well as the family's clothes, fruit and other foods. As in Venice as well, the ground floors were given over to stocking merchandise, while the merchants themselves lived upstairs on the *piano nobile*, usually lit with the most elaborate windows of the building. As you stroll through the lanes (an activity that becomes especially evocative in the evening), keep an eye peeled for the myriad sculptural details.

Figeac has no grand central piazza like Venice, but a dozen smaller ones that form the focal points of its old neighbourhoods, like Place Vival, site of the elegant 13th-century **Hôtel de la Monnaie**, one of the most beautiful secular buildings of the period in France. Philippe IV granted Figeac the privilege of minting its own coins, a dandy boost to commerce in those days; the ground floor with its pointed arches was used as a bank, while on top is a typical *soleiho*. Sharing the *hôtel* with the tourist office is the little **Musée du Vieux Figeac** (*t 05 65 34 06 25; open mid-Sept–June 10–12 and 2.30–6, closed Sun except May and June when it is open 10–1, July–mid-Sept daily 10–1 and 2–7; adm*), an eclectic collection including the beautiful Renaissance door from Sully's mansion, a set of stocks, a carving of a monk playing a drum, and more.

Just west of Place Vival runs **Rue Caviale**, one of Figeac's prettiest streets, where the **Hôtel de Marroncles** at No.30 hosted Louis XI in 1463. Rue Caviale gives into **Place Carnot**, Figeac's ancient market square, although since 1988 sadly lacking its 13th-

Getting Around

If you're flying from Paris, the nearest **airport** is at Rodez, a 45min drive away.

Figeac's **railway** station is on the Brive–Toulouse branch line, with direct connections to Gramat, Rocamadour and Capdenac.

The SNCF runs regular **buses** from Figeac to Capdenac, Toirac, Cajarc, St-Cirq-Lapopie, St-Géry and Cahors; private companies also link Figeac to Labastide-Murat, Toulouse, St-Céré, Cardaillac and Lacapelle-Marival – the tourist office has schedules.

Quercyrail excursions also depart from Capdenac several times a week in the summer; information and tickets from the Figeac and Capdenac tourist offices.

Hire a **bike** or mountain bike from Ets Larroque, 10 Quai Bessières, **t** 05 65 34 10 28.

Tourist Information

Figeac: at the Hôtel de la Monnaie, Place Vival, **t** 05 65 34 06 25, **f** 05 65 50 04 58. From early April to September they offer walking tours of the medieval centre day and night, and in July and August there are specialized tours on certain themes. You can also see the town from a 'train' which tours the old streets.

Capdenac-le-Haut: **t** 05 65 50 01 45.

Market Days

Figeac: Tues and Thurs mornings, and Sat all day; a fair on the second and last Sat of each month.

Activities

You can see Figeac and its lovely surroundings by **air**: hour-long flights for three people are only 700F at the Aérodome de Figeac-Livernon in Durbans (**t** 05 65 40 57 04; *closed Tues*).

You can hire a **canoe** or kayak to paddle down the Célé, with Eaux Vive, **t** 05 65 50 05 48; hire a **horse** at the Centre Equestre, Av de Nayrac, **t** 05 65 34 70 57; or **swim** in a wave pool at the Domaine du Surgié (**t** 05 65 34 59 00; *open April–June and Sept Sat, Sun and Wed 2–6, July and Aug 11–7*); it also has a playground, mini-golf and other kid-pleasers.

Where to Stay

Figeac ✉ 46100

******Château du Viguier du Roy**, Rue Droite, **t** 05 65 50 05 05, **f** 05 65 50 06 06 (*expensive*). A few years back, a Parisian couple, Anne and Philippe Secordel-Martin, fell in love with Figeac and the much ruined lodgings of Philippe le Bel's judge, built in 1302 and added to over the centuries, then

century grain *halle*. Note the well-preserved 13th–17th-century **Maison Cisteron** in the corner, with a turret: this was the residence of Pierre de Cisteron, master armourer of Louis XIV and a Huguenot. Just before revoking the Edict of Nantes, Louis sent down a special safeguard for Cisteron, to keep him from the persecutions he had in store for Protestants who weren't so dear to his heart.

To the east Place Carnot flows naturally into handsome **Place Champollion**. For centuries this held Figeac's chestnut market; until the 19th century chestnuts were staple in the local diet and ground into flour for bread. The butchers had their stands under the ogival arches, and the **Templars' commandery** (No.5), on the south side of the square, has little columns on the windows; note, too, the 12th-century **Maison du Griffon** at No.4. In nearby Rue Séguier is the **Musée Champollion** (**t** *05 65 50 31 08; open July and Aug daily 10–12 and 2.30–6.30, rest of year closed Mon; Nov–Feb 2–6 only; adm*). Audiovisual displays explain how Champollion cracked the code, and give

left to go to hell. Now it's a hotel including a cloister, several 18th-century houses, enclosed courtyard and terrace with a pool, all impeccably restored; there are 17 rooms and three suites, individually furnished with appropriate antiques; the 18th-century rooms have chimneys decorated with gold. *Closed Nov–early April*.

★★**Hostellerie de l'Europe**, 51 Allées Victor-Hugo, **t** 05 65 34 10 16, **f** 05 65 50 04 57 (*inexpensive*). A stylish place that offers full en suite baths, a winter garden, pool, garage and an Art Deco-kitsch touch in the public rooms.

★★**Les Bains**, 1 Rue du Griffoul, **t** 05 65 34 10 89, **f** 05 65 14 00 45 (*inexpensive*). A Logis de France with simple rooms directly over the waters of the Célé.

★★**Hotel-Bar Le Champollion**, 4 Place Champollion, **t** 05 65 34 04 37, **f** 05 65 34 61 69 (*inexpensive*). Small and very modern, with friendly staff and a bright bar where locals come to have their *café*.

★★**Le Terminus St-Jacques**, by the station at 27 Av Georges-Clémenceau, **t** 05 65 34 00 43, **f** 05 65 50 00 94 (*inexpensive*). Perhaps the nicest of all at the cheaper end, with a bit of a garden; the restaurant serves a tender slice of beef with Roquefort sauce (*menus 115–200F*).

Camping Les Rives du Célé, 1 km from Figeac, **t** 05 65 34 59 00, **f** 05 65 34 83 83. Basic bungalow accommodation, a beach, artificial lakelet and pool. *Open April–Sept*.

Eating Out

La Dinée du Viguier, in the Château du Viguier (*see* above). This new restaurant opened in 1996 and at once became the gourmet shrine of Figeac, hiring the fine chefs of the defunct Carmes, once Figeac's top hotel; the food features the finest of Quercy (*menus 140–360F*). *Closed Mon lunch May–Sept, Sun eve and Mon Oct–April*.

La Puce à l'Oreille, 5–7 Rue St-Thomas, **t** 05 65 34 33 08. In a 15th-century mansion. The name means 'flea in the ear', an expression meaning an awakened suspicion. They offer both traditional menus, featuring snails in flaky pastry and duck confits, and unusual dishes such as duck with *sabayon* (syllabub) and honey (*menus from 75–190F; book*). *Closed Sun eve and Mon, exc July and Aug*.

Chez Marinette, the restaurant attached to Hostellerie de l'Europe (*see* above), **t** 05 65 34 10 16. They do wonderful things with mushrooms and other traditional Quercy ingredients (*menus 78–190F*).

La Cuisine du Marché, 15 Rye Clermont, **t** 05 65 50 18 55. Eat out under the stone arches of this restored wine cellar, with a small but imaginative menu specializing in fish dishes such as *millefeuille de sandre sur un lit de mini-ratatouille* but also other delights such as *médaillon de veau en brioche*. The attentive Joel Centeno will be happy to explain it all to you (*menus 85–170F*). *Call for opening times in winter*.

Champollion and the Rosetta Stone

Son of Figeac's first bookseller, Jean François Champollion was born in a 14th-century house, now much-restored and a museum of his life and works, in 1790. He astonished all his teachers with his precocious aptitude for languages – by age 14 he could rattle away in Latin, Greek, Hebrew and Arabic. While still in his teens he discovered hieroglyphics; although common opinion held that they were mere decorations, Champollion suspected from the start that the 'pictures' were a form of writing, and he began a serious study of Oriental languages in the hopes of discovering a clue to their meaning. In 1799 the huge corps of scholars who accompanied Napoleon on his expedition to Egypt began the first systematic study of that country's antiquities (as well as scouting out the possibility of a canal through the Suez and inventing the lead pencil). It's a good thing they were around when French soldiers just happened to dig up a fragment of polished black basalt at Rosetta, covered with inscriptions in hieroglyphics, Greek and a cursive demotic script. They saved what became known as the Rosetta Stone and in 1814 it ended up in the British Museum. Attempts by Thomas Young to translate it were frustrated until Champollion got hold of a copy of the text and made the essential discovery in 1822 that the hieroglyphics were not only phonetic ideograms, but figurative and symbolic (as described in his *Précis du système hiéroglyphique*, 1824). Champollion made an expedition of his own to Egypt in 1828 and spent the rest of his abbreviated life as the curator of the Egyptian section in the Louvre, translating texts in Egypt and in Paris, and leaving behind a posthumously published dictionary and grammar of hieroglyphics.

the resulting translation of the Rosetta Stone; there are three mummies and a small but choice collection of ancient Egyptian and Coptic art, as well as a painting of the great linguist in Egypt, dressed in native costume, looking for all the world like a husky brigand with his bushy black beard and scimitar. Outside the museum in the **Place des Ecritures**, Champollion's bicentenary in 1991 was celebrated with the installation of a giant facsimile of the Rosetta Stone in the pavement and the planting of a papyrus garden, all designed by American artist Joseph Kosuth.

Notre-Dame-du-Puy and St-Saveur

Figeac's churches haven't withstood the trials of time as successfully as the mummies or even its secular buildings, but are nevertheless worth a look. From Place Champollion, Rue de Colomb passes some of Figeac's most aristocratic houses (note especially the fine courtyard off the pedestrian lane, Rue Malleville). You will also find here **Espace Patrimoine**, a permanent exhibition of the history and heritage of the town. To the right other lanes or steps lead up the hill to **Notre-Dame-du-Puy**. This much tampered-with 12th-century church replaces an ancient chapel built where the Virgin made a rose bloom on Christmas Day; the church's 14th-century portal retains its carving of animals, and inside there are some carved capitals from the same period. Perhaps best of all are the views over Figeac's medieval roofscape.

The most picturesque descent from Notre-Dame is by way of narrow medieval Rue Delzhens, past the seat of the king's judge, the **Hôtel du Viguier** (1300s, now a superb hotel, *see* above), to Rue Roquefort, where at No.12 are the elegant remains of the town house built by braggart Galiot de Genouillac (*see* pp.307–8). This street continues to **St-Sauveur**, encased in a forgettable 19th-century façade and bell tower crowned with a giant bread box; only its large size and some much knocked-about bits on the north and south flanks hint that this was Figeac's great, famous medieval church. The **chapterhouse** (now a chapel off the right aisle) was given its remarkable ogival vaulting in the 15th century; in the 17th century, to cover up some of the damage caused in the Wars of Religion, a local sculptor added the naïve painted reliefs of the Passion: don't miss the *Last Supper*, where the Apostles are served a platter of roast hamster, or the scene of baby Jesus sleeping sweetly on a cross, dreaming of his future torments. In the nave are medieval capitals from the original portal, transformed into holy-water fonts. In the adjacent riverside Place de la Raison stands a small obelisk, a monument to Champollion.

Just before the river, Rue du Balène winds past the **Hôtel du Balène** with its huge ogival door and flamboyant windows, a building now used as a theatre and cultural centre. From here Rue Orthabadial, once the realm of the medieval abbey gardener, returns you to the Hôtel de la Monnaie.

Around Figeac: Obelisks and Capdenac

The classic Figeac excursion is to its mysterious 26ft obelisk-needles or *Aiguilles*, erected in the 12th century on the summit of two nearby hills – the **Aiguille de Lissac** to the west and the **Aiguille du Pressoir** to the south, on the colline du Cingle. Their original purpose has long been forgotten, but they may have been set up by the abbey of St-Sauveur, either to lift the spirits of pilgrims approaching over the *causse*, or to set the limits within which fugitives were guaranteed the abbey's asylum.

After the death of Henri IV, Sully divided his time between Figeac and his 14th-century castle 8km south at **Capdenac-le-Haut**, a perched, medieval town fortified with ramparts; this was one of the keys to Quercy, and was constantly besieged throughout its history. Capdenac-le-Haut lays claim to the Uxellodunum title; digs have revealed artefacts dating back to Neolithic times, most notably the torso of the *Lady of Capdenac*, from *c.* 3000 BC, one of the oldest statues ever found in France. You can see a cast of her as well as Roman coins and other odds and ends in the little **museum** (***t** 05 65 50 01 45; open Tues–Sat June–Sept 10–12.30 and 2.30–7.30, Oct–May 2.30–6.30*). Capdenac's Gallo-Roman spring/fountain is claimed to be the very one cut off by Caesar. But Uxellodunum or no, Capdenac is a charmer, with a pair of Gothic gates, medieval lanes of sunny limestone houses and a belvedere, enjoying a bird's-eye view of the Lot and the village's own ugly stepsister, the industrial railway junction of Capdenac-Gare. East of here the corniche road leaves the Lot to wind into the chestnut forests of the Aveyron.

The Célé Valley

The Lot's merriest river, the Célé (from the Latin *celer*, or rapid) is born in the harsh lands of the Cantal, but once past Figeac this clear and shallow stream takes on a softer quality as it splashes through gentle valleys and steep colourful gorges protected by cliff forts, the so-called *châteaux des Anglais* left over from the Hundred Years' War. In the off-season the tiny hamlets along the river are almost deserted; come before the first tourist wave of Easter and you may think you've landed in a Quercy Brigadoon. Until the 1700s the valley was famous for its saffron, grown mostly as a dye and marketed by German merchants. Not a trace of a saffron remains, in spite of the local appetite for paella – a dish introduced by the many refugees from the Spanish Civil War who settled in southwest France. This is ideal walking country: pick up a copy of the latest literature describing walks in this area, from the *Promenades et Randonnées* series available at Figeac and other area tourist offices. You can take a walk guided by a portable CD player if you follow one of the routes designated by the **Communauté de Communes Lot-Célé**, **t** 05 65 31 40 42, and ask for the English-language *Walking, Riding and Mountain-Biking in the Lot Department*. The Célé is also an easy and lovely river to float down in a lazy canoe or kayak, and a number of places from Figeac (*see* above) on down hire them out to make the descent as far as St-Cirq-Lapopie.

From Figeac to Espagnac-Ste-Eulalie

Six kilometres west of Figeac, leave the D13 for the picturesque riverside D41 near the much restored fat-towered 15th–16th-century **Château Ceint d'Eau**. Soon to the right, just beyond a ruined Romanesque chapel, is a road leading up to tiny **Camboulit**, a charming medieval hill village as yet not given over to holiday homes. The valley narrows once past Boussac, where overhanging cliffs similar to those along the Vézère in Périgord were used as shelters or fortresses in the Middle Ages. In and around **Corn**, an old farming village, are fortified caves from the Hundred Years' War as well as a pair of 17th-century châteaux on either side of the river.

Espagnac-Ste-Eulalie, another 9km downstream, is the most photographed beauty spot along the Célé, a tiny hamlet watched over by a striking *clocher*, a slender tower crowned by an open-work timbered chamber with a bell from the 1500s and a pointy octagonal roof, the whole almost too quaint to be real. This belongs to a convent fittingly named **Notre-Dame-du-Val-Paradis**, founded in the 12th century but greatly expanded in the next by its benefactor, Aymeric d'Hébrard of Cajarc, a member of the valley's leading family and bishop of Coimbra in Portugal. The convent, which survived until the Revolution, incorporated all the buildings within the towered gateway, including the pleasant communal *gîtes*.

Once you've gone this far, chances are you will have met Madame Bonzani, the guide to the little church of **Notre-Dame** (her house is marked with a sign). The bell tower isn't the only quaint thing about it; note how the pentagonal apse rears up abruptly, a full storey higher than the rest of the church. The portal, decorated with carved ivy and fig leaves, leads into an interior half rebuilt after fires in the 15th century, and has ended up unusually short for its height. There are three tombs: those of Aymeric d'Hébrard, the knight Hugues de Cardaillac-Brengues (d. 1342), and his elegant wife, Bernade de Trian, niece of Pope John XXII. The lofty choir is decorated with the arms of the Cardaillacs and little mitred heads. On the high altar, a gilt wooden retable from the 1700s displays a badly restored copy of an altarpiece by Simon Vouet, showing Louis XIV's mum, Anne of Austria, floating up to heaven in the guise of the Virgin of the Assumption.

The next village, **Brengues** is an old Cardaillac fief, built on a bluff over the river that conceals a *château des Anglais*. The Hébrards came from the next village, **St-Sulpice**, partially built into and growing out of the curve of its cliff; its much restored 12th-century château is still in the Hébrard family. In the Middle Ages this was a cradle of bishops, soldiers and diplomats who served in important posts across Europe; the Hébrards owned so much of the Célé valley that it was nicknamed the 'Hébrardie'.

Marcilhac-sur-Célé

With a population of 240, **Marcilhac-sur-Célé** is one of the larger villages in the valley. It owes its existence to a powerful Benedictine abbey founded by Pepin the Short, which by the 12th century possessed over a hundred properties, including Rocamadour. Its abbots, however, had failed to foresee Rocamadour's potential – unlike the bishops of Tulle, who took it over and made it a prestigious pilgrimage site. When the pilgrims (and profits) starting piling into Rocamadour, Marcilhac naturally wanted it back, leading to an unseemly conflict that saw each side booting out the other's monks. In the end, Marcilhac surrendered its claim in exchange for cash. The

Tourist Information

Marcilhac-sur-Célé: at the *mairie*, **t** 05 65 40 68 44 , summer only.

Cabrerets: t 05 65 31 27 12, **f** 05 65 24 38 11, summer only.

Where to Stay and Eat

Boussac ✉ 46100

Domaine des Villedieu, between Figeac and Corn, **t** 05 65 40 06 63. A *ferme-auberge* offering delicious meals in its apple orchard: garnished duck dishes (*confit de canard, magret* grilled or on the spit), or the house speciality, *magret Rossini*, duck breast with truffles, foie gras and Madeira sauce (*menus 135F or the full whack with foie gras for 220F; book*).

Marcilhac-sur-Célé ✉ 46160

Restaurant des Touristes, t 05 65 40 65 61. Offers quality inexpensive meals (*in the 90F range*), served in summer under a pergola. *Best to book.*

Les Tilleuls, t 05 65 40 62 68 (*inexpensive*). A superb bed-and-breakfast in a Quercy house with a shady lawn and pretty rooms. *Book early. Closed mid-Nov–Dec.*

Cabrerets ✉ 46330

****Des Grottes, t** 05 65 31 27 02, **f** 05 65 31 20 15 (*inexpensive*). A pleasant hotel with a pool and restaurant. *Open April–Oct.*

****Auberge de la Sagne**, near the entrance to Pech-Merle, **t** 05 65 31 26 62, **f** 05 65 30 27 43 (*inexpensive*). A charming, tranquil old inn set in lovely gardens. *Open mid-May–Sept.*

Chez Bessac, opposite the *mairie*, **t** 05 65 31 27 04, **f** 05 65 30 25 46 (*inexpensive–cheap*). A friendly bed-and-breakfast.

abbey was badly pillaged in the Hundred Years' War. The Hébrards of St-Sulpice took it under their wing in 1451 and rebuilt the damaged bits in the Gothic style; this was in turn destroyed by the Protestants. A few monks stuck it out until the Revolution.

There are more ducks than people here now, but along the Célé they are still defended by the thick medieval buttresses topped with little carved figures mysteriously called 'conspirators' heads'. The path from Place des Platanes leads past the Romanesque chapterhouse, with curious capitals carved with scenes of heaven and hell in two distinct styles. The lofty, grandiose ruins of the bays and narthex of the abbey's Romanesque church form a kind of courtyard around what is now Marcilhac's parish **church**, rebuilt by the Hébrards in the Gothic style to replace the once-vast Romanesque apse and ambulatory. The interior is decorated with Hébrard coats of arms and 15th-century frescoes, 17th-century panelling and a copy of a Van Dyck *Virgin and Child* in the retable. Note the angel's head with a teasing smile on the pew with the heraldic carvings. The original Romanesque church's south portal has a rare Carolingian tympanum, a triangular composition of bas-reliefs. Christ on top is framed by symbols of the sun and moon, while two angels below grip instruments of the Passion, and at the bottom stand Saints Peter and Paul.

Two kilometres northwest of Marcilhac, a steep hairpin road zigzags up to the **Grotte de Bellevue**, discovered in 1964, full of curious red and white stalactites and stalagmites; one is called the 'jellyfish' (***t** 05 65 40 63 92; open mid-June–mid-Sept 10–6; adm*). Beyond the old village of **Sauliac-sur-Célé** (with a lovely place for a riverside picnic, overlooking a dilapidated château) is the narrow but well-signposted road up to **Cuzals** and the **Musée en Plein Air du Quercy** (***t** 05 65 22 58 63; open April–Oct Sun–Fri; June, July and Aug 10–7, rest of year 2–6; adm exp, ticket good for a week*). This re-creates two farms with original buildings, one pre-Revolutionary, the other from the early 1900s, along with 25 little museums of crafts, agriculture, water and natural sciences; there's a dentist's surgery from 1900, an antique carousel, working craftspeople (especially on Sundays), and more; there's also a picnic ground and snack bar.

Cabrerets and Grotte du Pech-Merle

Set back against the cliffs of the Célé, **Cabrerets** is the site of a dramatic, cliff-cut *château des Anglais*, begun in 745 by Waiffre, Duke of Aquitaine, although this one is better known as the **Château du Diable** – devils and Englishmen being frequently synonymous in medieval France. Downstream, on top of a high bluff is the much restored 14th-century **Château de Cabrerets**, owned until the Revolution by the Gontaut-Birons of Biron (*see* pp.361–2). Outside the centre of Cabrerets (signposted on the D41) the quirky **Petit Musée de l'Insolite**, 'little museum of the unusual' (***t** 05 65 30 21 01; open April–Sept daily 9–1 and 2–8, ring ahead out of season*), is precisely that, run by a slightly mad but charming surreal artist. Also down by the road, stop by **La Pescalerie**, an impressive resurgent spring that still powers a mill.

The main reason for visiting, however, is 4km up the road from Cabrerets, the **Grotte du Pech-Merle**, which rivals Font-de-Gaume at Les Eyzies as the finest prehistoric painted cave still open to the public since the closing of Lascaux (***t** 05 65 31 27 05; open mid-April–Oct, guided tours 9.30–12 and 1.30–5, get your time-stamped ticket when you* *arrive; adm*). While waiting for your tour, visit the **Centre de Préhistoire Amédée-Lemozi** (*same hours as Pech-Merle*) by the parking lot, with a fine collection of tools and art ranging from the Lower Palaeolithic to the Iron Age: engraved pebbles, tools, Bronze Age swords, pots and small works of art discovered in over a hundred sites, as well as photos of decorated caves and a film; there's also a snack bar, shady picnic area and a playground.

The original entrance to the cave had been blocked up at the end of the last Ice Age, and it was only rediscovered in 1922 by 16-year-old André David, son of the owner of Pech-Merle, and his friend Henri Dutertre. Inspired by the exploration of caves by Abbé Lemozi, a native of Cabrerets, they wormed and scrambled their way through a narrow 400ft passage and found exactly what they dreamed of finding – a magnificent cave, decorated with magnificent Upper Palaeolithic works of art. Some 80 drawings of animals and humans and hundreds of symbols decorate a third of Pech-Merle's mile of passageways, spanning three distinct periods, from the Solutrean to the Magdalenian periods (20,000–15,000 BC). The tour begins with the **Chapel of the Mammoths**, an arched gallery carved by an underground river with a great spiral frieze of mammoths, horses and bison outlined in black around a horse; one artist took advantage of the bulge in the rock to paint a mammoth in natural relief – a fine example of 'non-polarized' art, void of any north–south or up–down orientation. The frieze is believed to date from the Aurignacian or early Magdalenian age (15,000–14,000 BC), while the traces of red date back from the first cave users. Here too is the **Ceiling of Hieroglyphs** (what Abbé Breuil called 'macaroni'), covered with finger drawings of female and animal figures and mysterious circular signs dating from all periods.

From here the tour descends to the **Hall of Discs**, named after the rare calcite concentrations in upright concentric circles caused by water dripping slowing through hairline fissures in rock. Even more extraordinary are the **footprints** in the upper gallery, left by a woman and her 12-year-old child in the muddy clay of a natural dam at least 12,000 years ago. The next drawing is known as 'the wounded man' – a long figure hidden along the ceiling, pierced by arrows, with a bull and mysterious red signs, all from the Magdalenian age. Beyond are the famous white or red cave pearls (pisolites), part of the upper **Geological Network**, culminating in the magnificent **Red Hall**, with stalactites and columns formed by dripping limestone and oxides. Near another batch of cave pearls are curious figures, apparently an artistic synthesis of female forms and racing bisons.

The visit re-enters the prehistoric section by way of the **Bear's Gallery**, with signs of claw marks and a bear's head carved faintly in the wall. Beyond is Pech-Merle's best-known work, the two beautiful **spotted horses**, fat yet graceful beasts reminiscent of ancient Chinese figures, one with its delicate head drawn on a natural protuberance in the rock. The spots spill out of the outlines while six feminine 'negative hands' (made by blowing paint over hands) seem to be yearning to stroke or hold the horses. Over the horses is a rare picture of a fish – a large pike. Lastly, the **Combel Gallery** has the extraordinary root of a living oak drilling through its heart; bears' lairs are hollowed out in the floor and a cache of bear bones was discovered here.

Getting Around

The SNCF runs several **buses** a day between Cahors station and Figeac stopping at Vers, St-Géry, Capdenac or Cajarc, Montbrun and Toirac.

In 1990 the Lot was made navigable by **boat** again between St-Cirq-Lapopie and Luzech, thanks to the repair and installation of 14 locks. In Cajarc, the little *Schmilblic*, **t** 05 65 40 46 21, offers river tours every day in the summer. Safaraid at Bouziès, **t** 05 65 35 98 88, offers tour excursions (*daily April–Oct*) as far as St-Cirq or around Cahors, departing from the opposite Hôtel des Faliaises. They also hire out canoes, kayaks and *gabares*, for up to 12 people. Nicols Lot Navigations, at Bouziès, **t** 05 65 30 24 41, hires out houseboats sleeping up to 10 people by the week, and motorized catamarans with picnic tables for up to 12 passengers by the day.

Tourist Information

Cajarc: Tour de Ville, **t** 05 65 40 72 89, open summer only.

St-Cirq-Lapopie: Place du Sombral, **t** 05 65 31 29 06, **f** 05 65 31 29 06, *saint-cirq.lapopie@wanadoo.fr.*

Market Days

Cajarc: Sat afternoons, fairs on the 10th and 25th of each month.

St-Cirq-Lapopie: Wed mornings (July and Aug).

Where to Stay and Eat

Montbrun ✉ 46160

La Treille, t 05 65 40 77 20 (*inexpensive*). A pretty farm right on the river with four pleasant rooms, one equipped for the disabled.

Cajarc ✉ 46160

****Ségaliére**, Route de Cadrieu, **t** 05 65 40 65 35, **f** 05 65 40 74 92 (*inexpensive*). Named after the fields of rye (*siegle*) which used to cover the area. A modern hotel with well equipped rooms, some with a terrace. The restaurant opens out on to the swimming pool and serves regional dishes (*menus 70–210F*). *Closed Oct–mid-Mar.*

Down the Lot to Cahors

Sometime in the deep dark past the letters in the Celtic name *Olt* were jiggled to create the Lot, a river with more bends and curls in it than Goldilocks' ringlets; if you stretched it out from its source in the Lozère to Aiguillon, where it flows into the Garonne, it would measure 471km – all that to travel a mere 270km as the crow flies. Taking its own sweet way, the Lot wanders through three distinct landscapes. Above Vers it is closed in by blond and ochre limestone cliffs that the feudal lords of Quercy found convenient to carve out as nearly inaccessible *châteaux des Anglais* or to use as bases for their castles.

Beyond Vers the cliffs have been worn down into *cévennes*, rounded but arid rocky hills covered with scrub oak where vineyards were planted in the Middle Ages; in the rich alluvial soil of the meanders, tobacco and walnut farms are an important source of income. From Cahors west to Fumel, the typical Lot valley landscape is asymmetrical – *cévennes* on one bank, spacious valley on the other, cut by seemingly wayward loops, or *cingles*, similar to those of the Dordogne – much of it covered with oak forests, the rest with vineyards producing *vin de Cahors*. The scene changes again downriver at Fumel; the *cévennes* give way to isolated hills, locally called *pechs*. The river straightens its course in the wide valleys, and the vines give way to orchards, the source of the renowned prunes of Agen.

Tour-de-Faure ✉ 46330

★★Hotel Les Gabarres, just beyond the village near the bridge going over the Lot, **t** 05 65 30 24 57, **f** 05 65 30 25 85 (*inexpensive*). A modern, large and functional hotel in a quiet corner, not particularly pretty but with nice views of tree-covered cliffs from some of the rooms; there's a swimming pool, equipment for babies, and you can hire bikes. The hotel has no restaurant. *Open mid-April–Oct.*

St-Cirq-Lapopie ✉ 46330

★★★La Pélissaria, t 05 65 31 25 14, **f** 05 65 30 25 52 (*moderate*). Built in the 13th century, this intimate and friendly place has 10 wonderful rooms hanging on the cliff in the lower part of the village.

★★Auberge du Sombral, t 05 65 31 26 08, **f** 05 65 30 26 37 (*inexpensive*). In a medieval house in the centre, with eight charming rooms under its steep-pitched roof. *Closed mid-Nov–Mar.* The restaurant serves a delicious *gratin aux cèpes* and trout in old Cahors wine *à la carte* (*menus 75–220F*). *Closed early Nov–Mar.*

★★Le Causse, 2.5km out of St-Cirq on the D42 towards Concots, **t** 05 65 31 24 16 (*inexpensive*). Reduced room prices outside July and Aug. *Open mid-April–mid-Oct.*

Maison de la Fourdonne, t 05 65 31 21 51, **f** 05 65 31 21 48 (*cheap*). The municipality has restored this large Renaissance house in the centre of St-Cirq, with a kitchen corner (bring your own bedding); you can take a five-day woodworking course – the house includes a well-equipped workshop. Call for details of the courses.

Lou Bolat, on the side of the road as you start to climb out of the village, **t** 05 65 30 29 04. A pretty café-restaurant-crêperie, with a terrace looking out over the village, serving regional dishes such as *truite au vin de Cahors*, a range of savoury and sweet pancakes and ice cream desserts (*menus 60–170F*). There is also a bustling, shaded, terrace bar where people flock to try to escape the heat and rehydrate. *Open mid-Feb–mid-Nov, no evening meal in the winter.*

Camping de la Plage, at Porte Roque, **t** 05 65 30 29 51. By the river, with caravans, kayaks and bikes to rent. *Open all year. Book ahead.*

Capdenac to St-Cirq-Lapopie

To follow the Lot west of Capdenac, you'll have to cross over the bridge at Capdenac-Gare and take the scenic D86 along the south bank as far as the bridge to **St-Pierre-Toirac**, a pleasant village named after its 12th-century Romanesque church. In the 1300s, this doubled as the base for the town's defensive tower; the walls were thickened, and an upper rooom was added over the vaults. There are rustic carved capitals inside, and Merovingian sarcophaguses outside.

Larroque-Toirac is spread under the lofty donjon of its singular **château** (***t*** *05 65 34 78 12; open for guided tours 9 July–9 Sept daily 10–12 and 2–6; adm*). Dating from the 12th century, it passed to the Cardaillac family, whose stalwart fidelity to France in the Hundred Years' War invited numerous sieges before the English succeeded in taking the castle in 1372. It burnt down soon afterwards, but was rebuilt in the next century and restored in the 1920s. Incredibly, the high, pentagonal donjon, now cut off with a sloping roof, originally stood 100 feet higher before it was cut down to size in the Revolution; in the manor house, served by a spiral Romanesque stair, are some fine chimneypieces and furnishings. Prettily situated **Montbrun**, the next village, has the ruins of another Cardaillac castle, overlooking the grand belvedere on the south bank, known as **Saut de la Mounine** (Monkey's Leap). The cruel lord of Montbrun, furious at his daughter's choice of lovers, had ordered her to be thrown off the cliff; a kindly

La Truffière, Route de Concots, **t** 05 65 30 20 22. Campsite up on the *causse*, with many trees and a pool. *Open May–Sept. Book ahead.*

Bouziès ✉ 46330

****Les Falaises, t** 05 65 31 26 83, **f** 05 65 30 23 87 (*inexpensive*). A large country hotel overlooking the cliffs of the Lot; a heated pool and tennis court will keep you fit, and the hotel hires out mountain bikes. *Closed mid-Nov–April.* The restaurant serves good, reasonably priced Quercy cuisine (*menus 85–200F*).

Vers ✉ 46090

***La Truite Dorée, t** 05 65 31 41 51, **f** 05 65 31 47 43 (*cheap*). Good rooms in an old stone farmhouse and an amoeba-shaped pool; there is also a restaurant. *Closed mid-Dec–mid-Feb.*

Domaine du Bois Noir, on the Cahors road, **t** 05 65 31 44 50, **f** 05 65 31 47 10 (*inexpensive–cheap*). There are six pleasant *chambres d'hôte* set among the oak trees with a heated pool and meals on request (*from 75F*).

****Les Chalets, t** 05 65 31 40 83 (*inexpensive*). A modern hotel in a lovely spot by the river, some of the rooms with balconies taking full advantage of the view. There's a swimming pool and good restaurant too (*menus 55–230F*). *Closed Fri and Sat lunch out of season and Jan.*

Auberge Rustica, on the Figeac road at Cours, **t** 05 65 31 40 96. Combines modern cuisine with southwest tradition, and well-prepared ostrich dishes (*menus 60–130F*).

Lamagdelaine ✉ 46090

Claude Marco, just off the roundabout, **t** 05 65 35 30 64, **f** 05 65 30 31 40 (*expensive*). The gourmet star on this stretch of the river, in a 19th-century house, where M. Marco performs magic with local ingredients – *tartin de foie gras au jus de truffes crémées* is divine; excellent-value menus (*140–320F*). *Closed Sun night, Mon and Sat lunch out of season, and Jan, Feb and the last week of Oct.* There are four pretty designer rooms to rent, with a garden pool, and the chef's vegetable patch and flower garden at the back.

hermit dressed up a monkey in the girl's clothing and hurled it over in her place. The sight made the lord of Montbrun deplore his cruelty, and when he found out he had been duped he forgave his daughter. What she thought about him isn't recorded.

Next downriver, spread across a loop of the Lot is **Cajarc**, a pleasant riverside resort with a beach and extremely popular *plan d'eau* (man-made lake). Georges Pompidou had a holiday home in the village, and served on the town council when De Gaulle insisted that his ministers hold posts in local government to keep in contact with the people. Pompidou's strongest influence on Cajarc was an abiding passion for contemporary art, expressed in the changing exhibits in the **Maison des Arts Georges Pompidou** (***t*** *05 65 40 63 97; open Mar–May and Sept–Nov 10–12 and 2–6, closed Tues and Sun morning; June–Aug 10–12 and 3–7, closed Tues*). There are many fine medieval houses in the teardrop-shaped boulevard (especially the 13th-century Maison de Hébrardie) and, on the edge of town, the ruined 12th-century chapel of an asylum for lepers. Less than a kilometre north, there's a pretty waterfall, the **Cascade de la Cogne** (it dries up in the summer). The area north of Cajarc, between the rivers Célé and Lot, is rich in **dolmens**: there is a pair of good ones along the D82, west of Gréalou, and another two on the D17 just north of St-Chels; just south of St-Chels, there are beautiful views over both valleys from Mas-de-Laborie. Four kilometres south of Cajarc, a path off the D146 towards St-Clair leads to the deep **Gouffre de Lantouy**, with emerald-green water, and, according to the locals, a monster.

Château de Cénevières

Perched on a lofty cliff over the river, the **Château de Cénevières (t** 05 65 31 27 33; *open daily Easter–Sept 10–12 and 2–6, Oct 2–5; other times by appointment; adm*) marks a strategic point that has been fortified since the cows came home. Pepin the Short came here in 763, hunting down Waiffre, the last Merovingian duke of Aquitaine; in the 13th century, the lords of Gourdon constructed the first castle to spite the English. In the 1500s its lord was a master of the royal artillery, this one ripely named Flottard de Gourdon, who served François I with his buddy Galiot de Genouillac and married Marguerite de Cardaillac. The château was embellished and enlarged in the Renaissance style; Flottard's son Antoine converted to Protestantism, and in 1580 the future Henri IV stopped here, to plot his attack on Cahors. During the Revolution, local *sans-culottes* arrived ready to burn this symbol of feudalism and tyranny to the ground. The custodian opened the door and invited them in – to the wine cellar. They were soon drunk as skunks; afterwards they half-heartedly vandalized a bit here and there and staggered home, and Cénevières stands to this day.

Near the entrance to the château is the little Protestant temple added by Antoine Gourdon. Of the medieval castle, only the donjon remains, although it's hardly recognizable behind the ornate dormers and windows that stylistically meld it to the Renaissance sections added by Flottard and son. These are richly appointed with period furnishings and ancient tapestries; there's an ornate chimney, a complex stair, charmingly painted coffered ceilings, a vast kitchen and an unusual *Cabinet d'Alchimie* decorated with 16th-century frescoes; never fully explained, the paintings seem to express some alchemical allegory.

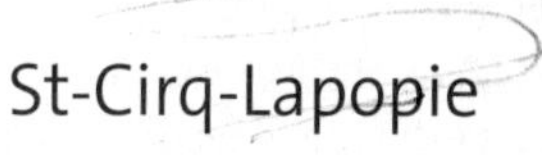

St-Cirq-Lapopie

Saint-Cirq appeared to me, embraced by Bengal fires – like an impossible rose in the night... I no longer have any desire to be anywhere else. I believe the secret of its poetry is related to certain of Rimbaud's inspirations, the product of the rarest balance in the most perfect gradation of relief. The enumeration of its other qualities can never exhaust this secret. Every morning when I get up, I have the impression of contemplating the very best of art, nature and life.

André Breton

If a hard-nosed urban surrealist like Breton melts at the sight, you can gather that the prettiest village in Quercy must be quite a looker. The setting is spectacular; St-Cirq (pronounced San-Seer) hovers 330ft above the Lot, overlooking the kind of dramatic, sheer cliffs beloved of Romantic poets. Its architecture is pure, harmoniously medieval – and rigorously preserved and protected. In season parking is nearly as difficult as at Rocamadour – there's a car park just west of St-Cirq, next to the belvedere. In the summer, get there early to avoid the disgorging coachloads; in winter you may well have it all to yourself.

St-Cirq began as a Gallo-Roman villa called Pompéjac, owned by the 7th-century bishop of Cahors, St Didier. It was the last possession of Waiffer of Aquitaine to be conquered by Pepin, and gave its name to the La Popie family who made it their bailiwick. In the 13th century, its strategic importance was such that the site was shared by the lords of Gourdon, Cardaillac and La Popie (later succeeded by the Hébrards), each of whom had their own castle, linked together at the top of the town. Such rare cooperation failed to keep the English out in the Hundred Years' War: not once but three times in the 14th century they played the same trick on the French barons, scaling the sheer cliff and surprising them. In 1471 Louis XI ordered the contiguous castles to be destroyed to punish the Hébrards for throwing in their cap with the English. Enough castle, however, remained intact to cause trouble in the Wars of Religion, until the future Henri IV ordered the site razed to keep out the Catholics. This time only a few crumbling but wonderfully panoramic **walls** survived above the church; many of the cut Gothic stones were reused in the houses of St-Cirq. These days many of St-Cirq's residents are artists and craftworkers, following in the footsteps of Man Ray and Foujita, who came to stay with André Breton.

The **church**, built by master mason Guillaume Capelle in 1522–40, is now the most prominent building in St-Cirq, its buttressed apse high on the bluff, its turreted watchtower running up the side of the stout bell tower. To the left of the portal are two medieval grain measures; inside, the church incorporates a Romanesque chapel, with a carved capital of Judith beheading Holofernes. The font is held up by a Gallo-Roman capital. Near the church you'll find St-Cirq's most medieval and picturesque lane, **Ruelle de la Fourdonne**, and the main street, the Grand-Rue, lined with 15th- and 16th-century houses; along the way look out for the lampholder with a head carved on it. The Château de la Gardette holds the **Musée Rignault** (***t*** *05 65 31 23 22; open daily exc Tues April–Oct 10–12.30 and 2–6.30, till 7 in July and Aug*) and a collection of art from Africa and Oceania, period furniture, and special art exhibitions every summer. The names of Rue de la Pélissaria and Rue de la Payrolerie recall two formerly important trades in St-Cirq: skin-dressing and copper-cauldron-making. Another was wood-turning: from 1810 to recently, the village was famous for the manufacture of boxwood taps for barrels; the **Musée de la Mémoire du Village**, in the Maison de la Fourdonne, has exhibits showing how it was done, as well as old photos (***t*** *05 65 31 21 51; open Mar–mid-Nov Mon–Fri 2–6, mid-June–mid-Sept daily 10–12 and 2–6, till 7 in July and Aug*). There is also a small **Musée du Vin** (***t*** *05 65 31 21 20; open in summer daily 9–7*).

St-Cirq-Lapopie to Cahors

One scenic way to continue downriver is to walk the towpath cut in the rock below St-Cirq that runs 5km west to **Bouziès**; it's part of the GR36, marked with red and white signs and decorated with a long relief in the living limestone, carved by sculptor Daniel Monnier. Little Bouziès is the chief pleasure-boat port on the Lot; here in the cliffs is another fortified cave or *château des Anglais*. Don't miss the lovely view from the belvedere on the D40, overlooking the confluence of the Célé and Lot, near a Renaissance château and ochre cliffs. Opposite is the little medieval hamlet of

Bouziès-Bas, while Pech-Merle is just north (*see* pp.316–17). **Vers**, where the little Vers river ripples down to meet the Lot, has impressive grooves cut in the rock left by the Roman aqueduct that follows the pretty Vers valley; the church under the cliffs, **Notre-Dame-des-Velles** ('of the sails'), was long a boatman's chapel and has a 12th-century apse decorated with *modillons*. In the afternoon you can visit the studio of artists Sally and Jeffry Stride, resident in France since 1967 (*Place Communal,* **t** *05 65 31 43 43*).

On the south bank, **Arcambal** has a castle, restored in the 19th century; the town marks the eastern limits of the region producing *vin de Cahors* (*see* below). The name of **Laroque-des-Arcs** on the north bank recalls the arches of the Roman aqueduct where it crossed the Lot. It had three storeys, like the Pont du Gard, but was demolished in 1370 by the consuls of Cahors to keep the English from seizing it. Nowadays Laroque's chief landmark is its little chapel of St-Roch on a bluff, with the wall of a *château des Anglais* below. Laroque-des-Arc's castle, **Château de Polminhac**, with its great round 13th-century donjon, began as a *borie*, or fortified country farm, built by a branch of the Gourdon family.

South of the Lot: Truffles and the Causse de Limogne

South of the Lot rises the dry, sparsely populated Causse de Limogne. More wooded and less dramatic than the Causse de Gramat, its rocky emptiness is dotted with dolmens, magnificent *pigeonniers*, abandoned walls and stone huts. Lavender is grown commercially here, and most of the Lot's truffles hide out near the roots of its twisted dwarf oaks. From November to February you can watch the locals in their berets with bulging jacket and trouser pockets (the better to fool plain-clothes tax inspectors) dickering with owners of the biggest restaurants in Paris at what is modestly claimed to be 'the world's biggest truffle market' at **Lalbenque** (*Dec–Mar Tues afternoon at 2 sharp*). Lalbenque is south of Arcambal and has a 15th-century altarpiece in its church and a fine carved 18th-century wayside cross by the fire station, but otherwise holds little of interest when the fungi aren't in season.

Five kilometres to the northwest are the pretty farms, Cahors vineyards (*see* below) and full-sailed windmill of **Cieurac**, as well as the ruined priory of **Pauliac**, a daughter of the abbey of Marcilhac, and the 15th-century **Château de Cieurac** (**t** *05 65 31 64 28; open July–mid-Sept daily exc Thurs 2–6.30; adm*), which has retained its sculpted

Where to Stay and Eat

Lalbenque ✉ 46230

*****L'Aquitaine**, west of town on the N20, **t** 05 65 21 00 51, **f** 05 65 21 08 33 (*moderate*). Modern and white with a pool, tennis and restaurant (*menus 80–160F*). *Closed Sun lunch, Sun night and Mon.*

***Lion d'Or**, in the centre, **t** 05 65 31 60 19 (*cheap*). Eight simple rooms and a little restaurant (*115–170F*). *Closed Sat, out of season.*

portal, carved stair and mullioned windows, all beautifully restored after being put to the torch by the retreating Germans in the last war. The château usually has an art exhibition, and there are pretty French gardens. The other main 'sight' in the area is the exceedingly vast public washbasin (*lavoir*) of **Aujols**. Are the locals laundry-proud, we asked, or do they indulge in too many dandelion (*pissenlits*) salads? 'No, no, that's just the way it is,' the little old lady assured us.

There's another seasonal truffle market on Fridays in **Limogne-en-Quercy**, the capital of the *causse*, but a town as dull as Lalbenque. It does have a pair of old-fashioned mills: a working windmill at Promilhanes (*see* below), and a walnut-oil mill, the **Moulin de Varaire**, operated by donkey power (***t** 05 65 31 52 34; open daily for visits by appointment*). The *bastide* **Beauregard** to the south was founded by the abbot of Marcilhac and possesses a very pretty 14th-century *halles* coiffed with a gorgeous *lauze* roof; you can still see the original grain measures cut into the stone. There are four dolmens near Beauregard and more in lavender-scented **Laramière**, including the *département*'s second largest dolmen (off the D55), the **Dolmen de la Borie du Bois**. Laramière's charming 12th-century **priory** was restored by the Jesuits after being damaged in the Wars of Religion. There are sculptures from the 1300s in the chapel, a room to put up pilgrims en route to Compostela, and a lovely chapterhouse,

The Poet of the Nipple

Cahors gave birth to several exceptional, obstinate men, with Pope John XXII and Léon Gambetta (*see* below) at the top of the list. A third was the poet Clément Marot (1495–1544), son of a Cadurcien mother and the Norman poet Jean Marot, *valet de chambre* of François I. Sent to Paris aged 11, Clément went into the service of the king's sister, Marguerite d'Angoulême, and soon made his mark at court for his elegant verse, if not for his personal charms; contemporaries described him as looking 'like a skinned rat'. Marguerite was known for protecting Protestants, and Clément Marot was often suspected of being one, especially in 1526 when he was chucked into prison for eating bacon during Lent. His eloquent plea to the king, the *Epître au roi*, got him out of the calaboose overnight, and the next year he succeeded his father as *valet de chambre*.

Although Marot remained faithful to the medieval forms of his father in his ballads and rondels, he was the first French poet to write in sonnets. When he got into trouble again in 1534, and was forced into exile in Italy, he regained favour with the invention of the *blason* (a short poem eulogizing an attribute of a lady) with his *Blason du beau tétin* ('to the beautiful nipple'). It was an immediate success: Clémont, 'the Prince of Poets', was welcomed back to court in 1536. But he was too honest to take much comfort in fashion; bored by his vast number of imitators that cropped up, he wrote the *Contre-blason du laid tétin* ('anti-blason to the ugly nipple'), setting a new fad for indelicate satires. Then he published *L'Enfer*, inspired by his stay in prison and today considered his greatest work. At the time, however, it caused such an uproar that he was forced to leave France yet again, and for the last time; he died alone in Turin in 1544.

decorated with geometric designs and effigies of St Louis and his wife, Blanche de Castille (***t*** *05 65 31 54 07; open daily 2–7, or by appointment*). To continue south of here into the Valley of the Bonnette, *see* pp.398–402.

Cahors

Towards Cahors the country changes, and has something of a savage aspect; yet houses are seen everywhere, and one-third of the area is under vines. That town is bad.

Arthur Young, *Travels in France* (1787–9)

The immediate surroundings of Cahors are some of the most discouraging landscapes in all France. In winter, the hardscrabble grey *causse* hills that glower over the town appear desertlike and eerie, and in summer they do not significantly improve. The anomic clutter of the newer parts of town matches them well, but persevere – in the middle you'll find a medieval city of surprising subtlety and character. Its star attraction is the Pont Valentré, which, as any Frenchman will tell you, is the most beautiful bridge on this planet.

History

A man from Cahors is a *Cadurcien*, just to remind us that the capital of the Lot *département* began its career as *Divona Cadurcorum*. Divona was the name of the sacred spring that still flows under the riverside cliffs, or perhaps of the Celtic goddess who presided over it. Cadurcorum refers to the Cadurcii, the fierce local tribe who probably had their capital here before the arrival of the Romans. Under Roman rule, Divona Cadurcorum was famous for exporting linen; the town boasted an aqueduct, well-appointed public baths, and a theatre with room for 1,000. It isn't known whether any of these were still working when the town became embroiled in a civil war among the Franks in the 570s and got thoroughly trashed. Fortunately, not long after, a strong-willed bishop named Desiderius took matters in hand; even more fortunately, this Gallo-Roman gentleman, later to be declared St Didier, was also royal treasurer to King Dagobert, and he found enough loose change to resurrect Cahors at a time when very little was being built anywhere else in Gaul. By the time he died, *c.* 650, Cahors's first cathedral was well under way, and its Roman bridges and aqueduct were restored.

Further insults were in store – unwelcome visits by Vikings, Magyars and Arabs – but Cahors survived to find a brilliant and surprising career in the Middle Ages. The bishops still ruled, and did quite well for themselves, gradually gaining control of most of the Lot valley and becoming a factor that even the French and the counts of Toulouse had to take into consideration. Under their stable rule, the town began to learn to make money. The founders of Cahors's great foray into modern capitalism seem to have been Italians, 'Lombard' merchants who fled north to the relative safety of the bishops' domains from the terrors of the Albigensian Crusade in the early

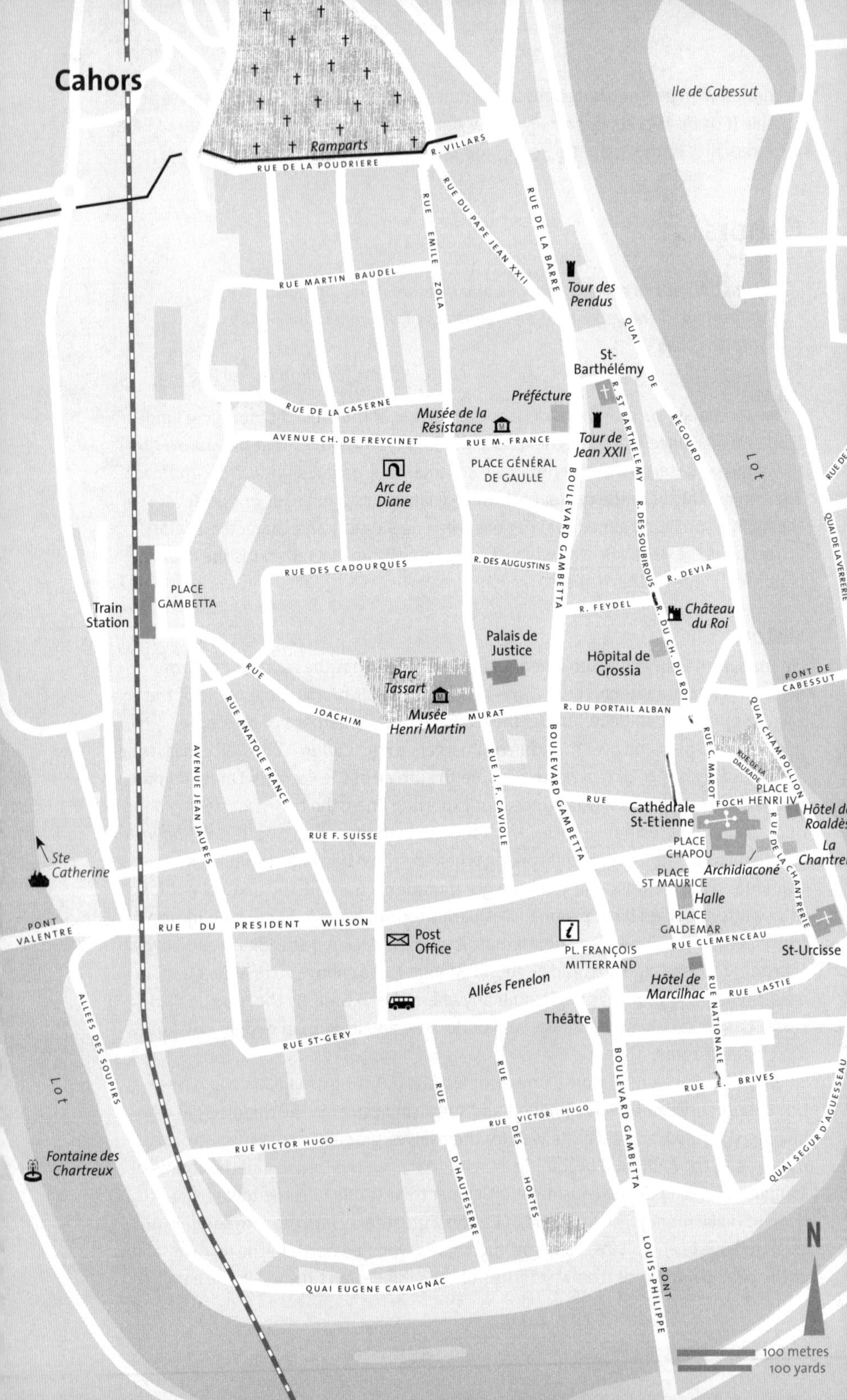

Cahors
Ile de Cabessut
Ramparts
RUE DE LA POUDRIERE
R. VILLARS
RUE EMILE ZOLA
RUE DU PAPE JEAN XXII
RUE DE LA BARRE
Tour des Pendus
RUE MARTIN BAUDEL
QUAI DE REGOURD
St-Barthélémy
Préfécture
Musée de la Résistance
Tour de Jean XXII
RUE DE LA CASERNE
AVENUE CH. DE FREYCINET
RUE M. FRANCE
R. ST BARTHELEMY
PLACE GÉNÉRAL DE GAULLE
Arc de Diane
Lot
BOULEVARD GAMBETTA
R. DES SOUBIROUS
QUAI DE LA VERRERIE
RUE DES CADOURQUES
R. DES AUGUSTINS
R. DEVIA
PLACE GAMBETTA
Train Station
R. FEYDEL
Château du Roi
R. DU CH. DU ROI
Palais de Justice
Hôpital de Grossia
PONT DE CABESSUT
Parc Tassart
Musée Henri Martin
RUE JOACHIM MURAT
R. DU PORTAIL ALBAN
RUE ANATOLE FRANCE
AVENUE JEAN JAURES
RUE J. F. CAVIOLE
RUE C. MAROT
RUE DE LA DAURADE
QUAI CHAMPOLLION
PLACE HENRI IV
RUE FOCH
Cathédrale St-Etienne
Hôtel de Roaldès
RUE F. SUISSE
PLACE CHAPOU
La Chantrerie
RUE DE LA CHANTRERIE
Ste Catherine
PLACE ST MAURICE
Archidiaconé
Halle
PONT VALENTRE
RUE DU PRESIDENT WILSON
PLACE GALDEMAR
Post Office
PL. FRANÇOIS MITTERRAND
RUE CLEMENCEAU
St-Urcisse
Allées Fenelon
Hôtel de Marcilhac
RUE LASTIE
ALLEES DES SOUPIRS
Théatre
RUE ST-GERY
RUE NATIONALE
RUE E. BRIVES
QUAI SEGUR D'AGUESSEAU
RUE VICTOR HUGO
RUE D'HAUTESERRE
RUE DES HORTES
Fontaine des Chartreux
QUAI EUGENE CAVAIGNAC
PONT LOUIS-PHILIPPE
N
100 metres
100 yards

1200s; among the old palaces of Cahors you will find family names like Dominici, Issalda and Grossia.

Throughout the 13th century these families and their native colleagues perfected their skill at merchant finance and moneylending. They became familiar figures in all the trade fairs and business centres of Europe, so prominent – and predatory – that *Caorsin* became a common word for a usurer. Dante mentions them in the *Inferno* (Canto XI, 50); he put the Caorsins down with the people of Sodom in the third circle of hell. No doubt they laughed all the way to the bank. The king of France needed them, whenever he was in the mood for a campaign; the noblemen and the Church needed them too, and they got on just fine with the town's bishops. In 1270, the bishop granted the merchants a city charter, establishing rule by elected consuls.

As their wealth piled up, the merchants translated it into impressive palaces along the main streets. Cahors's golden age, which lasted until the Hundred Years' War, produced not only these, but a new set of fortifications, magnificent bridges, a university and the completion of the cathedral. Even more money flowed in after 1316, when a Cahors merchant's son named Jacques Duèze became Pope John XXII. John reigned from Avignon, where he acquired a somewhat sinister reputation as an alchemist. One story has him bewitching the cardinals with a magic knife to secure his election. Another account has him quarrelling with a competitor in sorcery, another bishop of Cahors no less, and eventually having the man burned at the stake for trying to do him in with wax voodoo dolls and potions made of spiders and toads.

Cahors suffered from the Hundred Years' War only indirectly. Its new walls were good enough to keep the English out, but the disruption of trade meant a slow but inexorable strangling of its business affairs. The refined little city carried on, making a modest living off its rents and the wine trade and devoting its energies to higher things. During the Renaissance Cahors had a reputation as a cultured place, full of academies and libraries; its university lasted until 1751, when the jealous scholars of Toulouse succeeded in having it merged into their own.

During the religious wars, Cahors with its still-influential bishops remained stoutly Catholic. In 1560, there was a bloody massacre of Protestants; 20 years later, Henri IV stormed the city, and in retaliation the future king allowed his troops to give the place a thorough sacking. Not much has happened since; but there are signs that Cahors, after 600 years of decline and somnolence, is starting to look ahead to a more economically active future. Industry in the town is growing at a rate almost double the regional average, with some of the more successful businesses in electronics, printing, food and, of course, wine. Hardly an industrial boom town but moving in the right direction.

Orientation: Walking Cahors

Cahors's charms are discreet, and most tourists have little time for them. But a bit of knowledge and a careful eye can make this well-preserved and genteel medieval town come alive. First, pay no attention to the broad and leafy Boulevard Gambetta, pretending to be the centre of town. This is merely the course of the city's old walls; everything of interest is squeezed between it and the river. Instead, for a panorama of

Getting Around

Cahors is on Eurolines' **coach** route from London to Toulouse, an uncomfortable 20hr journey that beats the train in that you don't have to go through Paris and change stations; in Cahors buy tickets at Belmon, 2 Bd Gambetta, **t** 05 65 35 59 30. The **railway** station is near the centre, with frequent connections north towards Gourdon, Souillac and Paris, and south towards Montauban and Toulouse; this is the base of SNCF **buses** towards Fumel and Figeac. Although the Cahors–Capdennac tracks along the Lot are no longer used for regular service, **Quercyrail**, 'under the patronage of his Royal Highness the Prince of Denmark', juices up the 1950s omnibus Micheline and has excursions (*to Cajarc May–Oct Sun, July and Aug also Sat, at 9am; return at 6pm; to Château de Cénevières July and Aug Mon and Thurs afternoons; to St-Cirq-Lapopie Wed afternoons*). Check at the desk in the train station for details or the tourist office in Cahors. A little **train** can trundle you around old Cahor, departing from near Pont Valentré, **t** 05 65 30 16 55.

Safaraid runs frequent 1.5hr **riverboat** excursions from the Pont Valentré (*April–Oct*), and a 3hr trip to Vers (*July and Aug*), **t** 05 65 35 98 88. Babou Marine, **t** 05 65 30 08 99, hires out **houseboats** for up to nine people, as well as small motorboats by the day or half-day.

Tourist Information

Place François Mitterrand, **t** 05 65 53 20 65, **f** 05 65 53 20 74.

Market Days

Place de la Cathédrale, Wed and Sat mornings, though the covered market is open daily except Sun. Every first and third Sat there is a big *foire* spread all along Bd Gambetta and the Allées Fénelon; in the same place on Sat mornings from Nov to Mar there's a fattened duck and goose and truffle market.

Activities

See above for boat excursions along the river. The Île de Cabessut has been made into a big water park called **Archipel**, **t** 05 65 35 31 38, with a huge pool, whirlpool, children's area, beach, etc. (*open daily in summer 11–8; adm*).

Cahors's medieval skyline most people never see, start from across the river, over the Pont de Cabessut.

Long and narrow Cahors had a single main thoroughfare (Rue du Château du Roi north of the cathedral, Rue Nationale south of it). Along this are most of the merchants' palaces; to each side, the ranks of tiny alleys crowded with tall houses give an idea of how dense and urban the medieval town must have seemed. Many of these alleys are partially covered; if so they are not called *ruelles*, but *botes*, a word meaning 'vaults' that is peculiar to Cahors. The medieval palaces, built in grey stone, are spare and squarish, with big arches facing the street for the business façades and elegant twinned windows on the family quarters upstairs; less imposing buildings were made *en colombage*, in half-timbering, and scores of these survive. In the 1400s, Cahors developed a distinct style of decoration, surrounding doors and windows with carved rosettes and *bâtons écotés* (raised mouldings). Another feature is the *soleiho*, a Venetian-style sun porch on the top storey (as in Figeac); in Renaissance palaces they are often made of brick arches and called *mirandes*.

St-Etienne Cathedral and Around

A tour of Cahors should begin in Place Chapou, the elongated square in front of the cathedral, filled with vegetable stands on many weekday mornings. Note the bank

Where to Stay

Cahors ✉ 46000

Cahors's *luxury* hotel is 6km northwest of the city in Mercuès (*see* p.331).

Moderate

★★★**Le Terminus**, 5 Charles de Freycinet, opposite the station, **t** 05 65 53 32 00, **f** 05 65 53 32 26. Charming, resolutely retro and ivy-covered, this hotel has been in business for at least a century; it also has a garage, disabled access, TV in each cosy room, and Cahors's best restaurant (*see* below).

★★★**La Chartreuse**, St-Georges, **t** 05 65 35 17 37, **f** 05 65 22 30 03. Overlooking the Lot by the spring of the same name, not far from the Pont Valentré. The same facilities as the Terminus, less expensively. The rooms are modern, some air-conditioned; there's a pool, and a restaurant with a good set-price lunch.

Inexpensive

★★**Le Clos Grand**, 3km from the centre off the D8 at Labéraudie, in the suburb of Pradines (✉ 46090), **t** 05 65 35 04 39, **f** 05 65 22 56 69. The pick of the two-stars, a Logis de France country inn with cosy rooms, a large garden and pool; the restaurant serves hearty meals (*around 175F*). *Closed Sun night and Mon.*

★★**L'Escargot**, 5 Bd Gambetta, **t** 05 65 35 07 66, **f** 05 65 53 92 38. Simple but comfortable rooms in the big stone walls of the old palais Duèze, including two family rooms. The restaurant is popular with locals and serves, of course, snails as well as regional favourites (*menus 62–168F*). Friendly staff. *Restaurant closed Sun eve and Mon, hotel closed in Dec.*

★★**Le Melchior**, Place de la Gare, **t** 05 65 35 03 38, **f** 05 65 23 92 75. A functional place opposite the station.

Cheap

★**De La Paix**, 30 Place St-Maurice, **t** 05 65 35 03 40, **f** 05 65 35 40 88. Above a restaurant bar overlooking the market; tidy and budget-friendly.

Camping Rivière de Cabessut, near the Archipel water park, **t** 05 65 30 06 30. Camp in three-star luxury.

that has restored an old painted shop sign over its modern façade: *Bazar Genois – Gambetta Jeune et Cie*. This Italian immigrant grocer earned his immortality for being the father of Léon Gambetta, Cahors's great native son. As a lawyer and politician, Gambetta was a strong opponent of the tyranny of Napoleon III. After France's defeat in 1870, he declared the Third Republic in Paris, and then dramatically escaped from the city in a balloon while the Prussians were besieging it. After that, he raised new armies in the south (though the Prussians whipped them too), and eventually became premier; all France mourned in 1882 when he accidentally killed himself while cleaning a gun. The covered market is just down the square.

The **cathedral of St-Etienne** provides a sober backdrop. Begun in the 10th century on the site of St Didier's original cathedral, this is the second of the domed churches of Périgord and Quercy, directly inspired by St-Etienne in Périgueux. Not completed until the 1400s, its western and eastern ends were completely rebuilt, resulting in a not unlovely architectural mongrel, a kind of Romanesque-on-Gothic sandwich. The severe façade, the typical broad tower-façade of a Quercy church writ large, was redone in the 14th century, and the original entrance was moved around to the side. Now the **north portal**, this is one of the finest in southern France. In the centre, Christ in a mandorla is flanked by angels tumbling down out of the heavens and scenes of the martyrdom of St Stephen; below are the Virgin Mary and 10 apostles (there

Eating Out

Luxury

Le Balandre in the Terminus hotel, **t** 05 65 53 32 00. Long gripping the gourmet standard of Cahors, this restaurant has an elegant dining room with the woodwork and glass installed in 1910. They serve delectable Quercy dishes with a twist, accompanied by a great wine cellar; the restaurant's famous starter is poached eggs with an escalope of foie gras and truffles (*menus 195–450F, à la carte easily much more*). *Closed Sun and Mon except July and Aug.*

Moderate

La Garenne, 5km north on the N20 in St-Henri, **t** 05 65 35 40 67. In a 19th-century farm you can feast on imaginative, well-prepared land and sea dishes such as the delicate sole in puff pastry or duck with cèpes (*menus 95–250F*). *Closed Tues night and Wed exc in July and Aug, Feb and first half of Mar.*

Le Rendez-Vous, 49 Rue Clément Marot, **t** 05 65 22 65 10. A popular place in the heart of old Cahors; for a splurge try the ravioli filled with foie gras in truffle juice (*menu 125F*). *Closed Sun and Mon.*

Cheap

Au Fil des Douceurs anchored off Quai Verrerie, **t** 05 65 22 13 04. For a romantic evening on the Lot (literally), try the well-prepared regional and fish dishes aboard this floating eaterie (*menus from 75F*). *Closed Sun eve and Mon.*

Marie Colline, 173 Rue Georges Clémenceau, **t** 05 65 35 59 96. A real and rare treat for vegetarians: a proper vegetarian restaurant, offering a choice of two different *plats du jour* each day plus a choice of starters and delicious desserts. You may get *cannelloni aux carottes* or *gratin au chèvre* followed by *clafoutis aux fruits rouges* or *chocolat aux noix moelleux au chocolat* (*around 85F*). It has the air of a refined seaside café; in the summer you can sit outside on the pavement. *Closed Aug, only open Mon–Fri lunch.*

Auberge du Mont St-Cyr on top of the highest hill over Cahors, **t** 05 65 35 10 74. In the summer, you can have yourself a thoroughly French evening dining on old favourites, with pretty views and *guinguette* (accordion music and dancing) on Sat nights and Sun after 3 (*menus from 85F*).

Crêperie au Coeur du Lot, 71 Rue du Château du Roi, **t** 05 65 22 30 67. Crêpes, omelettes and salads with national labels; the English

wasn't room for 12). Of greater interest are the borders and *modillons*, with a full complement of monsters, scenes of war and violence, and unusual decorative motifs of roses that seem to prefigure the trimmings on Cahors's Renaissance palaces.

Once inside (through the main portal), turn around to see the finely drawn frescoes (*c.* 1320) high above the west door, a series of scenes from Genesis including the *Creation* and *Adam and Eve*. The other surviving original paintings are in an equally inconvenient spot, under the first of the two domes in the nave. These include figures of eight prophets, and in the centre the '*14 lapidateurs*' with their stones, ready to lapidate poor Stephen and ensure his status as the first Christian martyr. The large organ over the entrance has recently been restored and when in full throttle (the cathedral is a favourite concert hall) swells the domes with its magnificent sound.

In 1330, the original east end was replaced with a Gothic apse, an odd structure built on the plan of a pentagon that from the outside looks like a separate building. Inside, it contains some of the best of Cahors's sculptural work in its side chapels, done 1484–91. More of the same can be seen in the **cloister** (1509), lavishly spread with flowing flamboyant decoration. Tragically, Henri IV's lads did a thorough job of smashing up the capitals in 1580, but enough remains, or has been restored, to allow

salad is egg, corn and cucumber, the French Roquefort, apples and nuts. There is a wonderful array of ice cream desserts. You can eat out in a small courtyard in this atmospheric part of the old city. Popular with families (*à la carte, from 20–30F*). *Closed Sun and Mon.*

Le Bistrot du Cahors, 46 Rue Daurade, **t** 05 65 53 10 55. To toast the city head here: it's essentially an eatery (*menus under 100F*) but with an extensive list of local wines into which you can delve by the bottle or glass – an excellent way to sample the options. *Closed Mon eve and Tues and Oct–Mar.*

Le Montat ✉ 46090

Les Templiers, off the N20, 5km south of Cahors, **t** 05 65 21 01 23. In a 12th-century Templar priory, serving delicious regional specialities with an *haute cuisine* touch, such as *pigeonneau en cocotte, ail en chemise, échalote confites cèpes et feuille de sauge* (*menus 100–255F*). *Closed Sun eve, Tues except in Aug, half of July, and late Jan–late Feb.*

St-Pierre-Lafeuille ✉ 46090

La Bergerie, north on the N20, **t** 05 65 36 82 82. Delightful modernized versions of *cuisine quercynoise* that attracts hungry Cadurciens (*menus 95–250F*). *Closed Sun eve, Mon (except July and Aug) and mid-Jan–mid-Feb.*

Mercuès ✉ 46090

******Château de Mercuès, t** 05 65 20 00 01, **f** 05 65 20 05 72 (*expensive*). Sitting on a spur high above the valley, this Relais et Châteaux hotel has been sumptuously renovated into the last word in luxury. Rooms (two are in the towers) are fitted with large marble baths, canopy beds and other creature comforts; hanging gardens with a pool, and tennis courts are included in the lofty price. *Closed Nov–Easter.* The restaurant is equally classy, and the vast cellars feature owner Georges Vigouroux's famous wines; his Château de Mercuès 1990 won a gold medal in Paris (*menus 285–505F*). *Closed Mon, lunch Tues–Thurs and Nov–Easter.*

Le Mas Azemar, Rue du Mas-de-Vinssou, **t** 05 65 30 96 85 (*moderate–inexpensive*). At the foot of the mighty castle, an 18th-century farmhouse converted into a beautifully restored and very refined bed and breakfast (*meals 150F with wine*). *Book.*

you to appreciate one of the finest sculptural ensembles of the southwest. Note in one corner the winsome carved *Vierge des Litanies*. The carvings around the arches in the cloister's grassy centre have an M.C. Escher quality, metamorphosing from a leaf of curly kale into an ocean wave into a dog licking its hind legs. If you're lucky, the flamboyant entrance to the **Chapelle St-Gausbert** will be open, containing what remains of the cathedral treasure and 15th-century frescoes of a not very dire *Last Judgement*.

The back door of the cloister leads you to the handsome Renaissance ensemble of the **Archidiaconé**. Through here, in Rue de la Chantrerie, the growers of Cahors wine have beautifully restored the 13th-century **La Chantrerie**, the building containing the cathedral chapter's wine press, and made it into a wine museum (***t** 05 65 23 99 70; open July and Aug 10–12 and 3–7, closed Tues*). By the river here, along Quai Champollion in Place Henri IV, the handsome 15th-century **Hôtel de Roaldès** (a.k.a. Maison de Henri IV) has big stone fireplaces and a magnificent *soleilho*. King Henri stayed here during his pillaging of the Catholics; it has been furnished to match the period (***t** 05 65 35 04 35; tours mid-April–mid-Sept 10–12 and 2–6, closed Sun morning; other times ring for details*).

Vin de Cahors

Wine historians rate the deep crimson, full-bodied 'black' wine of Cahors as one of the last 'real' French wines, not drastically changed since the day Julius Caesar sent amphorae back to Rome after his victory over the Gauls at Uxellodunum. It went down so well in Rome that by the next century Italian vintners were whining about the competition, which in those pre-EU days resulted in an order from Emperor Domitian to uproot Cahors's vineyards, in AD 96. The vines were restored in 276 by a prince named Probus; they prospered, and in 1152 they became part of Eleanor of Aquitaine's dowry when she wed Henry Plantagenet. When John XXII of Cahors become pope at Avignon he further boosted the reputation of the wine by declaring it the papal communion wine. François I planted Cahors vines at Fontainebleau, and Peter the Great, finding *vin de Cahors* soothed his ulcer, planted vines in Azerbaijan along the Black Sea, which to this day produces its very own *Caorskoïe Vino*.

Knocked out in the 1870s by a phylloxera epidemic, Cahors wasn't replanted as quickly as other French wines. In 1947 a slow revival began with the founding of the excellent **Côtes d'Olt Cooperative** in Parnac (***t** 05 65 30 71 86; open Mon–Sat 9–12 and 1.30–6.30*) although it wasn't until after the vines froze in 1956 and '57 that the wine growers seriously began to replant the Cahors of yesteryear, at least 70 per cent Cot Noir, or Auxerrois, mixed with Merlot for bouquet and roundness, and Tannat, the great enhancer of Auxerrois. Their efforts were rewarded in 1971 with AOC status – partially thanks to the good offices of the then president Georges Pompidou, who had a summer residence in Cajarc. The immediate result brought the wine a fleeting popularity, soon tarnished by greed and local feuds that produced many a dire bottle of plonk. In the 1990s, however, the wine has enjoyed a great comeback (1999 and 2000 vintage promise to be superb as well), thanks in part to Cartier head and Cahors winegrower Alain Dominique Perrin (owner of the **Château La Grézette** in Caillac, **t** 05 65 20 07 42), who formed an association of châteaux-vineyards known as *Les Seigneurs du Cahors*. On the other end of Caillac, follow the signs to the friendly, family-run, award-winning **Domaine de Chatelle** (***t** 05 65 20 04 66; always open to visitors*), they do an excellent *vin traditionel* that never touches a splinter of oak.

If you want to do some serious wine exploring, pick up the free map to the vineyards and the leaflet *Le Livret du Vins de Cahors*, available at the local tourist offices: nearly all (there are some 200 altogether now) welcome visitors who just drop in, but outside of summer it never hurts to ring ahead to make sure someone's running the shop. The less hoity-toity ones sell the most recent *millésimes* by petrol pump (*en vrac*) if you bring your own container; a good way to try over 100 different *crus* is to visit Puy-l'Evêque in early August during the *Fête du Vin de Cahors*, where the only

Quartier des Soubirous

North of the cathedral extends what was the wealthy merchants' quarter in medieval times; *soubirous* means superior, for the way the area climbs uphill towards the citadel. It has been neglected for centuries, and only recently have the Cadurciens begun to restore some of its old mansions; a few of the old bankers' counting houses

expense is the special Cahors glass. In general, drink young, tannic Cahors with foie gras, duck, goose, meats in sauce, Roquefort cheese and charcuterie; a well-aged Cahors goes well with game dishes, red meats with wild mushrooms, and *cabécou* goat cheese. The year to look for is 1994. A leading member of *Les Seigneurs* is the **Château de Haute-Serre**, south of Cahors in Cieurac, **t** 05 65 20 80 20, where Georges Vigouroux has laboriously revived a famous medieval vineyard – planted not in the Lot valley as other post-phylloxera vines, but on the traditional limestone *causses*, where the wines take much longer to mature. His gamble paid off: Haute-Serre today is one of the top wines of the *appellation*, and he's even built his own huge shop at the south end of Cahors at Roc de Lagasse, **L'Atrium**, **t** 05 65 20 80 90, as well as adding the Château de Mercuès and its highly rated vineyard to his empire.

The oldest of the Cahors dynasties is now headed by the late Jean Jouffreau's daughter at Prayssac's **Clos de Gamot**, **t** 05 65 22 40 26, first recorded here in 1290 – a history traced in the frescoes in the cellars. The Jouffreaus have in their cellars the oldest known *vin de Cahors*, with bottles from the start of the 20th century; they also conserved Cahors stock predating the phylloxera scourge, which produced the exquisite '92 Vignes Centenaires. They have recently planted a new vineyard in the hills over La Bastide du Vert; the first results of this venture should now be ready for drinking. Besides the Clos de Gamot, the family also owns the elegant, early 17th-century **Château de Cayrou**, **t** 05 65 20 40 26, by the river in Puy-l'Evêque, where a botanist planted redwoods and other exotic trees 200 years ago. The Jouffreaus's wines are all organic and, unusually, 100 per cent Auxerrois: the Château de Cayrou '89 is ready to drink. Another Cahors thoroughbred is south of the river, the immaculately maintained vineyards of the 17th-century **Château de Chambert** at Floressas, **t** 05 65 31 95 75; in the same pretty area, Domaine de Paillas, **t** 05 65 36 58 28, also produces highly rated Cahors, as does nearby **Château de Cèdre** in Vire-sur-Lot, **t** 05 65 36 53 87.

In Puy-l'Evêque, **Château La Reyne**, **t** 05 65 30 82 53, must produce the jumpiest *vin de Cahors* – it is the official wine of BAC Mirande, one of France's top women's basketball teams. Another favourite of everyone in the area is Maradenne from **Château Nozières**, **t** 05 65 36 52 73, in Vire-sur-Lot, a few kilometres south of Puy-l'Evêque, signposted off the road to Maroux. Try the Cahors or refreshing *rosé* from the **Camp de Saltre Delbru et Fils** just north of Prayssac on the road towards Pomarède, **t** 05 65 22 42 40. At the **Domaine du Garinet**, **t** 05 65 31 96 43, south of Grézels at Le Boulvé, English owners Michael and Suzanne Spring will give you a warm welcome and offer tastings of their red and rosé; they also own a walnut orchard and sell the nuts as they are, shelled, or in bread or brownies.

now hold swish shops and antique dealers. **Rue du Château-du-Roi**, the spine of the neighbourhood, is an elegant street reminiscent of Siena or Perugia. Its most impressive façade is at No.102, the 13th-century **Hôpital de Grossia**. Take the alley to the right of it, the Bote de Fouilhac, which will bring you to a typically hidden Cahors surprise, a tiny, lovely courtyard decorated with modern murals and a musical fountain that works about half the time. Across from the Hôpital, the **Château du Roi** was one of Cahors' grandest palaces in the 1300s, though it was thoroughly wrecked in the 19th century when the state converted it into a prison and replaced the façade; the tall donjon inside, visible only from the riverfront, is all that survives.

Here the street changes its name to Rue des Soubirous, and continues its way to the northern edge of the city, with the austere church of **St-Barthélémy** and the adjacent **Palais Duèze**. Much degraded by the centuries, this was built by John XXII for his family; he also rebuilt the church, where he had been baptized. The best surviving parts can be seen from Boulevard Gambetta, including the solid and graceful **Tour de Jean XXII**, and, further north, the Barbacane with its massive **Tour des Pendus**, 'Tower of the Hanged Men'. At the top of the boulevard, by the large parking lot of Place Général de Gaulle, the **Musée de la Résistance** (***t*** *05 65 22 14 25; open daily 2–6*) has six rooms covering the role of the Resistance in the Lot from the beginning to the end of the war; most of the staff were themselves members.

The Badernes

This was the popular quarter of the city, south of the cathedral, though it too had its share of palaces, mostly along **Rue Nationale**, the southern continuation of Rue du Château-du-Roi. For one example, at the beginning of the street, there is the lovely Baroque carved door at the **Hôtel de Marcilhac** (No.116). The streets to the left off Rue Nationale are worth a digression, with a large number of well-restored half-timbered houses, and a few medieval palaces along Rue Lastié. The neighbourhood's church, **St-Urcisse**, stands at the end of Rue Clémenceau near the river. The 13th-century statue of the Virgin on the façade is one of the oldest sculptural works in Cahors; if the church is open, don't miss the set of carved capitals with fond naïve scenes of Adam and Eve and the life of Christ.

Pont Valentré

If anything is a sign of opulence in a medieval city, it's the bridges. Cahors had three, where one would have sufficed, and the two that have disappeared were almost as good as this one. The city demolished them in 1868 and 1907. Cahors in its decadence cared very little for its ancient monuments; the Roman theatre of *Divona Cadurcorum* survived to the 19th century, when the city fathers had it destroyed to make way for the railway.

The **Pont Valentré** (at the end of Rue du Président Wilson) survived because it was out of the way and carried little traffic. But it was built well enough for cars to continue to cross over it until 1996, when a new bridge, out of sight upriver, was built to replace it. Now you can happily cross without being squashed like a bug. Begun in 1308, and financed with the help of Pope John, the bridge nevertheless took nearly a century to complete. With the Hundred Years' War in full swing, it isn't surprising that defence became the major consideration. The three towers that look so picturesque are three rings of defences to keep the English out; each had its portcullis, and slits for archers and boiling oil.

Wherever in southern France you find a medieval bridge, you can be sure the Devil had something to do with it. Here, according to the legend, this master engineer made a deal for the soul of the Pont Valentré's builder in return for his aid. The builder tricked him, of course, by giving him a sieve with which to fetch water, but the Devil got his revenge by coming back each night to steal one of the corner stones of the central tower, which had to be replaced every following day. In the 19th century, restorers added the stone with the Devil carved on it to remind us of the tale (on the east side of the tower, near the top).

From the bridge, on the upstream side you may see the ***Ste-Catherine***, permanently moored here. This is a reconstruction ('5,200 hours of work!') of a medieval mill-boat, the only one in France. Nearby, 200 yards down on the riverbank, the medieval **Fontaine des Chartreux** is fed by the underground streams of the *causse*; recent explorations by archaeological divers, who discovered hundreds of ancient coins in the depths, seem to confirm the popular belief that this was Divona, the spring of ancient times around which Cahors grew up.

There isn't much else to see in the newer quarters of town. On Rue Caviole, just north of Rue du Président Wilson, the 17th-century Bishop's Palace now contains the **Musée Henri Martin** (***t*** *05 65 30 15 13; open Mar–mid-Oct daily 10–1 and 2–6, closed Tues; adm*), with a permanent collection of canvases of the Lot by *pointilliste* painter Henri Martin, a native of Toulouse who lived and painted in Labastide-du-Vert, a village to the west of town; it also holds temporary exhibitions. There's a pretty little park behind it, with a playground and a pair of swans. Nearby, on Boulevard Gambetta you'll find an appropriately flamboyant monument to Cahors' Republican hero, pointing dramatically, perhaps accusingly, north towards Paris. The only other reminder of the Roman town is the '**Arc de Diane**' in a schoolground, visible from Avenue Freycinet; this fragment of stone and brick was a part of the municipal baths.

Castles around Cahors

North of Cahors, visible off the N20 in St-Pierre-Lafeuille, the imposing **Château de Roussillon** is surrounded by a dry moat. It was begun in the 12th century and rebuilt in subsequent centuries as one of the city's chief defences. Cannibalized for its stone in the 19th century, it still makes an impressive sight and has been partly restored by its current owner (***t*** *05 65 36 87 05; open by appointment for a minimum of 10 people*). Even more striking is the **Château de Mercuès**, prominent, or rather unavoidable, on its hilltop over the D911 5km northwest of Cahors (note the 'medieval' railway tunnel beneath it). Begun in its present form in the 15th century as a stronghold and pleasure dome of the bishops of Cahors, this castle suffered sackings by the English and the Protestants. In 1563, the latter smoked the bishop out. He was caught climbing out of a window and made to ride backwards on a donkey dressed in mock papal regalia before being rescued; his embarrassment was so acute that he died shortly after. The castle burned in the 17th century; when a plague hit Cahors, the bishop offered hundreds of refugees shelter at Mercuès – in exchange for rebuilding his spread. The bishops gave Mercuès up in 1909, and since then it's settled down to its present career as the poshest hotel in the whole *département* (*see* above). It owes much of its present storybook appearance to 19th-century restorations; any bishop would be proud of the vast wine cellars.

South of the River Lot: Quercy Blanc

Quercy shows a markedly different, drier face south of the river, less hilly and forested, with fewer villages and farms. Conspicuous in the open countryside are the slopes where the poor soil has been washed away to expose the pale limestone underneath; this is also used to build the characteristic houses and simple Romanesque chapels, giving 'White Quercy' its name. Beyond the Provence-like sunbaked grandeur of its white hills, its fields of sunflowers and vineyards of Chasselas table grapes, attractions are few; if the sun isn't shining, it can be haunting, impatiently waiting its own Thomas Hardy to do it justice.

Montpezat-de-Quercy

Montpezat-de-Quercy, a half-hour due south of Cahors and west of the N20, may be the most rewarding destination in this area. This thoroughly medieval village retains its gate and arcaded square, as well as plenty of half-timbered houses, many of which are finally getting a long-overdue restoration.

Montpezat grew up in the 10th century. In 1257, its lord Alphonse of Poitiers granted it a charter as a free town, with rights to its own mill, a pigeon-house and an oil press. In the 1300s, the town was home to a dynasty of churchmen named Des Près. Well-

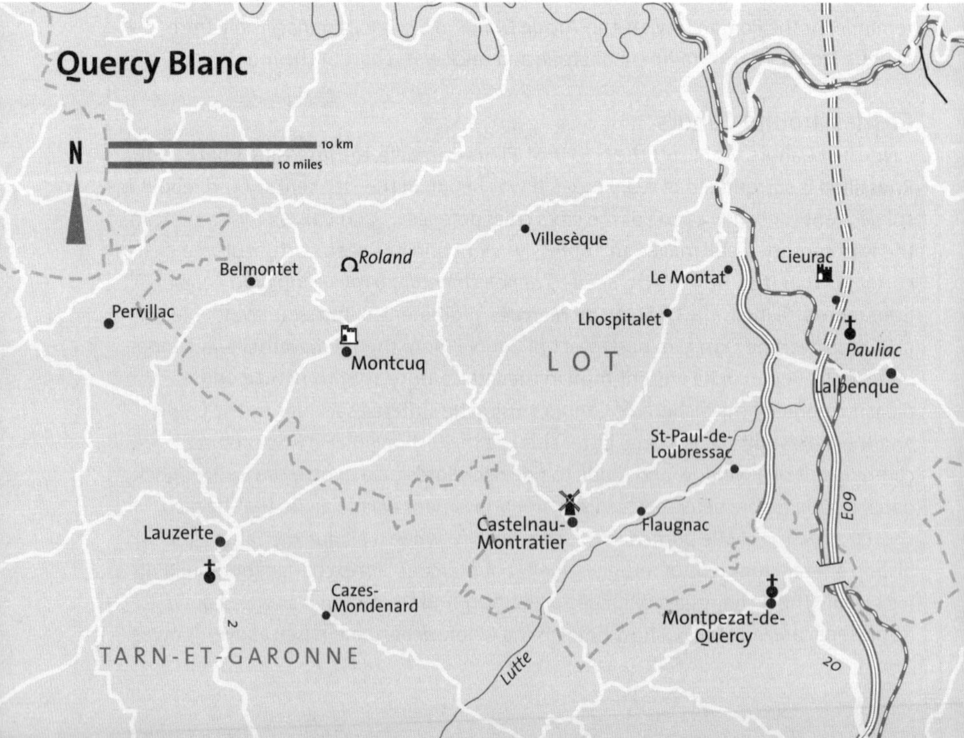

Getting Around

Raynal **buses** from Cahors run to Castelnau-Monratier; for times **t** 05 65 22 29 32.

Tourist Information

Montpezat-de-Quercy: Bd des Fossés, **t** 05 63 02 05 55.
Castelnau-Monratier: Place Gambetta, **t/f** 05 65 21 84 72.
Montcuq: La Promenade, **t/f** 05 65 22 94 04.

Market Days

Castelnau-Monratier: Sun, and fairs the second Tues of each month.
Montcuq: Sun, and Thurs in July and Aug, fairs the second Wed of each month.

Where to Stay and Eat

Castelnau-Monratier ✉ 46170

★★**Les Trois Moulins**, **t** 05 65 21 92 95, **f** 05 65 21 83 22 (*inexpensive*). Modern, with tidy rooms, pool and wide view. *Open all year.*

Les Arcades, Place Gambetta, **t** 05 65 21 90 22 (*inexpensive–cheap*). The restaurant offers a wide variety of tasty menus (*60F–180F with foie gras*). *Closed weekends and schools hols exc July and Aug.*

Montcuq ✉ 46800

★★**Du Parc**, Route du Fumel, **t** 05 65 31 81 82, **f** 05 65 22 99 77 (*inexpensive*). A sun-drenched country inn in a pretty garden (*meals from 65F/89F*). *Closed Nov–Easter.*

connected at the papal court at Avignon, they brought one of the popes' architects home to build the **Collégiale St-Martin** on a shady promenade at the edge of town. It makes a handsome setting for the Des Près Carrara marble tombs and the rich treasure they accumulated, including glittering medieval reliquaries and some lovely carved alabaster plaques from England. The collégiale's real prize, however, is the series of tapestries hung around the apse, perfectly preserved 16th-century Flemish works commissioned by Jean Des Près that tell the *Life of St Martin of Tours* with the colour and vivid directness of a comic strip. Woven to fit the very spot where they are displayed, each of the 16 scenes is accompanied by an Old French quatrain. A few minutes from Montpezat, off the D38 towards Castelnau, the woodland church of **Notre-Dame-de-Saux** has 14th-century frescoes of the legends of Sts George and Catherine, the childhood of Jesus and the Crucifixion (key at the Montpezat *mairie*).

Castelnau-Monratier and Montcuq

Northwest of Montpezat, **Castelnau-Monratier** had the honour of being razed to the ground in 1214 by Simon de Montfort during the Albigensian crusade. Rebuilt soon after as a *bastide*, it has an unusual, triangular arcaded market square and a handful of white stone houses from the 15th century. Castelnau's pride and its symbol, however, are the three venerable stone **windmills** on the hilltop above the village. Two centuries ago, when these were built, almost every village without a dependable river had them. Castelnau's are rare survivals; one, the Moulin de Boisse, is a historical monument. They provided a back-up for the 13th-century watermill, the **Moulin de Brousse**, still in operation with a 12ft waterfall (***t** 05 65 21 95 81; ring the miller to visit*). You can also poke around the **Roman ruins** of a sanctuary or village – no one is quite sure – among the weeds and wildflowers at the Moulin du Souquet, or play a round of golf at the beautiful course in nearby Sauveterre (nine-hole Golf des

Roucous, par 35 (**t** *05 63 95 83 70*); they also have a pool and tennis). Don't miss **Flaugnac**, a striking medieval hilltop village just east of Castelnau, or **St-Paul-de-Loubressac**, both perched over the valley of the Lupte.

North of Castelnau is an open, strangely empty part of Quercy Blanc. It was probably busier in Neolithic times; a number of tumuli can be seen, as at Lhospitalet and Villesèque. The people of the largest village, **Montcuq**, on the D653, claim that their village's name comes from the Latin *Montis Cuci* – Mount Cuckoo. Do pronounce the Q, unless you want to say 'My Arse' and hear the French giggle; a new range of silly postcards, mostly sold outside the village, exploits the joke, although the villagers aren't quite as desperate as the good folks of Condom, just south in the Gers, who are so fed up with the sniggers that they are opening a museum of birth control.

Montcuq's 85ft landmark, visible for miles around, is the 12th-century **Tour Comtale**, all that remains of the castle dismantled in 1229 by St Louis (*open July and Aug 3–7*). Impressive as it looks, with walls 7ft thick, this donjon wasn't strong enough to keep out Simon de Montfort; he called here too, and sacked the village. There are frescoes in Montcuq's 14th–15th-century church of **St-Hilaire**, with its striking octagonal bell-tower. In **Rouilhac** just to the south there are remarkable frescoes from the 12th century on the subject of Original Sin; one of the hamlet's main attractions in summer is a clean and pleasant *plan d'eau* with a playground. Three kilometres north on the D28, the pretty stalactite **Grotte de Roland** with an underground lake was a favourite abode of prehistoric bears and hyenas; there's a small museum on the subject and the guide makes sure you see every single scratch (**t** *05 65 22 99 90; open April–early May 2–5, closed Wed and Fri; May–mid-June and mid–end Sept Sat and Sun 2–5; mid-June–mid-Sept daily 10–12 and 2–7; adm*). The **Servat lavender distillery** is in **Belmontet** (**t** *05 65 31 90 17; open for visits July and Aug Wed 9–12 and 2–6*).

Down the Lot: Cahors to Soturac

Abruptly leaving the cliffs and *causse* behind, after Cahors the Lot valley becomes lush and fertile, the heart of the Cahors wine region. Among these landscapes, the river suddenly decides it is in no particular hurry to get to the sea, and winds around in big lazy loops. It contains more than its share of modest attractions, as well as plenty of wine châteaux and country inns.

Cahors to Caïx

Although the D911 is the obvious route, the scenery is much better near the river, carpeted with vineyards. You have several options, none straightforward, but then again, neither is the river. If you're in no hurry, leave Cahors by way of **Pradines**, now a suburb of Cahors but once a village in its own right, with an 11th–12th-century Romanesque church, **St-Martial**, containing a polychrome statue of the Virgin from the same period. The road then rises and skirts the river and heads west to **Douelle** ('barrel stave'), a favourite river port for barges in the old days, when all the cargo was loaded into enormous barrels. Douelle has seen better days, but has been decidedly

Getting Around

There is a regular SNCF **bus** service from the railway station in Cahors through Luzech and Prayssac to Monsempron-Libos.

For **boat** hire and excursions: Crown Blue Line in Douelle, **t** 05 65 20 08 79, hires out comfortable houseboats, sleeping up to four. Navilot at Caix, **t** 05 65 20 18 19, has excursions up the river to Cahors, with lunch, and hires out *gabares*, canoes, kayaks, pedalos and motor boats by the day or half-day; Locaboat Plaisance, in Luzech, **t** 05 65 30 71 11, hires out little barges for four by the week.

Tourist Information

Luzech: Maison des Consuls, **t** 05 65 20 17 27, **f** 05 65 20 17 27.

Prayssac: Place d'Istrie, **t** 05 65 22 40 57, **f** 05 65 22 40 57.

Market Days

Luzech: Wed, fair the first Wed of each month.

Prayssac: Fri. Also Sun morning farmers' market (summer only), and fair the 16th of each month (except Sun).

Where to Stay and Eat

Douelle ✉ 46140

***Auberge du Vieux Douelle**, in the centre, **t** 05 65 20 02 03 (*cheap*). Quiet rooms with TV (*menus from 70F*). *Closed the last three weeks of Dec.*

La Marine, in the centre, **t** 05 65 20 02 06. One of the best places in the area for seafood (*around 98–195F*).

Nuzéjouls ✉ 46150

L'Oasis, 10km northwest of Cahors on the D12, **t** 05 65 30 98 44. A chance to pretend you're in the Sahara desert; you can dress up like a Tuareg and ride a dromedary, by the hour or by the day. The main emphasis, however, is food: a delicious nomadic feast of couscous or tajines consumed in a genuine Tuareg tent. Otherwise, you can just camp here – there's a pool as well.

Caïx ✉ 46140

Le Capitan, t 05 65 20 18 19. Down by the river, beside a campsite and where you can hire the *gabares*. Enjoy a pleasant lunch or just a drink at the tables by the water. Most of the food is *à la carte* but there are three menus (*45–115F*), with a choice of fish or duck. There is a good choice of Cahors wine. *Closed Nov–Easter.*

Luzech ✉ 46140

Restaurant de la Poste Chez Dédé, Av Uxellodunum, **t** 05 65 20 10 07. There's not much in town, but you can eat a relaxed lunch here at a table overlooking the river. It's more of a café than restaurant, but serviceable (*menus 45–82F*). *Closed Sun and two weeks in the winter.*

Sauzet ✉ 46140

****Auberge de la Tour**, Route d'Agen, **t** 05 65 36 90 05, **f** 05 65 36 92 34 (*inexpensive*). In the 13th-century Château de Sauzet, now a handsome little hotel, with a restaurant devoted to the hallowed specialities of Quercy; in the summer dine out on the magnificent wisteria-covered terrace (*menus 85–196F*). *Closed Mon eve and Jan.*

Albas ✉ 46140

Auberge Imhoptet, 2km east in Rivière Haute, **t** 05 65 30 70 91. For a major but affordable duck feast, book at this little place, named for an ancient Egyptian genius who invented the force-feeding of ducks and geese in 2600 BC. The laid-back Jean-Jacques Kessler prepares these same ducks with a deft hand, accompanied by the elegant *vin de Cahors* from Château Eugenie just up the road (*menus 78–250F*). *Closed Sun eve and Mon.*

Prayssac ✉ 46220

Le Vidal, 3 Rue Garabets, **t** 05 65 30 66 00, **f** 05 65 30 89 49. A little Logis de France in the centre, with a popular, friendly bar and restaurant, with tables spilling out into the adjacent square (*menus from 60F*).

Ma Chaumière, in the west end of the village, **t** 05 65 22 40 52. Reasonably priced seafood on its pretty terrace (*menus 65–185F*).

more colourful ever since Didier Comizo painted the 400ft quay wall with a mural on the Creation, wine and humankind. The village has the Lot's *Ecole de Parapent*, if you want to learn to hang-glide (***t** 05 65 30 78 20; open all year*).

Cross the narrow suspension bridge in Douelle and head towards Mercuès, passing by way of two exceptional wine estates: **Caillac** and its handsome Renaissance château, **La Grézette**, beautifully restored down to the *pigeonnier*, overlooking a prestigious vineyard; and a bit further north, the 12th-century **Château Les Bouysses** (***t** 05 65 30 971 86; open by appointment*), donated by its builder, Raymond de Lard, to the Cistercians, who made it a priory (a rather nice one, with an orangery) until the Revolution, when the Count of Mosbourg purchased it and made it a wine business, and replaced the chapel with a *chai*. There's a small **museum** of ancient agricultural tools, art exhibitions in the summer, and excellent *vin de Cahors, bien sûr*. Caillac's Romanesque **church** is also worth a stop for its foursquare bell tower and 15th-century porch, with carvings, including Adam and Eve and floral motifs.

At Mercuès (*see* p.335), take the D911 west through **Espère**, 'a town called Hope' here in the Arkansas of France, and a noted speed trap. From the centre of town, signs point the way north to **Nuzéjouls** and its dromedaries, offering an unusual opportunity for *dépaysement* (the sensation of being somewhere else, perhaps more necessary for the locals than visitors). The D911 rises up the *causse* to Fred Flintstone's jobsite, the stone quarries of **Crayssac**, with neat piles of rocks for sale along the road. Here, however, in 1995, the quarries yielded a surprise: unique dinosaur footprints and fossils, dating back 140 million years, according to the palaeontologists at the CNRS. Turn south here past Crayssac church to the belvedere and narrow corniche road (a friend of ours calls it 'Snake Road') that loops down towards the river to **Caïx**, with a huge panoramic view over the valley. Queen Marguerite of Denmark, who married a local boy, Henri de Montpezat, comes down every summer; they stay at the 17th-century family château, where the surrounding vineyards produce the wine served at the royal table in Copenhagen; there's also a little wine **museum** (***t** 05 65 20 11 00*). Caïx also has an early Romanesque church with interesting naïve carvings, and a small recreational lake.

The prince consort's father, Comte André de Montpezat, was a rice planter in Vietnam before returning to the Lot to become a founding member of the Côtes d'Olt *Vin de Cahors* Cooperative in **Parnac**, the next village west, which still bottles the count's label. Next along the river, **St-Vincent Rive d'Olt** has a 16th-century church with many of its orginal fittings; nearby, Marcayrac has a curious tall **menhir** or *pierre levée* in the woods, pierced with natural holes.

Luzech

West of Parnac, **Luzech** enjoys the most striking setting of the river villages, on a narrow isthmus where two loops of the Lot nearly meet – an even more extreme version of Cahors' own setting. Once one of the four baronies of Quercy, captured by Richard the Lion-Heart in 1188, Luzech began as a Gallo-Roman citadel; some remains survive on the steep hill above the town at the **Oppidum d'Impernal**. This is yet another Uxellodunum contender, and pretty much fits the description in Caesar's *Gallic Wars*, althoughm if it once had the requisite spring, there's no sign of it now.

Below, medieval Luzech was held by its barons with the bishops of Cahors after the latter beat the local Cathars in the Albigensian crusade. Back then Luzech was defended at either end by castles, which successfully repelled every English siege in the Hundred Years' War. The barons' castle is gone, but what remains of medieval Luzech gathers itself under the stout ***donjon épiscopal*** (or *Tour Impernal*), all that survives of the bishops' fortress. In the village centre, the beautiful 13th-century **Maison des Consuls** now houses the *Syndicat d'Initiative* and the small **Musée Municipal Armand-Viré** (***t*** *05 65 20 17 27; open all year by appointment*) with Gallo-Roman finds from the oppidum, including a model of Trajan's column. The wide square that carries the main road, the D8 through the village, was once a canal, cutting off the loop of the river and dividing the village from its *bourg*; for a taste of old France, stop in for a drink at the Café Richard, with its old signs and lace curtains and original bar. From here, you can walk up to the teardrop-shaped hill that forms the river loop. The Flamboyant Gothic **church** on the top, **Notre-Dame-de-l'Isle**, was begun in 1505, in the same style as the Cahors cathedral cloister, with a Flamboyant portal; it replaces an older chapel venerated since the 13th century by river boatmen. In the winter, much of the local excitement is concentrated to the south, in the tiny village of **Sauzet**, where the basketball team, now joined with that of Cahors, is in the second division.

Albas to Prayssac

Albas, just to the west, occupies an exceptionally picturesque spot on a cliff over the river. The tiny fortified centre includes a church and yet another Cahors episcopal palace, much favoured by the wealthy bishops. **Castelfranc**, a few kilometres west on the opposite bank, is an austere *bastide* of the 13th century: die-straight streets and a central square with a spare, elegant church, typical of medieval Quercy architecture, with its *clocher-mur*, as wide as the church itself, serving as much for defence as for decoration. The village's small but elegant suspension bridge is typical of the structures the Ponts et Chaussées erected all around this area in the early 1900s.

The long ridge to the northwest of Castelfranc was an important Neolithic site. Leaving the village on the D911 west, take the first turn right, which climbs steeply up the hill for a fine view, and then pick up the marked ***circuit des dolmens***. There are only two dolmens, but in addition an unusual 'double' *garriote*, a rock-carved niche called 'Caesar's armchair', near an ancient well, and, at the summit of the hill, a circle of three huge menhirs amidst jumbles of rocks known as the Cromlech of Roquebert although everyone calls it 'Chaos'. Call the tourist office at Prayssac for information.

Prayssac, like Castelfranc, started out as a *bastide* – only a round one, a mere circle of houses around a marketplace; it has grown greatly since the 19th century, as the biggest producer of the *vin de Cahors* region. Prayssac is worth a mention for its addiction to marble statuary, starting with the quite unforgettable nude **Venus** on Venus Square, the vernal nymph in the lobby of the cinema, and the well-endowed sphinx-like creatures in the fountain by the post office. Also in marble is Jean-Baptiste

Bessières, the 'Duke of Istria', across from the *mairie*. One of Napoleon's henchmen, this son of Prayssac oversaw the military occupation of Moscow, and died with a cannonball in his brain at Lützen in 1814.

On the south bank, just west of Prayssac, **Pescadoires** has a fortified Romanesque church near the river, while **Bélaye** stands perched on the cliffs overlooking the valley. This ancient fortified place was one of the most important towns in the area before the English *routiers* raided it – several times – during the Hundred Years' War. The ruins of its episcopal castle remain, along with a strong-looking fortified church with a retable brought back by the souvenir-hunting Maréchal Bessières. Signs point the way to the Camping de la Tuque, one of the largest naturalist camping sites in France, completely lost in the woods, while below, on the D45 crossroads to Montcuq, there is an exceptionally pretty little castle, slowly, sadly, simply falling to bits.

Puy-l'Evêque to Soturac

Puy-l'Evêque and Grézels mark the end of the frontier of the lands owned by the count-bishops of Cahors, but *vin de Cahors* vineyards stretch all the way to the west end of the *département*.

Puy-l'Evêque and Around

The hills close in on the river again at **Puy-l'Evêque**, giving this village its exceptional riverside setting, best seen from the new bridge over the Lot. By now, you should be able to guess to which *evêques* this *puy* (an Occitan word for 'hill' or 'mount') belonged. The Cahors bishops defeated the Cathars to pick up this property in 1227, and soon after built the **donjon**, similar to Luzech's, at the highest point of the town. Not long after, many of the local nobles added their houses in its shadow – none is that impressive individually, but the whole makes a lovely ensemble. In the Revolution, there was a brief movement to change its name to Puy-Libre, but Napoleon changed it back. Though small, Puy-l'Evêque is worth a look around for its quiet medieval streets, the battered Flamboyant Gothic portal of its church **St-Sauveur** (near the top of the town), said to have been whacked by a hundred Protestant cannonballs in the Wars of Religion, and views over the valley.

To the north, the **church** of the pretty village of **Martignac** has remains of 16th-century frescoes, including large *Allegories of the Seven Deadly Sins* (not well preserved), some Italianate chiaroscuros, and in the apse a strange, looming figure like the king on a playing card that seems to be a pope, or God the Father himself. South of Puy-l'Evêque, the great square 18th-century **Château de Grézels** squats on its hillside like a fortified bunker, restored in the 1960s. You can spend the night there (*see* above).

The next village is **Duravel**, dominated by its massive 11th-century **church** atop a terrace, one of the most interesting pieces of Romanesque architecture in Quercy, but unfortunately also one of the most restored in the 19th century (*pick up the key at the tourist office*). The outside of its apse is decorated with perforated metopes – openings under the roofline, usually round, alternating with *modillons* or other carvings, a

Getting Around

Besides the Cahors-Fumel SNCF **bus** that serves the river's villages, Loca-Lot in Vire-sur-Lot, near Puy-l'Eveque, **t/f** 05 65 36 59 22, hires out all kinds and sizes of **bikes** and four-wheel-drive **cars**. If speed is no object, Les Roulottes du Quercy in Sérignac (near Maroux), **t** 05 65 31 96 44, **f** 05 65 31 93 41, hire out horse-drawn wooden **caravans**.

Tourist Information

Puy-l'Evêque: on the D911, **t/f** 05 65 21 37 63.
Duravel: in the centre, **t** 05 65 24 65 50, **f** 05 65 30 65 63.

Market Days

Puy-L'Evêque: Tues and Sat.
Duravel: Sat.

Where to Stay and Eat

Puy-l'Evêque ✉ 46700

****La Truffière**, **t** 05 65 21 34 54, **f** 05 65 30 84 47 (*inexpensive*). Small and simple, with a TV and full bath in each soundproofed room. A wide stone arch marks the entrance.

****Henry**, 23 Rue du Docteur Rouma, **t** 05 65 21 32 24, **f** 05 65 30 85 18 (*inexpensive*). At the bottom of Puy-l'Evêque. With a garden, room TV, and a restaurant. *Open all year.*

Grézels ✉ 46700

Château de Grézels, **t** 05 65 21 34 18, **f** 05 65 21 38 28 (*expensive–moderate*). Feel like the lord of the manor. Five *chambre d'hôte* rooms, each beautifully furnished and given an exotic name; meals served on request (*from 150F*).

La Terrasse, in the village centre, **t** 05 65 21 34 03. In spite of the notoriously grumpy owner, this is a favourite for miles around for a delicious country lunch under the oak beams with as much wine as you can drink (*85F*). *Book for the 135F Sunday lunch. Open July and Aug eve by reservation only, closed Sun night and Mon.*

Duravel ✉ 46700

Ferme-Auberge La Roseraie, 1km from the centre (signposted), **t** 05 65 24 63 82, **f** 05 65 30 89 79 (*inexpensive*). A bit newer than typical farms in the region, but the extraordinarily hard-working family who run it lay down as delicious and traditional a Quercy spread as any, though it now includes ostrich (*menus including their own* vin de Cahors *at 110–150F with foie gras*). *Open eves July–mid-Sept and Sun lunch, otherwise Sat eve and Sun lunch by reservation only.* It also has four *chambres d'hôte* and a pool.

conceit popular in this corner of the Lot. The occasion of this vast building project was the arrival in Duravel of an 11th-century sarcophagus containing 'three holy bodies' brought back from Palestine, by a crusader who perhaps bought them off some sharpsters with less imagination than the ones who peddled Geoffroi de Hardoin the Crown of Thorns. You can see their relics once every five years on the last Sunday in October (next display, 2005); at other times they are stored in the church's rare Carolingian crypt, with primitive but finely carved capitals, one showing a peacock. Upstairs, the capitals in the nave and chapels (scenes of misers in hell, St Michael pinning down the dragon) are among the very few that still wear their bright paintwork – a bit disconcerting at first, the way the Parthenon would be in all its original Technicolor tones. Also look for a Gallo-Roman relief of – aptly for this wine village – bunches of grapes.

From Duravel you can take the pretty back road by way of quaint **St-Martin-le-Redon** to the Château de Bonaguil (*see* pp.357–8). Alternatively, continue along the river until the signs point you back over the bridge to **Touzac**, site of a lovely deep-blue spring and 12th-century mill, the Moulin de Leygues (*see* below). Just west of the

Château La Gineste, just beyond La Roserai, **t** 05 65 30 37 00, **f** 05 65 30 37 01 (*expensive*). The *chambres d'hôte* are set in the middle of a vineyard and are sumptuous with high beamed ceilings and period furniture. Sit out in the lovely central courtyard under parasols: peace and calm guaranteed. Meals for guests only; château wine to drink. *Open all year*.

Domaine de Barry-Baran, signposted off the D911 between Duravel and Puy-l'Evêque, **t** 05 65 24 63 24 (*moderate*). One of Quercy's most delightful and friendly rural bed-and-breakfasts, run by a friendly American (*meals from 200F, eves only*). *Open all year. Book early.*

Le Pied de Mouton, in the centre, **t** 05 65 36 50 39. A little bar-restaurant where you can check out the local expat community on Fri nights.

Touzac ✉ 46700

******La Source Bleue***, **t** 05 65 36 52 01, **f** 05 65 24 65 69 (*moderate*). Next to the spring and bamboo forest, in a 12th-century mill. This was once owned by actress Marguerite Moreno, who used to entertain her friend Colette. Colette had an insatiable appetite for truffles cooked in the ashes (the way the locals used to eat them 50 years ago, when the annual harvest was 25 times what it is now). The 15 rooms are charming (try to get one of the large ones in the mill); a sauna, pool, and gym come with the deal; and you can still get truffles in the restaurant on occasion, along with foie gras and other regional delights (*menus 100–240F*). *Closed Wed, Jan and Feb.*

Le Clos Bouyssac, **t** 05 65 36 52 21. A delightful, shady campsite right on the Lot, with bungalows to rent, pool, boats and bikes. *Open May–Sept.*

Mauroux ✉ 46700

****Hostellerie Le Vert**, on the D5, **t** 05 65 36 51 36, **f** 05 65 36 56 84 (*inexpensive*). A pool and seven lovely, utterly tranquil rooms (one with a baby grand piano) in a country manor house and outbuildings; Bernard Philippe in the restaurant offers a good but limited menu, as well as *à la carte* dishes, all served with fresh herbs (*menus 120–220F*). *Closed Thurs and Fri lunch and mid-Nov–mid-Feb.*

Le Mas de Laure, 1km out of the village on the road to Sérignac and Montcuq, **t/f** 05 65 30 67 39 (*inexpensive*). These *chambres d'hôte* have only recently opened but have built up a good reputation; *book early*. The energetic and friendly Monsieur Trebossen will do everything he can to make your stay a success. *Evening meal 120F.* The rooms are fresh and airy with country charm and there's a pool. *Closed Jan.*

bridge, a dirt road leads to a simple bar and grill in one of the most idyllic locations on the river: no cars, no buildings, nothing but river, trees and a large colony of coypus – cute furry swimming raccoon-sized rodents from South America who have successfully invaded the lower Lot; someone introduced them thinking they might be good to eat, and then had a change of heart (at least, there's no sign of *terrine de coypu* in the shops).

The road from Touzac continues south up to the villages of Lacapelle-Cabanac and **Mauroux** (pronounce the 'x'). Between the two, to the right of the D5, is the striking Romanesque **church of Cabanac**, with a bell tower rebuilt in the 13th century (Penny and Colin Dunn of the nearby vineyard Château Latuc have the key). It stands at the highest point of the lost medieval town of **Orgeuil**. *Orgeuil* means 'pride', and an overweening insolence was the reason for its fall: in the 13th century the knights of Orgeuil, sworn enemies of the bishop of Cahors, terrorized the Lot valley, burning, pillaging and raping as far south as Moissac. Although the King of France took Orgeuil into hand by putting it directly under his rule with a charter in 1293, the

Hundred Years' War brought new troubles. The lords of Orgeuil sided with the English and gave nearby Puy-l'Evêque to the Duke of Derby. When they were banished the town became a robbers' den, occupied by English *routiers*. The count of Armagnac came and razed the pit of vipers once and for all in the mid-1300s. Orgueil is now the subject of one of the most important medieval digs in France: the finds (including a superb gold cross) are displayed in Maroux's *mairie* (***t*** *05 65 30 66 70; open May–Sept 10–1, July and Aug 10–1 and 4–7, closed Sun*).

North of the Lot: La Bouriane

Bories in Provence are dry stone huts, or what the southwest calls *cazelles* or *garióttes*; in this most Périgordian corner of Quercy *borie* means a farmhouse, especially a fortified medieval country retreat of Cahors' merchant élite; they give this mini-*pays* its name. Scattered farmhouses amid lush landscapes of chestnuts, pines and meadows are indeed the order of the day in the Bouriane, but there are some surprises, too: frescoed churches and modern Ukrainian art.

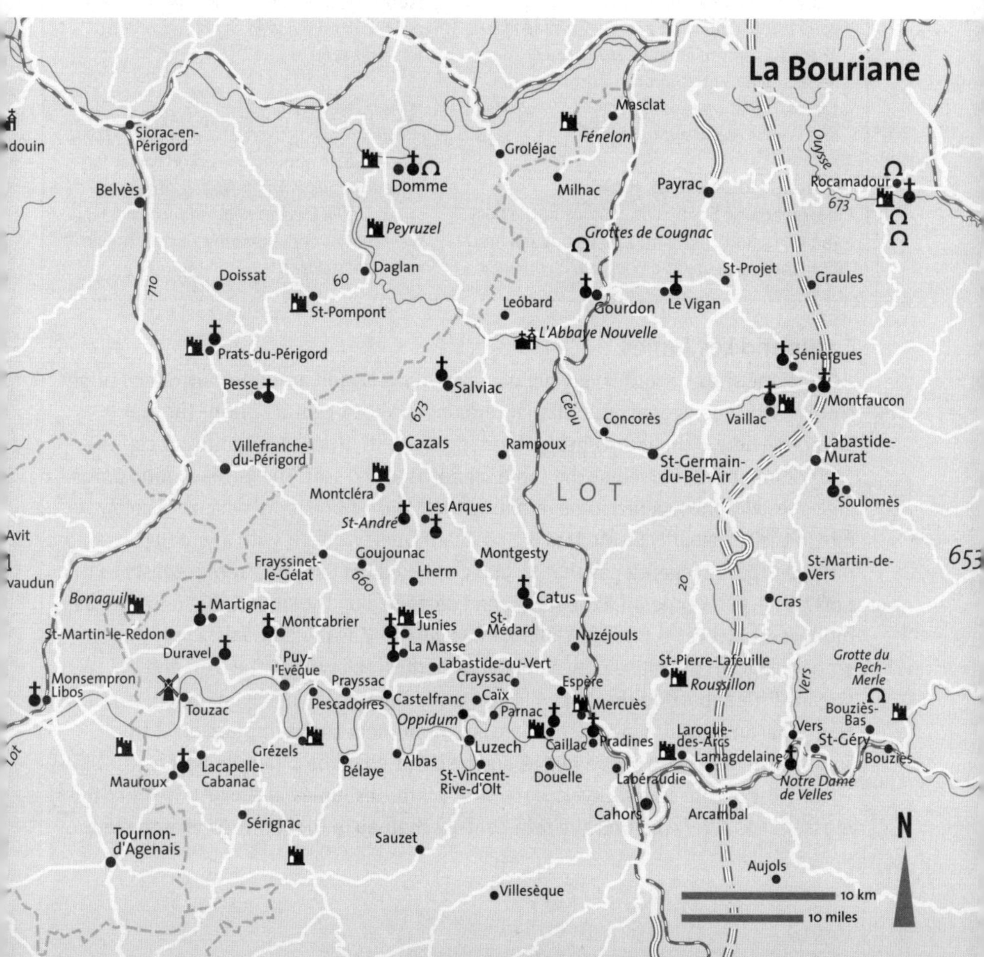

Tourist Information

Catus: Av Lac, **t** 05 65 21 20 06.
St-Germain-du-Bel-Air: Place Mairie, **t** 05 65 31 09 10.

Market Days

Catus: Tues, fair the last Tues of each month.
St-Germain-du-Bel-Air: Fri and Sun mornings in July and Aug.

Where to Stay and Eat

St-Médard ✉ 46150

Le Gindreau, **t** 05 65 36 22 27. The Bouriane's gourmet haven, in a building that originally served as the village school, with a pretty terrace overlooking the countryside. Alexis Pélissou prepares *elegantissimo* dishes with authentic ingredients – lamb from the *causse*, the freshest vegetables in season. There's a sommelier to help you select the correct wine, with Cahors naturally at the top of the list (*menus 165–420F*). *Closed Mon and several weeks out of season.*

Labastide-du-Vert ✉ 46210

Café-Tabac, **t** 05 65 36 21 86. For one of the best meals around, ring Mme Lasfargues, tell her how many you are and how much you want to pay per head, and she will suggest a meal using seasonal ingredients; be sure to ask for her famous walnut tart for dessert.

***Auberge de Vert**, just east in Pontcirq (✉ 46150), a stone's throw off the D911 crossroads at Rostassac, **t** 05 65 36 22 85, **f** 05 65 21 40 17 (*inexpensive*). An old stone country inn with seven rooms and economical meals (*menus 69–180F*). *Closed Sun eve, Mon and all eves Oct–Mar.*

Les Junies ✉ 46150

Château at Les Junies, **t** 05 65 36 29 98 (*moderate–inexpensive*). This delightful château has two *chambres d'hôte* on the second floor.

La Ribote, on the D660, **t** 05 65 36 25 55. The fancypants restaurant in the vicinity, in a pretty 12th-century mill. It serves elegant elaborate dishes and desserts, but is far too stuffy and formal for its own good (*menus 95–300F*). *Closed Wed out of season, also Jan–mid-Feb.*

Les Arques ✉ 46250

La Récreation, **t** 05 65 22 88 08. Set in the old schoolhouse, serving delicious food at fair prices (*menus from 90F lunch, otherwise 150F*). *Closed Wed and Thurs lunch; open weekends out of season exc Dec–Feb when completely closed.*

Catus and Les Junies

Catus, the site of another very popular *plan d'eau*, is built around a buttressed priory **church** with a polygonal apse, all that remains of a 10th-century priory; the star attraction here is the 12th-century chapterhouse with a dozen magnificent capitals and column bases, carved by the same school as at Moissac. The farms around Catus are especially photogenic, some retaining their *lauze* stone roofs, which are pretty rare in the Lot. Nearby **St-Médard** is a postcard Quercy village, with a famous restaurant (*see* above). Legends say that Roland clobbered the Saracens at **Montgesty** to the northwest, in revenge for a town they had destroyed on the site; all that digging has produced, however, is bits of a Gallo-Roman villa at Mas-de-Rieu. **Sals**, a very pretty stone village on the hill, is now half holiday homes; below it, on the D911 and the stream, little **Labastide-du-Vert** will look very familiar to anyone who has visited the Henri Martin museum in Cahors: there is a monument to the Impressionist from Toulouse in the centre of the village, and he is buried in the village cemetery.

Just west of Labastide-du-Vert is the turn-off for **Les Junies**, in the lush valley of the Masse. It has a very picturesque 14th-century **château** in the centre (one of the few you'll see that hangs the washing out on the line), given by the bishop of Cahors as a thank-you-for-stomping-on-the-Cathars present to Bertrand de Jean. The de Jeans built a nuns' priory nearby; the church has lovely 14th-century stained glass showing the founders, along with scenes of Christ and St John. The name de Jean was corrupted to form the village's name, Les Junies. Downstream, at **La Masse**, the **church** has the liveliest frescoes of any Bouriane church: a parade of the Seven Deadly Sins, each riding a beast guided by frisky devils and goaty satyrs. The spring water flowing into the basin in the centre of La Masse is delicious, and has never stopped flowing in living memory, even during the worst droughts.

Les Arques and Around

From the centre of Les Junies, a narrow road winds its way to the small old village of **Lherm**, a striking ensemble in stone, the site of an ironworks in the Middle Ages that was left so desolated after the passing of English Grands Companies in the 15th century that a wolf gave birth outside the church door. North of Lherm, **Les Arques** is a sleepy village that's always had an artist or two ever since the Cubist sculptor Ossip Zadkine of Smolensk bought a home here in 1934. Some of the works left by his widow to the city of Paris have been transferred here to create a little **Musée Zadkine** (*t 05 65 22 83 37; open June–Sept, school hols and weekends 10–1 and 2–7; otherwise 2–5; adm*). Zadkine is best known for his 1947 *Destroyed City* in Rotterdam, and in peaceful Les Arques his works – several are on public display – seem almost too searing and painful. Next to the museum is the superb 11th-century church of **St-Laurent**, which Zadkine loved; he initiated the restoration and contributed three sculptures. Once a priory of Marcilhac, the interior has been stripped down to its mellow ochre stone to reveal its essentials: a single nave ending in three tiny apses, divided by columns with primitive carvings and divided by little Mozarabic horseshoe arches, while below is a tiny, ancient crypt; on one of the exterior portals, note the carved Celtic spiral. At the museum, pick up the key for Romanesque **St-André-des-Arques**, 4km on the other side of the D45 (signposted). In 1954 Zadkine discovered its 15th-century frescoes under the plaster in the apse, interesting but damaged by the wet: *Christ in Majesty*, the *Annunciation* and the *Apostles*. St Christopher is painted on one pillar, and baby Jesus, waiting to be carried, on the other.

If your wanderings bring you further north, one of the many pretty routes to follow in the Bouriane is the D12 along the Céou valley, dotted with ruined castles at **Clermont**, **Concorès** and **St-Germain-du-Bel Air**.

Gourdon

Harmoniously piled on a lofty bluff, rose-coloured Gourdon, capital of the Bouriane, is easily spotted from miles around. Easily defended, the site has been inhabited for donkey's years. In 961 Count Raymond I of Toulouse gave the city to the Gourdon family. The clan, and Gourdon itself, were nearly wiped out in 1189 by Richard the Lion-Heart, who as Duke of Aquitaine often played the baddie – far more like the Sheriff of

Getting Around

Gourdon has a **railway** station with connections to Cahors, Souillac and beyond. To hire a **bike**, **t** 05 65 41 11 65.

Tourist Information

Gourdon: Rue du Majou, **t** 05 65 27 52 50, **f** 05 65 27 52 52. For information on Gourdon's July and August **Festival de Musique**, contact the Comité d'Animation Culturelle, 8 Bd du Docteur-Cabanes, **t** 05 65 41 20 06.
Payrac: **t/f** 05 65 37 94 27.
Cazals: Rue Notre-Dame, **t** 05 65 22 88 88.

Market Days

Gourdon: Tues and Sat in front of St-Pierre; Thurs farmers' market in Place Noël-Poujade in summer; big general fair first and third Tues of each month.

Where to Stay and Eat

Gourdon ✉ 46300

******Hostellerie de la Bouriane**, Place du Foirail, **t** 05 65 41 16 37, **f** 05 65 41 04 92 (*moderate*). A large country inn that has long been the place to stay in Gourdon, on the very edge of town; rooms are lovely, the food – including some fish dishes – delicious (*menus 85–250F*). *Closed Jan–mid-Mar and weekends out of season.*

******Domaine du Berthiol**, on the D704 towards Cahors, **t** 05 65 41 33 33, **f** 05 65 41 14 52 (*moderate*). Even more tranquil, occupying a large stone Quercy manor house in the woods, with a pool and tennis and games for the kids; here, too, the restaurant will win you over with a delectable seasonal menu (*100–280F*). *Closed Nov–Mar, restaurant also closed Thurs lunch.*

Bissonnier La Bonne Auberge, 51 Bd Martyrs, **t** 05 65 41 02 48, **f** 05 65 41 44 67 (*moderate–inexpensive*). Of the cheaper places, this is the nicest, in the medieval town and run by the same family since the early 18th century (*menus 86–190F*). *Closed Dec, Jan, Sun eve and Mon lunch in winter, Mon lunch only in summer.*

Le Paradis, on the road out to Salviac, **t** 05 65 41 09 73 (*inexpensive*).Popular *chambres d'hôte* run by Madame Jardin, in a large house in a big garden with pool; meals also possible.

Le Vigan ✉ 46300

Le Manoir La Battière, signposted off the D1, **t** 05 65 41 40 73, **f** 05 65 41 40 20 (*moderate*). Rather special *chambres d'hôte*. The bedrooms, all different, are huge and beautifully furnished; if you fancy sleeping in a

Nottingham than the good king of the Robin Hood legends. The story goes that the son who survived the massacre of Gourdon got his revenge with his crossbow 10 years later at the siege of Châlus, when he shot Richard fatally in the shoulder.

Gourdon in its medieval heyday had four monasteries, although one of its lords, a troubadour named Bertrand I, had a run-in with the Inquisition for protecting the Cathars. In the Wars of Religion the monasteries also made a juicy target for the fierce Protestant captain Duras, who spent a month razing them to the ground and slaughtering their inhabitants. Gourdon's once-mighty castle suffered a similar fate in 1651 when the lord of Gourdon foolishly supported the cause of Marie de' Medici over her son, Louis XIII. In the 18th century the city walls went down to make space for a circular boulevard.

Walking Around Gourdon

Start your tour of Gourdon at the top, with the massive church of **St-Pierre**, begun in 1302, its façade flanked by two 100ft towers, linked by a gallery over the rose window. The portal has some delicate carving on the capitals; inside, the vast single nave is the

four-poster ask for the Quercy room. The 13th-century manor house has all the old-world charm you would expect, set in a big garden with tailored lawns and a small pool (*175F for dinner*). *Book early. Closed Nov–Easter.*

Payrac ✉ 46350

****Hostellerie de la Paix**, on the N20, **t** 05 65 37 95 15, **f** 05 65 37 90 37 (*inexpensive*). Once a posthouse, this is a pleasant place to stop or stay, with a pool, sauna, garden and restaurant (*menus 85–240F*). *Closed Jan–mid-Feb.*

Frayssinet-le-Gélat ✉ 46250

La Serpt, signposted from the centre of Frayssinet, **t** 05 65 36 66 15. A *ferme-auberge* serving some of the best duck and goose *confits* and *magrets* in the Lot, also traditional dishes like *mique levée*, goose cooked in Cahors wine, or *pastis*, apple pie smothered in light flaky pastry like a pile of autumn leaves (*menus 80–170F*). *Book ahead.*

Goujounac and Around ✉ 46250

****Hostellerie de Goujounac**, **t** 05 65 36 68 67, **f** 05 65 36 60 54 (*inexpensive*). A handful of remodelled rooms in the village centre; reliable, generous menus, seasoned just right (*menus 75–230F*). *Closed Sun eve and Mon, exc July and Aug, and four weeks in the winter.*

Le Poule au Pot, **t** 05 65 36 65 48. A *ferme-auberge* with all the fixings, a keen rival to the aforementioned Serpt. The dining room is full of cycling trophies: the owner's son races in the Tour de France. Good for big fills (*menus 75–150F*). *Book, especially on Sun.*

Jeanne Murat, in Pomarède, 4km southwest, **t** 05 65 36 66 07. She lays down one of the most popular spreads around for a filling lunch (*80F*), using mostly home-grown ingredients. *Book on Sun.*

Montcabrier ✉ 46700

Ferme Auberge Lou Montaïcos, signposted from the D673, up on a hill, **t** 05 65 36 55 70. A friendly place that raises hundreds of geese and ducks and serves them in Cahor wine as well as in a dozen other ways, all good (*menus 66–162F*). *Open year-round, but by reservation only out of season.*

***Chambres d'Hôte* chez les Lemozy**, on the farm in the hamlet of Mérigou, on the D68 west of Montcabrier, **t** 05 65 36 53 43 (*cheap*). An Arcadian bed-and-breakfast, two *gîtes* also available in summer (*for four, from 3,000F*). (*Evening meal available at 70F.*) From 15 September to 15 May, sign up for a culinary weekend and learn all about preparing foie gras and *confits*.

most important venue of the town's summer music festival. For a view from Gourdon equal to the view of Gourdon from the distance, climb the stairs by the church for the esplanade that once formed the base of the castle: you can see the Dordogne valley, the green Bouriane and just about every roof in town.

Narrow little streets, like the famous Rue Zigzag leading up to St-Pierre, are lined with well-restored medieval houses. Near the church, the 13th-century consulate was converted in the 1700s into the **Hôtel de Ville**, with graceful arcades on the ground floor that shelter the farmers' market. Behind St-Pierre in Place des Marronniers, note the fine Renaissance portal and carved door of the **Cavaignac house**. The Cavaignacs were nationally prominent in the Revolution and 19th century; the father, Jean-Baptiste, served on the National Convention and ended up as a counsellor of Napoleon. His eldest son, a Republican journalist, created a society dedicated to the rights of man, while the younger, cast in the same mould as Richard the Lion-Heart, personally led the massacre of the Parisians in the revolt of 1848. The main street, **Rue du Majou**, is lined with relics of the Middle Ages – handsome houses, a fortified gate and chapel, and Gourdon's most interesting shops.

On Gourdon's ring boulevard, the Gothic church of the **Cordeiliers** survived Duras' monastic destruction. Although it's not much from the outside, the honey-hued interior is pure and lovely (*open for festival concerts; otherwise ask at the tourist office*) and has a beautiful 14th-century baptismal font carved with the figures of Christ and the 12 apostles. A third pretty church, **Notre-Dame-des-Neiges**, is 1km from the Hostellerie de la Bouriane (*see* above). Built near a water mill, the church stands on the site of a miraculous spring; the snow in its name refers to one of the Virgin's 4th-century miracles in Rome, when she caused a summer snowfall on the site of Santa Maria Maggiore. Although only the apse survives from the Romanesque church, the whole is simple and charming and contains an altar by Tournier, although it's always locked tight.

Around Gourdon

North of Gourdon are the two **Grottes de Cougnac** (***t*** *05 65 41 47 54; open Palm Sun–1 Nov 9.30–11 and 2–5, in July and Aug 9.30–6; adm*). One cave is full of stalactites and stalagmites. The second, 300 yards away, was discovered in 1952. Its entrance, blocked millennia ago, preserved inside the *département*'s second most important collection of prehistoric paintings: black and red outlines of goats, deer, mammoths, symbols and a number of humans, some pierced by lances. The cave walls around them look like trees and mutant cauliflowers. Amongst them, palaeontological detectives have found fingerprints believed to be 20,000 years old.

From the caves, the D17 continues north to **Milhac**, a delightful medieval village that was the cradle of the lords of Gourdon; another charmer is **Masclat** further north, built around a pretty château and church, only a few kilometres from Lamothe-Fénelon. **Le Vigan**, 6km east of Gourdon, is a busy village built around a massive **abbey church** with a giant belfry, founded by the canons of St-Sernin in Toulouse and especially favoured by the popes in Avignon, who gave it the relics of St Gall, uncle of St Gregory of Tours. The English in the Hundred Years' War so thoroughly pillaged the abbey that it never recovered, although stained glass was added to the church in the 15th century. Le Vigan is also the home to a private museum, **Musée Henri Giron** (***t*** *05 65 41 33 78; open May–June and Sept–Oct Tues–Sun 10–12 and 3–6, July and Aug Tues–Sun 10–6, Nov–April Sun and by appointment; adm*), where you can examine the landscapes, still lifes and nudes of the *inclassable* erotic, Modigliani-inspired Giron, a Frenchman who ran a hotel in Brussels in the 1930s, and gradually changed career; he still lives in Belgium, but many of his best works are here.

Further east, **St-Projet** has a naïve pilgrims' cross, in which the serpent represents evil, the heart triumphant love, the skull and crossbones unredeemed humanity; on the top Christ is crucified. The cross has an identical twin just to the east near **Graules**, en route to Rocamadour; the Graules cross, with its smiling Christ, has preserved its mysterious stone pendants. For a grand bird's-eye view, cross the N20 to Reilhaguet. **Payrac** to the north is a pleasant town unfortunately sliced in two by the big road, but the kids might like its **Aqua Folies** with slides, pools and mini-golf (*open May–Sept; adm*) or you can pay a visit at the **Musée Roger Thières** in the *atelier* of the eponymous artist-blacksmith (***t** 05 65 37 90 10; open June 9–12, July–mid-Sept 10-12 and 2.30–6, mid-Sept–Oct 2–6, closed Sun and Mon at the end of the season*).

Southwest of Gourdon: More Bouriane, along the D673 to Fumel

Just off the scenic D673, 8km west of Gourdon, stand the romantic ruins of the **Abbaye-Nouvelle** at Léobard. A Cistercian abbey (the 'old' one was at St-Martin-le-Désarmat), it was founded in 1242 on a rock overlooking the valley of the Céou on lands donated by Guillaume de Gourdon-Salviac, anxious to get back into good grace with the Inquisition. The Gothic church (1274–87) was damaged in the Hundred Years' War and never properly repaired, and by 1658 the abbey was abandoned. In 1950 it was dynamited by the farmers who owned it; the once elegant stairs were dismantled for a barn. Now only the lofty, ruined walls of the church stand, originally 90ft high – Abbaye-Nouvelle was the only known Cistercian church in France without a transept, and one of the few built with two storeys; the wooden upper floor has long since vanished. A local organization is dedicated to bringing the ruins back to life in some way.

The D673 to **Salviac** has its scenic merits as well; Salviac has a Renaissance château, some old houses, and a Gothic **church** built by Jean Duèze of Cahors, the future John XXII, which preserves some of its original stained glass. From Salviac a good navigator can get you through the narrow lanes to **Rampoux** to the southeast (easier, head south on the D6 from Dégagnac); the reward is a 12th–14th-century Benedictine priory decorated with naïve frescoes from the 15th century and a statue of St Peter from the 1200s.

Cazals

Back on the D673, the most important town in the area is **Cazals** next to a pretty *plan d'eau*. The town was a *bastide* laid out for the King of England by Guillaume de Toulouse in 1319. Only the main square serves as a reminder of its *bastide* origins, and the church (with some good capitals inside) is said to be built over a Roman temple. Cazals gave the world Hugues Salel (1504–53), one of the poets who drove Clément Marot crazy by imitating his *blasons*, preciously dedicated to pins and the like. **Montcléra**, the next village, has a most beguiling fat 15th-century château at the south end of town, best viewed when you head north up the D673; all it needs is a Rapunzel letting down her long hair.

Little **Frayssinet-le-Gélat** occupies the crossroads between Gourdon and Fumel, Cahors and Villefranche-du-Périgord. The only thing striking about it, besides its attractive medieval church, is the little monument next to it, with the inscription *TO THE MARTYRS OF GERMAN BARBARISM*, in letters big enough for everyone to notice. On 21 May 1944, a detachment of soldiers who had been attacked by the Resistance took their revenge on Frayssinet, rounding up villagers and shooting them; the old folks in the village still talk about it. If you take the D660 east from Frayssinet-le-Gélat, you'll pass through the golden village of **Goujounac** where the Romanesque church has a tympanum on its south side, carved with Christ and the four Evangelists

The D678 to Fumel follows the valley of the Thèze, passing under **Montcabrier**, a little *bastide* founded in 1297 by and named after Guy de Caprari, the seneschal of Quercy. Its church of **St-Louis** with its arcaded *clocher-mur* was given a pretty Flamboyant portal and rose window in the 14th century; inside its prize is a reliquary of St Louis, one of the few that portray the king with a beard. The steep heights on the opposite side of the D678 once held the town of **Pestilhac**, Montcabrier's bitter rival; some of its outer fortifications can still be seen from the valley. For three centuries, the two towns fought each other like Kilkenny cats; Pestilhac finally succumbed and disappeared in the 1500s. In its day it must have been one of the most important centres in the region. If you want to see the most evocative ruins in Quercy, climb up and make the acquaintance of the pleasant woman who lives in the smaller of the two houses on the site. The path leads through her back garden, up a wild, forested jumble of stones that includes parts of the walls and bastions, various buildings and best of all the church of Notre-Dame, still substantially intact, with some lovely carvings and an oak tree growing right through one of its Romanesque windows. From here it's only a few miles to the Château de Bonaguil (*see* pp.357–8).

Lot-et-Garonne

14

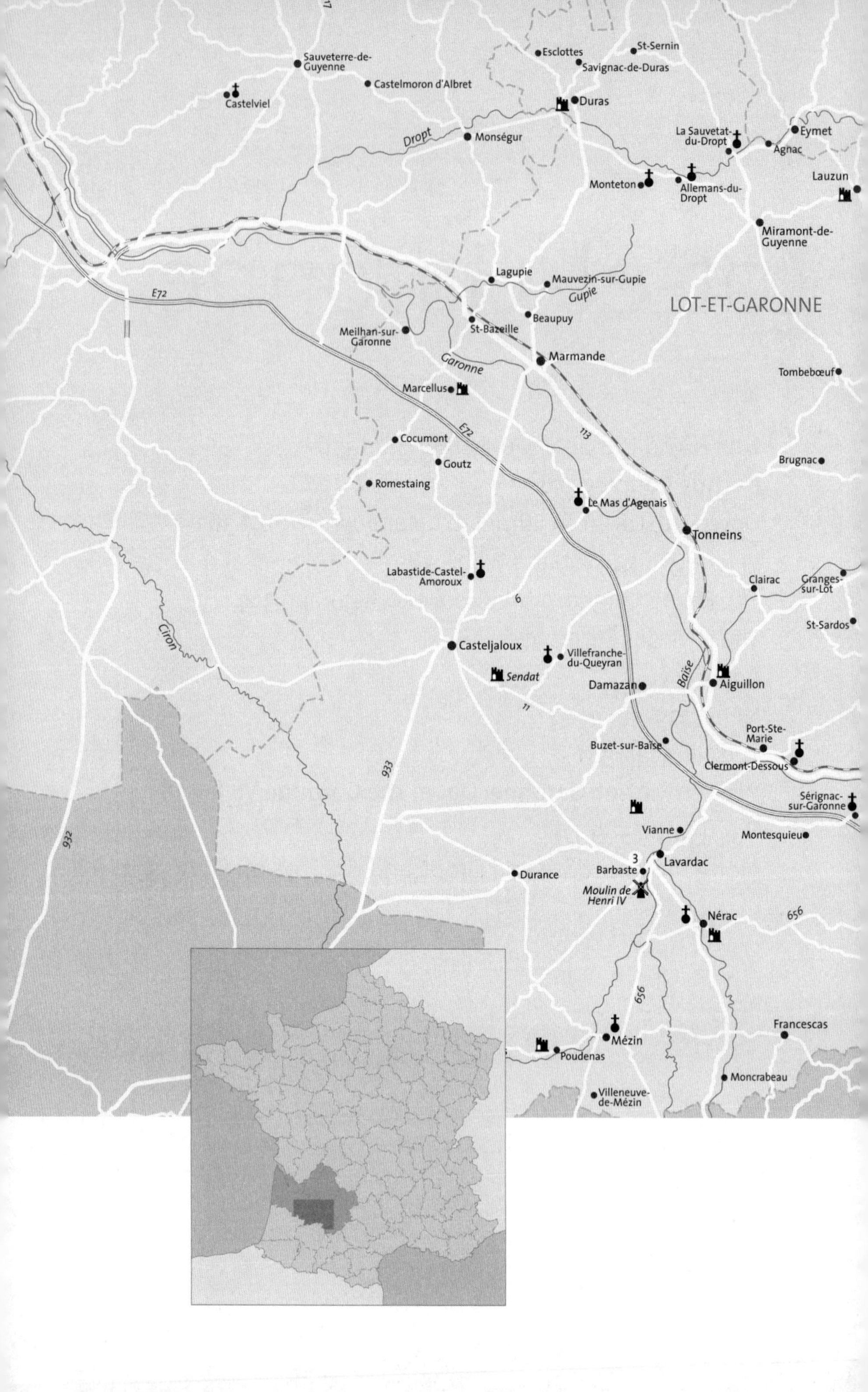

Sauveterre-de-Guyenne
Castelviel
Castelmoron d'Albret
Esclottes
St-Sernin
Savignac-de-Duras
Duras
Dropt
Monségur
La Sauvetat-du-Dropt
Eymet
Agnac
Monteton
Allemans-du-Dropt
Lauzun
Miramont-de-Guyenne
Lagupie
Mauvezin-sur-Gupie
Gupie
E72
LOT-ET-GARONNE
Beaupuy
St-Bazeille
Meilhan-sur-Garonne
Marmande
Garonne
Tombebœuf
Marcellus
113
Cocumont
Goutz
Romestaing
Brugnac
Le Mas d'Agenais
Tonneins
Labastide-Castel-Amoroux
Clairac
Granges-sur-Lot
6
St-Sardos
Ciron
Casteljaloux
Villefranche-du-Queyran
Sendat
Damazan
Baïse
Aiguillon
11
Port-Ste-Marie
Buzet-sur-Baïse
Clermont-Dessous
933
Sérignac-sur-Garonne
Vianne
Montesquieu
932
3
Lavardac
Barbaste
Durance
Moulin de Henri IV
Nérac
656
Francescas
Mézin
Poudenas
Moncrabeau
Villeneuve-de-Mézin

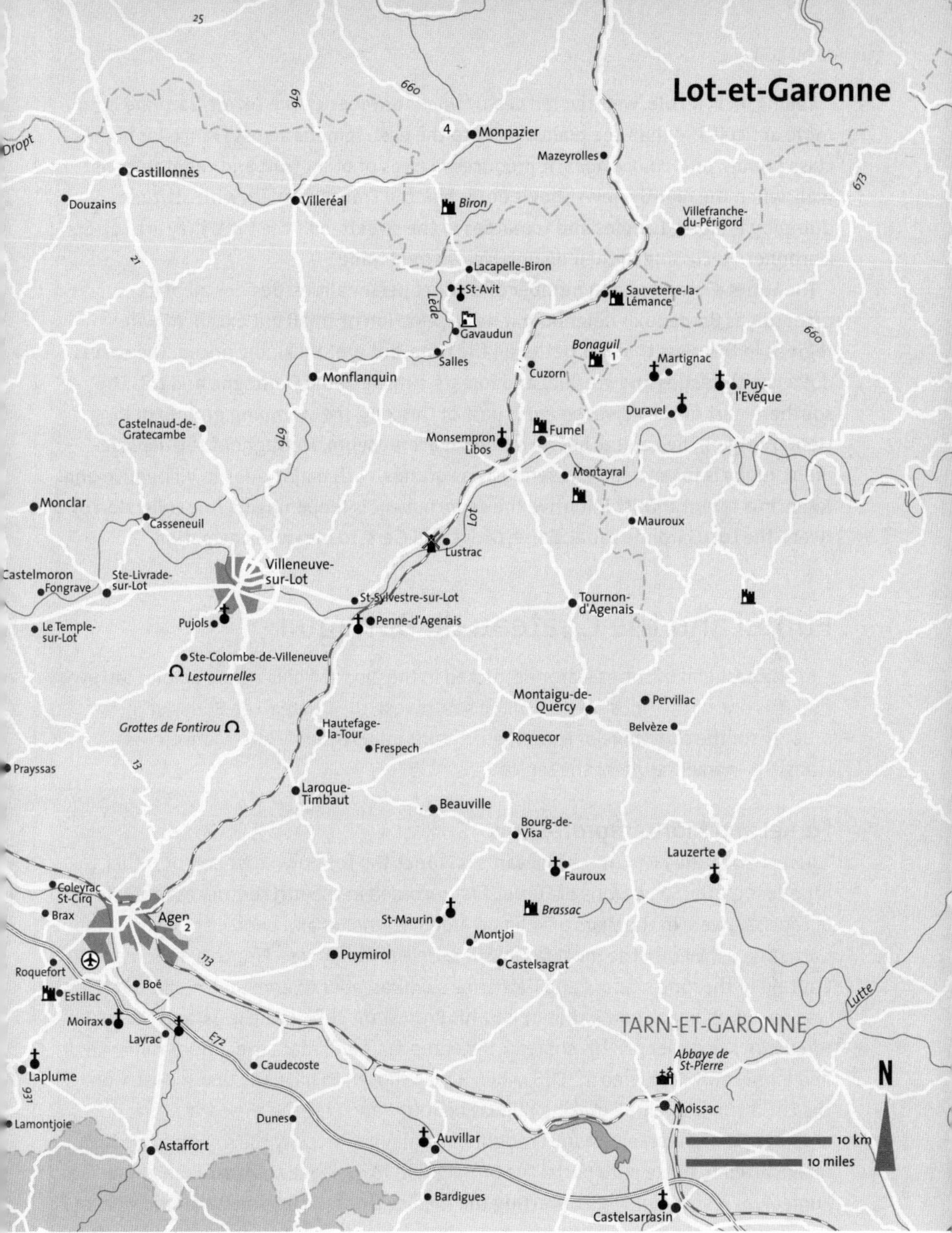

Highlights

1 The perfect stage-set castle, at Bonaguil
2 Five Goyas and a million prunes in Agen
3 Barbaste's august fortified mill, the Moulin Henri IV
4 Edward I's ideal *bastide* of 1284, Monpazier

Rolling, rich, fertile, well-rivered *département* number 47, the Lot-et-Garonne is far more agricultural than the plain old Lot to the east: famous across France for high-class prunes, *pruneaux d'Agen*, it produces masses of other fruit and vegetables as well; when the nightly news shows burly, bereted French farmers with attitudes dumping imported apples and tomatoes in the streets, half the time they are Lot-et-Garonners, a-cussing in their distinctive Gascon twang.

The Lot-et-Garonne has a number of distinct personalities. Besides all of its orchards, as Bordeaux's neighbour it has a selection of small but excellent wine regions in the west that get better all the time, but are still kindly priced. The east is dotted with castles and *bastides* and forests, similar to the Dordogne and Lot. The southern part of the *département* is part of Gascony, the stomping ground of King Henri IV. Agen, the capital, has an excellent art museum. Throughout the *département*, rugby is taken nearly as seriously as prunes, with major clubs in Villeneuve and Agen. In a recent tourist initiative the *département* is reopening its fine collection of rivers, the Lot, Garonne canal, Baïse, Dropt and Gers, to pleasure navigation.

Fumel and the Château de Bonaguil

At the east end of Lot-et-Garonne, tucked in the wooded hills where no one can ever find it, is one of the finest castles in the southwest, the Château de Bonaguil, now property of the *commune* of Fumel, which runs imperceptibly into Monsempron-Libos, the market town for the region.

Fumel and Monsempron-Libos

Just west of the last Cahors vineyards is **Fumel**, the Lot's own rust belt or, rather, little rust garter. The barons of Fumel, first recorded in the 11th century as protectors of Moissac, were in the Wars of Religion ardent Catholics and buddies of Henri II and Catherine de' Medici; the most famous leaf on the family tree, François de Fumel, was Captain of the King's Guard and Catherine's ambassador to Constantinople, but he was so unpopular at home that in 1562 his Protestant subjects rose up and slaughtered him like a sheep in his château. Bitter reprisals and mass executions followed, and Fumel only recovered in 1848, when it was chosen to have the first industry on the Lot, a small steelmill making railway bearings and pipes. In the early 1960s it employed 2,700 workers, many brought in from Algeria; today the mill has been reconverted to make auto parts. The one sight in town is the **château**. François de Fumel was responsible for converting the medieval donjon into an Italianate villa and, if you walk up the big steps to the library, there's a stucco of François over the door, his nose bust off in Fumel's proto-Revolution. Completed in the 1700s, with immaculately kept garden terraces overlooking the river, the château stayed in the family until 1950, when they sold it to the city to become the *mairie*. You can visit the gardens and take guided tours in English (*call the tourist office for information*). These days Fumel can hold its head a bit higher as the hometown of Jean Nouvel, architect of the exquisite Institut du Monde Arabe in Paris.

In recent years Fumel has reached out to touch its neighbours with its super- and hypermarket sprawl. If you can get past the car parks of **Montayral**, a former Templar fief across the Lot, look for its fortified mill built directly in the river, or its château, a 13th-century residence of the pirate lords of Orgueil just upriver, with bits added over the centuries. **Monsempron-Libos**, on the far side of the steelmill, is spread around a medieval *castrum* on a hill with the exquisite 12th-century church of **St-Géraud**. The exterior is decorated with perforated metopes, while the unusual plan inside has innovative vaulting and a special entrance under the choir to accommodate pilgrims who flocked to see the relics displayed in the crypt. The capitals in the nave (redone in the 14th century) are carved with masks and monsters.

The Château de Bonaguil

It's so perfect that it seems ridiculous to call it a ruin.

Lawrence of Arabia, 1908

Of all the castles bristling across France, few are as useless or as photogenic as the great prow-shaped Château de Bonaguil, 'the swan song of feudalism', born 200 years behind the times. Begun in the 13th century by a family of knights from Fumel, it passed in the 1460s to the hunchback Brengon de Rocquefeuil, who liked to be called 'the noble, magnificent and most powerful lord' of his assorted little possessions. Brengon was a perfect cartoon baddie, a proto-survivalist, as nasty and paranoid as he was vain. When Charles VII fined him for brutality towards his vassals, Brengon

Getting Around

The station at Monsempron-Libos has a few **trains** a day to Les Eyzies, Périgueux and Agen.

More frequent **buses** run up the Lot valley as far as Cahors. You can take a **boat** jaunt on the river at Fumel with La Gabare Fuméloise, **t** 05 53 71 13 70.

Tourist Information

Fumel: Place Georges-Escandes, near the *mairie*, **t** 05 53 71 13 70, **f** 05 53 71 40 91.

Market Days

Fumel: Sun.

Monsempron-Libos: Thurs, food and clothes.

Where to Stay and Eat

Fumel ✉ 47500

★★72nd Avenue, 72 Av de l'Usine, just across from the ex-steel mills, **t** 05 53 71 80 22, **f** 05 53 71 15 08 (*inexpensive*). A few comfortable rooms; they also have a reputation for serving some of the best seafood in the area (*lunch from 65F*).

Bonaguil ✉ 47500

Auberge Les Bons Enfants, just below the castle, **t** 05 53 71 23 52 (*inexpensive*). Reliably good meals for the tourists on its terrace lined with weeping willows (*menus 60–200F*). The inn also has three rather pricey rooms. *Closed 15 Nov–15 Mar.*

Sauveterre-la-Lémance ✉ 47500

★Le Centre, in the upper part of the village, **t** 05 53 40 65 45, **f** 05 53 40 68 59 (*cheap*). An old country inn, a blessing for the budget traveller, with good rooms and an excellent restaurant where you can feast on *duo de lotte et saumon aux girolles* and many more tempting offerings (*menus 75–240F*). *Closed Jan–Feb.*

ensconced himself at Bonaguil, in a massive donjon reminiscent of the Flatiron Building, filled with years' worth of provisions and weapons, and surrounded it with a moat and surging walls and towers, designed to deflect cannon fire from all sides (at the same time, all the other nobles of France, like the aforementioned François de Fumel, were abandoning their medieval castles or converting them into elegant Renaissance châteaux). 'I will raise such a castle that my villainous subjects will never take it, nor the English, nor even the most powerful soldiers of the King of France,' Brengon boasted. Never mind that none of the above ever showed the least interest in Bonaguil (although the Huguenots partially wrecked it in 1563, and it was rebuilt in 1572 by another Rocquefeuil). By the 18th century Brengon's lair was such a white elephant that it once changed hands for 100 francs and a bag of walnuts. Partially demolished in the Revolution, it was purchased by the town of Fumel in 1860.

Whether you approach it from Fumel or from above, via St-Martin-le-Redon (*see* p.343), it is as stunning as a Hollywood set; on summer nights it's illuminated until midnight. The interior (***t*** *05 53 71 13 70; open daily Feb–May and Sept–Nov 10.30–12 and 2–4.30, June 10–12 and 2–5, July and Aug 10–5.45, closed Jan and Dec except school hols 2.30–4.30*) can't match the exterior: there are fireplaces suspended in the void, objects found in the castle midden, graffiti (Rocquefeuil names, games, dirty doggerel and the magic square SATOR ROTAS), and views from the walls. The adjacent castle chapel, St-Michel, has an unusual cinquefoil window.

From Bonaguil, little winding roads will eventually bring you to **Sauveterre-la-Lémance**, dominated by a large, less glamorous but actually used **castle**, built by Edward I in the 13th century to defend the frontiers of Guyenne (***t*** *05 53 40 67 17; you can visit if you ring ahead*). Sauveterre was another popular prehistoric residence, and gave its name to the early Mesolithic period, the *Sauveterrien*; you can visit the excavations in the summer at Roc-Allan, and see what they've found at the little **Musée Préhistorique** (*at the* mairie, ***t*** *05 53 40 68 81; open Mon–Thurs 8.30–12.30 and 2.30–6.30, Fri till 5.30, Sat and Sun 2.30–6.30, mid-Oct–April closed Sat*) . The serene little valley of the Lémance is a pretty place to explore, with more reminders of the armies in the Hundred Years' War that raged up and down its length at **Cuzorn**, just south; here too are relics of the Lemance's old economic mainstays, forges and paper mills; **Montcabrier** with its frescoes is near by (*see* p.352).

Bastide Country

West of the Bouriane a similar landscape of rolling hills, woodlands and meadows continues into the *département* of Lot-et-Garonne and the southern bit of the Dordogne. Stendhal described this landscape as the 'Tuscany of France', and it's sprinkled with a superb collection of *bastides* and castles.

Monflanquin, Villeréal and Around

Monflanquin is a convenient starting point for exploring the *bastide* country, whether you approach from Fumel to the east or Villeneuve-sur-Lot to the west.

Tourist Information

Monflanquin: Place des Arcades, **t** 05 53 36 40 19, **f** 05 53 36 42 91.
Villeréal: Place de la Halle, **t** 05 53 36 09 65, **f** 05 53 36 63 58.
Castillonnès: Place des Cornières, **t/f** 05 53 36 87 44.
Issigeac: **t** 05 53 58 79 62.
Monpazier: **t** 05 53 22 68 59, **f** 05 53 74 30 08.
Lacapelle-Biron: Grande Rue, **t** 05 53 36 55 45, **f** 05 53 40 84 98 (*open summer only*).

Market Days

Monflanquin: Tues, Thurs and Sat in summer.
Villeréal: Sat, also a farmer's market on Wed during summer
Castillonnès: Tues.
Monpazier: Thurs.
Lacapelle-Biron: Mon.
Issigeac: Sun.

Where to Stay and Eat

Monflanquin ✉ 47150

★★**Moulin de la Boulède**, on the road to Villeréal, **t** 05 53 36 40 27, **f** 05 53 36 59 26 (*inexpensive*). You can stay very pleasantly in this restored mill over a stream, run by the same people for 47 years, or just enjoy one of its good menus (*70F–180F*).

Ferme-auberge de Tabel, on the same road, 5km from Monflanquin, **t** 05 53 36 30 57 (*cheap*). Lunch and dinner prepared from home-grown produce (*65–150F*); they also have three rooms and a large *gîte* to rent. *Book*.

Villeréal ✉ 47210

★★**Le Lac**, Route de Bergerac, **t** 05 53 36 01 39 (*inexpensive*). A fine un-gussied-up modern hotel in the trees by a little lake, popular with swimmers and fishermen, with a pool and a restaurant (*menus 95–160F*). *Closed mid-Oct–Mar*.

★**Europe**, Place Jean Moulin, **t** 05 53 36 00 35 (*cheap*). Simple rooms in the centre of the action.

Le Moulin de Labique, at nearby St-Vivien, on the way to Bourn, **t** 05 53 01 63 90, **f** 05 53 01 73 17, *www.moulin-de-labique.fr* (*moderate*). This *auberge-chambres d'hôte* is delightful. The traditional country rooms are colourful and pretty, with wooden beams and heavy furniture; the restaurant has the same cheerful feel and a lovely patio under a

Strategically planted atop a 594ft hill with views from miles around, the *bastide* of Monflanquin, 'one of the most beautiful villages in France', was founded in 1256 by St Louis' brother Alphonse de Poitiers. Alphonse's interest in these marches had much to do with his marriage to Jeanne, the only child of Raymond VII of Toulouse, which was part of his brother's strategy to Frenchify the lands recently devastated by the Albigensian Crusade; Alphonse and Jeanne further obliged by dying childless and leaving Toulouse to the Crown of France. Monflanquin has preserved most of its original *bastide* elements: the central square bordered with wide arcades, or *cornières*, a fortified church still bristling behind its original façade, its grid street plan and blocks of medieval houses; the exhibitions in the **Espace Bastides** (*Maison du Tourism, **t** 05 53 36 40 19; open July and Aug daily 10–12.30 and 2.30–7; Sept–June 10–12 and 2–6, closed Sun and Mon mornings*) will tell you all about them. Monflanquin's most recent vocation is art, and it fills the summer with events, exhibitions and festivals; it makes a drinkable *vin de pays de l'Agenais*, sold at the cooperative **Cave des 7 Monts** (***t** 05 53 36 33 40; open Mon–Sat*). It also has a rarity in this neck of the woods: a gym, heated pool and sauna at Espace Forme (***t** 05 53 36 47 35; some of the facilities can be used on a daily basis, call for information*). The late, not so great Robert Maxwell used to have a château on the outskirts of Monflanquin. There is a **Musée de la Vie Rurale** (***t** 05 53 41 90 19; open July and Aug daily 3–7, June and Sept Sat–Sun 3–7*) just outside town.

canopy of vines surrounded by flowers and butterflies. You get to choose between delicious regional options (*menu 150F*). *Book. Auberge closed in winter.*

Castillonnès ✉ 47300

******Des Remparts**, 26 Rue de la Paix, **t** 05 53 49 55 85, **f** 05 53 49 55 89 (*moderate*). Ten handsomely furnished rooms in a 19th-century house, overlooking the ramparts; dine out on the terrace around a fountain and plump for the superb 180F menu. *Closed Sun eve and Mon except in season, and half of Nov and Jan.*

Ferme du Bois de Mercier, **t** 05 53 36 81 97, **f** 05 53 36 71 10 (*inexpensive*). Located by a country pond you can swim in, this organic farm has lovely rooms at lovely prices.*Closed a week in May and Oct.* In the kitchen, owner Denise Bousquet will convert you to the charms of prune sauces. *Dinner only.*

Monpazier ✉ 24540

******Edward Ier**, 5 Rue St-Pierre, **t** 05 53 22 44 00 (*moderate*). The hotel occupies a 19th-century mini-château that the French call a bachelor pad (*gentilhommière*), with an attractive swimming pool added to where the moat might have been. The rooms are fitted out with every comfort – some with steam bath or Jacuzzi – and all have satellite TV and mini-bar; but there is no restaurant. *Closed Nov–Mar.*

La Bastide, 52 Rue St-Jacques, **t** 05 53 22 60 59. An old favourite with plenty of quirky French character, serving up the likes of *poulet au verjus* and trout with almonds; save room for the delectable *gâteau de noix* (*lunch menu 80–240F*). *Closed Mon out of season and mid-Jan–Feb.*

Les Peyrouliers, along the D660, **t** 05 53 22 66 10. Simple, well-prepared classics such as grilled salmon with dill (*menus 90–240F*). *Closed mid-Nov–mid-Dec, mid-Jan–mid-Feb.*

****Le St-Hubert**, 3km from Monpazier in the centre of tiny Capdrot, **t** 05 53 27 99 07 (*inexpensive*). A charming, quiet little hotel with a pool and tennis, and a good restaurant (*menus from 70F*). *Closed Oct–Mar.*

Gavaudun ✉ 47150

Le Donjon, **t** 05 53 40 82 32. For the best 65F lunch, join the crowds and put yourself in the hands of Christine and her mother (*more for the big Sun lunch, menus generally go up to 200F*).

It's a beeline 13km north up the D676 to another foundation of Alphonse de Poitiers, the 1269 *bastide* of **Villeréal** alongside the river Dropt (or Drot). Villeréal, with its agriculture (mostly orchards and tobacco) and commerce has a more solid air to it than artsy Monflanquin. The shop-filled arcades of the main square overlook the 14th-century *halle*, which has an upper storey added in the 16th century. The façade of the church is framed by two towers and retains the loopholes in the apse, from where the citizens shot at the rampaging English.

A decade before Villeréal, Alphonse had founded the handsome *bastide* of **Castillonnès** (13km west), down the Dropt and midway between Villeneuve and Bergerac, on the N21. Castillonnès has conserved its *cornières* and narrow medieval lanes, and, on Rue du Petit Paris, a fine 17th-century house. The church has a 17th-century gilded retable. The tiny village of **Douzains**, just to the southwest, is famous for its enormous oak tree that figures in several local legends.

Picture-postcard **Issigeac**, north of Castillonnès and Villeréal, has changed so little over the centuries that it's a favourite location for films; it also manages to be less austere than the other *bastides*. Among its charms are a late Gothic church with a good porch, a massive bishop's palace, and the half-timbered **Maison de Têtes**, decorated with leering faces.

Monpazier

Monflanquin, Villeréal and Castillonnès held the front lines against the English foundations at Beaumont and at Monpazier, 'the most perfect *bastide*', 15km up from Villeréal on the Dropt. Founded by Edward I in 1284, Monpazier had a perfectly rotten 14th century, when the town was a football kicked from side to side in the Hundred Years' War – even the Baron of Biron got into the act and put it to the sack, *routiers* pillaged it, and a streak of bad harvests was followed by a typhoid fever epidemic. The local lepers were blamed, and a few burned alive. Then in 1350 came the Black Death.

Amid the terrors of the next round of warfare, over religion this time, the duke of Sully recorded a story about Monpazier worthy of *Monty Python*: by sheer coincidence Monpazier decided to raid Villefranche-du-Périgord, the next *bastide* to the east, on the same night that Villefranche decided to do the same to Monpazier. By chance each militia took a different path; each was delighted to find their goal undefended and easy to plunder, and carried its booty back – to ransacked homes. An agreement was struck, and both sides gave back everything they stole.

Despite all the troubles, Monpazier has held itself together remarkably well, from its fortified church (still bearing its Revolutionary slogan, that 'The People of France believe in a Supreme Being and the Immortality of the Soul') to its 16th-century *halle*, complete with its original grain measures. Note that the regulation *cornières* around the square are irregular, and that narrow spaces were left between the houses – not to give the residents air or light so much as a place to throw their rubbish. In 1637 crowds stood under the arcades to watch Buffarot, the leader of the *Croquants'* revolt, broken on the wheel.

The Château de Biron

From Monflanquin or Villeréal you may have already sighted the superb **Château de Biron**, largest of all Périgord's castles (**t** *05 53 63 13 39; open Mar–April and Sept–Dec 10–12.30 and 2–5.30, closed Mon in Mar and Oct–Dec; May–June 10–12.30 and 2–6.30, July–Aug 10–7; closed Jan and Feb; adm*). The steep hill was a natural stronghold, and the first castle was built in the 11th century to command the northern approaches to the Agenais. In 1189 Gaston de Gontaut, chief of the four barons of Périgord (and an ancestor of Lord Byron) got his hands on it, and they were like glue – the Gontauts held on to the castle for 24 generations, until the early 20th century. Over the centuries the family created one of the most charmingly eclectic castles in France. The first Gaston built the square 12th-century keep, or Tour Anglaise, while Romanesque walls and the Tour du Concierge (with Renaissance dormers) date from after the 1212 siege of Biron by Simon de Montfort. Gaston de Gontaut was tainted with heresy after wedding his daughter to the Cathar captain, Martin Algaïs, England's seneschal of Gascony. Algaïs led a brave defence against the French crusaders, but de Montfort only agreed to go away when the young man was handed over for execution.

The next important building spree was initiated by Pons de Gontaut-Biron, who accompanied Charles VIII on his invasion of Italy in 1497. Pons returned to Biron determined to add some *quattrocento* grace to his muscular feudal domain with the delicate Pavillon de la Recette and a two-storey chapel – the ground floor built as a parish church for the villagers of Biron, and the upstairs reserved for the nabobs. This chapel long held two 14th-century masterpieces, a *Pietà* and *Mise au Tombeau*, which to the great outrage of many were sold by the Gontaut-Birons in the early 1900s to the Metropolitan Museum in New York; of the tombs, only two were priced too high for the New Yorkers, those of Pons de Gontaut-Biron, carved with the *Resurrection of Lazarus* and *Christ Appearing to his Disciples*, and his brother, Armand, bishop of Sarlat (d. 1531), with three dignified feminine *Virtues*.

A third round of building was begun by Baron Armand de Gontaut, a Maréchal de France (1524–92), who died fighting the Catholic League at the side of Henri IV. His hot-headed son Charles continued the fight, receiving 32 wounds in battle. Henri rewarded him by raising Biron to a duchy, and making Charles ambassador to England; but Charles found peace boring, and in 1602 he was un-duked and beheaded at the Bastille for conspiracy against the king (hence Biron's story of a headless ghost). The moat was filled in under Richelieu, who didn't like the great lords of France feeling safe or secure. Work was taken up again in the 18th century, but left incomplete at the time of the Revolution.

From the castle take the D150 south to **Lacapelle-Biron**, a village founded on the orders of Biron's baron to host the Monday market that used to take place under the château – the baron hated to be awakened by the noise. There is now a **Parc de Loisirs P'Arc-en-Ciel** (***t*** *05 53 71 84 58; open April–Oct 10–7; adm*) with animals, children's play area, picnic spot, gardens and walks. A little **Musée Bernard Palissy** in nearby **St-Avit** (***t*** *05 53 40 98 22; open daily*) covers the life and work of the great Renaissance potter and writer born here in 1510, famous for his superb enamels, before he was arrested for being a Protestant in 1589 and thrown into the Bastille, where he soon died. There is an annual exhibition of contemporary ceramics.

Gavaudun and Around

Lacapelle-Biron and St-Avit are near the head of the sweet leafy valley and mini-gorge of the Lède, a little stream that not only sounds like the mythological river of oblivion, Lethe, but really does make the cares of the world seem far away – deceptively so: St-Avit, for instance, was razed to the ground by the retreating Germans in 1944. Troops marched through in the Middle Ages as well: a striking 12th-century six-storey donjon dominates the ruins of the castle at **Gavaudun** (***t*** *05 53 40 82 29; guided tours June–Sept daily 2–6, weekends also 10–12*), set on a huge natural stone platform. The shelters in the cliffs around Gavaudun were densely populated from the Mousterian to the Magdalenian era, documented in the small **Musée de la Préhistoire** (***t*** *05 53 40 82 29; open July and Aug 10–6, or call*). Just above Gavaudun, **St-Sardos-de-Laurenque** has a pretty Romanesque church with fish carved on the portal. Another, more recent relic of the past is the old mill near **Salles** that spins wool the traditional way (*visitors welcome 9–12 and 2–6*).

Down the Lot: from Fumel to Villeneuve-sur-Lot

At **Fumel** the Lot moves into the 21st century, shedding its ringlets along with its pristine lack of industry, car parks and commercial sprawl as it meets flatter country en route to its confluence with the mighty Garonne at Aiguillon. From the valley road the scenery might seem unexciting, but take a short detour anywhere to the south and you'll find some of the most remarkable landscapes anywhere in the southwest: rank upon rank of flat-topped *mesas*, cut out of the limestone by little streams over the past few million years – the northern extremity of the Agenais *pays de serres* (the overlook at the top of Penne is a good place to see the whole of them). However dramatic, it is still a green and pleasant land, especially in the spring when its orchards burst into blossom.

Tournon-d'Agenais and Montaigu-de-Quercy

The hills here, at the crossroads of the *département* of the Lot-et-Garonne, the Lot, and the Tarn-et-Garonne, belong to the Haut Pays des Serres – the land of gentle undulations and valleys, a prelude to the Pays des Serres proper further downstream. Before leaving the Fumel area, there are two hill towns just to the south that merit a detour. **Tournon-d'Agenais**, the first, is a pretty mesa-top *bastide*, founded by the indefatigable Alphonse de Poitiers in 1270; there are several half-timbered houses, and arcades around the central Place du Marché. The vineyards in the area produce red *vin de pays Thézac-Perricard*, which was served to Nicholas II of Russia. Won over, Nicholas immediately ordered 1,000 bottles for a family party, and ever since then the wine has been known as the *Vin du Tsar*; try it at **Les Vignerons de Thézac-Perricard** on the D151 between Tournon and Puy l'Evêque, ***t** 05 53 40 72 76, www.vin-du-tsar.tm.fr.*

The second hill town, **Montaigu-de-Quercy**, 'Mount Sharp', was the site of a 12th-century castle built by Count Raymond V of Toulouse. Montaigu manages to look more Italian than French from a distance, but has a sufficiently large Brit contingent to support an English library. It also has a crystalline artificial lake, the **Plan d'Eau de Chênes**, with a white sandy beach. There's a pretty square with half-timbered houses, and some sharply steep streets in the centre. Ten minutes to the west, on an even higher hill, **Roquecor** is a sleepy, laid-back place with a Sunday morning market that attracts a jovial mix of twanging locals, squires in Rollers, bikers and expats. If you're continuing into the Tarn-et-Garonne *see* Lauzerte, pp.418–20. If you have small children, they'll probably love the **La Fermeraie du Jougla**, 8km away in **Belvèze** on the road to Lauzerte, a wooded park home to 200 animals from a llama down to a Vietnamese pig, with lambs and kids to bottle-feed (***t** 05 63 94 41 42; open mid-June to mid-Sept daily 10–7; adm*). Near Belvèze at **Pervillac**, on the D24, the church contains charming 16th-century frescoes.

Back on the Lot: Penne-d'Agenais and Around

On the river itself, **Lustrac**, 9km west on the D911 from Fumel, is a charming spot marked by one of France's most impressive fortified mills, the **Moulin de Montnavés**, founded in 1296; the adjacent château was a glorified river tollbooth. Further

Tourist Information

Montaigu-de-Quercy: Place du Mercaiel, **t** 05 63 94 48 50.
Penne-d'Agenais: Rue du 14 Juillet, **t** 05 53 41 37 80, **f** 05 53 49 38 37.

Market Days

Tournon-d'Agenais: Tues and Fri eves mid-June–mid-Sept.
Montaigu-de-Quercy: Sat.
Roquecor: Sun.
Penne-d'Agenais: Sun mornings at Port de Penne.

Where to Stay and Eat

Tournon-d'Agenais ✉ 47370

*__Le Midi__, **t** 05 53 40 70 08 (*cheap*). In the medieval centre, you'll find this family-run place with simple rooms. Tournon prides itself on its *tourtiéres* (flaky apple or prune pie), and this is a good place to try it with a cup of coffee; the other dishes don't get half as much attention. *Open daily May–Aug, closed Wed out of season* (get there early in the week: they sell out fast).

__Les Voyageurs__, **t 05 53 40 70 28 (*inexpensive*). On the roundabout at the foot of the *bastide*, quite worn in appearance, but with comfortable if simple rooms with small bathrooms which would be fine for an overnight stay. You can eat from the traditional menus (*67–150F*) either in the dining room or on the terrace. *Open daily in summer, closed weekends Oct–April and two weeks in Nov.*

Around Montaigu-de-Quercy ✉ 82150

Auberge de Filhol, near the centre, **t** 05 63 94 47 02. The best place to eat, with foie gras and other southwest specialities (*menus 130F–200F including apéritif, wine and coffee*).

__Château de l'Hoste__, 10km west at St-Beauzeil on the D656, **t 05 63 95 25 61, **f** 05 63 95 25 50 (*inexpensive*). An 18th-century *gentilhommière*, with well-restored, guaranteed-peaceful, homey rooms in the midst of a large park with a pool; the kitchen specializes in seafood and desserts (*menus 1140–185F*). *Book. Closed Feb.*

Penne-d'Agenais and St-Sylvestre-sur-Lot ✉ 47140

__Le Compostelle__, Rue Jean Moulin, **t 05 53 41 12 41, **f** 05 53 49 35 03 (*inexpensive*). Modern and tasteful, with a pair of rooms for the disabled (*menu 120F, then carte*). *Restaurant closed Sun and Mon eves, hotel closed Jan and Feb.*

__Le Moulin__, Rue du Port, **t 05 53 41 21 34, **f** 05 53 41 20 68 (*inexpensive*). Panoramic views over the Lot.

****__Château Lalande__, below Penne, in St-Sylvestre-sur-Lot, **t** 05 53 36 15 15, **f** 05 53 36 15 16 (*expensive*). This striking 13th–18th-century château has been given a complete overhaul and fitted with all the mod cons, including heated swimming pools cascading into one another, tennis courts, and a helipad for your chopper. The restaurant, one of the top in the region, offers a wide-awake cuisine combining traditional ingredients with exotic flavours, although beware: you can easily drop 500F dining *à la carte* (*menus 230–390F*).

downstream, rising high over the south bank, **Penne-d'Agenais** is a prettily restored artsy-craftsy *village perché* that has well earned its retirement from the affairs of this world. On a site inhabited since prehistoric times, by, among others, the Gauls (*penn* means hill crest in Celtic) and Romans, the medieval village grew up around a chapel of Our Lady of the Assumption first built around the year 1000 – one of the oldest churches in France dedicated to the Virgin. In 1182, Richard the Lion-Heart found the site inspirational in another way, and built a mighty castle here, making Penne 'the key of Guyenne'; he is locally recalled in the name of one of the three medieval gates, the **Porte Ricarde**, and in the nearby **Fontaine de Ricard**. Being chosen as the key of Guyenne was a mixed blessing at best: the town's other nickname was *Penne la sanglante*. Many inhabitants were Cathars, and in 1212 they were besieged for 50 days by the Albigensian Crusaders before they were captured and burned alive at the stake. In 1373, during the Hundred Years' War, the English set the town afire when du Guesclin was at the point of capturing it; in 1562, Blaise de Monluc captured it from the Protestants, then put them all to the sword. Shortly after, Henri IV ordered the destruction of the castle, probably to the great relief of the people of Penne: today only two towers by the deep 'English ditch' remain, and the prison, in the cellar of the *mairie*.

The famous church, now known as **Notre-Dame-de-Peyragude** (from *pierre aigue*, or sharp stone), was from the start an important stop along the road to Compostela; as it was outside the castle walls it took some hard knocks. It was rebuilt for the third time in 1653, in response to a vow, after floods from the Garonne set off a plague that killed half the population of the Agenais, then again in 1842 after the Revolution sold it off piecemeal for building stone. So many pilgrims kept turning up that in 1896 the local prelates built what you see today – a huge basilica in the kitschy neo-Byzantine taste of the time, but with a view in every direction.

Villeneuve-sur-Lot and Pujols

The bustling market city of **Villeneuve** grew out of yet another *bastide*, founded by Alphonse de Poitiers, Count of Toulouse in 1264. During a tour Alphonse had found the surrounding countryside in ruin and misery after the Albigensian Crusade, and, hoping to stabilize the area, he acquired the land for a new town from the Benedictine abbey of Eysses – hence the city's first name, Villeneuve d'Eysses. Although the town now spreads every which way, it has retained its simple *bastide* heart, as well as a pretty medieval neighbour, Pujols. Villeneuve likes its rugby *à treize* so much that it needs three stadiums to contain all the action.

A Walk around the *Bastide*

Enter by way of the 13th-century **Porte de Paris**, crowned with a 100ft tower, the bottom third made of stone, and the top two-thirds brick. The central market square, **Place Lafayette**, is still framed in its *cornières*, rebuilt in the 17th century after the riots of the Fronde. Near by, the elaborate brick **Ste-Catherine** was completed in the 1930s, replacing the original Gothic church which was in danger of collapse. The magnificent Gothic and early Renaissance stained glass of the latter (perhaps designed in part by Bernard Palissy) were incorporated in the modern church, depicting the *Life of Christ* and a bevy of saints associated with the city. St James the Greater appears three times, in honour of the many pilgrims who passed through en route to Compostela because Villeneuve was one of the few places on the Lot with a bridge, the **Pont Vieux**. This takes the Périgueux–Auch road, first tramped out in Neolithic times, and it made Villeneuve's fortune when the English built the bridge in 1282,

Getting Around

Trains run several times a day between Villeneuve and Agen. You can take a **boat** excursion, departing from Ponton de l'Aviron, Villeneuve, with Bateaux Promenades Electriques, **t** 05 53 36 17 30. You can also hire canoes and kayaks, **t** 05 53 49 18 27.

Tourist Information

Villeneuve-sur-Lot: 1 Bd de la République, **t** 05 53 36 17 30, **f** 05 53 49 42 98.

Pujols: Place St-Nicolas, **t** 05 53 36 78 69 (*summer only*).

Market Days

Villeneuve: Tues and Sat in Place Lafayette; farmers' market Wed in Place d'Aquitaine; Fri night farmer's market in July and Aug.

Pujols: Sun Mar–Nov.

Where to Stay and Eat

Villeneuve-sur-Lot ✉ 47300

Hotels here are geared mostly to prune merchants.

****La Résidence**, 17 Av Lazare Carnot, **t** 05 53 40 17 03, **f** 05 53 01 57 34 (*inexpensive*). Functional but pleasant.

****Le Terminus**, 2 Av Foch, **t** 05 53 70 94 36, **f** 05 53 70 45 13 (*inexpensive*). Well-preserved charm; it has a billiards room.

*Les Remparts, 1 Rue E. Marcel, **t** 05 53 70 71 63 (*cheap*). Decent if unexciting.

Aux Berges du Lot, 3 Rue l'Ancien Hôtel de Ville, **t** 05 53 70 84 41, **f** 05 53 70 43 15. Dine under the wisteria by the river. Welcoming, and by far your best chance for a memorable meal in the centre (including fish as well as duck, and *tourtière* for dessert); outdoor tables in summer (*menus 85–210F*). *Closed Sun eve, Mon and last half of Nov.*

Hostellerie du Rooy, Chemin de Labourdette, just east on the D661, **t** 05 53 70 48 48. Set back from the road, this is an attractive big inn with a pretty garden terrace, where the chef prepares seafood, mushrooms and cèpes with a deft hand that brings out their true flavour (*menus 98–250F*). *Closed Sun eve and Mon.*

Pujols ✉ 47300

******La Toque Blanche**, **t** 05 53 49 00 30, **f** 05 53 70 49 79 (*expensive*). Classic, cosy, intimate, gracious and elegant, attracting not only prune barons but gastronomes from across France. Set among the trees, panoramic views across to the medieval town are accompanied by some of the most delicious, delicately prepared duck dishes you've ever had, from the most traditional to the most innovative (especially the *magret* grilled with preserved pears); extensive wine list (*menus 145–450F*). *Closed Sun night and Mon exc in Aug, and mid-June–start July.*

*****Les Chênes**, on the hillside at Bel-Air, **t** 05 53 49 04 55, **f** 05 53 49 22 74 (*moderate*). Charming, with its refined rooms, warm family atmosphere and heated pool.

Auberge Lou Calel, **t** 05 53 70 46 14. La Toque Blanche's annexe, in a handsome medieval house with a big fireplace and terraces overlooking the valley and Villeneuve. For a good meal at less budget-busting prices try their delicious menus (*85–210F*). *Closed Tues night and Wed exc Aug, and the first half of Jan.*

Castelnaud-de-Gratecambe ✉ 47290

*****La Menuisière**, **t** 05 53 01 60 19 (*moderate*). Golfers can stay near the links, pool and tennis courts here; the rooms are functional but the food in the restaurant is excellent, with a fine 130F *menu golfeur* at lunchtime; try the *filet de bœuf à la fricassée de cèpes*. *Closed Fri and Sat lunch, Sun eve, Mon and two weeks in Nov.*

with three fortified towers similar to those of Cahors's Pont Valentré. Unfortunately these tumbled down when the bridge partially collapsed in a flood – hence the asymmetrical wide arch. Further evil has since been averted thanks to a frilly, dolled-up statue of Our Lady of Joy in the chapel overhanging at the north end, rebuilt in 1642.

Although the Benedictine abbey is gone, excavations have revealed bits of **Eysses**, originally the Roman *Excisum*, a pretty place with the remains of a tower and a villa 2km to the north on the Monflanquin road (***t** 05 53 70 65 19; guided visits in July and Aug 2.30–6.30*). Further north at **Castelnaud-de-Gratecambe** is a new golf holiday complex, with 27 holes and a driving range (***t** 05 53 01 60 19*).

Pujols and Two Caves

The main attraction around Villeneuve is its own mother, up on a hill, white, walled, medieval antique-dealing **Pujols**, 2km from the Pont Vieux . This was originally a Celtic oppidum that remained continuously inhabited until its allegiance to the Cathars earned it near-total obliteration in the Albigensian Crusade. To enter Pujols's ancient square, pass under the arch of the tower of 15th-century Flamboyant Gothic **St-Nicolas**. The church has star vaulting inside, and curious tribunes with little fireplaces so the barons of Pujols could attend Mass more snugly. A chapel on the left contains bits discovered and moved here during various remodellings – Gothic tombstones and a Renaissance mausoleum, originally in the choir. A second church in Pujols, **Ste-Foy la Jeune**, dates from the 1400s and contains some excellent murals from the period, one showing Ste Foy (Faith) of Agen, a 3rd-century maiden whom the Romans burned on a gridiron, just as they did St Lawrence. Although her cult centre is up at Conques (Aveyron), some of her relics were taken to Glastonbury and a number of English churches were named after her.

Ten kilometres south of Pujols on the road to Agen are the **Grottes de Fontirou** (***t** 05 53 41 73 97; open 10–12.30 and 2–6 daily July and Aug; 2–5.30 Sun and hols only Easter, May and the first half of June; 2–5.30 daily second half of June and first half of Sept; adm*), with extraordinary limestone formations. About 7km northwest, in **Ste-Colombe**, the **Grottes de Lestournelles** (***t** 05 53 40 08 09; open July and Aug 10–12 and 2–7, Sept–Jun weekends and hols only, same hours; adm*) are just as splendid.

The Prune Kingdom: Villeneuve to Aiguillon

Some 65 per cent of all French plums come from the Lot-et-Garonne and, dried as *pruneaux d'Agen*, are known around the world. As it happens, however, most of them do not come from Agen at all, but from the rich lands of this last stage of the Lot valley. It isn't a touristy area, but a businesslike, well-off agricultural paradise, packed tightly with not only plum orchards but strawberries, asparagus and all the other *primeurs* that decorate France's markets around the year.

Casseneuil to Granges

After Villeneuve, the first village on the Lot is medieval **Casseneuil**, a picturesque place built on a peninsula formed by the confluence of the Lot and Lède. Charlemagne himself apparently had a summer house there in the 9th century. Since good stone was lacking in this part of the Lot valley, nearly everything is made of brick, including most of Casseneuil's houses and its church, containing good

Pruneaux d'Agen

We all remember the episode in *Le Tour de Gaule d'Astérix* in which a treacherous Agenais innkeeper tries to capture Astérix and Obelix by slipping a Mickey into their prunes. And you will be as shocked as we were to learn that this is a flagrant anachronism. It seems that the first plums in the area were brought over from Damascus by the crusaders in 1148; they took at once to the local soil and climate, and people soon learned to dry them out for the famous *pruneaux d'Agen*, the prunes of Agen, which as every French gourmet knows are the finest in the universe. Most come from a fast-drying plum called *prune d'ente*, a word derived after the old French *enter*, 'to graft'. Go to any local market to discover the extraordinary variety of prunes. The Lot-et-Garonne produces, on average, 30,000 metric tonnes a year. You'll see a considerable portion of them prettily displayed in the purple shop windows of Agen: boxes of *pruneaux fourrés* (prunes stuffed with chocolate, etc.) jars of prune cream, and prunes in armagnac. There are also some really excellent prune liqueurs and *eaux de vie* made by small local producers – you'll see them on sale occasionally in pâtisseries. Local cooks bend themselves over backwards to come up with new ways to employ prunes in cuisine; recipes combine them with quail, rabbit, pork and even fish.

Alose aux Pruneaux (Shad with Prunes)

(from the Marmande tourist office)

Clean and cut 1.5kg of shad into sections. Soak 20 Agen prunes in warm water for 5mins, drain and stone them and cook for 8mins on low heat with a clove and orange peel in a cup of Côtes du Marmandais. Quickly brown the shad sections in a little oil in a large saucepan, sprinkle with armagnac, set alight and remove the fish. In the same pan sauté 150g chopped shallots, 50g thinly sliced carrots, 50g thinly sliced celery, and garlic, thyme, parsley and a bay leaf. Add the sauce from the prunes and two cups of red wine (minus a small glass) and then, when it's a quarter boiled down, add a half cup of *fumet de poisson* (or fish bouillon). Cook for another 5mins, then add the fish and prunes and cook for 20mins. When the fish is done, remove fish and prunes, strain the sauce and put back on the heat, add the glass of wine and season. Remove skin and bones of shad, arrange on a plate with the sauce ladled on top, sprinkle with chives, and then give it to the cat.

15th-century frescoes. The same goes for **Ste-Livrade-sur-Lot**, where there is an odd brick fortification called the Tour du Roi, the *roi* in this case being its builder, Richard the Lion-Heart. The bricks of Ste-Livrade's church are half eroded away, giving the building a strangely outlandish air. This was the church of an important priory, although the ambitions of its founders far outran the resources of those who followed. Look inside for some fine carvings in the 'Romanesque Chapel', now housing the main altar: on the capitals, a mermaid and her baby, a satyr and a monster or two. Down river, the humdrum church at **Fongrave** contains an unexpected masterpiece: a beautifully sculpted wooden Baroque altarpiece.

Next down the river on the south bank, **Le-Temple-sur-Lot** was named for the Templar headquarters that oversaw all the order's holdings in the Agenais; the red brick commandery building survives, along with its chapel, now the village church. Near the village, the century-old botanical gardens of the **Latour-Marliac** garden company (*open mid-Mar–Oct 9–6*) have over a hundred varieties of lotuses, water lilies and other water-loving plants, at their best between May and September.

In the hills to the south, off the D13, you can find your way to a delightful place called **St-Sardos**, a tiny, sleepy hamlet decked with flowers and sleeping dogs. The 12th-century church on the green has a lovely, well-preserved portal carved with beasts and floral designs. Where the D13 meets the river stands the unfortunately named **Castelmoron-sur-Lot**, where the Lot is backed up by a dam to make a little lake for swimming and boating; there's a beach along the river. The *mairie* occupies an Arabian Nights villa, built by the nostalgic wife of a former ambassador to Syria. The hills to the north of Castelmoron are quite pretty, though there is nothing to detain you there except another *bastide*, **Monclar d'Agenais**, built on a hill by Alphonse de Poitiers, enjoying lovely views in all directions. West of here, at **Brugnac**, you can visit **Le Chaudron Magique** (***t** 05 53 88 80 77; open daily Sept–June 3–6, July and Aug 10–6; adm*), where you can learn about raising angora goats, rabbits, other animals and natural plant dyes; there are baby goats for the kids to bottle-feed and a shop selling yarn, mohair pullovers and goat cheese.

In **Granges-sur-Lot**, just downstream from Castelmoron, one of the largest plum farms in the valley has created the **Prune Museum** (Domaine de Gabach, ***t** 05 53 84 00 69; open daily 9–12 and 2–7, Sun and hols 3–7, Nov–Mar closes at 6.30, closed last two weeks in Jan; adm*) for the curious and the constipated; a 35min prune video, old drying ovens, local costumes, a prune jammery and *chocolaterie*, free tastings and the plummiest shop in the hemisphere are only some of the attractions.

Clairac to Aiguillon

Clairac presents a beautiful panorama from the riverfront; from the inside, it is perhaps less beautiful, and has little to show from a busy history. Clairac once had a great abbey, where a roving monk brought back and planted the first *pétum* (tobacco) in France, beginning an important chapter in the local economy; the abbey itself was wrecked in the Wars of Religion, leaving only a bit called the Tour Ronde and bits restored from the ruins to become the **Abbaye des Automates** (***t** 05 53 79 34 81; open April–Oct daily 10–6, Nov–Mar Wed, Sat and Sun 10–6; adm*), where the clockwork monks work, pray and illuminate manuscripts, and dozens of other figures illustrate favourite fairy tales. Little kids think it's a gas. Upstairs there are scenes of celebrated characters who spent some time at Clairac. You can also see the **Forêt des Allumettes**, moved from Miramont-de-Guyenne, where you can visit all of France's best-known monuments made out of matchsticks; there is also a collection of model ships. Nearby you can visit other models, this time of trains, at the **Musée du Train** (***t** 05 53 88 04 30; same times and adm as Abbaye des Automates*) and something for the kids, **La Forêt Magique**, with gnomes and elves (***t** 05 53 84 27 54; same times and adm as Abbaye des Automates*). East of Clairac on the D911, follow the old blue historic marker

Getting Around

During the summer there are opportunities for **river** excursions of various kinds.

From Casseneuil you can hire a small *gabare* (**t** 05 53 95 69 77), a canoe, kayak, pedalo or other boat (**t** 05 53 41 12 22); from Castelmoron an electric boat (**t** 05 53 79 58 17), pedalo (**t** 05 53 84 27 41) or house boat by the week from Connoisseur for four to twelve people (**t** 05 53 79 58 17); from Clairac a motor boat (**t** 05 53 84 34 48) or take a trip on *L'Epervier* (**t** 05 53 84 34 48).

Tourist Information

Casseneuil: 45 Les Promenades, **t** 05 53 41 13 33, **f** 05 53 41 14 13 (*summer only*).
Aiguillon: Rue F. Sabatté, **t** 05 53 79 62 58.

Market Days

Casseneuil: Wed and Sun.
Ste-Livrade: Fri.
Monclar d'Agenais: Wed and Sat.
Clairac: Thurs in summer.
Castelmoron: Tues.
Aiguillon: Tues and Fri.

Where to Stay and Eat

Casseneuil ✉ 47440

*__Auberge La Résidence__, on the Route de Villeneuve, **t** 05 53 41 08 08 (*cheap*). A simple but sweet little place to stay, with restaurant and shady terrace; some rooms with bath (*menus 60–100F*). *Closed Sun and 10 days around Christmas.*

Ste-Livrade-sur-Lot ✉ 47110

__Le Midi__, 1 Rue Malfourat, **t 05 53 01 00 32, **f** 05 53 49 43 97 (*inexpensive*). A Logis hotel in the village with comfortable rooms and a restaurant serving, for a change, Basque meals, as well as the usual (*menus 70–135F*). *Closed Sun and Mon Oct–May and Nov.*

Le Temple-sur-Lot ✉ 47110

La Commanderie, **t** 05 53 01 30 66. A restored 12th-century building set among fountains and water plants, serving tasty dishes with verve – duck with quince, for instance (*menus 80–230F lunch, others more*). *Closed Sun eve and Mon exc July and Aug.*

Tombebœuf ✉ 47380

__Du Nord__, north of Monclar, **t 05 53 88 83 15, **f** 05 53 88 25 28 (*inexpensive*). A Logis hotel a

signs and with luck you will find your way to one of the most remarkable monuments of the region: an ornate monumental stone **fountain** most likely the work of Jean Goujon, France's master sculptor of the Renaissance, standing at the edge of a broad lawn (*private property; ask at the house to visit*).

The Lot meets the Garonne at **Aiguillon**, a town that began as a Roman encampment but knew its greatest fame as the residence of the wealthy Duc d'Aiguillon, a political figure of the last days of the *ancien régime* whose little court and decadent parties here made Aiguillon the hot spot of the Agenais in the summer, when lots of swells (including the duke's friend Madame du Barry) came down from Versailles. It is to him that the town owes its landmark **château** (1765), a stately work of early neoclassical architecture.

The Pays des Serres

A local geography teacher gets credit for naming the triangle between the Lot and Garonne the *pays des Serres*. It is a fitting word: *serres* means an eagle's talons (the

bit outside the usual circuit, useful in this area where hotels are thin on the ground. It has a restaurant (*menus 60–160F*). *Closed Fri and Sun eves out of season and the first two weeks of Jan.*

Castelmoron-sur-Lot ✉ 47260

Ferme de l'Isle, t 05 53 84 98 36. Book to get a table at this delightful riverside *ferme-auberge*, where you can idle the afternoon away over good-value, good-tasting lunches – try the *croq'agenais*, the *ne plus ultra* of *croque-monsieurs*, made with prunes marinated in armagnac and foie gras (*menus 89–149F, children's menu 40F*). The children can splash around in the kiddie pool, and there may well be a catapult lying around to admire: the owner's hobby is building medieval war machines. *Open Easter–1 Nov weekends only, daily in July and Aug.*

Monclar d'Agenais ✉ 47380

Ferme Auberge de Roussay, on the D667, **t** 05 53 41 82 10. Solid meaty fare (*menus 65–140F*) which you can eat in a large airy dining room or a smaller, more intimate one with a fireplace. There is a plesant garden. *Closed Sun eve. Book.*

Clairac ✉ 47320

Le Relais de Compostelle, t 05 53 79 77 11. Before or after the mechanical monks, dine on this nearby pretty terrace overlooking the river; duck- and goose-based menus on weekdays (*89F*). There's a pool. *Open early April–Oct daily, thereafter on weekends only.*

Chambres d'Hôte Le Caussinat, between Clairac and Granges-sur-Lot, **t** 05 53 84 22 11 (*inexpensive*). A big rambling farmhouse overlooking fields, which will make you think of your great aunt's large Victorian parlour. There is a pool and large garden. Eat in the evening with the family; meals from fresh farm produce (*90F*). *Closed Nov–Jan.*

Aiguillon ✉ 47190

****Le Jardin des Cygnes**, in the countryside along the Route de Villeneuve, **t** 05 53 79 60 02, **f** 05 53 88 10 22 (*inexpensive*). Simple rooms and a pool; the restaurant serves up some surprises, on the order of *confit de porc et chutney de pruneaux* (*menus from 78F*). *Closed Sat, except in mid-June–mid-Aug, and mid-Dec–mid-Jan.*

****La Terrasse de l'Étoile, t** 05 53 79 64 64, **f** 05 53 79 46 48 (*inexpensive*). Central hotel with stylish, individualized Art Deco rooms and a little pool and terrace (*menus from 78F*).

limestone looks as if it has been clawed by a huge bird, leaving gashes between its limestone 'tables'); coincidentally the word also means greenhouses, and there are plenty of these too – or more likely plastic tunnels for fruit and vegetable *primeurs*, which farmers have lately added to supplement the income from their wheatfields.

Little *Bastides* and Foie Gras

Many of the villages in the *pays des Serres* haven't changed much since the Middle Ages, places such as **Hautefage-la-Tour**, south of Villeneuve, with a Flamboyant Gothic church, hexagonal Renaissance bell tower and a village *lavoir* in the centre. Nearby **Laroque-Timbaut** has a 12th-century *halle* and tiny medieval lanes, especially the Ruelle de Lô, entered under the clock tower. According to legend, a church and fountain in the nearby Vallon de St-Germain cured Roland's army of a contagious disease on their way to Spain. You can visit a living museum of over 50 old breeds of poultry and other animals at **Les Vallons de Marennes** (***t** 05 53 95 97 32; open mid-June–mid-Sept 10–7; adm*). To the northeast, **Frespech** is a delightful little hilltop hamlet, where old gates and houses, and an 11th-century church with a partial *lauze*

Tourist Information

Puymirol: 7 Rue Maréchal Leclerc, **t** 05 53 95 32 10 (*summer only*).
Prayssas: Av Jean Jaurès, **t** 05 53 95 00 15.

Market Days

Beauville: Sun June–Sept farmer's market.
Castelsagrat: Sun.
Puymirol: Sun May–Oct farmer's market.
Porte Ste-Marie: Sat farmer's market.

Where to Stay and Eat

Laroque-Timbault ✉ 47340

Le Roquentin, opposite the church, **t** 0553 95 78 78. It can easily be missed as you pass through the village but if you make a point of looking for it you will be rewarded with a pleasant restaurant and fine food at reasonable prices (*menus from 60F*). The 140F *menu gourmand* includes *salade de St-Jacques aux crevettes, tournedos sauté aux deux poivres, chevre chaud au miel* and dessert. *Closed Sun eve, and Mon and Thurs eve out of season.*

Beauville ✉ 47470

*__Hôtel du Midi__, in the centre, **t** 05 53 95 41 18, **f** 05 53 95 47 12. A sweet little place, with good home-cooking (*menus 73–160F*). *Closed Mon eve and the first two weeks of Sept.*

Bourg-de-Visa ✉ 82190

La Marquise, overlooking the Château de Brassac, **t** 05 63 94 25 16 (*inexpensive*). The award-winning chef Michèle Dio prepares fragrant specialities mixing fowl and fruit (duck or goose stuffed with fruit, guinea fowl with prunes), as well as traditional cassoulet (*menus from 90F*). *Book*. It's also a bed-and-breakfast. Cooking classes available, if you want to learn how.

Ferme-auberge de Lasbourdettes, out in the country on the D7 south, 3km from the Château de Brassac, **t** 05 63 94 26 75. A delicious variety of menus including wine and

roof, still stand intact. Here you can learn all about the manna of the southwest at the **Musée de Foie Gras** (***t*** *05 53 41 23 24; open 15 June–Sept daily 10–7; other times daily 3–7; adm includes tastings*), on an hour-long guided visit of the history of *gavage* and modern techniques on the farm.

Further east are two baby *bastides*: **Beauville**, clinging to its promontory, complete with its arcades, vestiges of its walls and Gothic church with a pyramidal bell tower, and **Bourg-de-Visa**, near a sacred Gaulish spring now known as the Source de St-Quirin. Just southeast of Bourg at **Fauroux** (take the D43), there's a fine little Romanesque church of St-Romain and one of the prettiest places to swim in the region: the 'tropical' lagoon of **Rikiki Plage**, with a little waterfall and white sandy beach. South on the D7 bristles the moated, four-towered, military **Château de Brassac** (***t*** *05 63 94 59 67; open mid-June–mid-Sept 10–12 and 2–6, closed Tues*), built in 1180 by Raymond V of Toulouse.

In the same area you'll find **Castelsagrat**, another *bastide* (vintage 1270), with its old communal wells in the irregularly arcaded *place*, and a church of the Assumption with a wonderfully overripe 17th-century Baroque retable. Just west on its hill, half-timbered, 13th-century **Montjoi**, with only two streets, could win a prize as the tiniest *bastide* of all. **St-Maurin**, further west, is a charming, half-timbered village near the ruins of an abbey founded in 1097 by the abbots of Moissac and destroyed in 1802. Bits that were salvaged, including the altar, and a model of the abbey, may be seen in the church of **St-Martin d'Anglars**, as well as carved capitals telling the story of Maurin's martyrdom. The inhabitants of St-Maurin have put together a small but

coffee, featuring locally raised duck, goose and rabbit dishes (*90–200F*).

Puymirol ✉ 47270

★★★★**L'Aubergade**, 52 Rue Royale, **t** 05 53 95 31 46, **f** 05 53 95 33 80 (*expensive*). This little *bastide* once belonging to the Counts of Toulouse, 17km east of Agen, has something few one-horse towns ever dream of in their brightest moments: one of the top-rated restaurants in France. The beautifully medieval/modern place is run by master chef Michel Trama, who takes local ingredients – foie gras, *cèpes*, duckling, snails and so on – and combines them with the sure art, imagination and magic of an early Renaissance master, complete with all the pretensions that only the French can muster. Trama's desserts are legendary – warm chocolate cake with an exquisite sour sauce, or the *larme de chocolat* with tiny morello cherries (*weekday lunch menu 200F, also menus at 295 and 680F, easily much more à la carte or with a fine Bordeaux*). *Booking mandatory. Closed Sun eve , Mon and Tues lunch out of season*. L'Aubergade is also a Relais et Châteaux hotel, with 11 gorgeous rooms, all opening on to a garden courtyard.

Prayssas ✉ 47360

La Grangette, **t** 05 53 87 28 06. In a 17th-century *gentilhommière*, with five comfortable rooms; it's being taken over by new management in early 2001 so ring for details.

Clermont-Dessous ✉ 47130

Crêperie-grill Le Troubadour, on the main village street, **t** 05 53 87 24 45. Sit outside on the small terrace under the fairy lights and admire the scenery, whilst enjoying grilled meats or *galettes de sarrasin* and crêpes with any one of a large selection of fillings. Not exciting fare but the location is worth it (*100F menu, the rest à la carte, moderate prices*). *Closed Mon, and Tues out of season.*

intriguing **Musée de la Vie Agricole et Artisanale** in the abbey cellars, where they found the 13th-century tombs of the monks (***t** 05 53 95 36 45; open July and Aug 10–12 and 3–7, closed Tues; at other times ask the* mairie).

Puymirol, Prayssas and Around

Towards Agen is the *bastide* of **Puymirol**, built by Count Raymond VII of Toulouse in 1246. Located on a bluff, with a citadel and deep moat at its weakest point, Puymirol was believed to be impregnable until the Protestants shattered that illusion in 1574. Much of medieval Puymirol has survived – the counts' residence, the *cornières* and *halle* (now the village *salle de fêtes*), the 13th-century Gothic porch of the church, and the views from the Champs de Mars, site of the citadel before Richelieu had it razed. The most interesting part of the western *Serres* is around **Prayssas**, a round *bastide*, market town and Chasselas grape grower. North of Prayssas, there once stood another *bastide* called St-Sardos, founded in 1323 by pro-French monks connected with Sarlat. This founding angered the pro-English contingent at nearby Monpezat, who attacked and demolished the new town, put the monks to the sword and hanged the French seneschal from the maypole that had been set up to celebrate the founding of the *bastide*. Sorting out the incident caused the king of England to delay his homage to Charles IV for the duchy of Aquitaine, giving Charles sufficient reason to send in an army to confiscate Aquitaine and ignite the Hundred Years' War.

South of Prayssas, medieval **Clermont-Dessous** is clustered under a handsome 11th-century fortified church and ruins of a castle, and offers superb views down the

Garonne valley. In the 1950s the village was completely abandoned, but now it has been almost entirely restored. Catherine de' Medici and her daughter Marguerite de Valois spent time hiding out from the Protestants at **Port-Ste-Marie**, and met Henri of Navarre there – Marguerite's future husband. The 16th-century church of Notre-Dame was an important pilgrimage church for rivermen, who would pray here before braving the next particularly dangerous stretch of the Garonne. These days the village is known for its kiwis – at Sanz-Japienou, they even make kiwi wine and *eau de vie*.

Agen

Caesar made the first known mention of the future prune capital, then the humble hilltop *oppidum* of Aginnum, in his *Gallic Wars*. In the *Pax Romana* that followed, Aginnum re-located down into the Garonne valley, where it suffered the usual barbarian and Norman invasions. In the 13th century Agen found itself smack on the front lines between French and English territory. It changed hands 11 times in the Hundred Years' War, but it could have been worse – each new ruler would try to make the Agenais happy to see him by granting the town new privileges.

Even after becoming a *commune* in the 13th century, Agen was under the influence of its noble bishops. During the Renaissance many of these were Italian, and they gave the little provincial town a jump-start in art appreciation and the humanities. A booming textile trade, begun in the 17th century when Agen grew by leaps and bounds, was snuffed out by the Continental Blockade. These days it owes much of its prosperity to its location midway between Bordeaux and Toulouse; transport depots, fruit-packing and bureaucracy are the things that keep the money coming in.

Jasmin, the 'Hero of the Occitan Renaissance'

Jacques Boé (1798–1864), son of a humble tailor of Agen, was a wig-maker who liked to recite the poems he wrote in his native Occitan to his customers. In 1830 he published the fruits of his labours, the *Papillotos*, under the name of his grandfather, Jacques Jasmin; by chance the book was picked up by Charles Nodier, the author of *Trilby*, who made the verses the toast of Paris. The capital was then in the midst of a fervent, slightly retarded Romantic era, and the wigmaker-poet of Agen caught its fancy. Fellow poet Lamartine dubbed Jasmin 'the Homer of the Proletariat'; the Académie Française honoured him; he was received by Louis Philippe and Napoleon III, and embarked on a lecture tour across France, reciting his poetry and donating all the proceeds to charity. Provençal poet Frédéric Mistral (who went on to become the only Nobel prizewinner in literature in a minority language) idolized Jasmin and in 1854 asked him to lead his Occitan literary movement, the *Félibrage*. But Jasmin preferred to devote the rest of his life to poetry and charity. Perhaps his finest lyrics were his love songs to Agen: *Me fas troubà, pel sero de ma bito/Sourel del mèl et cami del belour*... (You found for me in the evening of my life/A sun of honey and velvet way...)

Getting Around

Agen's **airport**, La Garenne, **t** 05 53 96 22 50, to the southwest, is served by three flights a day to Paris with Air Liberté, **t** 0803 805 805. There are several **trains** a day to Monsempron-Libos, Penne, Périgueux and Les Eyzies, and TGVs to Bordeaux, Toulouse and Paris from the station at Place Rabelais. For a **taxi, t** 05 53 98 32 33. Or rent a **houseboat** from Locaboat Plaisance in the summer to sail along the Canal Lateral. Boat trips lasting 1.5hrs leave from Port de Plaisance, **t** 05 53 87 51 95.

Tourist Information

107 Bd Carnot, **t** 05 53 47 36 09, **f** 05 53 47 29 98.

For information on most conceivable aspects of the Lot-et-Garonne, contact the Maison du Tourisme, 4 Rue André Chenier, B. P. 158, Agen, **t** 05 53 66 14 14, **f** 05 53 68 25 42.

Market Days

Wed and Sun, Place du Pin; Sat Esplanade du Gravier and Place des Laitiers; annual prune fair in Place 14-Juillet in mid-Sept.

Sports and Activities

Parc Walibi, at nearby Roquefort, is one of the biggest amusement parks in southwest France, with rides, shows of various kinds, and a waterpark for a day out with the kids (*t 05 53 96 58 32; open May, june and early Sept week-ends and hols 10–6, July and Aug daily 10–7, sometimes until 9 at weekends*). Agen also has an outdoor heated Olympic-size pool and children's pools at Aquasud (*t 05 53 98 10 34; open July and Aug daily 10–8*).

Colayrac-St-Cirq, on the N113, has the tropical greenhouses of **Végétales Visions**, full of orchids, cacti and carnivorous plants (**t** 05 53 67 07 77; *guided tours daily 9–12 and 2–7, closed Mon and last two weeks of Jan; adm*). The local **golf course**, Bon Encontre, is nine-hole, par 70 (**t** 05 53 96 95 78; *open summer 9–8, rest of year 9–6*). Learn to pilot a ULM or have a go at karting at the **Base de Loisirs** at Caudecoste, 15km east of Agen (**t** 05 53 87 31 42; *open all year 10–12.30 and 2–dusk or 9, closed Tues*), or learn to **water ski** at Le Club Motonautique at Boé (**t** 05 53 96 77 65).

Where to Stay

Agen ✉ 47000

******Hôtel-Château des Jacobins**, Place des Jacobins, **t** 05 53 47 03 31, **f** 05 53 47 02 80 (*expensive*). Fifteen very comfortable rooms in central Agen, in a beautifully restored ivy-covered *hôtel particulier*, with private parking and a pretty garden.

*****Mariottat**, 25 Rue Louis Vivent, **t** 05 53 77 89 77, **f** 05 53 77 99 79 (*moderate*). Relocated from the outskirts of Agen to the centre, this now occupies a handsome town house; the chef-owner works wonders with the best the daily market provides (*menus 110–295F*). *Closed Sat lunch, Sun eve and Mon.*

*****Le Provence**, 22 Cours du 14 Juillet, **t** 05 53 47 39 11, **f** 05 53 68 26 24 (*moderate*). A pleasant little hotel in the centre, with spruce, soundproofed rooms.

****Atlantic Hotel**, 133 Av Jean Jaurès (the N113 going out to Toulouse), **t** 05 53 96 16 56, **f** 05 53 98 34 80 (*inexpensive*). A 1970s-style hotel on a busy road; the spacious rooms remain calm. Cool off in the swimming pool. No restaurant. *Closed end of Dec.*

***Les Ambans**, 59 Rue des Ambans, **t** 05 53 66 28 60, **f** 05 53 87 94 01 (*cheap*). One of the nicest of the cheaper places, recently remodelled, with showers in every room.

Admittedly these aren't big tourist magnets, but this shapeless, rather staid but very regular departmental capital does have an ace up its sleeve: one of the finest provincial art museums in France. Or come when the Agenais show their wild and crazy side, when their beloved rugby squad is thumping some hapless opponent. You'll know if they're doing well: all the shops in the town centre will have team photos and banners in their windows, next to all the displays of chocolate-filled prunes.

Around Agen

****Château St-Marcel, 3km south on the N113 towards Toulouse, at Boé (✉ 47550), **t** 05 53 96 61 30, **f** 05 53 96 94 33. (*expensive*). The château once belonged to Montesquieu, who may have given the order to plant the majestic cedars that line the entrance. There are sumptuous suites furnished with antiques in the 17th-century castle, or more modern (and far less pricey) rooms in the annexe; pool and tennis courts in the park. The restaurant serves imaginative, delicate combinations of local ingredients (*menus 120–250F*). *Closed Sun eve and Mon.*

La Table d'Antan, 41 Rue République, at adjacent Bon-Encontre (✉ 47240), **t 05 53 77 97 00, **f** 05 53 77 97 02 (*inexpensive*). A Logis hotel with 10 cosy country rooms opposite the shrine of the Virgin of Bon-Encontre.

Le Colombier du Touron, 187 Route des Landes, Brax, **t 05 53 87 87 91, **f** 05 53 87 82 37 (*inexpensive*). A Logis hotel west of the city with a good restaurant serving regional food, looking out over a park; or you can eat on the shaded terrace (*menus 95–250F*). *Closed Mon.*

La Corne d'Or, on the N113 towards Bordeaux, at Colayrac-St-Cirq (✉ 47450), **t 05 53 47 02 76, **f** 05 53 66 87 23 (*inexpensive*). Although on a busy road, this is a pleasant place to stay, modern and completely soundproof, with superb views over the Garonne, and an excellent restaurant, where you can become reacquainted with French classics among jovial crowds of Angenais (*menus 78–165F*). *Closed Sun eve, first week in Jan and the last two in July.*

Eating Out

Fleur de Sel, 66 Rue C. Desmoulins, **t** 05 53 66 63 70. The old Michelle Latrille has lost none of its charm and culinary expertise in the transition to its new incarnation. The food leans towards regional fare (*menus 120–210F*). *Closed Sat lunch, Sun and middle of Aug.*

Le Margoton, 52 Rue Richard Coeur de Lion, **t** 05 53 48 11 55. Another change in name, but what was once Le Petit Vatel again maintains standards. The 90F menu includes *blanc de pintade à la sauge et sa crème* (*menus 65–190F*). *Closed Mon and Sat lunch. Best to book.*

Le Grillée, 14 Rue des Cornières, **t** 05 53 66 60 24. A lively, local favourite in a cool spot under the arcades, offering on the whole regional food, but if you have had enough of duck opt for kangaroo or ostrich (*menus 63–160F*). *Closed Tues and Wed eves, Sun and bank hols.*

La Bohème, 14 Rue Emile Sentini, **t** 05 53 68 31 00. It may not have the classic appearance of a regional food haven but the chef will give you excellent southwest cooking with a personal slant; try the *magret aux épices*. There are also, for a change, Caribbean dishes (*menus 69–165F*). *Closed Sun, Wed eve, Sat lunch in winter, first half of Mar and first half of Sept.*

Le Buffet de la Gare, **t** 05 53 66 09 40. The cheapest good food, rather unusually, may be found in Agen's railway station. At lunchtime it's one of the most crowded places in town, and they make the best steak *bordelaise* you'll find anywhere.

Musée Municipal des Beaux-Arts

t 05 53 69 47 23; open May–Sept 10–6, Oct–April 10–5, closed Tues; adm.

This, the one great reason to visit Agen, is located in the centre of the city at Place du Docteur-Esquirol on the corner of Rue des Juifs, where its vast hoard occupies four beautifully restored 16th- and 17th-century *hôtels particuliers*. The collection begins with the Middle Ages – tombstones and effigies, goldwork, carved Romanesque and Gothic capitals and a 16th-century tapestry of the *month of March*. The star of the Gallo-Roman section is the *Vénus du Mas*, a 1st-century Greek marble dug up by a farmer at Mas d'Agenais in 1876, who, despite her lack of a head and part of an arm, is still a helluva tomato, a Venus de Milo in her early 20s; the special lighting perfectly shows off the exceptional cut of the drapery. Don't miss the fine small bronzes in the glass case – a Gaulish helmet, a Celtic horse head and a pawing horse. The next room, with a Renaissance chimneypiece, is devoted to hunting and warfare, with another fine tapestry and a Renaissance dagger carved with an intricate *danse macabre*. Prehistoric finds are kept downstairs where Agen used to keep its criminals – in the dungeon.

A beautiful spiral stair leads up to the 16th- and 17th-century paintings: two striking Renaissance portraits by Corneille de Lyon, a *Portrait of a Man* by Philippe de Champaigne and a *Virgin and Child* by the school of Raphael. There's a reconstruction of a pharmacy, and ceramic works by philosopher Bernard Palissy, born in 1510 in St-Avit, who desperately sought the ancient secret of enamel, burning even his furniture to light his kilns. Here too are brightly coloured plates from the same period by the Italian masters, especially from Urbino.

Beyond minor works by Tiepolo and Greuze are five **Goyas**, left to the city by Chaudordy, French ambassador to Madrid, who got them from Goya's son; they form a complement to the more important collection of Goyas at Castres. There's a powerful *Self-portrait* painted by the artist in his 40s, and one of the *Caprichos*, with a donkey, elephant and bull flying over a crowd of people. Another crowd follows the ascent of the *Mongolfière*, recording the 1793 launch of a hot-air balloon in Madrid. The *Study for an Equestrian Portrait of Ferdinand VII* was a royal commission; and Goya painted *La Misada Parida*, a picture of the first Mass of a newly delivered young mother, on top of an old painting that is slowly but surely leaching through. There's also a copy of Goya's *La promenade*, said to depict Goya and the Duchess of Alba. Other works here include *Le conteur* by Watteau.

The last rooms move on to the 19th century, first with ceramics, including those of Agen's own Boudon de St-Amas (1774–1856), who introduced English glazed-ware techniques to France. There's a fine landscape by Corot, another by Sisley, and seascapes by proto-Impressionist Eugène Boudin, the master of Monet and one of the first French painters to paint out of doors.

The Rest of Agen

Agen's cathedral, **St-Caprais** (north of the museum, a block from the station, in Rue Raspail), is named after a local boy who hid out during Diocletian's persecutions until he heard of the courageous martyrdom of Ste Foy, whereupon he outed himself as a Christian, only to get his head chopped off. There isn't much to see inside (just as well, because it's often closed) other than the Romanesque tri-lobe apse with *modillons* sculpted with heads of humans and animals. In the northwest corner of Agen an impressive 23-arch aqueduct, the **Pont Canal** built in 1839, carries the Canal Latéral over the Garonne.

Besides a stroll around Agen's prune-laden *pâtisseries* and *confiseries*, walk over to the banks of the Garonne and the city's favourite promenade, the **Esplanade du Gravier**. It offers a fine view of the Pont Canal, while just up Av du Général de Gaulle stands the **Monument to Jasmin**, honouring Agen's favourite poet.

South of Agen: the Brulhois, a little corner of Gascony

Vines take over from plums between Agen and the Gers in the hills of the Brulhois. Hilltop **Layrac**, 11km south of Agen, is the main town here, one that grew up around a priory consecrated by Pope Urban II in 1096, itself built over a Roman villa. Don't miss the 17th-century *fontaine-lavoir*, or the roadside cross, carved with indecipherable symbols. Its 12th-century church, **St-Martin**, has capitals on its façade adorned with intertwined demons and a striking Roman-Byzantine apse; the dome was added in the 18th century, and there's a fine marble altarpiece and 12th-century mosaic on the triumph of Samson.

Dunes and round **Caudecoste** to the east are other picturesque *bastides* to visit; **Moirax** to the west has a delightful 11th-century Romanesque **priory** with a pretty façade and more than its share of fine carvings both outside and inside, some by 17th-century master Jean Tournier. A French *bastide*, **Sérignac-sur-Garonne**, has an 11th-century church of **Notre Dame** with a peculiar spiralling bell tower, the *clocher hélicoïdal*, built in the 16th century, knocked down in 1922 and since rebuilt as it was. Nearby in **Montesquieu** you can visit the **Conservatoire Végétal Régional d'Aquitaine** (***t** 05 53 47 29 14; open 8–12 and 1.30–5.30, closed Sat afternoons and Sun; adm*) and learn about old varieties of fruit trees, see exhibitions of regional fruit and enjoy tastings. **Estillac** has a handsome 13th–16th-century château, one-time residence of Blaise de Montluc, *maréchal* of France and famous Protestant-crusher in the Wars of Religion. **Laplume** to the south was the old capital of the region and has a nice Renaissance church, with a *tour clocher*, but there's nothing feathery about it; *Penn* in Celtic means hill (the town stands on a steep one) and the Gallo-Romans called it

Where to Stay and Eat

Layrac ✉ 47390

La Terrace, Place de la Mairie, **t** 05 53 87 01 69, **f** 05 53 87 14 13. Five simple rooms and the eponymous panoramic terrace where you can dine very well indeed on quails and roast potatoes, or beautifully prepared river fish, with a good choice of wine (*menus 100–155F*). *Closed Sun eve and Mon in winter.*

Sérignac-sur-Garonne ✉ 47310

******Le Prince Noir**, **t** 05 53 68 74 30, **f** 05 53 68 71 93 (*moderate*). In a 17th-century convent, this is a comfortable place to stay, with traditional rooms and furniture and a classic southwest menu (*105–230F*). The speciality of the house is *escalope de foie de canard frais aux raisins*. Old farm machinery is dotted around a rather dry pond in the central courtyard. There's tennis and a pool.

Laplume ✉ 47310

******Château de la Lassalle**, in the hamlet of Brimont, **t** 05 53 95 10 58, **f** 05 53 95 13 01 (*moderate*). The posh place to stay in the environs, with beautiful airy rooms and a pool, and a terrace restaurant specializing in duck and its accessories, with an imaginative touch (*menus 180–330F*).

Astaffort ✉ 47220

******Le Square**, 5–7 Place de la Craste, **t** 05 53 47 20 40, **f** 05 53 47 10 38 (*moderate*). South of Layrac, Astaffort offers this big, amiable country house, with air-conditioning, TV, mini-bars and restaurant (*menus from 130F*). *Closed Sun eve and Mon.*

Une Auberge en Gascogne, 9 Fauborg Corné, **t** 05 53 67 10 27. With a good local reputation for serving traditional regional fare. In summer you can eat on the calm terrace (*menus 98–238F*). *Closed Wed and 1–20 Nov.*

Côtes-de-Brulhois

South of the Garonne, on the borders of the Gers, AOC Côtes-de-Brulhois is perhaps the least-known wine from the Lot-et-Garonne. Grown on the alluvial pebbles atop a clay and limestone bed, this well-structured, dark-red wine is made from Malbec, Tannat and Fer-savadou, as well as Merlot and Cabernet Franc. A favourite tipple of the Templars, it can be aged up to 10 years and goes well with game, rich meat dishes and cheeses. Best of all, it's much cheaper than Madiran or Cahors. Try it at the Cave Cooperative at Goulens, just south of Layrac by the N21, t 05 53 87 01 65. Or visiton the east end of the *appellation*, the Château de la Bastide, by the hilltop *bastide* Clermont-Soubiran, t 05 53 87 41 02 (*call first*), with a little museum and lovely views, as well as good bottles of Côtes-de-Brulhois.

Penna, which was eventually Latinized into Pluma. **Astaffort**, further south, grew up as a stop on a Roman and medieval thoroughfare, and has a handful of half-timbered houses, a fortified mill, and medieval churches.

Nérac

...an asylum sweeter than freedom

Clémont Marot

There's a pretty little river called the Baïse that starts up in the mountains near Lannemezan and bubbles down the Hautes-Pyrénées and Gers through rather unappreciative countryside; it doesn't pass anything particularly edifying until it gets to Nérac. This fat village counts scarcely more than 7,000 inhabitants, but its association with the d'Albret family in the 1500s has given it some fine monuments and the air of a little capital, if you see it from the right angle.

The Château

On a height over the Baïse, this is quite the most elegant thing in Nérac – at least what's left of it. Vengeful demolitions ordered by Cardinal Richelieu in 1621 have left only one side of what was once a stout, old-fashioned castle, hiding inside it a magnificent Renaissance courtyard built by Henri d'Albret's grandfather Alain. The side that remains has a lovely loggia of twisted columns. Inside, the **Musée Henri IV** (***t*** *05 53 65 21 11; open April–June 10–12 and 2–6, closed Mon morning and Tues; July–Sept 10–12 and 3–7, closed Tues; Oct–Dec and Feb–Mar 10–12 and 2–5, closed Mon and Tues; closed Jan; adm*) is largely devoted to explanatory exhibits of the town in its heyday, with models of the château as it originally looked; downstairs is the archaeology section, with everything from a mammoth's molar to scraps of Roman pottery with their manufacturers' trademarks.

A walk from here around the old centre of Nérac won't take long: it only covers some 15 blocks. Rue de l'Ecole was the old main stem; on it you can see the 17th-

Getting Around

Nérac is a lovely place to hop on a **boat**, ever since 45km of the Baïse were reopened to navigation in 1993, with 16 locks. You can hire your own *gabare* by the day or take an excursion on a barge at Croisière du Prince Henry, **t** 05 53 84 72 50. You can also hire a *gabare* at Gabares de la Baise, **t** 05 53 65 66 66.

Tourist Information

7 Av Mondenard, off Place de l'Hôtel de Ville, **t** 05 53 65 27 75, **f** 05 53 65 97 48.

Market Days

Sat morning in the Petites Allées, and Tues eve in summer.

Where to Stay and Eat

Nérac ✉ 47600

★★**Du Château**, Av Mondenard, **t** 05 53 65 09 05, **f** 05 53 65 89 78 (*inexpensive*). The acceptable hotel will put you up for a night you won't remember; much better, they can also fill you up royally with salmon in millefeuille pastry, a roast duck laced with strawberry vinegar and other *recherché* dishes (*good 68F menu, others up to 240F*). *Closed Fri eve, Sat eve and Sun eve out of season.*

★★**Hôtel d'Albret**, 40 Allées d'Albret, **t** 05 53 97 41 10, **f** 05 53 65 20 26 (*inexpensive*). Simple and proper, in the same family for three generations, with a much loved restaurant – a pure southwest confit, lamprey and foie gras palace with an outside terrace and a choice of menus (*68–240F*). *Closed Sun eve.*

Aux Délices du Roy, 7 Rue du Château, **t** 05 53 65 81 12. Rustic charm with its low, beamed ceiling and wood, and is a fish-lover's paradise with 15 or so different kinds on the menu plus shellfish (*menus 98–195F with a menu surprise at 250F*). *Closed Wed and two weeks in winter.*

Le Relais de la Hire, 11 Rue Porte-Neuve, south of Nérac, just off the Baïse in Francescas, **t** 05 53 65 41 59. One of the best places to dine in the area, in an 18th-century country squire's house, where all the freshest ingredients appear in elegant creations such as *artichaut de l'Albret soufflé au foie gras* (*menus 140–350F*). *Closed Sun eve and Mon.*

★**La Chaumière D'Albert**, Route de Nérac, at Lavardac (✉ 47230) to the north, **t** 05 53 65 51 75, **f** 05 53 97 23 17 (*cheap*). A small, simple and ivy-covered Logis hotel with a restaurant; you can eat on the terrace (*menus 50–165F*). *Closed Sun night and Mon out of season, most of Mar and beginning of Oct.*

century (former) town hall and a fine Renaissance palace, the **Maison des Conférences**. Nérac's church of **St-Nicolas**, like most French churches of the 18th century, hardly rates a notice in most books, but this one is a cut above the norm, a restrained neoclassical 'Greek' façade that is probably the better off for never having been able to afford the statuary that was intended for it, and a clean, airy interior with some 19th-century stained glass that impresses in the way such windows are supposed to impress: it tells the whole story, from Abel and Noah up to Jesus himself behind the altar.

Entering Nérac along the Allées d'Albret, you have probably already noticed the obligatory statue of 'Our Henry', Henri IV, with a twinkle in his bronze eye. Henri spent much of his time in Nérac after the St Bartholomew's Day Massacre until he became king; he especially enjoyed hunting boar in the pine forests of the Néracais. Even then the common people were fond of him, and it didn't bother Henri at all to learn that everybody in town called him 'Big Nose' (*Grand-nas*). The statue may not do it justice.

La Garenne

From the back of the château, an elegant stair descends to the Baïse, leading to the Pont Neuf and Nérac's cross-river *faubourg*, Petit Nérac. Henri's father, Antoine de Bourbon, laid out a royal park here for his family called **La Garenne**, stretching for over a mile along the riverfront, which has survived to become the town's outstanding civic embellishment. Everyone in Nérac comes here in the afternoon, to stroll along the Baïse, to fish, or just to take the kids to the playground. Near the entrance on Avenue Georges-Clémenceau, a small brick shelter covers a bit of **Roman mosaic**, excavated in an important villa that once stood near by. Further on you'll come to the **Fontaine de Fleurette**. According to the local legend, Fleurette was the daughter of Antoine and Jeanne d'Albret's gardener, and Henri's first love – when he abandoned her, she drowned herself in the river. If you like, you may take La Garenne as the setting for *Love's Labour's Lost*; most of the action of the play takes place in 'the king's park at Navarre'.

Petit Nérac's streets are as old as the town centre; the best part is along the river, picturesque **Rue Séderie**, site of the tanneries that were Nérac's main business in the old days. Now most of its houses have been restored (there's an art gallery). Around the corner on Rue Sully is the 16th-century **Vieux Pont**, and the **Maison de Sully**, a 16th-century house where Henri IV's great minister stayed when Henri was in Nérac.

The Néracais

This very pleasant *pays*, tucked between the Armagnac and the pine forests of the Landes, is also often called, along with parts of the neighbouring Landes, the 'Pays d'Albret'; its long history as the feudal domain of the d'Albrets has given it an identity that endures to this day.

Bastides, Castles and a Famous Mill

South of Nérac on the D656, where the road crosses the river Osse, there is a pretty medieval bridge called the **Pont Romain**. The next village, **Mézin**, was the home of Armand Fallières, president of France in 1906–13. Fallières's presidency caused no embarrassment to Mézin, and consequently the villagers have honoured him by naming their main square after him. The **Musée du Liège et du Bouchon** (***t** 05 53 65 68 16; open daily June–Sept 10–12.30 and 2–7, Oct and Feb–May Tues–Sun 2–6.30, Nov–Jan weekends and school hols 2–6.30*) has been given some zip: you can learn about the fabrication of corks through lively exhibition areas and the history of a family involved in the business. Mézin grew up around an important Cluniac abbey, and it retains the church of **St-Jean**, Romanesque in the apse and the rest strong and graceful Gothic – though the builders may have botched it: currently there are cracks in the vault and iron girders holding up a tilted column. On the vault over the altar, note the whimsical carving of a grimacing giant and pot of flowers. The tympanum on the north door must have been destroyed in the Revolution; replacing it you can

The Marguerite of Marguerites

It was no accident that the d'Albret family came into such spectacular prominence in the 15th and 16th centuries. They were in fact the agents of the French Crown. Their loyalty assured Paris an important ally in a Gascony that had few natural ties to France, made up of regions that had become accustomed to a large degree of independence under English sovereignty and the feudal anarchy that had preceded it. In return, the French kings showered every sort of prize on the family, not the least of which were advantageous marriages to increase the d'Albrets' wealth and influence. With their help Henri d'Albret became king of Navarre, at which point King François I found him a fitting match for his sister, Marguerite d'Angoulême (1492–1549).

Already a widow at 35, it was Marguerite's second go. Everyone at the time counted her the most eligible lady of France – not just for being the king's sister, but for a wit, charm and intelligence that stood out even in Renaissance courts. Henri d'Albret was no match for her, but he had sense enough to take care of political business and stay out of the way while Marguerite turned their favoured residence of Nérac into a brilliant court where poetry and the new humanistic learning were the order of the day. Though they never converted themselves, Henri and Marguerite welcomed many of the new Protestant thinkers to Nérac, including John Calvin; dissenters circulated Bibles and preached openly. Among the poets who enjoyed Marguerite's favour was Clément Marot of Cahors, who wrote some fulsome lines in her honour, describing her as *plus mère que maistresse*. Marguerite had literary ambitions of her own. Best known among her works, and widely popular throughout France, was the *Heptameron*, a collection of stories with a frame tale of travellers snowbound at Sarrance in the Pyrenees, inspired by Boccaccio's *Decameron*.

Marguerite and Henri had a cute little daughter, known to everyone in France as Mignonne, the nickname her uncle, King François, had given her. Sitting in at her parents' table, Jeanne must have been much more impressed with the fiery preachers than the poets. She grew up to be the redoubtable Jeanne d'Albret – 'nothing in her of a woman but the sex' – a dour, intolerant Protestant who enforced her theological opinions on most of her subjects, including the Néracais, and contributed as much as anyone in keeping the flames of the religious wars burning. As evidence for the argument that traits and qualities skip generations, consider Jeanne's son, the fellow who was brought up a good Protestant and fought across France for the cause, but finally found a way to use good sense and tolerance to put an end to the troubles – he was King Henri IV.

still (barely) make out some Revolutionary slogan about the 'Supreme Being'. These are common enough in French village churches; the radicals in Paris were telling the peasants that it was all right to believe in God, though not necessarily the god of the Christian Church – it's a mystery, though, that so many of these inscriptions survive.

Ask the tourist office for a copy of their leaflet on circuits of trees and chapels in the Mézin area. You could get lost for a long time in the lush, delightful countryside around Mézin and never mind it. On the stretch of the D656 that follows the valley of the Gélise, you'll pass pretty things like a country chapel and a traditional Agenais *pigeonnier* on stilts, and plenty of farmers hang signs out to sell you asparagus and *cèpes*, foie gras, and *Floc de Gascogne*, the 'Flower of Gascony' – the sweet apéritif wine, made since the 1500s and revived, uniquely for France, almost exclusively by women, the *Dames du Floc de Gascogne*.

Armagnac

Although the main growing area of that most Gascon drink of all, armagnac, is just south in the Gers, all the growers owe a debt to Armand Fallières of Mézin, who just happened to be a vintner before he became president of France, and who, in 1909, decreed the current AOC armagnac area, which actually extends as far north as Agen and nearly as far south as the Pyrenees, although in practice only a strictly limited 20,000 hectares are under production.

Armagnac is the oldest known *eau-de-vie* distilled from grapes. The first written record of the process goes back to 1411 (arch-rival cognac dates only from the 17th century); it proved by far to be the best way to treat the weak, local white wine nicknamed *picquepoul*, 'tingle-lips', for its principal feature: acidity. The Dutch provided the first market for the stuff; before setting out on a long voyage, they would outfit their ships with a great barrel of *vin brûlé*, or brandy. In the late 19th century, when armagnac was the rage, 100,000 hectares were planted – just in time to be totally devasted by phylloxera. Since then 10 different varieties of resistant white grapes are permitted to be grown, the leading one called bacco 22A, a hybrid of the original *picquepoul* and noah.

The essential technique for making armagnac hasn't changed since 1818, when the Marquis de Bonas patented an armagnac still that permitted a single-pass distillation process as opposed to the old two-step process still used in cognac. Some time between December and April, when the wine has finished fermenting, it is distilled; two specialists, the *brûleurs*, watch the still day and night to maintain a constant temperature. It is during distallation that the distinctive armagnac aromas are made in embryonic forms – violets, roses and plum flowers. Fresh from the still, the armagnac is a rough brandy with an alchohol content ranging from 58° to 63°; it is put in a 400-litre black oak cask and shut away in a dark storeroom. In the first decade of ageing, some six per cent is lost every year through evaporation ('the angels' share') and is carefully replenished by distilled water; meanwhile the brandy receives its distinctive golden hue by dissolving the tannins of the wood. The tannins make the brandy bitter, although after 10 years the bitterness gives way to the natural armagnac fragrance and the brandy is transferred into old tannin-less casks. The finest are aged for up to 40 years in oak barrels, demanding constant care and attention. When the *maître de chai* decides that at last the armagnac has achieved its quintessence, further evolution is stopped by transferring it to glass vats or bottles.

Tourist Information

Mézin: Place Armand Fallières, **t** 05 53 65 77 46.
Barbaste: Place de la Mairie, **t** 05 53 65 84 85.

Market Days

Mézin: Thurs and Sun farmers' market.
Barbaste: Mon.
Durance: Tues afternoons.
Vianne: Fri eve June–Sept.

Where to Stay and Eat

Poudenas and Environs ✉ 47170

*****Roi Henri**, just down the D656, **t** 05 53 65 72 57 (*cheap*). The bargain choice just happens to be a lovely half-timbered 17th-century post house, with basic rooms and a 55F menu.

Le Postillon, Place Delbousquet, in nearby Sos, **t** 05 53 65 60 27 (*cheap*). If you don't care for mills or stage stops, try this one in a restored smithy, with a few cosy rooms, and nice fat *magrets* and *confits* with *cèpes* out on the terrace (*menus 55–210F*).

La Ferme du Boué, southwest in Ste-Maure-de-Peyriac, **t** 05 53 65 63 94. Excellent rillettes, foie gras and more await. The full whack, with apéritif, wine and digestif, will set you back around 140F. *Book. Closed in winter.*

Sept Princes, Av J Bertrand, Mézin, **t** 05 53 65 83 04, **f** 05 53 65 15 60 (*cheap*). Simple but satisfactory rooms (with shower) and a restaurant serving traditional food; there's a shaded terrace for the summer (*menus 60–105F*).

Moncrabeau ✉ 47600

****Le Phare**, **t** 05 53 65 42 08, **f** 05 53 97 04 87 (*inexpensive*). France's finest liars bed down at this traditional provincial hotel with a garden (*see* below), but there's no fibbing or prevaricating in the kitchen: solid southwest cuisine rules OK (*menus 98–168F*). *Closed Sun eve, Mon out of season and Oct and mid-Jan–end of Mar.*

Poudenas, Moncrabeau and Around

Poudenas is famous for its good restaurants, its old bridge and a fine Italianate **château** to visit, with period furniture and paintings (***t** 05 53 65 70 53; open mid-May–Oct Sun 3–6, mid-July–Aug Tues–Sun 3–6; adm*). Built in the 13th century by the lords of Poudenas, vassals of Edward I, it was given its elegant Italian touches in the 17th century; the tour includes tastings of the château's *Floc de Gascogne*. There are Romanesque churches at **Sos** and **Gueyze**, and a fortified church with traces of frescoes from the 1200s at **Villeneuve-de-Mézin**, south of Mézin. **Meylan**, just inside the pine forest of the Landes, is a tiny village that seems to consist of a swing set, a *mairie* in a shed, a picnic table and a war memorial, yet it contains so many curiosities that the Meylanais have drawn out a little itinerary for them, posted in front of the *mairie*. The circuit includes the **château** and unusual Romanesque **church** of St-Pau, a small **cromlech** hidden in the pine woods, called Las Naous Peyros, and the **Lac Sans-fond**. As the name implies, no one has yet found the bottom of this mysterious little lake. There are a number of legends: about the phantom that haunts it, and about the church that once stood on its bank (the lake swallowed it up one Sunday, parishioners and all).

East and south of Nérac, the landscapes are much the same. You can visit the attractive *bastide* of **Lamontjoie** (they've got St Louis' hand in a reliquary in the church), or else swap some lies with the experts at **Moncrabeau**. Over 200 years ago, a jolly, tale-telling monk founded the Académie des Menteurs here, and ever since its 40 members (just like the Académie Française) have met every year on the first Sunday in August to throw the bull around and elect the King of Liars, consecrated in a solemn ceremony at the 'stone of truth'. Every three years this droll village also hosts the World Face-pulling Championship.

Barbaste and Vianne

North of Nérac, the D930 takes you to **Barbaste**, and one of the famous sights of the southwest, the **Moulin de Henri IV** (***t*** *05 53 65 09 37; open May–Sept 10.30–12.30 and 2.30–7.30*). If it looks more like a castle, it is that too; fortified mills are not uncommon in France, built in feudal times when grain was precious and there were plenty of enemies ready to try to grab it. This one, along with the bridge in front of it, is from the 1200s. The story has it that the nobleman who built it had four daughters of different ages, and made the mill's four towers different heights in their honour. In later times the mill belonged to the d'Albrets, and it passed from them to Henri IV, who liked being called the 'Miller of Barbaste', at least, better than he liked being called 'Big Nose'. It now has the 18-hole **Golf d'Albret** (***t*** *05 53 65 53 69*). To the west, on the D665, **Durance** is a 13th-century *bastide* surrounded by forests that were the hunting preserve of the d'Albrets and King Henri; the village has ruins of the castle they used for their hunting lodge.

Northeast of Barbaste is another *bastide*, **Vianne**, founded in 1284 by Jourdain de l'Isle, seneschal of King Edward I and named after his aunt, Vianne Gontaud-Biron – apparently it's the only *bastide* named after a woman. Vianne still has most of its walls and gates, along with the church of Notre-Dame and its austere tower, and a pretty churchyard full of cypresses. Today the village makes its living from faïence and crystal; there are some lovely things for sale in the shops on the main street, and at Faïence des Remparts, built into the village's wall. The **Atelier du Verrier d'Art** (***t*** *05 53 65 82 42*) offers tours. In the hills above Vianne is the **Château de Xaintrailles** (***t*** *05 53 65 51 49; tours by appointment*), once the home of Maréchal Poton, a companion of Joan of Arc.

Western Lot-et-Garonne: Down the Garonne Valley

In fact, it isn't just the Garonne: you have a choice of following either the river or the **Canal Latéral Garonne**, the 19th-century waterway that parallels the river, providing a complement to Languedoc's Canal du Midi and providing boats with a direct passage from the Mediterranean to the Atlantic.

From Aiguillon to Marmande

Starting from Aiguillon (*see* p.370), just across the river and the canal is **Buzet-sur-Baïse**, a village near the confluence of the Baïse and the Garonne, dominated by its castle, high on a hill with tremendous views. There are two things to do here: take a ride along the Baïse or the canal in a modern houseboat or a traditional boat called a *capucine* (Aquitain Navigation, **t** 05 53 84 72 50); or seek out a bottle of the local *vin*.

Buzet

A cousin of Bordeaux, red Buzet is a mainly Merlot wine that owed its AOC status in 1973 to the tireless work of the *Cave Coopérative de Buzet* (now called the *Vignerons Réunis*), created in 1955 in Buzet-sur-Baïse to bring back the winemaking traditions that made the wine important in the Middle Ages. Although the growing area stretches all the way down the Baïse beyond Nérac, the vineyards only exist in pockets among other crops, on the best-drained, pebbly land; many old mediocre family vineyards have been pulled up in the last two decades in favour of the more favoured modern varieties – Merlot, Cabernet Franc, Cabernet Sauvignon and Cot. Dedication, discipline and a unique interest in just the right type of oak cask (the cooperative has a coopery attached that makes 800 to 900 barrels a year, each with a five-year life span) have resulted in a fine, structured aromatic wine that goes beautifully with the region's rich dishes in prune sauces. At the top of the list of reds is the superb Château de Gueyze (especially the 1987 or '88, still perfect to drink), followed by Cuvée Baron d'Ardeuil, named by Napoleon after the Gascon soldier who offered him some from his gourd (he, too, was known henceforth as Baron). Another good year was 1990. The whites have improved lately and are well worth a try. L'Excellence 1998, light, fresh and fruity, is what it says and can be bought at *Les Vignerons de Buzet*, a union of 13 châteaux, which markets over 90 per cent of the wine – over 14 million bottles a year – and offers tours of its vast cellars (*t 05 53 84 74 30; open Mon–Sat 9–12.30 and 2–7*).

Damazan, another *bastide* of the 13th century, has creaky, leaning half-timbered houses, a little *mairie* over the market *halles*, and some of its walls and towers intact. Damazan, like Buzet, is one of the main centres for canal tourism, and there are cruises and boats to rent in season: try **Société Nautic** (***t** 05 53 79 59 39*). Down the Garonne, the large village of **Tonneins** offers a wonderful panorama over the Garonne valley from the top of the town, and it can claim the annual production of some ten billion of France's distinctively stinky home-grown cigarettes at the **Manufacture de Cigarettes**, the plant of the national tobacco monopoly. Gauloises and Gitanes, smokable only by Frenchmen and masochists, are made largely from Aquitaine weed; the *manufacture*, founded as a royal tobacco factory in 1726, cranks them out at the rate of 8,000 a minute. On the quay the **Espace Exposition a Garonna** tells tales of the river and its history (***t** 05 53 79 22 79; open July and Aug 3–7*).

Le Mas-d'Agenais

You'll reach this village by an elegant modern suspension bridge that crosses both the Garonne and the canal. Though the customary red-bordered sign announces the village, along with a floral arrangement of Mas's coat of arms (three gold hands on a red field), not a house is to be seen. Mas is up in the clouds, on a hill above the Garonne, a village closed into itself; it's special, and it knows it.

Known as *Velenum Pompeiacum* in Roman times, Mas was still one of the most important centres of the area in the Middle Ages. It isn't a large village, just a few

Getting Around

You can tour the Canal Latéral by **houseboat** from the Crown Blue Line, **t** 05 53 89 50 80, by the canal lock at Le Mas-d'Agenais, or from Aquitaine Navigation, at Le Coustet in Buzet, **t** 05 53 84 72 50.

For a **river** trip, there's Garonne Evasion, Quai de La Barre in Tonneins, **t** 05 53 88 28 58.

Tourist Information

Tonneins: 3 Bd Charles-de-Gaulle, **t** 05 53 79 22 79, **f** 05 53 79 39 94.

Casteljaloux: Maison du Roy, **t** 05 53 93 00 00, **f** 05 53 20 74 32.

Le Mas-d'Agenais: Place de l'Eglise, **t** 05 53 89 50 58 (*summer only*).

Meilhan-sur-Garonne: *mairie*, Place Neuf Brisach, **t** 05 53 94 30 04, **f** 05 53 94 31 27 (*summer only*).

Market Days

Tonneins: Wed and Sat, also night markets on Wed in summer.

Casteljaloux: Sat.

Buzet: Fri.

Where to Stay and Eat

Buzet-sur-Baïse ✉ 47160

Le Goujon qui Frétille, Rue Gambetta, **t** 05 53 84 26 51. 'The Wiggling Gudgeon' is cosy, with a lovely terrace, and serves wonderful variations on the old southwest themes, at very kind prices (*menus 85–150F*). *Closed Tues eve and Wed.*

Tonneins ✉ 47400

★★★★**Côté Garonne**, 36–8 Cours de l'Yser, **t** 05 53 84 34 34, **f** 05 53 84 31 31 (*expensive*). Not far from the centre, with five exclusive rooms hanging over the Garonne, and a superb restaurant with inventive, very seasonal cuisine (*menus from 165F*). *Closed Sun eve, Mon, the last half of Aug and first half of Nov.*

Le Mas-d'Agenais ✉ 47430

Jean Champon, right in the centre by the market stalls, **t** 05 53 89 50 06. For lunch you won't do better than the 68F menu here: four honest courses with maybe Bayonne ham for a starter, and for the main course perhaps a choice of *bœuf en daube* or *confit de poulet*.

Casteljaloux ✉ 47700

★★**La Vieille Auberge**, 11 Rue Posterne, in the old part of town, **t** 05 53 93 01 36, **f** 05 53 93 18 89 (*cheap*). Three rooms; delicious seasonal menus in the restaurant, with a number of dishes based on Aquitaine beef as well as *canard* (*menus 120–230F*). *Closed Sun eve and Wed out of season.*

★★**Des Cordeliers**, 1 Rue des Cordeliers, **t** 05 53 93 02 19 (*inexpensive*). A good budget choice in the centre; two rooms are equipped for the disabled. *Closed Sun eve in winter.*

Meilhan-sur-Garonne ✉ 47180

Le Tertre, Place du Tertre, **t** 05 53 94 30 28. For something different, an Italian touch to regional cuisine, all served in a charming setting with grand panoramic views over the laughing Garonne (*menus 140–260F*). *Closed Sun eve, Mon, two weeks in Oct and two in Jan.*

lovely streets and squares with many restored houses, a brick medieval gateway, a wooden market *halle* from the 1600s, and a beautiful view over the Garonne from its little park on the edge of the cliffs. It also has one of the region's most interesting churches, **St-Vincent**, begun in 1085, replacing an ancient church (*c.* 440) that itself was built on the site of a Roman temple. Tinkered and tampered with over the centuries, it isn't much to look at from outside; Viollet-le-Duc gave the main entrance its present appearance, and at about the same time the tall steeple over it was demolished. The interior, however, contains a wealth of excellent sculptural decoration, mostly on the capitals (nearby shops or the tourist office sell tokens for the lighting). In the south aisle, Old Testament scenes include *Samson, David and Goliath, The Sacrifice of Abraham* and *Daniel in the Lions' Den*. The capitals in the north aisle and choir are mostly New Testament vignettes, along with *St Michael and the Dragon* and the *Martyrdom of St Vincent*, while those high up in the nave itself have some surprising subjects: one is claimed to be the *Race of Atalanta* from Greek mythology and apparently the *Hunt of the Calydonian Boar* from the same story.

The church contains two ancient relics; one is an early Christian sarcophagus, said to be that of the obscure martyr St Vincent, which was on prominent display in Mas' original church. Hidden in the cemetery during the Norman invasions, it was only rediscovered in 1785. The other, a Roman *cippus* with a confusing inscription, may have originally been the base for the statue of a pagan god. Note also the beautifully carved **choir stalls**; these are believed to be a gift of Mary Stuart, originally intended for the church at La Réole. Mas' claim to fame, a painting by Rembrandt, was donated to the church in 1873 by a wealthy family from Mas who made it big in Dunkerque. Originally, this scene of *The Face of Christ on the Cross* was part of a series of seven on the Passion; all the rest are now together in Munich. For anyone who thinks Rembrandt only painted portraits, it will be a revelation (there are photographs of the others in the church); these are intense, remarkable paintings, in which Jesus goes up on the cross a man and comes down a god.

South of Mas, the D6 passes through the lovely Forest of Mas-d'Agenais, another old hunting preserve, on the way to **Casteljaloux**, a former possession of the d'Albrets and the gateway to the great piney Landes; the French immediately recall it as the base of the Cadets de Gascogne in Rostand's *Cyrano de Bergerac*. The name sounds as if it should mean 'jealous' but really comes from *gelos*, meaning perilous, a reality confirmed by the state of the castle itself, now a ruin but once a favourite hunting and love retreat of Henri IV. There are a few 15th-century buildings around the centre, but that's about it. However, it has the pretty sand-bordered Lac de Clarens just southwest, and, just southeast down the D11, the striking multi-towered **Château du Sendat**, first built in the 12th century, set amidst a tidy French garden. Among the Romanesque churches in the area, there's a good one at **Villefranche-du-Queyran** due northeast on the D120, with a score of carved capitals; **Labastide-Castel-Amouroux** to the northwest has another one, with some good monsters on the capitals.

Further northwest, **Romestaing** has the 12th-century church of **St-Christophe** with more mysterious capitals. **Cocumont**, a main centre of the Côtes-du-Marmandais growing area (*see* below), is just northwest of **Goutz** (or **Goux**), with a remarkable 11th-century Romanesque church built on top of a 2,000-year-old tumulus; deep below is the circular tomb of a local chieftain, never excavated. **Marcellus** is the site of a handsome 16th-century château, cradle of the count who bought the *Venus de Milo* from the Greek farmer who dug her up, and kept her from rival purchaser the Prince of Moldavia (the statue was on a Greek tender, ready to be placed aboard a ship for Romania just when the French vessel from Constantinople arrived; accounts say there was either some brisk bargaining, or a fight that the French sailors won – during which she may have lost her arms and pedestal). Further downstream, **Meilhan-sur-**

Tourist Information

Bd Gambetta, **t** 05 53 64 44 44, **f** 05 53 20 17 19.

Market Days

Tues, Thurs and Sat; flea market on the second Sun of each month.

Where to Stay and Eat

Marmande ✉ 47200

****Le Capricorne**, just outside town on Route d'Agen, **t** 05 53 64 16 14, **f** 05 53 20 80 18 (*inexpensive*). A modern motel with a pool, home to an excellent restaurant named for its chef, Thierry Arbeau, who does wonderful things at affordable prices with grilled pigeon, seafood and Garonne lamprey (*menus 90–280F*). *Closed Sat lunch and Sun.*

****Le Lion d'Or**, 1 Rue de la République, near Notre-Dame, **t** 05 53 64 21 30, **f** 05 53 64 77 39 (*inexpensive*). Adequate modernized rooms and a decent restaurant, where the chef is fond of tastefully combining meats and fruit (*menus 68–238F*).

L'Escale, at Pont-des-Sables, on the banks of the canal, **t** 05 53 93 60 11. A green refreshing backdrop for its good honest food, including shad and lamprey *à la bordelaise* (*menus 130–185F*). *Closed Sun eve.*

Auberge du Moulin d'Ané, 4km east by the river Trec in Virazeil, **t** 05 53 20 18 25. A romantic popular eatery just outside Marmande, where good country ingredients and fresh seafood create a delicate cuisine; sit on the terrace and let the apricot mousse with redcurrant sauce melt in your mouth (*menus 120–240F*). *Closed Tues and Wed.*

Garonne sits atop a natural balcony, overlooking the hills of the Entre-Deux-Mers and their famous vineyards.

Marmande

Marmande, the most important market town between Agen and Bordeaux, is currently on its third name. Originally it was Marmande-la-Royale, when it received its charter in 1182 from Richard the Lion-Heart. After being used as a kind of revolving door in the Hundred Years' War (when it changed hands eight times) and the Wars of Religion, it was Marmande-la-Sainte; now it's the more secular Marmande-la-Jolie, the queen of big red tomatoes.

A Walk around Marmande

Marmande's central Place Clémenceau, covering an underground car park, is decorated with a bronze statue called *La Pomme d'Amour*, a kneeling nude clutching a *tomate de Marmande*, in reference to an old belief that tomatoes were an aphrodisiac. The tomato maiden overlooks the new splashing **fountain** of Europa; near by is the **Musée Municipal Albert Marzelles** (***t*** *05 53 64 42 04; open Tues–Fri and Sun 3–6, Sat 10–12 and 3–6, closed Mon*) with a hotchpotch of local items, especially from the 19th century; don't miss the lavish firemen's helmets, which perhaps explain why pre-Impressionist French historical paintings were called *pompiers* (firemen). Rue Léopold Faye, lined with half-timbered houses, leads back towards the 13th-century **Notre-Dame**, where you can inspect a pretty rose window, a Baroque *Mise en tombeau*, a 16th-century retable dedicated to St Benedict and a beautiful topiary garden in the

Côtes-du-Marmandais

Rather unusually, Marmandais has two very distinct growing areas divided by the wide valley of the Garonne: the northern area has the same limestone-clayey soil as Entre-Deux-Mers, while the south is an extension of the sandy, gravelly Graves region just to the west. In the 18th and 19th centuries the lusty red and dry white wines grown here were in great demand in the Netherlands, but the 20th century saw a decline only halted in the last few decades. Like neighbouring Buzet, Marmandais owes its rise in status again to the cooperative efforts of its vintners, who after years of work achieved AOC status in 1990 for their bright, merry red wine that they promise 'will re-animate chagrined spirits and save an ordinary meal from insipidity'. One major change was the move from the somewhat obscure traditional grape varieties of the region (Boucalès, Abouriou, Fer-servadou). The reds, by far the majority, are now made from Merlot, Cabernet Franc and Cabernet Sauvignon; the whites are mostly Sauvignon, with Sémillon and Muscadelle. As in Buzet, most of the wine is produced in cooperatives like that of Beaupuy, just north of Marmande (*t 05 53 76 05 10; open 8.30–12 and 2–6.30*), a village with grand views in every direction: here the Rouge Presige '94 and the Blanc Sec '96 are two of the best. At the Cave de Cocumont, at Cocumont, south of the Garonne and A62 (*t 05 53 94 50 21; open 9–12 and 2.30–6.30*), the Rouge Tap de Per Bos is full of promise.

cloister of 1545. From here Rue de la Libération leads up to the **Chapelle St-Benoît** with an impressive 17th-century ceiling painted to imitate coffering.

Around Marmande

Down the Garonne, **Ste-Bazeille** was a Roman town, named after the daughter of a proconsul who was martyred for her faith; decapitated, her head bounced nine times, each bounce bringing forth a spring – now known as the nine fountains, *neuffonds* (St Paul suffered a similar fate in Rome, but his head, being full of weighty theology, bounced but thrice). There is a **Musée Archéologique** (*t 05 53 20 45 30; open July and Aug daily 2.30–6.30, closed Tues, Sept–June Sun afternoons only; adm*) with over 700 pieces from the Iron Age through Roman times to the Middle Ages. On a stream called the Gupie, **Mauvezin-sur-Gupie** has a 13th-century church covered by a remarkable roof shaped like a ship's keel. **Lagupie** has a 12th-century church with a sculpted tympanum; there's another, carved with Christ and the Elders of the Apocalypse, to the east of Marmande at **St-Pierre-de-Londres**, an English *bastide* project that never got further than this church. **Virazeil**, between Marmande and St-Pierre-de-Londres, has a neoclassical **château** built by Victor Louis, architect of Bordeaux's Grand Théâtre, in 1774.

Along the Dourdêze and Dropt, and the Pays du Duras

The low, rolling hills of this northwest corner of the Lot-et-Garonne *département* hold some of its most unusual sights, and some of its best wine. The French come here for *douceur de vie*, and the English, perhaps remembering Duras as one of the most pro-English corners of Aquitaine, have returned to buy large sections of it back.

Lauzun

Il n'était pas permis de rêver comme il a vécu.

La Bruyère, on the Duc de Lauzun

Lauzun owes its fame to Antonin Nompar de Caumont, born the younger son of an impoverished local baron in 1633 but so endowed with natural talent, good looks and charm that he quickly become Louis XIV's favourite. The Sun King promoted him to marshal and duke; one of his missions was to help James II's queen, Mary of Modena, and her son flee from England to France during the Glorious Revolution. On another occasion Lauzun hid under the king's bed to hear what Louis and his mistress were saying about him. Women adored him, most overwhelmingly the Big Miss herself, the *Grande Mademoiselle* – Louis' headstrong cousin – who fell head over heels for Lauzun, much to the astonishment of the court and to the fury of Louis, who sent Lauzun to the Bastille. Most accounts say that he secretly married the Grande Mademoiselle anyway, then proceeded to be terribly unfaithful to her. When she died, the spunky duke married a 15-year-old (he was 62), then to her horror lived to the ripe age of 90. One thing he did was add a domed pavilion to his golden half-medieval, half-Renaissance **château** (***t*** *05 53 94 18 89; open June–Sept on Sun and hols only*); it also has magnificent fireplaces. The Gothic **church**, next to an 11th-century tower, has a retable by Tournié of Gourdon, an elaborately carved altar, and two statues of the Virgin from the 13th and 15th centuries.

Just northwest of Lauzun, embraced by a meander of the Dropt, **Eymet** is another *bastide*, founded by Alphonse de Poitiers, with its arcades intact and a 13th-century donjon containing a small **Musée d'Archéologie** (*open afternoons July–Sept*), with prehistoric items from the area; a 300-acre *plan d'eau* is a favourite retreat in the summer. Eymet's chief rival, just to the south, **Miramont-de-Guyenne** was founded as a *bastide* by Edward I, but after grave damage in the Hundred Years' War and the Fronde it only retains some old houses (one once inhabited by Jeanne d'Albret) and a central arcaded square; the **church** is brand new, with stained glass by modern master Emile Wachter.

Allemans-du-Dropt

Supposedly named after the barbaric German tribe that pushed and shoved its way through in the Dark Ages (and made such an impression on the French that they still call the whole country on the other bank of the Rhine *Allemagne*), Allemans-du-Dropt

Tourist Information

Miramont-de-Guyenne: 1 Rue Pasteur, **t** 05 53 93 38 94, **f** 05 53 93 49 56.
Allemans-du-Dropt: Place de la Liberté, **t/f** 05 53 20 25 59.
Duras: Bd Jean-Brisseau, **t** 05 53 83 63 06, **f** 05 53 83 65 45.
St-Sernin-de-Duras: in the centre, **t** 05 53 94 76 94, **f** 05 53 94 77 63.

Market Days

Miramont-de-Guyenne: Mon; farmers' market Fri in summer only.
Lauzun: Sat.
Duras: Mon, Sat, and Thurs in summer.

Where to Stay and Eat

Allemans-du-Dropt ✉ 47800

★★L'Etape Gasconne, Place de la Mairie, **t** 05 53 20 23 55, **f** 05 53 93 51 42 (*inexpensive*). Pleasant, reasonably priced rooms, a pool for the weary and good food for the hungry; even the 70F weekday menu includes *hors d'œuvres* and wine. *Closed Sat lunch.*

Monteton ✉ 47120

Auberge des Treize Clochers, next to the church, **t** 05 53 20 24 50. A tasty *120F menu. Closed Mon and Nov–Mar.*

Château de Monteton, **t** 05 53 20 26 96, **f** 05 53 20 21 96 (*inexpensive–cheap*). A popular 18th-century château with lovely *chambres d'hôte* (not all with bath, ask when you book). The food is delicious and based on fresh ingredients, with several vegetarian dishes (*menus from 80F*). Be warned: in winter the château is often booked to the gills with conference-goers. *Book.*

Agnac ✉ 47800

Le Manoir du Pont, Le Bout du Pont, west of Eymet, on the D933, **t** 05 53 83 05 18. Set in a 12th-century pigeonnier and 17th-century manorhouse. At the time of writing it is a good restaurant (*menus 75F for lunch to 155F*). From 2001 there may be rooms, and cookery and wine courses with visiting lecturers. The owners and the team are English. *Closed Sun eve, Mon and a couple of weeks in the winter.*

Miramont-de-Guyenne ✉ 47800

La Poste, 31 Place Martignac, **t** 05 53 93 20 03, **f** 05 53 89 64 55 (*inexpensive*). Fourteen Logis de France rooms in an old posthouse, and the best restaurant in town: try the *éventail* (fan) of salmon and asparagus (*menus 62–275F*). *Closed Sat out of season, and one week in Oct.*

Duras ✉ 47120

★★Hostellerie des Ducs, Bd Jean-Brisseau, **t** 05 53 83 74 58, **f** 05 53 83 75 03 (*inexpensive*). You can stay amongst the vines in this early 19th-century convent, now transformed into a hotel with a pool and excellent restaurant: try the sturgeon fillets with leek fondue, and save room for the truly exceptional desserts (*menus 88–300F*). *Closed Sun eve and Mon out of season.*

has an ancient **church** given a neo-Gothic face-lift in the 19th century. The choir has a Mozarabic horseshoe arch, but best of all are the 15th-century **frescoes** in the nave, rediscovered in 1935 by the church bell-ringer. These are lively, colourful paintings – especially of the devils, one carrying off souls like a grape-picker in a basket on his back, another impaled by the armoured archangel in charge of separating baddies and goodies. All the damned appear to be either women or priests.

Nearby **La Sauvetat-du-Dropt** was yet another *bastide*, and one that saw a terrible blood-letting in 1637, when the Duc de la Valette brutally put down a peasant uprising by massacring 1,500 *Croquants*. From the 13th century there's **St-Gervais**, a church with an ornate portal and choir that survived a cyclone in 1242, and a charming bridge over the Dropt, near a picturesque *pigeonnier*. Don't miss the beautiful Renaissance house on the main street.

Southwest, at little **Monteton**, the delightful Romanesque **Notre-Dame** sits high on a terrace where the keen of eye should be able to pick out 13 belltowers on the horizon. One of the few churches to escape damage over the centuries, it has unusual interior buttresses, fine vaults, and a triumphal arch with carved capitals.

Duras

Spread out along a spur overlooking the emerald valley of the Dropt, **Duras** is said to be the only town in France that never built a Catholic church; the current one began as a Protestant temple. Having the same name as a famous French novelist hasn't hurt it, nor has the renown of its excellent wines. It has some fine old houses and arcades along the high street, Rue Jauffret. The **Musée Conservatoire du Parchemin et de l'Enluminure** (*Rue des Eyzins,* ***t*** *05 53 20 75 55; open April–Sept 3–7; adm*) is also now here having moved from Miramont, where they demonstrate how parchment was made from sheepskins, bound into books and illustrated with goose quills in the time of St Louis. They also run courses in case you want to learn.

But the main reason to stop is a visit to the great prow-shaped **Château de Duras** (***t*** *05 53 83 77 32; open April–May 10–12 and 2–7, June–Sept 10–7, Oct and winter hols 10–12 and 2–6, Nov–Mar 2–6*), which was first built in the 1100s, only to be completely redone in 1310 by a cousin of Bertrand de Goth, Pope Clement V. His niece married a Durfort, and from 1325 the castle belonged to that powerful pro-English family; in 1389 it was captured by du Guesclin. Henri IV's mother, Jeanne d'Albret, holed up here when Catholic Catherine de' Medici sent down the troops. In the late 17th century, its duke Jaques-Henri du Dufort served as a *maréchal* of France and helped capture the Franche-Comté for France, while his younger brother Louis went to England and became James II's top general. In 1794 the castle's surviving towers were cut down to

Côtes-de-Duras

Born during the Hundred Years' War, Côtes-de-Duras was one of France's first AOC wines, receiving the prized designation back in 1937. Of its gently rolling hills, only the sunniest slopes with the proper soil are under vines and they produce a mere 100,000 hectolitres of wine – a drop in the bucket compared to the various Bordeaux wines next door.

Côtes-de-Duras reds are often made from either 100 per cent Merlot or Cabernet Sauvignon; the whites are from Sauvignon, Mauzac or Sémillon. Domaine de Laulan in Duras, t 05 53 83 73 69, offers an expressive white wine and a great red Duc de Laulan '93. The pride of the Cave Coopérative de Duras (*t 05 53 83 71 12; open Mon–Sat 8–12 and 2–6, in summer 8–12.30 and 2–7, also open Sun*) is its standard-bearer, Cave Berticot, both red and white (especially the '95, Sauvignon Vieille Vignes). Among the sweet *blancs moelleux*, the soft, rich Château La Moulière is usually outstanding, the perfect accompaniment to foie gras.

size, and by the 20th century it was abandoned and falling to bits; the town purchased it in 1969.

After a 20-year restoration, it has been brought back to life, not only in its architecture – the grand halls, kitchen, the 'room of secrets', the oratory, the prison and moats, the tower with views that on a very clear day stretch to the Pyrenees – but also its troubadours, knights, ladies and music and boiling pots, thanks to lasers, video, sound and light and other high-tech gimcracks by the same wizards who created Futuroscope near Poitiers.

Around Duras

Romanesque churches share the *pays de Duras* with the grapes, and one of the best is to the north in **Esclottes**. Built in the 13th century, it has an unusually short nave, a false transept and skilfully carved capitals, one with a fish. Others are at **Savignac-de-Duras**, **Lubersac** and **Loubès-Bernac**. This last church has two doors; the one on the north was known as the **Porte des Cagots**. Loubès-Bernac also has a 14th-century château, completely redone in the 17th century. For a bird's-eye view, go for a ride in a **hot-air balloon**: Michel Fonvielhe's *Mongolfière* ascends from St-Jean-de-Duras (***t*** *05 53 89 02 23*).

Tarn-et-Garonne

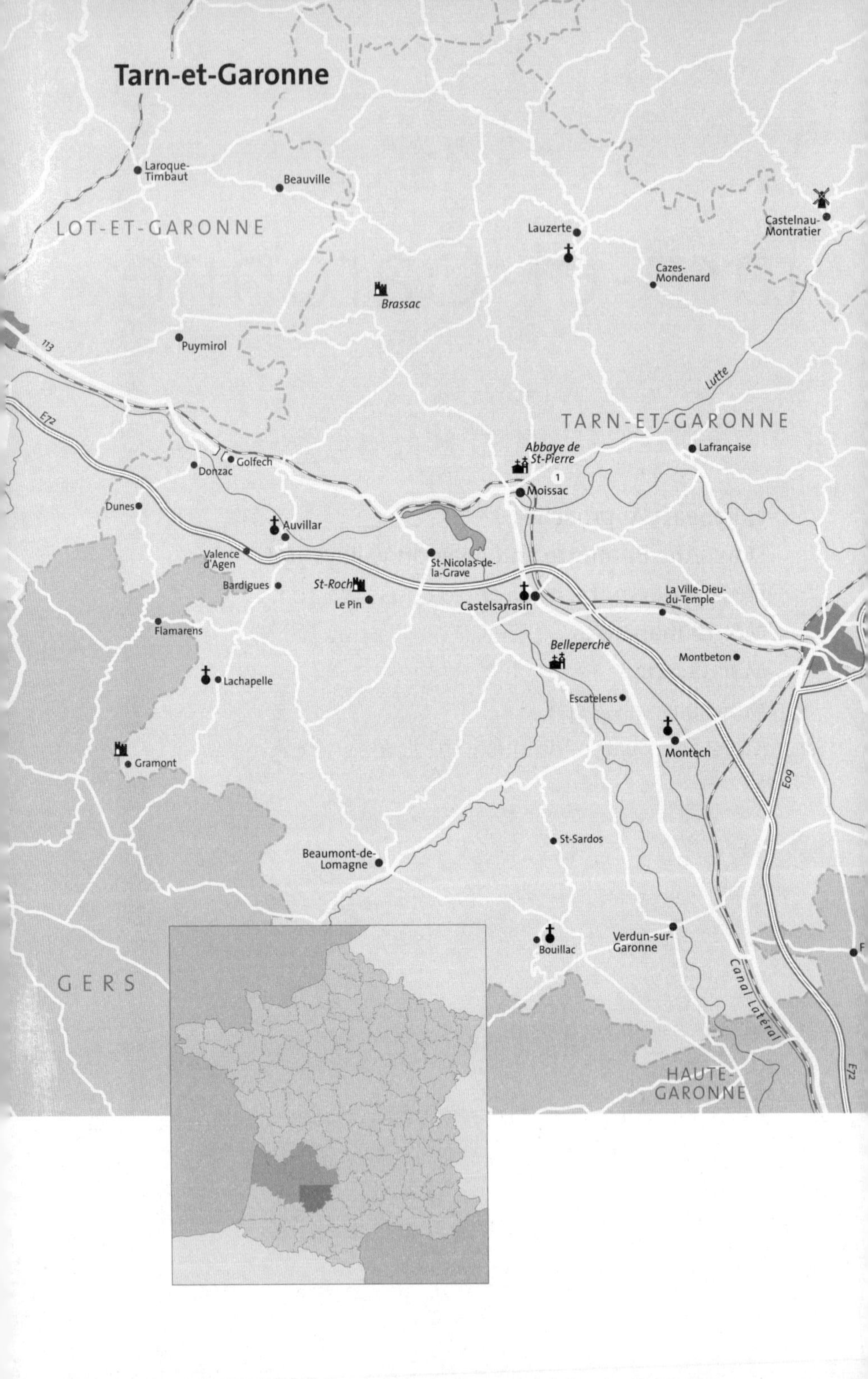
Tarn-et-Garonne
Laroque-Timbaut
Beauville
LOT-ET-GARONNE
Lauzerte
Castelnau-Montratier
Cazes-Mondenard
Brassac
Puymirol
113
Lutte
TARN-ET-GARONNE
E72
Abbaye de St-Pierre
Lafrançaise
Golfech
Donzac
1
Moissac
Dunes
Auvillar
Valence d'Agen
St-Nicolas-de-la-Grave
Bardigues
St-Roch
Le Pin
Castelsarrasin
La Ville-Dieu-du-Temple
Flamarens
Belleperche
Montbeton
Lachapelle
Escatelens
Gramont
Montech
E09
St-Sardos
Beaumont-de-Lomagne
Bouillac
Verdun-sur-Garonne
Canal Latéral
GERS
HAUTE-GARONNE
E72

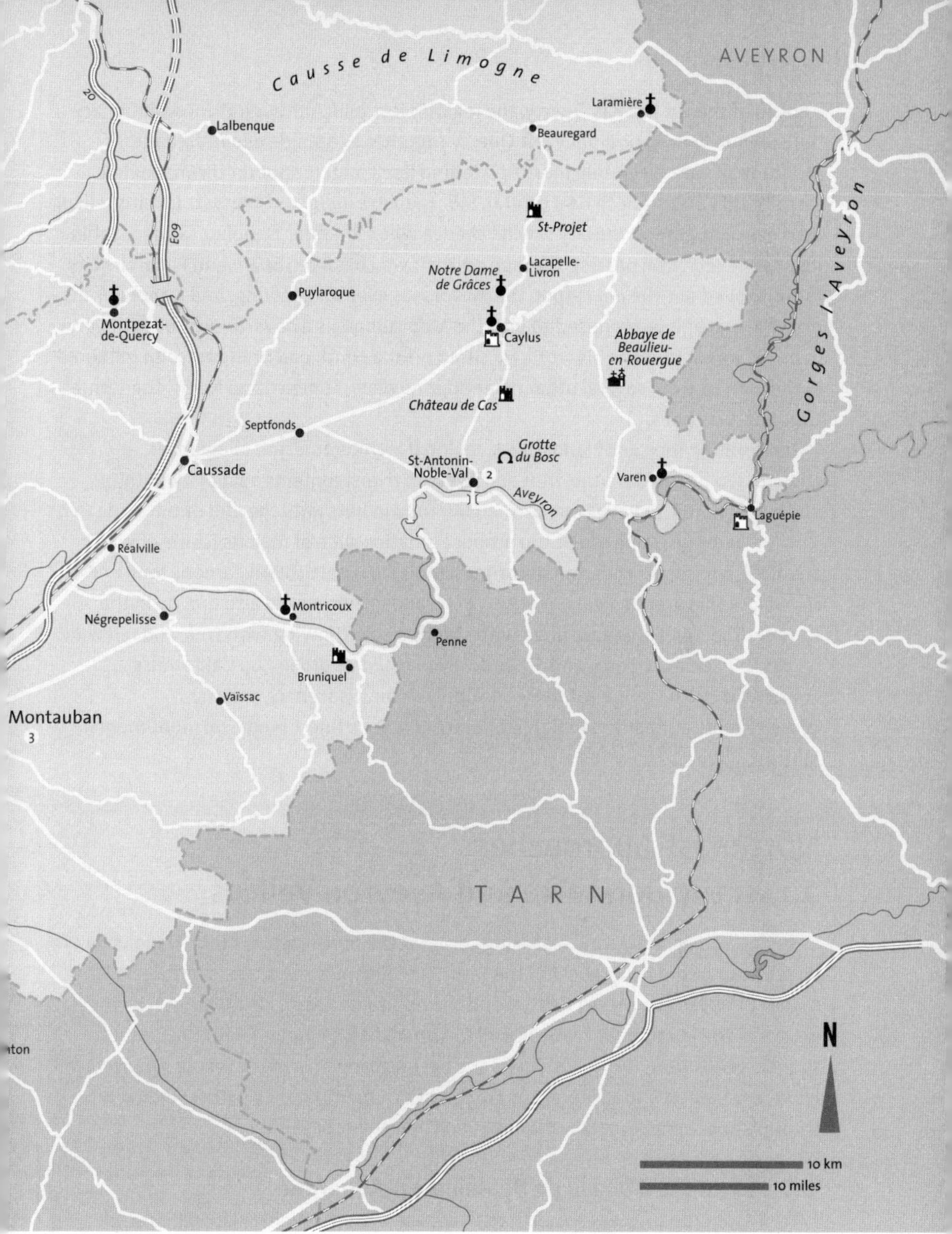

Highlights

1 Moissac, a crown jewel of French Romanesque
2 The labyrinthine lanes of St-Antonin-Noble-Val
3 Ingres and company at Montauban

South of the Lot lies Bas Quercy, the region's lost half. Although the Revolutionary bureaucrats in Paris originally left Quercy together as a single *département*, Montauban was absolutely mortified to find itself a mere spot on the map while rascally old Cahors got to be a capital. Montauban's indignant protests in Paris fell on deaf ears, but in 1808 the city saw its chance when Emperor Napoleon and Josephine just happened to be passing through on their way between Spain and Paris. The city fathers rolled out the red carpet, the mayor was ever so flattering, and Napoleon, his imperial ego aglow, promised to give the Montaubanais a *département* of their very own. He was as good as his word. He sliced off the south end of the Lot, and gathered in the corners from several other neighbouring *départements*, and No.82, the Tarn-et-Garonne, was born.

The resulting mosaic of landscapes, regional architecture and allegiances, crisscrossed by the Garonne, Tarn and Aveyron rivers, contains a bit of everything, and enough fruit to have kept Carmen Miranda in hats until the end of time. The Tarn-et-Garonne is one of the top producers nationwide of melons (some of which are AOC), apples, peaches and nectarines. Moissac is particularly famous for its AOC *chasselas* table grapes. Pears, cherries, kiwis and hazelnuts are also grown. In the summer the main roads are lined with stands so overflowing with fruit and red wine (VDQS Lavilledieu, Quercy and St-Sardos) you could be driving up California's Central Valley. The gorges of Aveyron supply dramatic scenery, and the *département* can thank Napoleon for one of France's finest medieval monuments: Moissac Abbey.

Northeast Approaches: down the Bonnette and Aveyron Valleys

The Tarn-et-Garonne's most striking corner is the northeastern bulge Napoleon gouged out of the Rouergue and the Tarn. Its rolling hills mark the transition in landscapes between the Massif Central and the Aquitaine Basin, sliced through by the gorges of the languorous Aveyron and its tributaries, beginning with the Bonnette that descends from the north. This is the best walking area in the whole *département*, crossed from north to south by the GR46, with numerous small paths winding off through fine scenery, medieval villages and ancient abbeys.

Caylus and the Abbaye de Beaulieu-en-Rouergue

From Montauban, the N20 north to Caussade then the main D926 will take you straight to Caylus; if you're coming from the Lot, find Beauregard and the Causse de Limogne (*see* pp.323–4) and drive south by way of the Renaissance **Château de St-Projet** where Queen Margot once took refuge from the Protestants (***t** 05 63 65 74 85; guided tours July–Oct daily 2–7; adm*). There are sometimes shows in July and August. **Lacapelle-Livron**, the next village south, has a Templar commandery (rebuilt in the 15th century) and a church so fortified that it looks more like a little castle. For a less bristling house of God, continue south a kilometre to 15th-century **Notre-Dame des**

Getting Around

Public transport exists, on a limited scale. From Montauban there is one **bus** daily to Caylus, one to St-Antonin-Noble-Val and one a day to most of the other villages. For information, call the Montauban tourist office on **t** 05 63 63 60 60.

Tourist Information

Caylus: Rue Droit, **t/f** 05 63 67 00 28.
Laguépie: Place du Foirail, **t** 05 63 30 20 34.
St-Antonin-Noble-Val: at the *mairie*, **t** 05 63 30 63 47.

Market Days

Caylus: Tues and Sat, fair first Tues of month.
Laguépie: Wed.
Varen: Sat.
St-Antonin-Noble-Val: Sun, food and flea market.

Ask at the tourist office for information about **night markets** in July and August.

Where to Stay and Eat

Caylus ✉ 82160

★★**La Renaissance**, Av Père Evariste Huc, **t** 05 63 67 07 26 (*inexpensive*). A simple place in the centre of town (*menus 70–200F*). *Closed Sun eve and Mon, one week in May and several weeks in Feb and Oct.*

★**De la Vallée**, 8km east at Cornusson, **t** 05 63 67 06 80 (*cheap*). With a pool and restaurant (*menus from 65F*). *Closed Sat and Dec.*

La Ferme du Mas de Monille, north, in Loze near St-Project, **t** 05 63 65 76 85. Meet the wild boar, and then dine *à la Obelix* (*open Sunday only out of season*). *Book.*

Les Vieilles Pierres, northeast at Parisot, 9km from Caylus on the D926, **t** 05 63 65 71 28. Big portions of *fondue bourguignonne* and other northern specialities, for a change (*around 120F*). *Closed Wed.*

Laguépie ✉ 82250

★★**Les Deux Rivières**, Av Puech Mignon, **t** 05 63 31 41 41, **f** 05 63 30 20 91 (*inexpensive*). Pleasant, modern and the nicest place to stay in the area; dine on well-prepared local dishes (*menus 65–185F*). *Closed Sun eve, Mon eve except Easter–Aug, and two weeks in Feb.*

Varen ✉ 82330

Le Moulin de Varen, on the D958, **t** 05 63 65 45 10. Set in a pretty old mill, preparing simple but delicious meals: goat-cheese lovers should order the *salade de chèvre chaud à l'huile de noix* (*menus 80–165F*). *Closed Mon and Tues, and mid-Nov–mid-Jan.*

St-Antonin-Noble-Val ✉ 82140

★★**Le Lys Bleu de Payrols**, 29 Place de la Halle, **t** 05 63 68 21 00, **f** 05 63 30 62 27 (*inexpensive*). Occupying several medieval houses in the heart of town; rooms have antiques and mini-bars. The little restaurant serves good pizza in the evening.

★★**Hotel des Thermes**, Place des Moines, **t** 05 63 30 61 08, **f** 05 63 68 26 23 (*inexpensive–cheap*). The exterior is pink and patchy in places and the bedrooms have been recently restored in a bright and young style; clean, serviceable, all rooms have a bathroom and phone and it has a cheerful restaurant and bar. It is superbly situated, opposite the cliffs and next to the river, and the room rate is reasonable. *Closed Jan.*

Bès de Quercy, on the D926 towards Caylus, **t** 05 63 31 97 61 (*inexpensive*). A *ferme-auberge* with four comfortable bed-and-breakfast rooms and menus (*90–190F*), based on chicken, duck or guinea fowl.

Brousses ✉ 82140

La Corniche, just off the D115 as it approaches St-Antonin-Noble-Val, **t** 05 63 68 26 95. This small restaurant run by the lively Michel Corbeau has a lovely view from its terrace of a tree-covered cliff; eat regional food with a few other things besides to the relaxing sound of a running stream (*menu du jour 90F, other menus 120–180F*). *Open July and Aug daily in the evenings, also midday Thurs–Sun. Open other times but call first to be sure. Booking obligatory; no cards.* Mr Corbeau also owns a rather rustic, but wonderfully cool apartment for two, nearly opposite the restaurant, which he hires out by the weekend and week. Phone for details.

Grâces, a miniature Flamboyant Gothic gem with a bird's-eye view across the *causse*; 4km south is another, built in 1302, called **Notre-Dame de Livron**, 'Our Lady of Liberation' in Occitan: a nearby cave was inhabited by a pesky dragon until a bold knight axed it and liberated the neighbourhood.

Caylus, the most important and certainly the prettiest town on the Bonnette, occupies an amphitheatre, most strikingly viewed from the west on the D926. The counts of Toulouse built a castle here in the 1200s, and its ruins still dominate the region. The medieval town, below the main road, is centred on the Place du Marché, with some arcades and a very sturdy *halle* with octagonal pillars. The church under the mighty stone steeple is **St-Jean Baptiste**, endowed with an elegant seven-sided choir of 1470 and the *Christ Monumental* by Zadkine, carved in 1954 from the trunk of an elm. Don't miss the 13th-century house near by, the **Maison des Loups** – as if to get back at these terrors of the Middle Ages, the wolves were made to do duty as rain spouts. Thirteen kilometres west of Caylus, the beautiful 13th- and 14th-century hilltop *bastide* of **Puylaroque** is a miniature version of the famous hilltown of Cordes near Albi.

Beaulieu-en-Rouergue

Southeast of Caylus in Ginas, Beaulieu-en-Rouergue, like most Cistercian abbeys, is prettily isolated at the bottom of a wooded valley. Founded in 1144 by 12 monks from Clairvaux, the present buildings were begun in the late 1200s; in the Wars of Religion, the whole was stripped and the cloister devastated. The *parlement* of Toulouse had much of it rebuilt in the 17th century, and the last Italianate stuccoes and marble chimneypieces were put in place just in time to be wrecked in the Revolution. Viollet-le-Duc had the idea of taking the church apart piece by piece and rebuilding it in St-Antonin-Noble-Val, a plan that fell through when St-Antonin couldn't come up with enough money for the job. Used as barns until 1960, the abbey was restored after 1974 and now houses a regional centre for contemporary art and music, with a permanent collection of late 20th-century works and annual summer art exhibitions. Although much rebuilt over the centuries, Beaulieu is an excellent example of the development of Cistercian architecture (and of the monks' increasing concern for

Vin de Coteaux-de-Quercy

The vines you see around here growing on the limestone terraces are destined for Vin de Coteaux-de-Quercy, which has recently achieved VDQ status. Grown in micro-climatic pockets between the AOC regions of Cahors, Moissac Chasselas, and Gaillac (to the east), over an area of about 400 hectares, Coteaux-de-Quercy wines are made from five varieties of grape: Cabernet Franc, Merlot, Cot, Gamay and Tannat in varying quantities. They are dark, well-structured and fruity wines that can be drunk young or aged – and with some of the escalating prices of Cahors, they're a bargain, too. You can learn all about them in English from Sarah or David Meakin at the Domaine du Merchien, just west of Puylaroque (*t 05 63 64 97 21; open daily 11–7*).

their physical comforts, a far cry from the original austerity of St Bernard of Clairvaux). The early 14th-century church is harmonious, with a beautiful portal and rose window. In the north crossing, a *porte des morts* survives – a door each monk went through but once in this vale of tears (***t** 05 63 24 50 10; open April–June and Sept–Oct 10–12 and 2–6.30, closed Tues, July and Aug daily 10–12 and 2–6*).

In the Gorges of the Aveyron: Laguépie to St-Antonin-Noble-Val

From the abbey of Beaulieu the D33/D20/D958 will take you down to **Laguépie** at the very corner of the Tarn-et-Garonne, a pretty village with a ruined castle standing at the junction of the Aveyron and Viaur rivers. Like **Varen**, the next village west, Laguépie is popular with riverside campers. But Varen has the added attraction of a well-preserved medieval core entered by way of a fortified gate called **El-Faoure**. The tiny lanes converge in the centre at a 10th-century Benedictine priory, **St-Pierre**, a barrel-vaulted, single-naved church from the late 1000s, which, unusually, has no door on its west front – originally the façade formed part of the town wall. The sculpted capitals on the north come from Varen's parish church, demolished in the 1700s, while the capitals in the choir, closed off by three mini-apses and two crypts, are among the most important from the early Middle Ages, decorated with sturdy knots, symmetrical face-to-face animals and biblical scenes. The adjacent 14th-century tower was the residence of the dean of the priory.

After Varen, the Aveyron flows below one of the oldest towns in the *département*, charming medieval **St-Antonin-Noble-Val**. Its setting first delighted the Romans, who named it *Nobilis Vallis*; the St-Antonin was tacked on when the body of the apostle of this area floated downstream in a boat and a monastery was founded to hold the relics. In the Middle Ages St-Antonin was a Cathar stronghold; in the Hundred Years' War, it was occupied by the English, who left their name behind in the tremendous cliffs of the **Rocher d'Anglars** that loom over the village. The monastery was wiped off the face of the earth by the Protestants, who were themselves clobbered in 1622 by Louis XIII; the king had failed to take Montauban after an 86-day siege, and in his pique came here to pick on someone smaller.

What it may lack in sacred architecture, St-Antonin more than makes up for in the civic, beginnning with the lovely Gothic **Place des Halles** and its **Maison des Consuls** of 1120, the latter Disneyfied by Viollet-le-Duc, who not only over-restored this rare example of Romanesque civic architecture, but added the incongruous Florentine belfry. On the first-floor gallery, note the pillar sculpted with Byzantine Emperor Justinian holding his famous *Code* of laws. The hollowed-out spaces on the second floor originally held Hispano-Moorish ceramic plates. Bits of these are now in the building's **Musée Archéologique** (***t** 05 63 30 63 47; open July–Sept 10–12 and 3–6, other times by appointment*), along with furniture and prehistoric items. The *halle* has a curious 15th-century *Crucifixion*, carved on a stone disc.

St-Antonin's labyrinthine lanes, many bearing pungent names like Rue Bombecul (what an American would call 'Shelf-butt street'), have such a rare assortment of medieval houses that the town has been called an outdoor museum of secular architecture, untouched by any recent attempts at restoration, much less the

Viollet-le-Duc beauty treatment. If you want to stock up on holiday reading visit the **English Bookshop** (*12 Rue Pelisserie, **t** 05 63 68 22 66*). Down by the river along the Promenade des Moines are the remains of the tanneries which once made St-Antonin's fortune, along with a working walnut-oil mill. Further along the river is a slate-roofed **spa** of 1913; the mineral spring here, the **Fontane de Saltet**, rich in copper, has been a popular cure for urinary infections since the 18th century. Since 1990 it has been commercially bottled so you can always keep some on hand.

The well-marked paths around St-Antonin make for exceptionally fine walking, especially along the Aveyron and up to the mighty 660ft **Rocher des Anglars** with its wide-ranging belvedere over the gorge. Stalactite spotters can aim for the **Grotte du Bosc**, 3km northeast (***t** 05 63 30 62 91, out of season **t** 05 63 56 03 12; open July and Aug daily 10–12 and 2–6, Easter–June and Sept Sun only 2–6; adm*), formed by a subterranean river; there are remarkable formations and a little museum of prehistoric finds. You can also visit at Bosc the **Musée du Machinisme Agricole de 1900 à 1950**, full of old farm machinery and tools (***t** 05 63 30 62 83; open June weekends 2–6, July–mid-Sept daily 10–12, 2–6*). Further north, the D19 leads to **Château de Cas** (***t** 05 63 67 07 40; open June–Aug 1.30–6, or by appointment at weekends April–Oct*), a rather austere citadel that defended the Bonnette valley, with a Merovingian chapel. Once the seat of a Templar commandery, it has been restored and refurnished after damage in the Revolution and the Second World War.

Further Down the Aveyron, to Caussade

Besides the kind of unspoiled beautiful scenery that makes this area a favourite for French film-makers, this section includes a surprise: an excellent museum full of works by one of France's early 20th-century masters, although the odds are 99 to 1 that you've never heard of him.

Bruniquel and Montricoux

After St-Antonin, the Aveyron cuts off a corner of the *département* of the Tarn, passing through a dramatic gorge; the best scenery and views are along the narrow corniche road, the D173, leading past the striking medieval village of **Penne**, with its castle hanging over the cliffs. Next down the river is **Bruniquel**, a picturesque hill town, Protestant stronghold and now artists' colony built under a large fortress, overlooking the cliffs at the confluence of the Aveyron and Vère. This, according to Gregory of Tours, was founded by Queen Brunehaut (d. 613), a Visigoth, married to Siebert, the grandson of Clovis. She was as fierce as a queen on a chessboard, fighting a relentless war with the neighbouring queen Fredegunda, personally eliminating 10 members of Fredegunda's family, until her own nobles tired of her cruelty and handed her over to her son, who, with a decided lack of filial devotion, tied her by the hair to a wild horse.

Story or not, the **château** (***t** 05 63 67 27 67; open April–June and Sept daily 2–6, July and Aug daily 10–12.30 and 2–7, Oct Sun and hols 10–12.30 and 2–6; adm*), rising 300ft

Tourist Information

Bruniquel: Rue d'Albi, **t** 05 63 67 29 84.
Caussade: at the *mairie*, **t** 05 63 26 04 04 or **t** 05 63 93 10 45.

Market Days

Caussade: Mon, farmers' market.

Where to Stay and Eat

Bruniquel ✉ 82800

Chambres d'Hôte chez Marc de Baudouin, Promenade de Ravelin, **t** 05 63 67 26 16 (*inexpensive*). Four rooms with bath in a grand old house with fine views (*evening meal 95F*).

L'Étape du Château, in the centre, **t** 05 63 67 26 16 (*cheap*). You can sleep for less and dine on good simple meals served in the panoramic dining room (*85F*). *Closed Nov–Feb.*

Montricoux ✉ 82800

★★**Terrassier**, in Vaïssac (to the southwest), **t** 05 63 30 94 60 (*inexpensive*). Modern and pleasant, with a pool; it has good food in the restaurant, especially in the autumn when most dishes include wild mushrooms (*menus 105–220F, childrens menu 55F*). *Closed Fri eve, Sun eve and a couple of weeks out of season.*

Relais du Postillon on the east edge of town, **t** 05 63 67 23 58, **f** 05 63 67 27 68 (*cheap*). Old-fashioned simple rooms; delicious meat and fish dishes on its delicious terrace – leg of lamb, salmon with sorrel, chicken with morels and more (*menus 95–180F*). *Closed Fri night and Sat lunch.*

***Chambres d'Hôte*, chez Johnny and Véronique Antony**, Brunis, 2km from Montrocoux and signposted off the D115, **t/f** 05 63 67 24 08 (*inexpensive*). A Gîte de France property and a delightful place to stay. There are two big rooms and two smaller ones, tastefully decorated, with an independent entrance. There is a large swimming pool in a pleasant garden. An evening meal is offered a couple of times a week (*100–130F*).

Les Gorges de l'Aveyron, **t** 05 63 24 50 50, **f** 05 63 24 50 52. A chic modern restaurant in its own private, shady park, complete with two aviaries, along the banks of the Aveyron offering such treats as *noisettes d'agneau sautées, simple jus réduit au Madère* (*menus 148–250F*) . Choice of about 150 different wines from all over France. A more relaxed grill is right next to the river, serving simple meat and fish dishes (*110F*); there is a bar for those dining here. *Closed end Oct–mid-March, except weekends. Reserve.*

Caussade ✉ 82300

★★**Larroque**, 17 Av du 8 Mai, **t** 05 63 65 11 77, **f** 05 63 65 12 04 (*inexpensive*). A welcoming, cosy small hotel in the heart of Caussade, with a pool and an excellent restaurant, presided over by a chef with an imaginative touch for regional ingredients (*menus 90–200F*). *Closed Sat midday and Sun eve out of season, and mid-Dec–mid-Jan.*

★★**Dupont**, 25 Rue des Récollets, **t** 05 63 65 05 00, **f** 05 63 65 12 62 (*inexpensive*). Occupies a 14th-century building in the centre, with comfortable rooms.

Réalville ✉ 82440

Le St-Marcel, **t** 05 63 67 14 27. In a former stable. Tasty *mélanges* of local ingredients with fruit: try the *tourtière* with apples and smoked *magret* (*menus 68–180F*). *Closed Sun eve and Mon out of season.*

Eskualduna, on the N20 just north of Réalville, in Albias, **t** 05 63 31 01 58. Packed every day at lunchtime for its Texas-size T-bones and other steaks, grilled in the fireplace as you watch (*menus from 85F, but true carnivores will do better à la carte*).

Négrepelisse ✉ 82800

Ferme Auberge de Belle Chasse, 2km out of Négrepelisse, on the D35 to Vaïssac, signed on the right, **t** 05 63 30 86 58. Lost along narrow lanes and among fields, large, rambling and relaxing; lovely view of the countryside from the terrace, surrounded by roses and wild flowers. The food is simple but generous and farm-fresh (*menus 95–155F*). Book two days in advance to enable the meat to be 'prepared'. *Closed Wed, except July and Aug.*

over the confluence of the Vère and the Aveyron, dates back only to the 12th century – the tour includes the keep, called the Tower of Brunehaut, the knights' room and chapel, and an elegant Renaissance gallery. The nearby **Maison des Comtes Payrol**, in Rue du Château, is a rare example of 13th-century civic architecture, with its original windows and a coffered ceiling (***t*** *05 63 67 26 42; open April–Sept daily 10–6, March and Oct weekends only; adm*). Two of Bruniquel's medieval gates are intact, including the picturesque ivy-swathed **Porte de l'Horloge**, at the top of a winding lane. Ask at Bruniquel's tourist office about visits to the **Grotte de la Madeleine**, a cave in the cliffs decorated with prehistoric engravings.

The gorge of the Aveyron begins (or peters out) at **Montricoux**, a town founded by the Templars. It has a 13th-century church, **St-Eutrope**, topped with a 16th-century Toulouse-style bell tower; inside is a fresco from the 1920s by Marcel Lenoir. Marcel Lenoir? The name doesn't ring a bell? Then find out more in the **Musée Lenoir**, housed nearby in Montricoux's château, built around the Templar keep and given a Tuscan facelift in the 18th century (***t*** *05 63 67 26 48; open April–mid-Oct 10–12.30 and 2.30–6, July and Aug till 7*). Briefly, Lenoir was born in Montauban in 1872 and died in Montricoux in 1931, although he spent most of his career in the artistic whirl of Paris, where his work was admired by Braque, Matisse and Rodin.

Since then, however, few artists have been more forgotten. Lenoir himself was partly to blame through his own stubborn integrity: he refused to accept any honours or scratch anyone's back, whether they be critics, dealers or even his own peers – and the art world responded by boycotting his work. Another difficulty is that Lenoir refused to be pinned down with an easily recognizable (and marketable) style; like Picasso, he had an endless capacity and need to change, moving on from his early days under the Symbolist influences of Gustave Moreau and Mucha, to later experiments in Cubism, Surrealism and abstraction. He approached each new change of style with religious intensity, sometimes in religious subjects, such as his *Descent from the Cross, with Orchestra*; the museum has examples from every period.

The largest town in these parts is **Caussade**, 'the city of hats', a pleasant, bustling place on the main Cahors–Montauban road, surrounded by small industries, including one that produced Maurice Chevalier's trademark boaters. Its landmark is a 15th-century brick bell tower in the Toulouse style, and there are some good medieval buildings, including the *halles*, in the centre.

The D5 from St-Antonin leads west to **Septfonds**, home of a good set of dolmens (including a jauntily tilted proto-Baroque model) and an austere Spanish Republican cemetery of 1939, near a vast camp set up for refugees of the Civil War. Just south, still on the N20, is a little *bastide* with the right name for our virtual times – **Réalville**. If you are desperate for a glass of beer after all that wine, pay a visit to the **Ferme Malterie Brasserie de St Martin** (***t*** *05 87 03 14 57 / 05 63 31 06 70; open all year, direction Mirabel from town) for a taste of La Désirée.*

Montauban

Originally covered with silvery willows, hence *Mons Albanus* ('white hill'), Montauban prefers to be known as 'the pinkest of the three pink cities' (pink, that is, as in brick; the other two are Toulouse and Albi). The capital of the Tarn-et-Garonne, Montauban was cast in an original mould from its foundation, a successful medieval experiment in city planning, a new possibility that caught on to spawn dozens of baby Montaubans, the *bastides*, in the 13th and 14th centuries. Not many of the others, however, have evolved into such pleasant medium-sized cities, or can claim a collection of art as prestigious as the Musée Ingres.

History

Montauban owes its origins to a crew of oversexed monks. These were the brethren of the 'Golden Hill', Montauriol, a monastery founded in 820 by St Théobard, who claimed the *droit de cuissage* (the right to select their bedfellows from the local population). The monks abused their privilege to such an extent that the people of Montauriol asked Count Alphonse-Jourdain for a new town. He complied, and in 1144 laid out the grid plan of the first new town in the southwest, essentially a *bastide* a hundred years before the others began sprouting like autumn mushrooms on the battle lines of the Hundred Years' War.

The counts allowed Montauban to elect its own consuls, and gave it so many privileges that it soon sucked up all the loose people in the area. In spite of being punished for loyalty to Toulouse during the Albigensian Crusade, Montauban quickly rebounded; as a new town with a relatively free, new population it had something of the enterprising spirit of an American frontier town. By the mid-14th century Montauban was bustling with the import and export of textiles – just when the Treaty of Brétigny (1360) ceded it to England. John Chandos came in person to take it for the Black Prince, who spent many months here, plotting and fighting on the frontiers of French territory.

After the Hundred Years' War Montauban's commerce quickly picked up again, and like other mercantile towns (Bergerac and Nîmes, for instance) it was very receptive to the new doctrines of Calvin. After a good deal of simmering, the pot boiled over on 20 December 1561; the Montaubanais en masse broke down the cathedral door, pillaged the building and burnt it to the ground, then did the same to all the other churches and convents in town, except for St-Jacques, which they converted into a Protestant temple. All the brick and stone of the churches immediately went into building walls, which were unusually efficient, twice repelling the concerted Catholic attacks.

The future Henri IV spent much time here, and when he became king his Edict of Nantes made Montauban a Protestant place of safety. His less tolerant and less capable son Louis XIII marched down in 1621 with an army of 25,000 and besieged Montauban for weeks, setting the outskirts on fire, but he found the Protestants too tough for his taste and went home feeling sorry for himself. His grand vizier Richelieu, however, waited until the fall of La Rochelle in 1629, which left Montauban isolated as the last Protestant stronghold in France, and diplomatically convinced it to surrender.

No dummy, Richelieu's first act was to demolish Montauban's walls. His second was to cajole the inhabitants not to emigrate to Protestant countries by offering them plums – money and job-generating bureaucracies, their own *intendants* and a regional bureau of finances; Richelieu may have been a cardinal but he knew well enough that it was the mercantile Protestants who generated much of the nation's wealth. His plan worked so well that by the 18th century Montauban could proudly claim to be the third city in the southwest. Its weavers produced a thick wool fabric called *cadis* that sold like hot cakes in France's American colonies. The *intendants* drew out new broad avenues and laid out the first parks.

Montauban's contribution to the Revolution was a woman about two hundred years ahead of her time: Olympe de Gouges, born in 1748, daughter of the obscure poet-magistrate Lefranc de Pompignan. Defender of the rights of all people, even women, to live without oppression, Gouges wrote a brochure called *Les Droits de la femme et de la citoyenne*, declaring that 'if a woman has the right to mount the scaffold, she has the right to ascend to the seats of justice'. For trying to obtain political rights for women and 'forgetting the virtues of her sex' she was guillotined in 1793. But if the Revolution was blind to the need for women's rights, the Napoleonic code that followed a few years later really put half the population of France in its place by ending rights (especially the right to buy and sell property) that even medieval women had enjoyed. Only since the 1970s have French wives been able to open bank accounts in their own names.

Another setback was in store for Montauban – its invaluable *cadis* trade began to decline when France lost her colonies in Canada and Louisiana, then disappeared altogether when the new industrial mills in the north undersold the city's artisan weavers. Napoleon's intervention, making Montauban a departmental capital, assured at least a bureaucratic vocation that kept the town from complete economic decline in the 19th century, although it was a century burnished by the reflected glow of the international fame of its native sons Ingres and Bourdelle, Rodin's chief assistant. Since the last war, Montauban has typified the turnaround of a *ville moyenne* – the proximity of dynamic Toulouse, and its key location on the southwest railways and highways, have attracted numerous small enterprises and led to, among other things, the thorough restoration of its old brick charms.

Place Nationale

The finest gift bestowed by old Alphonse-Jordain on the new town of Montauban is its central square, the Place Nationale. Although it was the prototype for the central *bastide* market square, none of the later squares can match its innovative, urbane sophistication. First off, it isn't even a square at all, but a more subtle, visually interesting irregular trapezoid with covered chamfered corners. The whole plan of the new town echoes this slight distortion of the plain, monotonous square grid. Its unique 'double cloister' arcades date from 1144 and were originally built in wood; after a fire in 1614, they were slowly rebuilt exactly as they were in warm brick, even though the style of vaulting was considered archaic at the time (you can see the year when each

bay was completed inscribed in the keystones of the vaults – the last reads 1708). The interior galleries functioned as covered lanes, the continuation of the streets that come into the angles of the Place Nationale; the outer galleries were given over to displays of merchandise. In the central square the Montaubanais bought their food, hanged their thieves and issued their proclamations.

During the 17th-century fashion for homogenous squares, the city ordered that all the façades of the buildings facing the Place Nationale should be rebuilt in the same style, with the attic storerooms lit by openings called *mirandes*. Note the sundial on the north side, with the legend *Una tibi* ('Your hour will come!'); the metal **metre bar** set vertically in the southwest corner of the square was put in place to instruct the locals when the Revolution standardized French measures.

St-Jacques and the Pont-Vieux

If you leave Place Nationale by the metre corner, you'll soon find yourself in Place Victor-Hugo, site of **St-Jacques**, a combination church, assembly and voting hall built by Montauban's consuls in the 13th century. During the repairs following the Hundred Years' War, it was given an octagonal bell tower, which, like St-Sernin in Toulouse, has a curious change in design halfway up and still bears scars from Louis XIII's cannonballs. The neo-Roman portal with its coloured-tile decoration dates from the 19th century; the interior is typically southern Gothic, with a large single nave.

Down from St-Jacques, **Place Bourdelle** is named after Bourdelle's dramatic 1895 ***Monument to the War Dead of 1870***, an early major work, showing the influence of his master Rodin. Here the neoclassical Tribunal de Commerce now houses two museums. The **Musée d'Histoire Naturelle** upstairs (***t*** *05 63 66 46 34; open 10–12 and 2–6, closed Sun and Mon*) has an immense collection of birds and animals, fossils (starring some unique Quercy primates from 65 million years ago) and minerals, among them phosphorites from Quercy – one of the places on earth where they are most abundant – and pieces of a meteorite that fell in the Tarn-et-Garonne in 1864 and excited much speculation about aliens from outer space. On the ground floor, the

Getting Around

Montauban's station off Av Mayenne, at the west end of town over the Tarn, is well served by **trains** between Paris and Toulouse with a stop at Angoulême, and between Toulouse and Bordeaux (stops at Moissac and Agen).

Autocars Barrière, 16 Rue du Châteauvieux, **t** 05 63 93 34 34, has **buses** twice a week direct to Barcelona, Valencia and Morocco. The largest coach company with routes to local towns and villages is Chauderon Jardel, **t** 05 63 22 55 00. Other routes are served by Barrière and Gau, **t** 05 63 30 44 45. It is probably easiest to telephone the tourist office first to check which goes where. Between them the companies serve most of the *département* and the big towns beyond.

You can hire **bikes** at Denayrolles, 878 Av Jean Moulin, **t** 05 63 03 62 02.

Taxis: t 05 63 63 20 02 or **t** 05 63 63 28 24.

From June to September you can rent your own little electric **boat** from near the Pont Vieux, by the car park, for a pleasant jaunt on the Tarn. Call the tourist office for more information.

Tourist Information

L'Ancien Collège, Place Prax-Paris, **t** 05 63 63 60 60, **f** 05 63 63 65 12.

Information for the whole of Tarn-et-Garonne from the Comité Départemental du Tourisme, Conseil Général de Tarn-et-Garonne, Bd Midi-Pyrénées, **t** 05 63 63 31 40.

Market Days

Sat mornings in Place Prax-Paris, farmers' and flea market. In winter, Wed and Sat mornings, *marché au gras* in Place Nationale.

Where to Stay

Montauban ✉ 82000

*****Hostellerie Les Coulandrières**, on the D958, 3km west of the city at Montbeton, **t** 05 63 67 47 47, **f** 05 63 67 46 45 (*moderate*). The prettiest place to stay in Montauban, a modern inn under a superb cedar tree, with a pool and park and bright rooms; the restaurant is one of the best, featuring delicious seafood (*menus from 110F*). *Closed Sun eve and Jan.*

*****Ingres**, 10 Av de Mayenne, near the station, **t** 05 63 63 36 01, **f** 05 63 66 02 90 (*moderate*). A fine modern hotel behind an older façade,

Musée du Terroir (*t 06 53 66 46 34; same hours*) is devoted to country life in Bas-Quercy and southwest ethnography in general. The interesting section on regional prehistory (*same hours*) is nearby in the former library at 8 Square du Général-Picquart (a street, incidentally, named after the army intelligence officer who went to prison for defending Dreyfus in 1898; Montauban is still a progressive town).

From Place Bourdelle the Tarn is spanned by the **Pont Vieux**, a bridge planned from Montauban's foundation by Alphonse-Jourdain. However, financial and technical difficulties prevented its erection until King Philippe le Bel was passing through Montauban in 1303, and the town consuls (as they would later buttonhole Napoleon) got the king to promise his assistance in raising taxes and providing wood for the brick kilns for the construction of their long-awaited bridge, promising in turn to name its towers after him. Work on the 677ft structure began in 1311 and was a technological *tour de force*; its seven uneven arches have stood up to the worst floods the unruly Tarn has sent down, including water so high in 1441 that it washed over the top of the bridge. Originally the bridge resembled the Pont Valentré in Cahors, with Philippe le Bel's three fortified towers; these were demolished early in the 20th century to let more traffic through.

with a garden, pool, but no restaurant; well-equipped rooms.

*****Mercure Montauban**, 12 Rue Notre Dame, **t** 05 63 63 17 23, **f** 05 63 66 43 66 (*moderate*). All the usual attributes of a chain hotel. The restaurant has a good reputation (*meals from 85F*). Worth considering for its very central location.

****D'Orsay**, Rue Salengro, opposite the station, **t** 05 63 66 06 66, **f** 05 63 66 19 39 (*inexpensive*). Very comfortable rooms, several air-conditioned, and the best food in Montauban (*see* below).

Eating Out

In the pastry shops of Montauban, look for ***montauriols***, chocolate truffles, with a cherry marinated in armagnac in the centre.

La Cuisine d'Alain, the restaurant in the Orsay hotel (*see* above). Warm and welcoming, offering local ingredients and traditions with an original slant; among the *à la carte* is the local version of cassoulet. Save room for a choice from the fabulous dessert cart. On Sat Alain Blanc concocts a special menu devoted to different regions of France (*menus 130–295F*). *Closed Sun, Mon lunch and mid-Aug.*

Le Ventadour, 23 Quai Villebourbon, **t** 05 63 63 34 58. In the brick vaults of restored 17th-century dyeworks, they serve an aromatic dish of beef with morels and other delicacies (*menus 140–220F*). *Closed Sun and Mon.*

Ambrosie, 41 Rue Comédie, **t** 05 63 66 27 40. A fair name, given the delicious dishes served in this up-to-date restaurant (tiny, so get there early for lunch). Menus offer alternatives for both seafood-lovers and fish-haters – try the duck in an onion fondue (*menus from 80F*).

Au Fil de l'Eau, 14 Quai Dr Lafforgue, **t** 05 63 66 11 85. In a pleasant and quite leafy spot on the banks of the Tarn, with a small children's play area opposite. There is a bias towards regional fare such as *magret de canard fourré de son foie gras* and a good selection of wines from the southwest (*menus 89–295F, children's menu 55F*). *Closed Sun eve, Mon and mid-Aug.*

Au Chapon Fin, Place St-Orens, just off the roundabout after crossing Pont Neuf, **t** 05 63 63 12 10, **f** 05 63 20 47 43. A local favourite, serving quite traditional food such as *cote d'agneau grillées* and *entrecôte au roquefort*. There is some fish too (*menus 95–180F, children's menu 60F*). *Closed end July–mid-Aug, Fri eve and Sat.*

The Musée Ingres

19 Rue de l'Hôtel de Ville, **t** *05 63 22 12 91; open daily 10–12 and 2–6, in July and Aug 9.30–12 and 1.30–6; mid-Oct–Easter closed Mon and Sun morning; adm.*

The museum is housed in the pretty bishops' palace at the eastern end of the bridge, built over the foundations of an unfinished medieval castle that had been the local headquarters for English rule. The bishop's palace, begun in the 1640s – a decade after the king's troops marched in – was a symbol of the new political and religious order. After the Revolution the building became Montauban's *mairie*, though later the mayor moved elsewhere, leaving the palace for what seemed a more fitting use: a monument to the city's favourite son, Jean-Auguste-Dominique Ingres (1780–1867).

This painter, whose donations to his home town make up the core of the museum's collection, was tremendously popular in his time, a technical virtuoso whose icily perfect religious and mythological works fitted the mood of Napoleonic neoclassicism; in fact many of his first paintings were kitsch propaganda pieces commissioned by the emperor. Ingres was an Academic artist from head to toe, the sort of dedicated conformist who believed in rules and precepts, and measured his success by the medals he won at competitions. His battles with the younger generation of Romantic painters, especially Delacroix, were legendary. The earlier paintings on display here were done when Ingres was still in the workshop of his master, the even more indigestible Jacques-Louis David.

The collection includes thousands of sketches and drawings, some of which are displayed in a way that shows up the contrast between the Academic painter and the suppressed artist within, as in the *Jesus among the Doctors* (painted when Ingres was 82), in which a lovely, almost Pre-Raphaelite study is juxtaposed with the stiff and silly finished work. Ingres did much better at portraits, of which several are offered here, and also in mythological scenes such as the *Dream of Ossian*, a colossal canvas of ghostly figures in the sky, painted for Napoleon's bedroom (Ossian was the supposed medieval Scottish bard whose 'rediscovered' works, all fakes, nevertheless made a great impression on poets at the dawn of the Romantic era).

The Salle Ingres, the bishops' bedchamber, was partially decorated by Ingres' father, also an artist. It houses a little shrine to Ingres, with the great man's desk, his paints, a view of his studio in Rome, and his violin (he was an accomplished musician as well as a painter) – all arranged the way Ingres himself planned it.

Not all the works present are by Ingres. From his collection are archaeological items – an Etruscan burial urn and a black-figure Greek vase with the *Battle of Centaurs and Lapiths* that may be the best work in the museum – as well as a few Italian paintings (a Masolino predella panel and a *Nativity* by Carpaccio), and one from Spain, a striking *St Jerome* attributed to Ribera. A flatulent historical echo is supplied by Ingres' spiritual ancestor, Charles Lebrun, the first director of the Académie: *Louis XIV in the Chariot of State*. Montauban's other famous son, the sculptor Antoine Bourdelle (1861–1929), gets a room, with portrait busts of figures as diverse as Ingres himself and Krishnamurti; Bourdelle's most acclaimed work, however, stands out in front of the museum on the square, the *Last Centaur Dying*.

Down below, in the Salle du Prince Noir – all that remains of the English castle – the museum keeps a small archaeological collection, including a Roman mosaic, and some medieval items, among them a nasty torture contraption subtly called the *banc à question*.

The Cathédrale Notre-Dame

From the Musée Ingres, Rue de l'Hôtel de Ville leads up to Montauban's cathedral, rebuilt between 1692 and 1739, when Louis XIV sent down his own architects to build a church worthy of the Counter-Reformation, celebrating the victory over heresy and, as always, his own glory. Unlike the warm red brick that epitomizes Montauban, the cathedral shows its foreign, Parisian origins in its white stone and frostily perfect classicism (not many cathedrals were built during this period in France; Versailles' is the most famous one).

The vast interior is full of equally frigid 18th–19th-century furnishings, and one of Ingres' major works, the enormous *Vow of Louis XIII*, commissioned for the cathedral and painted in Florence between 1820 and 1824. He exhibited the painting in the 1824 Paris salon, where it hung next to the *Massacre of Chios*, the Romantic masterpiece of Delacroix. To the neoclassical heirs of Jacques-Louis David, Delacroix's work was 'the massacre of painting' and Ingres was declared the champion and upholder of Academic values; Delacroix sniffed that Ingres' 'painting was pure Italian', and a life-long rivalry was born. It is certainly easy to see what Delacroix meant: the Virgin, Child and angels seem to have come straight out of Raphael's sketchbooks. Louis XIII is seen offering the Virgin his crown and sceptre, symbolizing the kingdom of France. The subject could only have been suggested by a rabid Catholic (or a Parisian), as Louis XIII certainly didn't do Montauban any favours.

Around Montauban

In 1679, Montauban's *intendant* Foucault initiated the greening of the pink city by planting thousands of elms on the banks of the Tarn, along the broad street that now bears his name, **Cours Foucault**. Enjoying a fine view of the historic centre, the Cours has been the city's most popular promenade ever since. Its focal point, closing the view between the long alleys of trees, is Bourdelle's *La France veillant sur ses morts*, a First World War monument inspired by the temples and sculpture of ancient Greece, typical of the sculptor's later career, when he moved from Rodin's romanticism to a more classical style. Curiously enough, a small piece of the Cours Foucault belongs to the Osage of Oklahoma. In 1829, some members of the tribe showed up in Montauban, exhausted and demoralized from a two-year tramp across Europe; white trappers back home had told them they could escape discrimination in America and become French citizens. The people of Montauban couldn't grant their wish, but they raised money to pay for their passage home. Some 160 years later contact was renewed, and a symbolic patch of France was donated to the Osage; every other year cultural exchanges take place in the summer. You can learn more from the Association Oklahoma-Occitania, 1096 Chemin du Coteau, **t** 05 63 66 89 98.

South of the centre, the **Jardin des Plantes**, created in 1860, has several rare species of tree, while to the east of Place Prax-Paris (with the mushroom-roofed market) is the **Espace François Mitterrand** (formerly the Parc Chambord), created in 1972; here, in May and June, 16,000 roses from around the world burst into intoxicating bloom. At the end of the garden you'll find the municipal Olympic-sized pool. Lastly, north of Place Prax-Paris, there's a little **Musée de la Résistance et de la Déportation** (*33 Grand Rue Villenouvelle,* **t** *05 63 66 03 11; open Tues–Sat 10–12 and 2–6*) with three permanent exhibitions on the period from the rise of Nazism to Liberation, internment camps in the region, and Free France. There are often temporary exhibitions as well.

Moissac

There's only one reason to make the trip to Moissac, but it's a solid five-star reason: the Romanesque Abbaye de St-Pierre, one of the crown jewels of medieval French sculpture. The town of Moissac, washed clean of most of its character in a tragic flood in 1930 that killed over a hundred people and destroyed over 600 buildings, now busies itself growing aromatic pale golden *chasselas de Moissac*, France's finest dessert grapes, first cultivated in the Middle Ages in the abbey's vineyards and the first French fruit to attain AOC status, in 1952.

The Abbaye St-Pierre

The first Benedictine monastery was founded here by Clovis in 506, commemorating his victory over the Visigoths. The battle had cost him a thousand men, whom Clovis declared would be remembered by an abbey of a thousand monks. Exactly marking the spot of such an important religious foundation being a very serious matter, Clovis, as the legend goes, climbed a hill and hurled his trusty javelin, telling God to guide it where he saw fit. Gshshloop! went the javelin as it struck the gooey muck of a marsh. Never questioning God's peculiar choice, Clovis ordered his builders to get on with it. He had to order them three times. In the end they had to sink deep piles to support the structure. No one knows if the story has a germ of truth in it, or if the monks made it up to explain their annoying problems with rising damp.

One of Clovis's successors, King Dagobert, put the abbey under royal protection, thanks to the influential bishop of Cahors, St Didier (AD 630–55), who according to some accounts was the true father of Moissac. Although royal protection was promised into the 9th century, the Merovingian and Carolingian kings proved to be too far away to be of much help when the abbey was sacked by the Arabs in 721 and 732 (the year of their defeat at Poitiers), then by the Normans in 850 and by the Magyars in 864. Fed up with royal 'protection', the abbots henceforth placed themselves under the counts of Toulouse. After a roof collapsed in 1030 and a fire in 1042, the monastery was in such spiritual and material disorder that the counts put it under the control of Cluny; they, noting its key position along one of the main pilgrimage routes to Compostela (from Puy-en-Velay), sent money for its restoration and a new abbot,

Getting Around

Moissac is on the slow **railway** line between Bordeaux, Agen, Montauban and Toulouse.

For **bus** information, call **t** 05 63 04 92 30.

An old barge, Le Grain d'Or, offers **cruises** of 2hrs or more of the Canal Latéral and the river Tarn, **t** 05 63 04 48 28 for information; most take in the unique *pente d'eau de Montech* (*see* p.425). Alternatively, hire your own boat, by the Uvarium.

Taxis are available: **t** 05 63 04 03 88 and **t** 05 63 04 02 28.

Tourist Information

6 Place Durand-de-Bredons, **t** 05 63 04 01 85, **f** 05 63 04 27 10. *Open mid-Oct–mid-Mar 9–12 and 2–5, mid-Mar–June and Sept–mid-Oct 9–12 and 2–6, July and Aug 9–7.*

Market Days

Sat and Sun mornings, farmers' market.

Where to Stay and Eat

Moissac ✉ 82200

****Le Pont Napoléon**, 2 Allées Montebello, **t** 05 63 04 01 55 (*inexpensive*). Named after the bridge commissioned by Bonaparte in 1808, although it had to wait for Napoleon edition no.III, in 1852, actually to be built. Delightful and old-fashioned, it has lovely rooms overlooking the Tarn. Purchased by master chef Michel Dussau, its reputation of serving the best food in Moissac on its lovely terrace will only increase (*restaurant menus from 139F*). *Closed Wed, Sun eve and two weeks in Jan.*

****Au Chapon Fin**, Place des Récollets, **t** 05 63 04 04 22 (*inexpensive*). A pleasant and central provincial hotel.

Ile du Bidounet, **t** 05 63 32 52 52. The municipal campsite, on the Tarn, a pretty place with a pool. *Open April–Sept.*

Bar de Paris, across from the market on Place des Récollets, **t** 05 63 04 00 61. Pizzas and brasserie-style dishes, including a fine plate of frogs' legs (*menus 70–150F*).

Durand de Brendon, who was also bishop of Toulouse and who consecrated the new church on 6 November 1063.

Because of Moissac's close links with Toulouse, Simon de Montfort sacked it during the Albigensian Crusade in 1212; although Raymond VII managed to recapture the abbey in 1222, he was helpless to save the 210 Cathars burned by the Inquisition here in 1234. These human bonfires seem to mark a turning point in the abbey's popularity; in 1466 a papal bull stripped the abbey from Cluny's jurisdiction and put it under absentee *abbés commanditaires* who sucked up most of the rents due to the abbey for their private pockets. By 1626 the monks had been replaced by a chapter of canons. Louis XIV's finance minster, Colbert, purchased Moissac's library and moved it to Paris, and many of the abbey buildings were demolished on the eve of the Revolution, which as usual could find no better use for the surviving monastery than as a saltpetre works, after taking care to surgically guillotine the carved figures of the greatest Romanesque cloister in France.

In 1847 Viollet-le-Duc was summoned by the then superintendent of historical monuments, Prosper Mérimée, to restore the majestic porch. He had hardly begun in 1850 when along came a cohort of philistines who made the sans-culottes look like schoolboys – the builders of the Bordeaux–Toulouse railway – who announced that the cloister was dead smack in the way of the line someone in Paris had drawn for the tracks. A huge battle ensued with the preservationists, and, although at the last moment the tracks were realigned, the railway men had their evil way with the splendid refectory and kitchens. A century and a half later, opinion has turned 180 degrees; now there are plans to cover up the railway tracks to enhance what remains of Moissac's medieval atmosphere.

The Porch

Given Moissac's record of trouble, the great abbot Ansquitil decided in 1115 to fortify the church's tower-porch. The tower is 12th century up to its first floor chapel; Viollet-le-Duc restored the brick steeple and crenellations. Sheltered underneath is the sublime porch, one of the most powerful and beautiful works of the Middle Ages; the men who commissioned it are remembered in the two statues on pilasters off on either side, Abbot Ansquitil on the left (or, some say, St Benedict) and on the right Abbot Roger (1115–35), who completed the work after Ansquitil's death.

The **tympanum**, originally vividly painted, rests on a lintel recycled from a Gallo-Roman building, decorated with eight large thistle flowers and enclosed in a cable or vine, spat out by a monster at one end and swallowed by another monster at the other. The main scene represents one of the key visions of the Apocalypse (Rev. 4: 2–8), of Christ sitting in the Judgment of Nations, with the Book of Life in his hand ('And he who sat there appeared like jasper and carnelian, and round the throne was a rainbow that looked like an emerald... and before the throne there is as it were a sea of glass, like crystal'). You might notice that this Christ has three arms, one on the book, one raised in blessing, and another on his heart, but please don't ask for an explanation: no one's come up with a convincing one yet.

The four symbols of the Evangelists twist to surround him, and two seraphim, carrying scrolls representing the Old and New Testaments, are squeezed under the rainbow. The rest of the tympanum is occupied by the 24 Elders, no two alike, each gazing up from their thrones at Christ, 'each holding a harp, and with golden bowls full of incense, which are the prayers of the saints'. Most writers describe the fear and awe in the Elders' eyes, but in actual fact they don't look frightened at all, and in place of harps they all play the medieval proto-violin, the rebeck. The whole wonderfully rhythmic composition could just as easily be an old-timers' band raising their glasses in an intermission toast to a stern but respected and beloved bandleader.

But that's not all. The central pillar of the door, the **trumeau**, is sculpted with three pairs of lions in the form of Xs symbolically guarding the church (others prowl about the capitals of the tower). Note the scalloped edges of the doorway, a design picked up from Moorish Spain. On either side of the door are tall relief figures: *St Peter* with his keys, stepping on a dragon (left); *Isaiah*, whose scroll prophesies the coming Messiah (right); and, on the outer sides of the porch, a severe *St Paul* and a gentle, dreamy-eyed *Jeremiah* (also holding a scroll), elongated, stylish, supple figures that sway and almost dance, most probably from the same anonymous chisel that sculpted the wonderful Isaiah at Souillac. To the right of the portal are scenes from the life of the Virgin – the *Annunciation*, *Visitation* and *Adoration of the Magi*; to the left, poor Lazarus' soul is taken into the bosom of Abraham, while, below, the soul of the rich, feasting Dives is carried off in the other direction. Below him, you can make out a miser with demons on his shoulder as he refuses alms to a beggar, while to the left is Lust, serpents sucking at her breasts while an amused, very Chinese demon looks on. Up above the porch on the cornice – hiding in plain sight – is a large figure blowing a horn, perhaps Gabriel. Few visitors ever notice him.

The Church

Inside the porch, the vaulted square of the **narthex** has some excellent Romanesque capitals, carved with voluptuous vegetation playfully metamorphosed into animals; one shows Samson wrestling with a lion. Above it is the mysterious **upper chapel**, built of a dozen arches linked in a central oculus. This has been interpreted as a symbolic representation of heaven, or more specifically the New Jerusalem. As in other, similar constructions around Europe, whatever ceremonial or liturgical functions it might have had are lost in time. There are two ways to enter it, the broad door for the many, and a narrow one leading into the cloister for the monks.

The **interior** of the church had to be rebuilt in 1430 and can't begin to compete with the fireworks on the portal. You can see the foundations of the single-naved 1180 church (along the bottom of the Gothic nave), which like that at Cahors was crowned with a row of Byzantine domes; unlike at Cahors they collapsed and have been replaced with Flamboyant Gothic vaults in brick. Only one chapel has managed to retain its 15th century geometrical murals, which inspired the restoration on the other walls. Some of the church's excellent polychrome sculpture survives, especially a 12th-century *Christ* and, from the 15th century, the *Flight into Egypt* with a serious-minded burro, the beautiful *Entombment* and a *Pietà* (the figure with the swollen head is Gaussen de la Garrigue, consul of Moissac). Note the Baroque organ consul, bearing the arms of Cardinal Mazarin, *abbé commanditaire* from 1644 to 1661 and one of the most successful grafters of all time.

The Cloister

***t** 05 63 04 01 85; open same hours as the tourist office, where tickets are bought; adm. Guided visits daily in July and Aug.*

Behind the church is the abbey's serenely magnificent cloister, built by abbots Durand de Bredons and Ansquitil. After Simon de Montfort sacked Moissac, the arches had to be rebuilt, and were given a gentle hint of a Gothic point (1260), but all the 76 magnificent capitals, set on alternating paired and single slender columns of various coloured marbles, come from the end of the 11th century; they are the oldest *in situ* in France. They also mark a major artistic turning point, away from the immobile, rather stiff, hieratical figures of the great Guilduin (as in Toulouse's St-Sernin) towards more fluid, stylized poses with a sense of movement, exquisite modelling, and a play of light and shadow hitherto unknown in Romanesque sculpture. The capitals are carved with foliage inspired by Corinthian capitals, but with luxuriant virtuosity; others have birds and animals intricately intertwined.

Some 46 capitals tell the lives of the saints – don't miss the dynamic martyrdoms: St Lawrence burning on the grill, while two Romans blow on the flames; St Martin

Moissac Abbey Cloister

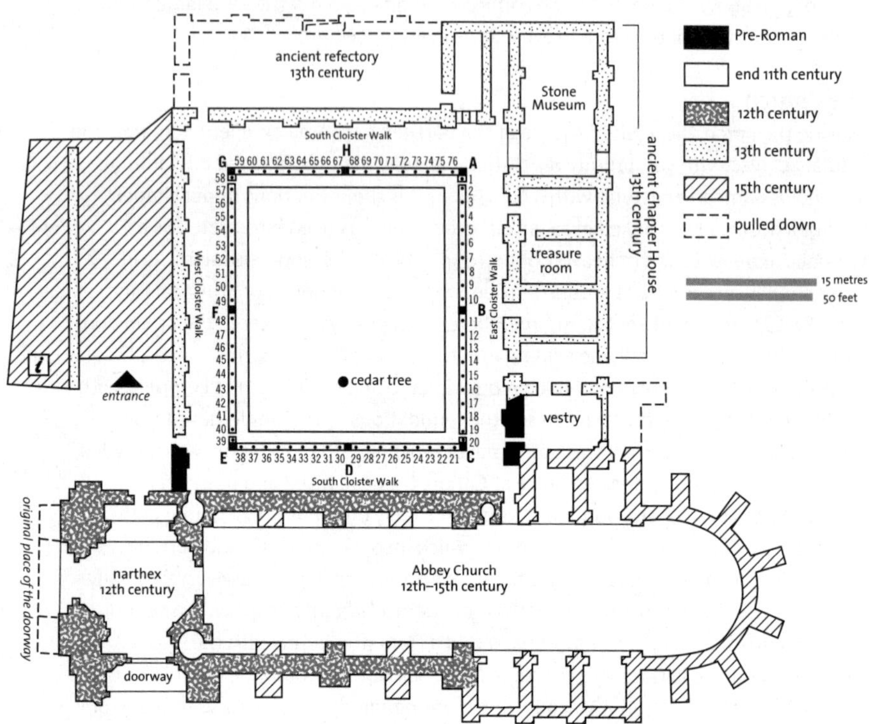

dividing his cloak with the beggar; St John the Baptist and the feast of Herod; St Stephen being stoned; St Peter upside down on his cross next to St Paul's beheading, a capital set near a little niche that once contained some of their relics. Other scenes are rare – the city of Jerusalem vs. unholy Babylon, the story of Nebuchadnezzar, and Shadrach, Meshach and Abednego in the furnace. At the corners and in the centre of each gallery are square pillars, covered with recycled tops of Roman sarcophaguses; the corners are carved with bas-reliefs of eight apostles, the 'pillars of the Church'; the central pillar in the east gallery has an effigy of Abbot Durand de Bredons, while on the west you can see the dedication inscription of the cloister: 'In the year of the Incarnation of the eternal Father 1100, this cloister was completed in the time of Lord Ansquitil, Abbot, Amen.'

Off the cloister, the 13th-century **chapel of St-Ferréol** has faint frescoes of its eponymous saint curing the ill; it now contains a museum of other capitals and the original reliefs from the lower part of the portal, damaged by the damp and replaced by copies. Near the entrance, a narrow stair leads up to the Upper Chapel.

Moissac Abbey Cloister

A Corner pillar: Sts John and James
1 Annunciation
2 Martyrdom of Sts Fructorosus, Eulogius and Augurius
3 Acanthus and vine decoration
4 Martyrdom of St Sernin
5 Acanthus decoration
6 Decoration, griffins and eagles
7 Adoration of the Magi; Massacre of the Innocents
8 Palm and vine decoration
9 Wedding at Cana
10 Decoration of eagles and human figures
B Central pillar: Abbot Durand of Bredons
11 Decoration of eagles and human figures
12 The rich man Dives and the beggar Lazarus (as on the portal)
13 Decoration of palms and birds
14 Jesus and the Apostles
15 Martyrdom of St Lawrence
16 Acanthus decoration
17 Adam and Eve
18 Decorations, alphabet and inscriptions
19 Martyrdom of Sts Peter and Paul, with Nero
20 Samson and the lion
C Corner pillar, Sts Peter and Paul
21 Baptism of Jesus
22 Liberation of St Peter
23 Transfiguration of Christ
24 Scenes from Revelations: the Reaper and the Four Horsemen
25 Temptations of Christ
26 Good Samaritan
27 Healing miracles of Jesus
28 The Four Evangelists
29 More Revelations: Michael defeats the Beast; Gog and Magog
D Central pillar: decorative
30 The New Jerusalem
31 David and his harp, and the other musicians
32 Lions and acanthus decoration
33 Martyrdom of St Stephen
34 Daniel and the punishment of Nebuchadnezzar
35 Eagles and floral decoration
36 Babylon (countertype to the New Jerusalem)
37 Dream of Nebuchadnezzar
38 Martyrdom of St John the Baptist
E Corner pillar: Apostles Matthew and Bartholemew
39 David and Goliath
40 Men and eagles with ropes
41 Vine decorations
42 Cain and Abel
43 Lions and figures
44 The Beatitudes (blessed are...)
45 Acanthus decorations
46 Lions and eagles
47 Decorations
48 Anointing of David
F Central pillar: dedicatory inscription of the cloister
49 Winged serpents
50 Acanthus decorations
51 The miracle of Lazarus
52 Musicians and archers
53 Acanthus and pomegranate decorations
54 Daniel in the lions' den; zodiacal sign of Capricorn
55 Birds and lions
56 Acanthus and floral decorations
57 The Cross
58 The sacrifice of Abraham
G Sts Philip and Andrew
59 Jesus and the Samaritan woman
60 Decorations
61 The story of St Martin
62 Shadrach, Meshach and Abednego in the furnace
63 Eagles and birds
64 The Four Evangelists
65 Arabesque decorations
66 The capture of Jerusalem on the First Crusade
67 Daniel in the lions' den
H Abstract designs
68 The Draught of Fishes, and Peter, John and James in the boat
69 Michael and Gabriel, seraphim and cherubim
70 Stags and horses
71 Miracles and Sts Peter and John
72 Birds and floral decoration
73 Miracles of St Benedict
74 Lions and griffins
75 Eagles and the sign of Pisces
76 St Michael and the dragon

Other Sights

Just behind the church, in the old abbots' palace in Rue de l'Abbaye, the **Musée Marguerite Vidal** (*t 05 63 04 03 08; open 9–1 and 2–6, closed Mon*) has a bit of everything from bonnets to bed-warmers in old-fashioned settings. In the 11th and 12th centuries the monks of Moissac were famous for their colourful illuminated manuscripts; in the former seminary, on Boulevard Léon Cladel (across the infamous train tracks) the **Centre d'Art Roman Marcel Durliat** (*t 05 63 04 41 79; open 9–12 and 2–6, closed Mon*) puts on exhibitions culled from its collection of photos of their works, nearly all of which have been carted off to the Bibliothèque Nationale in Paris.

South of the abbey is Moissac's market square, **Place des Récollets**. From here **Rue des Arts** (Rue Jean-Moura, lined with arts and crafts shops) leads to the deconsecrated church of St-Jacques, now the small **Musée St-Jacques** (*open Tues–Sun 3–7*), with tools, trains, religious art and other odds and ends donated by the Moissagais. The Canal Latéral à la Garonne passes just to the south, spanned by the **Pont St-Jacques**, one of the very last of the revolving bridges that permitted canal barges to pass. Upstream, an impressive 1,168ft **Pont Canal**, similar to that in Agen, takes the canal over the river Tarn. Under this in Place de l'Uvarium is the charming **Pavilion Uvarium** (1933), decorated with Art Deco frescoes. It was built for health seekers come to take 'the grape cure' to improve their complexion, offering fresh fruit from Moissac's orchards, and glasses of *chasselas* grape juice in September (*open May–Sept*). There are pretty views of the Tarn from the pavilion, its various old mills and the wooded **Ile de Beaucaire**, home of kingfishers and other birds.

On the western outskirts of Moissac, the medieval church of **St-Martin** has unfortunately been closed. A numbered plan from the tourist office will point you to the best spot for a fine view of the town; you may even see one of Moissac's herons.

Around Moissac

North of Moissac lies the realm of Quercy Blanc, with its sunflowers, vineyards of *chasselas* grapes and striking dovecotes. The Tarn-et-Garonne is said to have more of these bird hotels than any other *département* in France; if rural architecture tends to follow traditional forms, when it came to building the dovecote, or *pigeonnier*, the farmer let his imagination stray – they come in all forms, all postdating the Revolution. Before then, only the nobility were allowed to have them, and there was nothing the peasants could do if the *seigneur*'s bird gobbled his corn. Pigeons or doves had several very practical purposes: they kept down insects on the vines, they provided food for the table, but, most of all, they made a lot of guano, considered the best of all fertilizers and so precious that many a girl was married off with a dowry of pigeon poop.

North of Moissac: Lauzerte and Cazes-Mondenard

Above Moissac to the north hovers the memorable site of the *bastide* of **Lauzerte**, founded by Raymond VI of Toulouse in the 12th century and nicknamed 'the Toledo of Quercy' for its proud profile on the hill. Charmingly irregular *cornières* surround its

Tourist Information

Lauzerte: Place des Cornières, **t** 05 63 94 61 94.
St-Nicolas-de-la-Grave: Place du Château, **t** 05 63 94 82 81.
Auvillar: Place de l'Horloge, **t** 05 63 39 89 82.
Valence-d'Agen: 18 Place Sylvain-Dumont, **t** 05 63 39 61 67.

Market Days

Lauzerte: Wed and Sat mornings.
Valence-d'Agen: Tues and Sat, farmers' market.

Where to Stay and Eat

Lauzerte ✉ 82110

La Luzerta, in an cosy old mill at Vignals, **t** 05 63 94 64 43, **f** 05 63 94 66 67. Good south-west food with a *nouvelle cuisine* twist (*menus 100–220F*). *Closed Sun eve and Mon mid-Nov–Jan*. It has hotel rooms, too (*inexpensive*).

Cazes-Mondenard ✉ 82110

★★**L'Atre**, Place Hôtel de Ville, **t** 05 63 95 81 61. An especially nice little village inn, where the good cooking brings in a regular local clientele (*menus 120–210F*). *Closed Mon*.

Restaurant Yvan Quercy, **t** 05 63 95 84 02. This is in fact the hearse museum (*see* below); eating here is not only much better han it sounds, but in fact a pleasure, whether you opt for the traditional or classic menus (*150F, includes the museum and wine-tasting*).

Lafrançaise ✉ 82130

★★**Belvédère**, 16 Rue Mary Lafon, **t** 05 63 65 89 55, **f** 05 63 65 80 18 (*inexpensive*). A little Logis de France hotel in the centre, with good dining at its restaurant, **Au Fin Gourmet**; try the *civet de lotte* in Cahors wine (*menus 62–250F, children's menu 45F*). *Closed Sat and several weeks in winter*.

Ferme-Auberge des Trouilles, just north of town on the D20, follow the signs, **t** 05 63 65 84 46 (*inexpensive*). A huge farm with six delightful guest rooms and a pool; and superb farm meals (*menus 90–190F*) including Quercy salad, leek tart, grilled *magret* or lamb. *Book*.

Auvillar ✉ 82340

★★**Hotel de l'Horloge**, Place de l'Horloge, **t** 05 63 39 91 61, **f** 05 63 39 75 20 (*inexpensive*). A smart hotel with modern rooms with shower or bath. The restaurant is onsidered the best in Auvillar, with south-west favourites using fresh seasonal produce (*menus 155–320F*). Wines are mostly from the south. You can eat less formally at midday during the week on the terrace or in the bar from the bistrot menu. *Closed Wed mid-Oct–April and for a couple of weeks in Nov or Jan, phone for confirmation*.

Snack Café du Tourisme, just down the hill from the Hotel de l'Horloge. Good for a quick drink or sandwich under the parasols.

Bacchus, in the countryside on the road to Valence, **t** 05 63 29 12 20. A neoclassical location for traditional, good-value menus, with excellent duck dishes, and a chance to try ostrich prepared in the old southwest French style (*90–160F*).

Bardigues ✉ 82340

Auberge de Bardigues, **t** 05 63 39 05 58. The setting is lovely, in a pretty village entered through a line of plane trees, a couple of kilometres outside Auvillar. You can dine on regional fare in generous quantities while sitting on the wide terrace with a view of the green and pleasant countryside (*set menu 188F, menu du jour 58F, children's menu 50F*). The house speciality is salads, such as *salade gourmande with foie gras de canard, gésiers et magret séché*. The young couple who own the *auberge* are charming and welcoming. *Closed Mon in June and Sept, Mon and Tues the rest of the year, two weeks in Nov and three in Feb*.

central square, but one corner of the cobblestoned pavement looks as if it's been turned up, like the page of a book, with coloured tiles underneath. There's a fine selection of 14th- and 15th-century houses made from the white, sunbleached Quercy Blanc limestone. Below Lauzerte, visit the church of the **Carmes** for its extraordinary high altarpiece dated 1689. All Baroque is theatrical, but the action here happens on a genuine stage, starring the Virgin handing rosaries to St Simon Stock and St Teresa of Avila, while the prophet Elias and St John of the Cross stand by, all under God stage-managing from above.

Even more surprising is the museum to the east in **Cazes-Mondenard** – the only one in France dedicated to hearses, the **Musée des Corbillards**, on the D16 (***t** 05 63 95 84 02; privately owned, ring for an appointment; also* see *Where to Stay and Eat*). It had to be someone's hobby to take rusting old hearses out of junkyards and lovingly restore them; there are 80 of them, all horse-drawn, as well as old tractors and carriages; tastings of local produce and meals on request, and you can take a ride in a horse-drawn carriage. South of Cazes-Mondenard, and east of Moissac on the Tarn, is a French *bastide* of 1271. By that time they had run out of names for them and simply called this one **Lafrançaise**. It has a grand panoramic view over the Tarn, but good food is the main reason to stop by (*see* above).

St-Nicolas-de-la-Grave and Auvillar

Just west of Moissac where the Tarn flows into the Garonne is a region called La Lomagne – the bit Napoleon nicked off the Gers; it was also known, after its hills, as *Gascogne bossue*, hunchbacked Gascony. **St-Nicolas-de-la Grave** uses the swollen confluence of the big rivers as a recreational lake, a favourite for small sailboats as well as migratory birds. There's a castle with four towers built by Richard the Lion-Heart in the centre of the village, later inherited by the abbots of Moissac, and a church with a Toulouse-style bell tower and porch. St-Nicolas was the birthplace of the founder of Detroit, Antoine Laumet de Lamothe-Cadillac (1658–1713), a debt Motown has acknowledged by converting his birthplace, near the centre of the village, into the **Musée Lamothe-Cadillac** (*open July–Aug daily 2–6; other times contact the tourist office*). Lamothe had gone to Canada to explore and seek his fortune, and fought on the front lines against the English; the museum has exhibits on his deeds, and on how he founded Detroit as a French commercial base linking Louisiana to Canada. He borrowed the posh name 'Cadillac' from a château near Bordeaux (*see* pp.256–7), which General Motors also preferred for its most prestigious tall-finned gas-hogs, rather than 'Lamothe', which sounds lightweight and fly-by-night to American car-buying ears.

In this same area, south of the motorway at **Le Pin**, is the home of an extraordinary 19th-century neo-Renaissance folly set in an English park. The **Château St-Roch** is a precursor of Disneyland's Sleeping Beauty's Castle, built by a disciple of Viollet-le-Duc for an art lover who desperately wished he had inherited a château on the Loire and furnished it as if it really, really were. Unfortunately it cannot be visited.

Here in the heart of melon-growing country, the town to aim for is the lovely red-brick village of **Auvillar**, its name derived from the Latin *Alta Villa* – High House.

Auvillar's strategic location on the Garonne saw it badly battered in the Hundred Years' and Religious Wars, but it recovered nicely, and in the 18th century enjoyed a little economic boom based on goose quills for pens and painted ceramics, which you can see in the **Musée du Vieil Auvillar** (***t*** *05 65 39 89 82; open summer Tues–Sun 2.30–6.30, winter Sat and Sun only, same hours*). This is located in Auvillar's very fetching **Place de la Halle**, which, already defying the usual *bastide* geometry with its triangular shape, goes a step further in its unique circular market, rebuilt in 1828, with Tuscan columns, a tile roof and medieval grain measures intact and ready for use. (Back then, grain was measured by the *poignée*, or fistful, the equivalent of 28.6lbs – some fists! Next to the poignée measure you can see a 19th-century one in metal.) From the **Promenade du Château**, fine views down the Garonne unfortunately include the cooling towers of the nuclear plant at Golfech. Auvillar's war-scarred church of **St-Pierre**, by its sheer size, hints at the town's importance in the Middle Ages, when it produced the cantankerous Marcabru (*see* below).

Valence-d'Agen, a rather pretty town on the Garonne, started as an English *bastide* of 1283; today it gets on as best it can in the shadow of the steaming concrete towers of the nuclear plant at **Golfech**. A typical imposition of the EDF, the national electric monopoly, and its nuclear industry allies, Golfech was built to meet a demand that does not exist. For several years the EDF has been hoping to spin a new web of high-tension lines across the northern Tarn-et-Garonne and Lot to sell Golfech's power elsewhere, but the project has become the local environmentalists' public enemy number one. Meanwhile on television the EDF (which cleverly pays off residents whenever it wants to built a new nuke plant near the town) is trying to convince everyone to convert to expensive electric heating (while the government makes sure that all new public housing for the poor has it); at Golfech, they've opened a visitors' centre (***t*** *05 63 29 39 06; open daily 9–12.30 and 2–5.30pm, Sun 10–6; ring if you want to tour the reactors*). West of Valence on the D12 is the village of **Donzac** with a rather ambitious museum of the 'how we used to live' kind, the **Conservatoire de la Ruralité et des Métiers d'Autrefois** (***t*** *05 63 29 21 96; open daily 2–6, July and Aug 9–12 and 2–7; closed Jan*), with, among other things, reconstructed workshops, old farm machinery, equipment related to wine production, collections of regional pottery and minerals.

South of Auvillar and Valence d'Agen on the D11, lost in the middle of nowhere, **Lachapelle** is named after its **Oratoire de Templiers**, otherwise known as St-Pierre. The Templars originally built the oratory next to one of their castles, along the road to Compostela, and in the 15th century it became the parish church. Some time in the 18th century, Lachapelle acquired money to lavish on the interior, creating a church with opera décor, complete with boxes in the arcades. Further south, in the very corner of the *département*, **Gramont** has a 12th-century military **château** that was metamorphosed into a Renaissance residence in the 16th century; it has a lovely 12th-century statue of the Virgin in the chapel, 16th-century style garden and other fine features (***t*** *05 63 94 05 26; open May–Oct 9–12 and 2–6.30, Feb–April and Nov–mid-Dec 2–6, closed the last half of Dec and Jan*). You can also visit the **Musée du Miel** (***t*** *05 63 94 00 20; open June–Sept 10–12 and 2–7, by appointment the rest of the year*), which invites you to discover the world of bees and honey, offering free tastings.

Marcabru

The courts of love of Eleanor of Aquitaine in Poitiers had a role in changing European attitudes towards women, which until then had been influenced by the Church's opinion that women, the daughters of Eve, were the source of Original Sin and deserved to be nothing but the property of men. With an astute mix of what we might call today 'politically correct' translations of Ovid, Arthurian legend and Occitan troubadour poetry, Eleanor and her daughters (especially Marie de Champagne, her firstborn with Louis VI) formulated a startling alternative, that men were the property of women. The queen and her ladies were the judges of the new chivalric standards of behaviour of a knight towards his lady.

Auvillar's troubadour Marcabru (active 1129–50) offered the opposing view, to put it mildly. A foundling raised by Aldric d'Auvillar, he fought the Moors in Spain and had for a patron Eleanor's father, Guilhem X of Aquitaine (himself son of the first known troubadour, the bawdy Guilhem IX). Marcabru was a great innovator in rhymes, rhythms and metrical schemes and he used language in ways no one had ever done before, his vocabulary ranging from the most vulgar – even gross – realism to elegant, noble lyrics. Of his 41 surviving poems, a few are in a tender mode, especially *A la fontana del vergier*, beautifully depicting a young girl's sorrow for her lover crusading in the Holy Land, but the majority lambast women as fickle adulterous whores in language unfit for travel guides. 'He was one of the first troubadours within memory...and he spoke ill of women and of love,' wrote one of his biographers, in amazement. Eleanor must have frowned to hear his songs – or perhaps she laughed. Marcabru's *Dirai vos senes duptansa*, at any rate, is the medieval version of Louis Jordan's classic *Brother, You Better Beware*:

...Don't you think I know
when Love's cross-eyed or blind?
His words are sweet and polished
Listen! –
and his bite is gentler than a fly's,
but the cure is far more painful.

Men who follow women's wisdom
Will surely come to ill,
as the Scripture tells us.
Listen! –
Misfortune will bear down on you,
all of you, if you don't beware.

Translated by Anthony Bonner, in *Songs of the Troubadours*

Moissac towards Toulouse: the Lomagne

Once part of the Duchy of Gascony, this is one of the quieter corners of the *département* of fruit. Here, however, orchards give way to fields of little green sprouts – the Lomagne has the ideal climate and soil for garlic.

Castelsarrasin and Belleperche

Although the Arabs never built a castle here in their 8th-century thrust into France, **Castelsarrasin**, the largest town in the *département* after Montauban, did have a famous six-towered 12th-century stronghold built by the counts of Toulouse, who picked up a few stylistic tips during their many journeys to the Middle East; hence Castellum Sarracenum. The castle's defenders were so terrified of Simon de Montfort in

Tourist Information

Castelsarrasin: Place de la Liberté, **t** 05 63 32 75 00.

Beaumont-de-Lomagne: 3 Rue Pierre de Fermat, **t** 05 63 02 42 32.

Market Days

Castelsarrasin: All day Thurs.

Beaumont-de-Lomagne: Tues and Sat. Special garlic market on Tues in season.

Where to Stay and Eat

Castelsarrasin ✉ 82100

★★**Marceillac**, 54 Rue de l'Egalité, **t** 05 63 32 30 10, **f** 05 63 32 39 52 (*inexpensive*). A delightful place in the centre, with 12 well-equipped, antique-furnished rooms overlooking a central courtyard-garden.

Les Dantous, 3km south off the N113 on the D958, **t** 05 63 32 26 95 (*inexpensive*). The local postman runs a charming old farm bed-and-breakfast right off the Canal Latéral, with a pool and *boules* court, serving exquisite home-cooked meals (*also to non-guests, but book*). *Open all year.*

Auberge du Moulin, a country inn on the N113, Route de Toulouse, **t** 05 63 32 20 37. A great place to drop in for a dose of cassoulet, other regional food or wider choices (*menus 88–210F*). *Closed Wed eve.*

★★★**Château des Vicomtes Terrides** Labourgade, **t** 05 63 95 61 07, **f** 05 63 95 64 97 (*moderate*). For something more upmarket, head south to this 16th-century castle with 53 rooms and a restaurant (*menus from 145F*) near a golf course, pool and tennis courts.

Beaumont-de-Lomagne ✉ 82500

★★**Du Commerce**, 58 Av du Maréchal-Foch, **t** 05 63 02 31 02, **f** 05 63 65 26 22 (*inexpensive*). A reliable hotel-restaurant in the centre of the town, with good, filling menus (*85–160F*).

L'Arbre d'Or, 16 Rue Despeyrous, **t** 05 63 65 32 34, **f** 05 63 65 29 85 (*inexpensive*). A luxurious bed-and-breakfast in a 17th-century house with a *table d'hôte* in a garden setting run by a friendly English couple (*menus 100–120F, with wine*).

Auberge de la Gimone, Av du Lac, **t** 05 63 65 23 09. For a decadently overwhelming feast of delicious duck dishes, reserve, eat your way to gastronomic heaven, then pop like a balloon (*menu 185F*).

Montech ✉ 82700

★★**Notre-Dame**, Place Jean-Jaurès, **t** 05 63 64 77 45, **f** 05 63 64 75 36 (*inexpensive*). Comfortable rooms; puts on a good spread in a bright and pretty dining room (*menus 80–135F*).

Escatalens ✉ 82700

L'Estouffet, on the RN113, **t** 05 63 68 71 25. Fair enough for an overnight stay. Friendly owners. The restaurant specializes in grills (on the barbecue in the summer, over the fire in the winter) and cassoulet (*menus from 58F for the plat du jour, others 70 and 95F*). There is also a small shop.

1212 that they gave up without a fight when his army appeared at the gate. They were more stalwart in the Wars of Religion against the Huguenots of Montauban, only to have their exotic castle razed in the 1600s.

Castelsarrasin has kept the grid plan laid out by the counts of Toulouse, and, more unusually, the virtuous Revolutionary names of its oldest streets, reinstated in 1876 by a mayor in the Third Republic who had shared Victor Hugo's exile on Jersey: look for *rues* named Surveillance, Development, Peace, Friendship, Reason, Hospitality, Wisdom, Discretion and Equality, with Liberty Square in the centre. At 6 Place Lamothe-Cadillac lived the founder of Detroit, Antoine de Lamothe-Cadillac, who was so unimpressed with his new settlement in Michigan that he sold his title of *seigneur de Détroit* to purchase the governorship of Castelsarrasin. Castelsarrasin's main sight is **St-Sauveur**, a church founded by the monks at Moissac in 961 and rebuilt in 1260 in the southern Gothic style, all in brick, its heptagonal apse added in the 15th century. The magnificent Baroque woodwork, especially the elaborate organ console, crowned with wooden statues of angels and King David as conductor, the carved 17th-century choir stalls (only 39 of the original 80), the pulpit, and the pair of prayer-stools, one carved with a virgin and a unicorn, were originally at Belleperche.

The **Abbaye de Belleperche** (***t*** *05 63 95 62 75; open July and Aug Tues–Sun 10–6, June and Sept Tues–Sat 10–12 and 2–6, Sun 2–6; otherwise by appointment*) is true to its name, prettily perched directly over the waters of the Garonne, 5km south of Castelsarrasin. It was founded in 1143, when hermits living in the area decided to band together and sent a special request to the abbot of Clairvaux for permission to establish a branch; according to legend, when a group of Cistercians arrived to set things up, St Bernard himself came along to help the foundation. In its glory days the abbey had 200 monks and was noted for its magnificence; Pope Clement V and François I were among its guests. Nearly all was destroyed in the Wars of Religion, except for the vaulting in the library, the entrance to the refectory, and sections of the 13th-century painted tiled floor (partly removed to the Musée Ingres in Montauban). The church was rebuilt at the end of the 16th century; and the last work was done in 1760, just in time for it to be sold to speculators in the Revolution, who completely dismantled it (some of its furnishings may now be seen in the churches at the nearby village of Cordes-Tolosannes). The enormous monastery, however, was used as a farm and survived intact, although there's not much to see beside the walls and a few details. The *département* is in the throes of restoring the cloister.

South of Castelsarrasin

The pleasant *bastide* of **Beaumont-de-Lomagne** was founded in 1276 by the French and has kept its original fortified church, coiffed with an octagonal 14th-century Toulousain bell tower, a handful of old houses (one now sheltering the *mairie*), and an even rarer survivor – its enormous wooden *halle* from the 14th century. Beaumont is famous for garlic, and its garlic market, in business between July and October, claims to be the most important in France; everyone has good clean blood, although the town dentists wear a look of continual dismay. There is a garlic festival in July. The statue here of a 17th-century gentleman represents native son Pierre de Fermat

(1601–65), who was not only very, very smart, but was long suspected by many reputable mathematicians of being a smart aleck as well (*see* below).

Further south, lost in attractive rolling farm country, the village of **Bouillac** has a striking church, 17th-century **St-Sulpice**, a church with an unusual arcaded *clocher-mur* – all that survived the Wars of Religion. Inside, however, in a glass case next to the choir, it has a rare treasure: the golden reliquaries from the 13th-century Cistercian abbey of Grand-Selve, secreted out before the abbey was smashed and burned in the Revolution – beautifully worked caskets and mini-churches of gold, filigree and precious stones from the 13th century. One, a present from Alphonse de Poitier, contains a thorn from the Crown of Thorns purchased by his brother St Louis and installed in Paris's Ste-Chapelle. To the north begin the vineyards of **St-Sardos**, a pleasant *vin de pays* (tastings in the cooperative in the centre, ***t** 05 63 02 52 44; open Mon–Fri 8–12 and 2–6, Sat 8.30–12*); on the other bank of the Garonne, a velvety red wine, **La Ville-Dieu-du-Temple**, has been produced ever since the Templars planted the first vines (tastings at the **Cave de Lavilledieu**, ***t** 05 63 31 60 05; open Mon–Sat*).

Right on the Garonne, between the two wine-growing areas, **Montech** is also in the centre of the Tarn-et-Garonne's only forest, the **Forêt d'Agre**, which in the Middle Ages stretched from Castelsarrasin to the edges of Toulouse. Donated by a wealthy couple to the abbey of Moissac in 680, this mostly oak forest became the source of the abbey's prosperity; although now rather diminished in size and split by the railway and motorway, it has riding and walking paths to explore. Montech was an old stronghold of the counts of Toulouse and has a fine 15th-century **church** with an enormous bell tower. Montech is proudest these days of the world's first and only **Pente d'Eau** on its stretch of the Canal Latéral, a slope where barges are hauled up by a pair of engines, which replaces five canal locks.

South to Toulouse

There is little to detain you here, except perhaps a view of the Canal du Midi around Grisolles – unless you're feeling like a tipple or need a bite to eat.

Where to Stay and Eat

Verdun-sur-Garonne ✉ 82600

L'Oustal, follow small signs on the road going out to Bouillac, **t** 05 63 02 54 20. A popular local restaurant in a rectangular building covered in Virginia creeper. The usual south-west fare, accompanied by local wines. You can eat on the terrace to the tinkle of a fountain and there is a children's play area and ample parking (*menus 60–145F*). *Closed Sun eve and Mon.*

Grisolles ✉ 82170

★★Relais des Garrigues, Route de Fronton, **t** 05 63 67 31 59, **f** 05 63 64 13 76 (*inexpensive*). A modern little hotel a couple of minutes from the Canal du Midi, specializing in hearty *cassoulet de canard* and other south-west standbys (*menus 75–150F*). *Closed Mon.*

Ancre Marine at nearby Canals, on the RN20, **t** 05 63 02 84 00. An old farm specializing in superb seafood dishes, prepared in Breton style (*menus 75–180F*).

Fronton ✉ 31620

Lou Grel, 49 Rue Jules-Bersac, **t** 05 61 82 03 00, **f** 05 61 82 12 24 (*inexpensive*). In a garden environment, with 12 modern rooms, a pool, and an excellent restaurant that features dishes to go with the local wine (*menus 95–195F*). *Closed Sun eve and Mon.*

Côtes-de-Frontonnais

This is another ancient district, dating back to the 4th century BC, and made AOC in 1975. Now very much an up-and-coming wine, Frontonnais owes its distinction and unique character to the predominant use of the local Negrette grape (from 50 to 70 per cent of most vintages); grafted on to sturdier stock grown on tiered terraces between the Garonne and Tarn rivers, Negrette thrives on the kind of soil the French call *boulbènes*, silty pre-glacial soil on top, red clay subsoil, and, at two or three feet under that, pebbles that provide good drainage. A second factor is the local wind, the *autan* that usually assures fine weather in September and October. The resulting ruby-red wine, with a redcurrant fragrance, is either drunk quite young or after a few years in the cellar, when it is the perfect accompaniment to cassoulet; the rosés are a fruity summer drink. The two centres of the *appellation*, Fronton and Villaudric, both have cooperatives. The **Cave de Fronton**, in Fronton, **t** 05 61 82 41 27, is home to the floral Violette de Negret (the '94 is excellent), Exception du Comte de Negret (try the smooth 1997) and several good rosés. The **Château de Joliet**, Route de Grisolles in Fronton, **t** 05 61 82 46 02, produces some of the more interesting Frontonnais, especially the 100 per cent Negrette Vin de Printemps with a violet bouquet; try the '95. Also in Fronton, **Château Bellevue-le-Forêt**, **t** 05 61 82 43 21, sells an exceptional fine aromatic '95; **Château Le Roc**, **t** 05 61 82 93 90, does a fine velvety wine: taste the 1995 *cuvée réservée*.

On the south side of Toulouse itself, a very respectable red, rosé and white *vin de pays de la Haute-Garonne* comes from the **Domaine de Ribonnet** in Lagardelle-sur-Lèze, **t** 05 61 08 71 02. This vineyard used to be air-pioneer Clément Ader's hobby-horse, and has recently been revived by a Swiss owner. The *commune* of Toulouse, unique among the great cities of France, owns an 85-acre vineyard, the **Domaine de Candi**, that provides wine for its hospitals – although only the most manic oenophiles would consider having their tonsils out to try some.

Toulouse

16

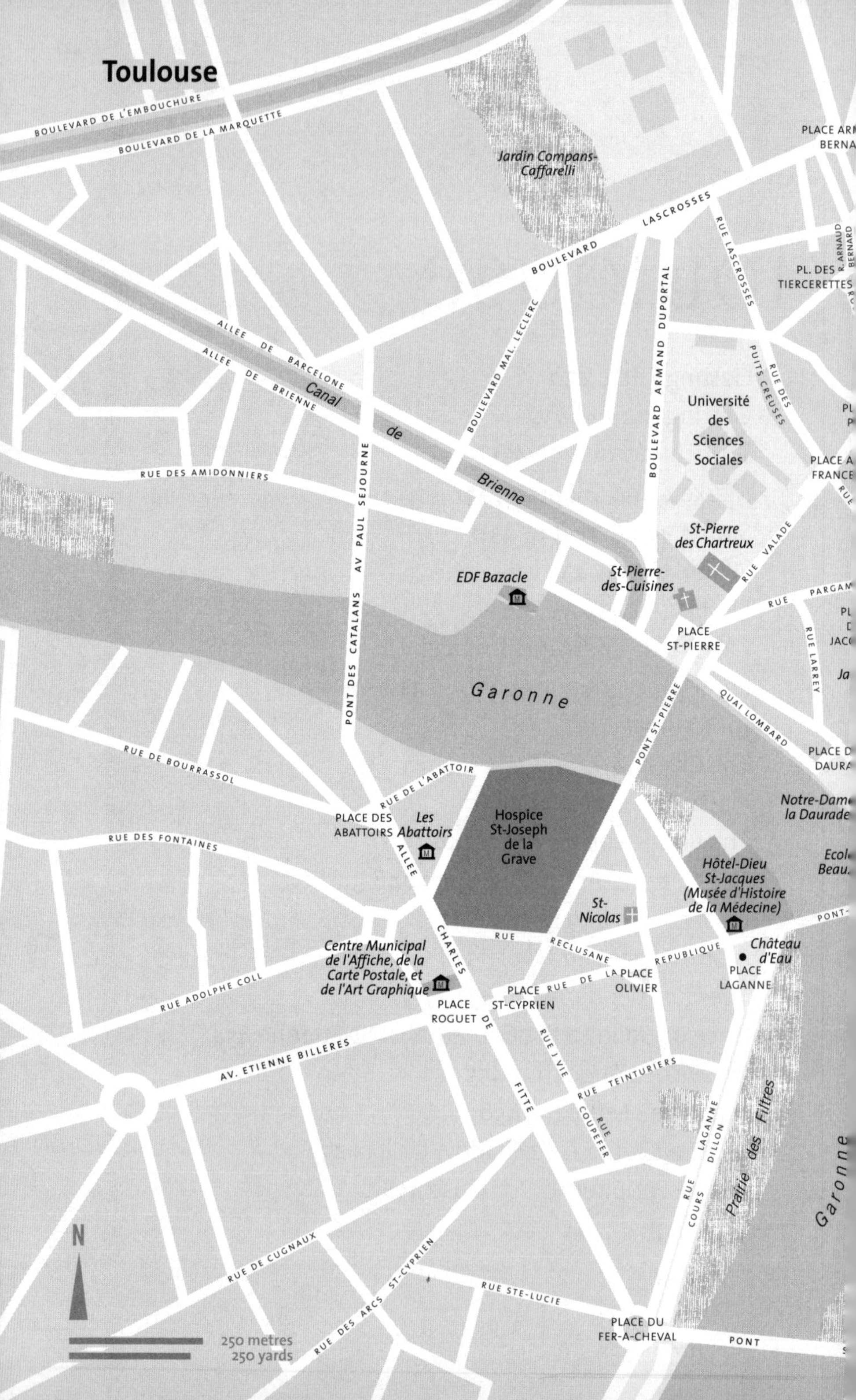

Toulouse
Boulevard de l'Embouchure
Boulevard de la Marquette
Jardin Compans-Caffarelli
Boulevard Lascrosses
Rue Lascrosses
Boulevard Armand Duportal
Boulevard Mal. Leclerc
Allee de Barcelone
Allee de Brienne
Canal de Brienne
Rue des Amidonniers
Université des Sciences Sociales
Rue des Puits Creuses
Pl. des Tiercerettes
Rue Valade
St-Pierre des Chartreux
St-Pierre-des-Cuisines
EDF Bazacle
Place St-Pierre
Rue Pargam
Rue Larrey
Quai Lombard
Garonne
Pont des Catalans
Av. Paul Sejourne
Pont St-Pierre
Rue de Bourrassol
Rue de l'Abattoir
Place des Abattoirs
Les Abattoirs
Hospice St-Joseph de la Grave
Notre-Dame la Daurade
Rue des Fontaines
Allee Charles de Fitte
Hôtel-Dieu St-Jacques (Musée d'Histoire de la Médecine)
St-Nicolas
Rue Reclusane
Rue de la Republique
Château d'Eau
Place Laganne
Place Olivier
Place St-Cyprien
Place Roguet
Centre Municipal de l'Affiche, de la Carte Postale, et de l'Art Graphique
Rue Adolphe Coll
Av. Etienne Billeres
Rue J Vie
Rue Teinturiers
Rue Coupefer
Rue Laganne
Cours Dillon
Prairie des Filtres
Garonne
Rue de Cugnaux
Rue des Arcs St-Cyprien
Rue Ste-Lucie
Place du Fer-a-Cheval
Pont
N
250 metres
250 yards

Bus station
(buses to airport)
Train Station
Lycée St-Sernin
Basilique du St-Sernin
Musée St-Raymond
Chapelle des Carmélites
Nôtre-Dame du Taur
Post Office
Clocher des Cordeliers
Hôtel de Ville
Tourist Information
Théâtre du Capitole
Les Jacobins
Hôtel de Bernuy
Musée du Vieux Toulouse
Fondation Bemberg/ Hôtel d'Assézat
Museé des Augustins
Cathédrale St-Etienne
Préfecture
Halle aux Grains
Nôtre-Dame
Halles
Musée Paul Dupuy
Hôtel de Malte
Hôtel de Pierre
Hôtel d'Ulmo
Hôtel du Vieux Raisin
Grand Rond
Jardin Royal
Palais de Justice
Théâtre Sorano
Jardin des Plantes
Musée d'Histoire Naturelle
Monument à la Gloire de la Résistance
Musée Labit
Canal du Midi
PLACE JEANNE D'ARC
PLACE DE BELFORT
PLACE ST-SERNIN
PLACE DU PEYROU
PLACE VICTOR HUGO
PLACE WILSON
SQ CH DE GAULLE
PLACE DU CAPITOLE
PLACE DES JACOBINS
PLACE OCCITANE
PLACE ST-GEORGES
PLACE DES PUITS-CLOS
PLACE DE LA BOURSE
PLACE ESQUIROL
PLACE DE LA TRINITE
PLACE DU PONT NEUF
PLACE ST-ETIENNE
PLACE DUPUY
PLACE MAGE
PLACE DES CARMES
PLACE DU SALIN
PLACE DU PARLEMENT
BOULEVARD D'ARCOLE
RUE DE LA CONCORDE
RUE MATABIAU
RUE RAYMOND IV
RUE DE BAYARD
RUE ST-BERNARD
BOULEVARD DE STRASBOURG
BOULEVARD DE BONREPOS
BOULEVARD P. SEMARD
RUE CAFFARELLI
ALLEES JEAN JAURES
RUE DE PERIGORD
RUE DE REMUSAT
RUE DU TAUR
RUE RIVALS
RUE LORRAINE
R. PORT SALDANE
R. AUSTERLITZ
RUE GABRIEL PERI
RUE DE L'INDUSTRIE
RUE CASTELLANE
RUE MAURY
RUE DE LA COLOMBETTE
RUE LA FAYETTE
RUE DES LOIS
RUE DEVILLE
RUE ROMIGUIERES
RUE MIREPOIX
RUE LAPEYROUSE
RUE M. FONVIELLE
BOULEVARD LAZARE CARNOT
RUE D'AUBUISSON
RUE DU REMPART ST-ETIENNE
BOULEVARD RIQUET
BOULEVARD DE LA GARE
RUE DE LA CHAINE
RUE LAKANAL
RUE GAMBETTA
R. DES GESTES
RUE ST-ROME
RUE D'ALSACE
RUE DE LA POMME
RUE ST-ANTOINE DU T
RUE ST-URSULE
R. DU MAY
RUE CHALANDE
RUE PEYROLIERES
R. PEYRAS
RUE CANTEGNI
RUE RIQUET
RUE DU PORT GULTHEMERY
RUE DES TOURNEURS
RUE DE METZ
RUE DES FR. LION
RUE CROIX BARAGNON
R. DE LA TRINITE
RUE DU COQ D'INDE
RUE DES ARTS
RUE TOLOSANE
RUE FERMAT
RUE DES PARADOUX
RUE DES FILATIERS
RUE DES COUTELIERS
RUE DU LANGUEDOC
RUE MAGE
RUE PERCHEPINTE
RUE NINAU
ALLEES F. VERDIER
RUE DES POTIERS
ST-ETIENNE
SAUVEUR
PORT SAINTE
R. PONT DE TOUNIS
QUAI DE TOUNIS
AV DE LA GARONNETTE
RUE DE LA DALBADE
RUE ST ROMESY
RUE PHARAON
R. PLEAU
RUE OZENNE
RUE NAZARETH
RUE DE LA FONDERIE
ALLEE P. SABATIER
ALLEE DES SOUPIRS
AVENUE M. HAURIOU
ALLEES J. GUESDE
RUE ALFRED DUMERIL
ALLEE P. FEUGA
ALLEE F. MISTRAL
RUE MONPLAISIR
RUE DES MARTYRS DE LA LIBERATION
ST-MICHEL

Getting There

By Air

Toulouse's international **airport** is at Blagnac, 10km from the centre, **t** 05 61 42 44 00.

The airport **bus**, **t** 05 34 60 64 00, departs from the bus station (next to the train station) every 20mins or so from 5.20am to 8.20pm during the week, a shorter time span at weekends and holidays. Tickets are 36F, 27F for under-25s; get them at the counter just inside the airport door.

By Train

Trains run from Paris-Austerlitz through Gourdon, Souillac, Cahors and Montauban to Toulouse in 6hrs30mins; TGVs from Paris-Montparnasse do the same in around 5hrs – by way of Bordeaux.

The slow trains to Bordeaux take 2hrs30mins and stop in Montauban, Castelsarrasin, Moissac, Agen and Aiguillon. Other connections include Albi (1hr) and Castres (1hr30mins), Auch, Carcassonne, Nice, Lyon and Lille (TGV, 7 hrs).

By Bus

The bus station is next to the railway station at 68 Bd Pierre Semard, **t** 05 61 61 67 67; there are buses to Foix, Albi, Gaillac, Auch, Nogaro and Montauban, and also to London, Madrid and Barcelona.

Getting Around

By *Métro* and City Bus

In 1993 Toulouse proudly opened its first *métro* line, running northeast to southwest from Joliment, the railway station and the Capitole to the Mirail. In the next couple of years this line is due to be extended and a new one built running north to south. The *métro* and city buses are run by SEMVAT, which has an **information office** at 7 Place Esquirol, **t** 05 62 11 26 11. Almost all the sites are within walking distance in the compact centre, though, so you'll hardly ever need either of these.

By Taxi

If you can't find one cruising the streets or at a taxi stand, try **t** 05 61 52 22 22, **t** 05 62 16 26 16 or **t** 05 61 42 38 38 (all 24 hours).

By Car

Toulouse's rapid growth and narrow streets have led to some major traffic tie-ups. Rush hour can be quite frustrating – you certainly don't rush. The most convenient pay **car parks** are at Place du Capitole, Place Wilson and Place St-Etienne; but it is quite expensive, 10F an hour.

Alternatively, you can battle to find a space in the free parking areas such as Place St-Sernin and Allées Jules Guesde (near the Grand Rond), trawl the streets looking for a free spot (easiest in the summer when people leave the city for the coast) or park at Joliment and take the *métro* in – the price of parking is included in the ticket price.

Car Hire

There are quite a few companies at the airport. ADA, **t** 05 61 30 00 33; Avis, **t** 05 34 60 46 50; Budget, **t** 05 61 71 85 80; Citer, **t** 05 61 30 00 01; Europcar, **t** 05 61 30 02 30; Eurorent, **t** 05 61 71 20 33; Hertz, **t** 05 61 30 00 26.

By Bicycle and Motorcycle

You can hire bikes, scooters and motorcycles from Rev Moto, 14 Bd de la Gard, **t** 05 62 47 07 08, and they organize tours. Phone for details.

By Boat

The system of aqueducts that enabled the goose Queen Ranachilde to paddle around the city in the 6th century (*see* p.55) is sadly long gone but you can still see some of the nicest corners of Toulouse by canal; Association Cap d'Ambre, **t** 05 61 71 45 95, offers 1hr30min tours departing from the Port de l'Embouchure (Ponts Jumeaux, bus 16 or 70) and taking you down the Brienne and around the Garonne. Other companies offer similar excursions: contact the tourist office for information.

You can also hire your own little electric boat to go up the Canal du Midi from Port St-Sauveur, near the Grand Rond.

Other Means

Other options for seeing the city include a **tourist train** which trundles around the main sites for half an hour or so (departs from Place Wilson daily June–Sept, **t** 05 62 71 08 51 for details during the winter), and a **tourist taxi** with drivers who know what they are talking about (**t** 05 34 250 250, currently 150F an hour for up to three passengers). The *mairie* has also put together some **routes** to follow either on foot or on bike to help you explore the city and around (available from the tourist office).

Tourist Information

Donjon du Capitole, Rue La Fayette, behind the Capitole, **t** 05 61 11 02 22, **f** 05 61 22 03 63; or check *www.mairie-toulouse.fr/*, the city's website.

The tourist office offers a range of themed **guided tours**; if you plan to do more than one buy a *passeport* which gives reductions on the price (at time of writing tours are about 50F, with the *passeport* two visits for 90F).

For information on the whole of the Midi-Pyrénées region, stop by the Comité Régional du Tourisme Midi-Pyrénées, 54 Bd de l'Embouchure, **t** 05 61 13 55 55 (ring first).

Central post pffice: 9 Rue Lafayette, **t** 05 62 15 33 51.

Night pharmacy: 17 Rue de Remusat, **t** 05 61 21 81 20 (open 8pm–8am).

Doctors on Duty (SOS Médecins de Garde): **t** 05 61 49 66 66.

Purpan hospital: Rond-Point de Purpan, **t** 05 61 77 22 33.

Rangueil hospital: Chemin du Vallon, **t** 05 61 32 25 33.

Markets and Shopping

There are regular **markets** at Place des Carmes (*daily exc Thurs 7–1*) and at Les Halles in Bd Victor-Hugo (*Tues–Sun 6–1*). On Wed mornings, Place du Capitole has a lively food and flea market, and on Tues and Sat an organic farmers' market. Sun (and to a lesser extent Sat) morning sees a huge flea market around St-Sernin and along the length of the boulevards, the 'relics' of modern Toulouse that draw thousands of 'pilgrims'.

With all the major French department stores – and a Marks & Spencer, just behind the Capitole, 28 Rue d'Alsace Lorraine – the Pink City is the shopping mecca of the southwest, although specifically local products, besides Airbuses, are mostly **violet** – violet-scented soaps, eau-de-cologne, and candied-violet **confits**, the last-named made since 1730 (along with superb chocolates) at Olivier, 27 Rue La Fayette; Maison Pillon, at 2 Rue Austerlitz and 2 Rue Ozenne, also produces delicious handmade **chocolates** which won the prize for the best in France in 1996. Or pick the ultimate Toulousain taste treat: rubbery aniseed- or mint-flavoured **Cachou pellets**, invented by a pharmacist named Lajaunie at 64 Av de Larrieu and sold all over France in the same little metal tins for the past 100 years or so.

Two **bookshops** have titles in English: Librairie Etrangère, 16 Rue des Lois, **t** 05 61 21 67 21, and The Bookshop, 17 Rue Lakanal, **t** 05 61 22 99 92. For **posters** and reprints, try the shop in the Centre Municipal de l'Affiche (*see* p.457).

If you fancy tasting some of the best **cheese** that France has to offer, head for Betty, 2 Place Victor Hugo; you smell it from fifty paces. There are 200 different types from all over the country, some of them quite special, such as the Vieux Salers, made in just one village in the Cantal and given a minimum of one year to mature. There is an assortment of goat cheeses made locally and even some good old Stilton. There is also a good selection of south-west **wines**. The shop also has a stall in Marché Victor Hugo opposite. For fine **preserves** and French classics such as **olive oil** and very dark chocolate go to La Boutique des Saveurs at 1 Rue Ozenne, **t** 05 61 53 75 21, a delightful shop that bombards you with tantalizing smells. Throughout the summer they have evenings for special tastings: call for details.

Sports and Activities

The **Toulouse Football Club** (T.F.C., pronounced 'tayfessay') plays in France's first division, and the city hosted matches in the 1998 World Cup, but the city's heart lies with its **rugby** team, the Stade, over a hundred years old, and frequent champion of France (and champion of Europe in 1996). They play on Sun afternoons at the stadium; local teams are divided into Rugby à XV and Rugby à XIII (heretical 'Cathar rugby').

You can swish out a figure eight at the Patinoire Olympique de Blagnac, an **ice rink** at 10 Av du Général de Gaulle, **t** 05 61 74 71 40 (buses 66 or 70). *Open Wed–Fri afternoons and evenings, all day Sat and Sun.*

Where to Stay

Toulouse ✉ 31000

Toulouse has chain hotels galore for its numerous business visitors as well as a short list of reliable independent establishments in the historic centre. Try to avoid the cheap fleabags near the station.

★★★★**Grand Hôtel de l'Opéra**, 1 Place du Capitole, **t** 05 61 21 82 66, **f** 05 61 23 41 04 (*expensive*). This, the most beautiful hotel in Toulouse, has 50 luxurious rooms and three suites set in a former convent, with sumptuous Italianate rooms, indoor pool, fitness room and a magnificent restaurant (*see* below).

★★★**Grand Hôtel Capoul**, 13 Place Wilson, **t** 05 61 10 70 70, **f** 05 61 21 96 70 (*expensive–moderate*). Large, light, air-conditioned rooms, a Jacuzzi and an excellent bistrot.

★★★**Des Beaux Arts**, 1 Place Pont-Neuf, **t** 05 34 45 42 42, **f** 05 34 45 42 43 (*expensive–moderate*). Set in an 18th-century *hôtel*, this is charming, warm and welcoming, with pleasant, soundproofed rooms overlooking the Garonne.

★★★**Parthenon**, 86 Allées Jean-Jaurès, **t** 05 61 10 24 00, **f** 05 61 10 24 20 (*expensive*). A pleasant, central residence hotel for longer stays.

★★★**Brienne**, 20 Bd du Maréchal Leclerc, **t** 05 61 23 60 60, **f** 05 61 23 18 94 (*moderate*). Ultra-modern, with well-equipped rooms, many with balconies.

★★★**Mermoz**, 50 Rue Matabiau, **t** 05 61 63 04 04, **f** 05 61 63 15 64 (*moderate*). Stands out as the exception to the hotels near the station, with delightful air-conditioned rooms overlooking inner courtyards, and perhaps the best breakfast in Toulouse.

★★★**De Diane**, 3 Route de St-Simon, **t** 05 61 07 59 52, **f** 05 61 86 38 94 (*moderate*). In a country setting, yet reasonably close to the centre; there's a pool and tennis courts, and an excellent restaurant serving a mean cassoulet (*menus 105–190F*).

★★★**Raymond IV**, 16 Rue Raymond IV, **t** 05 61 62 89 41, **f** 05 61 62 38 01 (*moderate*). Central, modern and comfortable, and all rooms have TV and mini-bar.

★★**Arnaud-Bernard**, 33 Rue de la Chaine, **t** 05 61 21 37 64, **f** 05 61 29 86 91 (*inexpensive*). in the centre of Toulouse's lively popular quarter near St-Sernin; has renovated rooms.

★★**St-Sernin**, 2 Rue St-Bernard, **t** 05 61 21 73 08, **f** 05 61 22 49 61 (*inexpensive*). In the same area; good rooms with bath, mini-bar, TV, and so on.

★★**Grand Hôtel d'Orléans**, 72 Rue de Bayard, **t** 05 61 62 98 47, **f** 05 61 62 78 24 (*inexpensive*). Near the station. Plenty of character, with its interior galleries, garden, and satellite TV too.

★★**Park Hotel**, 2 Rue Porte-Sardane, **t** 05 61 21 25 97, **f** 05 61 23 96 27 (*inexpensive*). Within easy walking distance of the Capitole; modern rooms with most creature comforts, including a sauna and Jacuzzi.

★★**Albert 1er**, 8 Rue Rivals, **t** 05 61 21 17 91, **f** 05 61 21 09 64 (*inexpensive*). Equally central, with convenient parking.

★★**Hôtel du Grand Balcon**, 8 Rue Romiguières, **t** 05 61 21 48 08 (*inexpensive*). At the corner of Place du Capitole, this is one of Toulouse's best-loved institutions. The phrase *grand balcon* is what early French pilots used to describe the view from the cockpit, and this is where St-Exupéry and friends stayed when on the ground. Three sisters ran it for 50 years, and the current owners have had it for the past 37, carefully preserving the rooms as they were, along with a fascinating collection of photos and memorabilia from France's early days of aviation. The author of *Le Petit Prince* always stayed in No.32. Bring your own soap. *Closed for Christmas and three weeks in Aug.*

★★**Hôtel Ours Blanc**, 25 Place Victor Hugo, **t** 05 61 23 14 55, and 2 Rue Victor Hugo, **t** 05 61 21 62 40, both **f** 05 61 23 62 34 (*inexpensive*). On two sites on opposite sides of Victor Hugo car park. The hotels offer quite small but neat rooms with TV, telephone, soundproofing and air-conditioning; their facilities are similar.

**Castellane, 17 Rue Castellane, t 05 61 62 18 82, f 05 61 62 58 04 (*inexpensive*). Down a quiet side street off Bd Carnot; light and spacious rooms with the usual gamut of facilities. There is private parking (for 40F a night) and the breakfast area is pleasant. It is also next to a good restaurant, L'Edelweiss (*see* below).

**Hotel de France, 5 Rue d'Austerlitz, t 05 61 21 88 24, f 05 61 21 99 77 (*inexpensive*). Huge, red, modern in places, other bits are Logis comfy: all in all it's a bit funky and a strange mix, but not without appeal. Try for the larger rooms with bath.

*Anatole France, 46 Place Anatole France, t 05 61 23 19 96 (*cheap*). Near the Capitole, with some of the nicest cheap rooms in Toulouse, all with showers and phones.

*Des Arts, 1 bis Rue Cantegril, t 05 61 23 36 21, f 05 61 12 22 37 (*cheap*). A friendly place near lively Place St-Georges: good rooms with showers.

*Croix-Baragnon, 17 Rue Croix-Baragnon, t 05 61 52 60 10, f 05 61 52 08 60 (*cheap*). A good bet near St-Etienne; all rooms have bath and shower.

Foyer de Jeunes Travailleurs, 3 Rue Gallois, St Michel, **t** 05 61 52 29 56 (*cheap*). This has replaced the Auberge de Jeunesse; ring ahead to make sure there is room.

Toulouse Outskirts

***La Flânerie, Route de Lacroix-Falgarde, Vieille-Toulouse (✉ 31320), 8km south on the D4, t 05 61 73 39 12, f 05 61 73 18 56 (*expensive*). If you're driving, you can sleep where the Tectosages once roamed. This is a pretty country house with grand views over the Garonne; pool, tennis and a golf course in the environs are added bonuses.

***La Chaumière, Ramonville-St-Agne (✉ 31520), 7km south on the N113, t 05 61 73 02 02, f 05 61 75 17 02 (*moderate*). Modern, air-conditioned rooms in a park with a pool, with a restaurant installed in an old farmhouse as centrepiece (*menus from 95F*).

**Les Chanterelles, Chemin Ramelet-Moundi, Tournefeuille (✉ 31170), t 05 61 86 21 86 (*moderate*). Out to the west by La Ramée golf course, seven spacious little suites in a garden, each with its own terrace.

Eating Out

Toulouse, one of the boom towns of France, has in recent years enjoyed a restaurant revolution that has trickled down from *les grandes tables* to the corner *bistrot*. Yet along with this leap in the quality of food, the city hasn't quite forgotten its key place in the southwest bean belt, and claims to make a cassoulet that walks all over the cassoulets of rivals Carcassonne and Castelnaudry. To the base recipe of white beans, garlic, herbs, goose fat, salt bacon, fat pork, and *confits* of goose or duck, the Toulousains like to chuck in a foot or two of their renowned sausage (*saucisse de Toulouse*), shoulder of mutton, and perhaps some ham. The final touch: sprinkle with breadcrumbs and bake in the oven. To aid in the long and tormented cassoulet digestion, the locals recommend a game of rugby, or a tipple of *eau de noix Benoit Serres*, the local walnut *digestif* (or *Get Frères*, if you like peppermint).

Expensive

Les Jardins de l'Opéra, 1 Place du Capitole, **t** 05 61 23 07 76. Toulouse's finest gastronomic experience is also one of the most beautiful restaurants in the southwest. It manages to stay light years from the hubbub just outside the door, a cool and refreshing glass-covered oasis overlooking a garden pool. The food matches the setting, orchestrated by the excellent Dominique Toulousy, who prepares aromatic mushroom dishes (morels stuffed with foie gras, when available), seafood cooked to perfection, a classic cassoulet and flavourful regional specialities, topped off by delicate desserts (*220F lunch menu with wine, other menus up to 540F*). *Closed Sun, Mon lunch, hols and most of Aug.*

Michel Sarran, 21 Bd Armand-Duportal, **t** 05 61 12 32 32. For a wonderful synthesis of sun-soaked southwest and Provençal cuisines.

Superb food in an elegant town house, and charming service too. *Closed Sat, Sun and Aug.*

Au Pois Gourmand, 3 Rue Emile-Heybrard, **t** 05 61 31 95 95. In a handsome old manor house with wooden galleries in Casselardit (just off the *rocade*, or ring road around the city). The perfect atmosphere for the refined and original cuisine that comes out of the kitchen, such as red mullet grilled in fig leaves with fresh-picked thyme and lemon (*menus 130–380F*). *Closed Sat lunch, Sun and Mon, and several weeks in the holidays.*

Le Pastel, 237 Rue de St-Simon, in a villa at Mirail, **t** 05 62 87 84 30. Make the extra effort to book lunch for some of the finest, most imaginative gourmet food in Toulouse at some of the kindest prices; the 155F lunch menu is exquisite (*evening menus up to 370F*). *Closed Sun and Mon.*

Le Frégate, 1 Rue d'Austerlitz (overlooking Place Wilson), **t** 05 61 21 59 61. Classy seafood (and superb game dishes, in season) in a classy setting (*menus 170–200F*).

Moderate

Le Cantou, 98 Rue Vélasquez, **t** 05 61 49 20 21. A lovely ivy-covered house in a beautiful garden, in the suburb of St-Martin-du-Touch, contains the very popular headquarters of some of the very best regional cuisine in Toulouse. Enormous southwest wine list (*menus 98 and 198F*). *Closed Sat and Sun.*

Chez Emile, 13 Place St-Georges, **t** 05 61 21 05 56. A city institution, preparing some of the finest seafood in Toulouse (ground floor) or a *confit de canard* or meat (first floor); in warm weather, there are worse things to do than sit out on the terrace (*menus 105 to 250F*). *Closed Sun and Mon, just Mon lunch in summer.*

Laurent Orsi, 13 Rue Industrie (off Rue de la Colombette), **t** 05 61 62 97 43. Cassoulet on the menu, as well as dishes from Provence and Lyon, all deliciously prepared in an Art Deco setting (*good-value menus 90–195F*). *Closed Sat lunch and Sun.*

Les Ombrages, 48 bis Route de St-Simon, **t** 05 61 07 61 28. A bit hard to find (take a taxi) but worth the effort for its fresh, sunny cuisine, immaculately prepared: try the *émincé de canard aux fruits rouges et foie gras* (*excellent lunch menu, prices up to 240F*). *Closed Mon.*

Le Bibent, 5 Place du Capitole, **t** 05 61 23 89 03. One of the most beautiful brasseries in Toulouse, strategically located, with a grand dining room last remodelled in the Roaring Twenties, and a terrace; excellent shellfish selection (*around 200F*).

Le Colombier, 14 Rue Bayard, **t** 05 61 62 40 05. One of the chief contestants in the 'best cassoulet in Toulouse' contest, with all the other southwest treats as well if you don't think you're up to the mighty beans (*menus 75–185F*). *Closed Sat lunch, Sun and a month in summer.*

L'Edelweiss, 19 Rue Castellane, **t** 05 61 62 34 70. It looks like nothing from the outside but don't let appearances deceive. Behind the concrete is a refined restaurant producing lovely meals, some of it classic southwest such as foie gras in five forms, other choices with a different slant, such as *pavé de thon*, *millefeuille de légumes* and gazpacho. A wonderful choice of ice creams and desserts (*menus 165–210F*). *Closed Sun, Mon and most of Aug.*

Sept Place St-Sernin, 7 Place St-Sernin, **t** 05 62 30 05 30. A large ivy-covered house in a perfect spot opposite the cathedral. The menus are delightful and varied: try *tournedos d'espadon lardée sur sa lasagne de courgette* or *foie gras de canard aux figues et salade d'herbes* (*menus 95–200F*). *Closed Mon lunch, Sat lunch and Sun.*

Cantaloupe, corner of Rue Mage and Perchepinte, **t** 05 61 55 34 01. Painted in Laura Ashley green and quite smart inside, offering something a bit different from the usual southwest fare, such as *travers de porc et crevettes poêlées, sauce au soja* (*menus 65–230F*). *Closed Sun and Mon, most of Aug and some of Jan.*

La Bascule, 14 Av Maurice-Hauriou, **t** 05 61 52 09 51. A popular brasserie a bit out from the centre and on a busy corner but set back enough that you can eat on the terrace lined with bamboo. Good selection of fish including oysters and traditional meat dishes plus some a bit different such as *gigot d'agneau des Pyrénées en croute avec* *jus d'estragon* (*à la carte only, but prices are moderate*).

L'Empereur de Hué, 26 Rue de la Fonderie, **t** 05 61 53 55 72. Toulouse's best Vietnamese restaurant, off Place du Salin and by common consent well worth leaving the centre of town for (*dinner only; à la carte, but moderate prices*). *Closed mid-July–mid-Aug and Sun.*

Inexpensive

Les Caves de la Maréchale, 3 Rue Jules-Chalande, **t** 05 61 23 89 88. Set in the immense cellar of a 13th-century Dominican priory off Rue St-Rome, and populated with copies of classical statues. Arrive early for the popular 70F lunch (*evening menus 110–145F*). *Closed Sun and Mon lunch.*

Les Beaux-Arts-Flo, 1 Quai Daurade, **t** 05 61 21 12 12. On the Garonne, this handsome *belle époque* brasserie offers well-prepared favourites: seafood platters, salmon and sorrel, cassoulet, good desserts (*menus 119F and 159F*).

Grand Café de l'Opéra, 1 Place du Capitole, **t** 05 61 21 37 03. Excellent versions of the classics in a cosy brasserie atmosphere – the original burnt to the ground, and it was rebuilt exactly as it was (*menus 129–200F*).

Le Belvèdére, 11 Bd des Récollets, **t** 05 61 52 63 73. Southwest classics in a modern setting south of the centre to accompany its grand panoramic views over Toulouse (*menu 90F*). *Closed Sun and Aug.*

Benjamin, 7 Rue des Gestes (off Rue St-Rome), **t** 05 61 22 92 66. In the centre of old Toulouse, serving up the likes of fennel and courgette terrine and steak with *cèpes* for some of the friendliest prices in town (*menus 65–134F*).

La Daurade, Quai de la Daurade, **t** 05 61 22 10 33. Dine on a barge (*péniche*) anchored in a magnificent setting. Book: the food is just as lovely (*menus 60–160F*). *Closed Sat lunch and Sun.*

Cosi-Fan Tutte, 8 Rue Mage, **t** 05 61 53 07 24. Book for an excellent Italian meal in an appropriately operatic setting (*menus dinner only 135 and 180F*). *Closed Sun, Mon and half of Aug.*

Le Bon Vivre, 15 Place Wilson, **t** 05 61 23 07 17. This place packs them in with its authentic southwestern cooking: *confits*, *magrets*, et al (*menus 70–175F*).

La Tatina de Burgos, 27 Av de la Garonnette, **t** 05 61 55 59 29. A zesty tapas bar and restaurant with lots of sherry and Spanish wines, a tasty *zarzuela* (Catalan fish soup) and other Spanish dishes (*menus 100–180F*). *Closed Sun and Mon.*

Cheap

The first floor of the **Marché Victor-Hugo** is chock-a-block with cheap little beaneries that daily attract Toulousains of every ilk for lunch (*exc Mon*).

A la Truffe du Quercy, 17 Rue Croix-Baragnon, **t** 05 61 53 34 24. The same family has been dishing out southwestern home-cooking for three generations; f*ormule menu 55F*, delicious regular menu for a bit more. *Closed Sun and hols.*

Chez Moi, 33 Rue des Frères Lion, **t** 05 62 73 01 69. By the Halle aux Grains east of the Grand Rond. Tasty Vietnamese delights; get there before 12.30 for the very pretty, filling three-course *59F lunch* – the menu changes daily. *Closed Sun.*

Mille et Une Pâtes, 3 Place du Peyrou, **t** 05 61 21 80 70. Pasta-lovers have a wide choice: some fairly orthodox and others more heretical, like chocolate and trifle lasagne (*menus 59–100F*). *Closed Sun and Mon eve.*

Cafés, Bars and Wine Bars

Le Père Louis, 45 Place des Tourneurs, between Rue Peyras and Rue de Metz, **t** 05 61 21 33 45. The most resolutely traditional bar in Toulouse has drawn Toulouse's *quinquina* drinkers for over a century; in fact, it's so traditional it's been declared a historical landmark (*open 9–3 and 5–10, closed Sun and Aug*).

Texas Café, 26 Rue Castellane, **t** 05 61 99 14 15. Tequila lubricates the clientele and keeps the guacamole dipped at Toulouse's oldest Tex Mex bar.

Le Nabuchodonosor, 15 bis Rue Coq-d'Inde, near Rue des Filatiers, **t** 05 61 53 65 00. Wide selection of wines and snacks. *Open till 8pm, closed Sat and Sun.*

Le Mangevins, 46 Rue Pharaon, **t** 05 61 52 79 16. Wide variety of wines accompanied by fancy snacks or light meals. *Open till 11.30pm, closed Sat, Sun and Aug.*

Dubliners, 46 Av Marcel-Langer. Toulouse's chief Irish pub, south of the centre.

Bagdam Café, 4 Rue Delacroix, **t** 05 61 99 03 62. Feminist and women-only. *Opens at 7pm Tues–Sat.*

Le Why not Café, 5 Rue Pargaminières, near Place St-Pierre, **t** 05 61 21 89 08. Be sure not to miss its inconspicuous entrance into an unexpected shaded courtyard filled with locals who also know the secret. *Open 11am–2pm.*

L'Ancienne Belgique, 16 Rue de la Trinité. Try a pint or two from their big selection.

Gay bars are clustered around Rue de la Colombette, east of Place Wilson.

Entertainment and Nightlife

The weekly ***Flash***, available at any newsstand, will tell you what's on in Toulouse. Also pick up a copy of John Sime's monthly English-language booklet ***Doings in Toulouse***, available at many hotels and from Mr Sime himself at his huge second-hand English bookshop Books and Mermaides, 3 Rue Mirepoix, behind Place du Capitole, **t** 05 61 12 14 29, **f** 05 61 23 66 14. He is a real character, very friendly and a mine of information. Make it one of your first ports of call.

Thanks to Toulouse's students, its Spanish blood and the do-re-mi provided by the city's high-tech jobs, there's plenty to do. Since the Second World War, the Toulousains have discovered **classical music** in a big way, with the gonfalon held high by the Orchestre Nationale du Capitole, under the baton of Michel Plasson; now one of the top symphony orchestras in France, they often play in the acoustically excellent La Halle aux Grains, Place Dupuy (just east of Cathédrale St-Etienne), **t** 05 61 62 02 70. In July and August, the city puts on a commendable **music festival**, including performances by the fine Orchestre Nationale de Chambre de Toulouse; in September the cloister of the Jacobins is the site of the **Festival International Piano aux Jacobins**; book early, **t** 05 61 23 32 00. From October to June, the prestigious Théâtre du Capitole, Place du Capitole, **t** 05 61 22 31 31, presents a series of **opera** and **dance**. The Le Sorano Théâtre National de Toulouse Midi-Pyrenées, 35 Allées Jules-Guesde, **t** 05 34 31 67 87, probably puts on the finest **plays** in Toulouse. For a listen to the current state of French **poetry**, ***chanson*** and **theatre**, there's La Cave Poésie, 71 Rue du Taur, **t** 05 61 23 62 00 (*every evening exc Sun and holidays*). **Concerts** and exhibitions of dance are now also given in the renovated auditorium of the old church of St-Pierre-des-Cuisines, Place St-Pierre, **t** 05 34 45 05 61.

Zenith, Av Raymond Badiou, **t** 05 62 74 49 49, is the biggest **stage and performance** venue in the area and hosts a range of events from displays of Basque sport to pop concerts, and more besides.

Toulouse likes its **movies** as well; the newly refurbished Cinémathèque, 69 Rue du Taur, **t** 05 62 30 30 10, is the second most important in France, and often shows films in V.O. (*version originale*), as do Le Cratère, 95 Grand Rue St-Michel, **t** 05 61 53 50 53, and ABC, 13 Rue St-Bernard, **t** 05 61 29 81 99.

Toulouse stays up later than any other city in this book, but places open and close like flowers in the night – check posters. Favourite music bars include:

Rag Time, 14 Place Arnaud-Bernard, **t** 05 61 22 73 01. Serving up jazz and Latin music as well as drinks (*open until 2am, 5am Sat, closed Sun and Mon*).

Eriche Coffie, 9 Rue Joseph Vié, **t** 05 05 61 42 04 27 (near St-Cyprien). A bar/German brasserie that puts on performance artists and lots of R & B.

Puerto Habana, 12 Port St-Etienne, **t** 05 61 54 45 61. A good venue for a lively night out *à la cubana*, with live salsa and great dance floor. *Closed Sun.*

El Barrio Latino, 144 Av de Muret, **t** 05 61 59 00 58. Another good Latin music venue; it is also a restaurant. *Closed Sun to Wed.*

Bikini, Route de Lacroix-Flagarde (*rocade* exit 24), **t** 05 61 55 00 29. Most of the up-and-coming rock or blues bands who pass through Toulouse play at this young and convivial venue with concerts every other night.

One thing that keeps southwest France from nodding off in its vats of goose fat and wine is this big pink dynamo on the cutting edge of the 21st century. Toulouse, called La Ville Rose for its millions of pink bricks, has 750,000 lively inhabitants, counting over 110,000 university students, and 70 per cent of the industry in the Midi-Pyrénées region, much of it high tech, related to aeronautics and space.

Toulouse should have been the rosy capital of a nation called Languedoc, but it was knocked out of the big leagues in the 1220s by the popes and kings of France and their henchman Simon de Montfort. Seven and a half centuries later, the Toulousains are finally getting their rhythm back. No star is too high. Spain, and in particular Barcelona, extends her cape here, distilling enough passion to give the heirs of medieval Toulouse's fat merchants a dose of madness. Toulouse is above all une ville d'émotion; listen to the Toulousains chant their national anthem, which they do at every possible occasion: '*O moun paiës, Toulouse, Toulouse! O moun paiës, Toulouse, Toulouse!*' over and over again. There aren't any other verses; according to the natives, there's nothing else to say.

History

The history of Toulouse is detestable, saturated with blood and perfidy.

Henry James

Toulouse was founded at a ford in the Garonne called the Bazacle, at the centre of what the ancient Greek geographer Strabo called the 'Gallic isthmus', the crossroads between the Mediterranean and the Atlantic, the Pyrénées and the Massif Central. Yet, confusingly, the original Toulouse (the name means 'elevated place') was on a hill, 10km from the modern city, at a spot now called Vieille Toulouse. The first Toulousains with a name came from the north: a Celtic tribe known as the Volcae Tectosages after their distinctive woollen cloaks (*tectus sago*). Because they controlled the roads through the Gallic isthmus, the Tectosages creamed profits from the silver mines to the south and from the trade in Italian wines. They mined the gold of the Ariège, but looked upon it as something too sacred to be minted into coins, and stored most of it at the bottom of a swamp. Despite their wealth, the insatiable Toulousains ranged far and wide ever searching for more; in 279 BC they even participated in the sack of the sacred treasuries of Delphi.

In 125 BC, Ligurian tribes in Provence asked Rome to defend them from the fearsome plunderers from Toulouse. This request was all the Romans needed to muscle in and do some plundering on their own account: they decreed the Tectosages were a 'new ally' and sent a Roman garrison to Toulouse to 'collaborate'. In 107 BC, when the Tectosages dared to give their unwanted new allies the boot, the Senate sent General Servilius Caepio to crush them and confiscate their fabulous swamp treasure – 110,000 pounds of silver and 100,000 pounds of gold. But only a fraction of this hoard ever made it to Rome. Caepio claimed his convoy was held up by Teutones near Massalia (Marseille); the Senate, suspecting another kind of highway robbery, confiscated all of Caepio's property, then sent him into exile and his womenfolk to the brothels. Hence the Roman expression *habebat aurum tolosanum* (to have the gold of Toulouse), i.e. ill-gotten gains seldom prosper.

If Rome cleaned out Toulouse's sacred swamp, it also brought years of peace. The Tectosages felt safe enough to come down from Vieille Toulouse to the plain of the Garonne, and by all accounts they were soon doing well enough again as one of the most important cities in the province of Gallia Narbonensis, with a population around 20,000. The city became known as *Palladia Tolosa* after its protectress, the goddess of wisdom Pallas Athena.

The Capital of the Visigoths

In 410 the Visigoths under Alaric captured Rome and took a valuable hostage – Galla Placidia, sister of Emperor Honorius. When Alaric died, Galla Placidia was inherited by his brother-in-law and new king Ataulf, who carried the young maiden off on his conquests in southwest France. Ataulf preferred Toulouse to Bordeaux, the Roman capital of Aquitaine, and made it the Visigothic capital. When his wife died, he married Galla Placidia. It was the love match of the Dark Ages, and her genteel Roman manners helped to tame his uncouth Visigothic temperament. Ataulf was later killed in a palace conspiracy and Galla Placidia returned to her brother in Ravenna, where she built herself a beautiful tomb of golden mosaics that can be seen to this day (she later remarried, gave birth to Emperor Valentinian III, and reigned for years as empress herself). Toulouse remained the elegant capital of the Visigoths until 507, when Clovis, the recently baptised king of the Franks, took it upon himself to wipe out the Arian heresy – the sect of the Visigoths. After Clovis defeated Alaric II in hand-to-hand combat, the Visigoths upped sticks over the Pyrénées for Toledo, which they made their capital until they were ousted in turn by the Arabs in 716.

Five years later these same Arab armies appeared at the gates of Toulouse. Although Clovis' successors, the Merovingian 'do-nothing kings' (*rois fainéants*), hadn't failed to neglect Toulouse, a brilliant resistance was organized by the city's Duke Eudes, who killed the emir and gave the Moors their very first taste of defeat on 9 June 721. The Arabs' later defeat at Poitiers marked both their northernmost incursion into France and the triumph of Charles Martel, founding father of the Carolingian dynasty that replaced Duke Eudes and the Merovingians in the person of his son, Pepin the Short.

Pepin, recognizing the danger of a renewed Arab attack from over the Pyrénées, spent years hunting down Waiffar, the last Merovingian duke of Aquitaine, in order to establish his authority and guarantee the frontiers of the Franks' empire. Pepin's son Charlemagne continued this policy by pampering Toulouse. The most able and loyal counsellors of his sons and grandsons who inherited these marches became in 849 themselves the counts of Toulouse, responsible for Languedoc – a vast territory extending from the Rhône to the Garonne and from the Pyrénées to the Dordogne.

The Counts of Toulouse

The counts of Toulouse are often called the Raymondine dynasty – because nearly all were named Raymond. The first to emerge from obscurity was Raymond St-Gilles, born in 1041, the younger brother of Count Guilhem. A mighty warrior, Raymond spent his youth battling the Moors in Spain with such audacity that the king of Castile married him to his daughter and put him under the wing of the great Cid himself. In 1090, Count Guilhem died without a male heir, and Raymond was summoned back to Toulouse, where he was so popular a ruler as Count Raymond IV that in 1095 Urban II asked him to lead the First Crusade. Before leaving Toulouse, Raymond IV oversaw the consecration of the great basilica of St-Sernin and, declaring he would never return, installed his son Bertrand as count. For his coat of arms in the Crusade, Raymond chose the 12-pointed red 'Cross of Languedoc', a symbol at least as old as the Visigoths and still used today by Toulouse and the Midi-Pyrénées region. As the leader of the Crusade, Raymond IV was offered the crown of Jerusalem in the Holy Land; to everyone's amazement he modestly refused and let the honour go to Godfrey of Bouillon. Before Raymond died in 1105, he saw the birth of a fourth son, Alphonse-Jourdain, and his baptism in the river Jordan.

Crusading quickly became a family pastime; little Alphonse-Jourdain was shipped home to Toulouse to take Bertrand's place as count when the latter succumbed to the itch. Alphonse-Jordain remained on the job long enough to found, in 1152, one of Toulouse's most enduring and original institutions, the *domini de capitulo* (lords of the chapter), or *capitouls*. Each parish in Toulouse had its own *capitoul* – in 1438 the number was fixed at eight – who were appointed each November by the count from a list of names provided by the outgoing *capitouls*, who had to wait three years to be eligible again. At first the *capitouls* were in charge of administering justice; by the time of the Revolution they ran the whole city.

The next Count Raymond, the fifth in the series, took over at age 14, when his father Alphonse-Jourdain could no longer resist the call of the Crusades. Raymond V was a troubadour who presided over a golden age of poetry for Toulouse; and continued his father's administrative reforms by granting the city municipal autonomy. Another charter, in 1192, established the very first concern, anywhere, managed by shareholders, the *Moulins du Bazacle*, for centuries one of the largest mills in Europe; Rabelais wrote that 'they filled the ears with the infernal racket of their wheels that rotated ten heavy millstones'. Although Raymond V is known among non-Toulousain historians as 'the weathervane', inconsistent and ambiguous in his diplomacy, his manœuvrings were all for the sake of his beloved Languedoc – a small but rich prize coveted by the most powerful rulers of Europe: France, England, Aquitaine and Barcelona all had tenuous claims and were ready to pounce. In 1190, the Duke of Aquitaine, Richard the Lion-Heart, did just that, capturing Cahors and 18 castles on the pretext of avenging alleged attacks on pilgrims passing through the lands of Toulouse. Raymond V quietly got his revenge by asking his Mediterranean allies to refuse a safe harbour for Richard's ship on his return from the Crusades, leading directly to his capture by Leopold of Austria.

To Lose Toulouse, Through Love

When Raymond V died in 1195, his son Raymond VI had already been through three wives (the first died, the second and third were repudiated) and was ready to patch things up with the troublesome Plantagenets by wedding a fourth, Joanna, sister of

Richard the Lion-Heart, who bore him an heir before she died. But the scandal of Raymond VI's private life was nothing compared to the reproach heaped on him for his ambiguous attitude towards the Cathars. In 1208, when one of his hotheaded Provençal vassals murdered the papal legate Pierre de Castelnau, Pope Innocent III demanded that the count, who knew nothing of the matter, do penance and let himself be stripped to the waist and beaten with rods. Even this humiliation, and the fact that he had undertaken the expense of constructing a new cathedral in Toulouse, failed to convince Innocent that he sufficiently hated the heretics. And he probably didn't. Raymond VI seems to have had quite a modern, tolerant attitude towards the Cathars: they lived honestly without harming anyone, and as their ruler he considered it his job to defend them. Such an attitude was so threatening to the Church that Innocent began recruiting in the north for what has come down in history as the Albigensian Crusade. Raymond and his barons soon enough recognized what it really was – an excuse to grab the south of France.

With the pope, the king of France and the crusaders' fanatical leader, Simon de Montfort, lined up against him, Raymond VI summoned his brother-in-law, Pere (Pedro) of Aragon, count of Barcelona, and offered to unite the counties of Barcelona and Toulouse into a kingdom of the south to defeat the northerners. Pedro was fresh from the great Catholic victory over the Moors at Las Navas de Tolosa, but he had no qualms about fighting against the pope's team – especially if he could combine war with a visit to his old flame, a certain Azalaïs de Boissezon. Simon de Montfort was near Toulouse at Muret when he intercepted the letter from Pedro, setting up a rendezvous with Azalaïs. 'How should I respect a king who, for a woman, marches against his God!' thundered de Montfort. Barcelona and Toulouse had 3,000 knights against de Montfort's 1,500, but what should have been an easy victory at Muret began ominously when King Pedro turned up for battle exhausted, barely able to sit in the saddle. One of his knights traded arms with him, hoping to conceal his identity, but from the beginning the Occitans were outmanœuvred by de Montfort. In the subsequent hand-to-hand combat, the king of Aragon, fearing to be labelled a coward, revealed himself and was quickly slain. The battle of Muret (12 September 1213) turned into a rout. It was the beginning of the end of the south's independence.

In 1215, with the king of France at his side, Simon de Montfort entered Toulouse, where he was made count in place of Raymond VI by the will of the pope. He ruled Toulouse with Bishop Folquet de Marseille, a former troubadour patronized by Raymond V who in 1195 got religion and became the most rabid bigot of them all (a contemporary wrote: 'And when he was elected Bishop of Toulouse he spread such fire throughout the land that no amount of water will ever suffice to extinguish it; he snuffed out, in body and in soul, the lives of more than fifteen hundred people...he is more an Antichrist than a messenger of Rome').

In 1217, when young Raymond, son of the count, orchestrated an uprising in Provence to draw de Montfort out of Toulouse, the city welcomed back Raymond VI 'as if he were the Holy Spirit', and diligently prepared against de Montfort's return and inevitable siege. It was to be his last hurrah. A woman operating a kind of homemade mini-catapult recognized de Montfort from the walls, took aim and lobbed a large rock on his skull, dashing out his brains.

Raymond VI died soon afterwards (his body was stolen while awaiting burial in a monastery corridor, and never found), and he was succeeded by his son, Raymond VII. His reign was a troubled one. Simon de Montfort's heir waged war on Toulouse for 17 years before he gave up and ceded his claim to Louis VIII, who embarked on another 'crusade', a fancy name for a scorched-earth campaign to crush the south once and for all. In 1229 Raymond VII, seeing the distress of his subjects, sued for terms from the king, now Louis IX. As put down in the subsequent Treaty of Paris these terms were: first, the public submission of Count Raymond in front of Notre-Dame in Paris and his promise to round up all the remaining Cathars in his realm; then the division of booty, eastern Languedoc for the king of France and the Comtat-Vénaissin for the pope (this later allowed the popes to install themselves in Avignon, and weighed in favour of Louis IX's canonization). Jeanne, Raymond's only child, was forced to wed Alphonse de Poitiers, the king's brother. In the spirit of the times, Jeanne and Alphonse also went crusading in the East, and died childless in 1271, and Toulouse reverted to the king of France as the chief city of his new province of Languedoc.

One spin-off of the Albigensian Crusade was the founding of the Dominicans (*see* 'Les Jacobins', pp.449–50). A second was the invention of the Inquisition. Raymond VII, in spite of his submission in Paris, had so little heart for persecuting the Cathars, that in 1233 Pope Gregory IX came up with the idea of creating a spiritual police force and put the Dominicans in charge of it. This went down like a lead balloon in Toulouse; the *capitouls* themselves ordered an assault on the monastery and forced the Grand Inquisitors to flee. Raymond VII was ordered by Rome to take them back, and one night a band of Cathars descended from their mountain fastness in the Pyrénées and slit their throats – an act that tragically sealed the fate of Montségur, the Cathars' last refuge. Another side effect was the founding of the University of Toulouse: the 1229 Treaty of Paris ordered Raymond to support 14 masters of theology and canon law for a decade. They stuck around to form the second oldest university in France, one controlled for years by Parisians and papal appointees to enforce orthodoxy on the wayward, far too tolerant southerners.

Yet another effect of the Albigensian Crusade was a boom in the slave trade: the French were not only buying up recalcitrant southerners, but they now found the path to Spain clear to capture Muslims to sell in the north. The *capitouls* found their behaviour revolting, and in 1226 struck a precocious blow for human rights by granting the right of asylum to any slave, whatever his country of origin. Despite considerable pressure from Paris, the law remained on the books in Toulouse until the Revolution.

A Second Golden Age, in *Pastel*

Although the city got through the Hundred Years' War fairly intact, a fire that started in a bakery oven in 1463 destroyed 7,000 buildings in the medieval centre. Toulouse rebounded from the disaster at once, thanks to a new cash crop – dyers' woad, locally called *pastel*. Cultivated in the hills of the Lauragais just southeast of

Toulouse, pastel leaves were pulverized and squeezed into balls called *coques*. Left to dry, these were then crushed into paste, fermented for a year, and then mixed with urine to produce the deep blue dye so fashionable in the Renaissance; mixed with other ingredients it became bright green or violet. For a century so much *pastel* money poured into Toulouse that the Lauragais, the land of the *coques*, became the *païs de Cocanha* or Cockaigne, the carefree land of abundance and pleasure. Merchants from across Europe speculated and dealt in *pastel* credits and futures, and in 1552 these activities were centralized with the founding of Toulouse's stock exchange – just before the *pastel* market collapsed in the 1560s with the import of a much cheaper substitute, indigo from South Carolina.

The 17th century brought Toulouse both deep economic depression and spiritual malaise. The clergy were openly corrupt, and many Toulousains, the Cathars of old, were receptive to the preachings of John Calvin. Although the *capitouls* tolerated the new religion (many of them were converts themselves), the *parlementaires* and *intendants* – representing royal power in Toulouse – stayed strictly in the Catholic camp, and conflicts were inevitable: a bloody riot broke out in 1562 when Catholic priests stole the body of a dead Protestant woman laid out in a temple, saying she had reconverted on her deathbed; by May it was open warfare in the streets. But the Catholics prevailed in the end, and Toulouse was one of the last cities to recognize Henri IV as king.

In 1632, with the dramatic execution of the governor of Languedoc, the duke of Montmorency (*see* p.445), Toulouse saw its remaining independence and privileges slowly gobbled up by the absolute monarchy. One bright spot was the digging of the Canal du Midi, linking the Mediterranean and the Atlantic, a project according to legend first envisaged by Charlemagne and brilliantly planned, financed and achieved by Pierre-Paul Riquet, scion of a prominent Italian family in the region. Louis XVI was pleased to take credit for uniting two seas and two worlds in record time (1666–81), but the cost – 3,600,000 livres – was borne by Languedoc and the dedicated Riquet, who died ruined.

The new prosperity and agricultural trade (mostly in wheat) brought about by Riquet's ditch may have improved local morale if not local morals. The most popular entertainments in Toulouse were public executions, to the tune of three or four a month, which may be why the population only grew 10 per cent (to around 60,000) while the rest of France shot up 40 per cent in the 1700s. The execution with the most repercussions was the 1761 *affaire Calas*: the son of a fervently Protestant cloth merchant was found strangled. The family claimed they had tried to keep his suicide quiet, to prevent the dishonour of having the body put on trial (as suicide was a crime), but the neighbours had often overheard father and son quarrelling over religion, and were convinced from the beginning that Calas *père* had murdered Calas *fils* rather than see him convert to Catholicism. Found guilty by the *parlement* of Toulouse, Calas *père* was brutally tortured, then had all his limbs broken with iron bars, and survived another two hours, the whole time stalwartly maintaining his innocence. Voltaire wrote of the case, and soon enough even the king of Prussia and Catherine the Great were expressing their great indignation. Funds were raised on the streets of Holland and England for a retrial; the *parlement* of Paris demanded the dossier, and three years later Calas was found innocent, his family rehabilitated. Encouraged by the result, Voltaire continued his sarcastic attacks on the inhumanity of French justice, until all the *parlements* in France were universally hated – adding another pile of kindling to the smouldering misery that ignited the Revolution.

Toulouse in the Sky with Diamonds

The mid-19th century found Toulouse a mere departmental capital, a sleepy provincial backwater where the élite invested in property and farms instead of joining the Industrial Revolution. In 1833 journalist Léon Faucher wrote: 'Life is too easy in Toulouse for the people there to feel pushed to be or do anything.' The arrival of the railway in 1856 shook things up a bit, or at least shook down branches of Paris's banks and department stores.

What proved to be the turning point for modern Toulouse literally fell from the sky. Clément Ader of Muret, born in 1841, gave a preview of coming events when one of his bat-winged, steam-powered *avions*, as he called them, hopped off the ground in 1873; in 1890 he flew a few dozen yards in the *Eole*, 13 years before Orville Wright's first flight at Kitty Hawk. In 1917, Latécoère founded the first aircraft factory in Toulouse – in honour of Alder, in part, but mainly because the city was far from the front lines of the First World War; at its peak it produced six combat aeroplanes a day.

After the Armistice, Latécoère continued production, for peaceful purposes, and on 12 March 1919 launched a Toulouse–Casablanca airmail route that soon extended to Dakar and eventually to South America. For this new airline, the now legendary Compagnie Générale Aéropostale, he recruited ace pilots – 'Archangel' Jean Mermoz, Daurat, Guillaumet and Antoine de St-Exupéry, the 'Lord of the Sands', who immortalized his comrades in his books. A second aircraft company, founded in 1920 by Toulousain Emile Dewoitine, was nationalized in 1937 and later became Aérospatiale, the birthplace of Ariane rockets and Hermès, the European space shuttle, as well as Caravelle, Concorde and Airbus jets. Aérospatiale is now part of EADS (European Aeronautical Defence and Space), which will be assembling at Toulouse the major part of the 3XX, the largest civil aircraft in the world. Toulouse fought hard to be accepted as the assembly site and now looks forward to even greater prosperity as a result. CNES, the French space agency, was transferred here in 1968 along with the French national weather service. Astrium, Europe's number one satellite manufacturer is also based here. The air and space industries have attracted scores of research centres, high-tech firms and élite schools of engineering and aviation.

The population of Toulouse has since grown apace, but not only with engineers. It was the principal centre for refugees during and after the Spanish Civil War, and, of the 360,000 or so civilians and Republican soldiers who passed through the city, a quarter stayed and became French citizens (in the 1970s, when Franco executed the Catalan anti-fascist Puig Antich, 3,000 protestors set fire to the Spanish consulate in Toulouse). Thousands came to work in the new post-war industries; 25,000 *pieds-noirs* from Algeria settled here in the 1960s. Then in 1964, when France decided to ever so slowly reverse the centralizing policies of Richelieu and Louis XIV, Toulouse was made capital of the largest of France's new regions, the Midi-Pyrénées, encompassing the western half of its old province of Languedoc. By then Toulouse, after its slow start, had become the fourth largest city in France. Although pink in its politics as well as its bricks for most of the 20th century, Toulouse since 1971 has been mayored by the central right-wing Baudises, first the father, and now his son, Dominique Baudis – a popular mayor with the majority of Toulousains, who thank him for the city's economic and cultural achievements in recent years and look to the municipal elections in March 2001, when he will certainly step down, with apprehension. Another local bigwig who has succeeded in making a bigger impact on the national stage is Prime Minister Lionel Jospin from L'Ile-Jourdain, just outside Toulouse. Jospin was elected for being a Socialist but also for being a Protestant, which, now that the Wars of Religion are over, carries with it a shining cachet of honesty and integrity in France's otherwise murky politics.

The City

Place du Capitole

This dignified front parlour of Toulouse dates from 1850, when the 200-year-long tidying away of excess buildings was completed and the edges rimmed with neoclassical brick façades. As a permanent memorial to the southern kingdom of nevermore, the centre of the pavement is marked by an enormous **Cross of Languedoc**. This same golden cross on a red background hangs proudly from Toulouse's city hall, the **Capitole**, or CAPITOLIUM as it reads, bowing to a 16th-century story claiming that ancient Rome got its Capitol idea from Toulouse's temple of Capitoline Jupiter.

Jupiter Poopiter! Everyone knows this Capitole is really named after the *capitouls*. In 1750, flush with money brought in by the Canal du Midi, these worthies decided to transform their higgledy-piggledy medieval buildings into a proper Hôtel de Ville. Parts of the original 12th–17th-century complex were saved, as much as could be masked by the neoclassical façade designed by Guillaume Cammas, who imported stone and marble to alternate with the homemade brick of Toulouse. Cammas's careful polychromatic effects were only briefly admired before the *capitouls* decided to order every building in the city to be whitewashed or covered with white stucco, the better to reflect the moonlight and make up for the lack of street lighting. The first building to get the treatment was the Capitole itself; the entire Place du Capitole lay under this dull make-up until 1946, when Toulouse decided to become the *Ville Rose* once more. Other critics have had trouble with the Capitole's height. '*C'est beau mais c'est bas*' was the only comment of Napoleon, an expert on the subject.

The portal on the right belongs to the **Théâtre du Capitole**, while over the central door eight pink marble columns represent the eight *capitouls*; the pompous historical rooms upstairs (*open Mon–Fri 10–12 and 2–5*) were decorated in the 1800s with busts of famous Toulousains. In the *Salle Henri Martin* is Toulouse's own contribution to the Impressionist movement, a painting of the great pre-First World War Socialist leader from nearby Castres, *Jean Jaurès on the banks of the Garonne*.

Pedestrians cut through the **Cour Henri IV**, with a statue of said king, who in 1602 gave his permission for the construction of the courtyard. He might not have said yes, had he known what was going to happen here 30 years later, thanks to the jealous rivalries and schemes of his two neurotic sons, Louis XIII and Gaston d'Orléans ('Monsieur' for short), and the prime minister and arch-puppeteer Cardinal Richelieu.

One back door of the Cour Henri IV gives on to Square Charles de Gaulle, defended by the **Donjon** of 1525, where the *capitouls* kept the city archives. The building, well restored by Viollet-le-Duc, now houses the city tourist office.

A Conspiracy's Martyr

Henri IV's companion-in-arms, Henri Duke of Montmorency, First Peer of the Realm and Governor of Languedoc, was succeeded in these titles by his son, Duke Henri II, a brave fighter and governor dedicated to the welfare of Languedoc. Richelieu, whose plans for creating an absolute centralized monarchy for Louis XIII necessitated tripping up the kingdom's mightiest barons, made it hot for Montmorency by choking Languedoc with taxes until it was at the point of insurrection. Montmorency hated Richelieu, and attracted the attention of 'Monsieur', who, in cahoots with his scheming mother, Marie de' Medici, was always ready to befriend an enemy of the cardinal. Monsieur offered to send down troops to liberate first Languedoc, then France from the high-handed cardinal's policies. After much soul-searching, Montmorency cast his lot with Monsieur.

Richelieu must have rubbed his hands with glee. With the king in tow he led an army south to snuff out the revolt. The promised military aid from Monsieur failed to materialize, and Montmorency, realizing he had made a terrible mistake, tried unsuccessfully to surrender, hoping to avoid battle. Richelieu refused. The royal troops surprised the hapless duke while he was reconnoitring the lines. Montmorency, fighting singlehandedly, was wounded 17 times; he might even have escaped, it was said, had he had his proper warhorse. Richelieu was careful to keep Montmorency alive, knowing he could make a much more memorable example *pour encourager les autres* by persuading the king to sentence the duke to death.

Montmorency's fate quickly became a *cause célèbre* across Europe – Charles I of England, the pope, the Republic of Venice and most of the nobles of France pleaded for mercy. Louis XIII turned a deaf ear, but on the appointed day of execution, 30 October 1632, popular feeling in Toulouse ran so high that the authorities decided to hold the execution privately in this courtyard of the Capitole rather than in public. In spite of his wounds, Montmorency walked alone to the chopping block (a slab in the pavement marks the spot), his eyes falling on the statue of Henri IV. 'He was a great and generous prince, and I had the honour to be his godson,' were Montmorency's last words. His blood splattered over the statue; the guard dipped their swords in the red pool; a throng of grieving Toulousains were allowed in to touch and kiss the sticky pavement. He was buried in St-Sernin, the basilica's first non-saint to receive such a high honour.

The Basilica of St-Sernin

Running north from Place du Capitole, narrow **Rue du Taur** was the road to Cahors in Roman times. The Taur in its name means 'bull', which features in the life of the city's first saint, Sernin, who died here in the 240s. Sernin (a corruption of Saturnin) was a missionary from Rome who preached in Pamplona and Toulouse. One day, runs the legend, he happened by the temple of Capitoline Jupiter, where preparations were under way for the sacrifice of a bull to Mithras. The priests ordered him to kneel before the pagan idol, and, when Sernin refused, a sudden gust of wind blew over the statue of Mithras, breaking it to bits. In fury the crowd demanded the sacrifice of Sernin instead, and he was tied under the bull, which, maddened by the extra weight, dragged his body through the city streets. Curiously, an identical martyrdom awaited Sernin's disciple Fermin in Pamplona, where he became the patron saint of matadors and is honoured each year by the famous running of the bulls, even though the official hagiography claims that Fermin died peacefully in bed as bishop of Amiens. One wonders: could Fermin really be Sernin, transformed long ago by a slip of a monastic quill?

After turning Sernin to pulp, the bull left his body where the 14th-century **Notre-Dame-du-Taur** now stands, replacing an oratory built over Sernin's tomb in 360. Its 135ft *clocher-mur* looks like a false front in a Wild West town; the nave is surprisingly wide, and has a faded fresco of the Tree of Jesse along the right wall. Sernin's tomb attracted so many pilgrims and Christians who desired to be buried near him that in 403 a *martyrium* was built 300 yards to the north. An imperial decree permitted the removal of the saint's relics to this spot, and over the centuries tombs lined the length of Rue de Taur, as in the Alyschamps in Arles. In 1075, just as the pilgrimage to Compostela was getting under way, Count Guilhem decided Sernin deserved something more grand. The construction of the **Basilique du St-Sernin** was continued by his famous brother Raymond IV, and of such import that in 1096 Pope Urban II, on tour that year preaching the First Crusade, came to consecrate its marble altar.

In 1220 St-Sernin was finished – at 380ft the largest surviving Romanesque church in the world (only the great abbey church of Cluny, destroyed in the Revolution, was bigger). It was begun at the same time, and has the exact same plan, as the basilica of St James at Compostela: a cross, ending in a semi-circular apse with five radiating chapels. In the 19th century the abbey and cloister were demolished, and in 1860 Viollet-le-Duc was summoned to restore the basilica. He spent 20 years on the project – and botched the roof so badly that rainwater seeped directly into the stone and brick. A century later the church was found to be in danger of collapse – hence a 22 million franc 'de-restoration' project to undo Viollet-le-Duc's mischief. Off came all his neo-Gothic ornamentation and heavy stone, to be replaced with tiles handcrafted in the 13th-century manner.

The Exterior

The apse of St-Sernin (seen from Rue St-Bernard) is a fascinating play of white stone and red brick, a crescendo culminating in the octagonal bell tower that is Toulouse's most striking landmark. New York had its war of skyscrapers in the 1930s; 13th-century Toulouse had its war of bell towers: St-Sernin's original three storeys of arcades were increased to five for the sole purpose of upstaging the bell tower of the Jacobins. The most elaborately decorated of the basilica's portals is an odd, asymmetrical one on the south side, the **Porte Miège-ville**. It faces Rue du Taur; apparently this street, called Miège-ville or 'mid-city' in medieval times, ran right through the spot before the basilica was built. Devotees of medieval Toulousain arcana – a bottomless subject – say that this portal is the real cornerstone of the kingdom of Languedoc that the 11th-century counts were trying to create; books have been written about its proportions and the symbolism of its decoration, even claiming that it is the centre of a geomantic construction, with 12 lines radiating from here across the counts' territories, connecting various chapels and villages and forming – what else? – Raymond IV's Cross of Languedoc. The tympanum was carved by the 11th-century master Bernard Gilduin, showing the *Ascension of Christ*, a rare scene in medieval art, and one of the most choreographic: Christ surrounded by dancing angels, watched by the Apostles on the lintel. On the brackets are figures of David and others riding on lions; the magnificent capitals tell the story of the Redemption (*Original Sin*, *Massacre of the Innocents*, *Annunciation*), all from the expressive chisel of Gilduin. The north transept door, now walled up, was the royal door; the south transept door, the **Porte des Comtes**, is named after the several 11th-century counts of Toulouse who are buried in palaeo-Christian sarcophagi in the deep *enfeu* nearby. The eight capitals here, also by Gilduin (c. 1080), are the oldest Romanesque works to show the torments of hell, most alarmingly a man having his testicles crushed and a woman whose breasts are being devoured by serpents, both paying the price for Lust.

The Interior

Begun in 1969, the 'de-restoration' of the barrel-vaulted interior stripped the majestic brick and stone of Viollet-le-Duc's ham-handed murals and fiddly neo-Gothic bits. In the process, some fine 12th-century frescoes have been found, especially the serene angel of the Resurrection in the third bay of the north transept, which also has some of the best capitals. In the south transpect, the shrine of St Jude, the patron saint of lost causes, blazes with candlelight in July – when French students take their exams.

For a small fee you can enter the **ambulatory** (*open daily 10–11.30 and 2–5, July and Aug 10–6, closed Sun morning*) and make what the Middle Agers called 'the Circuit of Holy Bodies', for the wide array of saintly anatomies stashed in the five radiating chapels. In the 17th century, bas-reliefs and wood panels on the lives of the saints were added to bring the relics to life, and although these were removed in the 1800s they were restored and replaced in 1980. Opposite the central chapel are seven magnificent marble bas-reliefs of 1096, carved and signed by Bernard Gilduin. The

Christ in Majesty set in a mandorla is as serene, pot-bellied and beardless as a Buddha, surrounded by the four Evangelists; the others show a seraph, a cherub, two apostles and a pair of hierarchic, extremely well-coiffed angels – scholars guess these were perhaps modelled after a Roman statue of Orpheus.

The Holy Bodies circuit continues down into the upper crypt, with the silver shrine of St Honoratus (1517) and the 13th-century reliquaries of the Holy Cross and of St Sernin, the latter showing the saint under the hooves of the bull. The lower crypt contains, more bodily, two Holy Thorns (a present from St Louis), 13th-century gloves and mitres, and a set of six 16th-century painted wooden statues of apostles. In the choir an 18th-century baldachin shelters St Sernin's tomb, remade in 1746 and supported by a pair of bronze bulls. In the south transept, note the big feet sticking out of a pillar, all that remains of a shallow relief of St Christopher effaced by the hands of centuries of pilgrims.

Around Place St-Sernin and the Quartier Arnaud-Bernard

At No.3, the Lycée St-Sernin occupies the **Hôtel du Barry**, built by Louis XV's pimp, the Roué du Barry. Du Barry married his charming lover, Jeanne de Bécu, to his brother and then in 1759 introduced her to the king. His pandering earned him the money to build this mansion in 1777; it would later earn the Comtesse du Barry the guillotine in the Terror. (The word *roué*, incidentally, was first used in the 1720s, to describe the bawdy companions of the regent, the Duke of Orléans; it was invented by some disapproving soul who thought they should have been broken on the wheel.)

On the south side of the square stood a pilgrims' hostel, founded in the 1070s by a chanter of St Sernin named Raymond Gayard, who was canonized for his charity to the poor. His hostel was succeeded by the *collège* of St Raymond (1505) for poor university students, and now by the rich archaeological collections of the **Musée St-Raymond** (***t** 05 61 22 21 85; open daily 10–6, June–Aug 10–7*). After much renovation the museum is once again opening its doors. This is the antiquities museum of Toulouse, with some exceptional pieces. The top floors concentrate on finds from the Roman region of Narbonnaise and one of its biggest towns, Tolosa, ancient Toulouse. One of the most interesting exhibits is the section of a relief depicting two Amazons in combat, one clearly with the upper hand over a man: this would have formed part of a temple or major monument. The collection of outstanding busts is small compared to the avenue of heads of emperors, men, women and children on the floor below: all found, with the other exhibits here, at Chiragan in Martres-Tolosane, 60km to the south of Toulouse. Don't miss the splendid marbles depicting the *Labours of Hercules*. Digs carried out in the basement of the museum have revealed the presence of a Christian necropolis dating from the 4th century which grew up around the tomb of St Sernin. Several of the tombs have been left not far from where they were found, close to a large, circular 5th-century lime kiln. Ornate sarcophagi from south-west France and other funerary objects are also on display. There are also vestiges of walls from an 11th-century hospital and 13th-century college. Temporary exhibitions allow the public to see other museum artefacts, principally from the Iron Age through the Middle Ages.

Just south of St-Sernin in Rue du Périgord, the atavistic southern Gothic **Chapelle des Carmélites** (1643) owes its existence to Anne of Austria, wife of Louis XIII, who laid the foundation stone on the day that she learned of the canonization of St Theresa. The walls are covered with paintings, and vaulting has been restored to bring out its lavish ceiling, covered with an unusual allegory on the *Glory of Carmel* by Jean-Baptiste Despax.

This northernmost medieval neighbourhood, the lively **Quartier Arnaud-Bernard**, has been the city's Latin Quarter ever since 1229, when the **University of Toulouse** was founded in Rue des Lois (part of it now occupies the old seminary of St-Pierre-des-Chartreaux to the west). Although forced down Toulouse's throat by Paris (*see* 'History', above), the university enjoyed a certain prestige in the Middle Ages; among its alumni were three popes and Michel de Montaigne. Rabelais started to study here, where he 'well learned to dance and to play at swords with two hands', but he quickly got out because its regents still had a certain problem when it came to free-thinkers; several were burned alive at the stake. 'It didn't please God that I linger,' Rabelais continued, 'me with my nature already rather parched, and not in need of any more heat.'

The three principal squares of the quarter – Place du Peyrou, Place des Tiercerettes and Place Arnaud-Bernard – became the centre of immigrant life in the last century; today they are quickly being gentrified, but are still quite lively after dark. North of the boulevard, the neighbourhood's 'lung', the **Jardin Compans-Caffarelli**, was laid out in 1982 with exotic plants, a Japanese garden and tea room.

Les Jacobins

t 05 61 22 21 92; open July–Sept 10–6.30, rest of year 10–12 and 2–6; closed Sun and hol mornings; adm for the cloister.

Just west of Place du Capitole stands the great Dominican mother church, **Les Jacobins**, the prototype for Dominican foundations across Europe and one of the masterpieces of southern French Gothic. The Spanish priest Domingo de Guzmán had tried hard to convert the Cathars before the Albigensian Crusade, although the persuasive powers of one man, even a saint, proved negligible in the face of an intellectual revolt against the openly corrupt, materialistic clergy. In 1206 Domingo had re-converted enough women to found a convent, which became the germ of his Order of Preaching Friars, established in Toulouse in 1215. Promoted by Folquet, the bishop of Toulouse, and confirmed by the pope in 1216, the new Dominican order quickly found adherents across Europe. In 1230, the Dominicans erected this, their third convent in Toulouse, which took the name of the Jacobins from the Dominicans' Paris address, in Rue St-Jacques (the very same convent where the fanatical party of Robespierre would later meet, hence the *Jacobins* of the French Revolution – a fitting name in light of the Dominicans' role as Inquisitors).

The magnificent Jacobins in Toulouse so impressed the popes that they made it the last resting place of the relics of the greatest Dominican of them all, St Thomas Aquinas (d. 1274). Confiscated in the Revolution, Napoleon requisitioned the church and convent as a barracks for his artillery, which built an upper floor in the nave. When Prosper Mérimée, inspector of historic monuments, visited Toulouse in 1845, he found the mutilated complex occupied by 500 horses and cannoneers, with a pig-ignorant military administration bent on demolishing the whole thing. In 1865 the military was finally convinced to leave the Jacobins to the city, and Toulouse spent a hundred years on its restoration.

The church is the perfect expression of the 13th-century reaction to Rome's love of luxury, which made the great preaching orders, the Dominicans and Franciscans, so popular in their day. Gargoyles are the only exterior sculpture in this immense but harmonious brick pile of buttresses, alternating with flamboyant windows; its octagonal bell tower of brick and stone crowned with baby towers is one of the landmarks of the city skyline. The interior is breathtakingly light and spacious, consisting of twin naves divided by seven huge columns, crisscrossed by a fantastic interweaving of ribs in the vault, reaching an epiphany in the massive flamboyant *palmier* in the apse. The painted decoration dates from the 13th to the 16th century, but only the glass of the rose windows on the west side is original. The 19th-century gilded reliquary shrine of St Thomas Aquinas was returned to the high altar in 1974.

A small door leads out into the lovely garden **cloister** (1309), with brick arcades and twinned columns in grey marble, used in the summer for the concert series *Piano aux Jacobins*. The east gallery gives on to the large **chapter house**, supported by a pair of slender marble columns. The walls of the adjacent **Chapelle St-Antonin**, the funerary chapel, were painted in the early 1300s with scenes from the life of St Antonin, while the ceiling is decorated with southwest France's favourite vision from the Apocalypse: the 24 Elders and angels glorifying Christ. In Rue Pargaminieres, the **Refectory** (*same hours*), nearly 200ft long, houses temporary exhibitions, often on historical themes.

West of Les Jacobins, near the Garonne's hog-backed bridge, **Pont St-Pierre**, are Toulouse's two churches dedicated to St Peter. **St-Pierre-des-Cuisines**, a little Romanesque priory associated with Moissac, is named after its kitchens where a person's bread could be baked at cheaper rates than at the counts' ovens; used as a warehouse from the Revolution until 1965, the church is still awaiting restoration. **St-Pierre-des-Chartreux**, to the north in Rue Valade, was founded in the 17th century by monks fleeing the Huguenots of Castres and, if open, has some fine works from the 17th and 18th century – the grand organ (1686; originally in Les Jacobins), elaborate sculpted wood panels, stuccoes and murals from the 1680s. Just west, along the **Canal de Brienne** that links the Garonne to the Canal du Midi, runs one of Toulouse's favourite leafy promenades, while, just beyond that, **Le Bazacle** was where the grumbling of the massive 12th-century mills so annoyed Rabelais. It is now a hydroelectric works supplying the city's bulbs with watts; you can visits its guts, its fish passages and special exhibitions, and enjoy a fine view of Toulouse (*open Oct–June 9–12 and 1.30–7, weekends and holidays 2–7; closed July–Sept*).

Pastel Palaces and Violets of Gold

Just south of Les Jacobins, to the south end of Rue Gambetta, is one of the city's most splendid residences, the **Hôtel de Bernuy**, built in 1504 by a *pastel* merchant from Burgos, Don Juan de Bernuy, a Spanish Jew who fled Ferdinand and Isabella's Inquisition and became a citizen – and *capitoul* – of Toulouse. Although Gothic on the outside, inside his master mason Loys Privat designed an eclectic fantasy courtyard, a mix of Gothic, Plateresque and Loire château, topped by a lofty tower rivalling those of all the other *pastel* nabobs. De Bernuy had a chance to repay France for the fortune he made when King François I was captured at the battle of Pavia by Emperor Charles V and imprisoned in Madrid; the king fell gravely ill, but no one could afford the ransom of 1,200,000 gold ecus demanded by the emperor – until de Bernuy bailed him out. In his distress the king had promised an ex voto to St Sernin if he survived, and in the ambulatory you can still see the black marble statue he donated when he came in 1533 to thank the saint and de Bernuy for his generosity.

Not long after de Bernuy's time the Jesuits converted his *hôtel particulier* into a college, now the prestigious **Lycée Pierre de Fermat**, named after its star pupil, the brilliant mathematician (1595–1665) who left his last theorem as a challenge to subsequent generations of mathematicians. Just to the east, another 16th-century *hôtel particulier* houses the **Musée du Vieux Toulouse** (*7 Rue du May,* ***t*** *05 61 13 97 24; open June–Sept Mon–Sat 3–6*) with a fascinating collection from the city's fragrant history and its former porcelain industry, as well as 19th-century paintings and etchings of Toulouse. Rue du May gives on to pedestrian-only Rue St-Rome, a street of many names that was the *cardo* of Roman Tolosa and the city's principal north–south axis in the Middle Ages and Renaissance, decorated with 16th-century mansions built by the *capitouls* and wealthy merchants. At its south end don't miss what was the very centre of Roman Toulouse, the triangular **Place de la Trinité**, with a 19th-century fountain supported by bronze mermaids. Near here, you can examine the popular artistic pulse of Toulouse in the ever-changing murals along narrow Rue Coq-d'Inde.

One of the finest private residences built in Toulouse, the **Hôtel d'Assézat** is just west, off Rue de Metz, a wide street rammed through the middle of medieval Toulouse in the 19th century. The *hôtel* was begun in 1555 by another *pastel* magnate, Pierre d'Assezat, who had a near monopoly on the dye in northern Europe. Designed by Nicolas Bachelier, Toulouse's master architect-sculptor-engineer, it consists of two buildings around a large square court, and a curious tower crowned with an octagonal lantern and dome that served the merchant as an observation post over the Garonne, enabling him to keep an eye on his fleet. The decoration, a rhythmic composition of Ionic, Doric and Corinthian columns, is so similar to that on the old Louvre that Bachelier was long thought to have copied the idea, although the records prove that both buildings went up at the same time. Facing the street, an Italianate loggia has seven brackets decorated with *pastel* pods. Inside, the **Fondation Bemberg** (***t*** *05 61 12 06 89; open 10–6, closed Mon; nocturnal visits Thurs 9pm, themed visits Thurs 7pm and Sat 11am; adm*) has a fine collection of art, specializing in Renaissance and modern French paintings; the latter includes over 30 works by Pierre Bonnard. Since the 19th century, the *hôtel* has also been the **Palais des Académies**, seat of the Académie des Jeux Floraux (***t*** *05 61 21 22 85*). Over the portico is a statue of Dame Clemence Isaure, the legendary patroness of the Floral Games.

The Eisteddfod of France

In November 1323, seven burghers of Toulouse met together in a monastery garden. Although not poets, these 'Seven Troubadours' were connoisseurs who regretted that good poetry in their town had died out with the counts of Toulouse. To inspire some new verse, the seven decided to invite all the bards of Languedoc to gather in the monastery garden to recite on 3 May; the poem the seven judged best would receive a violet made of gold. A big crowd showed up, and ever since then 3 May in Toulouse has hosted what has become known as the *Jeux Floraux*. The Seven Troubadours were soon succeeded by the 'Maintainers' of the *College du Gay Scavoir*, the world's oldest literary society, renamed the *Académie des Jeux Floraux* by Louis XIV.

Early on the Seven Troubadours added two other prizes, an eglantine and a marigold in silver. To cope with the bewildering disorder of entries in the competition, they commissioned a code from one of Toulouse's top jurists and humanists, Guilhem Molinier; the resulting *Las Leys d'Amors* in 1356 was widely read, and soon copied in Barcelona, which in 1388 started its own Jocs Florals. There the first prize was not a gold rose but a real rose, because, like the greatest poetry, a rose can never be imitated (it was also presumed that the winning poem would live forever and need no other reward). Although any true blue Toulousain would punch anyone in the nose for saying so, Barcelona's Floral Games actually produced the better poetry; so great was the fear of heresy or challenging accepted moral norms in the home town of the Inquisition that nearly all of Toulouse's entries were safe, bloodless praises of the Virgin Mary that hold little interest today. (Chaucer, a contemporary of the Seven Troubadours, would have told them the poetry might have been better had they chosen a different date for the contest: 3 May is the Invention of the Cross, traditionally the unluckiest day in the year.)

Along the Garonne

Rue de Metz continues to Toulouse's oldest bridge, which, as in Paris, is rather confusingly known as the new, or **Pont Neuf**. This Pont Neuf, with its seven unequal arches of brick and stone and curious holes (*oculi*), took from 1544 to 1632 to build, and links Gascony – the Left Bank – with the medieval province of Languedoc. Just down the quay stands the **Ecole des Beaux-Arts**, its façade larded with allegorical figures (1895). Hidden under the icing is a 17th-century U-shaped monastery connected to **Notre-Dame-la-Daurade**. Only the name recalls what was for centuries one of the wonders of Toulouse, the 10-sided, domed, 5th-century palatine chapel of the Visigothic kings, known as the Daurade ('the golden one') after its shimmering mosaics. Similar to the churches of Ravenna, it was destroyed in 1761, when the nitwitted monks who owned it decided to replace it with a reproduction of the Vatican. Plans for the new church collided with the Revolution and the building was only completed in the mid-19th century. The paintings in the choir are by Ingres's master, Roques. Don't miss the pretty **Place de la Daurade** just north of the church; it overlooked the Garonne until the rebuilding of the quays in the 19th century.

One of the finest views of the Pont Neuf and riverfront is to the south along the **Quai de Tounis**. Rue du Pont de Tounis, built in 1515 as a bridge over the Garonnette (a now covered tributary of the Garonne), leads back to the original riverbank and **Notre-Dame-la-Dalbade** (Our Lady the Whitened, after its medieval whitewash, in contrast to the Golden One). This church too has taken some hard knocks. It was rebuilt in the Renaissance with a 280ft spire, to show up St-Sernin's bell tower; the spire was chopped down in the Revolution, and rebuilt in the 1880s, using such cheap materials that it fell through the roof in 1926. It has a rich Renaissance door, under the tympanum's ceramic reproduction of Fra Angelico's *Coronation of the Virgin* (1874).

Rue de la Dalbade was the favourite address for the nobility; among its many *hôtels particuliers*, the standout is the sooty **Hôtel de Pierre** (No.25), which, extravagantly for the *ville rose*, is made of stone. In 1538 Nicolas Bachelier designed the façades around the courtyard, the doorway, framed by two bearded old men, and the monumental chimney. In the early 17th century, when the next owner, a president of the *parlement*, married a *pastel* heiress, he added the grandiose Baroque façade in imitation of one he saw in Italy. Just opposite is the grand **Hôtel de Malte** (1680), the headquarters of the Knights of St John in Toulouse since 1115; after 1315, they took over the wealth and duties of the Templars (who before their suppression were at No.13).

The Quartier du Jardin

At the south end of Rue de la Dalbade/Rue de la Fonderie in Place du Salin stood the fortified residence of the counts of Toulouse, the celebrated Château Narbonnais; it was also the site of the *parlement*, established in Toulouse in 1443. The whole complex was demolished in the 19th century for the Palais de Justice, with only the square brick tower, the 14th-century royal treasury (converted into a Protestant church), as a memory. In the adjacent Place du Parlement is an old house built on the Roman wall, donated to Domingo Guzmán for his new preaching order, and later converted to the use inscribed over the door: 'Maison de l'Inquisition'. In Roman times the south gate of the city stood here, at the end of the *cardo* (here Rue Pharaon).

South of the Place du Parlement, Allées Jules-Guesde replaces the walls torn down in 1752. Here, by the Théâtre Sorano, a plaque marks the exact spot where the hated Simon de Montfort was brained; nearby at No.35 is Toulouse's fascinating, fusty old **Musée d'Histoire Naturelle** (*closed for renovations; contact the tourist office for details*). Some very monumental architecture was planned here in the mid-17th century but never got built – the **Grand Rond** at the end of Allées Jules-Guesde was supposed to be the central garden in the midst of six wide radiating promenades, or *allées*, of which only four were laid out. The **Jardin Royal** was planted outside the walls, and in the 19th century Toulouse'sprettiest park, the **Jardin des Plantes**, was added. The garden's grand 16th–17th-century portal on Allée Frédéric-Mistral was salvaged from the original Capitole; just south of this is the **Monument à la Gloire de la Resistance**, with a crypt aligned to be illuminated by the sun's rays on 19 August, the anniversary of the Liberation of Toulouse (*open Mon–Fri 10–12 and 2–5, closed weekends and hols*).

There is one last museum in this quarter, and one not to be missed if you're fond of Egyptian, Coptic, Indian and Far Eastern Art. This is the **Musée Georges-Labit**, in a neo-Moorish villa (*43 Rue des Martyrs-de-la-Libération, off Allée Frédéric-Mistral,* **t** *05 61 22 21 84; open 10–5, till 6 in summer; closed Tues and hols*). Labit was a 19th-century traveller with plenty of money and a good eye who accumulated a choice Oriental collection, considered the best in France after the Guimet Museum in Paris.

Place du Salin to the Cathedral of St-Etienne

The parliamentarians liked to build themselves distingished houses in the homogenous quarter between the old *parlement* and the cathedral: all uniform pink brick, with light grey shutters and black wrought-iron balconies. In this mesh of quiet lanes, there are a few to pick out during a stroll, such as the sumptuously ornate **Hôtel du Vieux Raisin** (1515), 36 Rue du Languedoc, built by another *capitoul* in love with Italy. Another *hôtel* houses the **Musée Paul-Dupuy** (*13 Rue de la Pleau,* **t** *05 61 14 65 50; open 10–5, until 6 in summer, closed Tues and hols*), named after the obsessed collector – every city seems to have one – who left to Toulouse his hoard of watches, automata, guns, coins, fans, faïence, pharmaceutical jars and gems like the 11th-century 'horn of Roland' and other exquisite medieval ivories, as well as a silver marigold from the Jeux Floraux of 1762. Some of the exhibits can only be seen by appointment. In Rue Ninau the 16th-century **Hôtel de Ulmo** (with the marble baldachin in the courtyard) was built by Jean de Ulmo, president of the Toulouse *parlement*, whose motto *Durum patientia frango* (my constancy breaks adversity) hid a scoundrel to the core; caught selling every favour his office had to dispense, he was flogged, stripped of his possessions and sent off to prison, where he was given the task of keeping the accounts of the prison governor – which he falsified to his own advantage before he was hanged.

Rue Perchepinte and Rue Fermat, lined with antique shops, lead up to Place St-Etienne, with Toulouse's oldest fountain (1546) and the massive archbishop's palace (1713), now used as the Préfecture. All are overpowered by the **cathedral of St-Etienne**, begun in the 11th century by Raymond IV and, after various fits and starts, completed only in the 17th century. Fashions and finances rose and fell in the three major building campaigns, resulting in a church that seems a bit drunk. Have a good look at the façade: in the centre rises a massive brick bell tower with a clock, over the Romanesque base. To the right is a worn, asymmetrical stone Gothic façade, where the portal and rose window are off-centre; to the left extends the bulge of the chapel of Notre-Dame, a small church in itself stuck on the north end.

It's even tipsier inside. In 1211, Raymond VI inserted the oldest known representation of the Cross of Languedoc as the key in one of the vaults, just before 1215, when Bishop Folquet rebuilt most of Raymond IV's church in the form of a single nave 62ft high and 62ft wide, with ogival crossings, a style that went on to become the model for southern Gothic. In 1275, Bishop Bertrand de L'Isle-Jourdaine decided Bishop Folquet's bit of the cathedral was hardly grandiose enough for Toulouse's dignity and came up with a plan based on northern French Gothic that involved realigning the axis of the church. The choir was built, a fine example of flamboyant Gothic, with beautiful 14th-century glass on the west side, but the vaults, designed to be 132ft high, were cut short at 90ft due to limited funds. Money and energy ran out completely when Bishop Bertrand died, leaving a curious dogleg in the nave where his choir meets Raymond IV and Bishop Folquet's nave, marked by the massive Pilier d'Orléans, one of four intended to support the transept; it bears a plaque marking the tomb of Pierre-Paul Riquet, father of the Canal du Midi. Although many of the cathedral's best decorations are now stowed away in the Musée des Augustins, there are tapestries, faded into negatives of themselves, from the 15th and 16th centuries, and some interesting grotesques in the choir. The organ, a remarkable instrument from the early 1600s, was at the point of collapsing in the 1970s when it was restored and firmly bolted high on its wall bracket like an elephant in a flower vase.

Musée des Augustins

t 05 61 22 21 82; open 10–6, till 5 in winter, till 9 on Wed; closed Tues and hols.

Rue Croix Baragnon, opposite the cathedral, has two beautiful Gothic houses, especially No.15, decorated with a band of stone carvings. But the greatest medieval art in this part of town is in the **Musée des Augustins**, a block north at the corner of Rue de Metz and Rue d'Alsace-Lorraine. The museum, one of the oldest in France, is housed in a 14th-century Augustinian convent, beautifully restored in 1950.

During the Revolution, the *ville rose* went about gaily smashing up its fabulous architectural heritage, as ordered in 1790 by the Convention, 'to leave standing no monument that hinted of slavery'. Enter on the scene Alexandre Dumège, the self-taught son of a Dutch actor, who had such a passion for antiquities that he singlehandedly rescued most of the contents of this museum and opened its doors in 1794. Gothic sculptures occupy the Augustinians' flamboyant chapterhouse: the beautiful 14th-century *Virgin and Child* from Avignon, *Notre-Dame de Grasse* from the Jacobins, scenes from a 14th-century retable, the 'Group of three Persons one of which is strangled by a monster', and effigies from tombstones. A crooning choir of gargoyles from Toulouse's demolished Franciscan convent keep company with the sarcophaguses around the cloister; one is said to belong to the Visigothic Queen Ranachilde – *la reine Pédauque*, the goose-foot (*see* p.55), perhaps because of the web-footed bird carved in the side.

The nave of the convent church is devoted to religious paintings (Van Dyck's *Christ aux anges* and *Miracle de la mule*, Rubens's *Christ entre deux Larrons* and *San Diego in extase* by Murillo) and reliefs by Nicolas Bachelier. Best of all are the Romanesque works, most of them rescued from demolished cloisters: from St-Sernin, there's a capital sculpted with the *War of Angels* and an enigmatic bas-relief from the Porte des Comtes showing two women looking at one another, one holding a lion in her arms, the other a ram, an image that also appears on the main portal at Compostela. Other capitals, stylistically closely related to those of Moissac, come from the Romanesque cloister of the Daurade; the most beautiful of all are from Raymond IV's 11th-century cloister of St-Etienne – note especially the delicate, almost fluid scene of the dance of Salome and the beheading of John the Baptist. From the Romanesque portal of St-Etienne's chapterhouse are statue-columns of the Apostles that look ahead to Chartres.

The first floor of the convent is devoted to paintings, including two portraits of *capitouls*; one of their oldest prerogatives was the *droit d'image* – the right to have their portraits painted. In the 13th and 14th centuries this was exceptional: kings, emperors, the doge of Venice and the pope were among the few others were allowed to leave their likenesses for posterity. Other paintings include a 15th-century Florentine hunt scene, an extremely unpleasant *Apollo flaying Marsyas* by the 'Divine' Guido Reni, a typical froufrou portrait by Hyacinthe Rigaud, and works by Simon Vouet, Philippe de Champaigne, Van Dyck, Rubens (in the Augustins' church), the two Guardis, Delacroix, Ingres, Manet, Morisot, Vuillard, Maurice Denis and Count Henri de Toulouse-Lautrec.

From the museum, Rue des Arts Tolosane leads up to **Place St-Georges**, once the main venue for Toulouse's favourite, pre-rugby spectator sport, executions – including that of Jean Calas – as it could hold the biggest crowds (this was before Place du Capitole was enlarged). Nowadays the many spectators dawdling in the cafés mainly look at one another. The square lent its name to an inner-city development completed in 1982 called the Nouveau St-Georges, which stretches off to Place Occitane. Here, in Rue Lapeyrouse, the Nouvelles Galeries department store has a splendid view over Toulouse from its rooftop tearoom.

Rue St-Antoine-de-T (named after the *tau* symbol on the robes of the monks of St Anthony) leads from Place St-Georges to an early, cosier experiment in urban renewal, the elliptical **Place Président Wilson**, laid out by municipal architect Jean-Paul Virebent in the early 19th century, with a centrepiece monument to one of the last troubadours, Pierre Godolin (1580–1649).

Toulouse's Left Bank

Although the Left, or Gascon, bank of the Garonne has been settled since the early Middle Ages, the periodic rampages of the river dampened property values until the end of the 19th century, when flood control projects were completed. The main reason for visiting is just over the Pont Neuf: the round brick lighthouse-shaped tower of a pumping and filtering station, built in 1817 to provide pure drinking water to the city. In 1974 this found a new use as the **Galerie Municipale du Château-d'Eau** (***t*** *05 61 77 09 40; open 1–7, closed Tues and hols; adm*). The hydraulic machinery is still intact on the bottom level, while upstairs you can visit one of Europe's top photographic galleries – over and over again; exhibits change 10 times a year. An annexe has been installed in a dry arch of the Pont Neuf.

Opposite the water tower is the **Hôtel-Dieu St-Jacques**, a medieval pilgrimage hospital rebuilt in the 17th century. The grand Salle St-Jacques and Salle St-Lazare have magnificent ceilings, while down on floor level the hospital now houses a **Musée d'Histoire de la Médecine** (***t*** *05 61 77 84 25; open 9–5, closed Tues; adm free*). Nearby, a single arch survives of a 17th-century covered bridge over the Garonne, the Pont de la Daurade. Each of France's four great rivers has a nickname, and the Garonne is 'the Laughing'. Often enough, the joke has been on Toulouse. St Cyprien, the original dedicatee of the Left Bank's parish church (behind the Hôtel-Dieu), proved to wield so little celestial influence over the water that when his church was rebuilt in 1300 he was sacked in favour of **St Nicolas**, patron of sailors and protector of the flooded. The church is a small southern Gothic version of the Jacobins and boasts a grand 18th-century altar painted by Despax.

More visual arts, this time graphics, posters, ads and postcards from the 17th century to the present, are the subject of the changing exhibits at the **Centre Municipal de l'Affiche, de la Carte Postale et de l'Art Graphique** (*58 Allées Charles-de-Fitte,* ***t*** *05 61 59 24 64, St-Cyprien République métro; open Mon–Fri 9–12 and 2–6; adm*); there's an extensive book, film and record library, and, most popular of all, French commercials – those that used to be shown in the cinemas – from 1904 to 1968, on video cassettes. Just up the road is Toulouse's newest museum, **Les Abattoirs** (*76 Allée Charles de Fitte,* ***t*** *05 62 48 58 01; open Tues–Sun 12–8*), dedicated to modern art. No doubt about it, this is art at its most contemporary, illustrating all the main movements from the second half of the 20th century into the 21st. Some of it is quite disturbing stuff, such as Alberto Burri's *Sacco IV* with patched and tattered heavy sacking, holes in places resembling sores. The prize exhibit was created just outside the timeframe for most of the work; a stage curtain for the play *14 Juillet* by Romain Rolland, painted by Luis Fernandez in 1936 on the request of Pablo Picasso, copied from the great man's gouache of the corpse of a Minotaur in the costume of a Harlequin. It is massive and mirrors themes in Picasso's other works dispayed around the room. You would never guess the building's original purpose as the city's abattoir (of course): it is now large and airy with a sense of space throughout. You can take a turn about the landscaped grounds which look on to the Garonne.

Le Mirail, Toulouse's Shadow Utopia

In 1993, when Toulouse's new *métro* was inaugurated, it was with dire warnings of invasions from Le Mirail, now brought within a 10-minute ride of the Capitole. Le Mirail is the home to the last-off-the-boat in Toulouse, different nationalities, where many live together in an experiment in creative integration in the face of a high unemployment rate. This is a far cry from the experiment originally planned for Le Mirail.

Le Mirail ZUP (*zone à urbaniser en priorité*) was envisaged in 1960 as a *bis Toulouse* near the university, a futurist self-contained white-collar utopia for 100,000 people. This, of course, was back in the days when planners believed that architecture could modify behaviour and they were the great doctors who knew what was good for everyone else. Toulouse's Socialist government chose as its master builder George Chandalis, who had worked with Le Corbusier on the Cité Radieuse project in Marseille. Chandalis planned a star-shaped city of five separate neighbourhoods of 20,000 inhabitants, each with its own commerce, social and cultural services, with a regional centre in the middle. Cars and pedestrians were to be kept strictly apart, so children could play without danger: vehicles were banished to vast underground car parks under the large central squares of each neighbourhood. Each apartment was designed to have a view over the square, the ideal centre of urban life, and a view over the gardens at the back. Chandalis meant his 13-storey blocks or 'tripods' to be residential co-operatives, linked one to the other by long concourses (the *coursives*) or suspended streets with shops and other services that people would stroll past daily en route to the centralized lifts.

Two of Chanalis' five neighbourhoods, Bellefontaine and La Reynerie, were built as planned by 1971, when Pierre Baudis became mayor and radically changed the next stage of building to fit into a more traditional idea of a French *faubourg*. No one complained too vehemently; Le Mirail was already going awry. Toulouse's white-collar workers didn't care to be convivial and live in cooperatives, but instead bought bungalows in suburban dreamland, with their own little gardens and gates. Le Mirail's idealistic vision was altered: walls went up in the *coursives* to keep people in their own buildings, and new entrances and elevators have gone up to lower the amount of forced public interaction. In recent years the tenants' frustration with their lot has sometimes spilt over into violence.

On the Periphery of Toulouse

Aviation fans can delve into what makes Toulouse tick by watching Aérospatiale build its Airbuses at the **Usine Clément Ader** in Colomiers (***t** 05 61 18 06 01; Mon–Fri by appointment 5 days in advance, contact Taxiway to book*) or learn about the history of aviation in Toulouse at Aérospatiale's **Aérothèque** on Rue Montmorency (***t** 05 61 93 93 57; hours irregular so call first*). The **Cité de l'Espace** showcases the city's role as Europe's leader in the space race. They have a life-size model of *Ariane 5*, the *Mir* space station, the **Terradome** where you float in orbit and witness the earth's evolution from creation until today, all sorts of interactive exhibits, a planetarium and simulations (*4 Rue Mayrse Hilsz off the Rocade Est, between the Bordeaux and Montpellier autoroute* exits, **t** 05 62 71 48 71, *bus 19 from Place Marengo near the train station; open Tues–Sun 9.30–6, till 7 in July and Aug; adm exp*).

Out towards the airport, **Blagnac** (buses 66 or 70) has the tomb-oratory of the 5th-century bishop St Exupère, a friend of St Jerome, who on one occasion dispersed a besieging army of Vandals by sprinkling them with holy water; on another, he sold all the goods of his church to buy food for Palestine and Egypt during a famine. When the Toulousains proved to be impious ingrates in spite of his best efforts, Exupère stomped off to his father's farm in the Pyrénées. A delegation was sent from Toulouse to bring him back, but he angrily refused, saying he'd return only if the ox goad in his hand burst into bloom. It immediately did, of course, and back he went; hence the naïve 16th-century frescoes on the walls with their inscriptions in Occitan.

Glossary

Abbaye: abbey

Arrondissement: a city district

Auberge: inn

Aven: natural well

Bastide: a fortified new town founded in the Middle Ages; usually rectangular, with a grid of streets and an arcaded central square; sometimes circular in plan

Caryatid: column or pillar carved in the figure of a woman

Castelnau: a village, often planned, that grew up around a *seigneur*'s castle (often the parish church will be on the edge of a *castelnau* instead of at its centre)

Castrum: a rectangular Roman army camp, which often grew into a permanent settlement (like Bordeaux and many others); in Quercy, the word was often used in the same sense as *castelnau*

Cardo: a north–south street in a Roman castrum; a street running east–west was called a *decumanus*

Cave: cellar

Chai: wine and spirit storehouse

Château: mansion, manor house or castle. A strictly military castle is a *château forte*

Château des Anglais: a cave fortress along the cliffs of the Lot or Dordogne, first built by the English in the Hundred Years' War

Chemin: path

Chevet: eastern end of a church, including the apse

Cingles: oxbow bends in a meandering river, such as the Dordogne and Lot

Clocher-mur: the west front of a church that rises high above the roofline for its entire width to make a bell tower; a common feature in medieval architecture in many parts of southwest France

Cloître: cloister

Commandery: local headquarters of a knightly order (like the Templars or Knights Hospitallers), usually to look after the order's lands and properties in an area

Commune: in the Middle Ages, the government of a free town or city; today, the smallest unit of local government, encompassing a town or village

Cornière: arched portico surrounding the main square of a bastide

Cour d'honneur: the principal courtyard of a palace or large hôtel

Couvent: convent or monastery

Croquant: 'teeth grinder', a peasant guerrilla, especially from the Dordogne, in the anti-French revolts of the 17th and 18th centuries

Ecluse: canal lock

Eglise: church

Enfeu: niche in a church's exterior or interior wall for a tomb

Gare: station

Gariotte: small dry-stone building with a corbelled dome or vault for a roof; many were built as shepherds' huts, others as refuges for villagers in plague times; also called *bories*, *caselles* or *cabannes* in different parts of the Midi

Gentilhommière: a small country château, especially popular in Périgord in the 18th century

Gisant: a sculpted prone effigy on a tomb

Halle: covered market

Hôtel: originally the town residence of the nobility; by the 18th century the word became more generally used for any large, private residence

Lauze: heavy grey stones used for making steep roofs in the Dordogne, now mostly replaced by machine-made tiles; the rare *lauze* roofer these days manages to do about a square metre a day

Lavoir: communal fountain, usually covered, for the washing of clothes

Mairie: town hall

Marché: market

Mas: (from Latin *mansio*): a large farm-house, or manor, or hamlet

Mascaron: an ornamental mask, usually one carved on the keystone of an arch

Modillon: a stone projecting from the cornice of a church, carved with a face or animal figure

Mozarabic: refers to elements in art and architecure derived from Muslim Spain in the Middle Ages

Parlement: a French juridical body, with members appointed by the king; by the late *ancien régime, parlements* exercised a great deal of influence over political affairs

Pays: a region, or a village

Pech: hill

Plan d'eau: artificial lake

Puy: hill

Retable: a carved or painted altarpiece, often consisting of a number of scenes or sculptural ensembles

Rez-de-chaussée (RC): ground floor

Routiers: English mercenaries in the Hundred Years War.

Sauveterre: a village or town founded under a guarantee against violence in wartime, agreed to by the Church and local barons; *sauveterres'* boundaries are often marked by crosses on all the roads leading in to them

Soleiho: top story of a Quercy town house with an open loggia, especially in Figeac and Cahors

Tour: tower

Transi: in a tomb, a relief of the decomposing cadaver

Trumeau: the column between twin doors of a church portal, often carved with reliefs

Tympanum: semicircular panel over a church door; often the occasion for the most ambitious ensembles of medieval sculpture

Language

Even if your French is brilliant, the soupy southern twang may throw you. Any word with a nasal *in* or *en* becomes something like *aing* (*vaing* for *vin*). The last vowel on many words that are silent in the north get to express themselves in the south as well (*encore* becomes something like *engcora*).

What remains the same as anywhere else in France is the level of politeness expected: use *monsieur*, *madame* or *mademoiselle* when speaking to everyone (and never *garçon* in restaurants!), from your first *bonjour* to your last *au revoir*.

General

hello *bonjour*
good evening *bonsoir*
good night *bonne nuit*
goodbye *au revoir*
please *s'il vous plaît*
thank you (very much) *merci (beaucoup)*
yes *oui*
no *non*
good *bon* (*bonne*)
bad *mauvais*
excuse me *pardon, excusez-moi*
Can you help me? *Pouvez-vous m'aider?*
My name is... *Je m'appelle...*
What is your name? *Comment appelles-tu?* (informal), *Comment appellez-vous?* (formal)
How are you? *Comment allez-vous?*
Fine *Ça va bien*
I don't understand *Je ne comprend pas*
I don't know *Je ne sais pas*
Speak more slowly *Pouvez-vous parler plus lentement?*
How do you say ... in French? *Comment dit-on ... en français?*
Help! *Au secours!*
Where is (the railway station)? *Où se trouve (la gare)?*
Is it far? *C'est loin?*
left *gauche*
right *droit*
straight on *tout droit*
entrance *l'entrée*
exit *la sortie*
open *ouvert*
closed *fermé*
WC *les toilettes*
men *hommes*
ladies *dames* or *femmes*
doctor *le médecin*
pharmacy *la pharmacie*
aspirin *l'aspirine*
condoms *les préservatifs*
insect repellent *l'anti-insecte*
sun cream *la crème solaire*
tampons *les tampons hygiénique*
hospital *un hôpital*
emergency room *la salle des urgences*
police station *le commissariat de police*
tourist information office *office de tourisme*
How much is it? *C'est combien?*
Do you have...? *Est-ce que vous avez...?*
It's too expensive *C'est trop cher*
bank *une banque*
money *l'argent*
change *la monnaie*
traveller's cheque *un chèque de voyage*
post office *la poste*
stamp *un timbre*
postcard *une carte postale*
public phone *une cabine téléphonique*
shop *un magasin*
central food market *les halles*
tobacconist *un tabac*

Transport

airport *l'aéroport*
aeroplane *l'avion*
go on foot *aller à pied*
bicycle *la bicyclette/le vélo*
mountain bike *vélo tout terrain, VTT*
bus stop *l'arrêt d'autobus*
bus *l'autobus*

coach station *la gare routière*
railway station *la gare*
train *le train*
platform *le quai*
date-stamp machine *le composteur*
timetable *l'horaire*
left-luggage locker *le consigne automatique*
car *la voiture*
taxi *le taxi*
subway *le métro*
ticket office *le guichet*
ticket *le billet*
single to... *un aller* (or *aller simple*) *à...*
return to... *un aller et retour à...*
What time does the ... leave? *A quelle heure part...?*
delayed *en retard*
on time *à l'heure*

Accommodation

single room *une chambre pour une personne*
twin room *une chambre à deux lits*
double room *une chambre pour deux personnes*
bed *un lit*
cot (child's bed) *lit d'enfant*
towel *une serviette*
soap *du savon*
pillow *un oreiller*
blanket *une couverture*
booking *une réservation*
I would like to book a room *Je voudrais réserver une chambre*

Months

January *janvier*
February *février*
March *mars*
April *avril*
May *mai*
June *juin*
July *juillet*
August *août*
September *septembre*
October *octobre*
November *novembre*
December *décembre*

Days

Monday *lundi*
Tuesday *mardi*
Wednesday *mercredi*
Thursday *jeudi*
Friday *vendredi*
Saturday *samedi*
Sunday *dimanche*

Time

What time is it? *Quelle heure est-il?*
month *un mois*
week *une semaine*
day *un jour/une journée*
morning *le matin*
afternoon *l'après-midi*
evening *le soir*
night *la nuit*
today *aujourd'hui*
yesterday *hier*
tomorrow *demain*
day before yesterday *avant-hier*
day after tomorrow *après demain*

Numbers

one *un*
two *deux*
three *trois*
four *quatre*
five *cinq*
six *six*
seven *sept*
eight *huit*
nine *neuf*
ten *dix*
eleven *onze*
twelve *douze*
thirteen *treize*
fourteen *quatorze*
fifteen *quinze*
sixteen *seize*
seventeen *dix-sept*
eighteen *dix-huit*
nineteen *dix-neuf*
twenty *vingt*
twenty-one *vingt-et-un*
twenty-two *vingt-deux*
thirty *trente*
forty *quarante*

fifty *cinquante*
sixty *soixante*
seventy *soixante-dix*
seventy-one *soixante-onze*
eighty *quatre-vingts*
eighty-one *quatre-vingt-et-un*
ninety *quatre-vingt-onze*
hundred *cent*
two hundred *deux cents*
thousand *mille*

Deciphering French Menus

Many of the restaurants in this book don't translate their menus, so we've included the decoder below; try the section on regional specialities (*see* pp.58–62) if an item isn't listed below.

Hors-d'œuvres et Soupes (Starters and Soups)

Amuse-gueule appetizers
Assiette assortie Plate of mixed cold *hors d'œuvres*
Bisque Shellfish soup
Bouchées Mini vol-au-vents
Bouillon Broth
Charcuterie Mixed cold meats, salami, ham, etc.
Consommé Clear soup
Coulis Thick sieved soup
Crudités Raw vegetable platter
Potage Thick vegetable soup
Tourrain Garlic and bread soup
Velouté Thick smooth soup, often fish or chicken
Vol-au-vent Puff-pastry case with savoury filling

Poissons et Coquillages (Crustacés) (Fish and Shellfish)

Aiglefin Little haddock
Alose Shad
Anchois Anchovies
Anguille Eel
Bar Sea bass
Barbue Brill
Baudroie Anglerfish
Belons Flat oysters
Bigorneau Winkle
Blanchailles Whitebait
Brème Bream
Brochet Pike
Bulot Whelk
Cabillaud Cod
Calmar Squid
Carrelet Plaice
Colin Hake
Congre Conger eel
Coques Cockles
Coquillages Shellfish
Coquilles St-Jacques Scallops
Crabe Crab
Crevettes grises Shrimp
Crevettes roses Prawns
Cuisses de grenouilles Frogs' legs
Darne Slice or steak of fish
Daurade Sea bream
Ecrevisse Freshwater crayfish
Eperlan Smelt
Escabèche Fish fried, marinated and served cold
Escargots Snails
Espadon Swordfish
Esturgeon Sturgeon
Flétan Halibut
Friture Deep-fried fish
Fruits de mer Seafood
Gambas Giant prawns
Gigot de mer A large fish cooked whole
Grondin Red gurnard
Hareng Herring
Homard Atlantic (Norway) lobster
Huîtres Oysters
Lamproie Lamprey
Langouste Spiny Mediterranean lobster
Langoustines Norway lobster (often called Dublin Bay prawns or scampi)
Limande Lemon sole
Lotte Monkfish
Loup (de mer) Sea bass
Louvine Sea bass (in Aquitaine)
Maquereau Mackerel
Merlan Whiting
Morue Salt cod
Moules Mussels
Oursin Sea urchin
Pagel Sea bream
Palourdes Clams
Petit gris Little grey snail
Poulpe Octopus

Praires Small clams
Raie Skate
Rascasse Scorpion fish
Rouget Red mullet
Saumon Salmon
St-Pierre John Dory
Sole (meunière) Sole (with butter, lemon and parsley)
Stockfisch Stockfish (wind-dried cod)
Telline Tiny clam
Thon Tuna
Truite Trout
Truite saumonée Salmon trout

Viandes et Volaille (Meat and Poultry)

Agneau (de pré-salé) Lamb (grazed in fields by the sea)
Ailerons Chicken wings
Aloyau Sirloin
Andouillette Chitterling (tripe) sausage
Autruche Ostrich
Biftek Beefsteak
Blanc Breast or white meat
Blanquette Stew of white meat, thickened with egg yolk
Bœuf Beef
Boudin blanc Sausage of white meat
Boudin noir Black pudding
Brochette Meat (or fish) on a skewer
Caille Quail
Canard, caneton Duck, duckling
Carré The best end of a cutlet or chop
Cassoulet Haricot bean stew with sausage, duck, goose, etc.
Cervelle Brains
Chair Flesh, meat
Chapon Capon
Châteaubriand Porterhouse steak
Cheval Horsemeat
Chevreau Kid
Chorizo Spicy Spanish sausage
Civet Meat (usually game) stew, in wine and blood sauce
Cœur Heart
Confit Meat cooked and preserved in its own fat
Côte, côtelette Chop, cutlet
Cou d'oie farci Goose neck stuffed with pork, foie gras and truffles
Crépinette Small sausage
Cuisse Thigh or leg
Dinde, dindon Turkey
Entrecôte Ribsteak
Epaule Shoulder
Estouffade A meat stew marinated, fried and then braised
Faisan Pheasant
Faux-filet Sirloin
Foie Liver
Frais de veau Veal testicles
Fricadelle Meatball
Gésier Gizzard
Gibier Game
Gigot Leg of lamb
Graisse Fat
Gras Fat; a *foire* or *marché au gras* is the place to buy a fattened duck or goose for its *foie*, but also to make *confits* and *magrets*
Grillade Grilled meat, often a mixed grill
Grive Thrush
Jambon Ham
Jarret Knuckle
Langue Tongue
Lapereau Young rabbit
Lapin Rabbit
Lard (*lardons*) Bacon (diced bacon)
Lièvre Hare
Maigret (or *Magret*) (*de canard*) Breast (of duck)
Manchons Duck or goose wings
Marcassin Young wild boar
Merguez Spicy red sausage
Moelle Bone marrow
Mouton Mutton
Museau Muzzle
Navarin Lamb stew with root vegetables
Noix de veau (*agneau*) Topside of veal (lamb)
Oie Goose
Os Bone
Perdreau (or *Perdrix*) Partridge
Petit salé Salt pork
Pieds Trotters
Pintade Guinea fowl
Plat-de-côtes Short ribs or rib chops
Porc Pork
Pot au feu Meat and vegetables cooked in stock
Poulet Chicken
Poussin Baby chicken
Quenelle Poached dumplings made of fish, fowl or meat
Queue de bœuf Oxtail
Ris (*de veau*) Sweetbreads (veal)
Rognons Kidneys
Rosbif Roast beef
Rôti Roast

Sanglier Wild boar
Saucisses Sausages
Saucisson Dry sausage, like salami
Selle (d'agneau) Saddle (of lamb)
Steak tartare Raw minced beef, often topped with a raw egg yolk
Suprême de volaille Fillet of chicken breast and wing
Tête (de veau) Head (calf's). Fatty and usually served with a mustardy vinaigrette.
Taureau Bull's meat
Tortue Turtle
Tournedos Thick round slices of beef fillet
Travers de porc Spare ribs
Tripes Tripe
Veau Veal
Venaison Venison

Légumes, herbes, etc. (Vegetables, herbs, etc.)

Ail Garlic
Algue Seaweed
Aneth Dill
Anis Anis
Artichaut Artichoke
Asperges Asparagus
Aubergine Aubergine (eggplant)
Avocat Avocado
Basilic Basil
Betterave Beetroot
Blette Swiss chard
Bouquet garni Mixed herbs in a little bag
Cannelle Cinnamon
Céleri (-rave) Celery (celeriac)
Cèpes Ceps, wild boletus mushrooms
Champignons Mushrooms
Chanterelles Wild yellow mushrooms
Chicorée Curly endive
Chou Cabbage
Chou-fleur Cauliflower
Choucroute Sauerkraut
Choux de Bruxelles Brussels sprouts
Ciboulette Chives
Citrouille Pumpkin
Clou de girofle Clove
Cœur de palmier Heart of palm
Concombre Cucumber
Cornichons Gherkins
Courgettes Courgettes (zucchini)
Cresson Watercress
Echalote Shallot
Endive Chicory (endive)
Epinards Spinach
Estragon Tarragon
Fenouil Fennel
Fèves Broad (fava) beans
Flageolets White beans
Fleurs de courgette Courgette blossoms
Frites Chips (French fries)
Genièvre Juniper
Gingembre Ginger
Haricots (rouges, blancs) Beans (kidney, white)
Haricot verts Green (French) beans
Jardinière With diced garden vegetables
Laitue Lettuce
Laurier Bay leaf
Lentilles Lentils
Maïs (épis de) Sweetcorn (on the cob)
Marjolaine Marjoram
Menthe Mint
Mesclun Salad of various leaves
Morilles Morel mushrooms
Moutarde Mustard
Navet Turnip
Oignons Onions
Oseille Sorrel
Panais Parsnip
Persil Parsley
Petits pois Peas
Piment Pimento
Pissenlits Dandelion greens
Poireaux Leeks
Pois chiches Chickpeas
Pois mange-tout Sugar peas or mangetout
Poivron Sweet pepper (capsicum)
Pomme de terre Potato
Potiron Pumpkin
Primeurs Young vegetables
Radis Radishes
Raifort Horseradish
Riz Rice
Romarin Rosemary
Roquette Rocket
Safran Saffron
Salade verte Green salad
Salsifis Salsify
Sarriette Savory
Sarrasin Buckwheat
Sauge Sage
Seigle Rye
Serpolet Wild thyme
Thym Thyme
Truffes Truffles

Fruits et Noix (Fruit and Nuts)

Abricot Apricot
Amandes Almonds
Ananas Pineapple
Banane Banana
Bigarreau Black cherries
Brugnon Nectarine
Cacahouètes Peanuts
Cassis Blackcurrant
Cerise Cherry
Citron Lemon
Citron vert Lime
Coco (*noix de*) Coconut
Coing Quince
Dattes Dates
Figues (*de Barbarie*) Figs (prickly pear)
Fraises (*des bois*) Strawberries (wild)
Framboises Raspberries
Fruit de la passion Passion fruit
Grenade Pomegranate
Groseilles Redcurrants
Lavande Lavender
Mandarine Tangerine
Mangue Mango
Marrons Chestnuts
Mirabelles Mirabelle plums
Mûre (*sauvage*) Mulberry, blackberry
Myrtilles Bilberries
Noisette Hazelnut
Noix Walnuts
Noix de cajou Cashews
Pamplemousse Grapefruit
Pastèque Watermelon
Pêche (*blanche*) Peach (white)
Pignons Pinenuts
Pistache Pistachio
Poire Pear
Pomme Apple
Prune Plum
Pruneau Prune
Raisins (*secs*) Grapes (raisins)
Reine-claude Greengage plums

Desserts

Bavarois Mousse or custard in a mould
Biscuit Biscuit, cracker, cake
Bombe Ice-cream dessert in a round mould
Bonbons Sweets, candy
Brioche Light sweet yeast bread
Charlotte Sponge fingers and custard cream dessert
Chausson Turnover
Clafoutis Batter fruit cake
Compote Stewed fruit
Corbeille de fruits Basket of fruit
Coulis Thick fruit sauce
Coupe Ice cream: a scoop or in cup
Crème anglaise Egg custard
Crème caramel Vanilla custard with caramel sauce
Crème Chantilly Sweet whipped cream
Crème fraîche Slightly sour cream
Crème pâtissière Thick pastry cream filling made with eggs
Gâteau Cake
Gaufre Waffle
Génoise Rich sponge cake
Glace Ice cream
Macarons Macaroons
Madeleine Small sponge cake
Miel Honey
Mignardise Same as petits fours
Mousse 'Foam': frothy dessert
Oeufs à la neige Meringue
Pain d'épice Gingerbread
Parfait Frozen mousse
Petits fours Sweetmeats; tiny cakes and pastries
Profiteroles Choux pastry balls, often filled with chocolate or ice cream
Sablé Shortbread
Savarin A filled cake, shaped like a ring
Tarte, tartelette Tart, little tart
Tarte tropézienne Sponge cake filled with custard and topped with nuts
Truffes Chocolate truffles
Yaourt Yogurt

Fromage (Cheese)

Brebis (*fromage de*) Sheep's cheese
Cabécou Sharp local goat's cheese
Chèvre Goat cheese
Fromage (*plateau de*) Cheese (board)
Fromage blanc Yoghurty cream cheese
Fromage frais A bit like sour cream
Fromage sec General name for solid cheeses
Fort Strong
Doux Mild

Cooking Terms and Sauces

A point Medium steak
Bien cuit Well-done steak
Bleu Very rare steak

Aigre-doux Sweet and sour
Aiguillette Thin slice
A l'anglaise Boiled
A la bordelaise Cooked in wine and diced vegetables (usually)
A la châtelaine With chestnut purée and artichoke hearts
A la grecque Cooked in olive oil and lemon
A la jardinière With garden vegetables
A la périgourdine In a truffle and foie gras sauce
A la provençale Cooked with tomatoes, garlic and olive oil
Allumettes Strips of puff pastry
Au feu de bois Cooked over a wood fire
Au four Baked
Auvergnat With sausage, bacon and cabbage
Barquette Pastry boat
Beignets Fritters
Béarnaise Sauce of egg yolks, shallots and white wine
Bordelaise Red wine, bone marrow and shallot sauce
Broche Roasted on a spit
Chasseur Mushrooms and shallots in white wine
Chaud Hot
Cru Raw
Cuit Cooked
Diable Spicy mustard or green pepper sauce
Emincé Thinly sliced
En croûte Cooked in a pastry crust
En papillote Baked in buttered paper
Epices Spices
Farci Stuffed
Feuilleté Flaky pastry
Flambé Set aflame with alcohol
Forestière With bacon and mushrooms
Fourré Stuffed
Frais, fraîche Fresh
Frappé With crushed ice
Frit Fried
Froid Cold
Fumé Smoked
Galantine Cooked food served in cold jelly
Galette Flaky pastry case or pancake
Garni With vegetables
(*au*) *Gratin* Topped with browned cheese and breadcrumbs
Grillé Grilled
Haché Minced
Hollandaise A sauce of egg yolks, butter and vinegar
Marmite Casserole
Médaillon Round piece
Mijoté Simmered
Mornay Cheese sauce
Pané Breaded
Pâte Pastry, pasta
Pâte brisée Shortcrust pastry
Pâte à chou Choux pastry
Pâte feuilletée Flaky or puff pastry
Paupiette Rolled and filled thin slices of fish or meat
Parmentier With potatoes
Pavé Slab
Piquant Spicy hot
Poché Poached
Raclette Melted cheese with potatoes, onions and pickles
Sanglant Rare steak
Salé Salted, spicy
Sucré Sweet
Timbale Pie cooked in a dome-shaped mould
Tranche Slice
Vapeur Steamed
Véronique Green grapes, wine and cream sauce
Vinaigrette Oil and vinegar dressing

Miscellaneous

Addition Bill (the check)
Baguette Long loaf of bread
Beurre Butter
Carte Non-set menu
Confiture Jam
Couteau Knife
Crème Cream
Cuillère Spoon
Formule à 80F 80F set menu
Fourchette Fork
Fromage Cheese
Huile (*d'olive*) Oil (olive)
Lait Milk
Menu Set menu
Nouille Noodles
Pain Bread
Oeufs Eggs
Poivre Pepper
Sel Salt
Service compris/non compris Service included/not included

Sucre Sugar
Vinaigre Vinegar

Snacks

Chips Crisps
Crêpe Thin pancake
Croque-madame Toasted ham and cheese sandwich with fried egg
Croque-monsieur Toasted ham and cheese sandwich
Croustade Small savoury pastry
Frites Chips (French fries)
Gaufre Waffle
Jambon Ham
Pissaladière A kind of pizza with onions, anchovies, etc.
Sandwich canapé Open sandwich

Boissons (Drinks)

Bière (*pression*) Beer (draught)
Bouteille (*demi*) Bottle (half)
Brut Very dry
Chocolat chaud Hot Chocolate
Café Coffee
Café au lait White coffee
Café express Espresso coffee
Café filtre Filter coffee
Café turc Turkish coffee
Demi A third of a litre
Doux Sweet (wine)
Eau (*minérale, plate ou gazeuse*) Water (mineral, still or sparkling)
Eau-de-vie Brandy
Eau potable Drinking water
Gazeuse Sparkling
Glaçons Ice cubes
Infusion (or *tisane*) (*verveine, tilleul, menthe*) Herbal tea, (usually either verbena, lime flower or mint)
Jus Juice
Lait Milk
Menthe à l'eau Peppermint cordial
Moelleux Semi-dry
Mousseux *Sparkling (wine)*
Pichet Pitcher
Citron pressé/orange pressée Fresh lemon/orange juice
Pression Draught
Ratafia Homemade liqueur made by steeping fruit or green walnuts in alcohol or wine
Sec Dry
Sirop d'orange/de citron Orange/lemon squash
Thé Tea
Verre Glass
Vin blanc/rosé/rouge White/rosé/red wine

Index